BLUE GUIDE

ROME

ALTA MACADAM

WITH ANNABEL BARBER

SOMERSET • LONDON

CONTENTS

PRACTICAL INFORMATION

MAPS & PLANS

Eleventh edition 2016

Published by Blue Guides Limited, a Somerset Books Company
Winchester House, Deane Gate Avenue, Taunton, Somerset TA1 2UH
www.blueguides.com
'Blue Guide' is a registered trademark.

ISBN 978-1-905131-72-3

A CIP catalogue record of this book is available from the British Library.

Distributed in the United States of America by
W.W. Norton & Company, Inc.
500 Fifth Avenue, New York, NY 10110.

The authors and the publisher have made reasonable efforts to ensure the accuracy of all
the information in *Blue Guide Rome*; however, they can accept no responsibility for any
loss, injury or inconvenience sustained by any traveller as a result of information or
advice contained in the guide.

Statement of editorial independence: Blue Guides, their authors and editors,
are prohibited from accepting any payment from any restaurant, hotel, gallery or other
establishment for its inclusion in this guide, or for a more favourable mention than
would otherwise have been made.

Every effort has been made to contact the copyright owners of material reproduced in this
guide. We would be pleased to hear from any copyright owners we have been unable to reach.

Your views on this book would be much appreciated. We welcome not only specific
comments, suggestions or corrections, but any more general views you may have: how
this book enhanced your visit, how it could have been more helpful. Blue Guides authors
and editorial and production team work hard to bring you what we hope are the best-
researched and best-presented cultural guide books in the English language. Please
write to us by email (editorial@blueguides.com), via the comments page on our website
(www.blueguides.com) or at the address given above. We will be happy to acknowledge
useful contributions in the next edition, and to offer a free copy of one of our titles.

Maps: Dimap Bt. Floor plans and watercolours: Imre Bába
Architectural line drawings: Michael Mansell RIBA & Gabriella Juhász
All maps, plans and drawings © Blue Guides.

All images © Blue Guides except p. 57 (Jean-Pol Grandmont, Wikicommons)
and p. 252 (for which special thanks to the church of San Teodoro).
Drawing on p. 101 by Edit Nagy © Blue Guides.
Cover: The Pantheon, by Michael Mansell RIBA & Gabriella Juhász © Blue Guides.
All material prepared for press by Anikó Kuzmich.

Particular thanks to Marco and Gianna Fe' d'Ostiani and Stefano Donghi.
Thanks also to Natalie Arrowsmith (British School at Rome) and Katie McKain.
For comments on the previous edition, thanks to Karl Audenaerde, Giulia Cipriani,
Joan Gubbin, George Karpouzas, Frank Landgraff, Bosse Lanner, David Lown.

Printed in Hungary by Dürer Nyomda Kft., Gyula.

Alta Macadam is the author of over 40 Blue Guides to Italy. This is the tenth edition of Blue Guide Rome to come out under her authorship. She lives in the hills above Florence with her husband, the painter Francesco Colacicchi. She has worked for the Photo Library of Alinari and for Harvard University's Villa I Tatti. In 2003 her *Americans in Florence: a complete guide to the city and the places associated with Americans past and present* was published by Giunti (Florence). She is at present external consultant for New York University at the Photo Archive of Villa La Pietra in Florence. As author of the Blue Guides to Florence, Venice, Tuscany, Umbria and Central Italy, she travels extensively every year to revise new editions of the books.

Annabel Barber is Editorial Director of the Blue Guides. As well as this Blue Guide to Rome, she is the author of *Blue Guide Literary Companion Rome, Pilgrim's Rome: A Blue Guide Travel Monograph* and guide books to Budapest, Vienna and Dubrovnik.

Charles Freeman is a freelance academic historian who has known Rome since he worked as a volunteer at the British School in 1966 and has visited or led study tours there many times since. The third edition of his *Egypt, Greece and Rome*, widely used as an introduction to the ancient Mediterranean, was published by Oxford University Press in 2014 and is complemented by his *Sites of Antiquity, 50 Sites that Explain the Classical World* (Blue Guides, 2009). Both contain extensive material on Rome and its empire. As Historical Consultant, Charles has contributed to many Blue Guides.

Nigel McGilchrist is an art historian with a special interest in the Mediterranean. He worked for a period for the Italian Ministry of Arts and then as director of the Anglo-Italian Institute in Rome. He is the author of *Blue Guide Greece the Aegean Islands*. His contributions to this guide include the entry on the Sistine Chapel.

Mark Roberts joined the staff of the British Institute in Florence in 1977 and was Librarian from 1980–99. He has translated many art historical works for Pannini of Modena and other Italian publishers and has written a guide to the street names of Florence (Coppini, 2001). For New York University he has put in order the Harold Acton papers at Villa La Pietra. He lives at Badia a Passignano with his wife and family.

Introduction

Rome is one of the most celebrated cities of the world, and ever since her greatest days as the centre of the Roman Empire—and later as the home of the Roman Catholic Church—has had a role of the first importance in European history. The Eternal City was the *Caput Mundi* in the Roman era: from here law and the liberal arts and sciences radiated to the furthest reaches of the Empire, which covered the whole of the known western world. Ancient Rome, with a population of over one million, was built over the famous Seven Hills on the left bank of the Tiber. The walls built to defend it by the Emperor Aurelian in the 3rd century AD still defined the urban limits of the city in the late 19th century, and it was only in the 1940s that the population began to reach (and supersede) that of ancient Rome.

The city today preserves numerous magnificent ancient buildings. Some of these are very well preserved—such as the Pantheon and Colosseum—while others are picturesque ruins in the very centre of town. The Vatican, in the part of the city which from the 9th century onwards became the stronghold of the popes, has, since 1929, been the smallest independent state in the world. Amongst Rome's many churches there are still a number which preserve their fascinating early Christian mosaics. But most of the churches were decorated in later centuries, with Baroque masterpieces by Bernini and Borromini and then the elaborate splendour characteristic of the Counter-Reformation period. Superb ancient Greek and Roman sculpture is exhibited in the Museo Nazionale Romano (at four separate locations), at the Capitoline Museums on their hill and at the Centrale Montemartini. The vast Vatican Museums also have great Classical works as well as famous frescoes by Michelangelo and Raphael. There are also some fine private patrician collections of paintings open to the public.

No visitor can fail to notice the abundance of water in Rome, brought to it by aqueduct since ancient Roman times from springs many miles away. Almost every piazza has a lovely fountain and there are numerous street fountains which provide a continuous flow of drinking water for everyone. A special feature of the city are its numerous fine parks, including the huge Villa Borghese in its very centre. The distinctive atmosphere of Rome is perhaps best perceived today in the elegant streets around Piazza di Spagna, as well as in Piazza Navona, Campo dei Fiori, around the Pantheon and in Trastevere. Excavations continue in the Roman Forum, on the Palatine hill and in the Imperial Fora.

For centuries Rome has been visited by pilgrims and travellers; today mass tourism has arrived (over three million people see the Sistine Chapel every year). You are strongly advised to spend time exploring the quieter streets and squares and the smaller museums and palaces as well as the world-famous sights of this beautiful city.

View west from the Imperial Roman remains on the Palatine hill to the Baroque dome of Sant'Andrea della Valle.

History of Rome

by Charles Freeman

Rome the city, as both image and symbol, has penetrated so many layers of consciousness that an historical introduction can only scratch the surface. First, as capital of an extraordinary empire, which stretched from Britain to the Euphrates, it evoked a mass of different allegiances and meanings which lingered on, often in fresh or revived forms, long after its fall in the 5th century. Then, out of the Dark Ages, the city emerged as the capital of western Christendom, a spiritual focus which became global as Roman Catholicism spread to every continent. Since 1870, Rome has been a national capital, and there have been new challenges and tensions as the city sought to bring unity to a country where local loyalties have always been strong.

Within the city itself every period of history has been shaped by the past and has often deliberately echoed it. Classical architecture has been copied or adapted, often brilliantly, for the churches and palaces of Christian Rome (even reusing ancient materials) while the Roman Empire was invoked in the bombastic rhetoric and territorial ambition of Mussolini. Getting to know Rome—insofar as that can ever be achieved—depends as much on understanding these moods and resonances as on knowing its buildings and streets. 'As the wave of memories flows in,' writes the novelist Italo Calvino, 'the city soaks up like a sponge and expands.'

ORIGINS OF THE CITY

The historian Livy (59 BC–AD 17) summed up the advantages of Rome's position. 'Not without reason did gods and men choose this spot for the site of our city—the salubrious hills, the river to bring us produce from the inland regions, and seaborne commerce from abroad, the sea itself, near enough for convenience yet not so near as to bring danger from foreign fleets, our situation in the very heart of Italy—all these advantages make it of all places in the world the best for a city destined to grow great.' Rome lay on an ancient salt route, which ran inland from the coast, at its crossing of the river Tiber in the centre of the fertile plain of Latium. There was higher ground close to the crossing. The Seven Hills of Rome, as they are traditionally listed, are all on the east bank. Four of these, the Quirinal, Viminal, Esquiline and Caelian, are in fact outcrops of higher land divided by the courses of ancient streams while the Capitoline, Palatine and Aventine stand on their own closer to the river. On the west bank, there is the long ridge of the Janiculum with the Vatican hill immediately to the northwest of it. This high ground allowed escape for early settlers from the marshy and often flooded land between the Capitoline and Palatine hills (the future site of the Roman Forum) and the larger floodplain north of the Capitoline where the river swept round in an extended bend. Livy omitted to note the persistent problems of flooding, which were only solved by the building of embankments along the Tiber at the end of the 19th century.

In its earliest days, between 1000 and 750 BC, Rome was only one of many settlements on the plain of Latium. Its founding by Romulus is traditionally dated to 753 BC. The Romulus myth is much later than this, but the date itself is plausible: urban growth in Italy was certainly being stimulated in the 8th century through contacts between traders from Greece and the native peoples of Etruria to the north. Although early inscriptions show that the Romans were always Latin speaking, the city was something of a frontier town open to both Greek and Etruscan influences.

The area of the Regia in the Roman Forum (*see p. 84*) is traditionally identified as the site of a 'royal palace' dating from this period. This can be linked to early traditions that there were 'kings' of Rome acclaimed by the local population. At least two of these kings are said to have been Etruscans, and they brought with them models of city life from Etruria (themselves heavily influenced by Greek examples) as well as religious and military rituals. The last 'king' of Rome was the Etruscan Tarquinius Superbus (credited with building the temple of Jupiter on the Capitoline hill). His son is said to have raped Lucretia, the wife of a Roman aristocrat. She committed suicide as the result of her dishonour, and Tarquinius was driven out by a Roman counter-attack, led by a certain Brutus. The traditional date, which seems close to the historical record, is 509 BC. A republican government was now put in place, and a suspicion of any form of tyrannical power lasted throughout its 500-year history.

THE EARLY REPUBLIC

The chief magistrates of the new Republic were two consuls elected for one year. Their chief duty was to lead the Roman armies. They were supported by more junior magistrates, among them the praetors, who administered the law and stood in for the consuls when these were away on campaign; the quaestors who dealt with the city's finances; and the censors who kept the official list of citizens (with the right of 'censuring' any whose behaviour was unworthy). These were all elected posts, and an ambitious man would work his way up from a junior magistracy to the top. After their term of office, senior magistrates retired to the senate; and although this had little formal power, it became a repository of wisdom and experience that proved influential in the making of foreign policy and the supervision of the city. The magistrates were elected by councils of citizens. What was remarkable about Rome, certainly in comparison with the cities of Greece, was her generosity in granting citizenship. Even freed slaves received it automatically, as did most Italian communities who allied with Rome. Citizens could vote, if they could reach Rome, and received legal protection, but had to offer military service and pay *tributum*, a property tax, in return. This was the secret of Rome's success. Every victory was followed by the bringing of a mass of new citizens who could be recruited to serve in the armies and so bring on new victories. The cult of victory ran deep in the city's psyche. Spoils were brought into the city, dedications made to the city's gods, new temples built by successful generals (at least 14 are known from before 290) and an impetus for expansion sustained. No one was likely to be elected to a magistracy unless he had first proved his worth in war. (The exception which proved the rule was the brilliant 1st-century BC orator Cicero, who talked his way to power.)

IMPERIAL EXPANSION

The city inexorably expanded its power. In 396 came an important victory over the major Etruscan city of Veio; then a series of gruelling wars saw triumph over the Latin peoples (338 BC) and over a combined alliance of central Italian tribes at Sentinum in 296. The rigours of yearly campaigns in the rugged terrain of the Apennines gave the Romans a tenacity which was never lost. In the 280s Roman expansion moved south, to the decaying Greek cities of southern Italy. In conquering them, Rome came into conflict with the Carthaginian empire, which dominated the western Mediterranean. The two Punic Wars were more taxing than anything Rome had faced before and an invasion of Italy by Hannibal (218) brought her close to collapse. Hannibal was eventually defeated in 202. These hard-won wars left Rome with enormous confidence; a navy, which she had built from scratch; and control of Sicily, parts of Spain and north Africa. Troublesome Celtic tribes who had supported Hannibal in northern Italy were now suppressed and colonies of Roman citizens were imposed between them. The punishment of Philip V of Macedon, who had supported Hannibal, now extended Rome's grasp into Greece, and by the middle of the 2nd century BC, the whole peninsula had succumbed.

The impact of these sudden conquests on Rome was profound. A mass of booty was brought into the city in triumph. Much of it was Greek, and carried with it connotations of luxury and sybaritic living. Many traditional Romans looked back to earlier days, when the frugal, hard-working citizens had been tied to the land. Their ideal was Cincinnatus (c. 460 BC), who had left his farm to defend the early republic, then returned to it as soon as the war was over. Now the grander families were building fine houses (the Palatine hill was a favourite spot), employing a mass of slaves on their estates around Rome (and thus undermining the traditional economy of the peasant farmers) and flaunting Greek rather than Roman culture. In Rome itself the process can be seen in the city's building materials. Early Rome had been built of tufa, a volcanic rock which hardens with exposure. There are many kinds, and the Romans gradually discovered the more hard-wearing varieties, notably the blue-grey peperino, used from the 2nd century BC. By the 1st century BC a much harder white limestone, travertine, was being extracted from quarries east of Rome. Still an important building material in the city today, it allowed more detailed and enduring carving than the easily weathered tufa. However, the most coveted building material, for Romans as it had been for Greeks, was now marble. The earliest known marble building in Rome was a temple to Jupiter Stator (Jupiter the Saviour) in 146 BC. There was marble in Italy (at Carrara, its mines first exploited about 50 BC) but most had to come from further afield: Greece (Parian, the finest, and Pentelic, the marble used for the Parthenon), Turkey, Egypt and other parts of north Africa. By the 1st century BC, the wealthier Romans were beginning to import coloured marbles for their homes, as thresholds, wall coverings and columns. With the integration of Egypt into the empire by Augustus (30 BC) a mass of new marbles were to be discovered in the Nile valley and eastern desert (including the purple porphyry which became a symbol of imperial power), and vast columns were shaped and then shipped back to the capital. One of the fascinations of visiting Rome is to see these many marbles recycled.

CIVIL WAR: POMPEY AND CAESAR

By the end of the 2nd century BC there was increasing popular unrest in Rome. The city had expanded so fast that its water and food supplies were vulnerable, there was land hunger in Latium and all the time conscripts had to be found for the defence of the empire. Attempts to redistribute land in favour of the poor were quashed by an intransigent senate, and respect for this ancient institution plummeted. Eventually the traditional constraints on the consuls, which required them to retire after their terms of office, were subverted by a brilliant general, Marius, who got himself re-elected as consul from year to year, raised his own armies (the restriction of recruitment to property-holders had had to be abolished) and fought off Rome's enemies in North Africa and on the Italian borders. He had set a precedent. By the 50s BC two brilliant generals, Pompey the Great and Julius Caesar, were using commands—Pompey in Asia, Caesar in Gaul—to build up prestige, wealth, and loyal troops. They showered their wealth on Rome, the support of whose citizens was vital if their power was to be maintained at the centre. The focus for their building projects was the Campus Martius which, with its propensity to flood, was still undeveloped. Pompey built Rome's first stone theatre, a semicircle of steps surmounted by a temple to Venus Victrix (its shape can still be traced in the way Via Biscione curves into Piazza Paradiso; *map p. 654, B2*). Caesar also built a theatre, but his immediate ambition was to construct a marble-coated voting enclosure. It echoed his claims to be the voice of the citizens against the magnates of the senate.

An eventual showdown between Pompey and Caesar led, after a civil war fought across the empire, to the triumph of Caesar. Returning to Rome in 46, he continued his benevolence to the city. The Forum, traditionally the centre of political life, had been ravaged by unrest—even the senate house had been burned down in one riot. Caesar seized his chance to restore the area, rebuilding porticoes, temples (including one to himself), basilicas and rostra for public speaking. He went further in creating a completely new Forum, immediately to the north of the existing one and close to a new senate house. Yet his position was ambiguous. He had been granted a dictatorship—traditionally a short-term appointment during emergencies but in his case extended for life—and he seemed increasingly seduced by the trappings of power. There were still members of the senatorial aristocracy who clung to the ancient republican ideal of *libertas* and many feared Caesar would adopt the dreaded title of *rex*. Led by Brutus, the descendant of the Brutus who had overthrown tyranny in 509, the conspirators surrounded Caesar in the portico which fronted Pompey's theatre and stabbed him to death (March 44). However, when it was discovered that Caesar had left money and his gardens to the citizens of Rome in his will, Brutus and his co-conspirator Cassius were forced to flee the city. Shakespeare's *Julius Caesar* recreates this dramatic moment. Flowers are still left on the site of the funeral pyre in the Forum.

The assassination of Caesar might have been the moment when the Roman Empire collapsed, especially when Caesar's nephew, Octavian (whom he adopted as his son in his will) and Mark Antony, Caesar's fellow consul and close supporter, fell out and there was renewed civil war. At the Battle of Actium (31 BC), Octavian triumphed over the combined forces of Mark Antony and the Egyptian queen Cleopatra. The victory brought Egypt—and with it immense wealth—into the Empire.

THE EARLY EMPIRE

The glorification of Rome by Augustus (*see p. 127*) established the city as the imperial showpiece. Rome took on a mass of new symbolic meanings, and temples to the 'goddess' Roma became commonplace in the empire. The emperor Claudius (AD 41–54) was pragmatic and far-seeing. He realised that the survival of the city, whose population may now have been as high as one million, depended on efficient supplies of food and water. Two of Rome's greatest aqueducts, the Aqua Claudia (providing 184,000 cubic metres of water a day) and the Anio Novus (providing 190,000 cubic metres) were completed during his reign. Claudius also improved the grain supply. An estimated 200,000 tonnes of grain a year were needed, and it was brought in from southern Italy, Sicily, North Africa and above all Egypt, much of it coming into Rome via the port of Ostia. Even so the good order of the city was always precarious. The emperor had his personal Praetorian Guard, and there was also a city prefect with his own forces of law and order. Local government was centred on 14 'regions' set up by Augustus. Each had a magistrate chosen by lot and deputies usually chosen from freedmen, who welcomed the status. Their duties included care of local shrines, fire-watching and the maintenance of clean streets. Fire was the greatest threat to the city and Augustus organised a force of 7,000 nightwatchmen who were divided into smaller groups which were each responsible for two regions. They could deal immediately with residential fires and had the right to check that water buckets were kept on the upper floors of the *insulae*, the tenement blocks in which the mass of citizens lived. Even so fires quickly got out of hand: six major ones are recorded between AD 15 and 54 before the devastation of 64. Augustus' own house was destroyed by one in AD 3. The continuous supply of fresh water was also a priority, and a workforce of slaves was kept permanently working on the aqueducts.

Rome remained a city of extraordinary contrasts. The public areas, the old Forum and the great Imperial Fora built alongside it, the Capitoline hill and the Palatine, now the home of the emperors, were staggering in their magnificence. They were continually rebuilt and maintained and embellished with propaganda buildings such as the triumphal arches celebrating imperial victories over Rome's enemies. Yet among all this marble magnificence the mass of the population lived in poverty in the *insulae*. The higher the floor in a tenement, the more tenants were crammed into it, and the building thus became vulnerable to collapse. Political life was quiet as the emperors had displaced the popular assemblies, although there were still honorary posts such as the consulship and provincial governorships worth fighting over. In his *Annals* and *Histories*, the historian Tacitus provides a brilliant picture of a city where political life has atrophied and all depends on the will of the emperor.

The extravagance and megalomania of Nero ended in his suicide (AD 69). His successor, Vespasian, was more sensitive to the needs of the population. He built the Colosseum, one of the great achievements of Roman architecture, for the provision of mass entertainment. This entertainment was always brutal, featuring slaughter for slaughter's sake, and often grotesque, with strange combinations of animals and men set in conflict with each other, but it sucked in the energies of a restless populace.

Trajan (*see p. 129*) and Hadrian (117–38) were great benefactors of the city, even though Hadrian spent much of his reign wandering the Empire. His mausoleum, now the Castel San'Angelo, still broods across the Tiber and the Pantheon is a masterpiece of harmonious and sophisticated construction. His successor Antoninus Pius (138–61) stayed in Rome, 'like a spider in the centre of a web', as one observer put it. This is often seen as the moment when the Empire reached its height and when the identification between the name of Rome and its empire became complete. 'All nations look to the majesty of Rome', the Greek orator Aelius Aristides enthused in a panegyric to the Empire in 150 AD. 'You have made the word "Roman" apply not to a city but to a universal people...You no longer classify mankind into Greek or barbarian—you have redivided mankind into Romans and non-Romans...' New building went on, with the vast baths of the emperor Caracalla flaunting the magnificence of imperial patronage.

BARBARIAN INCURSIONS

However, the skies were clouding. From the mid-2nd century on increasing threats to the Empire from barbarian tribes on the northern borders and a revived empire of Persia in the East forced conscientious emperors to spend much of their time on campaign. Marcus Aurelius (161–80) was able to celebrate his triumphs in Rome and leave a column detailing his exploits there, but much of his reign was spent dutifully repelling raids along the Danube. Septimius Severus (193–211) spent a short time in the city (his triumphal arch celebrating a victory over the Parthians remains in the Forum) but campaigns took him from the Persian border to Britain, where he died in 211.

The century that followed almost saw the collapse of the Empire as barbarian raids reached ever deeper within it and emperor followed emperor in a desperate search for stability. It was a sign of the times that one of the more effective emperors, Aurelian (270–5), felt impelled to create a massive set of walls for Rome, large parts of which still stand (*see p. 296*).

The Empire was saved by the Balkan general Diocletian (284–305), who reorganised it under the tetrarchy of two senior emperors (the *Augusti*) aided by two junior ones (the Caesars) and restored stability. Diocletian had little time for Rome—he was busy constructing alternative imperial 'capitals' closer to the borders—and he only visited it once, in 303. However, he gave the city some form of recognition by rebuilding much of the Forum after a fire and constructing the greatest set of baths the pampered city had yet seen. After his abdication Maxentius, the son of one of his generals, seized Italy. He was generous to Rome, building one of the most stunning of the Roman vaulted basilicas at the edge of the Forum as well as another circus for chariot racing beside the Via Appia. He met his end in 312 at the Battle of the Milvian Bridge (Ponte Milvio; *see p. 559*), which crosses the Tiber just north of Rome. His antagonist was Constantine, son of one of Diocletian's Caesars. Constantine entered Rome in triumph and the senate acquiesced by granting the new ruler an impressive triumphal arch next to the Colosseum. Constantine completed Maxentius' basilica and had a vast seated statue of himself placed in one of its halls (fragments of it, including the head, still exist; *see p. 40*). He then restored the Circus Maximus and followed the imperial tradition of commissioning yet another set of baths. This all suggested a conventional emperor seeking to buy the support of his capital city: but it was only a façade. Constantine was about to alter the Roman way of life for ever.

CONSTANTINE AND THE NEW WORLD ORDER

Constantine announced that his victory over Maxentius was a sign of the favour of the Christian god. It was an astonishing revelation. The Christians were still only a small part of the city's population and they had kept a low profile. No more than 25 Christian meeting places are recorded from before 312, and it is clear that these were modest buildings. Christian burials had taken place in underground passageways cut into tufa rock around the city (although the earliest catacombs, from the 1st century BC, were in fact Jewish). In what must be one of the most important moments in western economic and architectural history, Constantine decided to shower the Christian community with vast, opulently decorated basilica buildings as if their God were equal to those pagan deities he was replacing. The earliest basilicas, St John Lateran and the neighbouring Santa Croce in Gerusalemme, were both built on imperial property. The first St Peter's, built over the traditional burial place of Peter on the Vatican hill, may also have been on an imperial estate. Constantine was sensitive to a city which was still overwhelmingly pagan, and while the interiors of these basilicas were beautifully decorated (it has been estimated that the cost of the gold for the apse of St John Lateran would have supported 12,000 poor for a year) the exteriors were kept plain. The bishops of Rome were nevertheless well supplied with estates and material resources. 'Enriched by the gifts of matrons, they ride in carriages, dress splendidly and outdo kings in the lavishness of their table,' was the comment of the historian Ammianus Marcellinus in the 380s. By the end of the 4th century most of the aristocratic families of the city had converted, adapting their traditional ways of life, and so their status, to fit with the new religion. A Roman identity for the Church was confirmed when Bishop Damasus transferred the liturgy from Greek to Latin in the 380s.

The world around Rome, meanwhile, was crumbling. The stretched Roman armies were finding it more and more difficult to deal with barbarian raids and the emperors had to compromise by allowing the invaders to settle within the empire in return for paying taxes. No emperor after Constantine lived in Rome. Constantine's successors had preferred Milan and Constantine himself had created another glittering capital, Constantinople, in the east. When the young emperor Honorius moved down to the well-protected city of Ravenna in 402, he left his generals to negotiate with Alaric, the leader of the Goths who were threatening Italy. After negotiations broke down, Alaric attacked Rome. The Goths were Christians and many treasures were saved by being gathered in St Peter's, but mansions were ransacked and the Forum looted. Even though the 'sack' only lasted three days, the impact on the Empire was profound. As far away as Bethlehem the Christian scholar Jerome recorded his shock and bewilderment at the news. The image of Rome as the inviolable *urbs sacra*—a name given it by Caracalla—was destroyed for ever.

THE PAPACY AND MEDIEVAL ROME

Among those who were stunned by the news of the sack of Rome was the great Christian theologian Augustine. In his *The City of God*, however, he gives his own gloss on events: the true City of God is the city in heaven. Rome, with its dependence on the pagan gods, had been bound to fall and the sack was therefore not to be mourned. This view was to be influential for a thousand years, until the Renaissance restored an awareness of the achievements of the Classical city and its civilisation.

The disintegration of the Western Empire allowed the more ambitious bishops of Rome to become prominent. Leo I ('the Great', 440–61) stressed his position as a direct legal heir of St Peter, thus finding new grounds for affirming the pre-eminence of the bishops of Rome, an authority which he asserted with confidence over his fellow western primates. When Attila and his Huns invaded Italy in 452, it was said that a personal confrontation by Leo forced him to withdraw. (Over a thousand years later Raphael recreated the scene in the Vatican for the Medici pope Leo X.) Less than 15 years later, in 476, the last emperor, Romulus Augustulus, abdicated, bringing the Western Empire to an end.

Decay set in in the next century. First there was a collapse in the Mediterranean economy (one account tells of the road between Rome and Ostia, once bustling with activity, being now covered in grass). A city such as Rome could never be sustained from its own resources, and the population began to shrink. More dramatic was the attempt by the eastern (Byzantine) emperor Justinian to recapture Italy for the empire. His general Belisarius entered Rome in 536, but protracted campaigns against the Ostrogoths led to the city being besieged, captured and recaptured. The aqueducts were cut and the population scattered—perhaps only 30,000 remained by the middle of the century. One Gothic leader massacred 300 children from senatorial families whom he had gathered as hostages, and the senate is heard of for the last time in 580. By the end of the century Rome was nominally back under the control of the Byzantine empire, but a new set of invaders, the Lombards, now held most of northern Italy. Refugees fled south, swelling the population of Rome to some 90,000, but the city was still a shadow of what it had been; churches and monasteries circled a decaying core. The collapse of drainage schemes on the plain appears to have led to the spread of malaria. (The disease was not to be eliminated until the 20th century.)

It was at this desperate moment that one of the great figures of Roman history, Gregory the Great (590–604), founder of the medieval papacy, appears. Gregory was the son of a former city prefect and he cared deeply for the people of his city. Instead of building new churches, he reorganised the papal estates so that they could feed the poor. As a pastor he was moderate, toning down the harsh asceticism of earlier Church leaders and endorsing the balanced monastic rule of St Benedict, of whom he was a great admirer. At the same time he refused to compromise on papal authority. While he accepted doctrines laid down by earlier church councils, he was adamant that 'without the authority and consent of the apostolic see [Rome] none of the matters transacted by a council has any binding force'.

Gradually the Church began infiltrating the historic centre. Patrician mansions were converted into monasteries, a hall from the Forum of Vespasian had taken on a new role as a church dedicated to two eastern saints, Cosmas and Damian (*see p. 90*). For a time pagan temples remained taboo areas, haunted by the malign powers of the pagan gods, but in 609 the Pantheon was made into a church dedicated to the Virgin Mary. The city was given new life through its relics, not only of Sts Peter and Paul, but of other early Roman martyrs (the remains of whom were brought into the city from the catacombs in cartloads) as well as imports such as the Titulus of the True Cross, to be seen (then as now) in Santa Croce in Gerusalemme. So began the history of Rome as a centre for pilgrimages. In 660 a monk from Ireland writes of sharing a hostel with pilgrims from Egypt, Palestine, Greece and even southern Russia.

Though the bishops of Rome had traditionally claimed supremacy over all the bishops of Christendom, this was clearly untenable when Rome was so isolated. The Goths, who had succeeded the imperial authorities in much of western Europe, were not even Catholic (they clung to what was now termed the Arian heresy, in which Jesus was seen as a lesser creation of God the Father). It took some time before Catholic rulers emerged in France and Spain so that with Ireland and England (which Gregory the Great had converted) a wider Catholic community was gradually consolidated in Europe. Within Italy itself the popes were consolidating control over their own estates in central and southern Italy and Sicily and were increasingly seen as the key figures in mediations between the Byzantine Empire and the Lombards. Strong links between the Empire and the papacy were retained—in fact 11 out of 13 popes between 678 and 752 were Syrian or Greek. However, disputes over doctrine, conflict over the relative powers of emperors and popes in spiritual matters, and the weakening of the Byzantine Empire as Islam gained sway in the 7th century could only strengthen the papacy as an independent force. When the Byzantine emperor Leo III launched a campaign against religious images (726), the popes refused to join in and, in retaliation, actually encouraged the worship of icons in Rome.

In the late 8th century, the West reasserted itself. It happened unexpectedly. In 751 the Lombards captured Ravenna, the seat of the Byzantine exarch, thus eliminating Byzantine control in Italy. Pope Stephen II (752–70) saw his chance to ask Pepin the Short, King of the Franks, for support against further Lombard expansion. Pepin and his successor Charles, later Charlemagne, defeated the Lombards and Charles took the crown of Lombardy (774). The papacy thus regained some of its old estates in the north, but was now dependent on Frankish military power. When a struggle over the papacy broke out in 795, the elected pope, Leo III, sought Charlemagne's help in resisting his opponents and on Christmas Day 800 he crowned Charlemagne as Roman Emperor in St Peter's. It was a clear throwback to the past. Charlemagne even took 'Augustus' as one of his titles and was spoken of as 'the new Constantine'. In a now lost mosaic in a hall of Leo III in the Lateran, the Apostle Peter was shown on a throne with Charlemagne kneeling on one side and Leo on the other. What was left unresolved, however, was which of the two, emperor or pope, had power over the other.

POPES AND HOLY ROMAN EMPERORS

The next three centuries were dominated by a power struggle between popes and emperors for ultimate spiritual and temporal jurisdiction. In 824 Charlemagne's grandson Lothar proclaimed in his *Constitutio Romana* that emperor and pope were to share judicial functions over the city and that the people of Rome had to swear allegiance to the emperor. The election of a pope had to be confirmed by the emperor. This went directly against the popes' view of their role, elaborated from a document, the so-called *Donation of Constantine*, which purported to show a transfer of imperial power by Constantine to the pope of his day, Sylvester (in the Chapel of St Sylvester in the convent of the Santi Quattro Coronati, a fresco shows Constantine giving his imperial crown to Sylvester). The struggle intensified when the Carolingian house disintegrated and it was a German, Otto of Saxony, who came to Rome in 962 to be crowned by the pope, only to impose a pope of his own choosing. The conflicts which followed were bitter, but slowly an accretion of papal power is discernible. A council held in the Lateran in 1059 reserved the election of a new pope to the cardinals, the procedure which is still followed today. This removed the process from the direct influence of the emperors and the powerful families of Rome, unless—as was often to happen—they had cardinals of their own. At the same time the papacy gradually increased its control over the patchwork of estates, ancient duchies and cities in central Italy, the so-called Patrimony of St Peter. In 1122 an agreement between Pope Calixtus II and the emperor Henry V, the Concordat of Worms, was in essence a recognition of the spiritual supremacy of the pope even over temporal rulers. The everyday lives of Romans in this troubled period are given prominence by Chris Wickham in his recent book *Medieval Rome, Stability and Crisis of a City, 900–1150.*

DISSENT AND SCHISM

In Rome itself the memories of an ancient republic based on the Capitoline hill had never vanished. They were taken up by an expanding class of professionals, lawyers attached to papal administration, craftsmen and agricultural entrepreneurs who instigated a popular revolt against the supremacy of the popes and the noble families in 1143. The insurgents 'assembled on the Capitol and, desiring to renew the ancient dignity of the city, again set up the senate'. They appealed to the emperors, who refused to support them, but their persistence eventually led to the popes agreeing to recognise a communal government. In 1188 the representatives of the city were given the right to make peace and war and to receive a share in papal revenues. The most outstanding pope of the period, Innocent III (1198–1216), in fact managed to achieve control over the appointment of the *senatore*, the chief executive of the city, whom he normally chose from a leading noble family. He consolidated the papacy with a vastly improved bureaucracy in the curia, or papal court. He built few churches but many public buildings including, after he had been disturbed by a dream in which fishermen dredged up the bodies of dead children from the Tiber, the Ospedale di Santo Spirito for foundlings and the sick. From Rome Innocent reached throughout Europe, claiming the right to intervene in disputed imperial elections, to combat heresy with force and to launch crusades (the notorious Fourth Crusade, which sacked Constantinople in 1204, took place in his reign). This was the climax of the medieval papacy. The 13th century saw the arrival of the Franciscans and the Dominicans and in Santa Maria sopra Minerva, Rome has one of its very few Gothic churches, modelled on the Dominican church in Florence,

Santa Maria Novella. Influences from the north were clearly still suspect, however, and when the Franciscans took over and rebuilt the church of Santa Maria in Aracoeli on the Capitoline hill from 1250, they chose the more traditional Romanesque style.

The end of the 13th century saw an outburst of new cultural and artistic activity, fostered by the popes, notably Nicholas IV (1288–92), and sustained by competitive showmanship from the city's cardinals. Many of Rome's churches were opulently redecorated. Tombs became more splendid and all the accoutrements of clerical life more gorgeous. Artists, including Cimabue and Giotto, were drawn southwards to Rome. The great new apse mosaic of the *Coronation of the Virgin* in Santa Maria Maggiore by Jacopo Torriti is perhaps the finest survivor from these years, which culminated in the announcement by pope Boniface VIII that 1300 would be a Holy Year, the first so proclaimed. An estimated two million pilgrims flocked to the city from throughout Christian Europe, bringing welcome amounts of offerings with them.

Despite the improved spiritual and temporal power of the papacy, it was still vulnerable to outside forces. Pope Clement V, elected in 1305, found himself under such strong influence from France that he was forced to move the papal court to Avignon (*see p. 178*). It remained there until 1377, but even then the return of the papacy to Rome was marked by the crippling dispute of the Great Schism and it was not until 1420 that papal control was resumed in Rome. One anonymous cleric noted that 'Rome without a pope is like a woman without a husband'. The city atrophied in the popes' absence, being reduced at one point to a mere 17,000 inhabitants. (Florence at this time had some 90,000, Venice a possible 100,000.) This was an unsettled time. Rome was, in theory, divided into 14 regions, as it had been in Augustus' time. Yet these divisions were made meaningless by the dominance of warring local families, whose power ranged across traditional boundaries. The Colonna lorded it over the Quirinal and Esquiline hills (and later appropriated the Mausoleum of Augustus). There were the Corsi on the Capitoline hill and the Frangipani on the Palatine, with control of both the Colosseum and the Circus Maximus. The Pierleoni were dominant on the Isola Tiberina and in Trastevere. The ruins of ancient Rome, such as still stood, were converted into fortresses and palaces, while a mass of towers (the 13th-century Torre delle Milizie near Trajan's market is a surviving example) acted as symbols of prestige and the readiness to defend territory.

Frustration with aristocratic infighting led to the most interesting event of the 14th century, the popular uprising masterminded by Cola di Rienzo in 1347. This man, an unbalanced opportunist of poor birth (it was typical of him that he claimed to be the illegitimate son of an emperor), was steeped in memories of the ancient Roman republic and having travelled to Avignon, he persuaded the pope that papal authority exercised through himself as a representative of the people needed to be asserted against the nobility of the city. Back in Rome, he took over the Capitol and in a wild but inspiring speech declared himself 'Illustrious Redeemer of the Holy Roman Republic'. Hatred of the fractious nobility was so great that for a short period Cola was triumphant. However, he was clearly unstable and extravagant claims that he was restoring the Roman Empire on behalf of himself and the pope soon lost him papal support. Despite a victory of his troops over the forces raised by the nobility, his increasingly tyrannical behaviour and a declaration by the embarrassed pope that he was a heretic led to his support slipping away. He was eventually clubbed to death by the mob in 1354. This bizarre episode showed, however, that ancient memories of the Roman Republic still lingered in the city: they were to reappear, in less dramatic form, in years to come.

RENAISSANCE ROME

The years in Avignon (1308–77) and the Great Schism which followed it were eventually settled with the election of Martin V, from the ancient—but often turbulent—family of the Colonna, in 1417. When Martin arrived in Rome in 1420 he found it so 'dilapidated and deserted that it bore hardly any resemblance to a city...Houses had fallen into ruins, churches had collapsed and whole quarters were abandoned'. It was the achievement of the popes who followed Martin to transform that desolate and fragmented place, which still bristled with its medieval towers, into a showpiece of Renaissance and Baroque art.

Papal Rome had two focuses. The ancient seat of the papacy remained St John Lateran, whose basilica was the cathedral of Rome. The Lateran, however, had no link to the foundations of Christianity. It was to the Vatican hill that pilgrims flocked to worship at the shrine over the supposed burial place of St Peter, and the core of the city's resident population remained in the Borgo, the immediate neighbourhood of St Peter's, and in the warren of medieval streets covering the former Campus Martius. Nicholas V (1447–55) decided to move to the Vatican. By doing so he strengthened the direct relationship of the papacy with St Peter's, while in times of trouble popes could enjoy the protection of the river, the walls built by Leo IV in the 9th century and the Castel Sant'Angelo (formerly the mausoleum of Hadrian). With the election of each pope, a *sacro possesso* was celebrated with a grand procession from the Vatican across the Capitoline hill, and down past the Colosseum to the Lateran.

The aim of the 15th-century popes was to create a city which reflected the spiritual and temporal power of the papacy as well as being accessible to the mass of pilgrims. The Holy Year of 1450 showed just how unsuitable the city was for large crowds when some 200 pilgrims drowned after a panic on the narrow Ponte Sant'Angelo. To relieve the pressure on the river crossing, Sixtus IV (1471–84) constructed the first bridge since antiquity, the Ponte Sisto (1475), together with a new street, the Via Lungara, connecting it with the Vatican.

Sixtus, in fact, was compared to Augustus for his mass of building projects, 'opening up and measuring out streets in accordance with the dignity of the empire,' as one inscription put it. Pilgrims were greeted as they entered through the Porta del Popolo with the grand façade of his Santa Maria del Popolo, the first church in Rome with a dome (Brunelleschi's great dome for Florence cathedral had been completed a few years before). It was Sixtus who built the Sistine Chapel, for his own private use and for the papal elections, which are still held there. Near to the Vatican he rebuilt Innocent III's decaying Ospedale di Santo Spirito, transforming it into one of the largest hospital complexes of its day. Sixtus also moved a collection of ancient bronzes which had accumulated around the Lateran palace to the Capitol, where they formed the core of the Capitoline Museums. Perhaps his most enduring legacy was his decision to allow clergy to pass on any palaces they had built for themselves to their families, even if they had used Church money to build them.

These projects were possible because of the underlying wealth of the papacy. It enjoyed the fruits of its own territory, which stretched across central Italy, in addition to an immense income from indulgences, from taxes on foreign churches, from special collections and the sale of offices. The Medici pope Leo X sold some 1,200 posts. The control of the popes over this wealth was absolute: at the death of Martin V, the papal treasury had to be retrieved from the Colonna's family palace. Some popes, for instance the Borgia Alexander VI, who had six illegitimate sons and a much-loved daughter, Lucrezia, to cater for, scattered it on their families; others on the glorification of the city. At the opposite extreme, the Venetian envoy complained of the austere Paul IV (1555–9): 'Life at court is mean...The clergy have withdrawn from every sort of pleasures... the state of things has been the ruin of artisans and merchants', a reminder that even though more spiritual Christians may have been shocked by papal excess, it did bring employment. Nevertheless, it meant that the ancient tradition of Rome as a city whose citizens lived off handouts was perpetuated and the mass of the population—judging from the anonymous notes which were left, in time-honoured tradition, by the statue of Pasquino (*see p. 202*)—showed a good deal of cynicism about their clerical masters. 'We have done the Carafa, the Medici and the Farnese families', sighed one wag on the accession of the Borghese pope Paul V in 1605, 'now we have to enrich the Borghese.'

Yet the pope had also to show theological and political skills if he was to keep peace in the Church and maintain his position among the secular rulers of Europe. The fall of Constantinople to the Ottoman Turks in 1453, and continued Ottoman expansion into central Europe, provided another challenge. In 1494 the wider political context within which the papacy operated was transformed when the rising nations of Spain and France began casting their eyes on the vulnerable and scattered Italian city states. In that year the French king Charles VIII marched down through Italy to claim the Kingdom of Naples. He forced his way into the centre of Rome while Alexander VI cowered in Castel Sant'Angelo. After this humiliation, it was little wonder that Alexander's successor, Julius II (1503–13), founded his own army, the Swiss Guard (which since 1806 has been only a papal bodyguard), and led them into northern Italy where he humbled Venice and then France and even enlarged the Papal States.

Julius, born Giuliano della Rovere and a nephew of Sixtus IV, was the *papa terribile*, tempestuous and uncompromising. Against the impassioned opposition of traditionalists, he announced he would tear down and rebuild St Peter's. His architect was Donato Bramante, who had already ushered in the Renaissance to Rome with his charming Tempietto (*see p. 404*). With Michelangelo diverted from work on a grandiose tomb for Julius to the repainting of the ceiling of the Sistine Chapel and Raphael at work in the papal apartments, this was an extraordinary moment in the history of European art. After the unearthing of the famous statue of Laocoön in Rome in 1506, there was a passion for ancient sculptures and soon sites were being quarried for examples. The collection of Alessandro Farnese (later Pope Paul III) was the most notable. The same passion inspired imitations of Classical models, both in architecture and in art and interior decoration.

THE REFORMATION AND THE SACK OF ROME

The worldliness of the papacy finally faced the challenge of Martin Luther, not over art or luxury but over the sale of indulgences. Leo X excommunicated the rebel monk in 1521, but papal control over medieval Christendom began to fragment as the Reformation caught hold. To make matters worse, Pope Clement VII (1523–34), like Leo X a member of the powerful Florentine Medici family, unwisely became entangled in politics. His backing of the French against the Emperor Charles V led to Charles sending his troops towards Rome after families such as the Colonna offered him active support. Charles' troops were joined by a band of Lutherans, who were eager to wreak revenge on the anti-Christ, as the pope was now dubbed by his enemies. Out of the control of their commanders, they stormed into the city in May 1527. While Clement took refuge in Castel Sant'Angelo and then had to flee north, the city was ransacked. Even the sick of the Ospedale di Santo Spirito were slaughtered in the mayhem, which one estimate suggests took 12,000 lives. The Vatican palace was only saved because one of the invaders' commanders protected it against his own men. When Clement, who was blamed for the disaster, finally made his way back, four fifths of the city was considered uninhabitable, trade was at a standstill and there were still unburied bodies among the rubble. 'Rome is finished,' wrote one observer. Michelangelo returned to the city to complete the Sistine Chapel but the pessimism of his *Last Judgement* (*see p. 471*) provided a strong contrast with the vitality and exuberance of the ceiling he had painted in happier times.

Yet amazingly, Rome was to revive. Clement's successor was the Farnese Paul III (1534–49), who was determined to restore some grandeur in the city, not least in the Palazzo Farnese, which he ordered to be enlarged as befitted the new status of his family. While Alexander VI and Clement VII had used the Castel Sant'Angelo as a refuge, Paul ordered new comfortable apartments to be installed there for everyday use. Bizarrely, in the frescoes with which they were decorated he linked himself, Alessandro Farnese, to Alexander the Great, a reminder of just how complex were the interactions between Renaissance and Christian present and Classical past. There was a real sense of a reconnection of Rome with its ancient roots. When the alarming news came that Charles V was on his way to Rome from the south (he had been fighting the Turks in Tunisia), Paul turned the situation to his advantage by laying on an imperial triumph. A route was cut through the city which echoed that of ancient times. The emperor entered along the Via Appia, passed the ruins of the Baths of Caracalla (from which Paul was busily looting statuary for his palace) and then processed through three triumphal arches: those of Constantine, Titus and Septimius Severus. Homage was paid to Trajan's Column before the imperial cavalcade made for the Vatican, where Charles dutifully kissed the papal foot. Some sort of redress had been made for the events of 1527.

ROME AND THE COUNTER-REFORMATION

The greatest challenge facing Paul was the reformation of the Church in the face of the inroads of Protestantism. (Henry VIII of England made his break with Rome during Paul's papacy.) It was Paul who called the Council of Trent (1545–63), which reformulated traditional Catholicism in such a way that it could offer an effective response to its enemies. In Rome he tightened papal control over dissidents by setting up the

Inquisition (1542); and in founding the Society of Jesus (1540) under the ascetic Ignatius Loyola, Paul created an intellectual battering ram for the Church. It was Farnese money which was to finance the great Jesuit church of the Gesù (1568–75), whose opulent decoration shows how overpowering emotional impact was central to the Counter-Reformation fightback (the Council of Trent in fact went so far as to insist that religious art should play on the emotions of the believer).

The most obsessive of the Counter-Reformation popes was the austere Paul IV (1555–9). Narrow and impetuous, he made a disastrous alliance with France against Spain, which led to the defeat of papal troops. It was only a generous peace which preserved the Papal States. He set up the Index of Prohibited Books and alienated all by his parsimony—which did not, however, extend to his own family, many of whom shamelessly exploited his nepotism. The citizens of Rome liked money to be spent on them and their city rather than on the worthless hangers-on of the papal family of the day and they showed their true feelings at Paul's death by sacking the Inquisition buildings and releasing their prisoners. Paul's successor, Pius IV (1559–65), took note and began spending on the city again.

Renaissance Rome was to be brought to fruition by five years of intense activity by Sixtus V (1585–90). Sixtus, who had spent his early years as a swineherd in the Marche, appeared so sickly at the papal conclave that he won election as a stop-gap pope. Once elected, he emerged with a will of iron and a fixed plan to transform Rome, especially by encouraging settlement in the sparsely populated east of the city (the French essayist Montaigne had noted in 1581 how desolate this area was). He hit on the happy idea of re-erecting the Egyptian obelisks—most of which had been brought to Rome by Augustus sixteen hundred years before—at focal points in the city, especially to help pilgrims find their way around the streets. Sixtus' favourite church was Santa Maria Maggiore (he was to be buried there), and it acted as a hub for a new set of broad radiating streets. They were well received because coaches were just coming into fashion, and needed space to move. More welcome to the mass of citizens must have been Sixtus' restoration of a 3rd-century AD aqueduct (known as the Acqua Felice after Sixtus' Christian name) so that a supply of fresh water could now be piped to 27 fountains in the city.

By the time Sixtus died, in 1590, the scholar Pompeo Ugonio was able to write that Rome is 'permeated with the light of peace, augmented with wider streets, adorned with buildings, refreshed by fountains, implanted with massive obelisks reaching to the highest heavens…Wheresoever Rome turns, she sees herself restored to a new golden age abounding with justice, fortitude, vigilance, liberality, magnificence…'. This was certainly an exaggeration. Behind the façade of magnificence Rome, now with a population of 110,000, was still a city of gross inequality and simmering unrest. Sixtus had launched campaigns against the mass of prostitutes and beggars who thronged the streets; in 1604 a famine led to rioting against the unpopular Aldobrandini pope Clement VIII (1592–1605). Ancient tensions between the French and Spanish communities were another focus for conflict. It seems a fitting backdrop to the turbulent life of the painter Caravaggio, who arrived in the city for the first time in 1592. Yet the trouble below the surface was effectively masked by a new outburst of building which was to transform central Rome into the city we recognise today.

BAROQUE ROME

The great façade of St Peter's is emblazoned not with any biblical quotation but with the name of Camillo Borghese, Pope Paul V, who completed it in 1614. The Borghese were a self-made family, originally from Siena, who had worked their way up through the papal administration, and Camillo emerged as a compromise candidate from the conclave of 1605. Paul spent lavishly, not only on St Peter's, but on the papal palace on the Quirinal. If Sixtus is remembered for his obelisks, Paul is remembered for his fountains. He rebuilt an aqueduct of Trajan so that fresh water now entered Rome on the Janiculum hill, bubbling into a fountain in the form of a triumphal arch (the Acqua Paola). From there it flowed downhill into Trastevere and across the Ponte Sisto to feed the fountains in front of Palazzo Farnese. Another branch was diverted to the Vatican fountains.

The two themes which run through 17th-century Rome, the Rome of the Baroque, are the consolidation of the grand family palaces as the centre of a glittering cultural and social life and, secondly, the contribution of a man who did more than any pope to create the public ambience of the city: the architect and sculptor Gian Lorenzo Bernini. The contrast with his rival, the less exuberant but equally imaginative Francesco Borromini, can be plotted through their Roman churches.

Grand society in Rome centred on those families lucky enough to secure the papacy. In the first half of the century, these were, notably, the Borghese (Paul V) and Barberini (Urban VIII). Paul V's nephew Scipione Borghese acquired enough wealth to become one of the great art collectors of the city: some of his acquisitions are still on view in the villa he built in the Borghese Gardens. The relatives of Urban VIII did even better, amassing a fortune that was estimated to be twelve times the annual income of the Papal States. Much of the wealth of these families was ploughed into their palaces. The Borghese acquired so much land for theirs they were able to create a piazza in front of it. The Barberini took advantage of the comparative emptiness of the Quirinal hill to plan an H-shaped *palazzo* with separate wings for the secular and clerical sides of the family.

Perhaps the finest architectural achievement of this century was the completion of St Peter's under the patronage of the Chigi pope Alexander VII (1655–67). His architect, Gian Lorenzo Bernini, had already enjoyed a glittering career. A consummate courtier and the favourite of Urban VIII, he had created sculptures of an emotionally charged but technically accomplished classicism, as well as fountains, tombs, palaces (including parts of the Palazzo Barberini), chapels, and his most important church, Sant'Andrea al Quirinale, begun in 1658. Inside St Peter's he was to raise the majestic bronze baldacchino over the central altar and create the brilliantly composed Cathedra of St Peter in the apse. Yet it was his sweeping colonnade, its arms reaching into the piazza to embrace the world of Christendom, that completed the magnificence of St Peter's.

YEARS OF DECLINE

This extraordinary outburst of patronage finally began to exhaust the resources of the papacy. In 1692 Pope Innocent XII (1691–1700) called an end to extravagance when he forbade popes to transfer wealth to their relatives. It had not been a happy century for Catholicism. In northern Europe the wars of religion, between Catholics and Protestants, had caused untold misery. The Ottoman Turks had made major inroads into eastern Europe and in 1664 Alexander VII had to sign a humiliating peace with France to stave off an invasion of the Papal States. Cultural supremacy shifted to France, now under the rule of the Sun-King Louis XIV (1643–1715). Even Bernini, who was particularly hard to detach from Rome, was found designing a grandiose façade for the Louvre (though it was never built). In Rome itself the 17th century had seen plagues and famines which only increased the resentment of the population over papal excess. Even if the Inquisition was not as ruthless as it is sometimes portrayed, it controlled freedom of thought. Italian translations of the Bible were banned. 'Don't you understand how so much reading of Scripture ruins the Catholic religion,' Paul V told the Venetian ambassador. The constraints within which dissent could be expressed were narrow, and it was in Protestant Europe that the scientific revolution which challenged the scholastic Aristotelianism of Catholic orthodoxy was able to take root.

There was still building in Rome in the 18th century. The Spanish Steps (1723–6) and the Trevi Fountain (1762) are two of Rome's most popular attractions. There was still room for more palaces, too, but imperceptibly Rome was losing its role as a centre of cultural activity and emerging as a place for foreigners to view. The first excavations at Pompeii and Herculaneum were arousing a new fascination with the Classical past. In response the popes banned the export of statues and then began instituting the great museums: the Vatican Museum was inaugurated by Clement XIV (1769–74) and the Capitoline Museums also took their present form in the 18th century, with new acquisitions and the rearrangement of their crowded galleries. In fact, several rooms still provide an example of what a museum of the period looked like.

The new visitors to Rome were often Protestants with a Classical education enjoying the Grand Tour. They were as much interested in Classical Rome as in papal display, and the impact of their first sight of original Roman ruins was often profound. James Boswell arrived in 1765 and 'experienced sublime and melancholy emotions' after he 'saw the place, now all in ruins, with the wretched huts of carpenters and other artisans occupying the site of that rostrum from which Cicero had flung forth his stunning eloquence'. Boswell summed up the variety of the experiences open to a traveller with the right connections: papal ceremonies, with visits to the Palazzo Borghese, Michelangelo's *Moses* in San Pietro in Vincoli and the Vatican Library. After a busy day sightseeing he boasted that he had found a different girl for every night of his stay—until a dose of venereal disease brought his nocturnal activities to a halt.

It was also in Rome that serious academic discussion of ancient art was beginning. Johann Winckelmann, a Prussian convert to Catholicism who became Librarian at the Vatican, published his *A History of Art in Antiquity* in 1764. Using examples from Rome, notably the *Apollo Belevedere* in the Vatican collection, which he believed the most sublime work of art ever conceived, he set out a history of ancient creativity which placed the Greece of the 5th century BC at the pinnacle of achievement, with decadence thereafter. Unfortunately many of the 'Greek' statues with which he chose to make his point turned out to be much later Roman copies, but at least he had fostered debate. A more committed champion for the art and architecture of Rome itself was the Venetian Giovanni Battista Piranesi. Piranesi travelled to Rome in 1740 'to admire and learn from those august relics which still remain of Roman majesty and magnificence, the most perfect there is of Architecture'. His famous *Vedute* of Rome; his *Capricci*, made up of imagined Roman buildings; and his meticulous measurement and drawings of those which survived gave him an international reputation and his prints helped inspire Classical buildings in the United States and beyond.

NAPOLEON IN ROME

In 1796 the Italian states were crushed by the armies of France, and in 1797 the forces of their leading general, Napoleon Bonaparte, surrounded Rome. Napoleon already conceived himself as the heir to the Roman conquerors of the past—but while they had brought their loot into Rome, Napoleon was to take his from Rome to Paris. Under the Treaty of Tolentino, imposed upon Pope Pius VI, Napoleon appropriated many of Rome's finest ancient statues, including the *Apollo Belvedere*, the *Capitoline Venus* and the *Laocoön*. Rome was declared a republic and the frail pope left the city to die in exile. Much of the Church's property was expropriated by the new regime.

Napoleon would not be the servant of the French revolutionary governments for long and, as he himself acknowledged, his rise to absolute power mirrored that of Augustus eighteen hundred years before. Starting with ancient titles such as first consul (1799), then consul for life (1802), he emerged in 1804 as Emperor of the French. While in 800 it has been Charlemagne who had travelled to Rome to be crowned emperor by the pope, now it was the new pope (Pius VII, elected under Austrian protection, in Venice) who travelled to Paris to crown Napoleon. With triumphal arches and even a sewerage system said to be Roman in inspiration, Napoleon attempted to create a new Rome in Paris. His looted treasures filled the Louvre, and Canova was obliged to create a large nude statue of Napoleon as Classical hero (it is now in Apsley House in London). Napoleon formally occupied Rome in 1808 and imprisoned Pope Pius the following year. Very little was achieved in Rome under French rule. Rather, the burden of heavy recruitment and taxation led to Pius being welcomed back with much rejoicing in 1815, when Napoleon's empire collapsed. The pope delegated Canova to join the peace negotiations in Paris, and with the support of the British government he secured the return of most of Rome's treasures. Although some Church property was lost for ever, the Papal States too were restored to the papacy.

REVOLUTION

The papacy exploited the mood of relief after the excesses of Napoleon to align itself with the reactionary Catholic regimes of France and Austria. In Italy, however, there were counter currents among liberal nationalists who, remembering the ideals if not the reality of revolutionary France, dreamed of the overthrow of the papal autocracy and the creation of a united Italy. The Church stood firm, and outbursts of disorder in the Papal States in 1831 were crushed when the new reactionary pope, Gregory XVI (1831–46), called in Austrian troops to support him. Gregory's successor, Pius IX appeared more open to change, however, not least in his acceptance of gas lighting and railways. His apparent readiness to foster some form of unity among the Italian states aroused great enthusiasm. It might be possible, many thought, for Italy to be brought together under his benevolent care.

It was not to be. In early 1848 revolutions spread throughout Italy, from Sicily and Naples in the south to Venice and Milan in the north. To the enormous disappointment of his supporters, Pius disowned them. The reaction in Rome was such that he was forced to accept a constitutional government in the city but even this was swept away in November and Pius was forced to flee to Naples. His attempts from there to demand the submission of 'the rebels' on pain of excommunication only led to a vote by an elected city assembly to bring papal rule to an end and declare a Roman Republic (February 1849). The messianic Italian nationalist Giuseppe Mazzini then declared that 'Rome, by the design of Providence, and as the People have divined, is the Eternal City to which is entrusted the mission of disseminating the word which will unite the world'. Then there arrived, at the head of an unkempt collection of guerrilla troops, Giuseppe Garibaldi, the charismatic revolutionary leader who had already been sentenced to death once for his part in an insurrection on behalf of 'Young Italy'. He had spent his exile in South America joining in local revolutions, and it was his luck to return to Italy in 1848, just when there was a cause adapted to his talents.

By 1849, however, the revolutions which had spread throughout Europe were losing their vigour and the forces of reaction were gathering strength. Pius IX found an ally in the new French President—later emperor—Louis Napoleon, the nephew of Napoleon Bonaparte. Louis Napoleon was anxious to secure the support of the French clergy and present the restoration of Austrian influence in Italy, and he saw his chance to do this by offering military help to Pius to regain his kingdom. A French army was dispatched to Rome and arrived ready to attack the city in April. Hectic preparations were made in Rome's defence, and Garibaldi and his followers managed to repulse some of the French attacks which came from the west, from the higher ground of the Janiculum hill. The streets which slope down into Trastevere from the church of San Pietro in Montorio on the hill still seem haunted by the skirmishing which took place here. The city fell, however. French troops entered it on 3rd July 1849.

Pius returned in 1850, but his survival depended on the French garrison which remained in the city. The movement for Italian unity was now led by the Kingdom of Piedmont and Sardinia whose chief minister, Camillo Cavour, masterminded the removal of Austrian control of northern Italy. By 1861 the Papal States were lost to the new Kingdom of Italy and its monarch Vittorio Emanuele II. Papal control of Rome, all that was left of its territories, remained precarious, and Pius' instinct was to show no sympathy with the forces of change. In the papal encyclical of 1864, *Quanta Cura*, he condemned religious freedom and any idea that 'the pope should reconcile himself to and agree with progress, liberalism and modern civilisation'. His spiritual authority might prevail; his temporal could not. Only two months later, under the pressure from the Franco-Prussian war, the French withdrew their garrison from Rome and Italian troops occupied the city. The Kingdom of Italy, with its capital now in Rome, was proclaimed in 1871.

ROME, THE SECULAR CAPITAL

Italian troops entered Rome near Michelangelo's Porta Pia on the 20th September 1870 and the Via Pia was renamed Via XX Settembre in memory of the event. Pius refused to recognise the regime which had taken his territory, and never again set foot outside the Vatican.

Rome now needed to be converted into a modern capital city. It is astonishing when looking at old maps to see how underpopulated the area within the old Aurelian Walls remained. Even in 1871 the population, at 212,000, was only just over a fifth of what it had been in Classical times. Rome was still a city close to the surrounding Campagna (old photographs show shepherds with their flocks by the gates of the city) with virtually no industry of its own other than simple craftsmanship. Now it had to be transformed into a capital with ministries, law courts and a palace for royalty: the Quirinal Palace was expropriated for them from the papacy. Émile Zola in his *Rome* (1896) speaks of 'the blood of Augustus rushing to the brain of these last-comers' (the Italian Government), urging them to a renewed desire to make Rome stately and great. There was a mass of new building in the western part of the city with grand new streets such as the Via Nazionale and the Via Cavour. Another new street, the Corso Vittorio Emanuele, ran up through the Campus Martius district to meet a new bridge Ponte Vittorio Emanuele (1911), so creating a completely new east–west axis. With the population rising fast, to 432,000 by 1891 and 660,000 by 1921, there was inevitably a great deal of scope for speculation, especially through the acquisition and conversion of former Church buildings.

Although the archaeological core of the city, from the Capitol to the ruins of the Baths of Caracalla, was made into a preserved zone, the rest of Rome was not so lucky and the carving up of the gardens of the Villa Ludovisi, now under the present-day Via del Tritone, caused an international outcry. Large numbers of apartment blocks for the expanding civil service took their place. Meanwhile the government's secular identity was affirmed through statues to Cola di Rienzo, by the Capitol; of Giordano Bruno, burned by the Church for heresy in 1600, in the Campo dei Fiori where the execution took place; and—perhaps most provocative of all—a Piazza del Risorgimento (the movement for Italian unity) alongside the walls of the Vatican (1921).

If the needs of the new Italian government (and the speculators who came its wake) predominated in the period before the First World War, after the war it was the ambitions of one man, Benito Mussolini, whose march on Rome in 1922 had led to an unexpected collapse of the Italian government, which took their place. 'Rome must be a city worthy of its glory, and that glory must be revivified tirelessly to pass on as the legacy of the Fascist era to generations to come,' he opined in 1924. For Mussolini Rome was there to be used as the backdrop for his imperialist fantasies. His desire to highlight the Classical monuments of the past by isolating them (the Mausoleum of Augustus is a good example) went hand in hand with his ambition to create 'the monumental Rome of the 20th century'. Central to his plans was to open Rome to the sea again. From the Piazza Venezia, the Via dei Fori Imperiali was cut through the ancient Fora— in the process destroying buildings and important archaeological evidence for the imperial Rome which Mussolini idealised—towards the Via del Mare.

Mussolini did solve one outstanding problem: the uneasy relationship between the papacy and the Italian state. Here was a nation made up largely of Catholics whose spiritual head, the pope, refused to recognise the very state to which they were supposed to give secular allegiance. Despite some tough talking between the representatives of Pius XI and Mussolini, the Lateran Pact of February 1929 produced a workable conclusion. The Vatican City was recognised as an independent state whose citizens were exempt from Fascist law. In return the pope accepted that the territorial losses of the 19th century were irrevocable—with financial compensation to be paid. Church authority over marriages and religious education within Italy was recognised. Mussolini is 'the man whom providence has sent us', said Pius XI, and it was indeed the Church which gained the long-term benefit from the pact.

Rome suffered little in the Second World War. The papacy took the opportunity to reassert itself as the true focus of civilisation after the collapse of Fascism but the image presented in films such as Fellini's *La Dolce Vita* (1960) is of a carefree amorality. There were deep-rooted problems facing the city, not least in how to deal with its future shape and identity. No city able to host the Olympics (1960), the Second Vatican Council (1962–5) and the World Cup (1990) could be considered moribund, but there was a feeling in the 1970s of life in Rome becoming out of control, not least through the proliferation of traffic which clogged the medieval streets and harmed its monuments. Piazzas pleasant to linger in in the 1960s became forbidding at night in the 1970s as Italy's political situation deteriorated. Perhaps the lowest point was the discovery of the murdered body of the prime minister, Aldo Moro, in the boot of a car in Via Caetani in 1978. Throughout the 1980s the discrepancy grew between the urbane and often civilised façade of Italian life and a chaotic and unregulated cronyism behind the scenes. Umberto Bossi's Northern League, founded in 1989, was able to portray the unwieldy bureaucracy and high taxation of Rome's politicians as an unhappy contrast with the energies of the entrepreneurial north.

A turning point seems to have come with the decision, in 1993, to appoint a directly elected mayor. The first incumbent, Francesco Rutelli (1993–2001), gave new energy to the city. Vigorous attempts to cut traffic together with the opening up of pedestrian areas allowed the centre to breathe again. Collections of the city's Classical art which had lingered for decades in storerooms were at last displayed. However, an attempt to sheath the old in the new, for instance in Richard Meier's museum for the Ara Pacis (2006), shows how difficult it is to preserve ancient buildings in ways that enhance them and the richly textured city that surrounds them. And the complexity of Rome's heritage is such that there is simply not enough money to sustain it. Hopes to create an archaeological park around the tomb of the 2nd-century AD general Marcus Nonius Macrinus on the Via Flaminia—one of the most important finds of the past 30 years—came to nothing for lack of funds and the monument had to be reburied. The visitor to today's Rome cannot ignore the many formidable challenges the city faces in finding a stable and effective government; but it remains 'eternal' in the way in which its varied pasts are in continuous interplay with one another. This provides the great fascination of Rome.

Popes & the Papacy

by Mark Roberts

The word pope (*papa* in Latin and Italian) is a childish diminutive of 'father', and was originally applied to the clergy in general; it is still used of ordinary priests by the Greeks, but in the West quite early on it was restricted to bishops. By the Middle Ages only the Bishop of Rome called himself pope, and in 1073 Gregory VII strictly forbade anyone else to do so.

The Bishop of Rome, according to Catholic teaching, is the successor of St Peter the Prince of the Apostles, and is the vicar (or representative) of Christ on earth, the visible head, in other words, of the Church. This teaching is based on a famous passage in St Matthew's Gospel (*16: 13–20*), describing the encounter between Jesus and his disciples at Caesarea Philippi. Jesus had asked them 'Whom do you say that I am?', and Simon Peter alone had replied that Jesus was the Christ, son of the living God. Jesus then said to him: 'Thou art Peter, and upon this Rock I will build my Church...and I will give to thee the keys of the kingdom of heaven'. The popes' claims to spiritual authority (the 'Petrine claims') are based on these very words of Christ, which are written in huge Roman capitals, two metres high, around the inside of the dome of St Peter's.

As well as Bishop of Rome, the pope is styled Metropolitan Archbishop of the Roman Province, Primate of Italy and the adjacent islands, Patriarch of the West, and head of the Universal Church. (In 2006 Benedict XVI dropped his title of 'Patriarch of the West' as a conciliatory gesture to the Eastern churches.) Additionally the pope is called *Pontifex Maximus* (the 'supreme bridge-builder', a title used by the pagan emperors but originally applying to the head of a college of priests, who was seen as building a bridge between earth and heaven) and—more humbly—*Servus servorum Dei*, the servant of the servants of God. In case some of the grander titles should go to his head, the new pope was reminded of his mortality during the ceremony of his coronation, when a quantity of tow was ignited by a kneeling priest. As the tow burned to ashes, the priest intoned *Beatissime pater, sic transit gloria mundi* ('Most holy father, even thus passes all earthly glory'). The present pope and his three predecessors, however, have chosen not to be crowned at all: the last papal coronation was Paul VI's in 1963.

The pope is elected by the cardinals, who form the 'parish clergy' of Rome and who comprise the Sacred College. The complicated rules for the conclave (from the Latin *con clave*, properly a chamber that can be closed with one key) were laid down in 1274 by Gregory X, though they have been adjusted several times since. The rules were designed to ensure that the election should not be unnecessarily delayed, should not be precipitated, should be free from any kind of external pressure. After the death of the pope, all the cardinals are summoned to the conclave, which is to begin on the tenth day following his decease. The election must be held in whatever city the pope dies: in 1800 Pius VII was elected in Venice. On the tenth day a Mass of the Holy Spirit is sung, and the cardinals form a procession and proceed to the conclave, where apartments have been prepared for them separated by wooden partitions. On the first day crowds of people swarm in and out, but in the evening everyone is compelled to leave ('*Extra omnes!*'), except for the cardinals and their authorised servants, who are known as conclavists. All the doors are bricked up except one, which is locked and carefully guarded. After three days, according to Gregory's rules, the supply of food was to be restricted, and if a further five days elapsed without an election only bread, water and wine could be sent in. Voting takes place twice a day. The practice of burning the ballot papers, so as to indicate by the colour of the smoke whether or not a pope has been chosen, would seem to be no older than the 20th century. The requisite two-thirds majority is generally obtained fairly quickly, though in 1799 the cardinals took three months to make up their minds. Attempts were often made to influence the result. As recently as 1903, the Imperial government used its veto to exclude the candidature of Cardinal Rampolla, thought to be anti-Austrian; Pius X, elected instead, immediately abolished the power of veto which had been possessed by certain secular powers. John Paul II altered the rules so that the physical separation of the voting cardinals is no longer insisted upon: in 2005 they were put up in comparative comfort at the newly built Domus Sanctae Marthae inside the Vatican, although the voting sessions still took place in the Sistine Chapel.

A winning candidate must be formally asked by the Cardinal Chamberlain whether he accepts the papacy. Sometimes he is very reluctant to do so: the infirm Leo XII, in 1823, pointed to his poor swollen legs and said 'Do not insist, you are electing a corpse'. Sometimes he is rather pleased: Benedict XIV, in 1740, said, 'Do you want a saint or a politician? Elect someone else. Do you want a good fellow (*un buon uomo*)? Very well then, elect me.'

Once he has accepted and has chosen his regnal name, the new pontiff is dressed in one of three different-sized outfits. The Cardinal Chamberlain makes the announcement to the waiting crowds: *Annuntio vobis gaudium magnum, habemus papam*; and for the first time the new pope gives his blessing *Urbi et orbi*, to the City and to the world.

Early popes are shown wearing a bishop's mitre, and sometimes the pallium, a circlet of white wool worn on the shoulders, worked with six purple crosses. The pope not only wears the pallium himself, he also sends it to patriarchs, primates and archbishops; it is woven from the fleeces of two lambs blessed in the church of Sant'Agnese fuori le Mura on St Agnes' Day (this ceremony, accompanied by the gentle bleating of the flower-garlanded lambs, still takes place every year on 21st January).

The triple crown, or papal tiara, has not been worn since the time of Paul VI (d. 1978). In any case it was not a liturgical head-covering and was never worn at Mass. Its form developed over several centuries. Nicholas I (858–67) is said to have been the first to unite the princely crown with the episcopal mitre. One coronet, around the lower edge, appears in art in the 12th century. Boniface VIII is said to have added a second crown, probably to symbolise the double monarchy—spiritual and temporal—which he claimed in his famous bull, *Unam sanctam*, of 1302, asserting the papacy's claim to be the only source of God-given authority, which kings must obey and to which royal power is merely ministerial. A third coronet was added in the early 14th century, either by Benedict IX or by Clement V, and the whole tiara was enlarged into its characteristic melon shape; it had a small cross on the top and two lappets at the back.

The triple crown has often been taken by commentators to symbolise the pope's threefold authority as Prophet, Priest and King, in other words his doctrinal, ministerial and jurisdictional powers. The doctrinal authority, or Magisterium, includes all the rights and privileges necessary for teaching divine revelation and for guarding the deposits of faith, and is held to be protected by 'Infallibility'. This teaching, defined by Pius IX in 1870, maintains that the pope's pronouncements on faith or morals, when made *ex cathedra* ('from the throne', i.e. addressed to the whole Church), are necessarily free from error. The ministerial authority involves, among other things, the appointment of cardinals, so that over a long pontificate a pope is able to pack the Sacred College with those *ab eo creati*, appointed by himself. The jurisdictional authority is very extensive and is held to be 'full, ordinary and immediate' over the entire Church. (It was George Bernard Shaw who pointed out that the infallible pope really claims very little: 'Compared with our infallible democracies, our infallible medical councils, our infallible astronomers, our infallible judges, our infallible parliaments, the Pope is on his knees in the dust confessing his ignorance before the throne of God, asking only that as to certain historical matters on which he has clearly more sources of information open to him than anyone else his decision shall be taken as final.')

The other great papal symbol is the crossed keys, always part of the pope's coat of arms. The scene of the *traditio clavium*, or handing over of the keys, is familiar in art and represents the power of binding and loosing, of locking and unlocking, given by Christ to St Peter and his successors at Caesarea Philippi. Perugino's fresco in the Sistine Chapel shows this scene, and so does Raphael's tapestry made for the same place (now in the Vatican Museums).

For much of their history the popes have been temporal sovereigns as well as heads of the Church. They ruled over the Papal States, or 'Patrimony of St Peter'. This papal monarchy came to a dramatic end during the pontificate of Pius IX in 1870, when King Vittorio Emanuele invaded the papal dominions: Pius refused to accept the settlement offered, and he and his successors became known as the 'prisoner of the Vatican', right up until the Concordat with Mussolini in 1929 (*see p. 30*). Since then the pope has ruled— as absolute monarch—over a tiny kingdom consisting only of the 109 acres of the Vatican City plus a few extraterritorial dependencies such as the Lateran and Castel Gandolfo. He has his own radio station and post office, so as to ensure freedom of communication with the outside world. The Vatican City, the smallest sovereign state in the world, should be distinguished from the Holy See, an entity which dates back to early Christian times and which maintains diplomatic relations with 177 states across the planet.

After the unexpected resignation of Benedict XVI in 2013, a conclave elected Cardinal Bergoglio, who took the name Francis. (It is unusual for a pope to adopt a name not used by any of his predecessors: before John Paul I in 1978, the last pope to do so was Lando in 913.) There are thus now two popes, as it were, a German and an Argentine, the former styling himself 'pope emeritus'.

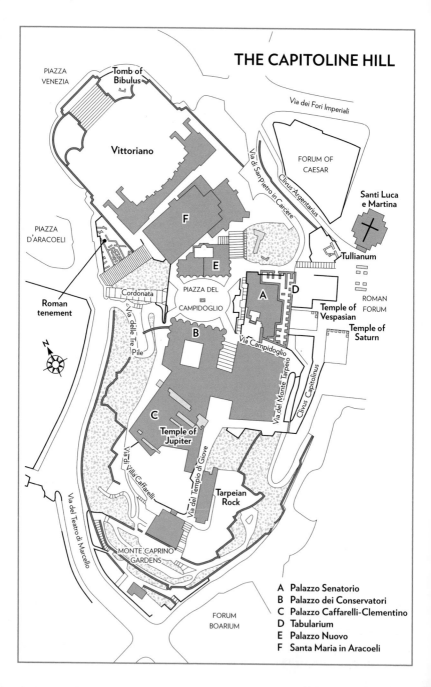

THE CAPITOLINE HILL

PIAZZA VENEZIA

Tomb of Bibulus

Via dei Fori Imperiali

Vittoriano

Via di San Pietro in Carcere

Clivus Argentarius

FORUM OF CAESAR

Santi Luca e Martina

F

PIAZZA D'ARACOELI

E

Tullianum

ROMAN FORUM

Cordonata

PIAZZA DEL CAMPIDOGLIO

A

D

Roman tenement

Via delle Tre Pile

B

Via Campidoglio

Temple of Vespasian

Temple of Saturn

Via del Monte Tarpeio

Clivus Capitolinus

C

Temple of Jupiter

Via di Villa Caffarelli

Via del Tempio di Giove

Tarpeian Rock

MONTE CAPRINO GARDENS

Via del Teatro di Marcello

FORUM BOARIUM

A Palazzo Senatorio
B Palazzo dei Conservatori
C Palazzo Caffarelli-Clementino
D Tabularium
E Palazzo Nuovo
F Santa Maria in Aracoeli

The Capitoline Hill

The political and religious centre of ancient Rome and the seat of civic government since the end of the 11th century of the modern era, this little hill, with views directly over the Roman Forum, has the city's historic collections of beautiful ancient sculpture.

L ocated in the heart of the city (*map p. 654, C3*), the Capitoline Hill (*Campidoglio*) is the best place to start a visit to Rome. Today it preserves its ancient feeling of pride, combined with a sense of intimate elegance provided by the little piazza created by Michelangelo on its summit. Here, around the famous equestrian monument to Marcus Aurelius, stand the town hall of Rome and the Capitoline Museums, with the city's superb collections of Classical sculpture—the arrangement still reflects their history as the oldest public collection in the world. There are delightful peaceful gardens off the quiet street which encircles the top of the little hill, from which there are superb views of the city and of the Roman Forum.

HISTORY OF THE CAPITOLINE HILL

The smallest of the seven hills of Rome, the Capitoline Hill is nevertheless the most important. Excavations have proved that it was the first place in Rome to be settled at the end of the Bronze Age (1300 BC). During the early 6th century BC the construction of a huge temple was begun on its southern summit (the Capitolium). It was dedicated to Jupiter, Juno and Minerva in 509 BC and remains of its foundations can still be seen (*see p. 44*). The northern summit of the hill was occupied by the Arx, or citadel of Rome, and in 343 BC, on the highest point of the hill here, a temple was dedicated to Juno Moneta. The temple was guarded by geese which were sacred to the goddess. In the middle of a dark night in the same century, it was their honking which alerted the Romans to an attempt on the hill by the Gauls, and all was saved, although the rest of the city was sacked. The name Moneta came to be connected with the mint established here (and hence our word 'money').

By the 8th century AD the site of this temple had been occupied by the church of Aracoeli, which was used as the meeting-place of the Roman Council. Because of its historic position, the fortress close by (now Palazzo Senatorio) was chosen as the seat of the newly-formed senate of the *comune* of Rome in the 12th century. From the mid-14th century onwards the governing magistrates (the 'Conservators') of the city carried out their administrative duties in Palazzo dei Conservatori, though they exercised effective power only for some hundred years, since Nicholas V saw to it that the papacy took control of the city in the middle of the following century, when he had the palace rebuilt. Incredibly, at the end of the 19th century, the city authorities permitted the construction of the huge Vittoriano monument at the hill's northern edge.

APPROACHES TO THE CAPITOLINE

At one time the hill was accessible only from the Roman Forum but since the 16th century the main buildings have been made to face north, in conformity with the direction of the development of the city. There are three approaches from Piazza d'Aracoeli. A long flight of steps mounts to the church of Santa Maria in Aracoeli, and on the right Via delle Tre Pile (a road opened for carriages in 1873) winds up past a fragment of Archaic tufa wall. In the middle the stepped ramp known as the **Cordonata**, designed by Michelangelo and modified around 1578 by Giacomo della Porta, provides the easiest way up the hill. At its foot are two Egyptian lions in black granite veined with red, dating from the Ptolemaic period (3rd century BC). They were formerly in the Temple of Isis which once stood near the Pantheon. The water they now blow from their mouths (except in winter) comes from the Acqua Felice, an aqueduct constructed to provide water for the hill in the late 16th century. In the garden halfway up on the left stands a rather sinister little **statue of Cola di Rienzo** in a cowl. This was set up in 1887 to mark the spot where the popular hero was killed in 1354.

COLA DI RIENZO

Cola di Rienzo (or Rienzi) led a successful rebellion against the warring barons of Rome during the absence of the popes in Avignon. From the church of Sant'Angelo in Pescheria in the Ghetto (*map p. 243*) he and his followers set out to seize the Capitoline on the night of Pentecost, 1347. A few days later he was proclaimed 'tribune' of a 'Holy Roman Republic', and crowned in Santa Maria Maggiore. He used the ancient *Lex Vespasiani* (still preserved on this hill in Palazzo Nuovo; *see p. 56*) in an attempt to demonstrate the greatness and the rights of the citizens of Rome. Claiming that Pope Boniface VIII had hidden it away beneath an altar, Cola had it installed inside St John Lateran for all to see. He addressed the assembly in the church of Santa Maria in Aracoeli here and 'ruled' from the Campidoglio, but his ambition to recreate a glorious period of republican governance modelled on ancient Rome only lasted a matter of months since the populace turned against him and he was killed by the mob, who decided to side with the nobility. His body was hung up by the feet in front of the church of San Marcello on the Corso and left there for two days to be mocked.

It was not until the 19th century that Cola was reinstated as a romantic figure, admired for his patriotic, utopian ideas of an empire led by the 'people'. An opera by Wagner was based on his life. Edward Bulwer-Lytton wrote a book on him, *The Last of the Tribunes*, which inspired a painting by the pre-Raphaelite painter William Holman Hunt. He is nowadays looked upon as a figure of 'a certain quaint glamour' but to this day he is the only person in Roman history since the glorious days of the Empire to have been allowed a memorial on the city's most important hill. (*For more on Cola, see p. 20*.)

PIAZZA DEL CAMPIDOGLIO

At the top of the Cordonata ramp is Piazza del Campidoglio, a superb piece of town planning, surrounded on three sides by stately palaces and with its open end defined by a balustrade. It is one of the most pleasing spaces in Rome, with the feel at once of an intimate courtyard and a terrace above the city. When Pope Paul III decided it was time to elevate the appearance of this spot to reflect its importance as the historical centre of the city, he ordered that the famous gilded bronze **equestrian statue of Marcus Aurelius** be moved here from the Lateran hill. He called in Michelangelo, who had just been made a citizen of Rome and was already working for the same pope on his huge fresco of the *Last Judgement* in the Sistine Chapel, to design the small and elegant base for it. The inscriptions record that the emperor was both '*pater patriae*' and '*pontifex maximus*' to the Senate and People of Rome. The magnificent original sculpture is now displayed (on a new base) inside the museums (*described on p. 44*). It has been replaced *in situ* by a disappointing copy.

Michelangelo seems to have envisaged the piazza paved in herring-bone brick with an oval in the centre around the statue; the attractive pavement was given its novel star design only in 1940.

The balustrade

In the 1550s Michelangelo designed a balustrade for the open side of the piazza. Flanking the top of the steps are colossal sculptures of the twin heroes Castor and Pollux (known as the Dioscuri; *see p. 82*) with their horses. They are much restored late Roman works that were found in the 16th century in the Ghetto (where a temple to them once stood). Beside them on the balustrade are two Roman sculptures modelled on the enemy arms and armour which used to be displayed as trophies in triumphs held in honour of victorious generals after battle. They have been known for centuries as the 'Trophies of Marius', since it was traditionally thought that they depicted the war booty of Gaius Marius after his victory over Germanic tribes in 101 BC, but in fact they date from the time of Domitian (late 1st century AD). The statues of the emperor Constantine and his son Constantine II came from the Baths of Constantine on the Quirinal hill, and the two columns were the first and seventh milestones of the Via Appia.

PALAZZO SENATORIO

At the back of the piazza is Palazzo Senatorio. In the 12th century the senate of the *comune* of Rome was installed in this building, and it is still today the official seat of the Mayor of Rome (and so normally closed to the public). In the Middle Ages one of the powerful Roman baronial families, the Corsi, built a fortress here using the remains of the ancient Tabularium and the Temple of Veiovis (*see p. 50*) as a foundation. The medieval building, with four towers, was restored over time, but in 1546 Michelangelo was called in to redesign it as part of his general plan for the hilltop. He regularised the façade and designed the steps in white travertine and decided to place the two Roman statues of reclining river-gods representing the Nile and Tiber in front of the double

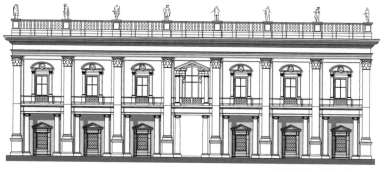

PALAZZO DEI CONSERVATORI

staircase. They were found on the Quirinal hill and the figure of the Nile to the left, in grey marble, is particularly successful and well proportioned. The figure to the right used to represent the River Tigris but was given the attributes of the Tiber in the 16th century (note the very damaged she-wolf). In 1589, when the Acqua Felice aqueduct reached the hill, the two Greek marble fountain basins were added and a colossal statue of Jupiter in the central niche was replaced by the small seated figure of Minerva, a Roman work in porphyry which was transformed into the goddess Roma.

Work on the palace was continued after 1549 by Michelangelo's little-known collaborator Mario Maccarone. Giacomo della Porta, who was extremely active in Rome as architect of churches and palaces and worked on several projects begun by Michelangelo (most famously the cupola of St Peter's), modified the design together with his collaborator Girolamo Rainaldi, when they provided it with its present façade in 1592.

The palace is crowned by a bell-tower (1582) with a clock, and another statue of Minerva; two bells (1803–4) replace the famous *Patarina*, which was installed in 1200 to summon the people to *Parlamento*.

PALAZZO DEI CONSERVATORI

This beautifully proportioned building by Michelangelo (aided by Guidetto Guidetti) has a very unusual design, with Ionic columns supporting horizontal architraves (rather than the more usual arches) to form an open loggia below, and handsome windows with coupled columns on the *piano nobile*, crowned by a prominent entablature with a balcony. The two storeys are united by very tall columns, which rise from the ground as far as the entablature, the earliest example of the giant order being used in secular architecture to produce an effect of dignified grandeur. Some of the engaged columns in the portico are set into the wall in very shallow niches, another extremely innovative architectural feature, later much copied.

PALAZZO NUOVO

Palazzo Nuovo, opposite Palazzo dei Conservatori, was also designed by Michelangelo (there are marked similarities in the two façades) but was not built until the mid-17th century.

THE CAPITOLINE MUSEUMS

Open daily 9.30–7.30 (last tickets 1hr before closing), museicapitolini.org. Ticket office in Palazzo dei Conservatori. The ticket includes entrance to Palazzo dei Conservatori, the Tabularium and Palazzo Nuovo. At least half a day is needed to do justice to this wonderful museum. The combined ticket (Capitoline Card, valid one week) includes entrance to the Centrale Montemartini, described on p. 491, which contains the rest of the Capitoline sculpture collection and should on no account be missed. The works are well labelled, also in English. Room numbers tend to change in situ: in the following description, the room numbers correspond to those on the plans in this text. There is a café on the delightful roof terrace of Palazzo Caffarelli-Clementino, with splendid views.

The collections housed in Palazzo dei Conservatori and Palazzo Nuovo (with the adjoining Palazzo Caffarelli-Clementino) are grouped under the comprehensive title of the Capitoline Museums (Musei Capitolini) and are famous for their magnificent Roman sculptures. Founded in 1471, they constitute the oldest public collection in the world. Today they provide a wonderful introduction to Classical sculpture, not only because of their numerous masterpieces, but also because they illustrate the way these were presented to travellers for centuries. The atmosphere in Palazzo Nuovo is particularly memorable. The itinerary through the museums in both buildings includes a visit to the Tabularium, a magnificent ancient Roman building which provides an unsurpassed view of the Roman Forum.

HISTORY OF THE SCULPTURE COLLECTIONS

In 1471 Pope Sixtus IV made over to the people of Rome five wonderful ancient bronzes (including the famous *Spinario* and the *She-wolf of Rome*), which were deposited in Palazzo dei Conservatori on the Capitoline hill. This nucleus was later enriched with finds made in the city of Rome and by various acquisitions, notably the collection of Cardinal Alessandro Albani in 1733. Today those masterpieces of sculpture are still to be found in several rooms of the Appartamento dei Conservatori and all the rooms in the Palazzo Nuovo.

In the 1990s a splendid new hall was built in a courtyard of Palazzo dei Conservatori for the display of the restored equestrian statue of Marcus Aurelius, and excavations beside it revealed imposing remains of the foundations of the most important temple on the hill, dedicated to Jupiter in the 6th century BC. At the same time the adjoining galleries were adapted to provide space for numerous pieces of sculpture which had once adorned the gardens of ancient Rome's patrician villas.

The tunnel beneath Piazza del Campidoglio, which now connects Palazzo dei Conservatori to Palazzo Nuovo, contains an excellent display of epigraphs.

More important sculpture from the collections can be seen imaginatively displayed in the superb exhibition space at the Centrale Montemartini, a former industrial plant near the basilica of San Paolo fuori le Mura (*see p. 491*).

PALAZZO DEI CONSERVATORI

Highlights of the collection include the fragments of the colossal statue of Constantine, the *She-wolf of Rome*, the *Spinario* and the original equestrian statue of Marcus Aurelius. The Picture Gallery (Pinacoteca) is also here.

Courtyard

Here are fragments of a **colossal seated statue of Constantine the Great**, including the head, hand and feet, which were found in the Basilica of Maxentius in the Forum (*see pp. 85–6*) in 1486 and which have been displayed here since then. It was about 12m high (the vault above it was twice that height) and was an acrolith, meaning that the body would have been made in wood (probably covered with bronze) while the extremities were of stone. The forefinger is raised apparently to hold a sceptre. The head, with its staring hooded eyes and hooked nose, is the best-known portrait of the emperor and would have been all the more imposing when it was crowned with a diadem. Despite the huge dimensions, the anatomical details of the arms and feet are carefully portrayed.

Opposite are **reliefs representing the provinces subject to Rome**, which once decorated the interior of the cella of Hadrian's temple in Piazza di Pietra (*see p. 163*): many of these were places visited by the emperor himself. Above is a fragment of the huge **inscription celebrating the conquest of Britain in AD 43**, from an arch erected by Claudius in AD 51 on Via Lata (now the Corso). The emperor is exhalted as the first ruler to have brought the 'barbaric tribes beyond the sea' under Roman dominion. Beneath the portico is a seated statue of a rather portly female divinity given the attributes of the goddess Roma, flanked by two colossal statues of barbarian captives in rare grey marble. All three were acquired by Clement XI in 1720 from the famous Cesi collection of ancient Roman sculpture formed in the 16th century. They had been the centrepiece of the garden statuary outside the Cesi palace in the Borgo district (mostly destroyed to make way for Bernini's colonnade in front of St Peter's).

Stairs and first-floor landing

Stairs lead up to a half-landing where there are **four splendid large reliefs:** the two on the end wall and the one to the right come from a triumphal arch set up to celebrate Marcus Aurelius in 176 after his military victory over the Sarmatian and German tribes. In the first panel the emperor is shown on horseback in the act of conquest, accompanied by Roman soldiers, dispensing clemency to prisoners kneeling at the foot of his horse. The second panel depicts the emperor in his triumphal procession up the Capitoline hill: he is transported in a quadriga with the symbolic figure of Victory above and preceded by a trumpeter. The third panel shows the emperor burning incense in a tripod before sacrificing, while the bull, above the heads of the crowd, looks on, unaware of his fate. The scene takes place in front of the Temple of Capitoline Jupiter (remains of which can be seen in this very museum; *see p. 44*): this is the most detailed representation we have of this famous sanctuary.

The panel on the left wall shows the emperor Hadrian entering Rome, welcomed by allegorical figures representing the senate and the *populus*, beside the goddess Roma.

On the first-floor landing is a **relief from the Arco di Portogallo**, another demolished arch across the Via Lata. The emperor is shown standing on a podium with figures again representing the senate (behind him) and the *populus* (the handsome young man holding out his hand to the emperor). The scene apparently records Hadrian's distribution of charity to the poor children of Rome (represented by the child at the foot of the podium).

Appartamento dei Conservatori

These rooms were decorated in the 16th century and later with scenes of Roman history. They have fine carved ceilings and marble doors, and are adorned with sculptures (*NB: Room numbers refer to the plan overleaf*).

(1) Sala degli Orazi e Curiazi: The room is frescoed with scenes depicting episodes in the early history of Rome, including the battle between the Horatii and the Curiatii (*see p. 524*) by the 17th-century Roman painter Cavaliere d'Arpino, in whose workshop Caravaggio first studied. From the 16th century onwards statues of popes were set up in this room in acknowledgement of papal power in the city. Today just two statues face each other at either end of the room: Urban VIII, a marble studio work begun by **Bernini**; and Urban's successor Innocent X, a bronze of some ten years later by **Alessandro Algardi**. It is interesting to compare the work of these two great rival sculptors.

It was in this room in 1957 that the Treaty of Rome, the foundation of the European Economic Community, was signed by Italy, Belgium, France, West Germany, Luxembourg and Holland. In 2004 the constitution of Europe was ratified here by 25 member states of the European Union.

(2) Sala dei Capitani: This room has colourful frescoes of scenes from Roman history (as recounted by Livy) by Tommaso Laureti, dating from 1594. At this time too statues of contemporary generals (*capitani*) who served the pontifical state, all of them members of Roman patrician families, were installed here, amusingly dressed as ancient Romans. The memorial to Virginio Cesarini has a marble portrait bust made in 1624: scholars recognise the hand of Bernini in the design, but it may have been carved by François Duquesnoy (*see p. 237*). Next to it Carlo Barberini (brother of Pope Urban VIII) is celebrated by a full-length ancient Roman statue restored by Alessandro Algardi (who added the cloak) and completed by Bernini (who supplied the portrait head). Other *capitani*, including Tommaso Rospigliosi with a typical 17th-century hairdo, are by Ercole Ferrata, who succeeded Bernini and Algardi as one of the most influential sculptors in late 17th-century Rome.

(3) Sala dei Trionfi: The frieze, painted in 1569, illustrates a triumphal procession on its way up the Capitoline hill in 167 BC, as described by Plutarch. The most famous of the bronzes presented to the *conservatori* by Sixtus IV in the 15th century are exhibited here. In the middle is the celebrated

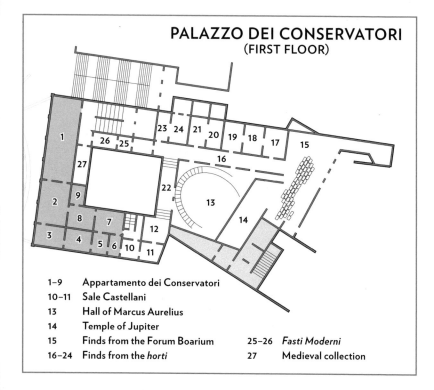

PALAZZO DEI CONSERVATORI
(FIRST FLOOR)

1–9	Appartamento dei Conservatori		
10–11	Sale Castellani		
13	Hall of Marcus Aurelius		
14	Temple of Jupiter		
15	Finds from the Forum Boarium	25–26	*Fasti Moderni*
16–24	Finds from the *horti*	27	Medieval collection

Spinario, a sculpture of a boy (with copper lips) plucking a thorn (*spina*) from his foot. This was for long thought to be a Greek original but it is now dated to around 50 BC or a little later, making it a Roman work based on a Hellenistic model. Recorded in Rome as early as the 11th century, it has probably never been buried underground—unlike so many other statues found in the city—and it was copied in countless small bronzes by Renaissance sculptors. Eight replicas of it exist in marble (and there are at least eleven replicas of its head).

Also here is a superb bronze head, with striking eyes, known as the ***Capitoline Brutus***. Since it shows Etruscan, Greek and Roman influences, its date is still disputed by scholars (4th–1st centuries BC) but it is usually dated to the 4th century as one of the earliest bronze portraits known (the bust was added much later).

A beautiful **bronze vase** bears an inscription recording that it was the gift of King Mithridates VI to a gymnastic association. This dates it to the 1st century BC: it must have been part of the booty from a war in Pontus in northern Asia Minor, when either Sulla or Pompey defeated Mithridates.

There is also an exquisite **statue of a boy** shown as if taking part in a religious ceremony (he would have held a cup for ritual libations in his hand): it dates from the 1st century AD.

The very fine **painting of the battle between Alexander the Great and Darius** is by Pietro da Cortona, on a monumental scale despite its relatively small dimensions (and dominated by one of Pietro's characteristic bright blue skies).

(4) Sala della Lupa: The famous *She-wolf of Rome*, shown baring her teeth as she turns towards us in fear, has been displayed here since at least the 16th century. The wolf is the symbol of Rome because of the story of the city's foundation by Romulus, who was saved from starvation together with his brother Remus by being suckled by a she-wolf. For centuries this was the most famous piece of sculpture in the entire city. It originally stood on the Capitoline Hill and was long considered to be an Etruscan bronze of the late 6th or early 5th century BC, attributed to the school of Vulca, a sculptor from Veio, just outside Rome. Restoration, however, has revealed that it was cast in one piece with the lost wax method, which has caused most scholars to date it to the Middle Ages. The discussion continues and *in situ* the sculpture is still attributed to the 5th century BC. The figures of the twins Romulus and Remus were certainly added c. 1471, and are attributed to Antonio Pollaiolo.

The Roman **mosaic floor** which illustrates a labyrinth was found beneath Via Nazionale. On the walls, in a simple frame designed by Michelangelo, are displayed fragments of the *Fasti Capitolini*, registers of Roman magistrates and of triumphs of the great captains of Rome in the period of 13 BC–AD 12, which are thought originally to have been set up on the inner walls of the Arch of Augustus which once stood in the Roman Forum.

(5) Sala delle Oche: The room takes its name from the two exquisite little **antique bronzes of 'geese'** (more probably ducks) displayed here on either side of a bust of Isis. The bronze **head of Michelangelo** is the most famous portrait of the great artist by his close friend Daniele da Volterra who, being with him when he died in Rome (*see p. 136*), made this from his death mask (a number of other versions of it exist; the marble bust was added later). The marble **head of Medusa** is a little-known work by Bernini showing the Greek monster with her terrible eyes mercifully closed.

(6) Sala delle Aquile: The '*aquile*' are two Roman eagles on cipollino columns. Also here is a Roman sculpture of Diana of Ephesus.

(7) Sala degli Arazzi: This room is decorated with tapestries made in Rome, one of them based on the painting of Romulus and Remus by Rubens in the Pinacoteca upstairs.

(8) Sala di Annibale: Here are the earliest frescoes in the palace, which date from the first years of the 16th century: they illustrate the Punic Wars, with Hannibal firmly seated on his elephant. The room also boasts the oldest ceiling in the palace (1519).

(9) Cappella: Decorated with frescoes and stuccoes in 1578. On the left wall is a *Madonna and Child with Angels*, attributed to the late 15th-century artist Andrea d'Assisi, L'Ingegno.

The Sale Castellani

Returning to Room 6, you enter the two Sale Castellani **(10–11)**, named after Augusto Castellani, the first director of these museums (and also a famous jeweller; *see p. 330*). Here are displayed part of his huge collection of finds made in excavations in the 1860s in southern Etruria and Lazio and which he donated to the museum. The ceramics dating from the 8th–4th centuries BC are particularly fine, including many Attic vases as well as bucchero and impasto Etruscan pottery. There are also bronze and silver artefacts from tombs. In the last room, the krater showing Odysseus and the Cyclops and a naval battle is signed by Aristonothos, a Greek potter who came to work in Cerveteri in the early 7th century BC. There is also a small terracotta statue of a seated dignitary, likewise from Cerveteri.

Room 12 has a bronze horse which dates from the 5th century BC, a fragment of the torso of a bull, also in bronze, and three bas-reliefs of animals in grey tufa which were made in the 6th century BC to decorate a tomb in Tolfa. The bronze *tensa*, a triumphal chariot which carried the images of the gods at the opening of the Circensian Games, was arbitrarily restored by Castellani.

The Hall of Marcus Aurelius

This splendid hall **(13)**, in a glass-roofed courtyard, was designed in the 1990s by Carlo Aymonino to provide an exhibition space for the **equestrian statue of Marcus Aurelius**, brought under cover from the piazza outside after its restoration. This magnificent colossal gilded bronze is a masterpiece of Roman art, thought to date from the latter part of Marcus Aurelius' reign (AD 161–80), or possibly from the year of his death; although we know there were some 22 equestrian statues in ancient Rome, this is the only one which survives. The sculpture of the horse and rider appears time and again in medieval representations of the city, and it is first documented in the 10th century when it was believed to represent the Christian emperor Constantine the Great (this is often given as the reason why it was preserved and not melted down for its metal). It is thought to have stood on the Lateran hill as early as 782 and it was greatly admired throughout the Middle Ages. On a visit to Rome in 1873 Henry James commented, 'I doubt if any statue of King or captain in the public places of the world has more to commend it to the general heart'.

The **colossal bronze head** is thought to be a portrait of Constantine (showing him as an older man than his portrait in the courtyard below), and the hand, foot and globe probably came from the same statue. The provenance of the head is unrecorded, although we know it was outside the Lateran Palace in 1200. It has recently been suggested that it is a portrait of Constantinius II (337–61).

Also displayed here is a sculpture of a lion attacking a horse, a Hellenistic work restored by a little-known pupil of Michelangelo, Ruggero Bascapè who, in 1594, added the head, hooves and tail of the horse and the back legs of the lion.

(14) The Temple of Jupiter: Below the hall can be seen the huge foundations of the Temple of Capitoline Jupiter, dedicated to the three gods known as

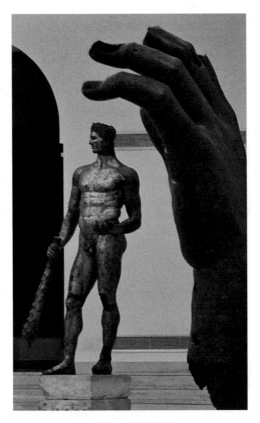

MUSEI CAPITOLINI
Gilded bronze statue of Hercules (2nd century BC) from his temple in the Forum Boarium,
and a colossal bronze hand, probably of Constantine.

the Capitoline Triad: Jupiter, Juno and Minerva. It was begun in the 6th century BC by Tarquinius Priscus and continued by his son Tarquinius Superbus, but not dedicated until 509 BC. This was the most venerated temple in Rome, since 'the best and greatest of all Jupiters' was regarded as the city's special protector. It became the symbol of Rome and replicas were built all over the Empire.

It was here that the investiture of consuls took place and where the triumphal procession awarded to victorious generals terminated. The largest temple known of this period (over 60m long and almost as wide, on a very high podium), it was destroyed by fire in 83 BC during the civil wars, rebuilt by Sulla, destroyed again in AD 69, rebuilt by Vespasian and again by Domitian, and was still standing in the 6th century. A model shows its vast scale, with just the tiny parts of it which survive here highlighted.

The colossal **cult statue of Hercules** in brightly gilded bronze was found in the time of Sixtus IV near the circular temple of Hercules Victor (*see p. 248*). It is derived from a Greek bronze.

(15) Finds from the Forum Boarium (Rome under the Tarquin kings):

Excavations in the 20th century in the area of the Forum Boarium at the foot of this hill towards the Tiber brought to light very interesting artefacts dating from the Bronze Age. Traces of hut dwellings of the 9th–8th centuries BC, similar to those on the Palatine, were found and the archaeological evidence has thrown new light on the origins of Rome and the presence of the Etruscans here in the 7th and 6th centuries BC.

Two Archaic temples (mid-6th century BC), dedicated to Fortuna and Mater Matuta and traditionally thought to have been founded by Servius Tullius, rested on an artificial mound in which were found Bronze and Iron Age shards and imported Greek pottery of the 8th century BC. Finds from the temple to Mater Matuta include ex-votos and fragments of terracotta sculpture from the pediment which has been reconstructed here. An exquisite tiny ivory plaque in the form of a lion dates from 616–578 BC and bears the oldest Etruscan inscription ever found in Rome.

There are also finds from the Bronze and Iron Age periods made during excavations for the construction of this hall, including pottery and artefacts from tombs.

Sculpture from the *horti* of ancient Rome

The two galleries overlooking the Hall of Marcus Aurelius (16 and 22) and the rooms off them (17–21 and 23–24) exhibit some magnificent pieces of sculpture found in the 19th century in the so-called *horti*, which were the gardens of grand villas built on the hills of Rome, and especially the Esquiline, and owned by the wealthiest citizens and members of the Imperial families.

(16) First Gallery: Here are two handsome large marble kraters, probably used as basins for garden fountains. One has Dionysiac scenes and the other a relief of the marriage of Paris and Helen.

Rooms 17–19: These rooms contain an excellent display of **finds from the Gardens of Maecenas** on the Esquiline hill, unearthed in 1874, although only one room of Maecenas' villa itself was discovered (the so-called Auditorium; *see p. 557*). In Room 17 is *Hercules in*

Combat, from an original by Lysippus; a colossal statue of Demeter; and a stele with a female figure in low relief. In Room 18 is the so-called *Auriga* or charioteer, a copy of a 5th-century original. The naked youth was probably about to climb into a chariot drawn by two horses. The seated dog is made of rare green Egyptian marble. There is also a group of herms and statues of Muses. In the last room (19) the rhyton, once used as a fountain, is an exquisite neo-Attic work signed by Pontius. The beautiful Head of an Amazon is a copy of a famous bronze by Polyclitus (*see p. 453*). The lovely *Dancing Maenad*, in low relief, is from an original by Callimachus. The statue of the flayed Marsyas is in pavonazzetto. Also here is a mosaic in miniature tesserae.

Rooms 20–21: These next two rooms exhibit **finds from the Taurani and Vettiani gardens**. In Room 20 the marble cow was probably a copy of a bronze by Myron made for the Athens Acropolis and brought to Rome at the time of Vespasian, and also here are reliefs of landscapes. Room 21 exhibits a colossal headless statue of Hygieia which was made in the late Republic period modelled on a 4th-century original. The huge sarcophagus from Vicovaro shows a wild boar hunt (the faces of the defunct couple shown lying on the lid were never completed).

(22) Second Gallery: Overlooking the Hall of Marcus Aurelius, this room exhibits some very fine **statues from the Lamiani Gardens** on the Esquiline hill (near the present Piazza Vittorio Emanuele), found in 1874. These include the torso of the reclining Dionysus, as well as the head of a centaur and the statue of an athlete (a copy of a work by Polyclitus), which is now headless and has only one leg. The very well preserved half-length portrait of Commodus shows the vain emperor in the guise of Hercules: a lion-skin bonnet encircles his curly hair and is tied at his chest, and he holds a club

and the apples of the Hesperides. The symbolism continues in the seemingly fragile carvings below, the orb and the cornucopia represent the Empire, and the shield and kneeling Amazons (only one of which survives) the Conquered. This must have been a public monument exalting the immortality of the emperor, and was made even more elaborate by the addition of two tritons in adoration on either side (remains of which are also exhibited). Despite the fact that the emperor appears to us today as rather ludicrous and anything but 'Classical', this work is recognised as a masterpiece of marble carving.

The ***Esquiline Venus***, the figure of a beautiful young girl probably connected with the cult of Isis, is an eclectic work dating from the 1st century BC. Although the arms are missing, we know that the girl was depicted tying up her hair before taking a swim. Nearby are two fine female statues (probably priestesses or muses), similar in style and date to the Venus.

Rooms 23 and 24: More **works from the Lamiani Gardens**. The first room has Greek originals: two funerary stelae (one with the relief of a young girl holding a dove) and a (very damaged) group of two young girls playing piggy-back. The second has magnificent decorative fragments from a villa, including part of its alabaster floor and inlaid coloured marble, gilded bronze, and beautiful gems which used to decorate its walls.

The *Fasti Moderni* and medieval works

Rooms 25 and 26, named after the *Fasti Moderni*, the lists on the walls of the chief magistrates of Rome since 1640, contain two Roman statues of athletes and a sarcophagus with Dionysiac scenes. They lead back to the first-floor landing of the main stairs outside the Sala degli Orazi e Curiazi and a small room (**27**) which contains **medieval works**. The seated statue of Charles of Anjou is by Arnolfo di Cambio (1275/77) and was originally in Palazzo Senatorio on this hill. Charles, King of Sicily, took power in Rome over the papacy. Arnolfo, a Florentine, produced numerous beautiful sculptural monuments for churches in Rome in the last quarter of the 13th century, aided by several assistants. As the Classical lines of this statue show, he was clearly influenced by ancient Roman sculpture, as well as by contemporary French masters.

Also here is a sculptural fragment from the church of the Aracoeli which was made by the Cosmati in the 12th century and incorporates an ancient Roman circular marble frieze. The bronze globe dating from the 1st century AD once decorated the obelisk in the piazza outside St Peter's.

The huge standard of St George, in red silk and leather, dates from around 1300 and was probably commissioned by Jacopo Caetani Stefaneschi, cardinal of San Giorgio in Velabro. It is said to be the oldest known 'flag' of its kind.

Second-floor landing

Another relief from the Arco di Portogallo (*see p. 159*) shows the ***Apotheosis of Sabina***. The solemn figure of Hadrian sits below his wife Sabina (who predeceased him in 136 or 137), who is being borne aloft by an allegorical female figure with huge, beautifully-carved wings, carrying a torch. The two splendid marble intarsia panels of a **bull attacked by a tigress** were found on the Esquiline hill. They are virtually all that remains of a basilica known to have been built there in the 4th century AD by a city prefect named Junius Bassus. It had its walls entirely decorated with opus sectile. It is interesting to note that the tradition of producing mosaics in marble and precious stones continued in Rome throughout the Middle Ages, and that when these panels were discovered in the 15th century, Roman artists came to emulate them. The taste for precious marble intarsia led to the founding of the famous workshop of the *pietre dure* in Florence. Junius Bassus' exceptionally fine sarcophagus is in the Treasury of St Peter's (*see p. 434*). More opus sectile panels can be seen in Rome in the Museo Nazionale Romano in Palazzo Massimo (*see p. 326*) and in the Museo Nazionale dell'Alto Medioevo in EUR (*see p. 504*).

Pinacoteca Capitolina

The picture gallery (on the second floor) is particularly important for its 16th–18th-century Italian and foreign paintings. The Emilian School, with Ferrara, is well represented, but its most precious possessions are two paintings by Caravaggio. The collection was founded in 1749 by Benedict XIV with the help of his Secretary of State Cardinal Silvio Valenti Gonzaga, a famous collector (his portrait hangs in the last room). They acquired the collections of Prince Gilberto Pio of Savoy and Cardinal Sacchetti. It was later enriched by the Cini bequest, and some interesting 14th–15th-century paintings from the Sterbini collection.

Since the labelling is good, only a few masterpieces have been mentioned here.

Room II: An *Annunciation*, by Garofalo, the leading painter in Ferrara in the early 16th century, is displayed here.

Room III: Works by the Venetian school include a *Portrait of a Lady as St Margaret* by Girolamo Savoldo, and others by more famous painters of the early 16th century: Palma Vecchio (*Woman Taken in Adultery*), Veronese (*Rape of Europa*) and Titian (*Baptism of Christ*, an early work).

Room VI: Works by the Bolognese school, including the Carracci (the *Head of a Boy* is a very fine early work by Ludovico) and Guido Reni (*St Sebastian*, *Cleopatra* and *Anima Beata*).

Room VII: Five works by Guercino including the huge canvas of *St Petronilla* which was formerly in St Peter's. The *Gipsy Fortune-teller* is one of the most delightful early works by **Caravaggio** (another version of it is in the Louvre). It shows the artist's typical mastery of light, and the clothes and head-dresses are superbly painted (in a style which recalls Venetian masters such as Giorgione and Titian). The expressions of the two young protagonists are a perfect mixture of timidity, affection and a sense of fun. The soldier is evidently the same model as the man who stood for one of the most prominent figures in the *Calling of St Matthew* in the church of San Luigi dei Francesi (*see p. 206*). Beside this is displayed one of a number of paintings by Caravaggio of *St John the Baptist* (a replica of which is in the Galleria Doria Pamphilj). Dating from 1602, the handsome young saint is portrayed in a pose which echoes one of Michelangelo's

ignudi on the Sistine Chapel ceiling and the iconography is totally innovative—with a mountain sheep complete with horns instead of the traditional meek lamb. On the opposite wall the painting of *Romulus and Remus Fed by the She-wolf* by Rubens was finished by pupils.

Room VIII (used for lectures): The room is named after **Pietro da Cortona** (*see p. 341*), represented here by a number of fine works (including the *Rape of the Sabines*).

Room IX (Galleria Cini): This room (with a view down into the Hall of Marcus Aurelius) contains part of the bequest of Count Giuseppe Cini (1881), including some fine ceramics. On the walls are mid-17th-century Flemish tapestries.

At the end of the room, beyond the columns and near the exit, are some beautiful paintings: portraits of the engravers Pieter de Jode, father and son, and of the painters Luke and Cornelius de Wael, by Anthony van Dyck. The latter work (1627) was of great importance in the development of portraiture in painting and sculpture. There is also a self-portrait by Federico Zuccari.

The attribution of the very fine *Portrait of a Man* has long puzzled art historians: some believe it to be a self-portrait by Velázquez; others demote it to an anonymous work by a 17th-century Roman artist. Beside it is displayed a small *Portrait of a Young Man* (c. 1500) traditionally attributed to Giovanni Bellini (but now believed to be by Giovanni Buonconsiglio). By the exit is a portrait of the portly Cardinal Valenti Gonzaga dressed in gorgeous clothes, by Pierre Subleyras.

MUSEI CAPITOLINI: EPIGRAPH COLLECTION
Third-century relief of footprints, a votive offering from a certain Jovinus,
for a safe journey out and a safe return home.

PALAZZO CAFFARELLI-CLEMENTINO

The upper floor of this building is connected to Palazzo dei Conservatori and can be reached either from a back staircase off the courtyard or from near the Hall of Marcus Aurelius. The roof terrace beside the café has a wonderful view. The **Medagliere**, a rich collection of Roman, medieval and modern coins and medals founded in 1872 by the jeweller Augusto Castellani (*see p. 330*), is displayed here, as well as jewels inspired by Hellenistic works made by his firm, and polychrome terracotta fragments from the pediment of a temple dating from the 2nd century BC.

THE EPIGRAPH COLLECTION AND TABULARIUM

From the portico of Palazzo dei Conservatori, stairs lead down to the tunnel beneath the piazza which connects Palazzo dei Conservatori and Palazzo Nuovo and which exhibits the **collection of epigraphs**. The display is introduced by the touchingly simple funerary stele of a certain Habib from Palmyra in the province of Syria, who died in Rome aged 32. It was set up on the Via Appia in the 2nd century AD by his brother, who had the inscription carved in both Latin and the Palmyrene language. The display in the tunnel proper is excellent (with labelling also in English), consisting of interesting ancient inscriptions (all of them transcribed) grouped according to subject matter: the languages of the Empire; burial rites; religion; legal texts; professions and trades; board games; roads and aqueducts; armies. They tell a fascinating story of Roman life.

Towards the end of the corridor a flight of steps on the right leads up to the impressive remains of the **Temple of Veiovis**, beneath Palazzo Senatorio. The temple was first erected in 192 BC and then rebuilt by Sulla after a fire in the 1st century BC. The pronaos is orientated towards the west and the podium and cella are well preserved. Also here is the colossal marble cult statue of the unknown god Veiovis (1st century AD, after a 5th-century BC type), found in the cella in 1939. In the passageway is displayed one of the most important epigraphs in the collection: the plinth of a statue dedicated to Hadrian by the *vicomagistri*, who were officials in charge of five of the regions of Rome.

The mighty external wall of the **Tabularium**, with its magnificent vaults, may be seen on two sides of the temple: only a small gap was left between it and the temple. The Tabularium was the depository of the Roman state archives. It had two storeys, built on a rectangular plan, and a central court. We know that it was erected in 78 BC: since an inscription stone of this date has survived. Part of the building was used from the Middle Ages onwards as a prison. In the corridor beyond are two large fragments of the friezes from the temples of Concord and of Vespasian, whose ruins are directly below in the Roman Forum. Today there is a magnificent view of the Forum through the arches of the Tabularium, constructed with great blocks of porous tufa built into the unhewn rock. If you lean out of the arched openings overlooking the Forum you can see the engaged columns which frame the arches (some of them strengthened by metal bands): this is the earliest surviving example of an applied architectural order which has no structural function.

PALAZZO NUOVO

Palazzo Nuovo contains a wonderful collection of ancient Roman sculpture begun by the extremely wealthy Clement XII (who at the same time was commissioning the Trevi Fountain) and added to by later popes. It was opened to the public during Clement's pontificate and still retains its old-fashioned, intimate aesthetic arrangement. The hospitable rooms are rarely overcrowded and are especially inviting in the evening when they are illuminated solely by magnificent chandeliers. You can get face to face with portrait busts of famous Romans, displayed in serried ranks on marble shelves. The memorable atmosphere is very special—quite different from the crowded Vatican Museums or the chilly displays of the state collection of Roman sculpture in Palazzo Massimo alle Terme.

In the portico at the foot of the stairs is a **colossal statue of Mars**, with fine bas-reliefs on the cuirass, dating from the 1st century AD. It was found in the 16th century in the Imperial Fora, so it is thought that it stood outside the Temple of Mars Ultor.

First floor

(1) Galleria: The statues, busts and inscriptions are still displayed as they were in the 18th century. At the top of the stairs a decorative krater of the 1st century AD rests on a very fine well-head from Hadrian's Villa at Tivoli, with archaistic decoration representing the procession of the twelve Dii Consentes, the most important of the Roman deities (*see p. 78*). When the colossal statue of Hercules was restored by Alessandro Algardi, he altered it (perhaps unintentionally) to show the hero slaying the Hydra instead of capturing the Hind. The *Eros* is a good copy of a celebrated Greek work by Lysippus (*see p. 453*). Another famous Greek masterpiece, the *Discobolos* of Myron (*also see p. 453*), clearly inspired the *Discus Thrower*—but only the torso is original; the rest is a late 17th-century restoration, when the statue was altered

PALAZZO NUOVO
(FIRST FLOOR)

I   Galleria
II   Sala delle Colombe
III Gabinetto della Venere
IV Sala degli Imperatori
V   Sala dei Filosofi
VI Salone
VII Sala del Fauno
VIII Sala del Gladiatore

to represent a fighting gladiator. Outside Room II is a statue of *Leda with the Swan*, a replica of a work attributed to Timotheos, another Greek master (4th century BC). Also here is a statue of a drunken old woman, apparently seated on the floor clutching a wine flask, typical of Hellenistic realist sculpture, and for long one of the most famous pieces in the museum. Near the door into Room VI, displayed opposite each other, are two colossal heads of female divinities; the one of Aphrodite is perhaps a Hellenistic original.

(II) Sala delle Colombe: Named after the exquisite small mosaic of four doves at a fountain, found in Hadrian's villa at Tivoli and inspired by a work of the famous mosaicist Sosus, who was at work in Pergamon in the 2nd century BC, when it was one of the most beautiful

of all Greek cities and had a flourishing school of sculptors. The other mosaic here, which depicts two striking theatrical masks, is probably of the same date. In a showcase below the windows is the *Tabula Iliaca*, a fragment of a plaque with miniature reliefs illustrating Homer's *Iliad* (1st century AD).

In the centre of the room is a charming statue of a young girl protecting a dove, a Roman copy of a Hellenistic work of the 2nd century BC (the snake is a later restoration). This is one of the most engaging statues in the museum.

Some 80 Roman busts (well labelled) decorate the walls. Displayed on a child's sarcophagus are two heads of infants, a rarity in Roman portraiture.

(III) Gabinetto della Venere: The **Capitoline Venus** turned up in the 17th century in a house near San Vitale and was purchased by Benedict XIV in 1752. But it had been mentioned for centuries as one of the most celebrated statues in the city. Superbly modelled in Parian marble and extremely well preserved, it is a Roman replica of a Hellenistic original. It is thought to be derived from the *Aphrodite* made by the great sculptor Praxiteles for a temple at Cnidos in Asia Minor, which became one of the most famous statues of antiquity and was reproduced in numerous replicas. The goddess is shown having just removed her clothes before taking a purifying bath and, taken by surprise, she attempts to cover her nudity with her hands. It is thought to be the statue admired by Master Gregory in the late 12th or early 13th century when it was probably on the Quirinal hill: in his *De mirabilibus urbis Romae* he describes how he went back to see her no fewer than three times during his stay, thoroughly seduced by her modesty. In 1835 a much later visitor to Rome, the French painter Ingres, complained that he was not admitted to the Capitoline Museum to see the statue since the prudish pope had locked her away because of her nudity; he tells us that Gregory XVI had also attached 'enormous vine leaves' to other sculptures on public display.

(IV) Sala degli Imperatori: Here is a splendid display of Roman Imperial busts, interesting as portraits of some of the most famous figures of Roman history. They are arranged chronologically, starting with a bust dated between 40 and 30 BC on the top shelf in the far corner by the door into Room V. Two excellent portraits of Augustus (one showing him wearing a wreath of myrtle) flank a portrait of his very plain wife Livia. In the next corner is a portrait of his granddaughter Agrippina the Elder. This beautiful lady suffered a tragic fate: she married Germanicus, a successful and charismatic commander who died young in Antioch. Their son, Caligula, was to succeed Tiberius as emperor, but on the death of Germanicus, Tiberius banished Agrippina and she starved to death.

Displayed on a pedestal is Marcus Aurelius as a handsome adolescent boy, long before he became emperor; the bust on the top shelf on the opposite wall (third from the right) shows him at least 30 years later as a much older man, bearded and already worn down by the cares of state. It is interesting to note that it was only with Marcus Aurelius that Roman portraiture began to depict psychological concerns in the faces of

its leaders. This is well illustrated on the shelf below, in the very fine portrait of the emperor Decius (who adopted 'Trajan' as his first name), who ruled for just three years from 249 to 251 but apparently long enough to give him the worried expression with which he is shown here. Displayed on a pedestal in front of the window is an unknown lady of the late Flavian period (late 1st century), with a splendid head-dress—one of the most beautiful of all the portrait busts in the museum. In the centre is a gracious seated figure of Helen, mother of Constantine, inspired by a Greek statue by Pheidias. Her portrait portrays her forceful character.

(V) Sala dei Filosofi: Another splendid display of busts, this time of Greek philosophers and poets, although only some of them are securely identified. On the left wall, the third and fourth busts on the top shelf are portraits of the famously ugly Socrates: he has a turned-up nose and protruding eyes. In the row below, Homer is shown as a blind bard. On the opposite wall, on the lower shelf is Pythagoras, the famous mathematician, shown with his characteristic cap, next to three portraits sometimes identified as Homer or the poet Hesiod, who was probably Homer's near contemporary. On the shelf above are two portraits thought to show the playwright Euripides, and two of an old man with his mouth slightly open, sometimes identified as Democritus, famous for his great wisdom, who is known to have died at a ripe old age. In the corner opposite the windows is a fine large bust of Cicero, in his toga. The double portrait portrays the Athenian philosopher Epicurus with his pupil Metrodorus.

ROMAN STATUES AND PORTRAITURE

Roman cities were filled with statues to an extent which is unimaginable today. One estimate is that Rome had some two million at the height of its glory. They would be found in temples, lining the fora, gracing public buildings, in gardens, and not least in private collections. For the cultured elite a favourite theme was busts of Greek poets and philosophers—many of the finest survivors are gathered in the Sala dei Filosofi in Palazzo Nuovo. For Roman connoisseurs the most prestigious statues were Greek from the Classical period (480–323 BC), many of which were looted during the Roman conquest of Greece. If original statues were not available, copies would be made. Hadrian reconstructed whole temples and porticoes from his favourite monuments of the Greek world in his villa at Tivoli.

The original media were bronze and marble (and occasionally gold or silver), although almost all the bronze statues have vanished. They were easier to carry off than marble, and also vulnerable to being melted down for other uses. In Rome the fine equestrian statue of Marcus Aurelius (*see p. 44*) shows the quality of what has been lost. Many marble statues are in fact copies of bronze originals—often a tell-tale strut or support records the transfer to the less tensile material. The problem for art historians is that these statues are very difficult to date. Most of the best-known statues in the Roman collections have been argued over for centuries. For instance, the famous

Developments in portraiture from the time of Caesar to the 4th century: Caesar (1) was first and foremost a conqueror and a tough statesman. Augustus (2) was concerned with images which could be recognised throughout the Empire and so his model is Greek Classicism. By the end of the 1st century the Flavian emperors, anxious to restore contact with the people after the megalomanic excesses of Nero, show themselves as down-to-earth men (the portrait here is of Vespasian; 3). Hadrian (4) sets a new tone by wearing a beard, as if he were a philosopher rather than emperor. All the emperors of the Antonine era followed this trend (also shown here is Lucius Verus; 5). In the 3rd century the pressures began to build and the emperors' faces show the challenges they faced from constant barbarian attack and political turmoil: Caracalla (6) is always shown looking tense and irascible. By the 4th century a further development has taken place. The Empire is now calmer but the emperors have removed themselves from the people. The colossal statue of Constantine (7) in the courtyard of Palazzo dei Conservatori represents the return to idealism: the emperor now transcends human life. We are on the way to the distanced and semi-divine rulers of the Byzantine world.

1   2   3   4   5   6   7

Clockwise from top left: (1) The *nodus* hairstyle, popular in the Republican and Augustan periods; (2) Elaborate hairdo of the Flavian age, with tight curls piled high in front; (3) A matron of the Antonine period with elaborate coiled braids and carefully arranged curls escaping at the front; (4) The Severan hairstyle of Julia Domna, wife of Septimius Severus. It was much imitated in Victorian times.

Laocoön in the Vatican (*see p. 454*) has been dated as early as the 4th century BC and as late as the 1st century AD. Is it a Greek original or a Roman original? A direct Roman copy of a Greek original or a Roman adaptation of a Greek original? Recently one scholar has even suggested it might be a deliberate forgery made by Michelangelo. The complexity of these problems can be shown in the famous Prima Porta statue of Augustus, also in the Vatican (*see p. 451*). It appears to be a marble copy of a bronze original which some suggest may have stood in a temple to Athena in Pergamon (a statue base which fits has been discovered there). Although the original was contemporary with the copy (just after 20 BC), Augustus affects the pose and demeanour of a Greek Classical hero of the 5th century BC, while his breastplate is designed to show off his victory over the Parthians as bringing peace and prosperity to the Empire. Other insignia emphasise his divine descent, via Julius Caesar, from the goddess Venus. The whole is a culmination of his successful rule as the blessed of the gods.

Within this plethora of styles and influences, it is possible to pick out a distinctive Roman art, typically expressed in a 'warts and all' portrait bust. Even here the influences are many. The Etruscans contributed a fine tradition of carefully observed bronzes, while funerary reliefs with the faces of the dead can be traced back to other pre-Roman cultures. The opulent Greek cities of southern Italy, conquered by the Romans in the 3rd century BC, were another influence, particularly in sculpture of the Hellenistic period (after 323 BC) when there was a concentration on themes of everyday life. All this provides a model for realism typical of Roman art but which does not in itself explain the popularity of the portrait bust. It may have originated with the practice of taking death masks of aristocratic Romans which were then made into busts to be carried in the family's funeral processions (see the statue of a man carrying the portrait busts of his ancestors in the Montemartini display; *p. 492*). Many of these busts were, of course, of older men, but it is clear too that the Romans preferred to show themselves off as elder statesmen, full of worldly experience. A magnificent early example, especially rare because it is in bronze, is the bust known as 'Brutus' (*see p. 42*) in the Palazzo dei Conservatori, perhaps (though by no means certainly) a portrait of Junius Brutus, the first Roman consul.   C.F.

(VI) Salone: The room was sumptuously decorated in the late 17th and early 18th centuries to display more very fine sculpture. Arranged in the centre are pieces in dark marble: the figure in green basalt shows Hercules as an infant: dating from the 3rd century AD, its huge dimensions make this an ugly piece, particularly because of the oddity of portraying a child as a colossus. Much more graceful, and beautifully proportioned, are the **pair of Centaurs**, which were found in Hadrian's villa at Tivoli, and are signed by Aristeas and Papias from Asia Minor, known to have worked as copyists of Greek masterpieces and who may have come to work in Rome during Hadrian's reign. The statues around the walls include (right of the far window) *Apollo*, a Roman copy of an Archaic Greek work, the stylisation of which reveals its early date. Very different in spirit is the frightened old woman (on the opposite wall), an extremely expressive work from the Hellenistic period, some two centuries later. It was probably part of a statuary group. The huntsman holding up a dead hare is an example of how Roman sculptors often mixed styles—the body is from the late Archaic period; the head is a portrait from the 3rd century AD.

The *Wounded Amazon* (right of the door out to the Galleria) is signed by the copyist Sosicles: her wound is only just suggested, close to her left hand. There are a number of other statues in Rome of wounded Amazons, derived from 5th-century originals (*see p. 453*). These hefty ladies, the survivors of a famous battle with the Greeks, lived in a distant country and had the habit of killing their male offspring. Their legend has been the subject of numerous works of art over the centuries, because their warlike nature contrasted with the stereotype of the woman who sat at home meekly spinning wool.

(VII) Sala del Fauno: The room is named after the delightful Imperial-era statue of the *Laughing Silenus*, in red marble, derived from a Hellenistic bronze, displayed in the centre. The room was decorated in the 18th century with Roman brick stamps and inscriptions. The bronze plaque known as the *Lex Vespasiani* has the end of a decree by which the Roman people and Senate conferred certain powers on the emperor Vespasian. Although only fragmentary, it is of great importance to historians, who have attempted through this document to determine whether by this law the emperor was given new sovereign powers, or whether this merely consolidated his position by reference to his eight predecessors. The two statues of young boys displayed here show one with a goose and the other with a mask (both copies of Hellenistic works).

(VIII) Sala del Gladiatore: The *Dying Gaul*, an exquisitely modelled figure of a moustached Celtic warrior who sits mortally wounded on the ground, dominates this room. It was discovered in 1622 near the Villa Ludovisi and is a copy from the Roman period of one of the bronze statues dedicated at Pergamon by Attalus I in commemoration of his victories over the Galatians (239 BC). It was beautifully restored in 1986 when the position of the right arm, altered in a 17th-century restoration, was corrected.

BYRON AND THE DYING GAUL

The *Dying Gaul* became particularly famous in the 19th century when it was thought to represent a victim of the contests in the Colosseum. Byron clearly took it to be such when he immortalised it in his *Childe Harold*:

> *I see before me the Gladiator lie:*
> *He leans upon his hand—his manly brow*
> *Consents to death, but conquers agony,*
> *And his drooped head sinks gradually low—*
> *And through his side the last drops, ebbing slow*
> *From the red gash, fall heavy, one by one,*
> *Like the first of a thunder-shower; and now*
> *The arena swims around him—he is gone,*
> *Ere ceased the inhuman shout which hailed the wretch who won.*
>
> *He heard it, but he heeded not—his eyes*
> *Were with his heart, and that was far away;*
> *He recked not of the life he lost nor prize,*
> *But where his rude hut by the Danube lay,*
> *There were his young barbarians all at play,*
> *There was their Dacian mother—he, their sire,*
> *Butchered to make a Roman holiday—*
> *All this rushed with his blood—Shall he expire*
> *And unavenged?—Arise! ye Goths, and glut your ire!*

The statue (between the windows) of the **Resting Satyr** shows a handsome and confident youth languishing against a tree trunk, a good replica of a beautifully composed original by Praxiteles, found in Hadrian's villa. It seems this was one of the Greek statues most admired by the Romans since some 70 copies of it are known. This is the 'Marble Faun' of Nathaniel Hawthorne's novel, the entire opening chapter of which takes place in this room, which today, some 150 years later, has the same statues 'still shining in the undiminished majesty and beauty of their ideal life'. Hawthorne goes on to give a detailed description of the Satyr and concludes: 'The whole statue...conveys the idea of an amiable and sensual creature, easy, mirthful, apt for jollity, yet not incapable of being touched by pathos.'

The other statues include another Amazon (much restored), and a charming group of **Eros and Psyche** embracing, a Hellenistic work. The statue of a nude youth glancing down as he steps forward, which is supposed to represent Hermes, was one of the earliest pieces to be displayed in this museum, acquired from the important collection of Cardinal Albani (*see p. 39*). It seems that Hadrian commissioned the sculptor to copy a 4th-century Greek work but to give it the features of his young lover Antinous (*see p. 554*).

Ground floor

The huge statue of a flaccid river-god (probably 2nd century AD) in the courtyard was moved in 1596 by Giacomo della Porta from the foot of the Capitoline Hill, where it had lain since the days of the Empire, and incorporated in the fountain here. It has always been affectionately known as '**Marforio**': its name is thought to be derived from *Martis forum*, since the statue came from the Forum of Augustus, dedicated to Mars. This was one of Rome's 'talking' statues, used for the display of satirical comments and epigrams. Marforio 'conversed' with another statue called Madama Lucrezia, still at the bottom of the hill (*see p. 143*).

Off the courtyard is a room which exhibits **Egyptian sculpture**, most of it from the Temple of Isis in the Campus Martius (*see p. 181*). At the entrance are two monumental columns in grey granite from the temple with reliefs of priests and musicians. Inside are a crocodile and sphinx in pink granite and a pair of grey granite monkeys. The sphinx in basanite shows the pharaoh Ahmose II.

Looking onto the courtyard from the atrium is a colossal statue of Minerva, a copy of a 5th-century Greek original. Beyond is Faustina, wife of Antoninus Pius, represented as the goddess Ceres (note the bas-relief beneath of a sow feeding her young), and at the end is a statue of Hadrian as *pontifex maximus*, in a toga which also covers his head.

A WALK AROUND THE HILLTOP

On the right of Palazzo Senatorio, take the very short Via del Campidoglio in order to see the splendid **view of the entire Roman Forum**, with the Colosseum in the background (and the Palatine hill on the right). From here Via del Monte Tarpeo goes uphill to a pine tree beside a former entrance to the Forum (*unfortunately today kept* *locked*) down the old Clivus Capitolinus, the Roman road which connected the Forum and Capitoline hill. The modern road then continues uphill to reach the delightful quiet **Via del Tempio di Giove** where, enclosed by a modern wall and very much below the level of the road, are the remains of the eastern corner of the façade of the Temple of Capitoline Jupiter (the rest of the foundations of the temple can now be seen inside the museums; *see p. 44*). The gardens here have sadly been closed for many years: the precipice below is thought to be the Tarpeian Rock (although it has also been suggested that this was on the north side of the hill).

THE TARPEIAN ROCK AND THE SABINE WOMEN

It seems that the entire Capitoline hill was once known as the 'Rupe Tarpea', and Milton, in *Paradise Regained*, referred to it thus:

The Tarpeian rock, the citadel
of great and glorious Rome, queen of the earth...

Legend relates that in the very earliest days of Rome, the city's founders, anxious to increase the population, invited the neighbouring Sabines to a party telling them to bring with them their daughters and sisters, and while the male guests were intent on enjoying games organised for their benefit, the women were 'raped' and locked up on the Capitoline hill. But the key of the fortress was unwisely entrusted to Tarpeia, who betrayed Rome by opening the doors to the Sabine men. However, the Sabines nobly disapproved of her traitorous behaviour and instead of being grateful, they promptly killed her. Ever afterwards, during the days of ancient Rome, traitors who were condemned to death were apparently flung from this rock. Its notorious fame has endured to this day in the imagination of visitors, even though so little is known about it, and the place tends to be ignored by modern scholars. Over the centuries it was often mentioned by poets, and the 'Rape of the Sabines' became a favourite subject for painters and sculptors in Europe from the 16th century onwards.

Via del Tempio di Giove continues past a little 19th-century temple down to the **gardens of Monte Caprino** on the edge of the hill (*steps, open 6–dusk, lead down to the bottom*). The name comes from the word for goat, since goats were allowed to graze all over the hill up until the 15th century, and the hill itself was often called Monte Caprino. Via di Villa Caffarelli continues right under an arch to skirt the side of the hill above the gardens and more paths which descend to its foot. In front of the 16th-century Palazzo Caffarelli (*with an entrance to the café in the Capitoline Museums and, to ticket holders, to the museum*) a little garden with pleasant places to sit provides another splendid panorama of Rome, this time towards St Peter's. A little fountain was installed here in 2010 to commemorate those Italian soldiers and civilians who have lost their lives in international peace-keeping missions overseas.

Between Palazzo Nuovo and Palazzo Senatorio there is another little garden planted with pines, cypresses and palms on several levels, where there are benches amidst a jumble of ancient ruins. Here **Via di San Pietro in Carcere** runs downhill to a terrace with an excellent view of the Roman Forum backed by the Colosseum. (Also off this road are the steps which lead down past a side entrance to the Carcer or Tullianum (*see p. 63*) and an exit from the Roman Forum.

Another narrow flight of steps (the Scale di Arce Capitolino) leads down the side of the hill skirting the Vittoriano. The much broader flight leads to the side door of the church of Santa Maria in Aracoeli. Near the foot of the steps can be seen the ruins of a **Roman tenement house** built in the 2nd century AD and over four storeys high. It is particularly interesting as one of the few remains found in Rome itself of a service building with shops on the ground floor and simple living-quarters above.

SANTA MARIA IN ARACOELI

Map p. 654, C3. Open 7.30–6.30. The most convenient entrance is by the inconspicuous south door, reached by steps just behind Palazzo Nuovo. There is also access from the Vittoriano, by a gate to the left of the church's west front.

This ancient church, on the highest point of the Capitoline hill, was certainly founded before the 8th century. The austere brick-built west front, which was never given a façade, is preceded by an extremely long and steep flight of 122 steps which rises directly from the foot of the hill and which was built in 1348 as a thank-offering for deliverance from a plague outbreak the same year.

The church stands on the spot where, according to a medieval tradition, the Tiburtine Sibyl appeared to Augustus to announce the coming of Christ with the words '*Ecce ara primogeniti Dei*' ('Behold the altar of God's first-born'): hence the name 'Aracoeli', or 'Altar of Heaven'. In the 10th century it belonged to the Benedictines; since 1250 it has been occupied by the Franciscans and the present building dates from that time.

Gibbon in Rome

'But at the distance of twenty-five years I can neither forget nor express the strong emotions which agitated my mind as I first approached and entered the eternal city. After a sleepless night I trod with lofty step the ruins of the Forum: each memorable spot where Romulus stood, or Tully spoke, or Caesar fell, was at once present to my eye; and several days of intoxication were lost or enjoyed before I could descend to a cool and minute investigation... It was at Rome, on the 15th October, 1764, as I sat musing amidst the ruins of the Capitol, while the bare-footed friars were singing Vespers in the Temple of Jupiter, that the idea of writing the decline and fall of the city first started to my mind...'

Memoirs of my Life and Writings (1795)

In the interior, almost the only conspicuous remains of the 12th-century church are the lovely **Cosmatesque pavement** and the 22 **ancient Roman columns** in the nave, from pagan buildings and in various different marbles. High up on the third column on the left can be seen an inscription '*a cubiculo Augustorum*' carved in beautiful large letters. This has been taken to refer to a bedroom in an imperial house which it may have once adorned. The church ceiling was decorated a few years after the famous naval victory over the 'infedel' Turks in the gulf of Corinth at Lepanto in 1571 by the papal troops and the Venetian fleet led by the Roman patrician admiral Marcantonio Colonna, who was here celebrated with a 'Triumph' modelled on those given on this hill to the victorious emperors and generals of ancient Rome (*see p. 114*).

The church, hung with pretty chandeliers, has a large number of very fine sepulchral monuments.

West wall: The tomb of Cardinal Ludovico d'Albret, with a reclining effigy (1465), is one of numerous tombs in the city by the 15th-century Lugano-born sculptor Andrea Bregno (there is another monument by his school, to a member of the Savelli family, in the apse). Beside it (set up on end against the west wall in the 19th century to try to preserve it) is the **pavement tomb, signed by Donatello**, of the archdeacon Giovanni Crivelli (1432): it is easy to miss and so worn that perhaps it is only by observing the feet that you can appreciate that this is indeed the work of this famous sculptor. It was probably made in Florence, together with the only other work by Donatello in Rome, a ciborium now in the Treasury of St Peter's (*see p. 434*), since Donatello spent almost all his long life in his native city. However, it is known that in the very first years of the 15th century he visited Rome with his close friend Brunelleschi, to study the ancient Classical art which was to have such a fundamental influence on his work.

On the other side of the west door is the tomb of the astronomer Lodovico Grato Margani: it was designed in the 16th century and is a studio production by Andrea Sansovino, although the figure of Christ is by Sansovino himself. There is another funerary monument by Sansovino, a Tuscan sculptor and architect who worked in Rome in the first years of the 16th century, on the left of the south door.

South aisle: The first chapel (*coin-operated light*) is entirely decorated with delightful **frescoes by Pinturicchio** (c. 1486) of the life of St Bernardino of Siena, the Franciscan missionary preacher who had died some 40 years earlier. Pinturicchio was an Umbrian artist who was much influenced by Perugino and was at work with him at this time on some of the frescoes on the side walls of the Sistine Chapel. It was in the Vatican that he carried out perhaps his most beautiful frescoes: those in the Borgia Rooms. He also frescoed two chapels in Santa Maria del Popolo (*see p. 354*). While in Rome he visited the Domus Aurea, which was rediscovered at that time (and left his signature there), and later often copied the *grottesche* he had seen in the vaults. He was an extremely skilled fresco painter and most of his works have survived in a wonderful state of preservation.

In the last chapel in this aisle are **fragments of frescoes by Pietro Cavallini**, discovered at the end of the 20th century. They include, on the altar wall, a lovely *Madonna and Child with Two Saints* and high up on the walls on either side very damaged scenes of buildings, and *Christ between Two Angels*. These are extremely important examples of Roman art of the late 13th and early 14th centuries, only very little of which survives. It has recently been suggested that the Madonna could be by the hand of Giotto, who is known to have worked in Rome before going to Assisi, and the influence of the Roman school of painters on his art is much discussed by scholars today. If you step out of the south door you can see (in the tympanum above) a mosaic of the *Madonna and Two Angels*, thought to be by the school of Cavallini.

Crossing: On the pilasters facing the high altar are two beautiful marble ambones from the earlier church, decorated by the Cosmati around the year 1200. The fine tomb of Cardinal Matteo di Acquasparta (d. 1302) in the north transept is another Cosmati work, incorporating a fresco by Pietro Cavallini.

COSMATI AND THE COSMATESQUE

The beautiful decorative revetment known as Cosmati work was developed in the 12th and 13th centuries, making use of abandoned and excavated ancient Roman coloured marble to create new and original designs. In part, it grew out of the Imperial Roman passion for opus sectile (fine polychrome marble and stone inlay), a tradition which had been transmitted through Byzantium and the areas of its influence, in particular in southern Italy. The characteristic of Cosmati work is the inlay into a plain marble slab of small triangles, squares and other shapes of cut porphyry, coloured marble, semi-precious stone and gold glass, in bold concentric, intertwined or rhythmically varying geometric designs. These patterns also had a practical purpose when used on the pavements of churches: they divided and mapped the floor into regular areas which facilitated the choreographing of processions on feast days. San Clemente, Santa Maria Maggiore and Santa Maria in Cosmedin are other good places to admire this effect.

The term 'Cosmati' comes from two craftsmen, both called Cosma, whose names are inscribed in some of their works; but it is used to refer to several families and generations of largely anonymous craftsmen who worked in this exquisite decorative manner, and who flourished for over a century from c. 1140. Their work is principally concentrated in Rome and its province, but the fashion spread rapidly, to centres as distant as London (see, for example, Edward the Confessor's monument in Westminster Abbey). Inspired perhaps by the descriptions in Revelation 21 of the walls and pavements of the New Jerusalem, it must have appeared to those who commissioned the works as a symbolically appropriate embellishment for floors, as well as for pulpits, screens, thrones, tombs, doorways and even whole cloisters. Cosmati work is elegant and durable, and its liveliness and beauty are particularly enhanced by the illumination of flickering candles and oil-lamps.   N.McG.

South transept: The Savelli Chapel contains 14th-century family tombs: that of Luca on the left, which incorporates a 3rd-century Roman sarcophagus, is attributed to the great sculptor Arnolfo di Cambio, while that on the right, of Luca's wife Vana, includes an effigy of their son, Pope Honorius IV (who died in 1287, the same year as his mother).

On the wall of the chapel to the right of the Chapel of the Holy Sacrament there is a beautiful small 13th-century mosaic: the *Madonna between St John the Baptist and St Francis*.

High altar: Over the altar is the *Madonna d'Aracoeli*, a tiny painting thought to be a very early work (attributed by some to a 10th-century master).

North transept: In the centre is a little circular 17th-century temple with eight marble columns above a **Cosmatesque altar** on which is depicted the legend of the founding of the church (*see p. 60 above*). On one side we see the figure of Augustus and on the other his vision of the Virgin and Child. The remains of an earlier altar and Roman masonry were found beneath this, as well as a carved 12th-century sandalwood coffer containing relics of St Helen (preserved in the Franciscan convent).

To the right is the **Cappella del Santissimo Bambino** (built at the end of the 19th century when alterations had to be made to the church during construction of the Vittoriano), where there is a popular devotional image of the Infant Christ, covered in jewels. The original, reputed to have been carved from the wood of an olive tree from the Garden of Gethsemane, was greatly venerated since it was solemnly crowned by the pope in 1897. It was particularly famous for its miraculous powers in the 19th and 20th centuries when it used to be carried (in a carriage provided by the Torlonia) to the bedsides of the sick. It was stolen in 1994 and had to be replaced by a copy but it seems to be no less revered for all that. It receives letters from all over the world (and paper and pencil are provided *in situ*) and it is a Christmas tradition for children to recite little poems in front of its crib. There is a procession with the Santissimo Bambino on the evening of 6th January, Epiphany.

MONUMENTS AT THE FOOT OF THE HILL

THE TULLIANUM OR CARCER

Open 9–5 (9–7 in summer), operaromanapellegrinaggi.org (listed as 'St Peter's Prison' under 'Roma Cristiana'). There are two tickets: if you want to see the multimedia exhibits you pay extra. The entrance at the time of writing is from the steps (one of the exits from the Forum) which begin on Via di San Pietro in Carcere.

This is thought originally to have been a cistern, like those at Tusculum and other Etruscan cities. In Roman times it was used as a dungeon for criminals and captives awaiting execution, hence its alternative names of Carcer (Latin for 'gaol') or

TULLIANUM
Detail of the 15th-century fresco showing Christ with St Peter.
The apostle was allegedly held prisoner here before his martyrdom.

Mamertine Prison. The lower level, which was the former prison cell, has now been adapted as a chapel, since according to Christian tradition, St Peter and St Paul were two of the celebrated inmates (a fresco dating from the 15th century shows Christ with his hand on St Peter's shoulder). Steps lead you down to a round building that may have had a conical dome, which could date it to as early as the 6th century BC. The prisoners kept here were typically of high status. Jugurtha, king of Numidia in north Africa, was brought to Rome as a captive by Sulla. He starved to death here in 106 BC. After Caesar's conquest of Gaul, the Gallic leader Vercingetorix lived incarcerated here for some years before being paraded through the Forum in Caesar's triumph in 46 BC (and put to death immediately afterwards).

Christian legend claimed that St Peter caused a spring to start from the floor so that he could baptise his gaolers. There is still a spring in the floor, which is paved with huge stones. The two apostles are supposed to have been tied up at the column here.

Since 2010 other parts of the little building have been used by the Vatican to show reconstructions of the prison and multimedia exhibits and a film on the life of St Peter. You can also visit the 16th-century Cappella del Crocifisso: the wood Cross was made by the Confraternity of Carpenters whose little church, San Giuseppe dei Falegnami (*only open on Sun*), was built on top of the Carcer in 1598.

Despite its associations with St Peter and St Paul and its consecration in the Middle Ages as the chapel of San Pietro in Carcere, this place has never taken on a hallowed or a comforting air. For centuries it retained its grim memories as the most ancient prison in the city. The Gemonian Steps close by were also associated with death: stories abounded of people being flung down them and of corpses being exhibited for ridicule.

SANTI LUCA E MARTINA

This church was probably founded in the 7th century by Honorius I, though the handsome building we see today is the result of a rebuilding in 1640 by the painter and architect Pietro da Cortona (*see p. 341*). It is considered his early masterpiece. Despite this, it is one of the most neglected churches in Rome, almost always closed (*officially open on Sat*). Nevertheless it is of the first importance for its architecture. The façade, built of travertine, and the dome are particularly fine. The interior is constructed partly on a centralised Greek-cross plan, although the two storeys, an upper dedicated to St Luke and a lower to St Martina, have an original and complex design.

The double dedication is the result of the patronage of two popes. The founder, Pope Honorius, was keen on erecting churches on the sites of martyrdoms, and for this one he chose the little-known Roman martyr Martina. The dedication to St Luke came about when Pope Sixtus V presented the church to the Accademia di San Luca, the artists' academy, in exchange for their original church beside Santa Maria Maggiore, which he had demolished to make way for his magnificent funerary chapel (*see p. 304*). Several academicians chose to be buried here, among them Pietro da Cortona himself.

In the upper church, above the high altar, there is a marble effigy of Martina, the titular saint, who is said to have been martyred under Alexander Severus in 228. It was made in 1635 by a minor sculptor, Niccolò Menghini, the year after a sarcophagus thought to contain her remains was found near here in the Roman Forum, and is clearly influenced by Stefano Maderno's effigy of St Cecilia (*see p. 397*). The altarpiece itself is a copy of Raphael's *St Luke Painting the Virgin*.

The lower church is reached by a staircase to the left of the high altar. Here is Pietro da Cortona's funerary monument (d. 1669), and the side chapel, with a pretty scallop motif, has a fine terracotta group of three saints by Alessandro Algardi (who also carved the bas-relief of the *Deposition* in the vestibule).

Outside the church you can see a well-preserved stretch of the **Clivus Argentarius**, the Roman road which ran between the Capitoline and the Quirinal hills and which is still open to pedestrians. Preserving some of its huge old paving stones, it is lined with the remains of shops where the money-lenders of the ancient city congregated, as well as a nymphaeum from the time of Trajan. It ascends to join the modern Via dei Fori Imperiali.

To the left, on a grassy lawn at the foot of the Vittoriano, are the remains of the **tomb of Gaius Publicius Bibulus**. The inscription, dating from the early 1st century BC, states that it was erected at the expense of the Senate and the Romans themselves. The sepulchre was reconstructed in the following century.

The Roman Forum

The Roman Forum is one of the most evocative places in Rome. Its ruins stand in the centre of the modern city as a romantic testament to her past greatness.

The Roman Forum (*map p. 655, D3 and plan on pp. 70–1*) was the heart of ancient Rome and served not only as a market-place but as a space for political assemblies throughout the Republic. These were held in front of the senate house, which is still one of the most conspicuous buildings here. Some columns and entablatures, podia and marble paving of the basilicas and temples erected at this time also survive. However, the most visible remains date from the Imperial era and include the very well-preserved triumphal arches of Titus and Septimius Severus and the magnificent vaults of the Basilica of Maxentius.

Planning a visit

Open 8.30–dusk. For information, see archeoroma.beniculturali.it. For advance tickets, T: 06 39 96 7700, coopculture.it. Combined ticket with the Palatine (for a single visit) and Colosseum (valid two days). For the Archaeological Card and reductions for young visitors, see p. 600.

At the time of writing there were two main entrances: on Via dei Fori Imperiali and Via di San Gregorio (on the side of the Palatine hill—usually the less crowded access). These entrances also function as exits and there are two further exits beside the Arch of Septimius Severus (convenient for the Capitoline hill) and from the Basilica of Maxentius to the church of Santa Francesca Romana (close to the Colosseum). Archaeological investigations often require the entrance and exit points to close or change, however. Check before you plan your visit.

There are lifts for the disabled at the entrances on Via dei Fori Imperiali and at the Arch of Titus, but the Forum remains a difficult place to visit in a wheelchair.

Restoration and maintenance work as well as new excavations mean that certain areas can be inaccessible for brief periods, while other buildings (notably Santa Maria Antiqua, the Oratory of the Forty Martyrs and the Lacus Juturnae) are accessible only sporadically. The Curia building is usually open only in the morning.

In the last few years more signs (also in English) have been installed discreetly in front of the main buildings, but the Forum is still a complicated place to visit because of its long history and the various layers of remains. There are no refreshments available but there are a number of drinking fountains with a constant supply of Rome's particularly good fresh water (the Palatine is a better place to picnic because it has some comfortable benches).

HISTORY OF THE ROMAN FORUM

The site of the Forum was originally a marshy valley between the Capitoline and Palatine hills. In the Iron Age it was used as a necropolis. The area was first paved as a market place c. 625 BC. The Etruscan king Servius Tullius (579–534 BC) made the area habitable by channelling its stagnant waters into a huge drain called the Cloaca Maxima. The first monuments of the Forum also date from the period of the kings.

The original Forum was a rectangle (about 115m by 57m), bounded on the north and south by shops (*tabernae*). Adjacent to it to the northwest was a second rectangle including the Comitium, for political assemblies; the Curia, or senate house; and the Rostra, or orators' tribune. Beyond to the east were the Regia, seat of the *pontifex maximus* (head of a college of priests who presided over the state cult), the Temple of Vesta and House of the Vestals. The Forum was therefore divided into three distinct areas: commercial, political and religious. It gradually lost its commercial character as it became more the scene of public functions. The greengrocers and other shopkeepers were moved to the Velabrum (*see p. 247*) and replaced by money-changers (*argentarii*).

In the 2nd century BC a new type of building, the basilica, was introduced. This was a large roofed hall used as law courts and for public administration when meetings could not be held outside. The first basilica to be erected in the Forum was the Basilica Porcia, built by the censor Cato in 185 BC (destroyed in 52 BC) and the last was the Basilica of Maxentius (4th century AD), which still partly survives (*see p. 85*). Inside they had aisles supported by columns and an apse at one end: their plan was adopted in Christian architecture for the earliest churches.

During the Republic new laws were proposed by a magistrate, who would address an assembly, open to all including women and slaves, in the Forum. All Roman citizens were then eligible to vote. How much the elite in Roman society counted in this process is still discussed by scholars, some of whom argue that a significant element of democracy was attained. It was also through assemblies that all consuls, praetors and other public officials were elected.

The Forum under the Emperors

After Julius Caesar's assassination in 44 BC, his body was cremated in the Forum. Caesar had begun the enlargement of the Forum which Sulla had planned some years before, and which was completed by Augustus. Between 44 and 27 BC the Basilica Julia, the Curia and the Rostra were completed, the Temple of Saturn and the Regia restored, the Temple of Julius Caesar dedicated and the Arch of Augustus erected. In his biography of the Roman emperors, *De Vita Caesarum*, published around AD 121, Suetonius states that Augustus found the city brick and left it marble: he also made the Forum a fitting centre of the expanding empire. Nevertheless, the area of the Forum soon became inadequate for the growing population and succeeding emperors were obliged to build their own Fora (*see p. 121*).

From the Middle Ages onwards

In later centuries the area reflected the general decline of the city. The temples and sanctuaries were neglected and robbed of most of their treasures. Medieval Roman barons used the tallest of the ruined buildings as foundations for their fortress-towers. A few churches were constructed but most of the Forum was used as cattle pasture, and so became known as the *Campo Vaccino*. Its monuments were used as quarries and its precious marbles were burned in lime kilns. In the Renaissance the Forum provided inspiration to numerous artists. Many buildings erected from the 15th–18th centuries took their plans from monuments here, and often architectural features of the Roman edifices were reused in these buildings. It is extraordinary to think that even in Augustus Hare's time (1883) the 'meek-faced oxen of the Campagna' were still to be found among the ruins.

First impressions of the Forum

As soon as he entered Rome, the home of the empire and all perfection, he went to the Rostra and gazed with amazement at the Forum, that sublime monument of pristine power. Wherever he turned he was dazzled by the concentration of wonderful sights.

The historian Ammianus Marcellinus, on the visit
to Rome of the emperor Constantius, AD 357

Excavations

At the end of the 18th century systematic excavations of the site began, and continued through the 19th century, especially after Rome joined the Kingdom of Italy in 1870. The distinguished archaeologist Giacomo Boni conducted digs from 1898 to 1925 and found Archaic monuments of great interest; his work was continued in the 1930s by Alfonso Bartoli, who also oversaw impressive restoration and reconstruction work. From 1980 onwards excavations were carried out at the west end of the Forum at the foot of the Capitoline Hill, near the Temple of Saturn, where both Archaic and 12th-century finds were made; around the Temple of Vespasian; in the area of Santa Maria Antiqua and the Temple of Castor; behind the Basilica Aemilia and the Curia; and on the northern slopes of the Palatine, between the Sacra Via and the House of the Vestals. Many of the monuments were well restored in 2000, including the Portico of the Dii Consentes and the Arch of Septimius Severus.

THE VISIT

NB: The following description begins from the entrance on Via dei Fori Imperiali. If you enter the Forum from a different entrance and wish to follow the described route, use the plan overleaf to find this point.

From the entrance on Via dei Fori Imperiali a broad path descends beneath the high cella wall of the Temple of Antoninus and Faustina with a good view right of the Basilica Aemilia, to the level of the original Forum and the round paving stones of the **Sacra Via**. This is the oldest street in Rome, traversing the length of the Forum, and it was once lined with important sanctuaries. The winding road, now at a lower level than the later monuments on either side and with its huge paving stones still visible in places, dates from the late Republican era; the later Imperial road probably took a slightly different course towards the Temple of Venus and Roma. It was along the Sacra Via that a victorious general awarded a Triumph passed in procession to the Capitol to offer sacrifice in the Temple of Jupiter.

(1) The huge **Temple of Antoninus and Faustina**, complete with its mighty cella walls and pronaos of ten huge columns above a flight of (reconstructed) brick steps, neatly encloses a church, and for this reason is one of the best-preserved temples left standing in the Forum today. It was a famous temple of Imperial Rome, which the Senate dedicated to the memory of the empress Faustina after her death in AD 141. When her husband, the emperor Antoninus Pius, died 20 years later, the temple received its double dedication. The pronaos has monolithic Corinthian columns (17m high) in green, grey and white-veined Greek marble (cipollino), six in front and two on either side, and a female torso has been placed here. You can see the huge blocks of tufa (peperino), which would originally have been faced with marble, of the side wall of the cella on its left flank, above which the architrave with a frieze of vases and candelabra between griffins survives.

The temple was converted into the church of San Lorenzo in Miranda (*the interior is always closed*) before the 12th century, and given a Baroque façade in 1602. The dedication to St Lawrence may commemorate the trial of the saint, which is thought to have taken place in this temple before his martyrdom in 258. Famous as one of the earliest Christian martyrs, Lawrence is frequently portrayed in Christian art being burned alive on a gridiron.

His death seems to have signalled an important moment in Rome for the advance of Christianity and decline of pagan worship.

Follow the Sacra Via right. On the southeast corner of the Basilica Aemilia is a large inscription (from a portico) with a dedication by the senate in 2 BC to the fourteen-year old Lucius Caesar, adopted son of Augustus and grandson of the deified Julius Caesar (he died just four years later).

(2) Three granite columns (one of them broken) of late Imperial date have been set up amidst various other architectural fragments scattered on the ground in front of a row of shops which used to be under a two-storyed portico of the **Basilica Aemilia**, the scant remains of which survive behind (you can walk through them). The basilica was built by the censors Marcus Aemilius Lepidus and Marcus Fulvius Nobilior in 179 BC, restored by members of the Aemilia *gens*—including another Marcus Aemilius Lepidus—in 78 BC and rebuilt in the time of Julius Caesar. It was again rebuilt in AD 22 after a fire and nearly destroyed by another fire during Alaric the Goth's sack of Rome in 410. Much of it was demolished in the 16th century in order to reuse the marble, but not before Sangallo documented its splendid decorations in drawings. Enough of it is left to show its original plan: a vast

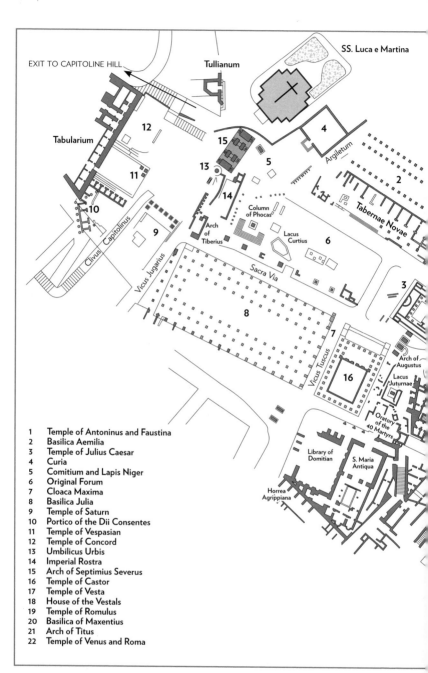

SS. Luca e Martina

EXIT TO CAPITOLINE HILL

Tullianum

Tabularium

Argiletum

Tabernae Novae

12

15

4

13

5

2

11

14

10

Column of Phocas

Lacus Curtius

6

9

Arch of Tiberius

3

Clivus Capitolinus

Vicus Jugarius

Sacra Via

8

7

Vicus Tuscus

Arch of Augustus

16

Lacus Juturnae

Oratory of the 40 Martyrs

Library of Domitian

S. Maria Antiqua

Horrea Agrippiana

1   Temple of Antoninus and Faustina
2   Basilica Aemilia
3   Temple of Julius Caesar
4   Curia
5   Comitium and Lapis Niger
6   Original Forum
7   Cloaca Maxima
8   Basilica Julia
9   Temple of Saturn
10 Portico of the Dii Consentes
11 Temple of Vespasian
12 Temple of Concord
13 Umbilicus Urbis
14 Imperial Rostra
15 Arch of Septimius Severus
16 Temple of Castor
17 Temple of Vesta
18 House of the Vestals
19 Temple of Romulus
20 Basilica of Maxentius
21 Arch of Titus
22 Temple of Venus and Roma

THE ROMAN FORUM

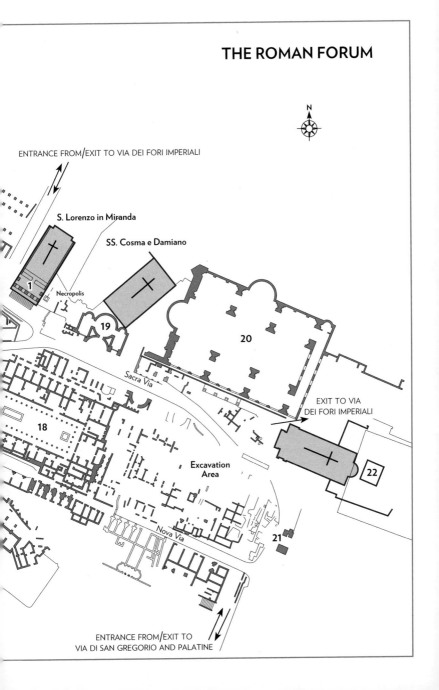

N

ENTRANCE FROM/EXIT TO VIA DEI FORI IMPERIALI

S. Lorenzo in Miranda

SS. Cosma e Damiano

1

Necropolis

19

20

Sacra Via

EXIT TO VIA
DEI FORI IMPERIALI

18

22

Excavation
Area

Nova Via

21

ENTRANCE FROM/EXIT TO
VIA DI SAN GREGORIO AND PALATINE

rectangular hall 70m by 29m, divided by columns into a central nave and aisles, single on the south side and double on the north. Only some broken marble columns and some of its coloured marble paving slabs (under cover) survive at the end nearest the Curia. If you look closely you can see some coins embedded in the marble: they fused with the bronze roof decorations which were thrown to the floor during the fire of AD 410.

(3) Protected by a roof is all that remains of the **Temple of Julius Caesar**. After his assassination on the Ides of March in 44 BC, Julius Caesar's body was brought to the Forum and it was probably here that it was cremated and his will read out by Mark Antony. The temple, which probably had only six columns in its portico, was preceded by a terrace which Augustus decorated with the ships' prows (or 'rostra') from the Egyptian ships of Antony and Cleopatra which he had captured at the decisive battle of Actium in 31 BC. Two years later he dedicated the temple to the Divus ('divine') Julius Caesar. In AD 14 Tiberius gave a funeral oration here over Augustus' own body before it was buried in his mausoleum (*see p. 170*).

Only a curving wall and the central block of the podium and the round altar survive: remains of foundations on the north and south sides of the temple are thought to be those of the arcaded Porticus Julia, which surrounded the temple on three sides.

Continue along the line of the Sacra Via. Beyond a small group of trees you will see the paved **Argiletum** diverging to the right. This was once one of the

Forum's busiest streets, which led north to the district of the Subura, a poor and unsavoury part of town, haunt of thieves and prostitutes, and described by Juvenal as home to 'the thousand perils of a savage city'. In the area to the north the **Macellum**, a market building paved in peperino and surrounded by columns, built in the late 3rd or early 2nd century BC, has been unearthed.

(4) The most impressive and conspicuous building in the entire Forum is the **Curia Senatus** (or Curia Julia), the senate house. Replacing the original Curia Hostilia said to have been built by Tullus Hostilius, traditionally held to be the third king of Rome (673–642 BC), it was begun by Sulla in 80 BC and rebuilt after a fire by Julius Caesar in 44 BC. Fifteen years after Caesar's death it was completed by Augustus, who dedicated a statue of Victory in the interior. The present building dates from the time of Domitian and was restored by Diocletian after a fire in 283. In 630 it was converted into the church of Sant'Adriano. In 1935–9 it was restored to the form it had under Diocletian.

The lower part of the brick façade was originally covered with marble and the upper courses with stucco. A simple pediment with travertine corbels crowns the building; it would originally have been preceded by a portico. The existing doors are copies of the originals, removed by Alexander VII in the 17th century to St John Lateran, where they still—incredibly enough—serve as the main entrance to the basilica (an example of the famous 'plundering' of the ancient buildings in the Forum which in fact probably saved these historic works from destruction in later centuries).

JULIUS CAESAR

Julius Caesar (100–44 BC) is perhaps the best known of all Romans, his name transmitted into later European history as Kaiser and Czar and incorporated into the western calendar (July). His assassination lingers as a powerful folk memory, and even today admirers commemorate with flowers the supposed site of the burning of his body in the Forum. Caesar's family was an ancient one which claimed descent from the goddess Venus, though when Caesar was born its influence was limited, and Julius had to make his own way in the tricky political climate of the late Republic. He was a brilliant speaker and cleverly associated himself with the *populares* (those politicians claiming to represent the demands of the ordinary citizen) against the senatorial elite. One early achievement was election to the prestigious post of *pontifex maximus*, the head of the priesthood, in 63.

However, his success left him deeply in debt, and to recoup his losses he took on a command in Spain, where a successful campaign against local tribes brought him both plunder and prestige. Back in Rome he was elected consul, and he worked with another prestigious general, Pompey, to boost his position further. A consulship lasted only a year, and rather than retire from political life, Ceasar acquired another command, this time to subdue the Celtic tribes of Gaul. His accounts of the campaigns (*The Commentaries on the Gallic War*) were carefully composed to present him as a man of calm determination, resolute in adversity and decisive in command. They were complemented by a building programme in Rome which included the extension of the Roman Forum to the north with a porticoed square and a temple to Venus, his family deity.

All this time the political situation in Rome was disintegrating. The senate, which had been revered a century before, was now openly attacked. Its members called on Pompey to restore order. By now Pompey's alliance with Caesar had broken down, and Caesar looked as if he had been isolated. Ruthlessly ambitious as ever, he decided to launch a direct attack on Rome. In the civil war that followed Caesar gradually eliminated Pompey and his supporters. Pompey was hunted down to Egypt, where the authorities arranged his murder. Caesar, in an uncharacteristic lapse of duty, dallied with the charismatic and sensual queen Cleopatra, who bore him a son. He was finally back in Rome in 45, where he was awarded four successive Triumphs for his victories.

The question now was whether Caesar could forge a political settlement in Rome. Although the republican system had collapsed, fears of dictatorship ran deep in the Roman consciousness. Caesar, however, let power go to his head. He gradually adopted the trappings of monarchy, appearing in public on a throne and dressed always in a triumphal robe. He began to see himself as semi-divine and acquiesced in having a temple dedicated to him. For the senatorial class, who still prided themselves on their ancient status, this was too much. In 44 BC a plot was hatched and Caesar was struck down by a band of aristocratic conspirators.   C.F.

The remarkable interior of the Curia is usually only open in the mornings. It preserves a beautiful green-and-maroon pavement in opus sectile, and contains a porphyry statue found in excavations behind the building at the end of the 20th century as well as the two extremely important **Plutei of Trajan**, balustrades or parapets, carved with reliefs of emperors carrying out public duties in the Forum, and the so-called *suovetaurilia*, the traditional trio of sacrificial animals: bull, ram and sow.

In recent excavations (*at present closed*) behind the Curia, remains of the Augustan building have come to light. Two doors at the rear end opened into a columned portico of the Forum of Caesar (*see p. 124*), providing an entrance from the old Republican Forum to the new Imperial one. Connected to the Curia was the Secretarium Senatus, used by a tribunal set up in the late Empire to judge senators.

(5) The area in front of the Curia building has been inaccessible for a number of years since excavations are in progress: it includes the **Comitium**, where the earliest political activity of the Republic took place and which very early on was on an artificially raised site to protect it from the marshy ground. Here also is the site of the **Lapis Niger** ('Black Stone'), where a pavement of black marble was laid to indicate a sacred spot, now identified as the ancient sanctuary of Vulcan. Here a stele provides the most ancient example of the Latin language (probably mid-6th century BC) and seems to refer to a *lex sacra* (holy law) warning against profaning a holy place. Recent excavations nearby (*in another area not at present accessible*) have revealed some remains of the **Republican Rostra** and two marble bases, one with an inscription to the emperor Constantius II (one of Constantine's sons) and the other, which bore a column, with reliefs.

(6) The open space to the south was the **original Forum**. As the meeting point of the whole population and a market-place, it was kept free of obstructions in Republican days (up to 31 BC). All important ceremonies and public meetings took place here. The Forum was where the main religious festivals were held, where political offenders were executed, and where the funerals of important people took place. During the Empire (27 BC–AD 395), the Forum lost its original character and new buildings encroached on it. It remained merely an official centre and was to a great extent replaced by the new Imperial Fora (*see p. 121*).

The best view of this area can be had by returning past the Temple of Julius Caesar and following the Sacra Via north. To the right is a row of **seven brick bases** dating from the 4th century. These were the 'Columnae Honorariae', which used to bear columns with statues of illustrious citizens: two of them have been re-erected. They mark the southern limit of the original Forum, which was first paved in the Etruscan period. In one of the pavement slabs is incised the name of Lucius Naevius Surdinus, *praetor peregrinus* in the time of Augustus, who possibly had his tribunal here. This legal dignitary had to deal with cases involving *peregrini*, in other words, those who were not Roman citizens.

Beyond, the low fence opens out on the right and you can see the covered, paved area of the **Lacus Curtius**, with the substructure of the parapet of a well surrounded by a twelve-sided structure of peperino blocks. The 'lake', or pond, was presumably a remnant of the marsh drained by the Cloaca Maxima (*see below*), but the name was traditionally explained with the charming story that in 362 BC a great chasm opened here which the soothsayers said could only be closed by throwing into it Rome's greatest treasure. A young Roman called Marcus Curtius, announcing that Rome possessed no greater treasure than a brave citizen, rode his horse into the abyss, which promptly closed. A bas-relief of a horse and rider was found here: a cast is shown *in situ*. (Livy much more prosaically suggests that it was merely named after a consul named Curtius, who fenced off this area in 445 after it had been struck by lightning.)

To the left rises the **Column of Phocas**, not only a conspicuous feature of the Forum but the last of its monuments to be dedicated. The fluted Corinthian column, probably taken from some building of the best Imperial era, is 13.5m high. It stands on a tall base, formerly faced with marble and surrounded by steps. A long inscription states that it was crowned with a golden statue which was placed on its summit in 608 by Smaragdus, exarch of Italy, in honour of the centurion Phocas who had seized the throne of Byzantium after assassinating the Emperor and his five sons; its erection may have been a mark of gratitude for the usurper Phocas's gift of the Pantheon to Boniface IV in the same year.

Behind and slightly to the left of the Lacus Curtius is a small, square, unpaved space, which may be where a statue of Marsyas once stood next to the fig tree, the olive and the vine (all replanted in 1956) recorded by Pliny the Elder as being in the centre of the Forum. All three were plants sacred to the ancient Romans; the fig was a symbol of fertility.

(7) The ancient road called the Vicus Tuscus leads north past an entrance to the **Cloaca Maxima**. This was part of an extensive hydraulic system which reclaimed the stagnant marshy land in the valleys between the Esquiline, Viminal and Quirinal hills, as well as the area of the Roman Forum, which was little more than a swamp. At first a natural watercourse to the Tiber, it was canalised by Tarquinius Priscus and Servius Tullius (c. 616–535 BC), and arched over in c. 200 BC. It crossed the Forum from north to south before emptying into the Tiber, and also helped eliminate the stagnant marshes in the area of the Velabrum. A great engineering feat, it vastly improved the living conditions of the inhabitants and provided the city with a central area where the most important religious and political activities could take place, and markets could operate.

On the other side of the Vicus Tuscus can be seen a fenced-off area accessible only occasionally (though there are long-term plans to open it permanently). The church of **Santa Maria Antiqua** is the oldest and most important Christian building in the Forum and its 7th–8th-century wall-paintings are of the first importance in the history of early Christian art. The **Oratory of the Forty Martyrs** also

BASILICA JULIA

Tabula lusoria, or game board, etched into the former top step of the basilica.

has very early frescoes. Before it was converted into a church it is thought to have served as a vestibule to the **Imperial Ramp**, a remarkable barrel-vaulted corridor which could be used by horses and which winds up to the Palatine. It was built by Domitian in the late 1st century as a means of descending from his palace to the Forum (a drop of some 35m). Domitian also built the huge building clearly to be seen against the hill of the Palatine, with three of its walls still standing, in which niches high up in the walls are still visible (it is thought that they were accessed by walkways around the walls). This seems to have been a library built by Domitian after Vespasian had introduced a state salary for teachers of rhetoric.

Also on the Vicus Tuscus is a vast brick building known as the **Horrea Agrippiana**. This was a grain warehouse built (by Agrippa) around three courtyards, each provided with three storeys of rooms. The round church of San Teodoro (which can be seen from here, but which is entered from outside the Forum enclosure; *see p. 252*) stands in the second courtyard.

(8) Raised above a stepped basement is the huge platform of the **Basilica Julia**, which occupied the area between two ancient roadways, the Vicus Jugarius (or Vicus Unguentarius) and the Vicus Tuscus. All that remains of this large building are the steps and some column bases.

The basilica, built on the site of the Basilica Sempronia (170 BC; named after its builder, the censor Tiberius Sempronius Gracchus), was begun by Julius Caesar in 54 BC and finished by Augustus. Reconstructed after a fire, it was rededicated by Augustus in AD 12. It was again damaged by fire in AD 283 and reconstructed by Diocletian in 305. It was damaged yet again in the sack of Rome by the Goths in 410 and was restored for the last time by the prefect of the city, Gabinius Vettius Probianus, six years later.

The Basilica Julia was the meeting-place of the four tribunals of the *centumviri*, a special court of justice which dealt with civil cases. In the Middle Ages a church (Santa Maria in Cannapara) was built at its west side. The surviving remains mostly date from

305; the brick piers of the central hall are 19th-century reconstructions.

The basilica was even larger than the Basilica Aemilia, measuring 101m by 49m. It had a central hall 82m long and 18m wide, bordered all round by a double row of columns which formed aisles. On the long side, facing south, was a colonnade of arches and piers with engaged columns; this contained a row of shops. Graffiti on the marble steps show that the Romans used to while away their time here playing 'board' games.

In recent excavations beneath the basilica a building has been unearthed which may prove to be part of the residence of Scipio, the famous general dubbed 'Africanus' after the territory he conquered following his defeat of Hannibal in 202 BC. Tiberius Gracchus was his grandson.

Facing onto the **Vicus Jugarius** are remains of shops and offices dating from around 12 BC and an early medieval building. The ancient road (the paving stones survive) ran south towards the Tiber and the Velabrum.

At the junction of Vicus Jugarius and the Sacra Via stood the **Arch of Tiberius**, erected in AD 16 in honour of the emperor and of his nephew Germanicus after a victory over German tribes. Its foundations can be seen below ground level.

Behind the Temple of Saturn there is a newly excavated area where more medieval houses have been found.

THE WESTERN PART OF THE FORUM

(9) In the westernmost part of the Forum, at the foot of the Capitoline hill, are remains of a number of temples. Eight columns, nearly 11m high, with part of the entablature, survive of the pronaos of the **Temple of Saturn**, raised on a high podium. Six columns in grey granite are in front; the other two, in red granite, are at the sides. The Ionic capitals were added in a 5th-century restoration. This was one of the earliest sanctuaries in the Forum, possibly inaugurated in 498 BC in honour of the mythical god-king of Italy, whose reign was the fabled Golden Age. There is still some mystery about this ancient deity, whose name suggests he was the god of sowing but who is sometimes also associated with the Kronos of Greek mythology. The 'Saturnalia' was the most important day of festivities in the Roman year, an occasion when temporary freedom was given to slaves and presents were exchanged. It was always celebrated here on 17th December: it later came to be associated with New Year's Day and Christmas. The temple was rebuilt, after several previous reconstructions, by Lucius Munatius Plancus in the year of his consulship, 42 BC, and the columns we see today survive from that time. It was again restored after fires in AD 283 and c. 400. The temple was the state treasury, where gold and silver ingots and coined metal were kept. The treasury itself (*aerarium*) was a room east of the narrow stairway: the holes for the lock can still be seen. In front of it today there is a fragment of a huge column lying on the ground.

Beside the Temple of Saturn, the ancient road known as the **Clivus Capitolinus** turns steeply uphill. Built in the 2nd century BC, it preserves many of its huge old paving stones. It was the western continuation of the Sacra Via and the only way up to the Capitol in ancient times. It was used for triumphal and other processions to the Temple of Capitoline Jupiter at the top of the hill.

Behind a fence on the left, a marble fragment with a carved frieze of palmettes marks the site of the **Miliarium Aureum** ('golden milestone'), a bronze-covered column set up by Augustus in 20 BC as the symbolic starting-point of all the roads of the Empire, with the distance from Rome to the chief cities engraved in gold letters on its base. Ever since, there has been a familiar saying that 'all roads lead to Rome'. There was a *curator viarum*, an official whose duty it was to oversee the upkeep of the roads, in recognition of the fact that they were of such fundamental importance to the smooth running of the Empire.

(10) The **Portico of the Dii Consentes** preserves twelve white columns forming an angle: the seven original columns are in marble, the restorations in limestone. Rebuilt on the pattern of a Flavian structure in AD 367 by the prefect Vettius Praetextatus (known for his opposition to Christianity), this was the last pagan monument in the Forum. It was decorated with statues of the twelve deities, the Dii Consentes (literally, 'consenting gods'), who were the object of the state cult. The Etruscans had recognised six male and six female deities who assisted Jupiter in directing his thunderbolts, and the Romans came to identify these gods with the great Greek gods: Jupiter (Zeus), Neptune (Poseidon), Mars (Ares), Apollo (also called Apollo by the Greeks), Vulcan (Hephaistos), Mercury (Hermes), Juno (Hera), Minerva (Athena), Diana (Artemis), Venus (Aphrodite), Vesta (Hestia) and Ceres (Demeter).

The portico was reconstructed in 1858. Beyond, on the side of the Capitoline hill, you can see the mighty wall of the Tabularium (*see p. 50*) with Palazzo Senatorio towering above. On the right is an area newly excavated, where a deposit of ex-votos from the Archaic period, probably connected with an ancient cult of Saturn, has been found, and an interesting 12th-century district of the city has been revealed.

(11) Three high columns are all that remain of the hexastyle pronaos of the sumptuous and elegant **Temple of Vespasian**, erected at the foot of the Tabularium staircase by his sons Titus and Domitian after his death in AD 79. The front part of the basement has also been excavated.

(12) Only the pavement remains of the **Temple of Concord**, a reconstruction by Tiberius (7 BC–AD 10) of a sanctuary traditionally thought to have been built in 366 BC by Camillus, a famous military leader and politician in early Roman history, to commemorate the concordat between the patricians and the plebeians. It is more probable, however, that the temple was first built in 218 BC. It was then rebuilt in 121 BC with the consent of the consul Lucius Opimius after the murder of the plebeian Gracchus. But it did anything but symbolise concord: Gracchus, a great reformer who was twice elected tribune, had tried to undermine the authority of the senate by uniting the *plebs* with the *equites* (members of the business community) and lost his life in a riot provoked by Opimius and the senate. He is also remembered for his far-sighted—but unsuccessful—attempt to extend Roman citizenship to Latins and Italians. The temple became a museum and gallery of paintings and sculptures by famous Greek artists. Part of the temple frieze can be seen in the Tabularium when visiting the Capitoline Museums (*see p. 50*).

(13) Opposite the Temple of Concord is a cylindrical construction in brick, the **Umbilicus Urbis** (?2nd century BC), supposed to mark the centre (the *umbilicus* or navel) of the city, and hence of the known world. In front of it is a quadrangular area protected by a little roof, thought to be an **Altar of Saturn**, dating from before the 6th century BC. Two trees grew here in Republican times, a lotus and a cypress, said to be older than the city itself.

(14) The **Imperial Rostra** platform was moved from its original site in front of the Curia during a restoration by Caesar: it is marked by the low brick wall visible to the right of the Arch of Septimius Severus. This was the orators' tribune, from which magistrates' edicts, legal decisions and official communications were proclaimed. The original structure, of very early date, can only be seen from the other side of the Arch of Septimius Severus, but all that is left of it is a mound of rubble supported by brick arches (and with a fragment of a carved frieze on top). The *rostra* were the iron prows of the ships captured at the battle of Antium (modern Anzio) in 338

BC, when Rome finally subjugated the Volsci, who had controlled the territory in southern Latium. On the platform rose columns surmounted by commemorative statues, and the parapet was probably decorated with the sculptured Plutei of Trajan (now inside the Curia). At the north end was the Rostra Vandalica, a 5th-century AD extension; the modern name is taken from an inscription commemorating a naval victory over the Vandals in 470.

The Rostra tribune was famously profaned by the emperor Augustus' sensual daughter Julia, who used it at night for her notorious carnal encounters. Despairing of her incorrigible ways, Augustus eventually exiled her to the island of Pandateria.

(15) The triple **Arch of Septimius Severus** has survived its 1,800 years remarkably well. It is nearly 21m high and over 23m wide, and entirely faced with marble. It was erected in AD 203 in honour of the tenth anniversary of the accession of Septimius Severus. The inscription in the attic dedicated by SPQR (the Senate and People of Rome) to '*pater patriae*' and '*pontifex maximus*' refers to his military victories in Parthia (present-day Iran). His elder son, known as Caracalla, became joint emperor in 198 and when Severus died in York in 211 his younger son Geta stood in as joint emperor until Caracalla had him murdered the following year. The orginal inscription included Geta's name but this was eliminated in *damnatio memoriae* and replaced by flattering words recording just Severus and Caracalla: the original text can be reconstructed from the holes where the bronze letters used to be attached.

On the well-proportioned arch the four large reliefs depict scenes from the two Parthian campaigns: in the small friezes are symbolic Oriental figures paying homage to Rome, and at the bases of the columns are captive barbarians.

An interior staircase led up to the four chambers of the attic. Unfortunately it is not at present possible to walk under this great arch. (*There is an exit from the Forum here up modern stairs directly to the Capitoline hill*).

ROMAN GODS AND THEIR WORSHIP

The relationship between the Romans and their gods was a very powerful one. From the earliest history of the city it was believed that the community should participate in a variety of rituals which would win divine support. These rituals had to be followed exactly and all involved some kind of sacrifice. Surviving religious calendars suggest that there were at least 40 major festivals in Rome, celebrating the changing seasons of the year or important moments in the evolution of the state. Indeed, religion was so closely tied up with the needs of the state that priesthoods were often political offices.

The Roman gods themselves have their roots deep in the earliest history of Italy. So Jupiter, the sky god, is found in different forms in most Italic (pre-Roman) societies, as is Mars, the god of war. Among female deities Juno is an ancient goddess of fertility. With a strong Greek presence in southern Italy from the 8th century BC, Roman equivalents of Greek divinities appear, such as Venus for Aphrodite and Ceres for Demeter. Minerva, an ancient Italian goddess of handicrafts, becomes associated with Athena. Dionysus, the god of wine and sexual abandon, emerges, via the Greek cities of southern Italy, as the Roman Bacchus—but his rites were so wild that the senate banned them in 186 BC. His worship survived in a more restrained form. Some Greek gods were directly transferred to Rome. So Apollo, whose attributes included the ending of plagues, was introduced specifically for that purpose in 433 BC. Asclepios, the god of healing, was 'summoned' to Rome for the same reason in 291 BC and as Aesculapius was given a temple on the Isola Tiberina (where a hospital stands to this day). The Etruscans too had an important influence on Roman religion. It was the Etruscan kings who founded the great Temple of Jupiter on the Capitoline hill (it was dedicated to the triad of Jupiter, Juno and Minerva in the first year of the Republic) and who introduced the ritual of the Triumph, which ended with sacrifice at its steps. Books of prophecies by a Sibyl (whose origins are unknown) were reputedly brought to Rome by one of the Etruscan kings and were consulted at times of crisis. The Sibylline Books became so intimately connected with the city that even Christians consulted them for prophecies of the coming of their faith to Rome.

Although new festivals could appear, the most ancient were virtually impossible to eradicate. The Lupercalia (15th February), associated with fertility, probably predates the foundation of Rome but was still being celebrated (to the disgust of Christians) as late as AD 494. The ancient rituals of the state were clung to with intense conservatism and any sensible emperor respected them. However, the Romans would never have ruled an empire of so many cultures without a readiness to innovate, adapt and compromise. By the 1st century BC the Greek practice of offering cult worship to leaders had spread to Rome. Julius Caesar appears to have been offered a temple and his own priesthood in Rome itself, although this offended traditionalists. He was accepted as a god only after his death, as were Augustus and other 'good' emperors such as Trajan. The linking of an emperor to the 'goddess' Roma, in a temple dedicated, say, to Augustus and Roma, became an important feature of Roman imperialism. However, it remained essential for an emperor not to claim divinity during his lifetime. Domitian was assassinated in 96 after he had insisted on being addressed as 'Lord God', as was the emperor Marcus Aurelius Antoninus (218–22) when he unwisely took on the name and cult of the Syrian sun-god Elagabalus. By the end of the 3rd century emperors were linking themselves closely to traditional gods such as Jupiter or Hercules, and they would elevate themselves above their people as if the chosen god's patronage had given them a semi-divine status while they were still alive.

The cosmopolitan nature of Rome can be seen in the wide range of foreign cults which were accepted into the city. Cybele, the great mother goddess of Anatolia, known to the Romans as *Magna Mater*, was brought to Rome in 205 and a temple exotically served by Oriental priests was built to her cult on the Palatine hill. A large temple to the Egyptian goddess Isis was built near the present church of Santa Maria sopra Minerva in the 1st century AD (an obelisk found on the site stands on Bernini's charming elephant in the square outside the church). The cult of Mithras from Persia was also enormously popular (*see p. 539*).

In the long run, of course, it was the Christian community, first attested in the 1st century, which was to provide the most dominant of these foreign cults. The Christians actively denigrated existing Roman religion, and their refusal to sacrifice to the traditional gods made them the target of persecution; motivated, it would appear, by the ancient fear of losing the gods' support. The motives for Constantine's adoption of Christianity are difficult to fathom, but his transference of immense imperial resources into church-building was revolutionary. At first the new foundations (largely on the burial sites of martyrs outside the city walls) did not threaten the ancient pagan centre, but in a *cause célèbre* of the 380s, the Church forced the removal of the ancient winged statue of Victory from the senate house. Power now shifted. The Christian scholar Jerome captures the changing mood well: 'The golden Capitol now falls into disrepair; dust and cobwebs cover all Rome's temples. The city shakes on its foundations, and a stream of people hurries, past half-fallen shrines, to the tombs of the martyrs.' Even if ancient pagan festivities continued for some time, Rome was nominally a Christian city.

The office of *pontifex maximus* has a long and interesting history. In republican Rome it was an office to be competed over, and Julius Caesar's election to the office in 63 was an important moment in his political career. Under Augustus its power and status were absorbed by the emperor and every emperor held the title until the Christian emperor Gratian (375–83). In the 15th century the popes took it as one of their titles: '*pont. max.*' follows the names of popes on public inscriptions.   C.F.

THE RELIGIOUS CENTRE OF THE FORUM

(16) Three tall columns with their entablature are all that survive of the **Temple of Castor**, or Temple of the Dioscuri (also known as the *Castores*). The temple was almost certainly built in 484 BC by the dictator and general Aulus Postumius in honour of the twin heroes Castor and Pollux (who had been revered in Greece as sons of Zeus and brothers of Helen of Troy). In Rome their cult was adopted after the Battle of Lake Regillus (496 BC), where they led the cavalry charge directed by Postumius which resulted in victory for the Romans over the Etruscan Tarquins and their Latin allies. During the fighting they miraculously appeared calmly watering their horses in the Forum by the Temple of Vesta to announce the victory. Roman knights regarded the Dioscuri as their patrons; every year, on 15th July, they staged an impressive parade in front of the temple. The temple had three *cellae* and a deep pronaos, built on a high podium, and was restored after 200 BC. It was reconstructed by the consul Metellus Dalmaticus in 117 BC, when a tribune for orators was installed, and, according to Cicero, it was also used by money-changers. This temple was destroyed by fire in 14 or 9 BC, and the present building was inaugurated by Tiberius during the reign of Augustus (AD 6).

Peripteral in plan, and approximately 26m by 40m in area, the temple had eight Corinthian columns at either end and eleven at the sides. The wide pronaos, excavated in 1982–5, was approached by a flight of steps. The three remaining columns, which are 12.5m high and have a beautifully proportioned entablature, date from the time of Tiberius. The twins are usually depicted as giants with white chargers: the most famous statues of them are on the Quirinal hill (*see p. 331*) and another pair are on the balustrade of Piazza del Campidoglio.

The excavations in the 1980s clarified that a large atrium was built by Caligula in front of the Temple of Castor which also provided an extension to the imperial palace on the Palatine above. Traces were found of the 26.5m by 22.3m perimeter wall, built of blocks of travertine. On a lower level were Republican buildings facing the Vicus Tuscus, demolished to make way for Caligula's atrium.

Beyond the fence behind the temple are the remains of the restored shrine of the **Lacus Juturnae** (Pool of Juturna), closely connected to the story of the Dioscuri. Juturna, the nymph of healing waters, was venerated in connection with the springs here, which were of great importance in the time of the Republic. In the 4th century, fittingly enough, this became the seat of the city's water administration.

(17) A number of columns on high bases support a fragment of entablature, as well as part of the curving cella wall of the **Temple of Vesta**. This temple was a circular edifice of 20 Corinthian columns, its design recalling the form of the huts used by the Latin people, traces of which have been found on the Palatine and elsewhere in Rome. The first temple on this site was possibly made, like these, of straw and wood. It was burned down several times, notably during Nero's fire of AD 64 and in 191, and rebuilt as often, the last time by Septimius Severus and his wife, Julia Domna. It was closed by Theodosius and was in ruins by the 8th century. The circular basement surmounted by tufa blocks and some architectural fragments survived until 1930, when it was partially reconstructed.

Here the Vestals guarded the sacred fire and Vesta, goddess of the hearth, protected it. In the interior was an *adytum*, or secret place, containing the *Palladium*, a statue of Pallas Athena supposedly taken from Troy by Aeneas. No one was allowed inside the adytum except the Vestals and the *pontifex maximus*, and its contents were never shown. The *Palladium* was an object of the highest veneration, as the safety of the city depended on its preservation. When the emperor Elagabalus tried to steal it, the Vestals are supposed to have substituted another statue, keeping the cult statue of Vesta in a small shrine near the entrance to the House of the Vestals.

THE VESTAL VIRGINS

The task of the Vestals, the virgin priestesses of Vesta, was to keep the fire that symbolised the perpetuity of the state constantly alight: its extinction was the most fearful of all prodigies, as it implied the end of Rome. The origin of the cult is supposed to go back to Numa Pompilius, second king of Rome, or even to Aeneas, who brought the eternal fire of Vesta from Troy, together with the images of the *penates* (household gods).

There were six Vestals, who were chosen by the king, and later, during the Republic and Empire, by the *pontifex maximus*, a post held by the emperor himself. Girls between six and ten years of age from patrician families could be candidates. After her election, a Vestal lived in the House of the Vestals for 30 years: ten learning her duties, ten performing them and ten teaching novices. During this period she was bound by the vow of chastity. At the end of the 30 years she was free to return to the world and even to marry. The senior Vestal was called *vestalis maxima* or *virgo maxima*. If a Vestal let the sacred fire go out, she was whipped by the *pontifex maximus*, who then had to rekindle the fire by the friction of two pieces of wood from a *felix arbor* (propitious tree).

The Vestals' other duties included making offerings to Vesta, sprinkling her shrine daily with water from the Egerian fountain (*see p. 516*), assisting at the consecration of temples and other public ceremonies, and guarding the *Palladium* (*see above*). Maintained at public expense, they had many privileges, such as an exalted order of precedence and the right of intercession. Wills—including the emperor's—and treaties were entrusted to their keeping. If a Vestal broke her vow of chastity, she was immured alive in the 'Campus Sceleratus', the present Piazza Indipendenza (*map p. 655, F1*) and the man was publicly flogged to death in the Forum.

(18) The **House of the Vestals** is immediately east of the temple (*you can usually walk into it, but if not, it is partly visible from two marble corner steps*). A rose garden is planted in its ruined courtyard. The house seems too large for just six Vestals, and part of it may have been reserved for the *pontifex maximus*, whose official seat during the Republican era was in the Regia (*see below*). It dates from Republican times but was rebuilt after Nero's fire in AD 64, and was last restored by Septimius Severus.

The spacious courtyard, 61m long and 20m wide, has three ponds. The central pond was once partly covered by an octagonal structure of unknown purpose. The statue bases and statues of Vestals date from the 3rd century AD onwards. A two-storey portico surrounded the courtyard, off which are the remains of numerous rooms (some of which had more than two storeys) including a dining room and kitchen, and a mill.

As you retrace your steps, to the right of the Temple of Castor, the paving of the old road which ran through the **Arch of Augustus** has been uncovered. Only the foundations of this triumphal arch remain: it had a central span flanked by lower and narrower side passages surmounted by pediments. Excavations have dated it to 20 BC, after the standards captured by the Parthians had been returned (*see p. 126*). The *Fasti Capitolini* (*see p. 43*) may have belonged to the arch. Another, single, triumphal arch is known to have been erected by Augustus in another part of the Forum in 30 BC to commemorate his victory over Antony and Cleopatra at Actium two years earlier.

Between the Temple of Vesta and the huge Temple of Antoninus and Faustina was the site of the **Regia**, identified by very scanty remains. This was traditionally supposed to be the palace of Numa Pompilius, the second king of Rome, and the official headquarters of the *pontifex maximus*. Primitive huts, similar to those on the Palatine (*see p. 102*) were found here, and the earliest permanent construction excavated dates from the 7th century BC. The edifice, known to have been rebuilt after a fire in 36 BC, retained its 6th-century form over the centuries: the elegance of its architecture can be seen from the few scattered fragments here. The Regia may have been the depository of state archives and of the *Annales Maximi*, written by the *pontifex maximus*. It also included the Sacrarium of Mars, with the *ancilia* (sacred shields) and the Chapel of Ops, goddess of harvests. The foundations of a triumphal arch, erected in 121 BC by the censor and military commander Quintus Fabius Maximus Allobrogicus to span the Sacra Via, have been discovered at the southeast corner of the Regia.

THE EASTERN PART OF THE FORUM

The Sacra Via runs east (note the pretty drain-cover in the paving) past an **Archaic necropolis**. This was the cemetery of the ancient inhabitants of the Esquiline and Palatine, dating back to the early Iron Age, before the traditional foundation of Rome. Tombs were found for both cremations—with ashes in urns surrounded by tomb furniture, in small circular pits—and for burials—either in tufa sarcophagi, hollowed-out tree trunks or trenches lined with tufa slabs. From here the Sacra Via begins to ascend the low ridge of the Velia, which connected the Palatine hill with the Esquiline. On either side of the road are the ruins of private houses and shops.

(19) Conspicuous on the left is the so-called **Temple of Romulus**. The curving pronaos has two porphyry columns supporting an architrave (taken from another building) which flank the doorway, which still has its splendid original bronze doors, a remarkable survival from ancient Rome. The edifice is circular, built of brick, and still covered by a cupola. It was once flanked by two rectangular rooms with apses, each originally preceded by two cipollino columns (only those on the right survive). A 4th-century building, it was formerly identified as a temple dedicated to Romulus, son of Maxentius, who died in AD 309, but its precise identification is still discussed: various hypotheses include a temple of Jupiter, or the audience hall of the city prefect. In the 6th century it became the vestibule of the church of Santi Cosma e Damiano (*you can sometimes enter it from here; otherwise its interior can be seen from the church; described on p. 90*) and that is why it is so well preserved.

(20) Beyond a medieval portico on the left of the road, an old shady path with huge ancient paving stones leads up left and left again to the amazing remains of the huge **Basilica of Maxentius** (also called the Basilica of Constantine and the Basilica Nova), which dominates the Forum. The three vast barrel-vaulted niches—20.5m wide, 17.5m deep and 24.5m high—are one of the largest and most impressive examples of Roman architecture to have survived anywhere. The skill and audacity of their design inspired many Renaissance builders, and it is said that Michelangelo studied them closely when he was planning the dome of St Peter's. They formed just

the north aisle of the basilica, which was begun by Maxentius (AD 306–10) and completed by Constantine—who considerably modified the original plan—after he had defeated Maxentius in the famous Battle of the Milvian Bridge (*see p. 559*).

This enormous building was a rectangle 100m long and 65m wide, divided into a nave and two aisles by massive piers supported by buttresses. As first planned, it had a single apse on the west side. Against the central piers were eight Corinthian columns 14.5m high; the only survivor was moved by Paul V in the 17th century to Piazza Santa Maria Maggiore, where it still stands. The original entrance was from a side road to the east; on the south side Constantine added a portico with four porphyry columns (which partly survive), which opened onto the old Roman road. The basilica was used as the seat of the city prefects and, in the 4th century AD, of the *Secretarium Senatus*, the tribunal which heard cases against senators, formerly connected to the Curia. In the middle of the north wall Constantine built a second apse, which was shut off from the rest of the building by a colonnaded balustrade; here the tribunal probably held its sittings.

The interior walls, decorated with niches, were faced with marble below and with stucco above. The arches of the groin-vaulted nave, whose huge blocks have fallen to the ground, were 35m high and had a radius of nearly 20m. Parts of a spiral staircase leading to the roof can also be seen on the ground, having collapsed in an earthquake. A tunnel was built under the northwest corner of the basilica for a thoroughfare which had been blocked by its construction. The entrance to the tunnel, walled up since 1566, can still be seen. In 1487 a colossal statue of Constantine was found in the west apse; fragments of it are now in the courtyard of Palazzo dei Conservatori (*see p. 40*). The bronze plaques from the roof were removed in 626 by Pope Honorius I to be used for St Peter's Basilica.

On the right of the Sacra Via is a large open space with just two olive trees, which covers an area of recent excavations, still in progress in the summer months. From here there is a good view across the entire Forum towards the Capitoline hill.

(21) The well preserved **Arch of Titus** was presumably erected by Domitian just after the death of Titus (his brother) in AD 81, in honour of the victories of Titus and his father Vespasian in the Judaean War, which ended with the sack of Jerusalem in AD 70. Father and son shared a joint triumph on their return to Rome. In the Middle Ages the Frangipani family incorporated the arch into one of their castles; its buildings were partly removed by Sixtus IV (1471–84) and finally demolished in 1821. When Pius VII was pope in the first decades of the 19th century, the arch was dismantled and then carefully reconstructed by Giuseppe Valadier, who used travertine instead of marble so that his restorations are easily distinguishable (this is recorded in the inscription on the west face). In the attic of the east face the prominent dedication is from SPQR (the Senate and People of Rome) to the 'divine' Titus, son of the 'divine' Vespasian.

The beautiful, perfectly-proportioned single archway with Composite columns is covered with Pentelic marble. The two splendid reliefs inside are very worn. One of them shows the goddess Roma guiding the Imperial quadriga with Titus and the winged figure of Victory; and the other shows a triumphal procession bringing the war booty from Jerusalem, which includes the altar of Solomon's Temple, decorated with trumpets, and the seven-branched golden candlestick (or Menorah), the symbol of Judaism. In the centre of the panelled vault is the *Apotheosis of Titus*, showing the deified emperor mounted on an eagle. On the exterior frieze is another procession in which the symbolic figure of the conquered Jordan is borne on a stretcher.

(22) On the left of the Arch of Titus is a terrace on the summit of the Velia overlooking the Colosseum, where the enormous **Temple of Venus and Roma**, the largest temple (145m by 100m) ever built in Rome, stood. Probably designed by Hadrian himself, it occupied the site of the vestibule of the Domus Aurea (*see p. 115*). It was built in honour of Venus, the mother of Aeneas and the ancestor of the *gens* Julia, and of Roma Aeterna, whose cult appears to have been localised on the Velia. Begun c. 125 and dedicated in 135, it dominated this end of the Roman Forum. Its Classical proportions show how strongly the emperor was influenced by Greek architecture. Damaged by fire in 283, it was restored by Maxentius in 307. It is said to have been the last pagan temple to remain in use in Rome: it was closed in 391 by Theodosius. It remained virtually entire until 625, when Honorius I took

ARCH OF TITUS
Relief showing Roman soldiers carrying off war booty from Jerusalem.

the bronze tiles from its roof for the old basilica of St Peter's.

To counteract the unevenness of the ground, it was necessary to build a high platform. This was of rubble, with slabs of peperino and marble-faced travertine. The temple had ten granite Corinthian columns at the front and back and 20 on each of the sides. It had two cellae placed back to back; that facing the Forum was the shrine of Roma Aeterna and the other that of Venus. The visible remains date from the time of Maxentius. The two *cellae* (the apses and diamond-shaped coffers were added by Maxentius) are still standing. The brick walls were formerly faced with marble and provided with niches framed with small porphyry columns. The apse contains the base of the statue of the goddess. The floor is of coloured marbles. The temple was surrounded by a colonnaded courtyard, with two entrances on the north and south sides; in 1935 some of the columns and column fragments on the south were re-erected.

THE LOWER SLOPES OF THE PALATINE

Excavations since 1985 in the area between the Arch of Titus and the House of the Vestals have revealed evidence of the destruction of numerous buildings by Nero for his huge Domus Aurea (*see p. 115*). Remains have been found of its large portico, which Domitian reused when he built the **Horrea Piperataria**, a bazaar for Oriental goods, pepper and spices, and the area gradually became commercialised, as part of a general plan of the Flavians to reinstal public edifices after the death of Nero. The visible remains belong to large warehouses on several floors and to the **Horreum Vespasiani**, a market which fronted the Horrea Piperataria.

The building nearest the House of the Vestals probably dates in its present form from the time of Hadrian. A row of shops against the Palatine hill is prominent: almost in the centre a well-preserved vaulted edifice can be seen, beside which steps led up to the Nova Via and the upper floors. Also in this area, the servants' quarters attached to the **residence of Marcus Aemilius Scaurus** is thought to have been identified **(23)**. This was frequently mentioned by Roman writers as being the most splendid on the Palatine at that time. Scaurus was a quaestor who had judicial and financial powers under Pompey. He married Pompey's former wife and is thought to have lived here in 58 BC before he fell into disgrace and was exiled in 52 BC.

The excavations also seem to have revealed **Archaic walls** on three levels: the oldest traces have been dated to 730–675 BC; above these a wall constructed in large blocks of red tufa defended by a ditch was identified (c. 600 BC), and the fortifications on this site appear to date from 530–50 BC. Subsequent levels have shown interesting remains of at least four Archaic houses and four from the later Republican era.

THE POMERIUM

The *pomerium* is the name given to the sacred boundary of an ancient Roman city founded with the help of omens. It consisted of a wall and/or the sacred strip of land between the wall and the city's outermost buildings: when a Roman colony was founded a simple ploughed furrow would encircle it in order to define the pomerium. Within the enclosed precincts, burials were forbidden.

Founding a city: relief from the Museo Nazionale Romano in the Baths of Diocletian.

The name of 'Roma Quadrata' was also used by ancient authors in connection with the city founded by Romulus, since the line of its pomerium seems to have formed an approximate rectangle. However studies by archaeologists and scholars of ancient texts are still underway to locate the precise area of the first pomerium and its gates. It has been suggested that the Scalae Caci on the Palatine are on the site of one of the three gates (in the southwest corner overlooking the valley of the Circus Maximus, where traces of a wall of tufa have been found) and another part of the Archaic wall has been identified by some scholars as that unearthed in the Roman Forum at the northern foot of the Palatine (*see above*). This may suggest that the sacred area was limited more or less to the area of the Palatine (as described by Tacitus), but neither the Porta Mugonia (northeast) nor the Porta Romanula (northwest) have yet been identified. Many archaeologists believe that a corner of the pomerium has been identified in recent excavations on the northeast lower slopes of the Palatine (*see below*), together with remains of the ancient shrine known as the 'Curiae Veteres' mentioned by the Latin authors (other scholars suggest that it is the little shrine in the form of a temple set up by Augustus in memory of his wife Livia).

Marcus Terentius Varro (116–27 BC) describes a much larger pomerium which enclosed the Capitol, Quirinal, Viminal, Oppian, Caelian and Palatine hills. Under the emperors the boundaries extended to include the Aventine and other parts of the city.

Very important excavations are in progress on the **northeast lower slopes of the Palatine** (seen from the Forum behind railings and a row of cypresses). The earliest finds date from the 6th century BC and include an oval structure thought to be a sanctuary founded by Romulus (it was repeatedly restored up until the 4th century AD). There are also ruins of the Curiae Veteres (*see Pomerium, above*) and a domus built in the late Republican era (destroyed in Nero's fire). The sceptres, flagstaffs and lances used in ceremonies by the emperor Maxentius in the early 4th century AD were found here (now exhibited in Palazzo Massimo; *see p. 327*). On the Palatine beneath the Vigna Barberini (*described on p. 105*) you can see remains of markets and porticoes built under Hadrian and Septimius Severus.

TWO CHURCHES JUST OUTSIDE THE FORUM

SANTA FRANCESCA ROMANA

Map p. 655, D3. Open 10.30–12.30 & 3.30–6. The church is outside the exit from the Roman Forum through the Basilica of Maxentius and is also reached by a short road up from the Colosseum. Part of the former conventual buildings now contain the excavation offices of the Roman Forum (entered from inside the Forum).

The church of Santa Francesca Romana is also known as Santa Maria Nova because in 847, after grave structural damage to the church of Santa Maria Antiqua in the Roman Forum, that church was abandoned and the diaconate was transferred to the oratory here, which became the 'new' St Mary's.

There is a fine stretch of ancient Roman road (which led up to the Velia hillock) on the approach to the west door. The church encroaches on the ruins of the Temple of Venus and Roma (*see p. 86*) and incorporates an oratory of St Peter and St Paul built by Pope Paul I (757–67) in the west portico of that temple. The campanile was added before the church was reconsecrated in 1161. The façade, by Carlo Lombardi, dates from a second reconstruction of the building in 1615 when a monastery for the Olivetans, of the Benedictine Order, was provided.

St Francesca Romana (1384–1440)—Francesca Bussa de' Leoni, wife of Lorenzo Ponziani—founded the Congregation of Oblates here in 1421, and joined it herself after her husband's death in 1436. Canonised in 1608, she is the patron saint of motorists, and on her festival (9th March) the street between the church and the Colosseum is congested with cars lining up for a blessing. The painter Gentile da Fabriano was buried in the church in 1428.

The interior

There is a restored Cosmatesque pavement at the raised east end where the little marble **confessio**, which has a marble group of Santa Francesca Romana and an angel carved in 1866, is particularly interesting as it is a documented early work by Bernini. The statues of angels on either side of the sanctuary are by his workshop. Above the high altar is a 12th-century *Madonna and Child*, detached in 1950 from another painting found beneath it. The earlier painting, a very large and beautifully-painted *Virgin and Child*, which may have come from Santa Maria Antiqua, is now kept in the sacristy (*sometimes shown on request; you can also try ringing at the convent door outside at the top of the steps on the left of the façade*). Probably dating from the end of the 6th century (it was already described as 'an ancient image' by the middle of the 8th), it is one of the earliest Christian paintings in existence. It belongs to the type known as *Glykophilousa*, from the Greek for 'sweet love', and shows the Madonna embracing the Child with her arm as the Child reaches up to caress her face. The sacristy also has fragments of medieval frescoes, and early 16th-century paintings (attributed to Perino del Vaga) of Paul III and Reginald Pole, whom the pope made cardinal after his refusal to condone Henry VIII's divorce. The beautiful **apse** mosaics of the *Madonna and Saints* were probably completed in 1161.

In the vestibule of the side entrance are the tombs of Cardinal Marino Bulcani (d. 1394) and Antonio da Rio (or Rido), castellan of Castel Sant'Angelo (c. 1450), who is shown in relief mounted on his charger.

In the south transept is the tomb of Gregory XI by Pier Paolo Olivieri, set up in 1585 by the Roman people in honour of the pope who had restored the seat of the papacy to Rome from Avignon in 1377. Let into the south wall here behind grilles are two flagstones from the Sacra Via which supposedly show the imprint of the knees of St Peter, made as he knelt to pray for the punishment of Simon Magus, a legendary figure who tried to demonstrate his wizardry to Nero by flying; this was a sacrilegious act since it imitated the Ascension of Christ.

From here stairs lead down to the **crypt**, with the gruesome 'body' of St Francesca Romana, wrapped in a white shroud with just her skull and black slippers showing. Messages are left for her. The 17th-century bas-relief shows her with an angel.

SANTI COSMA E DAMIANO
Map p. 655, D3. Usually open 9–13 & 3–6.30. Entrance just outside the entrance to the Roman Forum on Via dei Fori Imperiali.

In 527 the so-called Temple of Romulus (*see p. 85*) in the Roman Forum was used by Pope Felix IV as a vestibule for his church dedicated to two brothers from Cilicia, Cosmas and Damian, who were miraculous healers (they are now the patron saints of doctors). At the west end a huge window provides a **view of the temple interior**.

The beautiful **mosaics on the triumphal arch and in the apse** were commissioned by St Felix (*coin-operated light*) and include a likeness of him holding a model of his church. His inscription proudly points out how the brightness of the mosaics makes the church 'shine' in splendour. They inspired other such decoration in early Christian churches in Rome, especially in the 9th century. The detail is astonishing, and the style of expression more personal than the static mosaics of the later Byzantine tradition. On the triumphal arch is the *Lamb Enthroned*, surrounded by seven candlesticks, four angels and the symbols of two Evangelists. In the apse are Sts Cosmas and Damian being presented to Christ at His Second Coming by St Peter and St Paul; St Theodore (on the right); and St Felix IV (on the left, restored). There are also mosaics of palms (symbols of life and of victory over death) and the phoenix (sym-

SANTI COSMA E DAMIANO
Detail of the 6th-century apse mosaic. In this early Christian work, Christ is portrayed
clad in the *toga praetexta*, the purple-banded toga of Roman magistrates. On it is the
letter iota, tenth letter of the Greek alphabet thought to symbolise the
Ten Commandments, hence the Law and the Word made Flesh.

bol of the Resurrection). Below the word *Iordanes* is the Lamb on a mount from which four rivers, symbolising the Gospels, flow; twelve other lambs represent the Apostles, with Bethlehem and Jerusalem on either side.

The church was rebuilt in 1632, when the pavement was added to make it a two-storey building, and the frescoes and painted altarpieces mostly date from that time. On the Baroque high altar is a 13th-century *Madonna and Child* and in the first south chapel (right aisle) is an unusual fresco of Christ on the Cross wearing a crown and with open eyes, which may also date from the 13th century. It seems to be derived from the *Volto Santo* in Lucca (an ancient wooden likeness of Christ which is still a famous devotional image) and was probably repainted in the 17th century by an artist from that Tuscan city.

Off the early 17th-century **cloister**, decorated with a fountain and palm trees, is part of an 18th-century Neapolitan *presepio* (crib). The models and figures in wood, terracotta and porcelain are of exceptionally fine workmanship.

The Palatine Hill

The Palatine Hill, inhabited by the 9th century BC, was chosen as a place of residence during the Republic and then as the site of the palace of the Roman emperors. Today it is a beautiful park with the ruins of these ancient buildings.

I t was on the Palatine Hill (*map p. 655, D3–D4 and plan on pp. 96–7*) that the primitive city of Rome was founded, and splendid Imperial palaces were later built over its slopes, so that the word Palatine came to be synonymous with the palace of the emperor (and provided the derivation for our word 'palace'). The gardens are nicely kept, with a profusion of wild flowers and fine trees, and are inhabited by many birds (and cats). There are wonderful views from the edge of the hill. Remarkably isolated from the traffic-ridden streets below, the Palatine is one of the most romantic and charming spots in the centre of the city.

Planning a visit

Open 9–1hr before sunset. For information, see archeoroma.beniculturali.it. For advance tickets, T: 06 39 96 7700, coopculture.it. Ticket (valid 2 days) includes (a single) admission to the Palatine Museum and Roman Forum, as well as to the Colosseum. For the Archaeological Card and reductions for young visitors, see p. 600. Access is from the Forum or from Via di San Gregorio (see plan on pp. 96–7).

At the time of writing it was necessary to book the combined visit to the Casa di Augusto (Domus Augustae) and the Casa di Livia, both of the highest interest for their exquisite bright wall-paintings, although off season you can also sometimes arrange a visit directly at the entrance. To book and buy your ticket: prenotazioni@ coopculture.it or T: 06 39 96 7700.

The gate that gives access to the so-called 'Arcate Severiane' (near the Via di San Gregorio entrance) was only open on Tues and Fri at the time of writing; to check opening times, see coopculture.it or telephone as above.

HISTORY OF THE PALATINE

Recent research suggests that the Palatine Hill was inhabited sporadically by the Late Bronze Age (13th–12th centuries BC), and traces of occupation going back to the 9th century BC have been discovered during excavations. The earliest Palaeolithic material has been found in the area of the Temple of Victory (near the Temple of Cybele) and at the northern foot of the hill.

The northern slopes of the Palatine, in the area nearest to the Forum, were for centuries considered one of the most prestigious residential districts. During the Republic many prominent citizens lived here, including the great orator and writer Cicero, the statesman and philosopher Quintus Lutatius Catulus, the orators Crassus and Hortensius, the demagogue Publius Clodius and the triumvir Antony. Remains of some of these residences have recently been unearthed. Augustus was born on the Palatine and as emperor built himself a residence here. The Temple of Apollo, with Greek and Latin libraries attached, also dates from his time. Succeeding emperors, especially the Flavians, chose to build their private residence and official palace on the summit of the hill.

Odoacer, first king of Italy after the extinction of the Western Empire in 476, lived on the Palatine; so for a time did Theodoric, King of the Ostrogoths, who ruled Italy from 493 to 526. The hill later became a residence of the representatives of the Eastern (Byzantine) Empire. From time to time it was favoured by the popes, and some churches were built here. In the course of time, after a period of devastation, the Frangipani and other noble families erected their castles over the ruins. In the 16th century part of the hill was laid out as a villa for the Farnese, and in the following century the Barberini planted a vineyard on the huge terrace which had supported the eastern wing of the Flavian palace.

LEGENDS ATTACHED TO THE PALATINE

According to tradition the hill was first settled from Greece. Sixty years before the Trojan War (traditional date 1184 BC) Evander, son of Hermes and an Arcadian nymph, led a colony from Pallantion in Arcadia, and built a town at the foot of a hill near the Tiber, naming it after his native village. Aeneas, who escaped from burning Troy after the Trojan War, sailed to Italy, and according to Virgil was welcomed here by Evander.

Some Classical authors give quite another explanation of the name *Palatium*: that it is derived from Pales, the goddess of flocks and shepherds, whose festival was celebrated on 21st April, the day on which the city of Rome is said to have been founded by Romulus and Remus in 754 or 753 BC. The story goes that the twins were found on the hill by the shepherd Faustulus, and the cave where they were nursed by the she-wolf was located at its foot. When they grew up and decided to found a new city, they contested its site, with Remus advocating the Aventine and Romulus the Palatine. It was decided that the first to see a flight of birds as an omen would be given the choice, and when twelve vultures flew over the Palatine Romulus was given the honour of naming the city. After killing his brother to remove all threat of opposition, he became the first king of Rome.

EXCAVATIONS

Systematic excavations were started about 1724 by Francesco Bianchini, shortly after Duke Francis I of Bourbon-Parma had inherited the Farnese Gardens. Little more was done in a scientific way until 1860; in that year the gardens were bought by Napoleon III, who entrusted the direction of the excavations to Pietro Rosa, an extremely skilled archaeologist who preserved the finds by founding the Palatine Museum. He continued his work after 1870, when the Palatine was acquired by the Italian Government.

In the early 20th century Giacomo Boni directed excavations in the area of the Imperial palace and he was succeeded between the two world wars by Alfonso Bartoli, who also brought to light much information about the earliest inhabitants. In the 1960s important work was done in the House of Augustus and the adjacent Temple of Apollo was identified. Excavations are still in progress on the lower northern slopes of the hill, as well as on the eastern slopes near the Vigna Barberini and near the Domus Severiana on the hill's eastern limit.

The most extensive digs have been carried out in the southwest corner of the hill in the area of the Temple of Cybele. Since 1998 new studies have been in progress in an attempt to date the various stages of the building of the imperial palace in the areas on the eastern side of the hill and to understand how the different groups of buildings were used and connected to each other.

VISITING THE RUINS

It is now generally accepted that the entire summit of the hill was covered with buildings used by the emperor of the day, and he would sometimes add a new edifice or radically rebuild an old one. The first grand buildings are thought to have been built by Augustus, but it was the Flavian emperors, and in particular Vespasian and Domitian at the end of the 1st century AD, who first designed the buildings as a great Imperial palace. This included the following areas: to the south the so-called Domus Flavia, Domus Augustana, Stadium and Domus Severiana; and to the north the Domus Tiberiana. The visible remains date from modifications made right up to the time of Diocletian, making it difficult to appreciate the appearance of the Flavian palace.

NB: It is not always easy to identify the ancient ruins, some of which are under cover, some reduced to little more than fragments of their marble paving, others far below ground level and only viewable from above, and still others over-planted with gardens. The plan overleaf shows their layout.

The description below is divided into five distinct areas:
- Open ruins of the imperial palace on the summit of the hill: Domus Augustana, Domus Flavia and Domus Severiana (*opposite*);
- Covered excavations in the southwestern part of the hill (*p. 102*);
- Domus Tiberiana: Farnese Gardens and cryptoporticus (*p. 104*);
- Vigna Barberini (*p. 105*);
- Casa di Augusto and Casa di Livia (*p. 105*).

THE ANCIENT APPROACH TO THE PALATINE

The ancient approach from the Forum, which can still be taken today, followed the so-called **Clivus Palatinus** near the Arch of Titus. It then crossed the Nova Via, the ancient road which ran parallel to and above the Sacra Via and provided a means of communication between the Forum and the Palatine. The visible remains on either side of the Nova Via probably date from the Flavian period, but at the point where it crosses the Clivus Palatinus, recent excavations have revealed paving which seems to date from the Republican era. Considerable ruins of shops and buildings which faced onto the road can be seen here. The Clivus Palatinus continues uphill. On the right are the steps which ascend to the Farnese Gardens and cryptoporticus. At a point where the round paving stones of the Clivus Capitolinus are still preserved, an archway on the left leads into the Vigna Barberini.

THE OPEN RUINS OF THE IMPERIAL PALACE

Beyond a row of olive trees, the path on the site of the Clivus Palatinus reaches a T-junction. Take the path to the left, where there is a little fountain with running water, and turn towards the solitary pine on a little mound in an area of the hill covered with romantic ruined Roman buildings, left standing above fragments of their once-sumptuous marble paving. The most conspicuous remains are those of the imperial palace, the grand residence of the emperors of the Flavian dynasty. It was begun by Vespasian and continued by Domitian, who employed the famous architect Rabirius.

It is divided into three areas: the buildings used in a private capacity by the emperors, named in the 20th century the 'Domus Augustana'; the garden area in the so-called 'Stadium' and to the south where the 'Domus Severiana' (or recently named 'Arcate Severiane') faced onto the Circus Maximus; and the so-called 'Domus Flavia', where the official life of the emperor took place.

THE PRIVATE QUARTERS OF THE EMPEROR (DOMUS AUGUSTANA)

The design of the Imperial domicile is not easy to appreciate today, but it was built on two levels with two peristyles, one on the upper level and one much lower. On the **upper level**, only the bases of the columns of the open peristyle, in front and to the east of the Palatine Museum building, and various small rooms survive. A path leads towards the southwest edge of the hill between the museum and the triclinium, from where there is a splendid view of another court on the **lower level** (*no access but well seen from above*), some 10m below the ground, in the middle of which is a large basin with a quadrangular shrine, surrounded by numerous living-rooms and fountain courts. A doorway in the bottom wall led to the exedra of the palace overlooking the Circus Maximus; this was originally decorated with a colonnade.

THE AREA OF THE GARDENS AND THE DOMUS SEVERIANA

The gardens laid out in the time of Domitian adjoining the eastern part of the palace, included a sunken garden, today still known as the **Stadium (1)**, since it has the appearance of a hippodrome. There is a splendid view of it from above, although there is no admission to the ground level. It is a huge enclosure 160m long, with a series of rooms at the north end and a curved wall at the south. The interior had a two-storeyed portico on three sides with engaged columns covering a wide ambulatory or shady clois-

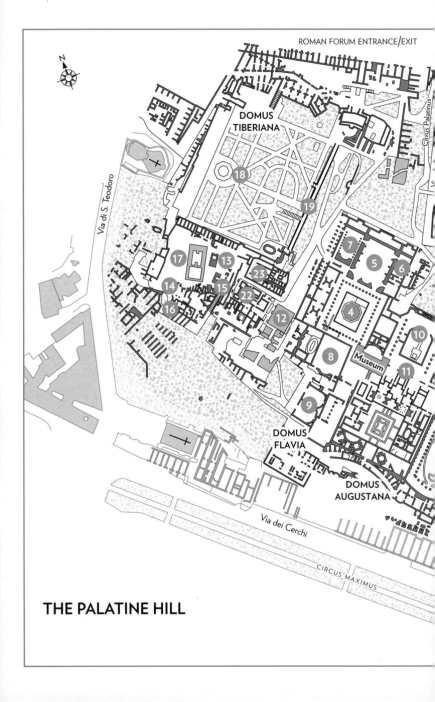

ROMAN FORUM ENTRANCE/EXIT

DOMUS
TIBERIANA

Clivus Palatinus

Via di S. Teodoro

DOMUS
FLAVIA

DOMUS
AUGUSTANA

Museum

Via dei Cerchi

CIRCUS MAXIMUS

THE PALATINE HILL

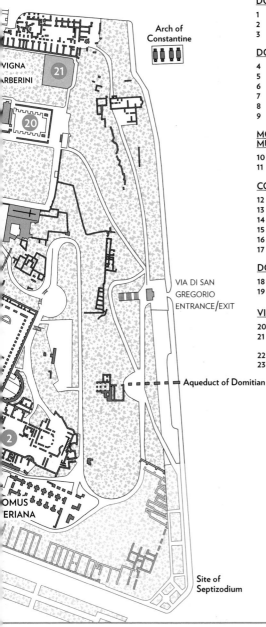

Arch of
Constantine

DOMUS SEVERIANA

1 'Stadium' (garden)
2 Arcate Severiane
3 Site of imperial box

DOMUS FLAVIA

4 Peristyle
5 Aula Regia
6 Lararium
7 Basilica Jovis
8 Triclinium
9 Rooms with apses

MONUMENTS OPENED BY THE MUSEUM

10 House of the Griffins
11 Loggia Stati Mattei/ Aula Isiaca

COVERED EXCAVATIONS

12 Temple of Apollo
13 Temple of Victory
14 Hut village
15 Scalae Caci
16 House of Romulus
17 Temple of Cybele

DOMUS TIBERIANA

18 Farnese Gardens
19 Cryptoporticus

VIGNA BARBERINI

20 Excavations (Temple of the Sun)
21 Excavations (Circular hall)

22 Casa di Augusto
23 Casa di Livia

VIA DI SAN
GREGORIO
ENTRANCE/EXIT

Aqueduct of Domitian

Site of
Septizodium

ter. In the centre are two rows of piers of a portico. Towards the south are the remains of an oval construction inserted in the early Middle Ages which blocked the curved end. Columns of granite and cipollino, Tuscan, Corinthian and Composite capitals, and fragments of a marble altar with figures of divinities now lie on the ground. In the middle of the east wall is a wide two-storey exedra shaped like an apse and approached from the outside by a curved corridor.

East of the Stadium was the area of the so-called **Arcate Severiane (2)**, which was built over a foundation formed by enlarging the southern corner of the hill by means of enormous substructures that extended almost as far as the Circus Maximus. Built by Septimius Severus this included an **imperial box (3)** from which the emperor could watch the contests in the Circus. It is now thought that these buildings, more extensive than previously assumed, were all part of Domitian's imperial palace, and would have included a lake and hanging garden. At the time of writing the area was open on two days a week (*see above*), reached through a gate on the far side of the 'Stadium' where a path leads behind the exedra through the reception area of this wing of the palace. There is a wonderful view left towards the interior of the Colosseum. The Severan buildings dating from AD 193–211 include a reconstruction of the terrace, and baths built by Septimius Severus. Recent excavations have revealed a large pavilion overlooking a porticoed garden which was decorated with fountains. The baths were built above these. From the fence you can see them far below the present ground level and in the distance the view of St Peter's is framed by a group of cypresses and a Roman wall (and on the right you can see the dome of Sant'Andrea della Valle). If you continue up across a bridge you reach a huge (reconstructed) terrace (supplied with nice benches) directly overlooking the Circus Maximus. The wider view remains more or less as it was in ancient times: you can see the Aventine and Caelian hills on the left, with the Alban Hills in the distance and the Baths of Caracalla on the skyline. On the right was the area of the Forum Boarium and, beyond, the Vatican and the ridge of the wooded Janiculum (today marked by the white monument to Garibaldi). At the end the grassy slope below the terrace is near the site of the famous Septizodium (*see p. 559*).

Lower down are remains of the **aqueduct built by Domitian** to provide water for his palace; it was an extension of the Aqua Claudia which ran from the Caelian hill to the Palatine. The aqueduct was restored by Septimius Severus.

THE OFFICIAL QUARTERS OF THE EMPEROR (DOMUS FLAVIA)

The public part of the Flavian Palace, which covered the Palatium summit, was a vast collection of buildings, brilliantly planned for Domitian in AD 81–96 by the architect Rabirius, who levelled the central part of the hill to fill up the depression on the west. In the process he demolished or buried numerous earlier constructions, from private houses to imperial palaces, some of which have been revealed by excavations. The splendour of the palace was praised by numerous Roman poets.

The original entrance was to the north, towards the Forum, by a monumental staircase of three flights. Recent excavations have confirmed that the palace extended as far as the area of the Vigna Barberini (*see p. 105*), and there was a magnificent library hall connected to it on the other side of the Palatine hill.

In the centre of this palace is the spacious **peristyle (4)**, with an impluvium in the middle in the form of an octagonal maze surrounding a fountain. A box hedge reproduction of this maze is in the Farnese Gardens (*see below*). The peristyle was surrounded by a portico, and because of Domitian's constant dread of assassination he is thought to have had the walls covered with slabs of Cappadocian marble, the mirror-like surface of which enabled him to see anyone approaching. On the west side is a series of small rooms with apses, statue bases and baths; on the east side are traces of three more rooms.

To the north of the peristyle are three large halls facing north (*at present fenced off*). The central hall is the so-called **Aula Regia (5)**, or throne room, originally decorated with 16 columns of *pavonazzetto* and twelve black basalt statues: two of the statues were found in 1724 and are now in Parma. In the apse was the imperial throne where the emperor sat when he presided over meetings of his council and received foreign ambassadors. To the east is the so-called **Lararium (6)** (*under cover*), not as was once thought a shrine to the *lares* but more probably another room used for public ceremonies, or a guardroom protecting the main entrance to the palace. To the west is the **Basilica Jovis (7)**, divided by two rows of columns of *giallo antico*; it has an apse at the further end, closed by a marble screen. This may have been used as an auditorium for political and administrative meetings. A flight of steps (*no admission*) connects the basilica to the cryptoporticus in the Farnese Gardens. A portico of cipollino columns, also on the north, may have served as a loggia.

To the south of the peristyle is the **triclinium (8)** or banqueting hall. It has an apse reached by a high step; in it was placed the table where the emperor dined. The hall was paved with coloured marbles, which are well preserved in the apse. Leading out of the hall on either side was a court with an oval fountain. Around the fountain on the west side, which is also well preserved, is a magnificent pavement in opus sectile. The conspicuous pavilion here, with a double loggia, was constructed by the Farnese in the 16th century as part of their gardens (*see below*). A staircase (*no admission*) leads down from the triclinium to a court beneath it with a partly restored nymphaeum, decorated with rare marbles; the exquisite mid-1st-century AD frescoes from the vault, attributed to Fabullus, have been detached and are now exhibited in the Palatine Museum.

Behind the triclinium is a row of partly-restored columns belonging to the Flavian palace. Further south are two **rooms with apses (9)**, probably reception rooms used by Augustus for legates.

THE PALATINE MUSEUM

Roughly in the centre of the hill is a former convent building which has been home to the Palatine Museum since 1868 (*same opening times as the hill itself*). It houses wall decorations and frescoes, stucco, marble intarsia and sculptures from excavations on the hill, including material found only a few years ago dating from the earliest settlements here. It was re-opened in 2014 with an excellent new display and good labelling and interactive supports.

Ground floor: The earliest prehistoric hut villages found on the hill (9th–8th centuries BC) are well illustrated; finds from the area near the Temple of Victory include Palaeolithic artefacts.

Upper floor: Room VI is dedicated to Augustus. There is a fragment of a wall-painting which shows Apollo with his lyre against a bright blue ground.The four exquisite terracotta heads (three of Apollo and one of Venus, derived from Greek bronzes) were made from moulds but finished by hand. The beautiful painted terracotta panels with reliefs of paired figures (38–28 BC) were found in the area of the House of Augustus and Temple of Apollo. The four herms (three in black marble and one in red marble) were part of the series of the 50 Danaïds which decorated the temple portico. These were the daughters of Danaus who, according to a complicated Egyptian myth, were ordered by their father to kill their Egyptian husbands on their wedding day, and were sent to Hades and condemned to carry leaking jars of water. Also found near the temple is the damaged but very lovely basalt statue of an ephebus. Two marble statues of vestals come from the House of the Vestals in the Roman Forum. The extraordinary pair of marble wings (from a statue of Victory) and the statue of a prince of the Julio Claudian family were found very recently in the excavations on the site of the Domus Tiberiana. Room VII contains beautiful marble intarsia pavements and exquisite frescoes of Homeric subjects, all found beneath the triclinium of the Palace of Domitian.

Room VIII has marble intarsia panels, a fragment of a colossal statue of a river god from the Septizodium, the torso of a tiger which once had inlay in its coat, and a graffito caricature of the Crucifixion which shows a young man standing before a cross on which hangs a figure with a donkey's head. The blasphemous inscription in Greek reads 'Alexamenos worships his god'.

Room IX has a display of Imperial portrait heads including Nero, Trajan and a girl identified as a daughter of Marcus Aurelius (mid-1st century AD). The last room, Room X, has a graceful statuette of a satyr turning round to look at his tail, a Roman copy of a Hellenistic bronze, and numerous other very fine statues including an elegant female figure of the 5th century BC in shining white Thasian marble, two statues of seated nymphs and a statue of Aphrodite, all three found in the 'Stadium'. The headless seated statue of Cybele from her temple is also displayed here between two very unusual but moving portrait heads, one known as the *Dying Persian* and one of a woman, also close to death.

MONUMENTS OPENED ON REQUEST AT THE PALATINE MUSEUM

The **House of the Griffins (10)** is named after the two griffins in stucco which decorate a lunette in one of the rooms. It is the oldest Republican building preserved on the Palatine (2nd or 1st century BC). A steep staircase leads down to its lower floor where the best preserved room is the large hall with its paintings in the second Pompeian style, which simulate three planes of different depth, and the columns imitate various marbles. Round the top of the walls runs a cornice and the ceiling is stuccoed. In the centre of the mosaic floor there is an opus sectile pavement.

PALATINE MUSEUM

Graffito from the early Christian period mocking the new religion. A man given the Greek name Alexamenos is shown worshipping a donkey-headed figure on the Cross. Crucifixion was a humiliating punishment in Roman eyes, reserved for the lowest of the low; that a sect could have grown up around the worship of an executed felon is ridiculed here.

Next to the museum building is the **Loggia Stati Mattei (11)**, a winter loggia formerly part of the Villa Mattei, built in 1520 with a vault decorated with *grottesche* on a white background by the circle of Baldassare Peruzzi, clearly showing the influence of Raphael. The tondi with the Signs of the Zodiac were detached in 1846 and ended up in the Metropolitan Museum of Art in New York: the museum has recently generously returned them here. The frescoes from the walls found their way to St Petersburg at the same time and are still in the Hermitage.

The loggia overlooks a room which contains murals detached in 1966 from the **Aula Isiaca** (Hall of Isis) beneath the Basilica Jovis of the Palace of Domitian. This was a large rectangular hall with an apse at one end, erected in the Republican era and modified probably under Caligula, and dedicated to the cult of Isis. The fantastic architectural paintings, with Egyptian motifs, were painted just before the edict of 21 BC banning the worship of Isis, but their style was much in vogue at this time, after Octavian's victory over Antony and Cleopatra at Actium. They were discovered in 1724 and were copied in the same century by Francesco Bartoli. His watercolours of them (when they were in much better condition) are preserved in the Topham Collection at Eton College in England.

THE COVERED EXCAVATIONS ON THE SOUTHWESTERN PALATINE

From the ruins of the triclinium of the royal palace a few steps (*signposted for the Casa di Augusto and Casa di Livia*) descend to the ruins in the western part of the hill, which have been covered with protective roofs, making them much less romantic to visit, though they include very beautiful wall-paintings in the Casa di Augusto and the Casa di Livia.

THE TEMPLES OF APOLLO AND VICTORY

The **Temple of Apollo (12)** was initiated by Augustus in 36 BC and dedicated eight years later, after the Battle of Actium. This famous building has only been identified recently but all that survives of it is its basement, 44m by 24m, reached on the south side by a long flight of steps (the existing flight is a modern reproduction). It was surrounded by the Portico of the Danaïds, on which were statues (or herms) of the 50 daughters of Danaus (*for the finds see p. 100*). A corridor thought to have connected the temple to the House of Augustus has been excavated here, and wall-paintings have been discovered near the temple podium. A building of the late Republican era was found beneath the temple. Nearby were the renowned Greek and Latin libraries, rebuilt by Domitian.

The path continues past a round cistern (under cover), and it is flanked on the right by arches which belonged to the Domus Tiberiana (*see below*). On the right is the modern building which protects the Casa di Livia (*open by appointment; described on p. 106*).

From the pathway there is a fine view of the dome of St Peter's beyond that of the synagogue. On the left a path leads down past (right) the base of the small **Temple of Victory Virgo**, dedicated by Marcus Porcius Cato (Cato the Elder) in 193 BC. Cato was well known for his wise politics while serving as censor, and is also famous for his writings. On the left is the larger **Temple of Victory (13)**, one of the earliest temples so far found on the hill, built in 294 BC. The path ends on the left at the gate into the Casa di Augusto (*open by appointment; described on p. 106*).

THE ARCHAIC HUT VILLAGE AND LUPERCAL

In the large (covered) area on the southwestern edge of the hill the earliest traces of habitation have been discovered. Excavations have been in progress here since 1978 and access is limited, but from the end of the walkway you can just make out some holes and channels in the tufa marking the site of a **hut village (14)** of the Early Iron Age (9th century BC). This is clearly explained in the Palatine Museum (*see above*): each hut was about 18 square metres in size. We know that the land here was farmed at the time (grain was cultivated and animals used). The village was destroyed in the 7th century BC.

Traces of a wall of tufa and the site of the **Scalae Caci (15)**, probably one of the three gates of the ancient city (*see Pomerium, p. 88*), have been found in the vicinity. The gate is named after Cacus, a giant monster who, according to legend, had his den in the Forum Boarium at the foot of the hill and terrified the populace by his pillaging. It was only when he dared to steal the cattle which had belonged to the monster Geryon, and which Hercules had obtained as one of his Twelve Labours, that he was finally put to death by the Greek hero.

It is known that the **Lupercal** was also in this part of the hill. This was the cave sanctuary of the she-wolf connected with the legend of Romulus and Remus and sacred to Rome. There was an altar here which was surrounded by a grove sacred to the god Lupercus, and at the annual festival of the Lupercalia, held on 15th February, the priests of the god, the *luperci*, dressed in goatskins, would process around the hill whipping whomever they met (it was believed that the castigation of women encouraged fertility). The Latin *februarius* means purification and expiation.

In 2008 investigations on the lower part of the hill here, some 16m below ground level, revealed the presence of a circular domed edifice decorated with shells and pebble mosaics, with a white eagle in the central tondo of the vault, which some archaeologists claimed might be this very grotto. Others have strongly contested this claim, suggesting that it was, instead, a nymphaeum, probably part of the Imperial palace here which had already been identified in the 16th century. Discussion continues.

A hut at the top of the Scalae Caci near the Temple of Cybele is known as the **House of Romulus (16)**: it was restored periodically and up until the 4th century AD was mentioned as being the hut that belonged to the shepherd Faustulus who found the legendary twins and brought them up.

THE TEMPLE OF CYBELE

On a mound covered with a thicket of dark ilex trees is all that is left of the base of the Temple of Mater Matuta or **Temple of Cybele (17)**. Cybele, the Magna Mater, mother of the gods, was the great Asiatic goddess of fertility and was worshipped in the town of Pessinus in Phrygia (Asia Minor). She and her young lover Attis were served by eunuch priests, and their festival was celebrated annually (22nd–24th March) with primitive orgies. During a critical period of the Second Punic War, an oracle had foretold that the battle could only be won if the Romans obtained from Phrygia the black stone which was the attribute of the goddess Cybele. Once in possession of this sacred cult image the Romans were in fact victorious, and the temple was built in 204 BC and consecrated in 191. Burned down in 111 BC, it was rebuilt by Quintus Caecilius Metellus (consul in 109) and restored again after another fire in the reign of Augustus (AD 3). The temple, raised on a high podium, had six Corinthian columns in antis, as can be seen on a Roman relief now on the garden façade of the Villa Medici. Excavations in the late 20th century clarified the various stages of its building history. The podium and the walls of the cella date from after the fire of 111. At this time a large platform for athletic games and theatrical performances in honour of the goddess was built in front of the temple, providing room beneath it for an area of shops and baths served by an underground road. Pavements and external architectural decorations were found from the Augustan period. The cult statue of Cybele and fragments of a marble lion from the temple are exhibited in the Palatine Museum.

THE DOMUS TIBERIANA

The northwestern area of the hill was covered by the so-called Domus Tiberiana, very little of which is visible, although its substructures are clearly seen from the Forum. Recent excavations have revealed that the first grand buildings on this site, which was formerly occupied by Republican houses, were probably part of Nero's Domus Aurea. This was reconstructed by Domitian (who seems to have called it the Domus Tiberiana), and extended by Hadrian to the northwest towards the ancient road known as the Clivus Victoriae. A cryptoporticus with entrances (*now blocked*) on Via di San Teodoro and dating from the period of Nero was found, as well as traces of the Imperial Ramp built by Domitian to connect the Domus Tiberiana with the Forum (*see p. 76*). There are plans to open this permanently to the public.

The buildings were transformed into a monumental palace by the elderly Claudius (AD 41–54). Important excavations are still underway in this area and finds (including a pair of marble wings from a statue of Victory) are on view in the Palatine Museum. Claudius, who was an educated man, had his first wife Messalina murdered when she proved unfaithful to him. He then married his niece Agrippina whose son, Nero, Claudius adopted. Nero became emperor aged 17 and during the first years of his reign he lived here. The site is occupied by the Farnese Gardens.

THE FARNESE GARDENS

These gardens **(18)** were laid out by Vignola in the middle of the 16th century for Cardinal Alessandro Farnese, grandson of Paul III. They are still a lovely place to wander or to relax on the old-fashioned benches. They extended from the Nova Via on the level of the Forum, then much higher, to the slopes of the Palatine; the various terraced levels were united by flights of monumental steps with a nymphaeum and a water cascade. Vignola's work was completed by Girolamo Rainaldi at the beginning of the 17th century. The twin pavilions were used as aviaries. These pleasure-gardens were modelled on the Classical *viridarium* of ancient Roman villas (now the subject of important studies) and they were replanted at the end of the 19th century by the great archaeologist Giacomo Boni. They are still very beautiful and well-kept, and contain orange trees and pools of papyrus between the paths. Boni's tomb stands beneath a solitary palm tree in the part overlooking the Roman Forum (the view of the three immense arches of the Basilica of Maxentius is particularly striking from here). You can take the monumental flight of steps down from between the two aviaries back to the Roman Forum, or return towards the Arch of Titus to visit the Vigna Barberini (*described below*). But whichever you choose, don't miss the cryptoporticus, reached by steps from the gardens.

THE CRYPTOPORTICUS

This is a tunnelled gallery **(19)**, 130m long, built by Nero, which was used to link the main buildings of the imperial palace to the area called the Domus Tiberiana. Today it is one of the most impressive structures on the Palatine since it is relatively well preserved: the vault is decorated for part of its length with casts of fine stuccoes (the originals are kept in the museum; *see p. 100*), and parts of the tiny herring-bone paving and simple mosaic floor also survive. It is a perfectly proportioned space, inducive to taking a cool stroll on a summers' day, and it receives light and air from windows set high up on the east side. At the end it bends right and emerges near the Clivus Palatinus.

THE VIGNA BARBERINI

Entered from an archway off the Clivus Palatinus, on a large artificial terrace created at the time of the Flavian emperors, this is a lovely walled garden named after a vineyard planted here by the Barberini in the 17th century. It is the probable **site of the Adonaea**, or gardens of Adonis, where the god was worshipped. Outside the walls can be seen two churches: the small medieval **San Sebastiano al Palatino**, near the site where Sebastian is supposed to have been martyred, and San Bonventura (they are both approached by Via di San Bonaventura). The excavated area close to San Sebastiano and its palm tree has revealed the **foundations of a Temple of the Sun (20)**, built by Elagabalus in AD 218–22 in the centre of a hanging garden created at the time of Domitian. Elagabalus placed here numerous treasures from the most ancient cults of the city, including the sacred stone from the Temple of Cybele (*see p. 103*) and what he took to be the *Palladium* (*see p. 83*). The district thus acquired the name 'Palladii' or 'in Pallara' in the Middle Ages. The temple was re-dedicated to Jupiter Ultor by Alexander Severus, who succeeded Elagabalus.

Beyond two huge old ilex trees excavations are still in progress. There is a **circular hall (21)**, thought to have been part of Nero's Domus Aurea. In the centre a round pillar some 4m in diameter has been found and some scholars believe this could have been the mechanism for a rotating pavement, since this exotic and unique feature of a room in Nero's palace is mentioned in the ancient sources. The view from here is excellent.

Excavation in this area has also revealed a **semicircular exedra** with the same dimensions as the south exedra of the so-called Domus Augustana overlooking the Circus Maximus, and which therefore seems to have been part of Domitian's imperial palace, confirming that its extent was huge. The excavations have been covered over but the exedra's shape is reflected in the curve of the gravel path near the entrance.

CASA DI AUGUSTO & CASA DI LIVIA

Augustus, Rome's first emperor (*see box on p. 127*), who was born in his father's house on the other side of the Palatine hill, acquired the orator Hortensius' house here around 40 BC and incorporated it into his new palace four years later. The house **(22)** was reconstructed by the emperor (at public expense) after a fire in AD 3, and included his private quarters as well as rooms for public ceremonies and two libraries. He also built a wing for his wife, Livia Drusilla. Here can be seen the most important wall paintings which have survived on the Palatine. They are in the second Pompeian style (1st century BC), which imitated, in painting, the marble of Greek and Roman domestic architecture and introduced figures, with red, purple and yellow as the dominant colours.

NB: Admission is by appointment only (see p. 92). The houses are unlocked for you and you can then visit them on your own.

CASA DI AUGUSTO

The wall-paintings date from 25 BC–AD 25 and are remarkable for their vivid colours (mostly red, yellow and black), their intricate designs, including architectural and theatrical motifs, and refined figure studies.

The **ground-floor rooms** can be visited, where red and green hues predominate. On the left (seen through glass) is a room decorated with pine-cones in front of a painted portico (note the shadows cast by the columns). The adjoining room has red walls with masks and curious figures decorating architectural features.

The long **library**, visited on a modern walkway, has festoons agains a black ground. At the end, from outside, you can look into a magnificent hall, its barrel vault with green, maroon and red-painted coffers. A small room here is the best preserved of all: the bright red walls have painted Corinthian columns in front of walls in perfect perspective, and above imitation marble painted panels there is a delicate frieze of tritons and sea horses.

Modern iron stairs lead up to the exquisite little **studiolo**, the emperor's private study, which you can see through a glass door. The refined decoration has been beautifully restored. It has an even better-preserved barrel vault, *grottesche* with winged figures, and sophisticated architecture and painted figures on the deep red walls. The peristyle outside, with its pool of aquatic plants, has been reconstructed.

'CASA DI LIVIA'

A modern flat-roofed brick building encloses the so-called **House of Livia (23)**, also famous for its wall-paintings. An original staircase descends to the rectangular **atrium**, or courtyard, in which there are two pillar bases and architectural paintings. The most important rooms open onto it: they are thought to belong to the **tablinum**, or reception suite. The frescoes have been detached but are exhibited *in situ*. The paintings in the central room are the best preserved, especially that on the right wall. It has panels separated by columns of fantastic design in a free interpretation of the Corinthian style. In the central panel Hermes is seen coming to the rescue of Io, the lover of Zeus, who is guarded by Argus of the hundred eyes; in the left panel is a street scene; the right panel is lost. In the intercolumniations are small scenes of mysterious rites. The central painting on the rear wall of this room, now almost obliterated, shows Polyphemus pursuing Galatea into the sea; on the left wall, which lost its paintings in ancient times, are exhibited the lead pipes bearing the inscription '*Iulia Augusta*' which gave the house its name when it was discovered by Pietro Rosa in 1869.

On the right is a room which was probably the **triclinium**. It has red walls painted with columns supporting vases, and buildings crowned with statues.

The Colosseum
& Domus Aurea

The Colosseum is the most famous and most visited monument in Rome. It is one of the most magnificent buildings ever erected by the ancient Romans and still incredibly well preserved. Another remarkable survival close by, Nero's Domus Aurea, can also be visited. A short distance away is the church of San Pietro in Vincoli, with Michelangelo's famous statue of Moses.

The Colosseum stands in the centre of the city, just outside the Roman Forum and next to the well-preserved Arch of Constantine. Its setting is not particularly attractive today, in part the fault of development in the 1930s and because there are busy roads all around it. The area is usually crowded with tour groups and souvenir stalls, all of which detract from the grandeur of the building. Nevertheless, the interior still retains an extraordinary atmosphere, made all the more remarkable by the excellent guided tours (*advance booking necessary*) of the vaults below the arena, the arena itself, as well as the topmost surviving tier.

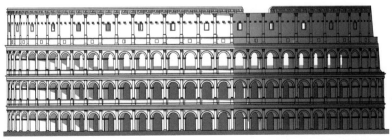

THE COLOSSEUM: NORTH ELEVATION

Map p. 655, E3. Open 8.30–dusk. For information, see archeoroma.beniculturali.it. For advance tickets, T: 06 39 96 7700, coopculture.it. Ticket includes (a single) entrance to the Roman Forum and Palatine and is valid for two days. Since there can be long queues, it is a good idea to visit the Palatine first and with that ticket you can go straight to the entrance of the Colosseum and do not need to wait in line. For the Archaeological Card and reductions for young visitors, see p. 600. On no account should you miss joining a guided tour (advance tickets as above).

Despite its fame, the Colosseum is one of the least-studied works of the Roman period and only recently has a detailed elevation been carried out of the entire building. It is the largest Roman amphitheatre ever built and its design was copied in similar buildings all over the Empire. Though pillaged for centuries for its marble, the huge edifice preserves its remarkable grandeur and the northeast side appears almost undamaged.

The Colosseum has been an emblem of Rome's eternity for centuries. The Venerable Bede (c. 673–735) is supposed to have quoted a prophecy made by Anglo-Saxon pilgrims whereby the fate of Rome will stand or fall by the Colosseum: if the amphitheatre falls, Rome will fall with it, and if Rome falls, the world will follow.

HISTORY OF THE COLOSSEUM

The amphitheatre was begun by Vespasian in AD 70 and completed by his son Titus some ten years later. It is significant that the site chosen was where there had been a large ornamental lake in the gardens of Nero's huge Domus Aurea, the palace he built all for himself in the very heart of Rome on land which had formerly been public space in a valley between the Velia to the west, the Esquiline to the north and the Caelian hill to the south. Vespasian, by contrast, here provided a place for the Roman populace, who had been outraged at Nero's megalomania. The expense was in part covered by the sale of war booty. The inaugural festival lasted 100 days, during which many gladiators and 5,000 wild beasts were killed. The name 'Colosseum' referred to a colossal statue of Nero, which stood beside the amphitheatre; however it soon became the popular name applied to the building itself. Its original name, the Flavian Amphitheatre, commemorated the family name of Vespasian, who began the building, and of his son Titus, who completed it.

This was the first amphitheatre in the city to be built in stone, and it was surrounded on three sides by a quadrangular portico and by the numerous buildings needed to support the spectacles for which it had been built. These included four barracks, places where the gladiators could practice, including even a miniature amphitheatre, deposits for arms and the machinery used for the sets, stables for the wild beasts, and the store for the huge awning (the *velarium*). Of these 'outbuildings' only the Ludus Magnus (*see p. 115*) has been fully excavated.

The Colosseum was restored after a fire in 217 under Alexander Severus and in 248 the thousandth anniversary of the foundation of Rome was celebrated here. The damage from an earthquake in 443 was probably repaired by Theodosius II and Valentinian III. The building was again shaken by earthquakes in 1231 and 1349. It was converted into a castle by the aristocratic families of the Frangipani and the Annibaldi.

In 1312 the Colosseum was presented to the senate and people of Rome by the Holy Roman Emperor Henry VII. By the 15th century it had become a quarry for building material. Its travertine (limestone) was used during the construction of Palazzo di Venezia and Palazzo della Cancelleria. Other parts of the building were reused in St Peter's and Palazzo Barberini.

At the end of the 19th century the Colosseum was freed from obstructive buildings and undergrowth and the structures beneath the arena were uncovered. Further clearances were carried out after the construction in 1933 of Via dei Fori Imperiali.

EXTERIOR OF THE COLOSSEUM

Today the total circumerence measures 545m and in the pavement which encircles it a white line shows the dimensions of the original building. It is built of travertine outside and of brick-faced concrete and tufa in the interior (once covered with travertine). The travertine blocks were originally held together with iron clamps; these were torn out in the Middle Ages but their sockets are still conspicuous. Today the mighty exterior wall, which supports the complicated interior, has four storeys (there were originally six). The lower three have rows of arches decorated with engaged columns of the three orders superimposed: Tuscan Doric on the lowest, Ionic in the middle and Corinthian on the top. The fourth storey, dating from the restoration of Alexander Severus, has no arches but is articulated by slender Corinthian pilasters. Some 152 statues originally occupied the arches of the second and third storeys. At the four main entrances there were quadriga groups and there was more statuary in the interior. However very little is known about these decorative elements since they had virtually disappeared by the 5th or 6th century. The projecting corbels at the very top supported the poles used for the *velarium* (*see overleaf*).

Admiration for its ruined state

The Colosseum was particularly admired by 19th-century travellers to Rome because of its romantic ruined state. Lord Byron dedicates many stanzas of *Childe Harold's Pilgrimage* (*Canto IV, 1818*) to this 'vast and wondrous monument...a ruin—yet what ruin!'. Dickens in 1846 declared: 'It is the most impressive, the most stately, the most solemn, grand, majestic, mournful sight, conceivable. Never, in its bloodiest prime, can the sight of the gigantic Coliseum, full and running over with the lustiest life, have moved one heart, as it must move all who look upon it now, a ruin. God be thanked: a ruin!' Augustus Hare was disgusted by the 'tidying up' of the Colosseum in 1882 and the eradication of its 'marvellous flora' (in fact, the monument used to be covered with an extraordinary variety of plants and flowers, some of them unknown elsewhere in Rome).

THE INTERIOR: UPPER LEVEL

From the ticket check, continue straight ahead through the magnificent arched passageway which affords wonderful glimpses of the interior. Beside the lift you are signposted up the stairs on the right (over 65s can take the lift here). On the upper level, there is an excellent small **exhibition** illustrating the building history of the monument, with some archaeological fragments as well as bits and pieces dropped on the ground by spectators, including remnants of food (such as oyster shells), dice and spindles, all found during excavations. Beyond there is space for temporary exhibitions, usually on a certain aspect of life in the ancient world and of the greatest interest.

From here you can go outside and follow the open walkway around the interior of the vast **cavea**. It provides an extraordinary view of the interior, which could probably hold around 75,000 spectators, even though more than two-thirds of the original masonry of the seats has been removed over the centuries. In the centre was the **arena** (83m by 48m), so called because the wooden floor used to be covered with sand (*arena*) in order to prevent combatants from slipping and to absorb the blood: all subsequent stages of this sort took on the name. The **substructures** which would have been covered by the floorboards are now visible beneath: they provided space for the mechanism operated by slaves by which scenery (we know that some of this consisted of depictions of landscapes in north Africa and Egypt, where the exotic animals brought here had come from) and other apparatus, as well as the gladiators and wild beasts themselves, were hoisted up through trap doors into the arena above (there were no fewer than 60 of these elevators). The underground rooms included passages for the animals and gladiators while waiting their turn to 'perform'.

Today a wooden stage has been constructed at one end to show how it would have looked, and near it you can see a small section of the seats which were restored (using ancient pieces of marble from elsewhere) in the 1930s. In 2015 this part of the building was used for a performance of drama for an audience of some 700.

THE *VELARIUM*

One of the most remarkable aspects of the Colosseum was the vast awning (known as the *velarium*) which was stretched across the building to protect the audience from the sun. It has been estimated that a whole week would have been needed to erect it, a task performed by some 300 sailors. It weighed around 80 tons and there would have been complicated calculations to ensure that it resisted gusts of high wind.

It protruded over the top of the building, where it was attached to 240 wooden poles which were inserted through the holes in the cornice and supported by the projecting corbels (still visible on the exterior). There was a narrow platform encircling the summit where the sailors could stand during the installation and dismantling of the *velarium*, and to ensure the safety of the crowd during spectacles. All around the outside of the building was a paved area some 18m wide, and on its outer rim there was a circle of stone bollards (one or two of them still survive) which served to attach the guy ropes and anchor the awning to the ground.

THE INTERIOR: LOWER LEVEL

On the ground floor are some original paving stones near the Cross set up here in 1749 by Benedict XIV when he dedicated the Colosseum to the Passion of Jesus and pronounced it sanctified by the blood of martyrs (though there is no scholarly consensus that the arena was explicitly used as a place of Christian execution). Since the time of Paul VI the pope has visited the Colosseum on Good Friday to re-enact Christ's journey to Calvary (the *Via Crucis*), an event televised throughout the world.

On this level is exhibited a fragment of an equestrian statue in Luni marble dating from the 1st century AD (found in 2008 on the southeast side of the building, and the most precious piece of sculpture yet unearthed in the vicinity). You follow the walkway for part of its length to exit on the south side towards the Caelian hill.

A VISIT TO THE COLOSSEUM IN ANCIENT ROMAN DAYS

According to the famous phrase of the satirist Juvenal, what the Roman populace needed above all to keep them happy and placid were two things: bread and entertainment. Throughout the Empire, animal hunts or fights between wild beasts would take place in the Colosseum in the mornings, and later in the day gladiatorial combats. To watch one of these free spectacles put on by the emperor of the day, you would go through one of the 80 entrance arches on the ground floor. All the arches were numbered: you would look for the one which corresponded to the number on your wooden *tessera* (ticket). You would then follow a concentric vaulted corridor as far as the appropriate staircase, which led up to one of the three landings separating the tiers in the cavea, where you would find your place along one of the numerous passageways (160 in all) inserted between each *cuneus* (wedge of seats). If you were an *eques* (from the equestrian class), you would be seated on the lowest tier (but above the terrace) and therefore closest to the arena; Roman citizens had their seats on the tier above. If you were a member of the populace (*plebs*), a woman, child or slave, then you would find your seat (less comfortable and constructed of wood) at the topmost level. The only women who could sit near the arena were the Vestal Virgins. The sailors responsible for the *velarium* (*see below*) would stand on the narrow platform at the summit of the building, above the colonnade on the topmost tier.

The emperor himself entered through the wider arch on the northeast side, which opened into a foyer decorated with stuccoes. From here he would go out to his couch (*pulvinar*) on the podium of the broad parapeted terrace, and here he would ensconce himself among senators, pontiffs, Vestals and foreign ambassadors. A wall some five metres high protected him and these other dignitaries from the violent action taking place in the arena.

All the spectacles would be preceded by grand ceremonies and processions. When the Colosseum was first opened, and for the ten years following, the arena was sometimes flooded for mock sea-battles (*naumachiae*), but these ceased when the wooden floor was installed. The gladiatorial combats involved mostly prisoners of war, slaves or condemned convicts and the gladiators would fight man to man in single combat. When a winner was declared, if his defeated opponent had shown particular courage, he was sometimes granted mercy by the public (with the consent of the emperor) and his life would be spared, but at other times the contest only ended when one of the contenders was killed. Another form of popular entertainment were the wild animal hunts (*venationes*), or spectacles in which animals were left to fight each other: bears, crocodiles, lions, ostriches, elephants and tigers were shipped to Rome for these. There are terrible accounts of the quantity of humans and animals who died in the Colosseum: we learn that during Trajan's reign no fewer than 11,000 animals and 10,000 gladiators lost their lives. By the end of the empire some animal species had become extinct because of the numbers which had been killed here. At last gladiatorial combats were suppressed in the 5th century and fights with wild animals in AD 523.

THE SUBSTRUCTURES AND HIGHEST TIER

These are visited on a guided tour, which lasts about 75mins and is conducted by an archaeologist: highly recommended (*for ticket information, see p. 107*). You are first taken out onto the (reconstructed) stage so that you can see the view the performers would have had of the spectactors. An iron stair leads down to part of the substructures where the tunnel from the outbuildings used by the gladiators and wild animals to reach the amphitheatre (now blocked) is pointed out. The barrel-vaulted boat houses used for the vessels which took part in the mock sea battles can also be seen, as well as the way the water was channelled here from underground streams. The rails and the holes for the winches survive. The tour continues right up to the highest storey where there is a very well preserved barrel-vaulted passageway. It is interesting to note that the steepness of the stairways would have been even more challenging for the short-statured Romans; it is thought that they were designed with such high risers for structural engineering reasons. The tour ends on the balcony beside the highest part of the external wall, with magnificent views of the interior as well as the townscape.

THE ARCH OF CONSTANTINE

The triple Arch of Constantine (*map p. 655, D3*) was erected in AD 315 by the senate and people of Rome in honour of Constantine's victory in 312 over a rival emperor, the 'tyrant' Maxentius, at the Milvian Bridge, which crosses the Tiber to the north. A triumphal arch of excellent proportions, it was partly decorated with fine sculptures and reliefs reused from older Roman monuments. Because of this it is often taken as an example of the decline of the arts in the late Imperial period. The inscription mentions the 'divine inspiration' which served Constantine in his victory over Maxentius, which seems to refer to both pagan and Christian beliefs. Indeed scholars have suggested that the idea of a supreme god (Jupiter) already existed in pagan Rome.

Decorations from the time of Constantine: The decoration in the spandrels of the arches **(a)**, the oblong reliefs above them **(b)**, the victories and captives at the base of the columns **(c)**, and the two roundels and oblong friezes on the two short sides of the arch **(d)**.

Decorations from the time of the Antonines: The large medallions on each of the two long faces **(e)**, with finely-carved hunting scenes and pastoral sacrifices, belonged to an unknown monument erected by Hadrian. The high reliefs in the attic **(f)** were taken from a monument to Marcus Aurelius, and represent a sacrifice, orations to the army and to the people, and a triumphal entry into Rome.

Decorations from the time of Trajan: The splendid reliefs on the inside of the central arch **(g)** and on the upper sides **(h)** are from a monument commemorating Trajan's victories over the Dacians, probably by the sculptor who carved Trajan's Column. The eight statues of Dacians **(i)** are of the same date.

ARCH OF CONSTANTINE: NORTH SIDE

THE EXCAVATIONS BESIDE THE COLOSSEUM

Close to the entrance to the Colosseum is an area of excavations near a little garden which has been planted with three cypresses. The slightly raised lawn with four ilexes marks the site (7m square) of the huge **brick base of the colossal statue of Nero** from the vestibule of his Domus Aurea, which apparently gave its name to the Colosseum. It was melted down in the Middle Ages and all other remains of it were demolished in 1936 by order of Mussolini. This gilt-bronze statue of the emperor as god of the sun, by the Greek sculptor Zenodorus, is thought to have been nearly 35m high and thus the largest bronze statue ever made (it had a concrete core); it was even larger than its model, the Colossus of Rhodes. The statue was given a new base and moved here on the orders of Hadrian—carried by no fewer than 24 elephants—when he built the Temple of Venus and Roma on the site of the vestibule of Nero's palace (*the temple ruins on their raised terrace can be seen from here; for a description, see p. 86*). A long stretch of **Roman road** has recently been unearthed here, with its huge paving stones intact.

On the other side of a square lawn is a fenced area of recent excavations planted with five olive trees. The visible ruins belong to part of the vestibule of the Domus Aurea, beneath which were found remains of a temple.

TRIUMPHS

The original Triumph was a way of allowing a Roman general to celebrate victory without giving him lasting political dominance. The elaborate ritual appears to be Etruscan in origin, adopted by the Roman Republic after the expulsion of the kings in 509 BC. Once a major battle had been won (so many generals applied for triumphs that it was later stipulated that 5,000 of the enemy had to have been killed in a victory which effectively brought a war to an end), the victor gathered his troops, captives and booty outside the walls of Rome. Behind the general stood a slave who held a laurel wreath over his head and who reminded him continually of his mortality. Dressed as the god Jupiter for the day and riding in a four-horse chariot (four horses were always a symbol of heroic status), the general led the procession into the city through the Porta Carmentalis. It wound its way across the major public spaces so as many citizens as possible could see it. Finally it would enter the Forum and move along the Sacra Via and up to the Temple of Jupiter on the Capitoline hill, where the general would place his wreath and sacrifice to the gods. His prisoners were led away for execution. After his day of triumph a general was supposed to retire from active political life, but by the end of the republic, powerful men such as Pompey the Great and Julius Caesar were subverting the rules and a Triumph proved a stepping stone to permanent power.

After the fall of the Republic (27 BC), only emperors were able to celebrate full-scale Triumphs, although victorious generals could be granted triumphal insignia. As there was by now no question of a Triumph leading to political quiescence, it could be recorded in permanent form in a triumphal arch. In the Roman Forum the arches erected to commemorate the victory of Titus over Jerusalem (erected after his death, in AD 81), of Septimius Severus over the Parthians (erected in AD 203) and of Constantine over the rival emperor Maxentius at the Milvian Bridge (erected in 315) survive from the 34 recorded in the city. On Titus' arch reliefs show the emperor enjoying his Triumph with the booty from the temple at Jerusalem carried in procession with him. In the Capitoline Museums there is a fine relief of the emperor Marcus Aurelius in a Triumph of AD 176. Other arches were scattered through the Western Empire, especially in Italy, Africa and Gaul.

Triumphal arches were traditionally surmounted by a four-horse chariot, sometimes with the emperor inside (all have long since disappeared). In 1797 the French general Napoleon Bonaparte seized Rome. He saw himself as the heir of the Roman conquerors of the past, and like them wished to carry off plunder. Many of the city's finest Classical statues were transported to Paris, where they entered the city in a triumphal procession. Napoleon constructed two triumphal arches: the Arc du Triomphe and the Arc du Carrousel. On the latter he placed the only surviving quadriga from the ancient world, the four horses of St Mark's (returned to Venice after his downfall).   C.F.

Also here can be seen the circular base of the **Meta Sudans**, a marble-faced fountain, probably around 17m high, which was erected by Domitian and marked the boundary of four regions of the Augustan city (II, III, IV and X). It was the largest monumental fountain in the ancient city, surrounded by a circular basin, and its shape is known from its representation on Roman coins. It was restored by Constantine, and received its name from its resemblance to the conical turning-post for chariot races in circuses (*meta*), and from the fact that it 'sweated' water (from *sudare*, to sweat) through numerous small orifices. In 2002 another circular structure made from red tufa, about 3m in diameter, was found here and dated to the time of Augustus.

On the east side of the Colosseum, between Via Labicana and Via San Giovanni in Laterano, are remains of the **Ludus Magnus**, the principal training-school for gladiators, constructed by Domitian. Part of the curved wall of a miniature amphitheatre used for practice can be seen, as well as remains of buildings used to house the wild beasts and the gladiators.

THE DOMUS AUREA

Map p. 655, E3. At the time of writing important work was in progress on consolidating the building. It is only open at weekends, when the worksite is closed, for excellent pre-booked guided visits (which last about 90mins). Visitors are lent protective helmets. For up-to-date information, T: 06 39 96 7700, coopculture.it. Entrance above the Colosseum from Via Labicana (at its junction with Viale Colosseo and Via Nicola Salvi) through the gates of the Parco Oppio. Inside the park follow Viale della Domus Aurea for a few metres, and then take the first path to the left.

In the heart of the city Nero built this huge suburban villa which came to be called his 'Golden House'. With its outbuildings and gardens, it extended over part or all of the Palatine, much of the Caelian and part of the Oppian hills, an area of about 50 hectares. When it was completed Nero is reputed to have commented that at last he was beginning to be housed like a human being.

He employed Severus as architect and Fabullus as painter, and produced what has been called the first expression of the Roman revolution in architecture. The understanding and use of vaulted spaces in the palace was quite new. It is thought that nearly all the rooms were vaulted. The atrium or vestibule, with the colossal statue of the emperor (*see p. 113*), was on the summit of the Velia; the main part of the palace was on the site of the so-called Domus Tiberiana on the Palatine; the gardens, with their lake, were in the valley now occupied by the Colosseum.

This grandiose edifice did not long survive the tyrant's death in 68, and his successors hastily demolished or covered up his buildings, and returned the huge area they had occupied to the city. In 72 Vespasian obliterated the lake to build the Colosseum; Domitian (81–96) buried the constructions on the Palatine—except the cryptoporticus—to make room for the Flavian palaces; and Hadrian (117–38) built his Temple of Venus and Roma on the site of the vestibule and moved the statue. When Trajan chose to build his baths on this hill, as a clear act of *damnatio memoriae* he poured tons of mud and rubble into the halls of the palace so they could serve as foundations for his baths. All this is clearly visible during the visit to the Domus Aurea.

When the rooms with their stuccoed and painted walls and vaults were first discovered underground in the 1490s, they at once became famous and their decorations were called 'grotesques' (from *grotto*, an underground room). This delicate type of decoration, normally on a light ground, is characterised by fantastical motifs with intricate patterns of volutes, festoons, garlands and borders of twisted vegetation and flowers interspersed with small winged human or animal figures, birds, masks, griffins and sphinxes. Renaissance artists came to see and study the rooms—some left their names scratched on the walls—and this type of decoration became very fashionable and was widely copied: it clearly inspired Raphael when decorating his Loggia in the Vatican. Finds from the Domus Aurea include the great porphyry vase now in the Circular Hall of the Vatican (*see p. 456*).

In 2010 it was decided that it had become necessary to consolidate the architecture (in some cases reconstructing the upper parts of the walls using the same materials). This work is now well underway. The tree-roots of the Parco Oppio above are attacking the masonry of the vaults so that a metre-thick protective layer between them and the soil will have to be inserted. Sadly the invasive vegetation and oriental-type trees introduced in 1936 will need to be eradicated but there are plans to redesign the hill as an ancient Roman pleasure-garden. In the meantime some of the frescoes have had to be detached, but they are stored here and will not be removed from the building.

INSIDE THE DOMUS AUREA

The vaulted rooms in this wing of the palace, now deep underground, are extremely important for their architecture as well as for the remains of their fresco and stucco decorations. Today it is hard to imagine these as they used to be: open pavilions, garden rooms, courtyards, cryptoportici, peristyles: places in which to wander and converse.

The **nymphaeum** has a vault mosaic, the earliest one known, depicting Ulysses and Polyphemus, and remains on the walls of a shell decoration and artificial stalactites. A room which once had stucco work on the vault covered with gold leaf is known to have been studied by Renaissance artists: they made holes in the ceiling (still visible) and let themselves down through them and, standing on the rubble which almost filled the room, they were able to see the vault decoration at close quarters (some of their signatures survive here).

A **cryptoporticus** has remarkably effective lighting provided by a series of windows high up on the left wall, through which the natural light is directed onto a second series of lower windows on the right wall. The graceful decoration features grotesques of plants and animals as well as Egyptian motifs. There are also signatures here of 16th-century artists (including Giovanni da Udine) on the vault.

The **Room of Achilles on Skyros** has perhaps the best-preserved decoration of all the rooms in the palace so far discovered (it was only found in the 20th century). The barrel vault has exquisite stucco and painted decoration, probably by the hand of Fabullus. In the centre, surrounded by refined decorations, is a well-preserved scene of Achilles on Skyros (his mother Thetis, hearing that her son was fated to die in Troy, sent him to Skyros disguised as a girl so that he would not go away to war; Odysseus retrieved him).

The **Octagonal Hall** has an entirely original design, made possible through the novel use of concrete. In fact the Romans at this time perfected a mix of local volcanic ash, known as *pozzolana*, with lime to make a mortar which would set even under water. Mixed with stones it was formidably strong and could be built up in layers to create vaults and domes. This room brilliantly shows how this concrete could be used to create great architecture: the light effect is masterly both from the wide central oculus in the dome, and from the side rooms. There is an opening for a cascade to the north, and some painted stucco decoration just survives in places.

BATHS OF TRAJAN

The Parco Oppio was instituted in 1871 but was only planted in 1936 by Antonio Muñoz (*but see opposite*): it still has scattered remains of the huge Baths of Trajan which were built over Nero's Domus Aurea after a fire in 104. They were designed by Apollodorus of Damascus and opened in 109, and were taken as a model by later builders of Imperial baths. Beneath a building thought to have been a library (*not yet open to the public*) a fascinating Roman fresco of a city was discovered in 1998 and two mosaics of satyrs gathering grapes and poets or philosophers received by the Muses. A reservoir which supplied water to the baths, called the Sette Sale (*entrance at Via Terme di Traiano 2; for admission, see sovraintendenzaroma.it*), also survives: this is a remarkable large vaulted building divided into nine compartments for the collecting tanks. The famous sculpture of Laocoön, now in the Vatican Museums (*see p. 454*), was discovered in a vineyard nearby in 1506.

SAN PIETRO IN VINCOLI

Map p. 655, D3–E3. Open 8–12.30 & 3–6 or 7. The most pleasant approach is from above the Colosseum, up the steps from Via Nino Salvi along Via delle Terme di Tito uphill past the Parco Oppio and then into Largo della Polveriera with its cafés. Via Eudossiana continues past the huge building of the Engineering Faculty of Rome University to reach the piazza in front of the church. NB: The church can get very crowded with tour groups, who come here only to see Michelangelo's famous statue of Moses.

The church, named after the chains of St Peter (*see overleaf*), was restored in 1475 under Sixtus IV by Meo del Caprina, who was responsible for the façade, with its beautiful colonnaded portico. The elegant simplicity is echoed in the basilican interior. Though much affected by restoration, it preserves its 20 ancient fluted columns with Doric capitals (the Ionic bases were added in the 17th century). The nave, almost four times as wide as the aisles, has a ceiling painting representing the cure of a person possessed by an evil spirit through the touch of the holy chains.

MICHELANGELO'S *MOSES*

The tomb of Pope Julius II, the famous unfinished masterpiece of Michelangelo, who was so harassed while working on it that he called it the 'tragedy of a sepulchre', is at the end of the south aisle. Hindered by quarrels with the pope and by the jealousy of his successors, Michelangelo finally abandoned work on the tomb and the great pontiff, who had contemplated for himself the most splendid monument in the world, lies uncommemorated in St Peter's. Some 40 statues were to have decorated the tomb, including the two *Slaves* now in the Louvre and the four unfinished *Slaves* in the Accademia Gallery in Florence, but no idea of the original design can be gained from the surviving unsatisfactory grouping. Only a few statues remain here, notably the magnificent *Moses*, in whose majestic glance is seen the prophet who spoke with God. The satyr-like horns represent beams of light, a traditional attribute of the prophet in medieval iconography, based on a mistranslation of the Hebrew word for the radiance that emanated from Moses' head after his interview with the Almighty (it was confused with the Hebrew word for horns). The figures of *Leah* and *Rachel* on either side— symbols of the active and contemplative life—are also by Michelangelo. The rest is his pupils' work, although the effigy of the pope himself was attributed by some scholars to Michelangelo during restoration work in 1999. The pose is based on the reclining figures on Etruscan tombs. The *Prophet* and *Sibyl* are by Raffaello da Montelupo.

THE TOMB OF POPE JULIUS II

The project for the tomb of Pope Julius II stretched over 40 years of Michelangelo's career (between 1505 and 1545) and was in constant transformation during that period. The changes it underwent are documented in six surviving contracts, each of which successively reduced the scale of the original scheme. At its inception, the plan was to create one of the grandest Christian tombs ever built, to be placed above the sepulchre of St Peter at the centre of St Peter's basilica. It was Pope Julius who had conceived and begun the building of the new St Peter's; after his death it was to become an everlasting mausoleum to himself. What we see now is a deflated and ill-proportioned shadow of that project: the artist himself would acknowledge as much.

The exact design of the original plan is not clear: but we know that it was to have been a massive, free-standing structure with three tiers in pyramidal arrangement, surrounding an internal chamber. At the summit was to have been either the pope's sarcophagus or a seated effigy of the pope. Below this, on the middle level, were the figures of Moses and St Paul (emblems of the two Testaments), paired with a sibyl and a prophet: of these, the *Moses* (1515) alone remains. On the lowest level was an allegorical arrangement playing on the way Classical and antique architecture uses human figures as architectural elements: in Michelangelo's conception, the figures were not just supporting the cornice but were miraculously coming to life and breaking free of their bonds. Sometimes called 'slaves' or 'prisoners', sometimes referred to as 'dying' and at other times as 'awakening', these powerful figures of male nudes are seen by some as representing the provinces subjugated by Julius, the warrior pope, and by others as personifying the Liberal Arts, awakened during his enlightened reign. For the artist, they were expressions of the soul's struggle against mortal flesh, and they were to be alternated with figures of Victory (one was partially realised and is in Palazzo Vecchio in Florence). The programme of the whole structure could be seen therefore as an allegory of the ascent of the soul, from its battles against the bonds of the flesh, up through the purification afforded by the teachings of the Church, to its final emancipation in death.

After Julius died in 1513, the project lost momentum and was eventually reduced to no more than a small façade on a wall, in which assistants contributed major elements. Only the *Moses*, on the insistence of the trustees of the will, was included from the original project.

N.McG.

OTHER WORKS OF ART IN THE CHURCH

In the chapel to the right of the sanctuary (behind glass) is a beautiful painting of *St Margaret* by Guercino. The bishop's throne in the apse is a marble chair brought from a Roman bath. The 19th-century baldacchino over the high altar is by Virginio Vespignani. In the confessio below are the **Chains of St Peter** displayed in a 19th-century casket in a tabernacle with beautiful bronze doors (1477) attributed to Caradosso—however these are not usually visible since they are kept open.

THE CHAINS OF ST PETER

The two chains with which St Peter was supposedly fettered in the Carcer (or Tullianum; *see p. 63*) are said to have been taken to Constantinople. In 439 Juvenal, Bishop of Jerusalem, gave them to the Empress Eudoxia, wife of Theodosius the Younger. She placed one of them in the Church of the Holy Apostles at Constantinople and sent the other to Rome for her daughter, also Eudoxia, the wife of Valentinian III, who was Emperor of the Western Empire (425–55). In 442 the younger Eudoxia gave the chain to St Leo I (pope 440–61) and built this church (called the Basilica

Eudoxiana or St Peter ad Vincula: 'St Peter in Bonds') to house it. Later the second chain was sent to Rome. On being brought together, the two chains are said to have miraculously united. They have ever since been amongst the most revered relics in any church in Rome.

In the tiny **crypt** (*closed*) there is a fine late 4th-century Roman sarcophagus with New Testament scenes, for long thought to contain the relics of the seven Jewish Maccabee brothers (1st century BC). These martyrs are interesting as the only figures in the Old Testament (apart from the archangels) who had a liturgical cultus in the Roman church. However, investigations carried out in the 1930s found the bones to be those of dogs.

In the **north aisle**, the third altar has a framed well-preserved 7th-century mosaic icon of the bearded St Sebastian. The first altarpiece has a *Descent from the Cross* by Pomarancio. Near the west wall, the tomb of Cardinal de Cusa has a good coloured relief, attributed to Andrea Bregno. The cardinal philosopher was titular of the church from 1449 until his death in 1464; his coat of arms of a crayfish also appears on one of the huge beams above the columns on the south side of the nave.

On the end wall near the entrance door is the little **tomb of Antonio and Piero Pollaiolo**, with two expressive portrait busts of the two brothers attributed to Luigi Capponi. They were Florentine and their family name was Benci, but they were always known as 'Pollaiolo' since their grandfather and father had both been poultry vendors in the Florence market (*pollo* = 'chicken'). Antonio, the elder brother, was a brilliant goldsmith, sculptor and painter: he died two years after Piero who was a painter (most of his works are in Florence). The inscription, devised by Antonio, mentions his two famous papal monuments in bronze of Sixtus IV and Innocent VIII (in St Peter's) and the fact that he expressly wished to be buried here with his brother. Above is a very worn fresco of the plague of 1476 by an unknown 15th-century artist, and lower down to the left, an early fresco of the *Head of Christ* (behind glass).

In the **south aisle** the first altarpiece is a *St Augustine* by Guercino. By the second altar there is a tomb designed by Domenichino, who painted the small portrait in an oval above; the second altarpiece is a copy of his *Deliverance of St Peter*, now outside the sacristy. The **sacristy** itself has a pretty 16th-century frescoed vault by Paris Nogari and a small 15th-century marble bas-relief of the *Madonna and Child*.

The **cloister** (*entered at Via Eudossiana 16 on the right*) is attributed to Giuliano da Sangallo. The well-head is by Simone Mosca.

An archway in the piazza leads to a flight of steps called **Via San Francesco di Paola**, on the site of the ancient 'Via Scelerata', which apparently received its name—the 'Wicked Way'—from the impious act of Tullia, who here drove her chariot over the dead body of her royal father Servius Tullius in 535 BC. According to legend she was responsible for ordering her brother-in-law Tarquinius Superbus to murder both her husband and her father, so that he would become king and she could marry him. Tarquinius, indeed, became the last of the six Etruscan kings who ruled Rome after Romulus.

The attractive Doric loggia above the archway was once part of the house of Vannozza Cattanei (1442–1518), the beautiful mistress of Pope Alexander VI (*see p. 142*). The steps lead down to the busy Via Cavour.

The Imperial Fora

The Imperial Fora are a succession of ever more splendid public spaces laid out
by Julius Caesar and the emperors Augustus, Vespasian, Nerva and Trajan,
as extensions to the Roman Forum. Most of them can only be viewed from walkways
but the Markets of Trajan, part of his Forum, can be visited and they house
a museum of finds from all the Fora. Dominating the site is the perfectly preserved
Column of Trajan, with a sculptural frieze said to be the most beautiful work
of its kind ever produced by Roman artists. The nearby Domus Romane,
remains of ancient Roman houses, are visited on an interactive tour.

The Imperial Fora (*map pp. 654–5, C2–D2 and plan overleaf*) occupy the huge area next to the Roman Forum. Most of them were only uncovered in 1933, when Mussolini constructed the wide Via dell'Impero, now Via dei Fori Imperiali, between Piazza Venezia and the Colosseum. The road is now closed to through traffic except for buses, taxis and service vehicles and the area will become an archaeological park. The most impressive monument is the beautiful Column of Trajan. The Markets of Trajan are also particularly well preserved and contain a very fine museum with finds from all the Imperial Fora. One of Rome's most recently excavated areas, the Domus Romane, close to Trajan's Column, is a very exciting place to visit, but you have to book in advance. Details are given in the description below.

HISTORY OF THE IMPERIAL FORA

With the population of the city ever increasing, by the end of the Republican era the Roman Forum had become too small for its purpose. It was congested with buildings and overcrowded by citizens and by visitors from abroad. The purpose of any new forum was to be the same as that of the Roman Forum: namely to serve as a judicial, religious and commercial centre. The only direction in which expansion was possible was to the north, even though numerous buildings had to be demolished to allow it.

The first step was taken by Julius Caesar, who built his forum during the decade preceding his death in 44 BC. In it he placed the Temple of Venus Genetrix, in commemoration of the victory over Pompey at Pharsalus in Thessaly (48 BC). Caesar's example was followed by his successors, most of whom erected temples in memory of some outstanding event in Roman history for which they took the credit. The Forum of Augustus, with the Temple of Mars Ultor, commemorated the battle of Philippi (42 BC), in which Augustus avenged the murder of Caesar by Brutus and Cassius. The Temple of Peace was erected by Vespasian with the spoils of the campaign in Judaea

(AD 70); and the Forum of Trajan, completed by Hadrian, had a temple to the deified Trajan in honour of his conquest of Dacia (AD 106). All the Fora were connected and the whole area was arranged in conformity with a definite plan, as can be seen from the plan on the facing page.

In the early 9th century orchards and cultivated fields covered the ruins of the Fora. Two wealthy citizens decided to build their residences right in the middle of the Forum of Nerva, and more humble dwellings gradually invaded the Forum of Caesar. The Temple (or Forum) of Peace seems to have been denigrated to a knacker's yard. When marshes formed here in the late Middle Ages the area was abandoned, and it was only at the end of the 16th century that Cardinal Michele Bonelli built a new residential district in the area, called the 'Alessandrino' after his birthplace (Alessandria in northern Italy). Throughout this period, and especially in the Renaissance, the Fora were pillaged for building material and robbed of their marbles and bronzes, although fragments of the Fora of Trajan and Augustus have always been visible.

Ruthless clearance of the area was begun in 1924 to make way for Via dei Fori Imperiali, built to add dignity to Fascist military parades. The Alessandrine buildings were totally demolished, the Velia hill was levelled, and the Imperial Fora were hastily and inconclusively excavated, leaving only about one fifth of them visible.

The whole area has been in the process of systematic study and excavation since 1985. The new excavations have revealed important information about how the Forum of Augustus was linked to that of Trajan, as well as about the form of the portico which lined the southern end of the Forum of Trajan (fragments of huge columns of *giallo antico* and a statue of a Dacian in Luni marble have been found here). Considerable new areas of the fora of Caesar and Nerva have been uncovered, including stretches of original pavement in grey granite, as well as Republican houses. The ground plan of the Temple (or Forum) of Peace has been revealed. In addition, extremely interesting traces of the medieval city, about which relatively little is known, have also been found.

Excavations are in progress in front of the church of the Madonna di Loreto, where a complex of buildings constructed for Hadrian has been found, as well as a flight of steps connected to buildings near Trajan's Column. Digging began on this site in 2009 for Rome's new Metro line C—but clearly the Piazza di Venezia station planned here will have to be moved.

Planning a visit

The following is a description of what you see from outside and above starting beside the earliest of the Fora, that of Caesar, and describing the others not in strict chronological order, but as you can most logically and conveniently see them from Via dei Fori Imperiali and the modern walkways that traverse the site. Trajan's Column and his forum and market buildings are described at the end (the Museum and Markets of Trajan can be entered rather than simply viewed from a distance). After that the description takes in the Domus Romane and the two churches that flank Trajan's Column. In spring there are usually excellent son-et-lumière productions in the Forum of Caesar and the Forum of Augustus (see viaggioneifori.it).

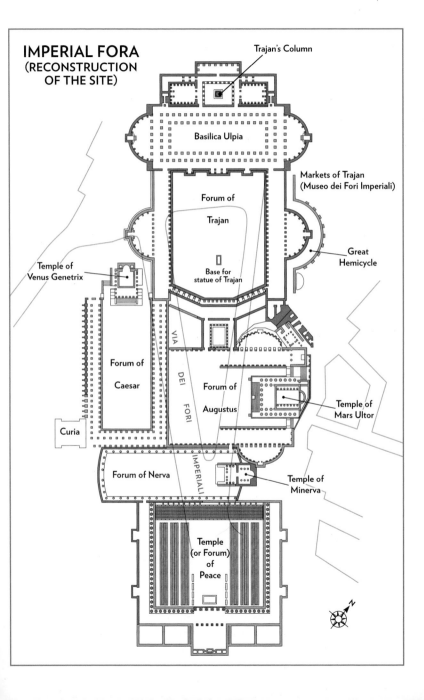

IMPERIAL FORA
(RECONSTRUCTION
OF THE SITE)

Trajan's Column

Basilica Ulpia

Markets of Trajan
(Museo dei Fori Imperiali)

Forum of
Trajan

Great
Hemicycle

Temple of
Venus Genetrix

Base for
statue of Trajan

Forum of
Caesar

Forum of
Augustus

Temple of
Mars Ultor

Curia

Temple of
Minerva

Forum of Nerva

Temple
(or Forum)
of
Peace

VIA DEI FORI IMPERIALI

FORUM OF CAESAR

Well beneath the level of Via dei Fori Imperiali are the remains of part of the Forum of Caesar, the first of the Imperial Fora. Excavations have shown that Caesar created an entrance to it from the Roman Forum (behind the Curia building, which is clearly seen from here). The forum was completed by Augustus.

The focal point of the new Forum was the **Temple of Venus Genetrix**, the most important building erected in the city by Julius Caesar, who claimed descent from the goddess. 'Genetrix' was not one of Venus' known manifestations; instead it was an attribute given by Caesar designating her as the one who gave birth to his family (although it has also been suggested that Caesar intended a double meaning with the epithet, wanting also to claim Venus as the mother of the Roman people as a whole). The temple's high base remains (although it has lost its marble facing) and three of its fluted Corinthian columns have been re-erected. The temple was dedicated in 46 BC, two years after Caesar's decisive defeat of Pompey at the Battle of Pharsalus (after which Pompey fled from Thessaly to Egypt where he was stabbed to death on his arrival). In front of the temple stood an equestrian statue of Caesar.

Inside were exhibited works of art by well-known contemporary artists: a statue of the goddess, the best-known sculpture by Arcesilaus who worked in Rome and was encouraged by his friend Lucullus who had been a successful commander as a young man but who, on retirement, took a great interest in art. Here also Caesar hung two pictures, of Ajax and of Medea, which we know he purchased (for 80 talents) from the painter Timomachus who was born in Byzantium. Next to a statue of Julius Caesar stood a gilded bronze statue of Cleopatra, who had lived in Rome for a while with Caesar, as his mistress and mother of his son, at the time when the temple was dedicated. It is thought that Augustus plundered the statue in Egypt after his famous defeat of Antony and Cleopatra at Actium, and erected it here as a spoil of war.

Cassius Dio, who was twice consul under Commodus and Alexander Severus and who wrote a history of Rome from the earliest times up until his own day (2nd century AD), vividly imagined the scene at the dedication of the temple by Caesar: '...when the people had finished dinner, Caesar entered his Forum shod with slippers and garlanded with flowers of all kinds. From there he continued home, escorted by almost the whole population, and by elephants bearing torches'. Cassius goes on to state categorically that this forum was more beautiful than the Roman Forum.

The forum itself was an open piazza which was surrounded on three sides by two rows of columns raised on three steps and paved in white marble. Well below the level of the temple, the three steps of the southwestern colonnade can clearly be seen, and most of the columns are still standing. Behind them are remains of *tabernae*, or shops, on two floors. Trajan rebuilt the temple and forum and added the Basilica Argentaria, or exchange building, as well as a large heated public lavatory (*forica*), remains of which survive above the shops. Excavations in 2006 found Iron Age tombs of the 10th century BC as well as various strata of a medieval district of the city (and interesting evidence of the destruction of the city by the Gauls in 390).

FORUM OF NERVA

A terrace adjoining the Forum of Caesar provides a fine view of the extensive area of new excavations in the southwestern part of the Forum of Nerva. Begun by Domitian, who was assassinated in AD 96, this forum was completed by his successor Nerva in AD 97, whose brief reign of less than two years was marked by enlightened and humanitarian government. It was also called the Forum Transitorium, because it led into Vespasian's earlier Forum of Peace (*see below*) and was traversed by the Argiletum, the street that led from the Roman Forum to the rowdy Subura district. Excavations have revealed clear evidence of the various uses of this land over time. From the terrace can be seen all that remains of it today: just a few large cracked marble slabs which provided the paving. Directly below, the modern yellow wall belongs to a 17th-century sewer and on the right you can see a cobbled medieval road (overlooked by a 9th-century house). Below ground level are the scant remains of foundations of dwellings dating from the 2nd century BC. Straight ahead a 9th-century house with arches is conspicuous. Towards the Roman Forum can be seen part of the Cloaca Maxima drain (*see p. 75*). A sewage conduit laid in the 15th century was also discovered, and this has been restored and now serves to connect the new excavations with those done in the 1930s on the other side of Via dei Fori Imperiali, adjoining the Forum of Augustus. Nerva's Forum included, in its centre, the **Temple of Minerva**: only its massive basement survives. It was still standing at the beginning of the 17th century, when it was pulled down by Paul V to provide marble for the fountain of the Acqua Paola on the Janiculum.

FORUM OF PEACE

The Temple of Peace (later called the Forum of Peace) was built by Vespasian with the spoils of the Jewish War and inaugurated in AD 75 to commemorate peace at the end of the civil wars which followed the death of Nero. During the Republican era there was a large food market (*macellum*) on this site, which was destroyed in the fire of 64 AD. The temple was preceded by a large piazza which it now seems was really a garden decorated with six low brick walls, on the top of which water constantly flowed along marble channels. Over 30 flower pots have been found, which apparently contained 'Gallic' roses. On three sides of the piazza there was a portico above marble steps (part of the one at the southwest side, towards the Roman Forum, can be seen), and these were decorated on two sides with quadrangular exedrae (one of which is preserved beneath the Torre dei Conti). The temple itself is being partially reconstructed.

A rectangular hall flanking the temple, probably a library used to house the city plans and public property registers, had one of its walls decorated with the ***Forma Urbis***, a famous plan of the ancient city commissioned by Septimius Severus between 205 and 208. It was carved in some 150 marble blocks which made up a detailed map of Rome (showing public buildings, streets, etc. all marked with their names), about 18m by 13m in overall size, today considered the most important document for our knowledge of the topography of the city. The first fragments of it were found here in 1562 and another 24 pieces were unearthed in 1999. Though the most important pieces are not on public display, a part of it can be seen in the Crypta Balbi (*see p. 144*).

Recent excavations have revealed a fragment of the perimeter wall of the Forum (beside a lovely broken mottled marble column), continued by a modern fence, and beside another column of the same marble there are remains of the pavement of the square. The form of the garden has been reconstructed with low concrete walls, beside which a few original fragments of the 'gutters' which were used for the rivulets of water have been left *in situ*. At the far end are rows of plants in (modern) pots above a stack of all the other pieces of columns which were found during excavations.

FORUM OF AUGUSTUS

The Forum of Augustus was built to commemorate the victory of Philippi (42 BC). It was dedicated to Mars Ultor (the 'Avenger'); at the battle Caesar's assassins, Cassius and Brutus, were defeated.

TEMPLE OF MARS ULTOR

The forum was dominated by this octastyle temple, which has columns on three sides. It was dedicated in 2 BC, when Augustus was named *Pater Patriae*, and had a large pronaos and an apsidal cella. Three tall fluted columns with Corinthian capitals supporting an architrave, at the end of the right flank, are still standing. A broad flight of very high steps ascends to the capacious pronaos, where four of the eight Corinthian columns in front (the two middle and the two end ones) have been partly reconstructed from antique fragments. The effect of undue width in the cella was lessened by a colonnade on either side, and here are stepped bases of statues (probably of Mars, Venus and the *Divus Julius*). Behind is the curve of the large apse.

This was one of the most honoured temples throughout the Empire. As a centre of solemn ceremonies and the Imperial sanctuary, it became a museum of art and housed miscellaneous relics, including the sword of Julius Caesar. Also kept here were the Roman standards which had been lost to the Parthians in a war in 54 BC in which Crassus and his son died and the Roman army suffered a humiliating defeat. Caesar had planned to lead a campaign to Parthia (accompanied by Octavian; Augustus' name before he became emperor) in 44 BC just before his murder, but it was not until 24 years later that Augustus achieved their surrender, signifying a temporary reconciliation with them and the establishment of a Roman protectorate in what is now Iran. However, the Parthians remained a continual threat to the stability of the Roman Empire and numerous campaigns were organised against them by Trajan, Marcus Aurelius and Septimius Severus' sons: their well-organised army (with its formidable horsemen) was the only force able to offer serious resistance to the Empire up until the 3rd century, before the Parthian empire fell to the Sasanids and the Persians took over as Rome's arch enemies.

THE EMPEROR AUGUSTUS

Octavian, known to history by his title *Augustus*, 'the revered one', was one of the most remarkable figures in Roman history and certainly the most influential (ruled 27 BC–AD 14). Emerging as the adopted son of Julius Caesar, he exploited his position ruthlessly as the Republic collapsed after Caesar's assassination. He cooperated at first with Mark Antony but the rivalry between them soon turned to open conflict. Mark Antony, who had taken command of the empire in the East, allowed himself to become entangled with the ever-opportunistic Cleopatra, and this enabled Octavian to brand them both as enemies of Rome. In 31 BC at the Battle of Actium their navy was routed and both committed suicide in Egypt.

Back in Rome, now enriched with the wealth of Egypt and backed by a large army, Octavian could easily have become a dictator. However, that was not his way. Despite the ruthlessness of his youth, he now showed himself to be measured and balanced. His favourite god Apollo was, after all, the god of reason. Knowing that the senate was desperate for respect and peace, he disbanded his army and let the senate acquiesce in his growing influence. His title, *Augustus*, was awarded him in 27 BC and he gradually absorbed other ancient republican titles too, as if the old political system were still intact. Behind this façade he was spending his booty fast. He claimed to have restored no fewer than 82 temples in Rome. He completed the Forum of Caesar and then embarked on a massive one of his own, centred on a temple to Mars Ultor: Mars as the avenger of his adoptive father's murder. Statues of the heroes of Rome's past lined the porticoes and led up to a great bronze of himself in a four-horse chariot. Other statues played on ancient traditions: Augustus appears as military commander, youthful hero or veiled priest as circumstances dictated. The statues were distributed throughout the empire—one estimate is that there were originally between 30,000 and 50,000 in total. One notable legacy of Augustus in Rome is the large number of obelisks, which he brought back from Egypt. By the time his projects were complete, he could rightly boast that he had made Rome into a city of marble.

The empire prospered under Augustus' steady control: poets such as Virgil and Horace praised his rule and there was no challenge to his growing influence. Further recognition of his success came in in 9 BC when the senate dedicated the Ara Pacis, the Altar of Peace, to him after he had returned from campaigns in Spain and Gaul. (In its reconstructed form it stands close to a massive mausoleum Augustus had created for himself and his family in 28 BC.) In 2 BC he was granted the honorary title *Pater Patriae*, Father of the Fatherland, an honour which left him deeply moved. Still his reign continued, although by now Augustus was ailing. He died in AD 14 and it was observed at his cremation that his body had been seen ascending through the smoke towards heaven. The senate forthwith decreed that he should be ranked as a god. By now the Republic had been irrevocably transformed into an empire, and emperors ruled Rome for the rest of its history.   C.F.

THE PORTICO AND EXEDRAE

The high wall behind the temple, some 30m high and still partly standing, was built to isolate the Forum of Augustus from the Subura, a crowded, insalubrious residential district of ancient Rome. The temple itself was surrounded by a portico raised on three steps (as in Caesar's Forum) which enclosed a large piazza, in the centre of which there was a statue of Augustus in a triumphal chariot. On either side of the temple the three marble steps survive which led up to the porticoes where there were rectangular niches (the remains of some of which can still be seen) decorated by Augustus with statues of his ancestors (members of the Julian clan), and including both Aeneas and Romulus as founders of Rome, and Roman heroes from Republican days. On the ground between the surviving columns of the temple and the right-hand portico are numerous interesting architectural fragments (others are preserved in the museum; *see p. 132*). The left portico has an extension at the north end where you can still see part of a large hall which was big enough to contain a colossal statue of Augustus: the base remains with the striking imprint of one of its huge feet (remains of the statue and the decorations from the hall are displayed in the museum).

Large semicircular exedrae decorated the exteriors of the two porticoes but these were almost completely destroyed during the Renaissance for their marble. The southwestern area of the Forum (seen on the right), where there must have been two more exedrae—which scholars now think could have belonged to a square in front of the temple or even a covered basilica—has been studied in excavations which were completed in 2006 but which unearthed only later buildings.

On the left, beyond the temple, are two enormous Corinthian columns in purple and white marble, which have survived over the centuries from the northeast colonnade and have always been known affectionately by the Romans as the **Colonnacce**. In the attic between the columns is a high-relief of a female figure wearing a helmet (usually identified as Minerva/Athena) and in the rich frieze of the entablature women are shown sewing and weaving. After the discovery in 1999 of another female figure, scholars believe the iconographical programme of this temple may have centred on the personification of the provinces symbolising the success of the Roman Empire in bringing peace and unification. In front of the Colonnacce is a section of the Argiletum, which was repaved in the 9th century when it was still one of the busiest roads in the city. Behind you can see the base of the massive **Torre dei Conti**, all that remains of a great tower erected above one of the exedrae of the Temple of Peace probably in 1203 by Riccardo dei Conti, brother of Innocent III, as part of a fortified residence. It was damaged by an earthquake in 1348 and reduced to its present state by Urban VIII in the 17th century.

FORUM OF TRAJAN

This forum was built between 107 and 113 to celebrate Trajan's military victories and was the last and most splendid of the Imperial Fora. It is the most famous work by the Greek architect Apollodorus of Damascus, whom the emperor called to Rome from his native Syria. To make room for the monumental buildings, the site had to be excavated to a depth of some 30m in the saddle between the Capitoline and Quirinal hills.

THE EMPEROR TRAJAN

Trajan (ruled AD 98–117) is often seen as the ideal Roman emperor. Born in Spain, probably in 53, he made his way up through military campaigns in Syria, Spain and Germany until the elderly emperor Nerva adopted him as his son and thus made his succession inevitable. It was a good example of the way talent could be rewarded, and Trajan more than repaid the compliment. He was a stable and restrained man, scrupulous in his dealings with the powerful senatorial class and his provincial governors, and built up a reputation for administrative competence. Pliny praised him for being open to all petitioners and giving replies quickly, and the correspondence between the two, when Pliny was governor of Bithynia, is full of practical common sense. Trajan's humanity was shown through schemes to help impoverished and abandoned children. Gregory the Great even said that Trajan deserved to be admitted to heaven as an honorary Christian.

Like all successful Roman emperors Trajan knew the importance of military victories, and his campaigns were wildly popular. The most successful in the early 2nd century were against the Dacians who, under their king Decabalus, threatened the empire from north of the Danube. When they were finally subdued (105–6) and Decabalus's palace was sacked, there was immense booty to be brought back to Rome. The victory was celebrated with 123 days of games, after which Trajan set about building a massive Forum alongside that of Augustus, with porticoes, libraries, a vast basilica and eventually a huge temple constructed by his successor Hadrian to the now deified emperor. When the emperor Constantius visited the Forum in 357, the historian Ammianus Marcellinus described how 'the emperor stood transfixed with astonishment, surveying the gigantic fabric around him...Its grandeur defies description and can never again be approached by mortal men'. At its heart stood, then as now, a 30-metre column with reliefs showing the Dacian campaign. Yet there was a practical side to Trajan, and he appreciated that vast buildings did not in themselves provide for the needs of Rome's citizens. So, even before he had built the Forum, Trajan had constructed his great market complex, numerous shops on three levels in the hillside, to the east of the existing Fora; had created a canal to stop the Tiber flooding; and built a new port at the Tiber mouth.

In his later years Trajan headed east. There had been peace with the Parthian empire for 150 years, but the emperor may have feared revived enmity (or, as ancient sources suggest, he may have been searching for even greater glorification). There were more astonishing victories and Trajan marched through Mesopotamia, adding it as a province of the empire before arriving at the Persian Gulf in 116. Here news of revolts behind him forced him to give up and he died the next year, always regretful that he had not equalled the conquests of Alexander. His popularity back in Rome remained intact and in later years the senate used to greet a new emperor with the words 'May you be even luckier than Augustus and even better than Trajan'.   C.F.

The buildings of Trajan's forum included Trajan's Column, the Basilica Ulpia, an open forum beyond, and a great hemicycle to the north (always known as the Markets of Trajan). In the opinion of ancient writers these constructions made up a monumental group unequalled in the world.

TRAJAN'S COLUMN

A columned vestibule provided the original north entrance to the Forum of Trajan, close to Trajan's Column. The Column, still almost intact and carefully restored in the 1980s, is generally considered to be the masterpiece of Roman sculptural art. It was dedicated to Trajan by Hadrian in memory of his conquest of the Dacians, the inhabitants of what is now Romania. Around the column shaft winds a spiral frieze 200m long and between 0.89m and 1.25m high, with some 2,500 figures in relief illustrating in detail the various phases of Trajan's remarkable military achievements in the Dacian campaigns (101–2 and 105–6). The carving was carried out in less than four years by an unknown Roman master and his workshop. The scenes show the emperor himself as well as his soldiers and those of the enemy, both always depicted with great delicacy and intent on showing the dignity of the defeated as well as the victors. Numerous naturalistic details include plants and animals. It is presumed that the column could originally be seen from the neighbouring buildings, which surrounded it on various levels. On the left and right of it were two twin edifices, sometimes identified as libraries, which had at least three storeys. From ground level it is difficult to appreciate the beautiful details of the carving with the naked eye, but a fascinating **photographic reproduction** of the entire column, describing each scene, is exhibited here in front of the church of the Nome di Maria.

The column, 100 Roman feet (29.7m) high, is constructed in a series of marble drums and it has an internal spiral stair which ascends to the top of the Doric capital, on which the statue of Trajan—replaced by St Peter in 1588—once stood. (The idea of a statue surmounting the column gave the model for the adulation of later heroes, such as Nelson in Trafalgar Square in London.) The ashes of the emperor, who died in Cilicia (in modern-day Turkey) in 117, and of his wife Plotina, were enclosed in a golden urn and placed in a vault below the column. Trajan was the first and probably the only emperor to be buried in the centre of the city. An inscription at the base has been taken to indicate that the top of the column reached to the original ground level, thus giving an idea of the colossal excavations necessary for the construction of the forum (i.e. how much of the hill had to be cut away).

BASILICA ULPIA

Behind the column are fragments of colossal grey granite columns, one with its marble Corinthian capital, some of the largest ever found in Rome, and now thought to have belonged to the monumental entrance to Trajan's Forum. Beyond, crossing the entire site, are the extensive remains of the **Basilica Ulpia** (Trajan's family name was Ulpius), dedicated to the administration of justice, and the largest in Rome. Like all basilicas, it was once roofed with bronze tiles and may have been some 50m high. It was divided by colonnades into a nave and four aisles: some of the columns of this section of the inner colonnade are still standing (the rest of it is under the modern roads). The back entrance, with two doors, was here, but the main approach was from the other side (from the open forum), where traces of three doors have been found. Part of the pavement in coloured marbles has survived, as has a fragment of the entablature, with reliefs of scenes of sacrifice.

On each short side was an extensive apse or portico; the north portico was found under Palazzo Roccagiovine beside Via Magnanapoli. It conforms to the semicircular shape of the markets. In the Middle Ages the portico was stripped of its precious marbles: all that survives are the remains of three steps of *giallo antico*, a column base, traces of the polychrome marble pavement and a column of the apse. Behind the portico part of the wall of the enclosure is visible. The site of the south portico is under Via dei Fori Imperiali.

FORUM OF TRAJAN

Stretching beyond the modern raised walkway which now crosses the site is the area of the open **Forum of Trajan**, itself in the form of a rectangular piazza which covered some 9,000 square metres and had a portico and exedra on each of the long sides. In the centre but towards the lower end was a colossal equestrian statue of Trajan (over 12m high), the travertine base of which was found during excavations in 1999.

The broad modern pathway follows the line of Via Alessandria (*see p. 122*), laid out in 1570 but destroyed in the 20th century. Recent excavations have revealed some remains of the old district, including a monastery (on the right).

To the north of the forum and virtually adjoining it rises the huge semicircle of the so-called Markets of Trajan, which you can visit together with the Museo dei Fori Imperiali (*described below*). There is a raised iron walkway at the end of the hemicycle of Trajan's markets below the 16th-century loggia of the Casa dei Cavalieri di Rodi.

On the right, dug up in 2000, are remains of a porticoed three-sided court which had a monumental arch which served as a vestibule into Trajan's Forum and also connected Trajan's Forum with the adjoining Forum of Augustus.

On the left, beyond a high wall, you can look over the Forum of Augustus.

MUSEO DEI FORI IMPERIALI & THE MARKETS OF TRAJAN

Entrance at Via IV Novembre 94 in Largo Magnanapoli (map p. 655, D2), reached by steps close to the Column of Trajan, or by an iron walkway from Via dei Fori Imperiali. Open daily 9.30–7.30. T: 060608, mercatiditraiano.it. Labelling is excellent, also in English, with very helpful interactive screens, including a fascinating Admotum virtual-reality game.

The area known as the Markets of Trajan was built in the first years of the 2nd century AD and became an integral part of the monumental group of buildings which made up the Forum of Trajan. Although always known as 'markets', many of these vaulted rooms are likely to have been used for official ceremonies and as administrative offices. In addition there were individual shops and workshops, most of which were in the Great Hemicycle, which is the most conspicuous part of these buildings, with its superimposed rows of arcaded fronts, set into the slopes of the Quirinal hill. Part of these ancient buildings is now occupied by the Museo dei Fori Imperiali, which traces the history of the Imperial Fora and preserves finds from them, including some ancient sculpture unearthed only in the last few years while excavations continue.

THE MUSEUM

Ground floor

The entrance leads straight into an ancient rectangular vaulted hall, two storeys high, with six rooms off each side of each floor. The exhibits here provide an introduction to the history of the Imperial Fora. In the centre of the hall is a fine reconstruction of part of a portico from the Forum of Augustus (the caryatid is a cast).

The side rooms contain a particularly significant piece of sculpture from each of the Fora. The first room to the right displays a colossal marble head found in the Forum of Trajan in 2005, dating from the 1st century AD (and reused three centuries later to provide a portrait of Constantine). In the second room is the torso of a colossal statue in armour (AD 112) and the third room has a charming frieze of cupids from the temple in the Forum of Caesar (reconstructed by Trajan in AD 113). The fourth room is dedicated to the Forum of Augustus, and a gilded bronze foot from a winged female statue of Victory thought to have decorated the exterior of the temple there is strikingly displayed.

In the rooms off the opposite side are fragments of a huge Egyptian porphyry basin, 3.5m in diameter, dating from the 2nd century AD, and a tiny bronze portrait bust from AD 75 of Chrysippus the Greek Stoic philosopher, who died in 297 BC. Both these were found in the last years of the 20th century.

Upper floor

On the upper floor are finds from the Forum of Augustus. These include (first room on the right) a delicate capital with winged horses from the temple, and fragments with lions' heads.

The rooms on the other side are dedicated to the Forum of Caesar, with fragments of external friezes and reliefs with *amorini*.

In the ancient rooms above the hemicycle are more finds from the Forum of Augustus, including a hand from the colossal statue of the deified Augustus, which was 12m high and was kept in a room beside the temple in his Forum (an interactive screen shows a reconstruction of the statue and where the various pieces fitted). Here also are what survives of the very unusual painted decoration, with blue and bright red festoons, made on the white marble slabs which lined the walls of the room. The beautiful pavement was made from different coloured marbles.

The next series of rooms, also dating from ancient Roman times, has some of the most impressive sculpture in the museum, very well displayed. These include the

MUSEO DEI FORI IMPERIALI
Marble rosette with egg and dart border from the
Temple of Mars Ultor (dedicated in 2 BC).

beautifully-carved capitals from the portico and exedra of the Forum of Augustus, and fragments of some huge fluted columns.

TORRE DELLE MILIZIE

From the upper floor of the museum a door leads out to the ancient paved Via della Torre, which can be followed to the garden at the foot of the Torre delle Milizie (*no admission*). Thought to date from the mid-13th century, with a crenellated summit, this tower is one of the highest buildings in the centre of the city and a conspicuous feature on the skyline. It originally had three storeys; two of them survive. It stood on the edge of this part of the medieval city and so would have been visible from miles around. It acquired its lean after an earthquake in 1348 and may have belonged to the Conti, the same family who owned the other even earlier tower in this district (*see p. 128*)—they are among the most important civic medieval buildings to have survived in Rome. In 1914 the Torre delle Milizie was restored and isolated from the convent of Santa Caterina by Antonio Muñoz, an architect who showed great skill in restoration projects (best known for his work on the church of Santa Sabina).

In the other direction, Via della Torre leads to a terrace high above the markets beside the little Renaissance loggia of the Casa dei Cavalieri di Rodi, the ancient seat of the Roman priorate of the Order of the Knights of St John of Jerusalem (*see p. 573*). From here there is the best view of the Fora, and you can also see the dome of St Peter's above the fortified roof of Palazzo di Venezia.

THE HEMICYCLE AND ANCIENT ROADS

The rest of the market buildings and the roads which connected them to the level of the Forum of Trajan can be explored through a labyrinth of stairs and corridors. Steps lead down from below the terrace to the ancient **Via Biberatica**, with its huge round paving stones in front of the façade of the **Great Hemicycle** of the markets, off which can be seen a series of rooms (the framed doorways are restorations). Follow the old road to the left and take more steps down to the lower level. Here you can follow a semicircular barrel-vaulted corridor (which has a floor covering to protect its ancient herring-bone paving) and through the open arches look down to the forum. Opening off it are a series of vaulted rooms presumed to have been used as public offices, some of which still preserve their black and white mosaic floor. At the end, another flight of steps continues down to the level of the forum and another ancient paved road. Here you can see the exterior of the two well-preserved apsidal halls at either end of the Great Hemicycle. Stairs are signposted back up to the exit, through more ancient rooms in the two-storey **Small Hemicycle**.

SANTA MARIA DI LORETO & THE NOME DI MARIA

Two little domed churches, of similar design but different date, flank Trajan's Column. **Santa Maria di Loreto** (*map p. 654, C2*) is a good building erected in 1507 by the bakers' guild of Rome, enlarged in 1520 by Antonio da Sangallo the Younger and given a lantern by Giacomo del Duca (1582). It contains an altarpiece on a gold ground attributed to Marco Palmezzano with four female statues in niches around it, including *St Susanna* (1630), a little-known saint who was martyred under Diocletian (*see pp. 321–2*), shown pointing towards the altar and dressed as a Roman Vestal, by the Flemish-born Baroque sculptor François Duquesnoy (*see p. 237*). Standing in Classical *contrapposto*, with a supple grace and exquisitely executed drapery, the statue carries with it a mood of serene calm and modesty.

The second church (1738), dedicated to the **Santissimo Nome di Maria** (Most Holy Name of Mary), is one of just two churches in the city by the little-known Antoine Dérizet, who had the good taste to match the architectural style of the much earlier church close by. The *Madonna and Child*, both with golden crowns, over the high altar, may date from the 13th century. Dérizet's other church in Rome is that of Santi Andrea e Claudio on Piazza San Silvestro (*see p. 165*). He also contributed to the decorations in the French church of San Luigi (*see p. 206*).

In front of these churches is an area of excavations. While digging was in progress for a planned station of Metro line C, remains were found of the **Auditoria of Hadrian**, his so-called 'Athenaeum', with three large halls with stepped seating on two sides, used for poetry recitals and contests of rhetoric. After the fall of the Empire the area was turned into a huge workshop specialising in the production of copper alloys and later still, in the Middle Ages, lime for the building trade.

THE DOMUS ROMANE

Map p. 654, C2. Entrance through the courtyard of Palazzo Valentini, Via IV Novembre 118 (the headquarters of the Province of Rome, palazzovalentini.it). Admission by previous appointment only, daily except Tues. To book a tour (also in English), T: 06 32 810 or see tosc.it. The visit (max. 15 people) takes 1hr 40mins.

This is one of the newest archaeological sites in Rome and will impress even those who tend to have misgivings about interactive displays.

Excavations carried out beneath this 16th-century palace in the first decade of this century have revealed important remains of ancient Roman residences which over-looked Trajan's Column. One dates from the 4th century AD and has its own private baths as well as remains of some very fine floors and walls in precious marbles (opus sectile), mosaic pavements and a surprisingly grand staircase. There are also remains of an earlier house (1st–2nd century AD). By the 5th century AD the houses were abandoned and there is evidence of medieval buildings on a higher level before the present *palazzo* was constructed. However the most remarkable feature of this site is the way it has been displayed: glass floors throughout provide wonderful views of the various rooms and their history is vividly explained by a recording (also in English) as the various features are illuminated or reconstructed beneath your feet. This makes the remains all the more fascinating to visit (and a place also for young children). The Roman city comes alive through this 'performance' as perhaps nowhere else, even though—as the narrator readily admits—some of the reconstruction can only be conjectural.

The visit ends with the extraordinary sight of two vast Roman columns (two metres in diameter and probably once 15m high) and the suggestion that these are almost certainly remnants of Trajan's Temple, known to have been in this area beside his column and forum. You then sit to watch a fascinating film which tells the story of the reliefs on Trajan's Column before seeing the base of the column itself from close range, from a little door which gave access to an air-raid shelter used in 1939.

Around Piazza Venezia

Piazza Venezia, a huge square always full of traffic and dominated by the colossal monument to Vittorio Emanuele II, is usually considered the centre of Rome. The name of the piazza comes from the Renaissance Palazzo Venezia, which is now a museum of decorative arts. The Crypta Balbi, just west of the piazza, is particularly important for the evidence it provides of the medieval city.

Although there was a piazza here by the mid-15th century, Piazza Venezia (*map p. 654, C2*) was transformed at the end of the 19th century when parts of the Renaissance city were demolished and the Capitoline hill itself was encroached upon to make way for the huge Vittoriano, the vast and rather ugly monument to Italy's first king, Vittorio Emanuele II. It is one of the tallest buildings in Rome; and though the views from its terraces are superb, it is an unforgivable intrusion on the city.

Opposite the Vittoriano on the left are Palazzo di Venezia, built for a Venetian cardinal (*see overleaf*) and the basilica of San Marco, which has a remarkable early mosaic in its apse (*see p. 142*). Behind them the Via del Corso runs in a dead straight line all the way to Piazza del Popolo, some two kilometres away. At the busiest times of the day a policeman still regulates the immense volume of traffic which converges on the piazza. Standing on a little round podium at the head of the Corso (let into the pavement when not in use), he conducts this operation with great elegance and is usually watched by a little group of people who justly consider this 'ballet' to be one of the sights of the city—though it is equally fascinating to see how the traffic manages to avoid congestion at times when it is given no directions at all.

On the site now roughly occupied by the huge Palazzo delle Assicurazione Generali (built in 1906), in the district called Macel de' Corvi, stood the **house where Michelangelo lived** for the last 30 years of his life. The name of the district is derived from a slaughterhouse (*macello*) which used to be here and *corvi* refers to the crows sold at a market on the site. Michelangelo received his lodging here from the della Rovere when he came to the city to work on the tomb of Julius II (*see p. 118*), and through the good offices of the later pope Paul III he was allowed to continue living in the house. While living here he painted the *Last Judgement* in the Sistine Chapel. He died here in 1564 and his body was taken to Santi Apostoli close by (where there is a memorial to him, *see p. 157*), but his funeral service and burial took place in Florence. At his death his nephew generously decided that his devoted friend and pupil Daniele da Volterra, who sculpted the most famous portrait we have of Michelangelo (now in the Musei Capitolini; *see p. 43*), should take over the house.

THE VITTORIANO

Map p. 654, C2. Open 9.30–4.30 (9.30–5 in summer). Free, but you have to buy a ticket for the lift (Mon–Thur 9.30–6.30, Fri–Sun 9.30–7.30) to the very top terrace—which is well worth taking. Entrances are through the gate at the front of the building or on each side, through the Museo Nazionale Emigrazione Italiana in Piazza Aracoeli and the Museo Centrale del Risorgimento in Via di San Pietro in Carcere. There is also a convenient entrance from the Campidoglio, in front of the façade of the church of Santa Maria in Aracoeli, to an upper terrace close to the lift shaft. There is a café near the lift.

This overwhelming monument was inaugurated in 1911 to symbolise the achievement of Italian unity and of the nation's first king, Vittorio Emanuele II. Some 80m high, the building changed irrevocably the aspect of the city, throwing out of scale the Capitoline hill itself and causing indiscriminate demolition. Familiarly known as 'the wedding cake' or 'Mussolini's typewriter', it can only be described as a colossal monstrosity. However, since 2000 when it was opened to the public, it has taken on a more friendly aspect and now has an air much less hostile to its surroundings.

It was begun in 1885 by Giuseppe Sacconi, winner of an international competition in which there were 98 entries. He used an incongruous dazzling white *botticino* marble from Brescia, which further alienates the monument from its surroundings. It was only completed in 1937.

EXTERIOR OF THE VITTORIANO

The monument is decorated with rhetorical allegories of the homeland, unity and liberty, and the individual sculptures are interesting examples of official Academic Italian art of the period. The two fountains represent the Tyrrhenian Sea (by Pietro Canonica) and the Adriatic. At the foot of the wide flight of steps are two colossal groups in bronze: *Action* by Francesco Jerace on the right, and *Thought* by Giulio Monteverde on the left. Midway are two winged lions and at the top sculptured bases for flagstaffs with bronze Victories. The four sculptural groups on the extreme left and right represent *Law* by Ettore Ximenes, *Sacrifice* by Leonardo Bistolfi, *Concord* by Ludovico Poliaghi and *Strength* by Augusto Rivalta.

The grave of **Italy's Unknown Soldier** (*il Milite Ignoto*), from the First World War, is perpetually guarded by two sentinels (each one is on guard for an hour). Official military ceremonies take place here, often in the presence of the President of the Republic.

Above is the 'Altare della Patria' by Angelo Zanelli, with a figure of Rome enshrined in the pedestal and classical friezes on either side: the *Triumph of Patriotism* on the right and the *Triumph of Labour* on the left. Steps to right and left flank the **equestrian statue of Vittorio Emanuele II** in gilt bronze, 12m high, by Enrico Chiaradia, completed by Emilio Gallori. (It is interesting to think that there were a number of statues as large as this and even larger in the days of ancient Rome in the nearby Imperial Fora). Around the base are figures by Eugenio Maccagnani representing historic towns of Italy. From the centre to the left they are Turin, Florence, Naples,

Amalfi, Pisa, Ravenna, Bologna, Milan, Genoa, Ferrara, Urbino, Mantua, Palermo and Venice. On the pedestal are military emblems. Decorating the portico are a frieze with eagles and a cornice with lions' heads and 16 colossal statues symbolising the Italian provinces.

If you keep to the steps on the right (*signposted*) you reach the ticket office for the **glass lift**, discreetly installed at the back of the building (*for opening times, see above*). It ascends to the **panoramic terrace**, just ten metres below the two quadrigae crowning the monument symbolising Liberty and Unity. The view is spectacular: to the right you can see the Quirinale, with flags always flying from its tower, then the twin towers of the Villa Medici in trees on the Pincio ridge. To the left is the Corso and the top of the Column of Marcus Aurelius, with the dome of the church of Santi Carlo e Ambrogio al Corso behind it. Further left and nearer at hand is the flat dome of the Pantheon, and the small dome of the church of the Gesù and, on the skyline, St Peter's. In the other direction the Campidoglio is directly below (we are higher than the belltower of Palazzo Senatorio) and then the trees of the Palatine hill can be seen above the Forum. The Colosseum is visible, and the statues on the facade of St John Lateran on the skyline, and the Alban Hills in the distance.

INTERIOR OF THE VITTORIANO

The vast halls and monumental staircases are on an even grander scale than you would expect from the outside and have a certain fascination for their period. They contain a collection of flags as well as two important museums (with excellent labelling, also in English). The **Museo Centrale del Risorgimento** (*open daily 9.30–6.30; free; entrance on the left side, reached from Via di San Pietro in Carcere; T: 06 67 93 598, risorgimento.it*) covers the 19th-century Risorgimento (literally the 'resurgence', the political renaissance of Italy) as well as the First World War, after which Italy made substantial territorial gains from Austria-Hungary (notably the South Tyrol). Stairs, hung with prints, lead up past a small theatre where fascinating early films (*Film Luce*) of the First World War are shown. Up more stairs is a grand rectangular room with mementoes of Garibaldi, Mazzini and Cavour, the prime movers of the Risorgimento. In the long curving corridor, with busts of war heroes, are various well-labelled sections on moments of historic significance in Italian history from 1848 onwards.

The **Museo Nazionale Emigrazione Italiana** (*open Mon–Thur 9.30–6.30, Fri–Sun 9.30–7.30; free; entrance on Piazza d'Aracoeli; T: 06 67 80 664, museonazionaleemigrazione.it*) beautifully documents the history of emigration from Italy. Fourteen million Italians emigrated between 1876 and 1914, most of them to Europe, but from 1886 onwards many also went to Argentina, Brazil and the United States. The total number of emigrants who had left Italy by the mid-20th century was a staggering 29 million. There are touching accounts of their lives, as well as of the prejudice and discrimination they encountered and the few possessions they took with them, all against a background of the songs they sang and evocative film footage. This extraordinary part of Italian history is very well recreated, and at the end there is a reminder that 6.5 percent of the population of Italy today are immigrants. The problems they now encounter are also discussed.

PALAZZO DI VENEZIA

The battlemented Palazzo di Venezia (*map p. 654, C2*) was the first great Renaissance palace in Rome. The famous architect Leon Battista Alberti may have been involved in its design, but it has also been attributed to the little-known Francesco del Borgo. The palace was begun in 1455, partly using stone from the Colosseum, for the Venetian cardinal Pietro Barbo. It was enlarged in 1464 when he became pope, and finally finished in the 16th century. The finely-carved door on Piazza Venezia is attributed to Giuliano da Maiano.

Cardinal Barbo is said to have built the palace in order to view the horse races in the Corso. When he became pope he used it as his residence and rebuilt the church of San Marco, providing it with a loggia for papal benedictions. The palace was often occupied as such even after Pius IV (1559–65) gave it to the Venetian Republic for its embassy. Charles VIII of France stayed here after entering Rome with 20,000 soldiers in 1494. From 1797 (when Venice was ceded to Austria by Napoleon) until 1915 it was the seat of the Austrian ambassador to the Vatican. In 1917 Italy resumed possession and the palace was restored. During the Fascist regime it was occupied by Mussolini, who made the huge Sala del Mappamondo his office. Some of his most famous speeches were given from the balcony overlooking Piazza Venezia.

Adjoining the palace in Piazza di San Marco is the Palazzetto di Venezia (c. 1467). This originally closed the south end of Piazza Venezia but was moved to its present position in 1911 because it obstructed the view of the Vittoriano.

MUSEO NAZIONALE DEL PALAZZO DI VENEZIA

Open 8.30–7.30. Closed Mon. T: 06 69 99 4318, museopalazzovenezia.beniculturali.it. Entrance in Via del Plebiscito (ticket office on the first floor). The arrangement is subject to change and some of the later rooms are often kept closed. The state rooms are open only for exhibitions.

The Museo del Palazzo di Venezia is Rome's museum of decorative arts and one of the least-visited museums in the city. It was founded in the first years of the 20th century and several important collections were donated in the 1930s: that of George Wurts and his wife Henrietta Tower, who lived in the Villa Sciarra (*see p. 577*) in the early 20th century, and the Barsanti collection of small bronzes. It includes treasures from churches and later acquisitions and donations, such as the Odescalchi collection of arms and armour left to the museum in 1976.

It occupies the rooms used by the cardinals of San Marco in Palazzo di Venezia, and many rooms in the Palazzetto di Venezia. The main state rooms are sadly only open during exhibitions. The picturesque inner courtyard, with its tall palm trees, has a large, unfinished 15th-century loggia on two sides, of beautiful proportions. The fountain dates from 1730.

First floor

The monumental staircase in Renaissance style, by the Venetian architect Luigi Marangoni, was installed in 1924–30 when he was called in to make modifications to the building. It has 150 capitals carved with patriotic citations. At the top is the **loggia**, with early medieval architectural fragments, off which there is a room which displays a sculptured female head of Nike, thought to be an original Greek work dating from the late 5th century BC.

Appartamento Cybo: These rooms were used by Lorenzo Cybo, cardinal of San Marco from 1491–1501, and they became the residence also of his successors. They were very well restored in Renaissance style in the first years of the 20th century, when the floors in terracotta and polychrome majolica were installed and the pretty ceilings were designed by Ludovico Seitz.

Room 1: A 15th-century marble bust of Pietro Barbo by Paolo Romano is displayed beside his wooden coat of arms.

Room 3: A late 13th-century painted Crucifix by the Roman school, and the *Madonna of Acuto* (a little town in southern Lazio), a wood polychrome seated statue, the earliest known work of its kind dating from the first years of the 13th century.

Room 4: The display cases contain particularly precious small treasures: *Christ Pantocrator*, an unusual Byzantine work in metal and enamel (13th century from southern Italy); a Byzantine ivory casket decorated with the story of David (10th–11th century); a gilded bronze incised lunette, thought to be an early 13th-century German work; the door of a tabernacle in Limoges cloisonné enamel dating from the mid-13th century with a relief of an angel in gilded bronze; a 10th-century ivory triptych of the *Deësis* (Christ enthroned as judge, with the Virgin and St John the Baptist beside him); reliquary caskets of the 11th century; and the *Head of a Lady* by Nicola Pisano in pyrite, a very hard mineral. Amongst the paintings here is a *Mystic Marriage of St Catherine between Saints* attributed to the 'Master of the Christ Church Coronation of the Virgin', who was at work in Florence from c. 1360.

Room 5: 14th- and 15th-century paintings by the Tuscan school include a fresco fragment of the *Head of the Redeemer* recently attributed to Fra' Angelico. Four panels in low relief by Mino da Fiesole (1463) illustrate episodes in the life of St Jerome.

Room 6: 17th- and 18th-century works and a gilded terracotta group of the *Baptism of Christ*, by Alessandro Algardi (acquired in 2004). In the little niche is a bust of Innocent X also by Algardi (in terracotta, but skilfully painted white to look like marble).

Room 7 (Salone Altoviti): The ceiling, by Giorgio Vasari, dates from 1553: it was salvaged from the Roman residence of the celebrated Florentine banker Bindo Altoviti, which had to be demolished in 1888 when the Tiber embankments were created. Delicate grotesques surround illustrations of Ceres and the Months. The painting of the *Holy Family* here, also by Vasari, is on a long loan from a private collection. The late 16th/early 17th-century altarpiece in gilded bronze, ebony and lapis lazuli with a Crucifix and statuettes of saints and prophets is by the workshop of Bernini (acquired in 2005). The marble bust of Marino Grimani was carved by the great Venetian portraitist Alessandro Vittoria, just before Grimani became doge of Venice in 1595.

Room 8: Here are displayed works from the Veneto and the Sterbini collection. These include an exquisite early 14th-century diptych by an artist named from this work, the Master of the Sterbini Diptych; a fragment of a frescoed head of a woman by Pisanello; an orchestra of angels by Paolo Veneziano; and a double portrait attributed to Giorgione.

Room 9: The charming pastel portraits of ladies (17th–19th centuries) are mostly by English and French painters.

Room 10: German wood sculptural reliefs and a statuette of St Michael defeating Satan by Michael Pacher. The painting of the *Death of the Virgin* dates from the early 16th century.

PALAZZETTO DI VENEZIA

A long **corridor** (**11**) overlooking the delightful courtyard connects the Cybo apartment to the Palazzetto di Venezia. Displayed here is a representative collection of Italian ceramics with examples from all the main workshops—including Faenza, Urbino, Montelupo, Deruta, Pesaro and Casteldurante. In the second half of the corridor there is porcelain, including Meissen and Sèvres. The display continues in **Room 12** which has Bow, Wedgwood and Staffordshire ware.

Room 13: In the centre of the room is an extraordinary Islamic statue of a gazelle in damascened gilt bronze, made in the 11th or 12th century, presumably for a fountain. Also here is late 17th-century porcelain from Turkey and Persian bronzes, including a pair of doves (late 18th century).

Room 14 (left) displays silver tableware and Church silver.

Room 15 has a circular 16th-century Flemish tapestry showing the *Rape of the Sabines* and a showcase of majolica from the Castelli (Rome), Urbino, Faenza and Montelupo.

In **Rooms 16 and 17** is a splendid display (in showcases designed in the 20th century by Franco Minissi) of small-scale bronzes: there was a tradition in ancient Roman times of collecting such works and this was revived in the Renaissance, when it was the fashion to commission statuettes which were copies of antique pieces, small replicas of contemporary statues or bizarre figures and animals. Some of the 16th- and 17th-century masters of this artform are represented here, including Il Riccio, Nicolò Roccatagliata, Girolamo Campagna, Giovanni Francesco and Antonio Susini, Pietro Tacca, Pietro Bracci, Il Moderno, Tiziano Aspetti, Giambologna,

Duquesnoy, Algardi, Bernini and Alessandro Vittoria.

Rooms 18–20 display models and *bozzetti* in terracotta, including two reliefs of the *Miracle of St Mark* by Jacopo Sansovino (models for the bronze reliefs in the chancel of the basilica of San Marco in Venice).

From Room 20 a door leads out into the top loggia of the cloister, planted with orange trees and cypresses and full of birdsong, and nicely arranged as a **lapidarium**. This includes Roman pieces as well as medieval sculptures.

Rooms 21–26 (*often kept closed*) continue the display of terracottas, with numerous busts, statuettes and *bozzetti* by Bernini (including models for an angel on Ponte Sant'Angelo and for details of his Roman fountains), Algardi (bust of Giacinta Sanvitali Conti and *St Agnes Appearing to St Constance*) and Bartolomeo Mazzuoli (bust of Benedict XIII, c. 1725).

Room 27 (*closed at the time of writing*) has an important collection of 15th–16th-century arms and armour.

SAN MARCO

Map p. 654, C2. Open Tues–Fri 10–1 & 4–6; Sat, Sun and holidays 10–1 & 4–8.30; Aug 4–8. Closed Mon. sanmarcoevangelista.it.

The basilica was founded in 336 by St Mark the Pope, making it the earliest place of public Christian worship in the heart of the city. The campanile is Romanesque and the façade an elegant Renaissance work with a loggia added by Paul II for the papal benediction ceremony when he moved into Palazzo di Venezia and rebuilt the church.

The ancient **well-head** under the portico, its marble rim worn down over the centuries by the ropes, may date from the 9th or 10th century. Behind it is the large **tomb slab of Vannozza Cattanei**, broken in three places, with damaged lettering. Vannozza was the mistress of Cardinal Borgia (later Pope Alexander VI), to whom she bore four children. The inscription reads: 'To God the greatest and most high. To Vannozza Cattanei, mother of Cesare of Valentinois, Giovanni of Gandia, Goffredo of Squillace and Lucrezia, Duchess of Ferrara. Distinguished by her probity, her piety and a discretion befitting her age. Benefactress of of the Lateran Hospice. This stone was placed by Girolamo Pico, hospice commissioner, in accordance with her will. She lived 76 years 4 months and 13 days. She died in the year 1518, 26 Nov.'

The **central door frame** has a relief in the tympanum of *St Mark Enthroned* attributed to Isaia da Pisa (1464), who was born in Pisa but worked principally in Rome and Naples. The doorway is flanked by two stone lions, the symbol of of St Mark.

The interior
Steps lead down to the interior, 17th-century in appearance but retaining its ancient

basilican form with a raised sanctuary. The apse still has the beautiful **mosaic** (*light inside the sanctuary, left of the high altar*) commissioned c. 829 by Gregory IV when he reconstructed the ancient church. The large figure of Christ, dressed in purple, is flanked by six saints including Gregory IV himself—with a rectangular halo signifying that he was still alive at the time—holding a model of his church. Below are the familiar twelve sheep representing the Apostles: these ones are particularly woolly and stand in a flowery meadow. Below is an inscription in gold lettering. On the outer arch are three mosaic roundels with Christ between St Peter and St Paul.

The bright columns of Sicilian jasper, which have a pinky-red tint, and the stucco reliefs in the nave (between 17th-century frescoes) date from a Baroque restoration in the 18th century, although the Renaissance ceiling survived the changes as did part of the Cosmatesque pavement at the east end. The altarpieces date from the 17th century. The best is the one in the third south chapel—the beautiful *Adoration of the Magi* by Carlo Maratta, who painted numerous other altarpieces for Roman churches. The domed chapel to the right of the presbytery, which was designed by Pietro da Cortona, contains a painting of *St Mark the Pope* by Melozzo da Forlì and later frescoes by Borgognone. By the steps down to the crypt in a niche decorated with a scallop shell, is the elegant Neoclassical **tomb of Leonardo Pesaro**, in the form of a cippus. It is the work of Antonio Canova. Leonardo, the long-haired 16-year-old son of one of the Venetian ambassadors who lived in the palace next door and who died in 1796, is shown in profile in a medallion.

The **crypt**, a curving passageway behind the high altar, is said to preserve the relics of two Persian noblemen called Abdon and Sennen who found themselves in Rome as prisoners of war in the 3rd century and are supposed to have helped the early Christians before they were martyred and became (rather doubtful) saints.

MADAMA LUCREZIA

At the corner of Piazza San Marco is a colossal mutilated bust of Isis with a shawl at her neck, dating from the 2nd or 3rd century AD, probably once part of a statue of the Egyptian goddess in her temple in the Campus Martius (*see p. 181*). It was Cardinal Lorenzo Cybo who decided around 1500 to set it up in front of the basilica of San Marco, and a little later it was moved to its present position. It became known as 'Madama Lucrezia', after the mistress of Alfonso V of Aragon, Lucrezia d'Aragno, and it used to be decorated at festivals with a necklace of garlic, chilli peppers and onions. It was one of Rome's 'talking' statues: she carried on witty 'conversations' with Marforio on the Capitoline hill (*see p. 58*). When Lucrezia fell from her pedestal in 1799 and broke into eight pieces she was said to declare: 'I've seen enough!', but she was put back together again in 1806 and was restored in 2009. One wonders what she makes of the contemporary world. In the garden in front is a fountain (1927) with a pine cone, the emblem of this district, the Rione della Pigna.

CRYPTA BALBI (MUSEO NAZIONALE ROMANO)

Map p. 654, C2. Via delle Botteghe Oscure 31. Open 9–7.45; closed Mon. For informa-
tion, T: 06 48 0201, archeoroma.beniculturali.it. For advance tickets, T: 06 39 96 7700,
coopculture.it. Tickets are valid for three days and give entry to the four museums of the
Museo Nazionale Romano (this one, Palazzo Massimo, Palazzo Altemps and the Baths
of Diocletian). For the Archaeological Card and reductions for young visitors, see p. 600.
When you buy the ticket you are told when you can visit the excavations below ground
level. The more important recent excavations, including a Mithraeum, can only be visited
at weekends, every hour from 10.45 until 3.45. There are excellent explanatory panels,
also in English.

The so-called Crypta Balbi is a museum of medieval Rome, on a site where systematic
excavations were begun in 1983 to study the various levels of development in the city's
urban history, above a Roman theatre built by a certain Balbus and a cryptoporticus
(known as the Crypta Balbi). Opposite the museum entrance are the ruined columns
of a temple, the Temple of Via delle Botteghe Oscure. Apart from the scant Roman
remains on this site, the finds from later buildings, including a church and monastery, are particularly interesting as illustrations of the early medieval period in Rome,
about which relatively little is known since excavations in other parts of the city have
tended in the past to concentrate on unearthing ancient remains, destroying the later
levels of occupation above them. The medieval exhibits, beautifully displayed, include
finds made here, as well as from other collections in the city.

GROUND FLOOR

The exhibits here illustrate the archaeology and history of this urban site, from Roman
times to the present day. Two delicately carved ancient Roman altars found during
excavations are displayed near the ticket office. The display begins with the history of
the district called the **Campus Martius** (Field of Mars; *see p. 183*), then moves on to
trace the building of the small **Theatre of Balbus**, inaugurated in 13 BC and adjoined
to the west (behind the stage) by a cryptoporticus, remains of which have been uncovered (in the courtyard the excavations and a pilaster from the portico can be seen).
This theatre was the smallest of the three theatres which were built at this time in
Rome (the other two were the Theatre of Marcellus and the Theatre of Pompey). Also
on the ground floor is a fragment, showing this area, of the ***Forma Urbis***, an important
marble 'map' of ancient Rome (*see p. 125*).

The display continues with **medieval finds**, both domestic and ecclesiastic,
including documents relating to the Conservatory of Santa Caterina, built on this site
in 1549 by Nanni di Baccio Bigio, to house the daughters of Roman prostitutes.

The final section deals with the history of the site in the **19th century**, the widening
of Via delle Botteghe Oscure in 1935, and the archaeological investigation of the entire
area from 1983 to the present day, a remarkable project intent on revealing all periods
of the history of this urban area. Architectural fragments found on the site are also

shown, including a very fine huge Corinthian capital, probably once part of the theatre. Part of the wall of the Roman cryptoporticus can be seen in the last room.

FIRST FLOOR

Here are finds from the **Mithraeum**, with wall paintings, some of which show traces of the fire in AD 80. There are also very lovely wall decorations from the buildings unearthed southeast of the exedra dating from the 2nd century AD, one with a dancing figure. The head of Livia, Augustus' wife, also emerged from ruins on this site.

SECOND FLOOR

The general history of **Rome in the Middle Ages** (5th–10th centuries) is illustrated in a large hall with a fine wood roof. Exhibits include household objects, including cutlery and kitchen utensils; jewellery; some 6th-century ceramics found recently in the House of the Vestals in the Roman Forum; oil lamps, glass and coins; and finds from tombs.

The second room is devoted to the **Byzantine period** and in the third room are interesting 7th–9th-century frescoes detached from a building below the church of Santa Maria in Via Lata (*see p. 160*) on the Corso. Earlier frescoes from a diaconia in the Roman Forum are also preserved here. Also in the third room are exhibits related to **papal Rome** from the 8th century onwards. These include commemorative inscriptions, 8th- and 9th-century architectural fragments from Roman churches, and pilgrims' phials (made out of lead, terracotta or glass). These phials were sold at sacred shrines and contained the oil which was used to illuminate holy relics and which was considered to have miraculous powers.

The upper balcony displays medieval finds from the area of the Imperial Fora and Roman Forum, which show that these areas were densely inhabited in medieval times. There is a hoard of over 80 glazed vases found by Boni in 1900 in the Lacus Juturnae and dating from the 8th–10th centuries.

There is also a reproduction of the famous *Einsiedeln Itinerary* dating from the 9th century (the name comes from the monastery in Switzerland where it is preserved). This is a 'walking guide' for pilgrims divided into ten different areas of Rome, where some 100 religious buildings are recorded. It constitutes the most important document we have on the topography of the early medieval city.

ROMAN REMAINS BELOW GROUND LEVEL

These are only shown at certain times and include a huge cistern and warehouses. The most interesting of the recent excavations include the exedra in the centre of the Balbi cryptoporticus and a Mithraeum (*for the cult of Mithras, see p. 539*).

SANTI APOSTOLI
Monument to the engraver Giovanni
Volpato, by his pupil Canova (1807).

ANNO · DOMINI · MDCCCVII

Galleria Doria Pamphilj & Galleria Colonna

These two collections represent the most important private concentrations of art and sculpture in Rome that are open to the public. They are housed in the families' sumptuous palaces, which are still their residences. The power of both the Colonna and Doria Pamphilj families was enhanced when two of their members became pope (respectively Martin V, in 1417; and Innocent X, in 1644). In the 18th century the families were united when Olimpia Pamphilj married Filippo II Colonna.

GALLERIA DORIA PAMPHILJ

Map p. 654, C2. Entrance at no. 305 on the Corso, next to the church of Santa Maria in Via Lata. Open every day 9–7 (last tickets 1hr before closing). T: 06 67 97 323, doriapamphilj.it. Ticket includes free audio guide. There is a little tea room on the ground floor. There is no heating in winter so it can be extremely cold.

The huge Palazzo Doria Pamphilj on the Corso has since the 17th century been the residence of the Doria Pamphilj and the period rooms, richly decorated in white, red and gold and attended by uniformed staff, provide a sumptuous setting for the family's fine paintings (although some of the rooms are now a little shabby and the rear façade is in need of cleaning).

The palace was first built in 1435. Its façade on the Corso (1731–4) is by Gabriele Valvassori, who is known exclusively for the work he carried out for the Doria Pamphilj family, both here (also inside the palace) and in the church of Sant'Agnese in Agone. Built at a time when Roman architecture tended towards a Classical style, it shows the influence of European art and is usually considered the finest and most balanced Rococo work in the city. The north façade, which faces onto Piazza del Collegio Romano and has two handsome wings, is earlier (by Antonio del Grande, 1663).

The collection was initiated in 1651 by the Pamphilj pope Innocent X, who decreed that the pictures and furnishings in Palazzo Pamphilj in Piazza Navona were to be inherited by his nephew Camillo, son of the pope's acquisitive sister-in-law Olimpia Maidalchini. Important additions were made to these works of art when Camillo married Olimpia Aldobrandini, widow of Paolo Borghese. In 1760 Prince Andrea (IV) Doria added his family bequests, and the present arrangement follows that of his time. The collection has been officially listed by the state since 1816.

A grand staircase leads up to a landing from which you can look into the **Sala di Giove (1)**, with its 18th-century furniture.

(2) Sala del Poussin: The walls are covered with 17th-century landscapes by Gaspard Dughet, brother-in-law of Nicolas Poussin and often known as 'Il Poussin'. The rooms at the side can be seen (but not entered) when the family is not in residence (*so they are usually closed at weekends*).

(3) The **Sala dei Velluti** is named after its late 18th-century red velvet wall-hangings. It contains two fine busts by **Alessandro Algardi** of Innocent X and Benedetto Pamphilj.

(4) The **Sala da Ballo**, with the adjacent smaller ballroom, was decorated in 1903; the silk hangings date from that time. It was designed for electric light, and the parquet floor (which now creaks delightfully) was laid for dancing. The musicians' podium survives. The smaller room has an 18th-century ceiling fresco of *Venus and Aeneas* and a Gobelins tapestry woven for Louis XIV from a 16th-century Flemish design, representing the month of May.

(5) The **family chapel**, the dimensions of which give it the appearance of a small church, was designed by Carlo Fontana (1691) and the altar of rare marbles and the ivory Crucifix by Ercole Ferrata date from the same century. Alterations were made to Fontana's work in the 18th and 19th centuries.

(6) The **Sala di Cadmo**, even though hung with paintings, is used as a bookshop.

In the four magnificent galleries around the courtyard, redesigned by Valvassori in 1731–4, paintings crowd the walls. Here the family would stroll with their guests to show off their most precious possessions.

(7) Galleria Aldobrandini: On the left wall are a number of works by **Annibale Carracci**, a famous member of the Bolognese school of painters who came to work in Rome in 1595. His very fine *Flight into Egypt* (236) shows a new Classical concept of landscape painting. His work was to have a great influence on **Claude Lorrain**, born in France but who worked all his life in Rome, where he was considered one of the finest painters of his time and worked with Poussin and Dughet. He too is represented here with several landscapes, including *Mercury Stealing the Oxen of Apollo* (281), one of the most lyrical of his typical idealised scenes. There are also a number of works by 16th-century painters: Garofalo (206, 270), Lodovico Cigoli (246), Paris Bordone (321, 363) and Carlo Saraceni (239, 261). On the window wall is a work by the Netherlandish painter **Quinten Massys**, born in 1465. Entitled *The Usurers* (307), this is one of several satirical genre scenes by this artist who, influenced by Erasmus,

GALLERIA
DORIA PAMPHILJ

1   Sala di Giove
2   Sala del Poussin
3   Sala dei Velluti
4   Sala da Ballo
5   Chapel
6   Sala di Cadmo
7   Galleria Aldobrandini
8   Galleria degli Specchi
9   Cabinet
10 Galleria Pamphilj
11 Galleria Doria
12 Sala Aldobrandini
13 Sala dei Primitivi

was intent on laying bare the negative qualities of his avaricious and acquisitive contemporaries. The tiny portrait of Agatha van Schoonhoven (216; on the window wall) by another Netherlander, Jan van Scorel, shows how the artist combined the qualities of his native school of painting with those of the great Venetian masters. It was painted in 1529 and Van Scorel is known to have been in Rome earlier in the same decade.

(8) Galleria degli Specchi: This is the loveliest part of Valvassori's design, resplendent with gilded mirrors and lined with Roman statues on a small scale, chosen to fit their setting. The portrait of a lady, thought to be Isabella de Requesens of Naples, is a copy of a painting by Raphael.

In the Cabinet **(9)** is the superb **portrait of Innocent X**—the gem of the collection—commissioned by that pope in 1650 from the great Spanish painter Velázquez. It was painted during Velázquez' second stay in Rome and is among his most powerful portraits. Displayed beside it is a sculpted bust of the same pope by **Bernini**.

(10) Galleria Pamphilj: On the left, *The Triumph of Virtue* (265), an unfinished sketch for the painting now in the Louvre, is a good work by Correggio.

Here are more works by Claude Lorrain (266) and Garofalo (108, 300); a *Madonna* (288) by Guido Reni; and two works (*The Return of the Prodigal Son*; 279 and *St John the Baptist in the Desert*; 293) by Guercino, who succeeded Reni as the leading painter of the Bolognese school in the mid-17th century. The scene of a battle in the port of Naples (546) was painted by **Pieter Brueghel the Elder** the year before he visited Rome in 1553. On the window wall are a *Madonna and Child with St John the Baptist* (98) by **Giovanni Bellini** and his *bottega*; landscapes by Paul Bril; scenes from the Old Testament by the Bassano family; and works by Boccaccio Boccaccino (558) and Federico Barocci (*Study of a Head*; 247).

(11) Galleria Doria: Here are five works by **Jan Brueghel the Elder** (449, 341, 274, 634, 273). The charming little Saletta degli Specchi was decorated in the early 18th century. The extraordinary **bust of Olimpia Maidalchini Pamphilj**, sister-in-law and opinionated advisor of Innocent X, is by Algardi (*see p. 191*).

(12) Sala Aldobrandini: The most famous paintings in the collection hang here. *Salome with the Head of St John the Baptist* (517) by **Titian** and a double portrait by **Raphael** (130). There are also two early masterpieces by **Caravaggio**. *The Rest on the Flight into Egypt* (241) is a tender work with charming naturalistic details, the scene dominated by the incredibly graceful figure of a young angel playing the Child to sleep, providing a totally innovative element in the iconography of this famous biblical scene, which was much favoured by painters. *The Penitent Magdalene* (357) shows the desolate figure of the saint (Caravaggio used the same model as for the Madonna in the other painting) abandoned in a bare 'room'. The iconography is also entirely new, and indeed it is only the exquisitely-painted flask of oil on the floor (her customary attribute) which suggests this is intended to portray the Magdalene. The *Young St John the Baptist* (349), attributed to Caravaggio, is a replica of the painting in the Pinacoteca Capitolina.

Also exhibited here are a number of paintings by Guercino and a portrait by Lorenzo Lotto thought to be a self-portrait. Here too are displayed the most important pieces of antique sculpture—not yet fully catalogued so unlabelled. In the centre stands a *Centaur* in red and black marble. Around the walls are three large sarcophagi, busts and statues, including a young *Bacchus* made from red basalt. On the far wall are marble reliefs by François Duquesnoy.

(13) Sala dei Primitivi: Panel paintings include a lovely *Annunciation* (668) by **Filippo Lippi** (with two predella panels below by Pesellino; 666, 667). There is also a tondo by Beccafumi (672) and 15th-century works by the Ferrarese painter Lodovico Mazzolino (including his *Massacre of the Innocents*, 428) and by Gian Battista Benvenuti Ortolano and Bernardino Parentino. There is another satirical genre work by **Quinten Massys**, two monks in prayer entitled *The Hypocrites* (417), and a *Lamentation over the Dead Christ* (592), one of the best works by the famous Flemish painter **Hans Memling**, painted at the height of his career in the 1470s.

GALLERIA COLONNA

Map p. 654, C2. Open only on Sat 9–1.15. Closed Aug. T: 06 67 84 350, galleriacolonna.it.
Entrance at Via della Pilotta 17. The apartment of the Principessa Isabelle is shown on a
guided visit by appointment. A list of the paintings with their numbers is lent to visitors,
since not all the paintings are labelled.

Palazzo Colonna occupies the whole of one side of Piazza Santi Apostoli and incorporates the church of Santi Apostoli. It is the largest private palace in all Rome, covering some 60,000 square metres. It is connected to its beautiful garden by four flying bridges which span Via della Pilotta.

The very fine collection of paintings is arranged in magnificent Baroque galleries, sumptuously decorated with frescoes, mirrors and antique sculpture. The setting, with its marble floors and huge columns (to suit the family name), is truly splendid. The magnificent chandeliers provide light and there is particular attention to other details to ensure that the grand atmosphere survives: the clocks are kept wound and chime the hours; visitors are provided with plush red seats (and even the old-fashioned bathrooms survive, hidden discreetly behind ingeniously painted doors).

THE PALACE AND ITS COLLECTION

There were numerous palaces on this site, one of which was built by the only pope in the family, Oddone Colonna, who lived here as Pope Martin V from 1424 until his death in 1431. There were a number of Colonna cardinals, but by far the most famous member of the family was Marcantonio, the victorious admiral at the Battle of Lepanto in 1571. Cardinal Girolamo I Colonna employed Antonio del Grande in 1654 as architect to enlarge the palace, which was rebuilt in 1730, and here, on 4th June 1802, after the cession of Piedmont to France, Carlo Emanuele IV of Savoy, King of Sardinia, became a Jesuit and abdicated in favour of his brother, Vittorio Emanuele I.

The collection of paintings was begun by Lorenzo Onofrio Colonna (1637–89), who was advised by the famous painter Carlo Maratta on the purchase of contemporary works and others from the 16th century. Many of the best of these paintings (including Titian's *Venus and Adonis*, now in the National Gallery in London) were sold by the family at the end of the 18th century to help fill the papal coffers. More Florentine works joined the collection after the marriage of the Florentine Caterina Salviati to Fabrizio Colonna in 1718; in the 19th century important 15th-century works were purchased by the family as there had been few acquisitions from that period.

Entrance Hall: The charming old gate for visitors survives in the 19th-century hall, which is decorated with ancient Roman reliefs. On the stairs are portraits of famous men, copies of those by Cristofano dell'Altissimo in the Uffizi.

Vestibule: The lovely (?unfinished) *St Julian* (142) is attributed to Perino del Vaga. The window shutters are usually kept closed so you can see the landscape painted on them, which has been lovingly preserved since the 17th century.

Hall of the Colonna Bellica: Named after a 16th-century column of *rosso antico*, decorated with reliefs and surmounted by a statue of Pallas Athene, there is a view of the splendid main hall, and of the little bridge across to the terraced garden with orange trees. The ceiling frescoes of the ***Reception into Heaven of Admiral Marcantonio II Colonna***, who commanded the papal contingent at the Battle of Lepanto (1571), are by Giuseppe Chiari, pupil of Maratta. On the wall opposite the entrance is the *Madonna and Child with St Peter and Donor* (139) by Palma Vecchio and *Holy Family with St Jerome and St Lucy* (25) by Bonifacio Veronese. The two very fine paintings of *Venus and Cupid* are by Bronzino (between the windows, 32) and, opposite (117), Michele di Ridolfo del Ghirlandaio. Also by Ghirlandaio are *Night* (116) and *Dawn* (115), both inspired by Michelangelo's sculptures in the Medici Chapel in Florence. At the top of the wall opposite the entrance is *Narcissus* (189) by Jacopo Tintoretto. On the right and left of the steps are two splendid portraits: *Cardinal Pompeo Colonna* with his dog (106), attributed to Lorenzo Lotto, and *Pius V* (147) by Scipione Pulzone.

From here a door leads out onto the spacious **terrace** overlooking a courtyard with a fountain, where you can sit in the shade.

Great Hall: On the steps leading down to this room is a cannon ball which fell here on 24th June 1849, during the siege of Rome (when Garibaldi held the city against the French) and which has never been removed. It graphically demonstrates how impervious the great Roman family was to the events going on outside the walls of their palace. The Great Hall is superbly decorated with pilasters and columns of *giallo antico*, mirrors, chandeliers, antique sculpture (fine bas-reliefs and sarcophagus fragments are set into the walls beneath the windows, and into statue pedestals), as well as paintings. Work was carried out on the room by four generations of the family and was only completed in 1725. The ceiling paintings, by Giovanni Coli and Filippo Gherardi, depict incidents in the life of Marcantonio II Colonna; the central panel illustrates the Battle of Lepanto. On the walls are four Venetian mirrors decorated with flower paintings (the putti are by Carlo Maratta).

The paintings here include, high up on the right wall, a very fine painting of *St John the Baptist* by **Salvator Rosa** (162), once thought to be a self-portrait, and (next to it) an equestrian portrait of Carlo Colonna, Duke of Marsi (165), a copy of a work by Rubens. On the opposite wall is *St Irene Taking the Arrows from St Sebastian* (46) by Giovanni Domenico Cerrini.

Room of the Desks: This room derives its name from two valuable desks. The first, in ebony, has 28 ivory bas-reliefs by Franz and Dominik Steinhart after drawings by Carlo Fontana; the central relief is a copy of Michelangelo's *Last Judgement*, the other 27 are copies of works by Raphael. The second desk, in sandalwood, is adorned with lapis lazuli, amethysts and other semi-precious stones; in front are twelve small amethyst columns and at the top, gilt-bronze statuettes representing the Muses and Apollo seated under a laurel tree. The ceiling frescoes, by Sebastiano Ricci, once again depict the Battle of

Lepanto. On the walls on either side of the columns and on the right wall is a fine series of landscapes by **Gaspard Dughet** (54–65), distinguished by their pale colours. There is a further series by J.F. van Bloemen, with figures probably by Placido Costanzi (21–24), on the left and end walls. Other landscapes include works by Borgognone (49, 50). There is a miniature bronze copy of the *Farnese Bull*, by Susini.

Room of the Apotheosis of Martin V: This room, from which there is a good view of the grand formal courtyard planted with palms, takes its name from the subject of the central ceiling painting by Benedetto Luti; the other ceiling panels show *Fame Crowning Victory* by Pietro Bianchi and *Time Discovering Truth* by Pompeo Batoni. The paintings by the Venetian school are particularly fine. On the entrance wall: *Man in Venetian Costume* (197), a splendid portrait by **Paolo Veronese**, is displayed beneath another good male portrait (170) by Francesco Salviati. The portrait of the Augustinian Onofrio Panvinio (190) by **Jacopo Tintoretto** was formerly attributed to Titian. On the console table here there is also an amusing bust of the portly cardinal Girolamo I Colonna. This cardinal purchased the *Guardian Angel* (83) by Guercino which hangs here.

Between the windows are two portraits by Domenico Tintoretto (187, 188). By the door into the Throne Room, *Peasant Eating Beans* (43) is a well-known genre work by **Annibale Carracci** (also attributed to Bartolomeo Passarotti).

Throne Room: The pope of the day would be received by the family here. As in other princely houses, the chair is turned to the wall so that no one else can sit in it. Facing it is a portrait of Martin V, Oddone Colonna (144), a copy from a work by Pisanello: the poor pope seems to be almost submerged by his heavy vestments. On either side are *Madonna and Child Enthroned with Angels* (179), a very elegant work in the International Gothic style by **Stefano da Zevio** (one of the most delightful paintings in the collection), and a *Crucifixion* (10), the only signed work known by Jacopo Avanzi, a Bolognese painter of the early 15th century. The nautical chart was presented by the Roman people to Marcantonio II and the parchment diploma given him by the Roman senate after the Battle of Lepanto.

Room of Maria Mancini or **Room of the Primitives:** On the wall opposite the windows is a *Resurrection of Christ* by **Pietro da Cortona** (143), with no fewer than five members of the Colonna family being helped out of their tombs by angels in order to follow the Saviour to heaven. Also on this wall is a fine portrait of a young man in profile (154), traditionally identified as Guidobaldo della Rovere, Duke of Urbino, and attributed to Rocco Zoppo (who worked closely with the more famous Umbrian painter Perugino). Next to it are Madonnas by Giuliano Bugiardini (35) and Bernardino Luini (107). On the wall opposite the entrance is another Madonna by Bartolomeo Vivarini (198). On the window wall is the *Massacre of the Innocents* by Jacopo del Sellaio (232).

Beyond the **Yellow Room**, with pretty country scenes painted on its walls, the **Hall of the Tapestries** is named after four tapestries illustrating the story of Artemisia, made in the 1560s. The adjoining room has just one large tapestry, the last of the Artemisia series, made in Paris in 1623. Amongst the little paintings here is one by Cosmè Tura. The walls of the last room are entirely covered with lovely 17th-century Indian embroideries. The vestibule of the **Chapel** has three works by Guercino: *Moses and the Tablets of the Law* (84) and the heads of the *Virgin Annunciate* (85) and *Angel Gabriel* (86).

Apartment of Princess Isabelle and the Gardens (*for admission, see p. 151*): The apartment consists of a suite of ten rooms on the ground floor, named after Isabelle Sursock, wife of Marcantonio Colonna, who restored it in the early 20th century. The rooms are sumptuously decorated and furnished. The contents include paintings by the Dutch painter Gaspar van Wittel, known as Vanvitelli, who carried out 107 works for the Colonna between 1681 and 1732, including numerous views of Rome.

In the **Sala Rosa** are exquisite small paintings on copper by Jan Brueghel the Elder dating from the 1590s. Part of the vault of the **Sala della Fontana** is painted in gold and blue by Pinturicchio (c. 1485–92). On the floor there is a red granite crocodile dating from the 3rd century AD. The superb painting of *Two Saints with Abbot Niccolò Roverella* (part of a polyptych; the other panels are in the Louvre and the National Gallery in London) is by Cosmè Tura. On the screen are self-portraits by Sofonisba Anguissola and Annibale Carracci.

The **Sala del Tempesta** is named after the artist who painted the seascapes on the walls in the 17th century. The adjoining room is decorated with landscapes by Gaspard Dughet.

The **Winter Dining Room**, formerly used by Ascanio Colonna as a library, has a vault decorated in the late 16th century by a group of artists including Pomarancio, Giovanni Baglione, Jacopo Zucchi and Ferraù Fenzoni. The **Sala del Mascherone** has a Roman pavement (4th century AD) and various ancient marble fragments.

A door leads out to a **garden** planted with clipped tangerine trees, and with lemons in pots and two magnolias. The pilasters and arches in the wall on one side date from the 15th century. The beautiful **main garden**, with its tall cypresses, is across Via della Pilotta. Here you can see remains of the huge **Temple of Serapis**, built at the time of Caracalla, but which Urban VIII gave the Colonna permission in 1625 to demolish.

SANTI APOSTOLI

Map p. 654, C2. Open 8–12 & 4–7; Bessarion Chapel only open Fri and Sat 9–12.

This basilica dedicated to the apostles may have been founded by Pelagius I and the Byzantine general Narses around 560, to commemorate Narses' conquest and final expulsion of the Goths from the Italian peninsula. At this time Rome was under the control of the Eastern Empire, ruled from Ravenna, and the joint dedication to the

Apostles Philip and James was borrowed from Constantinople, where these two apostles had always been highly venerated. The church was restored and enlarged from the 15th century and given its Baroque appearance when it was almost completely rebuilt by Carlo Fontana in 1702–14 as part of the Colonna family palace.

The unusual **façade**, which indeed has the appearance of a palace rather than a church, is in a mixture of styles. The stately Renaissance double loggia of nine arches, attributed to Baccio Pontelli, was built at the expense of Cardinal Giuliano della Rovere, afterwards Pope Julius II (who lived next to the church in Palazzo dei Santi Apostoli and whose father is buried in the church). Baroque windows were installed in the upper storey by Carlo Rainaldi c. 1665. Rainaldi also provided the balustrade above with statues of the Apostles. Behind this and above it, the Neoclassical upper façade of the church, added by Valadier in 1827, can be seen.

In the **portico**, on the left, is the tomb of the engraver Giovanni Volpato, by his much more famous pupil Antonio Canova (1807). On the right is an exquisite bas-relief found in Trajan's Forum, dating from the 2nd century AD and representing an eagle holding an oak-wreath in its talons. Also here is a lion, signed by Pietro Vassalletto, member of a family of sculptors active in Rome in the 12th century. The two red marble lions flanking the entrance portal date from the same period.

INTERIOR OF SANTI APOSTOLI

The Baroque interior is on a vast scale, with an exceptionally broad nave. The effect of immensity is enhanced by the manner in which the lines of the vaulting continue those of the massive pillars, and the lines of the apse those of the nave.

From the end near the entrance the surprising effect of relief achieved by the little-known painter Giovanni Odazzi in his contorted group of *Fallen Angels*, on the vault above the high altar, can be seen. On the ceiling of the nave is the *Triumph of the Order of St Francis*, a late work (1707) by Baciccia (the Angels and Evangelists were added in the late 19th century by Luigi Fontana). Baciccia, born in Genoa, spent most of his life in Rome (where he died in 1709) and—as a friend of Bernini—was given numerous commissions for altarpieces and portraits, though he is best remembered for his vault decorations. The most successful is in the Gesù (*see p. 213*).

South aisle: The first chapel contains a beautiful ***Madonna and Child* by Antoniazzo Romano**, the most important Roman artist of his time, who continued to paint Madonnas in an archaic Byzantine style against a gold ground in the late 15th century. It was commissioned by Cardinal Bessarion (1403–72) for his chapel in this church.

Chapel of Cardinal Bessarion (*for admission, see above*): Bessarion was a native of Trebizond and as Bishop of Nicaea he accompanied the Greek Emperor John Palaeologus to Italy in 1439 in an attempt to bring about a union between the Greek and Roman churches. But once in Rome he joined the Roman church and was made a cardinal; this was his titular church and the place he chose for his burial. He was a famous Humanist scholar and bequeathed his remarkable collection of Greek and Latin manuscripts to the

Biblioteca Marciana in Venice in 1468.

In this chapel (only rediscovered in 1959) excavations of the pavement of the original 6th-century church, carried out in 2005, can be seen beneath glass, beyond a lovely little spiral stair. On the lower level of the frescoed wall is a late 16th- or early 17th-century copy of Antoniazzo's *Madonna and Child* (*see above*). An iron spiral staircase leads up to a walkway where you can view the frescoes which Bessarion commissioned from Antoniazzo Romano and which were executed with the help of Melozzo da Forlì. They depict two stories from the life of St Michael Archangel and are extremely interesting for their unusual iconography: the Archangel is depicted as a bull in both scenes, perhaps an allusion to a legend from 5th-century Puglia of a bull which disappeared into a cave and could not be retrieved by its owner. St Michael appeared in a vision and commanded that the cave be turned into a church. The tiny cases protect finds made during excavations dating from the Roman and medieval periods, and there is a precious ancient Roman red porphyry sarcophagus embedded in the wall.

The cardinal is also recorded elsewhere: there is an epitaph of 1682 (and a delightful relief portrait in a medallion) on the second pillar in the north aisle; and in the second cloister (*see below*) there is a Latin and Greek inscription which he dictated for his own tomb.

Against the second south pillar is a **monument to Clementina Sobieska**, wife of James Stuart, the Old Pretender (*see overleaf*), by Filippo della Valle. The chapel at the end of the south aisle preserves eight free-standing large columns from the 6th-century church.

Sanctuary and confessio: Here are the tombs of several members of the Riario family, which supplied numerous cardinals over the centuries: that of Cardinal Pietro, on the left, is a particularly beautiful work by the school of Andrea Bregno, with a *Madonna* by Mino da Fiesole. Fragments of the famous frescoes by Melozzo da Forlì, which formerly covered the 15th-century apse, are preserved in Palazzo del Quirinale (*see p. 332*) and in the Vatican (*see p. 444*).

Steps in front of the sanctuary lead down to the confessio. The **relics of the Apostles Philip and James** are preserved here, and in the chapel to the left is the beautiful **tomb of Raffaele della Rovere** (d. 1477), brother of Sixtus IV and father of Julius II, with a serene effigy by Andrea Bregno. The other chapels here were decorated in 1876–7 in the style of the catacombs, and foundations of the earlier church can be seen.

High altar: The *Martyrdom of St Philip and St James* is by Domenico Muratori, who produced very few paintings after this one—thought to be the largest in Rome (14m by over 6.5m).

North aisle: At the east end of the aisle, around the door into the sacristy, is the first important work in Rome by Canova, the **monument to Clement XIV**, a masterpiece of Neoclassical art (1783–7), showing the pope extending his hand in blessing over those who enter. When it was completed it won Canova renown throughout Europe.

HIC CONDITA SVNT CORPORA SS. APOSTOLOR. PHILIPPI ET IACOBI MIN.

SANTI APOSTOLI
Reliquary chest of the apostles Philip and James the Less.
The carving shows a scene from the miracle of the loaves and fishes.

Something of the state of Italian art at the time can be guessed from the French writer Stendhal's comment that Canova 'had emerged quite by chance out of the sheer inertia which this warm climate imposed...nobody else in Italy is the least like him'. The mourners are personifications of Humility and Temperance and add to the gravity of the monument.

In the second chapel is a surprising **altarpiece of St Joseph of Copertino**, showing him 'flying' as he celebrates Mass. This St Joseph (from Copertino near Lecce in southern Italy) became a Franciscan and was widely known for his powers of levitation, but the official Church was sceptical and he was only canonised some hundred years after his death in 1663 (when this painting by Giuseppe Cades celebrated the event). The two columns flanking the altar are reputedly the largest known works in *verde antico*, a marble found only in Thessaly in Greece.

The two **Renaissance cloisters** (*entered at no. 51; ring*) can be visited. In the first (in the left walk) is an unusual three-tiered bas-relief by the school of Arnolfo di Cambio: it shows the *Annunciation to the Shepherds*; the *Nativity* (with the Madonna lying stretched out in front of the crib); and the *Washing of the Child* (by two midwives as Joseph sits taking a nap). In the second cloister is a quaint **memorial to Michelangelo**, whose body was temporarily placed here after his death in Rome in 1564 before it was transported to Florence less than a month later for his funeral service and burial in Santa Croce. The great artist is shown lying on a sofa in the company of two cherubs.

On the opposite side of Piazza dei Santi Apostoli from the church is **Palazzo Odescalchi**, which extends to the Corso. The façade on the piazza is by Bernini, with additions by Niccolò Salvi and Luigi Vanvitelli (1750). The orange-coloured Baroque **Palazzo Balestra** (formerly Muti) was once owned by the Stuarts of Scotland and England (*see below*).

THE JACOBITES IN ROME

The exiled house of Stuart was descended from James I of England (James VI of Scotland), whose grandson James II was forced to abdicate from the English throne in 1688 because of his Roman Catholic sympathies. Members of this royal line and their supporters became known as Jacobites. James II's son, James Stuart (1688–1766), nicknamed the 'Old Pretender', first lived in France and then came to Rome, where Clement XI presented him with Palazzo Balestra on the occasion of his marriage in 1719 to Clementina Sobieska. Although his wife died in 1735 he continued to live here until his own death, when he was given a grand funeral in St Peter's with no fewer than 22 cardinals present. A portrait of him survives in the Galleria Doria Pamphilj.

His son, Charles Edward (1720–88; the 'Young Pretender' or 'Bonnie Prince Charlie'), who was born in Palazzo Balestra, led the last Jacobite rebellion in Scotland in 1745–6. It ended in his decisive defeat at Culloden, after which he was forced to escape to France, from where he returned to Rome. Here he married Louise de Stolberg and they moved to Florence, where the Prince led a dissolute, drunken life and his wife escaped to a convent with the help of the poet Count Vittorio Alfieri. Years later, when Alfieri was giving a private performance of one of his plays in the Spanish embassy in Piazza di Spagna, he met Louise again and they lived together for the rest of their lives. Bonnie Prince Charlie died in Palazzo Balestra in 1788.

The Young Pretender's younger brother was Henry, 'Duke of York' (also born in Palazzo Balestra, in 1725), who was made a cardinal, and as 'Henry IX' was the last of the Stuarts. Known as Cardinal York, he was given the bishopric of Frascati, just outside Rome in the Alban Hills, where he died in 1807. When the Young Pretender died, his brother saw that his body was buried in the Duomo of Frascati (where his cenotaph remains) before it was moved to the Vatican Grottoes. Cardinal York built a convent on Monte Cavo near Frascati and restored a chapel in Santa Maria in Trastevere. The three last Stuarts are commemorated in St Peter's with a magnificent monument by Antonio Canova (*see p. 428*), paid for in part by King George IV.

On & Around the Corso

The long, straight Via del Corso has been an important throughfare since ancient times and is still one of the streets which best characterises the city. Also described in this chapter is the Ara Pacis, a beautiful monumental altar set up by the emperor Augustus, just a short distance from the Corso.

Via del Corso (*map p. 654, C2–C1 and p. 652, B3*), now called simply Il Corso or 'the Corso' is relatively narrow and always busy; the pavements are hardly wide enough to accommodate the almost incessant stream of pedestrians in either direction during working hours and at weekends. From Piazza Venezia it runs past the Italian prime minister's official residence, in a square decorated with the splendidly carved Column of Marcus Aurelius, and, just beyond, the Italian parliament. About halfway along, delightful pedestrian streets open on the right with vistas of the Spanish Steps; the most elegant and fashionable shops in Rome are concentrated in the area between the Corso, Piazza di Spagna and Piazza del Popolo.

HISTORY OF THE CORSO

The Corso represents the urban section of the Via Flaminia (221 BC), which was the main road to Rimini and northern Italy in the days of ancient Rome. At that time it was called the Via Lata ('broad way') because of its exceptional width compared to the other roads in the ancient city. It was spanned by a series of triumphal arches: one built by Claudius in AD 51; and another, which became known as the Arco di Portogallo, to celebrate Hadrian (reliefs from it are preserved in the Capitoline Museums; *see p. 41*). They were demolished in 1662 by Alexander VII to perfect the straightness of the street between Piazza Venezia and Piazza Colonna. A third, the Arcus Novus, was built by Diocletian in 303–4 (but it was destroyed in 1491). A number of churches were erected along the street in the earliest years of Christian Rome and by the Middle Ages the Corso had become an important area to live. Today its appearance is characterised by the many palaces which were built to front the road in the 16th–18th centuries.

Its present name is derived from the riderless horse races inaugurated here by Paul II in 1466 (up until then they had taken place on Monte Testaccio), which became a celebrated event (*corso* means race; the pope would watch the finish from Palazzo Venezia, which he had built while still a cardinal). The Corso has since given its name to the principal street in numerous other Italian cities.

The carnival celebrations in the street from the 17th century onwards became famous spectacles: John Evelyn, Goethe, Dickens and Henry James all left vivid descriptions. James found it all a bit too much, and glumly complained that the celebrations were not what he had hoped for or expected. Dickens, on the other hand, fully entered into the spirit, declaring 'anything so gay, so bright, and lively as the whole scene there, it would be difficult to imagine'.

THE SOUTHERN CORSO

At the beginning of the Corso both sides are lined by grand 17th-century palaces: on the left corner is **Palazzo d'Aste Rinuccini Bonaparte**, where Napoleon's mother, Letitia Ramolino, came to live after her son's fall from power in France. She remained in Rome until her death here in 1836. Further down on the other side is **Palazzo Salviati** (1662; now a bank building) by Carlo Rainaldi, the most important architect working in Rome in the late 17th century, and best known for his church façades. The great Rococo **Palazzo Doria Pamphilj** (*described on p. 146*) is the grandest of all the palaces on the Corso. Alongside it rises Santa Maria in Via Lata.

SANTA MARIA IN VIA LATA

This small church (*open Tues–Sun 4–7pm; 3–6 in winter; Sat also 10–1; closed Mon; T: 06 83 39 6276, cryptavialata.it*) is of ancient foundation, rebuilt in 1491 when Diocletian's Arcus Novus (*see above*) was demolished to make way for it. The graceful **façade and vestibule** are by Pietro da Cortona (1660). The pretty little **interior**, which dates from the late 17th and early 18th century, has decorative marbles, which are particularly colourful in the sanctuary (which was once attributed as an early work of Bernini but is now thought to be by a certain Santi Ghetti). Over the high altar is an ancient image of the Madonna inscribed '*Fons lucis stella maris*'. At the end of the left aisle is the tomb (only set up in 1776) of the poet Antonio Tebaldeo (1463–1537), tutor of Isabella d'Este, secretary to Lucrezia Borgia, courtier of Leo X and friend of Raphael (who painted his portrait now in the Vatican, a copy of which is placed in the oval here, surrounded by gilded putti). The church also contains tombs of the families of Napoleon's brothers Joseph and Lucien Bonaparte (whose palace was nearby).

Beneath the church are a few (fairly modest) **Roman remains** (*open at the same time as the church; fee*): they are just a small part of a huge ancient building, some 250m long, thought to have been used as a warehouse, which was converted in the 5th century into a Christian chapel and welfare centre and then into a church (the early murals discovered here are exhibited in the Crypta Balbi; *see p. 144*). Claims have been made that this was once the house of St Luke and that St Paul was kept here under guard after his arrival in Rome.

Just inside Via Lata, low down on the right, is the **Fontanella del Facchino**, with the figure of a sturdy porter holding a barrel: water issues from the bung-hole. Water-sellers are supposed to have resold Tiber or Trevi water from their barrels. *Il Facchino* was one of Rome's 'talking' statues (*see p. 202*); with his flat beret, he was once thought to be a caricature portrait of Martin Luther, but the figure more probably represents Abbondio Rizio, a heavy drinker. In 1751, Vanvitelli surprisingly attributed the sculpture to Michelangelo.

The next palace on the left, **Palazzo Simonetti** (no. 307), was for many years in the 18th century a centre of the political and cultural life of the city as the residence of Cardinal de Bernis, ambassador of Louis XV at the papal court. In 1833 it was purchased by the prominent Roman Boncompagni Ludovisi family.

SAN MARCELLO

Set back on the opposite side of the Corso is the church of San Marcello (*map p. 654, C2; open 7.45–6, Sat 11–6; sanmarcelloalcorso.eu*), of ancient foundation, dedicated to the very early pope Marcellus, who reigned for a year or so in the first decade of the 4th century. A popular legend survives which suggests that the emperor Maxentius ordered him to work as a stable-boy in the farm once on this site and that he died in the job. The very fine concave **façade** (1683) is perhaps the best work in the city by Carlo Fontana, who succeeded Bernini as papal architect. Delightful details include leafy palm fronds tied with ribbons on either side of the upper storey (instead of the more usual rigid scrolls) and the two playful but graceful angels which support the tondo over the doorway.

After a fire in 1519 the **interior** was rebuilt to a design by the Tuscan sculptor and architect Jacopo Sansovino, although today it has a rather gloomy Baroque appearance, probably acquired after restoration in 1867. Sansovino carved the double **tomb on the west wall** of Cardinal Giovanni Michiel (d. 1503, poisoned by Cesare Borgia) and his nephew Bishop Antonio Orso (d. 1511), below. The bishop's effigy is supported by a pile of books wedged under his couch since he was specially remembered for his donation of a large collection of manuscript volumes to the library of the convent. Sansovino left the city for Venice in 1527, where he spent the rest of his life designing Classical buildings for the doge derived from the ancient monuments he had seen in Rome. Most of the frescoes in the main body of the church date from the 17th century.

The **wooden ceiling** has carved reliefs by Giovanni Battista Ricci (1594), who also painted the scene of the *Crucifixion* on the west wall in 1613 as well as many of the paintings between the windows in the nave and in the chapels.

In the **third south chapel** (on the left wall) is a monument to Cardinal Thomas Weld (1773–1837); his very English-looking Neoclassical bust is by a certain Thomas Hill. On the ceiling of the **fourth south chapel** are frescoes of the *Creation of Eve, St Mark* and *St John the Evangelist*, begun by Perino del Vaga and completed after the 1527 Sack of Rome by Daniele da Volterra and Pellegrino Tibaldi. Beneath the altar, which has a fine 14th-century Crucifix (said to be miraculous), is an ancient Roman cippus, re-worked in the Middle Ages with geometric marble inlay. The precious reliquary on the altar of this chapel, enriched with lapis lazuli and agate, dates from 1689. The **fourth north chapel** opposite, with frescoes and an altarpiece of the *Conversion of St Paul* by Taddeo Zuccari, commemorates six members of the Frangipani family with busts: those on the right wall are by Alessandro Algardi.

THE PIAZZA & CHURCH OF SANT'IGNAZIO

Just off the left side of the Corso (reached by Via del Caravita) is the delightful Rococo **Piazza di Sant'Ignazio** (*map p. 654, C2*), a theatrical masterpiece by Filippo Raguzzini (1728). The buff-coloured buildings with numerous windows all have curving façades of the same height which fit into a careful decorative scheme in relation to the streets between them. The effect is that of a stage-set rather than a piazza. The central building is used by the Cultural Ministry and by the special *carabinieri* police force in charge of safeguarding Italy's cultural heritage.

THE CHURCH OF SANT'IGNAZIO
Map p. 645, C2. Open 7.30–7pm; Sun 9–7pm. santignazio.gesuiti.it.
The Jesuit church of Sant'Ignazio rivals the Gesù in magnificence. It was begun in 1626 by Cardinal Ludovico Ludovisi as the church of the Collegio Romano (*see p. 573*) to celebrate the canonisation of St Ignatius Loyola, founder of the Jesuits, by the cardinal's uncle Gregory XV.

The church was designed by Carlo Maderno and others, and was executed by Orazio Grassi, a Jesuit mathematician from the college, who is also responsible for the fine **façade** (his only architectural work).

The spacious aisled interior is sumptuously decorated. In the **vaulting of the nave and apse** are remarkable paintings, the masterpiece of Andrea Pozzo. Pozzo, himself a Jesuit, was the greatest exponent of the *quadratura* technique, which uses painted architectural elements to provide illusionistic decorations on walls and ceilings, and which became extremely popular in the Baroque period. These works, his most brilliant achievement, represent the missionary activity of the Jesuits and the triumph of St Ignatius. The amazing *trompe l'oeil* perspective projects the walls of the church beyond their architectural limits, and Pozzo even provided a cupola, never built because of lack of funds, in a canvas 17m in diameter. The vaulting and 'dome' are best seen from a small yellow disc set in the pavement in the middle of the nave.

On the **west wall** are two allegorical figures by Alessandro Algardi. The **second south chapel**, lavishly decorated with rare marbles, has an altarpiece of the *Death of St Joseph*, one of numerous altarpieces carried out by Francesco Trevisani for churches in Rome in the early 18th century. In the sumptuous **transept chapels**, both also designed by Andrea Pozzo, with marble barley-sugar columns, are large marble high-reliefs: on the south side, the *Glory of St Aloysius Gonzaga*, a member of the Jesuit Order, by Pierre Legros (a French sculptor who worked in Rome for the Jesuits), with a lapis lazuli urn containing the remains of the saint; on the north side, the *Annunciation* by Filippo della Valle (one of the best works by this early 18th-century sculptor), and a lapis lazuli urn with the relics of St John Berchmans (d. 1621, another Jesuit) and two 18th-century angels by Pietro Bracci (who worked with Filippo della Valle on the Trevi Fountain). In the chapel to the right of the high altar is the elaborate funerary monument to Gregory XV and his nephew Cardinal Ludovisi, the founders of the church, also by Legros.

COLUMN OF MARCUS AURELIUS
The miraculous rainstorm spreads its dripping wings over the rival armies, preventing
a rout of the Romans by their German adversaries.

THE TEMPLE OF HADRIAN

In front of Sant'Ignazio, Via de' Burrò leads to the pleasant, peaceful Piazza di Pietra with the splendid remains of the huge Temple of Hadrian, built by Antoninus Pius in 145 and dedicated to his adoptive father. Now incorporated in the façade of the Chamber of Commerce building, the high wall of the cella survives, along with the peristyle of the right side with eleven disengaged fluted Corinthian columns (15m high). The houses in front follow the line of the portico which used to surround the temple. The Caffettiera café at no. 65 is famous for its Neapolitan pastries.

PIAZZA COLONNA & PIAZZA MONTECITORIO

Piazza Colonna (*map p. 654, C1*) was for centuries (before motor traffic) considered the centre of the city. It is now the official residence of the Prime Minister. Beside a graceful fountain with a particularly attractive veined pink-and-grey marble basin designed by Giacomo della Porta (the dolphins are a 19th-century addition by Achille Stocchi) rises the monument from which the piazza derives its name, the majestic **Column of Marcus Aurelius**, or 'Colonna Antonina'. It is made entirely of Italian marble from Luni and is formed of 27 blocks. The ancient level of the ground was nearly 4m lower than at present, so the original base is now hidden. The shaft measures 100 Roman feet (29.6m) and the total height of the column, including the base and the statue, is nearly 42m. In the interior (*no admission*) are 203 steps lit by 56 tiny windows.

The column was erected between AD 180 and 196 in honour of Marcus Aurelius' victories over the Germans (169–73) and Sarmatians (174–6), and dedicated to him and his wife Faustina. The philosopher-emperor Marcus Aurelius led his troops in all these important battles, which delayed the barbarian invasions of Italy for several centuries. The column was inspired by that of Trajan (*see p. 130*), but instead of being the focal point of a forum it was in the centre of an important group of monuments of the

Antonine period. The ancient base was decorated with Victories, festoons and reliefs. The summit was originally crowned with figures of Marcus Aurelius and Faustina, but during its restoration in 1589 Domenico Fontana replaced the imperial statues with one of St Paul.

Around the shaft a bas-relief ascends in a spiral of 20 turns, interrupted halfway by a Victory; the lower part of the relief commemorates the war against the Germanic tribes, the upper that against the Sarmatians. On the third spiral (east side) the Roman soldiers are represented as being saved by a rainstorm, which in the 4th century was regarded as a miracle brought about by the prayers of the Christians in their ranks.

Since 1961 the huge **Palazzo Chigi** has been the official residence of Italy's prime minister. It was built in the 16th century and enlarged (and given a fine courtyard) in the following century, when it was acquired by the Sienese Chigi family. The family moved to Rome and became celebrated at this time when Fabio Chigi became Pope Alexander VII. The splendid library founded by him remained here until the palace and its contents were sold by the Chigi to the state in 1917 (and in 1923 the library was donated by the state to the Vatican).

When **Palazzo Wedekind** was built on the west side of the piazza in 1838 eleven ancient Roman Ionic marble columns which had been excavated a few years earlier at Veio were incorporated into its handsome portico. One of Rome's daily newspapers, *Il Tempo*, has its offices here. The little church in the piazza is **San Bartolomeo dei Bergamaschi** (1561). Across the Corso is a huge, Y-shaped **shopping arcade** built in 1914 in an eclectic style with polychrome skylights. Formerly called the Galleria Colonna, it was renamed in 2003 after the great film star Alberto Sordi, who had died the previous year. Much beloved by Romans, Sordi's long and successful career began when Fellini chose him for his film *Lo Sceicco Bianco* in 1951.

Piazza di Montecitorio, adjoining Piazza Colonna but on slightly higher ground, is named after the huge **Palazzo di Montecitorio** (*usually open on the first Sun of the month 10–5.30; T: 06 67 601, en.camera.it*) which, since 1871, has been the seat of the Camera dei Deputati, the Italian Parliament. The 630 members, who have to be at least 25 years old, are elected at least every five years by Italian citizens over the age of 18. A constitutional reform of the Senate was going through parliament at the time of writing.

The original palace was begun for the Ludovisi family in 1650 by Bernini, who was responsible for the general plan of the building and for the idea of enhancing the effect of the façade by giving it a convex, slightly polygonal form. In 1904–26 it was enlarged by Ernesto Basile and given its new red-brick and travertine façade on Piazza del Parlamento. The sculptural decoration of the grand entrance and the decorative lamp-posts are derived from the Art Nouveau style.

In the interior the chamber, also designed by Basile, is panelled in oak and brightly illuminated from above by a row of windows in the cornice, below which is an encaustic frieze by Aristide Sartorio, begun in 1908, representing the history of Italian civilisation. The fine bas-relief in bronze in honour of the royal House of Savoy is by Davide Calandra.

The **obelisk** (22m high) in the centre of Piazza di Montecitorio, was originally erected at Heliopolis by Psamtik II (c. 590 BC). It was brought to Rome by Augustus to celebrate his victory over Cleopatra, and set up in the Campus Martius, where it served as the gnomon of an immense sundial. In 1748 it was discovered underground in the Largo dell'Impresa (an open space north of Palazzo di Montecitorio) and in 1792 it was erected on its present site.

PIAZZA SAN SILVESTRO

The church of **San Silvestro in Capite** (*map p. 654, C1; open 7–7, Sun 9–12.45 & 3.30–6.30; entrance at 12 Via del Gambero beneath the lovely campanile; T: 06 69 77 121*) was founded by Pope Stephen III (752–7) on the site of a Roman building, possibly Aurelian's Temple of the Sun. It was bestowed on the English Roman Catholics by Leo XIII in 1890, and has been administered by the Irish community of the Pallottines since then (*there are services in English at 10 and 5.30 on Sun*). The *capite* refers to a relic of the head of St John the Baptist which is preserved here, in a chapel on the north side. The 12th-century bronze cockerel which used to surmount the campanile (it recalls the cock which crowed three times when St Peter betrayed Christ) is now kept here too. The interior is shabby but atmospheric, with age-faded 17th-century works: the *Assumption* in the nave vault is by Giacinto Brandi; the second south chapel has an altarpiece of *St Francis* by Orazio Gentileschi (all the works are well labelled in Italian and English).

The church of **Santi Andrea e Claudio**, on the other side of the square, is dedicated to St Andrew and Claude (or Claudius) of Besançon, a monk and later abbot who lived in the late 7th century. Built by Antoine Dérizet, the church was consecrated for the French community in 1731.

THE NORTHERN CORSO

After Via Convertite the Corso narrows. **Via Frattina**, on the right, is the first of several long, straight pedestrian streets, lined with fashionable shops, between the Corso and Piazza di Spagna (one of the pleasantest is **Via della Vite**, totally closed to wheeled vehicles).

SAN LORENZO IN LUCINA

Map p. 654, C1. Open daily 8–8.

The basilica, in a pretty, irregularly-shaped piazza with a number of cafés, probably originally dates from the time of Sixtus III (432–40) or even earlier. It is said to have been constructed on the site of the house of an early Christian called Lucina. The church was rebuilt in the 12th century and again in 1650. The restored campanile and the **portico** with its six Ionic columns remain from the 12th-century church.

Inside the church, the first south chapel has a reliquary purporting to contain part of the gridiron on which the titular saint, Lawrence, is said to have been martyred

NICOLAS · POUSSIN
NE AUX ANDELYS EN MDLXXXXIV
MORT A ROME EN MDCLXV
ET INHUME EN CETTE EGLISE

SAN LORENZO IN LUCINA
Detail of the tomb of Poussin, showing a relief carving of
one of his own paintings: *Et in Arcadia Ego.*

in 258. In the second chapel is the **tomb of Nicolas Poussin**, who lived in Rome for many years: the monument was commissioned in 1830 by the great French writer of the Romantic movement, Chateaubriand, when he came to Rome as a minister in the French government. The fourth chapel, **designed by Bernini** for Gabriele Fonseca, Innocent X's doctor, is decorated with pretty stuccoes and has a fine portrait bust (1664; left of the altar), one of numerous such expressive works in which the great sculptor faithfully portrayed his famous and less famous contemporaries. The ***Crucifixion* on the high altar** is by the prolific Bolognese artist Guido Reni, who was at work in Rome at the turn of the 16th century. The work was greatly admired in the 19th century. The poet Browning, in *The Ring and the Book*, calls it 'second to nought observable in Rome'. On the north side, the decorative fifth chapel was designed by Simon Vouet, a French painter who came to Rome at the beginning of the 17th century. His paintings on the side walls, of two stories from the life of St Francis, are considered amongst his best works. Although he was greatly influenced by the work of Reni, the atmosphere here is far removed from the deeply religious high altarpiece.

Excavations (*open for a guided tour on the first Sat of the month at 5*) have revealed remains of the early Christian basilica built above Roman edifices, including a private house and a market building of brick-faced concrete, thought to date from the time of Hadrian.

SANTI AMBROGIO E CARLO AL CORSO

The Corso widens at the church of Santi Ambrogio e Carlo (*map p. 654, C1; open daily 7–7*), dedicated to two great bishops of Milan, St Ambrose and St Charles Borromeo, who lived in the 4th and the 16th centuries respectively and were both the most influential prelates of their day. This is the only work in Rome by Onorio Longhi (1612), and was completed by his son Martino (the Longhi were an important family of architects and Onorio's father, also called Martino, carried out numerous works in the city).

The **cupola** is a fine late work (1668) by Pietro da Cortona, recalling Michelangelo's dome of St Peter's; it is also an important feature of the city skyline. The heavily restored **façade** was completed at the end of the 17th century.

In the grand Baroque **interior**, the poorly-lit high altarpiece, *The Madonna Presenting St Charles Borromeo and Ambrose to Christ*, is a particularly good painting by Carlo Maratta, who was the most important painter at work in Rome in the late 17th century. He was an extremely prolific artist and his altarpieces can be seen in numerous churches all over the city. He interpreted the spirit of the Counter-Reformation on a grand scale and had the assistance of many pupils who came to work in his studio. On the altar behind is a rich urn containing the heart of St Charles Borromeo.

THE ARA PACIS

Map p. 652, A3. Open daily 9.30–7.30. Last tickets 1hr before closing. T: 060608, arapacis.it. Excellent bookshop.

Via dei Pontefici leads left towards the Tiber to the conspicuous white building protecting the Ara Pacis, a monumental 'altar of peace' consecrated by Augustus in 13 BC. It is one of the most beautiful examples of ancient Roman relief carving to have survived anywhere.

Since 2006 it has been exhibited in a pavilion of white travertine and glass designed for it by Richard Meier. Its inauguration caused quite a stir and not everyone was pleased with it; but apart from some details (such as the banal fountain at the bottom of the steps, which are rather too close to the façade of the church here, and the perhaps unnecessarily high wall built out of huge blocks of tufa) it provides a very pleasant, well-lit environment in which to view this great work of art. There are comfortable seats and the atmosphere is peaceful, as the hall is well insulated from the noise of the traffic on the busy Lungotevere outside. Exhibition space for temporary shows is discretely hidden on the floor below.

DISCOVERY OF THE ALTAR

The Ara Pacis Augustae, built of Luni marble, was consecrated in the Campus Martius, and dedicated in 17 BC, in celebration of the peace that Augustus had established within the Empire. This much is known from the document (*Res gestae Divi Augusti*) which the emperor had had engraved on bronze tablets a year before his death in AD

ARA PACIS
Detail of the altar's rear entrance showing the earth goddess Tellus and symbols of bounty above a luxuriant acanthus plant.

14. The excellent plans and models in the new building clarify its history and location in the ancient city.

In 1568, during excavations for the foundations of Palazzo Fiano on the Corso, nine blocks belonging to the frieze of the altar were found and bought by Cardinal Ricci da Montepulciano for the Grand Duke of Tuscany. To facilitate transport to Florence, each block was sawn into three pieces. The cardinal overlooked two other blocks unearthed at the same time. One of these passed to the Louvre, the other to the Vatican Museums. Three hundred years later, during a reconstruction of the palace, other parts of the altar were found, and acquired in 1898 by the Italian government for the Museo Nazionale Romano. In 1903 and 1937 excavations brought to light the basement of the altar and further fragments. The pieces from the Museo Nazionale Romano and the Uffizi were recovered; those in the Louvre, the Vatican and the Villa Medici were copied, and in 1938 the altar was reconstructed, as far as possible in its original form, though its original position was further south, close to the Via Lata, between the present Piazza del Parlamento and Piazza di San Lorenzo in Lucina.

THE ALTAR TODAY

The rectangular altar is decorated inside and out with wonderful carvings influenced by Classical Greek and Hellenistic models and representing the supreme achievement of Augustan art. The **lower part of the walls** has an intricate and beautiful composition of acanthus leaves and a great variety of plants and flowers, including lilies and campanula, above which are swans with outstretched wings. Between the jambs of the **main entrance** are two scenes illustrating the mythical origins of Rome, one with Aeneas and the other, almost totally destroyed, with the She-wolf. The imposing figure of Aeneas is shown at sacrifice outside a temple, and the sow is here because an oracle in Troy had prophesied that it would be waiting for him on his arrival in Latium.

In the **interior**, where sacrifices took place, there are beautifully carved bucrania, with garlands of pine cones, pomegranates, acorns and all kinds of plants above the bare walls. On the altar itself, framed by winged griffins, are reliefs of the sacrifice with the *suovetaurilia*, the three animals which were always used in sacrifices: the sow, ram and bull.

At the **rear entrance** there is a panel with Tellus, the earth goddess, possibly intended as an allegory of Peace, which is the best preserved panel, and the other panel (fragmentary) shows a seated warrior. But it is on the **upper register of the two exterior side panels** that the greatest interest lies: they illustrate the ceremony that took place during the consecration of the altar itself: the long procession includes Augustus, state officials and priests, as well as many members of his family, including children. All the participants are evidently portraits, and they are depicted sometimes in conversation, or attending to the children, or looking back to find a friend, or just contemplating life. It is interesting to remember that the sculptures would have been coloured.

Beside a model of the altar, drawings of the frieze explain exactly who is who. There is also a model showing how the altar related to the Pantheon and the Mausoleum of Augustus in the Campus Martius, as well as a family tree of the Julio-Claudian imperial family, together with a video in English.

PIAZZA AUGUSTO IMPERATORE

This square (*map p. 652, A3–B3*) was laid out in 1936–8 in monumental Fascist style with square colonnades around the remains of the huge circular **Mausoleum of Augustus**. There are long-term plans to reopen it to the public and possibly also redesign the piazza, which still retains (on the north side) its dedicatory plaque in Latin to 'Mussolini Dux 1940'.

THE MAUSOLEUM OF AUGUSTUS

Only the exterior can be viewed; the interior is not at present open (*for information, see www.sovraintendenzaroma.it*). This is the tomb of Augustus and of the principal members of his family, the *gens* Julia-Claudia. It was one of the most sacred monuments of the ancient city, but has been very much neglected for decades while sporadic excavations and restoration projects have been carried out. It is the only important building of ancient Rome to have survived to this day which is not adequately looked after.

The mausoleum dominated the north end of the Campus Martius and in ancient times was surrounded by a huge public park. Erected in 28 BC, it has a diameter of 87m (330 Roman feet), the largest mausoleum known. The smaller cylinder above was originally surmounted by a tumulus of earth some 45m high, planted with cypresses and probably crowned with a bronze statue of the emperor. The circular base, which incorporated a series of large niches, was built of opus reticulatum and was once faced with travertine. On either side of the entrance were two obelisks—one of which is now in Piazza del Quirinale and the other in Piazza dell'Esquilino—and pilasters on which was inscribed in bronze lettering the official will of Augustus, a copy of which was found at Ankara in Turkey.

In the interior a corridor leads to the centre of the building. There are numerous abandoned marble architectural fragments that once decorated the upper part of the mausoleum, and some finely-carved pieces of inscriptions. The sepulchral cella in the centre had three niches; two survive: that on the left preserves an inscription to Augustus' sister Octavia and his beloved nephew Marcellus, who was the first to be interred here in 23 BC (the Theatre of Marcellus is dedicated to him; *see p. 243*). The other niches contained the cinerary urns of Augustus himself and of his wife Livia, and of his nephews Gaius and Lucius Caesar, who also predeceased him. The last Roman emperor to be buried here was Nerva in AD 98.

In the Middle Ages the tomb was used as a fortress by the wealthy Colonna family. Later it was pillaged to provide travertine for other buildings, and a wooden amphitheatre was built on top of it, where Goethe watched animal-baiting in 1787. In the 19th century a theatre was constructed on the site, which was used as a concert hall from 1908 to 1936. When these structures were demolished and excavations began, it was left open to the sky. It awaits restoration.

NB: The far northern part of the Corso and Piazza del Popolo are described on p. 352.

The Pantheon & District

*The Pantheon survives virtually intact as the most magnificent symbol of the
Roman Empire. Close by, near the site of a temple to Minerva, stands Rome's
finest Gothic church, Santa Maria sopra Minerva, with frescoes
by Filippino Lippi and a sculpture by Michelangelo. The district is a lovely place
to wander (this chapter contains three short guided walks).*

Piazza della Rotonda, dominated by the huge Pantheon, is almost always crowded and has a delightful atmosphere, typically Roman and relaxed. The fountain (1575), on a model by Giacomo della Porta, was surmounted in 1711 by an obelisk of Ramesses the Great, which formerly belonged to the Temple of Isis (*see p. 181*). Horse carriages wait here for fares, and there is a medley of small houses painted in pale blue and buff colours, almost all of them with cafés or restaurants outside them. On the house at no. 7, a marker records the level reached by the Tiber waters in the 1870 flood. The grandest house in the square is the old-established Albergo del Senato, with its lovely roof terrace. The large plaque on the house in front of the Pantheon informs us in self-congratulatory terms that it was Pius VII who in 1823 found the piazza occupied by '*ignobilibus tavernis*' and ordered their demolition in due respect for the ancient building.

THE PANTHEON

*Map p. 654, B2. Open Mon–Sat 8.30–7.30, Sun 9–6, public holidays 9–1. Free.
pantheonroma.com. The interior can become uncomfortably crowded and the intrusive
recorded calls for silence are usually ignored.*

A pedimented pronaos precedes a gigantic domed rotunda, with a rectangular feature as wide as the pronaos and as high as the cylindrical wall inserted between the two. This combination of pronaos and rotunda gives the building a special place in the history of architecture. Dedicated to all the gods (*pan theon*), it was conceived as a secular Imperial monument as much as a shrine. In 609 it was converted into a church, the first temple in Rome to be Christianised. The word 'Pantheon' came to be used for places where illustrious people are buried.

The original temple, apparently of travertine, was built during the third consulate of Agrippa (27 BC) to commemorate the victory over Antony and Cleopatra at Actium.

This building was damaged by fire in AD 80, restored by Domitian, only to be struck by lightning and destroyed by another fire in 110.

It has been conclusively proved by examination of the brick stamps that the existing temple, including the pronaos, is not that of Agrippa, but a new one, built and probably also designed by Hadrian, on a larger scale and on different lines. This second building, begun in AD 118 or 119 and finished between AD 125 and 128, received and retained the name of Pantheon. Hadrian characteristically set up the dedicatory inscription (the bronze letters were remade at the end of the 19th century) on the pediment of the pronaos—M. AGRIPPA L.F. COS. TERTIUM FECIT ('Marcus Agrippa, son of Lucius, consul for the third time, had [this building] made')—in honour of Agrippa.

The Pantheon was restored by Septimius Severus and Caracalla. Closed and abandoned under the first Christian emperors and pillaged by the Goths, it was given to Boniface IV by the Byzantine emperor Phocas, whose column is in the Roman Forum. Boniface consecrated it as a church in 609 with a dedication to Santa Maria ad Martyres—there was a legend that some 28 wagonloads of martyrs' bones had been transferred here from the catacombs. On a twelve-day visit to Rome in 667, Constans II, Emperor of Byzantium, robbed the temple of what the Goths had left and stripped off the gilded roof tiles, which were probably of bronze. Benedict II restored it (684), Gregory III roofed it with lead (735), and Anastasius IV built a palace beside it (1153).

When the popes took up residence in Avignon, the Pantheon served as a fortress in the struggles between the rival Roman aristocratic families of the Colonna and the Orsini. In 1435 Eugenius IV isolated the building, and from then on it was the object of such veneration that a Roman senator on taking office swore to preserve 'Maria Rotonda' intact for the pontiff, together with the relics and sacred treasures of the city.

The monument was greatly admired during the Renaissance. Pius IV repaired the ancient bronze door and had it practically recast (1563). The Barberini pope Urban VIII unwisely commissioned Bernini to add two bell-towers in front: however they looked so clumsy that the Romans derided them, calling them the 'ass-ears of Bernini' (they were only taken down in 1883). Urban also melted down the bronze ceiling of the portico to make the baldacchino for St Peter's and 80 cannon for Castel Sant'Angelo, an act of vandalism that prompted a stinging gibe from the 'talking' statue (*see p. 202*) Pasquino: '*Quod non fecerunt barbari fecerunt Barberini*' ('What the barbarians did not do, the Barberini did').

Alexander VII had the portico restored in 1662 and lowered the level of the piazza to provide a better view of the façade; Clement IX surrounded the portico with an iron railing (1668); Benedict XIV restored the interior and the atrium.

THE PORTICO (PRONAOS)

Take time to savour the experience of standing in the portico, where the mighty columns dwarf the scale of the human figure: here you can imagine what it must have been like to have been a visitor to the ancient city, filled as it was with so many vast monumental buildings. Originally the Pantheon would have produced an even grander effect, since it was raised by several steps and preceded by a large rectangular paved forecourt much larger than the present piazza.

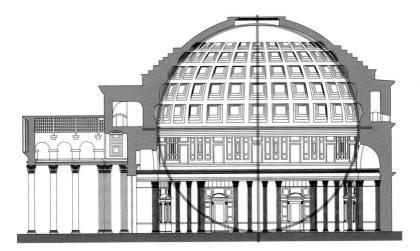

THE PANTHEON
The proportions of the building are so harmonious because the distance from the floor
to the centre of the dome is exactly the same as the building's diameter. The interior contains,
in fact, a perfect sphere.

It is nearly 34m wide and 15.5m deep, and has 16 monolithic Corinthian columns of red or grey granite, without flutings, each 12.5m high and 4.5m in circumference. Eight of them stand in front, and the others are disposed in four rows, so as to form three aisles, the central one leading to the bronze doors, and the others to the two great niches which may formerly have contained colossal statues of Augustus and Agrippa. The superb capitals and the bases are of white marble.

The three columns on the east side are replacements, one by Urban VIII (1625), the other two by Alexander VII (1655–67); the arms of these popes can be seen in the decoration of the capitals.

THE INTERIOR
The huge dome was designed not to be visible from outside and so the visual impact that it produces once you enter the Pantheon is unforgettable. The use of light from the open oculus, which measures almost 9m across, displays the genius of the architect. The great dome has five rows of coffers diminishing in size towards the centre, and their intricate design contributes to the effect of space and light. They were probably originally ornamented with gilded bronze rosettes.

The height and diameter of the interior are the same—43.3m. The diameter of the dome, the largest masonry vault ever built, exceeds by more than one metre that of the dome of St Peter's. Its span, which contains no brick arches or vaults, begins at the level of the highest cornice seen on the outside of the building, rather than, as it appears in the interior, at the top of the attic stage.

The cylindrical wall is 6m thick. It contains seven great niches, or recesses: except for the central apse, each is preceded by two Corinthian columns of *giallo antico* and flanked by pilasters; the apse has two free-standing columns. Between the recesses, which originally contained statues, are eight shrines (*aediculae*), those flanking the apse and entrance with triangular pediments and the others with segmented pediments. These are supported by two Corinthian columns in *giallo antico*, porphyry or granite. Above the recesses is the entablature with a beautiful simple cornice, and still higher is an attic, unfortunately restored in 1747, making this stage more pronounced than was intended. But a small part of the original decoration and its dimensions can be seen over the recess to the right of the apse: between the rectangular openings (fitted with grilles) were shallow pilasters of reddish marble alternating with three marble panels. More than half of the original coloured marble revetment on the walls is still in place. The floor, though restored, retains its original design. Over the high altar there is a 7th-century icon of the *Virgin and Child*.

THE TOMBS

Raphael was the first person to be buried in the Pantheon, on his specific request: he died in 1520 aged only 37. Pope Leo X had tasked him with the preservation of Rome's ancient monuments, so it is particularly fitting that he should repose here. His tomb is below the statue of the *Madonna del Sasso*, probably designed by Raphael but executed by his devoted pupil Lorenzetto (perhaps with the help of Raffaello da Montelupo). Pietro Bembo wrote the epitaph, which was used by Alexander Pope in his *Epitaph on Sir Godfrey Kneller*: 'Living, great Nature feared he might outvie Her works, and dying, fears herself may die.' Today a fresh red rose usually honours the tomb. A roundel bears a bronze bust of the artist, added in the 19th century by Giuseppe de Fabris; the roundel on the right remains empty since Maria Bibbiena, niece of Cardinal Dovizi da Bibbiena, who was to have married Raphael, predeceased him (she is recorded in a short epitaph).

PIETRO BEMBO AND RAPHAEL IN ROME

It was natural that Bembo was chosen to write Raphael's epitaph since he had been a devoted friend of the painter. Born in Venice, Bembo became a cultivated scholar, writer and collector. After a period at the court of Urbino where he enjoyed the company of Baldassare Castiglione and first met Raphael (who painted his portrait), he left for Rome in 1512, hoping to pursue a career in the church. Just a year later the Medici pope Leo X appointed him his secretary, attracted by his erudition and his skills in Latin. Raphael was at work for the pope at the same time, painting the Stanze in the Vatican and designing cartoons for the tapestries for the Sistine Chapel. Bembo recognised the 'universal' qualities of Raphael's art and travelled to Tivoli with him and Castiglione to study the ancient Roman monuments there.

The year after Raphael died Bembo left Rome for Padua, but he returned to the city when he was finally appointed cardinal (by Paul III). By now unquestionably the most famous 'man of letters' of his time, he befriended Michelangelo and the poet Vittoria Colonna and remained in Rome until his death in 1547 (he is buried close by in Santa Maria sopra Minerva).

Among other artists buried in the Pantheon are Giovanni da Udine, Perino del Vaga, Taddeo Zuccari, Annibale Carracci and Baldassare Peruzzi, all close contemporaries of Raphael.

The tombs of the two first kings of Italy lie opposite each other: **Vittorio Emanuele II**, who died on 9th January 1878; and **Umberto I**, assassinated at Monza on 29th July 1900 (and his consort, Margherita of Savoy, first Queen of Italy who died in 1926). The tombs were designed by Manfredo Manfredi and Giuseppe Sacconi respectively.

SANTA MARIA SOPRA MINERVA

Map p. 654, C2. Open weekdays 7.30–7, Sat 7.30–12.30 & 3.30–7, Sun 8–12.30 & 3.30–7. santamariasopraminerva.it.

This church stands on the site of a small oratory probably built before AD 800 close to the ruins of a temple of Minerva. It was rebuilt in 1280 by the Dominicans, who modelled it on their church of Santa Maria Novella in Florence (according to Vasari it was by the same architects). This explains its Gothic style, an extreme rarity in Rome. It was altered and over-restored in 1848–55. The simple façade dates from 1453. The delightful elephant monument in the piazza is described on p. 179.

In the very dark interior, the vault, rose windows and excessively colourful decorations date from the 19th-century restoration. The church contains some fine monuments and works of art, many of them either by Florentine artists or commemorating Florentines, since, before San Giovanni Battista dei Fiorentini was built in the 16th century, this was their 'national' church. There are important frescoes by Filippino Lippi, as well as one of Michelangelo's lesser-known statues. Fra' Angelico and the two most famous Medici popes are buried here.

South side: The baptistery **(1)** has a *Noli me Tangere* by Marcello Venusti and the bust of Ladislao di Aquino (d. 1621) by Francesco Mochi. Outside is a memorial to Virginia Pucci Ridolfi (1567) **(2)** with a fine bust.

The fourth chapel was designed by Carlo Maderno. The altarpiece of the *Annunciation* **(3)** is by Antoniazzo Romano (1500): the painting also shows Cardinal Juan de Torquemada (uncle of Tomás de Torquemada, the Inquisitor) presenting three poor girls to the Virgin, and commemorates the Confraternity of the Annunziata, founded in 1460 to provide dowries for penniless girls.

The fifth chapel **(4)** has an altarpiece of the *Institution of the Eucharist* by Federico Barocci. The tombs **(A)** and **(B)** of Clement VIII's parents are by Giacomo della Porta and there is a statue of Clement **(C)**, who was the son of a Florentine lawyer.

South transept: The Cappella Carafa **(5)** is entered under a fine marble arch, attributed to Giuliano da Maiano, with a beautiful balustrade. The chapel contains celebrated **frescoes by Filippino Lippi**, who had temporarily

SANTA MARIA SOPRA MINERVA
Detail of Michelangelo's *Risen Christ* (1514–21).

to interrupt his work on his other great fresco cycle in the church of Santa Maria Novella in Florence when he received this commission from Cardinal Oliviero Carafa in 1489. On the right wall, below, is *St Thomas Confounding the Heretics*, the central figures being Arius and Sabellius. Sabellius' heresy tried to confute the idea of the Trinity, maintaining that God was not 'one in three' but a single 'unity'. Arius denied the divine nature of Christ, which caused one of the most serious crises in early Christianity. The two youths in the right-hand group are probably portraits of the future Medici popes Leo X and Clement VII, both buried in this church (*see below*). In the lunette above is *St Thomas Aquinas at Prayer*. On the altar wall is the *Assumption*, with a splendid group of angels, and an altarpiece of the *Annunciation*, with *St Thomas Aquinas presenting Cardinal Carafa to the Virgin*, also by Filippino. On the left wall is the funerary monument of Paul IV (d. 1559).

Outside the chapel is the tomb **(6)** of Guillaume Durand (d. 1296), bishop of Mende, by Giovanni di Cosma, with a beautiful 13th-century mosaic of the *Madonna and Child*.

The Altieri Chapel **(7)** has decorations of 1671 commissioned by Pope Clement X (Emilio Altieri). His pontificate saw numerous canonisations: the altarpiece of the *Madonna and Saints* by Carlo Maratta, also commissioned by the pope, is dedicated to them. The saint on the left, shown holding a Crucifix with a pistol at its other end, is St Louis Bertrand (Luis Beltrán), who was a missionary in South America. His attribute alludes to his miraculous escape from a murder attempt.

Sanctuary: At the foot of the sanctuary steps is a **statue of the *Risen Christ* (8)** by Michelangelo (1514–21), for which the great artist was paid 200 ducats (a princely sum). Standing in marked *contrapposto*, Christ carries the instruments of the Passion (rod and vinegar sponge, scourge and Cross); the small size of the latter gives it a purely symbolic value. Michelangelo's original figure was nude, although it has distinctly unclassical proportions; the bronze drapery is a later addition. Designed to be seen from below, it used to stand in a tabernacle.

Under the 19th-century high altar **(9)** lies a marble effigy of **St Catherine of Siena**, marking the place where her decapitated body is buried (her head was returned to her native Siena three years after her death and is preserved in a reli-quary there in San Domenico). It was St Catherine who persuaded Gregory XI to return from Avignon to Rome, and her remarkable letters are preserved. She was proclaimed a patron saint of Italy in 1939 and became a patron saint of Europe in 1999.

In the apse behind are the **tombs of the two most famous Medici popes (10)**: Leo X (left) and Clement VII, designed by Antonio da Sangallo the Younger, with statues by Raffaello da Montelupo and Nanni di Baccio Bigio respectively (but they are both without inscriptions). In the pavement is the **tomb slab of Cardinal Pietro Bembo** (1547; *see p. 174*).

North transept: In a passageway which serves as an exit, is the pavement **tomb**

SANTA MARIA SOPRA MINERVA

1 Baptistery
2 Ridolfi memorial
3 *Annunciation* altarpiece
4 *Institution of the Eucharist*
5 Cappella Carafa
6 Tomb of Guillaume Durand
7 Altieri Chapel
8 Michelangelo's *Risen Christ*
9 High altar (tomb of St Catherine of Siena)
10 Tombs of the Medici popes
11 Tomb of Fra' Angelico
12 Bonelli monument
13 Pimentel monument
14 Frangipani Chapel
15 Sacristy
16 Chapel of St Dominic
17 Tomb of Andrea Bregno
18 Memorial to Maria Raggi
19 Vigevano tomb
20 *Redeemer* altarpiece
21 Naro tomb
22 Tornabuoni/Tebaldi tombs
23 Diotisalvi tomb

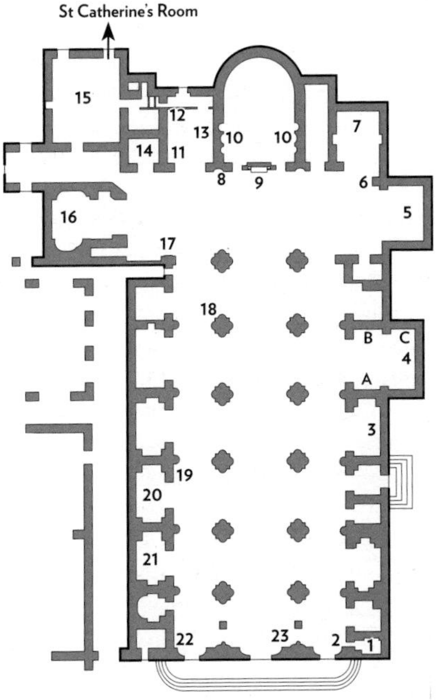

St Catherine's Room

of Fra' Angelico (11), with an effigy taken from his death mask, attributed to Isaia da Pisa. The great Florentine painter and Dominican friar died in the friary of this church in 1455 (he was in Rome because he was at work on the frescoes in the chapel of Nicholas V in the Vatican, *see p. 466*). Further into the corridor are several large monuments, including those of Cardinal Michele Bonelli (Alexandrinus) **(12)** by Giacomo della Porta, and of Cardinal Domenico Pimentel **(13)**, designed by Bernini.

The Frangipani Chapel **(14)** has a 15th-century altarpiece (a processional standard painted in tempera on silk) of the *Madonna and Child*. To the right of the altar is the charming **epitaph of Fra' Angelico**, composed by Pope Nicholas V (*see above*). The tomb of Giovanni Arberini (d. c. 1470) on the left is by a Tuscan sculptor (?Agostino di Duccio), who incorporated a splendid bas-relief of *Hercules and the Lion*, probably a Roman copy of an original Greek work of the 5th century BC.

From the 17th-century sacristy **(15)**, there is access to a **room in which St Catherine of Siena died** in 1380 (it was brought here from Via di Santa Chiara by Cardinal Barberini). The poorly-preserved frescoes are by Antoniazzo Romano and his school (1482).

The **Chapel of St Dominic (16)**, contains (on the right) the monument of Benedict XIII (d. 1730), with sculptures by Pietro Bracci.

POPES, ANTIPOPES AND THE GREAT WESTERN SCHISM

For 70 years in the 14th century the popes abandoned Rome for the south of France, causing a scandal in the rest of Christendom. This 'Avignon period' began when the archbishop of Bordeaux, who had been elected pope *in absentia* in 1305, was persuaded by the French king Philip the Fair to set up his court in Avignon. Political disturbances in Italy made this seem a good idea to Clement V (as the archbishop now was), and he and his seven successors ruled from the comfortable Palais des Papes. Shocked contemporaries—such as the poet Petrarch and St Catherine of Siena—begged these French popes to return to Rome, but it was not until 1377 that Gregory XI re-established papal government in the Eternal City, by then in a pitiful state of abandon and neglect. (Since this Gregory, there has never been another French pope.)

The Avignon interlude contributed to an even worse disaster: the Great Schism, which lasted from 1378 to 1417. This rupture of ecclesiastical unity produced a situation whereby there were two or even three popes at once, each claiming to be the true successor to St Peter and denouncing his rival or rivals. The Church has since decided which were the true popes (Urban VI, Boniface IX, Innocent VII, Gregory XII) and which were the so-called antipopes (*listed on p. 618*); but it was by no means clear at the time, and indeed it was not until 1958 that the status of Baldassare Cossa, 'John XXIII', was finally determined: in that year Angelo Roncalli took the same name and regnal number, thus indicating that his 15th-century predecessor had never been true Bishop of Rome.

M.R.

North aisle: At the corner of the nave and transept is the charming small **tomb of Andrea Bregno (17)**, with his bust and, in very low relief, tools of the sculptor's trade (he produced numerous tombs for Roman churches in the 15th century). On the second nave pillar is a showy **monument to the nun Maria Raggi (18)**, an early work by Bernini.

Between the fourth and third chapels is the tomb of Giovanni Vigevano (d. 1630) **(19)**, with a bust by Bernini (c. 1617). The third chapel has a tiny altar-piece of the *Redeemer* **(20)**, attributed to Perugino or Pinturicchio. In the second chapel the tomb of Gregorio Naro **(21)**, showing the cardinal kneeling at a priedieu, has recently been attributed to Bernini.

On the west wall is the tomb **(22)** of Francesco Tornabuoni (1480) by Mino da Fiesole, and above is that of Cardinal Tebaldi (1466) by Andrea Bregno and Giovanni Dalmata, as well as the tomb of Nerone Diotisalvi **(23)**, a Florentine exile (d. 1482).

THE FRIARY

The friary, once the Roman headquarters of the Dominicans, was the scene of Galileo's trial in 1633 when he was condemned by the Inquisition for his contention that the Earth was not at the centre of the Universe (he was only rehabilitated in 1992 by John Paul II). The Dominicans were left a library by Cardinal Girolamo Casanate, which they opened in the friary in 1701. Today the Biblioteca Casanatense (*entrance at Via Sant'Ignazio 52*) specialises in theological texts and works on the history of Rome.

THREE SHORT WALKS NEAR THE PANTHEON

WALK ONE

THIS FIRST WALK BEGINS BEHIND THE Pantheon, in **Via della Palombella**. Here there are considerable remains of a Roman structure, which was named the Basilica of Neptune when it was unearthed in 1938, and attributed to Agrippa. It has similarities to the pronaos of the Pantheon and although it is now known to date from Hadrian's time, its purpose is unclear. Today you can see fragments of a Classical frieze with dolphins and scallop shells, one of which is supported by a single tall columns which still has its entablature and its base.

Via della Palombella leads into **Piazza Minerva** in front of the church of that name (*described above*). On the corner of the church façade are numerous plaques which register the heights reached by the waters of the Tiber in flood before it was canalised. In the centre of the piazza is a marble **elephant supporting an obelisk**. This is a bizarre but delightful work by Bernini (1667), commissioned by Pope Alexander VII, who was inspired by a woodcut in a famous book entitled *Hypnerotomachia Poliphili*, a Renaissance allegory of love. The inscription on the plinth underlines the significance of the ensemble, namely that a strong mind nourishes sure-seated hope. The small obelisk once belonged to the Temple of Isis that stood here. It has a hieroglyphic inscription relating to Apries, the last of the independent pharaohs of Egypt, the Hophra of the Bible (*Jeremiah 44:30*), ally of Zedekiah, King of Judah, against Nebuchadnezzar in the 6th century BC.

The **Grand Hotel de la Minerve** stands on the site of Palazzo Conti, where Stendhal stayed in 1834–6. The commemorative plaque adds that his *Promenades dans Rome* make him worthy to be called a true Roman. One suspects he would have been delighted

with the compliment, despite his scalding criticism of the Church and his inordinate love of Napoleon.

Another remnant of the Egyptian sanctuary can be seen if you follow the side of the church, past the Barbiconi clerical vestments emporium (there are a number of other old-established shops in this area which sell liturgical articles and grand attire for the clergy who come to visit the Vatican), and two bookshops, as far as **Via del Piè di Marmo** (the street 'of the marble foot'). On the right, on the corner of the narrow Via di Santo Stefano in Cacco (and in front of Moriondo & Gariglio, a smart confectioners shop named

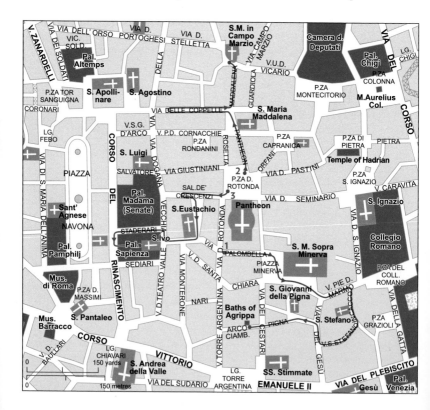

after two cousins who served the Royal House of Savoy in Turin in the 19th century before moving to Rome; it sells jellied friuts, chocolate, and all sorts of delicious sweet things and you can sit here and enjoy them), there is a **colossal marble foot** shod in a sandal which is thought to have been part of an ancient Roman statue of Isis (or Serapis). It is an arresting sight, and typical of the haphazard way ancient pieces of sculpture still survive in the modern city—it even gave the street its name. The name of the perpendicular street, Santo Stefano 'in Cacco', is thought to come from '*macaco*', the epithet given to a statue of the Egyptian god Thoth, which stood in the vicinity until the 14th century (its remains are now in the Vatican; *illustrated below*). Thoth was portrayed either with the head of an ibis or of a monkey (*macaco*).

EGYPT AND ROME

The Temple of Isis was erected in 43 BC in the Isaeum Campense, located in the area to the east of Santa Maria sopra Minerva. This was the most important Roman sanctuary dedicated to Egyptian deities, restored in AD 80 by Vespasian and his sons. In addition to the Temple of Isis there was another dedicated to Serapis.

Egypt was annexed as a Roman province in 30 BC and soon became essential to Rome because it supplied most of the grain needed to feed Rome's vast population. The obelisk above the fountain in Piazza della Rotonda outside the Pantheon, and the smaller obelisk outside Santa Maria sopra Minerva, both came from the Isaeum Campense. Another obelisk found here in 1883 is now incorporated in the Dogali monument (*see p. 319*). Numerous Egyptian statues were transported to Rome and are today preserved in the Capitoline Museums, Palazzo Altemps, the Egyptian Museum in the Vatican, and the Museo di Scultura Antica Giovanni Barracco. There are now more Egyptian obelisks in Rome than in Egypt itself.

Lower half of the statue of the Egyptian god Thoth, in simian guise, which once stood in a sanctuary near the Pantheon. The Italian word *macaco*, meaning a rhesus monkey, has given its name to the local street, Via di Santo Stefano in Cacco. The statue fragment is now preserved in the Egyptian Museum in the Vatican.

Turn up the street past the foot to the little piazza in front of the church of **Santo Stefano Protomartire**, its façade set into a monastery of Silvestrine monks. Cars are kept from its portal by a row of plants in pots: until Michelangelo decided to remove them to the foot of his Cordonata (where they have become one of the most photographed sculptures in Rome; *see p. 36*), the portal was guarded by two Egyptian lions, formerly inside the Temple of Isis. A church was founded on this spot by Paschal I in the 9th century. The present building is a 17th-century successor.

Via di Santo Stefano in Cacco continues past a repairs garage and then a house with two old vines reaching almost to its roof near the Teatro Flaiano. There is a lovely portal at no. 61 and a Roman sarcophagus used as a fountain, carved with winged genii, a Medusa head, and two overturned vases with squirrels enjoying the contents. A plaque records that in 1874 it was moved out of the palace so the public could enjoy its water. Turn right on **Via del Gesù**, past a palace where in the courtyard you can see a curious clock fountain and a modern glass lift, the bottom of the shaft discreetly hidden behind two Roman baths. The portal at no. 85 is beautifully decorated with griffins.

Turn left into the wide **Via della Pigna**, which is probably named from the huge ancient bronze pine cone which topped a fountain of Isis and is now in the Vatican (*see p. 449*). The entire *rione* or district which extends to the south retains its name. The pretty little church of **San Giovanni della Pigna** (*open 7–12.30 & 3.30–7*) has a Baroque interior with a fine chandelier and interesting 14th-century tomb slabs on either side of the doorway. One, rather primitive, with a mosaic border and a mosaic Cross, commemorates a certain Julianus Porcarius. The two others, very similar to each other, with incised decoration, commemorate a father and son of the same family (the pig, or '*porco*' is prominent in all three). The Porcari were an important local family in the Middle Ages, tracing their lineage from Marcus Porcius Cato (the 'Censor').

Via della Pigna leads past the Porcari house (no. 19), which is opposite the grander 16th-century Palazzo Maffei Marescotti (now owned by the Vatican), into Via dei Cestari, across which, in Via dell'Arco della Ciambella, is part of the central hall of the **Baths of Agrippa**, charmingly incorporated into the street architecture. The owners of the house have difficulty in opening one of their shutters as a result of this massive ruin—a typical sight in Rome, where ancient remains make their presence felt in the later urban development. These were the first public baths in Rome, begun by Agrippa in 29 BC and restored by Hadrian. The brick-faced concrete dates from the 3rd century. Agrippa was a close friend of Augustus and supported the emperor by financing numerous ambitious building projects in Rome, including the original Pantheon, these baths, three aqueducts and hundreds of fountains. He married Augustus' only child, Julia (they feature, with one of their sons, as figures on the Ara Pacis; *see p. 167*). Wanton and wayward though she was, Julia enjoyed the prospect of becoming empress (Agrippa was considered Augustus' obvious successor); but Agrippa and his two children all predeceased Augustus, and Julia and her mother ended their lives in exile.

WALK TWO

THIS WALK BEGINS IN PIAZZA DELLA Rotonda. The short **Via del Pantheon** leads north out of the piazza (note the plaque on no. 57–58 on the right, recording Thomas Mann's stay here in 1896–7). The street ends in a little piazza in front of the Rococo façade (by Giuseppe Sardi, 1735) of the church of **Santa Maria Maddalena** (*open 7.30–11.45 & 5–7.45; 9–11 on Sun*). The pretty interior (1695–9), on an original plan where all the lines are curving, is encrusted with marble and entirely decorated with statues of the Virtues (candelabra shaped like sprays of lilies burst from beneath them) and with paintings and frescoes from the 1730s in the vault and cupola. The elaborate cantoria (still used) and the organ were installed at the same date. The lovely old confessionals survive. The third south chapel has an elaborate reliquary urn beneath the altar by Luigi Valadier (1770), with a vault fresco by Sebastiano Conca. In the chapel to the right of the sanctuary is an unusual wooden statue of Mary Magdalene (15th century). On the north side there are altarpieces by Baciccia and Luca Giordano (1704). The sacristy, entered from the left aisle, is a charming room which preserves intact its Rococo decoration and furnishings from 1741. The church contains a much venerated image of the *Madonna della Salute* (a good 16th-century copy of an earlier work).

In **Via delle Coppelle** (at no. 35) is Palazzo Baldassini, a smaller version of Palazzo Farnese (*see p. 228*), built by Antonio da Sangallo the Younger (1514–23), with a handsome courtyard and loggia. Garibaldi lived here in 1875. Next door is an old-fashioned shop for household goods with a cavernous interior which looks as though it might stock everything you could ever possibly want. The street has two very good restaurants (Le Coppelle and I Maccheroni).

Retrace your steps and turn left into **Via della Maddalena**. At the end of it, the apse of Santa Maria in Campo Marzio is conspicuous (and to the right you can see **Giolitti**, a very old-established café). The church of **Santa Maria in Campo Marzio**, of ancient foundation but rebuilt in 1685 by Giovanni Antonio de Rossi on a Greek-cross plan, has a courtyard, unusual in shape, with two porticoes. Over the high altar is a *Madonna*, part of a triptych probably dating from the 12th–13th century. Since 1920 the church has belonged to the Roman Catholic Patriarchate of Antioch of the Syrians. Outside is a lovely old Roman altar.

THE CAMPUS MARTIUS

The name of the church and its piazza recalls the Campus Martius, or Field of Mars, a district of the ancient city which at first included the whole area between the Capitoline hill, the Tiber and the Quirinal and Pincian hills, but which came to refer more precisely to the low-lying ground enclosed in the Tiber bend. It was said originally to have been the property of the Tarquins and to have become public land after the expulsion of the kings. The area at first had a predominantly military nature: it took its name from the sacred enclosure devoted to Mars, the god of war, to whom an ancient altar was dedicated. After the 2nd century BC many temples and edifices for public entertainments were built, and on other parts of the land military exercises and athletic competitions were held. Since the low-lying area to the north was subject to flooding, Hadrian raised the ground level and made numerous other improvements. The southern part of the Campus Martius was the Prata Flaminia, with the Circus of Flaminius. The area was not brought within the walls of Rome until Aurelian built his famous wall round the city in AD 272–9.

WALK THREE

NB: Because of the restricted opening times of the church of Sant'Ivo, the best time to do this walk is on a Sunday morning.

FROM PIAZZA DELLA ROTONDA, ON A line with the portico of the Pantheon, take **Salita de' Crescenzi**. Just to the left is a piazza (in fact called Via di Sant'Eustachio) which has a house overhung with Virginia creeper and two tall free-standing ancient Roman granite columns (restored in brick) with a fragment of a Classical cornice between them. The notice on the wall is one of many in the centre of Rome from past centuries forbidding the local inhabitants to litter the streets. To the right, in Via della Palombella, there is a good view of the delightful spiral Baroque tower of Sant'Ivo (*see below*) as well as the (nearer) squat medieval campanile, decorated with green ceramic basins, of **Sant'Eustachio**. This church has two huge columns flanking the portico gate. In the dark interior, the two altarpieces of 1737 in the crossing of *St Jerome* and the *Visitation* are by the little-known Giacomo Zoboli, born in Modena, and the high altarpiece of the *Martyrdom of St Eustace* (1727) is by the equally obscure Francesco Fernandi, born in Milan in 1679. These are surprisingly good paintings by these two near contemporaries who both died

in Rome. Fernandi took the name of his Roman patron Cardinal Imperiali, and he taught both Allan Ramsay and Pompeo Batoni. He was apparently popular with English milords on the Grand Tour and many of his works ended up in Britain.

The piazza has no name since it is really just a little open place where numerous roads meet. But it has the atmosphere of a piazza since it has a number of cafés, much frequented by politicians from the Italian Senate nearby. One of these, called **Sant'Eustachio, Il Caffè**, is extremely famous for the quality of its coffee, which you can try here or purchase (along with plenty of other branded goods in the trademark bright yellow), but if you want to sit in more comfort and also eat something then you can go across the road to **Camilloni**, which has more tables outside. For a very simple and delicious quick snack, try a piece of pizza at the tiny 'hole in the wall' called **Zazà**. (NB: if you are a coffee fiend, you may want to retrace your steps for a moment, since Romans hotly dispute where the best coffee in the city is to be found. The contenders are

Sant'Eustachio, Il Caffè and La Casa del Caffè, also known as **La Tazza d'Oro**, which is just out of Piazza della Rotonda in Via degli Orfani).

Across the broad Via della Dogana Vecchia, which has a number of handsome palaces, take **Via dei Staderari**, which separates the huge Palazzo Madama from Palazzo della Sapienza. The splendid huge **antique basin** was set up here as a fountain in 1987 by the Senate to commemorate the 40th anniversary of the Italian Constitution; it is one of the most recent fountains to be inaugurated in central Rome. Against the side wall of Palazzo della Sapienza is a small **wall-fountain** featuring volumes of books (symbolising the erudition of the university close by), carved in 1927 to mark the *rione* or district of Sant'Eustachio.

Cross Corso del Rinascimento and look back. On the left of Via Staderari is the main Baroque façade of **Palazzo Madama**, where the Italian Senate sits (*open for guided visits of c. 40mins on the first Sat of the month, except Aug, 10–6; T: 06 67 061, senato.it*). Originally the palace belonged to the powerful Roman Crescenzi family, and it passed to the Medici in the 16th century as part of the dowry of Alfonsina Orsini (who married Piero, brother of the Medici pope Leo X). In the 17th century the building was enlarged and given its façade. It owes its name to the residence here of 'Madama' Margaret of Parma, illegitimate daughter of the Holy Roman Emperor Charles V. She married first Alessandro de' Medici and afterwards Ottavio Farnese, and was regent of the Netherlands from 1559 to 1567. Benedict XIV bought the palace in 1740 and it became successively the residence of the governor of Rome and the seat of the Ministry of Finance (1852–70). The right wing was added in 1931. The palace has been the seat of the Italian Senate since 1871. This, together with the Camera dei Deputati in Montecitorio (*see p. 164*), comprises the parliament of Italy. A constitutional reform of the Senate was going through Parliament at the time of writing.

To the right of Via dei Staderari is the fine Renaissance façade of **Palazzo della Sapienza**, by Giacomo della Porta. Until 1935 it was the seat of the University of Rome, founded by Boniface VIII in 1303 (one of the three universities in Rome is still known as La Sapienza after this palace). It now houses the Archivio di Stato and exhibitions are held in a library designed by Borromini. The door is open all day, so you can visit the beautiful courtyard. This was also designed by Borromini and has porticoes on three sides and the church of **Sant'Ivo** (*only open on Sun 9–12*) at the far end. Begun for the Barberini pope Urban VIII, both the courtyard and the church incorporate his device (the bee) into their design, as well as Alexander VII's Chigi device of mounds. The dome is crowned by an ingenious spiral tower, a unique feature of the city skyline and later copied many times, especially in German architecture. The church is a masterpiece of the Baroque, with a remarkable light interior painted in white and entirely devoid of decoration. There were once steel mirrors over the altar which increased the light effects, but these were later gilded.

Piazza Navona
& its District

*The delightful Piazza Navona is one of the places which best illustrates the spirit
of Rome: an ancient circus successfully adapted to a later urban framework.
The centrepiece is Bernini's famous Fountain of the Four Rivers. The piazza is
always full of people who come to enjoy the scene, and it has a relaxed, festive
atmosphere. A few steps away is Palazzo Altemps, with its beautifully displayed
collection of ancient sculpture, and the lovely church of Santa Maria della Pace.*

The form of Piazza Navona (*map p. 654, B2*), preserving the dimensions of the
Stadium of Domitian, a building which could probably hold some 30,000 spectators, represents a remarkable survival within the modern city. Its appearance, surrounded by stately palaces and churches and with fountains in its centre, has
remained almost totally unchanged since at least the beginning of the 18th century, as
numerous paintings and prints of old Rome attest. It is the most animated square in
Rome, beloved of the Romans as well as visitors, and the cafés and restaurants have
tables outside for most of the year. It is usually very crowded and many street artists,
buskers and performers of all kinds are always at work here.

Its name is derived from the athletic games, the *Agones Capitolini*, held here after
the stadium was inaugurated in AD 86. The remains of the north curve of the Stadium
of Domitian can be seen beneath modern buildings on Piazza Tor Sanguigna, where
the entrance gate to the stadium stood. In the Middle Ages the piazza was called the
Campus Agonis; hence *agone, n'agona* and *navona*. Festivals, jousts and open-air
sports took place here, and it was also used as a market-place from 1477 until 1869.
From the 17th to the late 19th century the piazza was flooded every weekend in August
for the entertainment of the populace; the nobles enjoyed the spectacle from their carriages. Nowadays, in December, statuettes for the Christmas crib are sold here, and the
fair and toy market of the *Befana* takes place during Epiphany.

THE FOUNTAINS

Three monumental fountains decorate the piazza. The central **Fountain of the Four
Rivers** (*Fontana dei Quattro Fiumi*) represents the triumph of Bernini's Baroque
style. It was Innocent X who had the idea of decorating Piazza Navona with a fountain to provide a support for the tall obelisk. But he deliberately excluded Bernini from
the list of sculptors when he asked for designs. Bernini decided to produce a model

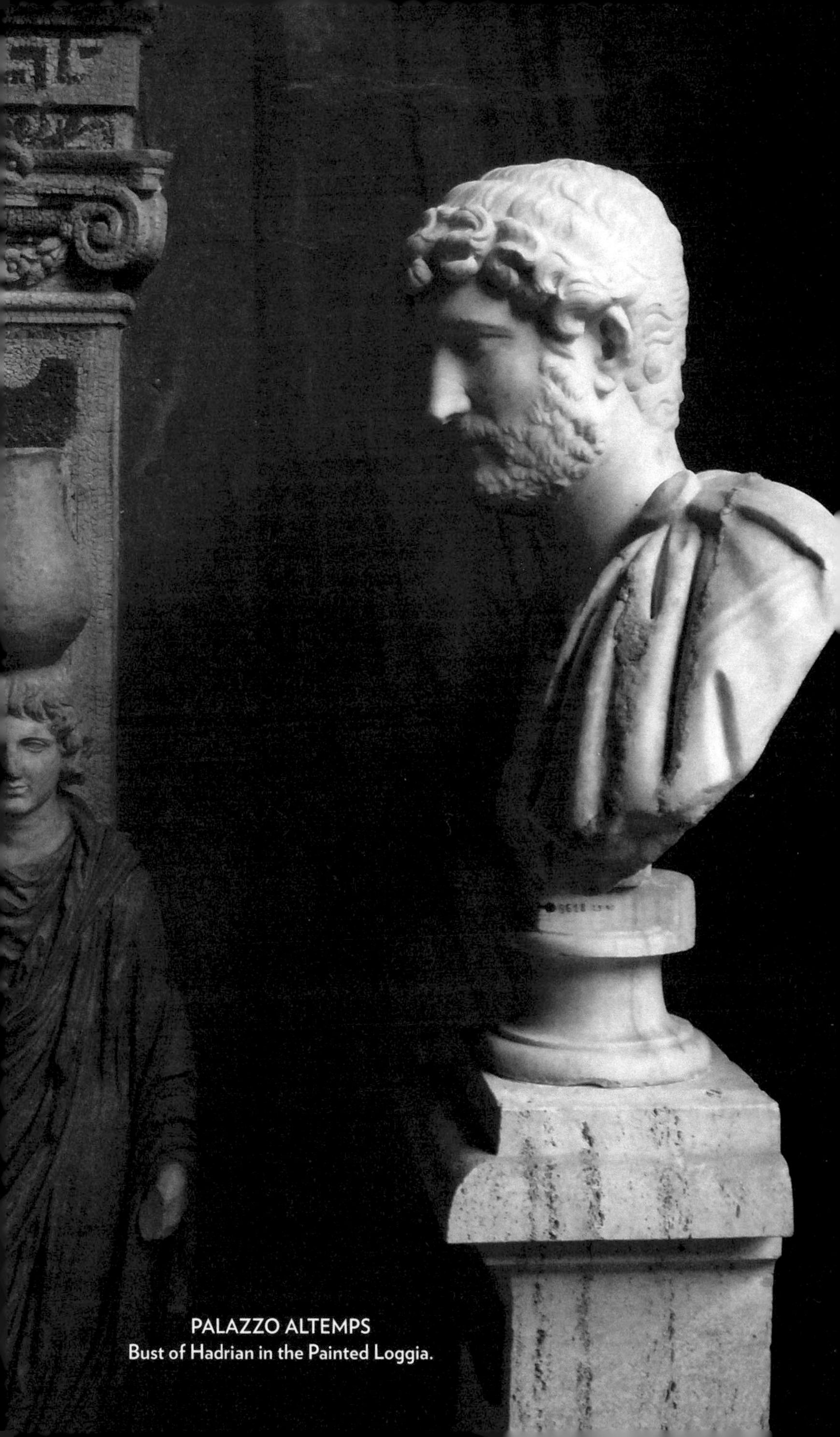

PALAZZO ALTEMPS
Bust of Hadrian in the Painted Loggia.

anyway, and a nephew of the pope managed to show it to Innocent, who was unable to resist giving Bernini the commission in 1648. Four colossal allegorical figures are seated on a triangular base of travertine rock. They represent the four most famous rivers of the four continents then known and were carved by Bernini's assistants, Antonio Raggi, Giacomo Antonio Fancelli, Claude Poussin and Francesco Baratta. The bearded figure with a punt pole and an elephant beneath him represents the Ganges. The Danube is personified by a figure with his hair tied back, a huge fish beneath him and a horse below. The Rio della Plata (holding his arm up) has a pile of coins beside him, a reference to the riches of the New World. Lastly comes the Nile (veiled), with a lion on the rocks beside a palm tree. The popular story told to illustrate the rivalry between Bernini and Borromini—that the Rio della Plata is holding up an arm to block out the sight of Sant'Agnese—is apocryphal, since the fountain was finished in 1651, before Borromini started work on the church.

The **obelisk**, which was cut in Egypt, was brought to Rome by order of Domitian, where the emperor had Roman stonemasons carve hieroglyphs referring to himself as 'eternal pharaoh' and to Vespasian and Titus (his father and brother) as gods. For centuries it lay in the Circus of Maxentius on the Via Appia, in five pieces, until moved here by Pope Innocent. It is crowned with the dove, the Pamphilj (Innocent X's) emblem.

The **Fontana del Moro** at the south end of the piazza was designed by Giacomo della Porta in 1576, with sculptures by Taddeo Landini and others. In 1874 these were replaced by copies made by Luigi Amici, and in 1909 the originals were moved to the Giardino del Lago in Villa Borghese. The fountain was altered by Bernini in 1653 when he designed the central figure, known as *Il Moro* (the Moor), executed by Antonio Mari. The fountain at the north end of the square, the **Fontana di Nettuno**, showing Neptune struggling with a marine monster or giant octopus, surrounded by nereids and sea-horses, is by Antonio della Bitta and Gregorio Zappalà (1878).

SANT'AGNESE IN AGONE

The church of Sant'Agnese (*open Mon–Sat 9.30–12.30 & 4–7, Sun 10–1 & 4–8; santagne-seinagone.org*) is an ancient church built on the ruins of the stadium which Christian tradition marks as the spot where St Agnes was exposed (*see p. 482*). It was reconstructed for Innocent X by Girolamo Rainaldi and his son Carlo in 1652, who were still at work on the Pamphilj pope's palace next door; the following year they were substituted by Francesco Borromini, who provided the splendid concave façade, which adds emphasis to the dome. Innocent X died in 1655. Borromini was out of favour with his successor, and by 1657 he had abandoned work on the church. His collaborator Giovanni Maria Baratta completed the façade and the twin bell-towers.

The small Baroque interior has an intricate Greek-cross plan in which a remarkable effect of spaciousness is provided by the cupola. Innocent X's family crest, the dove, is ever present in the decorations. The dome fresco is by Ciro Ferri, Pietro da Cortona's able pupil; the pendentives are by Baciccia, famous for his Baroque ceiling paintings. Above the seven altars, 17th-century bas-reliefs or statues (including an antique statue of St Sebastian, altered later) take the place of paintings. These are by Algardi's followers including Ercole Ferrata and Antonio Raggi. Above the main west door is an

SANT'AGNESE IN AGONE

early 18th-century monument to Innocent X, who is buried here. On the left is a chapel which preserves the skull of St Agnes. The sacristy (*used for concerts*) was designed by Borromini. The Oratory of St Agnes, built before 800 in a vault of the Stadium of Domitian, survives beneath the church. It contains badly-damaged 13th-century frescoes and the last work of Alessandro Algardi, a bas-relief of the *Miracle of St Agnes*.

To the left of the church is the splendid façade of **Palazzo Pamphilj**, which, like the church of Sant'Agnese, was started by Girolamo Rainaldi and completed by Borromini for Innocent X in the mid-17th century. Pamphilj doves decorate the stones flanking the doorway. (*For the interior, not open to the public, see p. 574.*) On the opposite side of the piazza is the church of the **Madonna del Sacro Cuore**, formerly San Giacomo degli Spagnoli, which was rebuilt in 1450 and restored in 1879. It has a strange alignment since you enter through the façade but emerge at the east end. The chapel off the north side is by Antonio da Sangallo the Younger.

PALAZZO ALTEMPS
(MUSEO NAZIONALE ROMANO)

Map p. 654, B1. Open 9–7.45; closed Mon. T: 06 68 4851, archeoroma.beniculturali.it.
Ticket valid for three days for all four museums of the Museo Nazionale Romano (this
one, Crypta Balbi, Palazzo Massimo and the Baths of Diocletian). For the Archaeological
Card and reductions for young visitors, see p. 600. Room numbers given in the text below
correspond to the plans on p. 193 (the rooms are not numbered in situ).

Palazzo Altemps contains some of the Museo Nazionale Romano's most important collections of ancient Roman sculpture once in private hands. It also has Egyptian sculpture. The arrangement of the works attempts, as far as possible, to illustrate 17th-century antiquarian taste and the unusually spacious display is extremely pleasing. Diagrams show where the antique statues have been restored.

THE PALACE AND ITS COLLECTIONS

The palace which houses the collections was begun before 1477 by Girolamo Riario. Building was continued by Cardinal Francesco Soderini of Volterra (1511–23) and completed after 1568 by Cardinal Marco Sittico Altemps and his descendants, for whom Martino Longhi the Elder worked. Longhi was responsible for the charming turret-shaped belvedere, an innovative architectural feature and later much copied.

In the 16th century Cardinal Altemps began to collect antique sculptures in this palace. The 16 statues that survive from his collection are preserved here. All the rest have been dispersed and some of the finest are now in the collections of the Vatican, the British Museum and the Louvre.

The Ludovisi collection was begun in 1621 by Cardinal Ludovico Ludovisi, nephew of Pope Gregory XV, to decorate his villa and garden near Porta Pinciana (*see p. 380*). He acquired part of the Altemps collection and other pieces from the Cesi and Mattei families. The collection was further enriched by finds from excavations, some of which were carried out in Ludovisi's own garden. He employed Bernini and Algardi to restore and integrate the statues. A fashion grew up for copying the statues and making casts of them: Goethe was able to obtain a cast of the colossal head of Juno when he visited the city (*see p. 356*). His friend Johann Winckelmann, the distinguished German scholar who was considered the greatest expert on Classical works in Rome during the 18th century, made a detailed study of the statues, and the collection continued to grow in the 19th century. In 1883, however, the Villa Ludovisi and its garden were destroyed for building land. In 1901 the state bought 104 pieces of the collection, which include some very fine Greek and Roman works, although their provenance is mostly unknown. The collection is particularly interesting as a reflection of 17th-century taste for the antique, and shows the skill with which so many of the pieces were restored at that time.

Palazzo Altemps is also home to the antiquities collection of the tenor Evan Gorga: many of the pieces were unearthed during building work in the late 19th century.

ALESSANDRO ALGARDI

Algardi (1598–1654) would be Rome's most important sculptor of the 17th century were it not for the dominating presence of Bernini. His studio was large and, under Innocent X, when Bernini was out of favour, Algardi received numerous official commissions. His art is an interesting counterbalance to that of his great contemporary: introspective rather than extrovert; static, more than dynamic; timeless, rather than ephemeral. His innate solemnity (particularly in his fine portraits) also distinguishes him from two other great contemporaries, Francesco Mochi and François Duquesnoy. He was called to Rome in 1625 by Cardinal Ludovico Ludovisi, a fellow Bolognese, and spent the next six years restoring his collection of antique sculpture, imbibing in the process a Classicism that appealed to his sober nature. Many of these statues can be seen in Palazzo Altemps, as well as the *Dadoforo*, which he created from an antique Greek marble torso.

Less adventurous than his contemporaries in varying the surfaces of the marble and in evoking a plasticity from the stone, his pieces can have a glassy frigidity to them—a characteristic he used to superb effect in his portrait bust of Donna Olimpia Maidalchini in the Doria Pamphilj collection. In his greatest work, however, the high-relief of *Leo the Great Arresting the Progress of Attila* (1646–53) in St Peter's, Algardi overcomes this tendency: here, through a vibrant and dramatic surface, he pulls the viewer into this determining moment in Rome's history.

Ground floor

The handsome courtyard **(1)** was begun by Antonio da Sangallo the Elder in 1513–17, continued by Baldassare Peruzzi and completed by Martino Longhi at the end of that century. Some statues which were part of the original Altemps collection, and some very damaged statues which formed part of the Mattei collection, removed from the Villa Celimontana, are displayed under porticoes **(2)**. The *Dacian Prisoner* is carved in *giallo antico*: the black marble face and hands are later alterations.

(3) The Evan Gorga collection of antiquities: Two large rooms off the courtyard (on this floor and on the floor above) display part of the huge collection amassed in the late 19th and early 20th centuries by the tenor Evan Gorga. It was acquired by the state from Gorga in 1950, seven years before he died (he was by then destitute) and is here displayed more or less as Gorga himself classified it. Only about a fifth of Gorga's antiquities (he possesed some 10,000 pieces) is on show but the ingenious arrangement (and video) give a fascinating picture of the objects in bronze, alabaster, glass, *pietre dure*, terracotta, bone, ivory (as well as painted plaster and marble wall veneers, statuettes, inscriptions, coins, architectural fragments, etc.) which he managed to acquire in Rome at a time when so much was being unearthed during the chaotic building activity necessitated when Rome first became capital, and when the Tiber embankments were laid out. The collection is also famous for its musical instruments, now housed in the Museo Nazionale di Strumenti Musicali.

Room 4: In the atrium, a statue of Antoninus Pius, which was in the Mausoleum of Augustus in the 16th century and was restored in 1621, begins the exhibition of pieces from the Ludovisi collection.

Rooms 5–6: Here are displayed a head of Zeus in high relief (2nd century AD) and a bust of Pluto. Many of the portrait busts have been restored. The colossal **bronze head of Marcus Aurelius** is one of the most famous pieces of the collection: the porphyry bust dates from the 4th century AD but the bronze cloak and other additions were made in the 17th century. The portrait of Antinous, although originally Roman, mostly dates from a 17th-century restoration.

Room 7 (Sala della Torre): Part of a medieval tower built on the site of the palace can be seen beneath the floor— hence the room's name. There is a case of exquisite fragments of Roman wall-paintings on a bright red ground found during the excavations (2nd half of the 1st century AD), and a case of 16th–17th-century ceramics also found here.

Room 8 (Salone delle Erme): The room takes its name from six herms from the 2nd century AD. In the centre are an antique vase and a Roman fountain basin in rare Egyptian marble. Also here are two seated statues of Apollo with his lyre.

Room 9: Once the palace entrance. It displays three sculptures, but only the central one is a Roman original.

Room 10: Here is a Roman statue of Athena, but the head, hands, feet and serpent's head are all by Algardi.

Room 11: The statue of Athena is one of the very few copies of the renowned statue made by Pheidias for the Parthenon in Athens to have survived: it was made by an Athenian sculptor called Antiochos (the arms are 17th century).

Room 12: A fine sarcophagus with Dionysiac scenes includes a charming procession with an elephant (AD 190–220). It is very ruined as it was formerly used as a fountain. Also here are two graceful small statues of the seated Muses (1st and 2nd centuries AD); the heads, although ancient, do not belong.

Room 13: The statue of a maenad, probably dating from the 1st century BC, was found in 1777 in Via Prenestina, and two years later was acquired by George Strickland when he was in Rome. It then passed to Thomas Jenkins, a well-known antiquarian and dealer, who restored it, adding the head so that it would impress visitors to his residence in England, Boyton Hall. When it was sold in the 1950s, it returned to Italy and in 1982 was acquired by the Italian state from a private collection, in lieu of taxes.

Room 14: The colossal torso, from the Altemps collection, probably represents Polyphemus or Atlas.

Room 15: The room is filled with a colossal group with Dionysus, a satyr

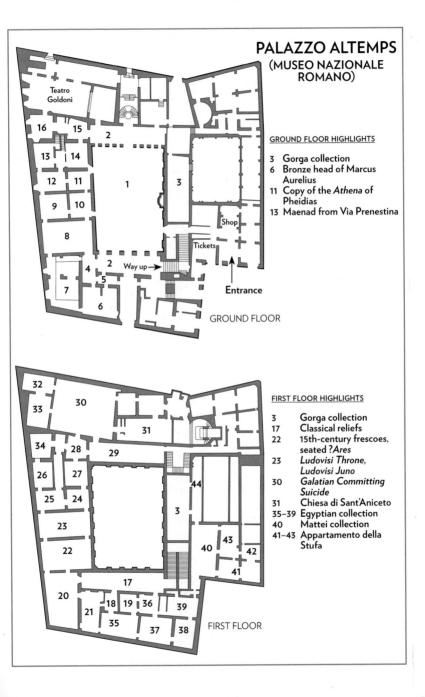

PALAZZO ALTEMPS
(MUSEO NAZIONALE ROMANO)

Teatro Goldoni

16   15   2

13   14

12   11

9   10

8

1   3

Shop

Tickets

4   2   Way up→

5

7

6

Entrance

GROUND FLOOR

GROUND FLOOR HIGHLIGHTS

3   Gorga collection
6   Bronze head of Marcus Aurelius
11   Copy of the *Athena* of Pheidias
13   Maenad from Via Prenestina

32

33   30

31

34   28   29

26   27

25   24

23

22

17

20

18   19   36   39

21

35   37   38

3

44

40   43

42

41

FIRST FLOOR

FIRST FLOOR HIGHLIGHTS

3   Gorga collection
17   Classical reliefs
22   15th-century frescoes, seated ?*Ares*
23   *Ludovisi Throne, Ludovisi Juno*
30   *Galatian Committing Suicide*
31   Chiesa di Sant'Aniceto
35–39 Egyptian collection
40   Mattei collection
41–43 Appartamento della Stufa

and a panther. This was found on the Quirinal hill during the late 16th century. The satyr and torso of Dionysus are mostly original Roman works.

Room 16: The two busts here are of the emperors Lucius Verus and Gallienus.

The **Teatro Goldoni**, which preserves its 17th-century decoration, is usually kept closed: it was one of the first private theatres in Rome, known to have been rebuilt in 1575. After restoration in 1890, it was opened as one of the first cinemas in the city in 1905.

First floor

From the other side of the courtyard, stairs lead up to the first floor. In the **loggia (17)** are important reliefs from the Del Drago and Brancaccio collections. They were known and studied as early as the 15th century, and were published by Winckelmann. The Italian state acquired them in 1964. A relief shows divinities and *Zeus Enthroned*, derived from a work by Pheidias, but with late additions. The relief from the end of a sarcophagus (of uncertain significance), with two female figures, one washing the feet of the other, who is covering her face, was made in the same century. This piece was well known in the Renaissance—drawings of it by Andrea Mantegna and Raphael survive—and the round hole was made when it was adapted for use as a fountain. The relief of a funerary banquet (which includes the dead man's horse) dates from the 4th century BC, and the one which depicts the Dioscuri (Castor and Pollux) and their sister Helen is a Greek work (5th–4th century BC), found in 1885 on the Esquiline hill.

Room 18: This small room contains a kneeling statue of Venus made in the Hadrianic era but derived from a 4th-century BC work.

Room 19: The statue of Osiris (3rd century AD) was found on the Janiculum hill, and the one of Dionysus has traces of gold in his hair.

Room 20: Here a bust of a satyr in grey *bigio* marble, thought to have been restored by Bernini, is displayed on top of a funerary urn and altar from the 1st century AD. The beautiful figure of Hermes, dating from the late 1st or early 2nd century AD, was carefully restored by Algardi, whose workshop probably also restored the statue of Aesculapius (late 2nd century AD) in 1627.

Room 21: Two statues of Bacchus: the one with a panther was made up from antique pieces in the 17th century, and the other dates entirely from the 17th century and was made as a fake Classical work. The satyr dates from the 2nd century AD but the arms are modern.

Room 22: Delightful **15th-century frescoes** (appropriate to a dining room), attributed to the circle of Melozzo da Forlì, show a tapestry covered with wild flowers behind a sideboard on which are displayed plates, ewers and candlesticks which were wedding presents given to Girolamo Riario (nephew of Sixtus IV) and Caterina Sforza when they married in 1477. Riario was assassinated ten years later, having been involved in the Pazzi conspiracy against the Medici in Florence. Nothing daunted, Caterina married Giovanni de' Medici; their son (known as Giovanni delle Bande Nere) was the father of Cosimo I. Caterina was a woman of character (admired by Machiavelli), remembered also for her experiments with alchemy which she recorded in a book of secrets, with recipes for producing medicines, cosmetics and perfumes, as well as household tips.

The **Roman statue of a seated male** is thought to represent Ares. The statue of Achilles was found in the early 17th century and restored by

Bernini. The standing group of *Orestes and Electra* is signed by the Greek artist Menelaus, pupil of Stephanos. Pliny mentions Stephanos as being the assistant of Pasiteles (early 1st century AD). Winckelmann was the first to identify the figures as Orestes with his sister Electra at the tomb of their father Agamemnon.

Room 23: The famous ***Ludovisi Throne*** was found at the end of the 19th century in the Villa Ludovisi.

THE LUDOVISI THRONE

The central subject of the *Ludovisi Throne* is apparently the birth of Aphrodite, who rises from the sea supported by two figures representing the Seasons. It is thought to have been intended for the statue of a divinity, and is usually considered to be a Greek original of the 5th century BC. On the right side is the figure of a young woman sitting clothed on a folded cushion; she is taking grains from a box and burning them in a brazier. On the left side is a naked flute girl, also sitting on a folded cushion, playing a double pipe.

The Throne is, nevertheless, the subject of fascinating debate. Only one other such 'throne' is known: the *Boston Throne*, now widely held to be a fake. The *Ludovisi Throne* has not been so stamped, but its provenance, purpose and iconography continue to bewilder scholars. In form and size it is most like a sarcophagus, yet its iconography is not matched on other funerary monuments. What is more puzzling are a number of apparent illogicalities: the figures are not as naturalistic as one would expect from late Archaic sculpture. Aphrodite's ear is in the wrong place, for example; the anterior arms of the two Seasons are longer than the near arms, and the folds of their garments descend from the near flank and fall on the inside of the anterior ankle. The feet are akin to what we know from vase painting, but not otherwise from sculptural relief. All in all, the mood of the design is impressionistic. It is, indeed, more design than representation, and this, some scholars argue, suggest that it might well be a forgery.

And yet the 5th-century BC bas-reliefs found at the Greek city of Locri in southern Italy bear many stylistic resemblances to the Throne. Locri was a known cult centre of Aphrodite and there is even a claim that its temple has a 'gap' in it, where the Throne could once have been.

Also displayed here are two colossal heads: one of them, the ***Ludovisi Juno***, three times natural size. Winckelmann supposed this to be a Greek work and it was greatly admired by Goethe on his visit to Rome: he had a cast made of it which is now in the Casa di Goethe. Its subject has now been identified as Antonia, mother of the emperor Claudius, who deified her as Augusta after her death. The other colossal head of an acrolith is a Greek original of 480–470 BC, possibly from Locri in southern Italy.

The painted frieze is by Pasquale Cati (1591).

Room 24: This room has another 16th-century frescoed frieze, attributed to Antonio Viviani, and two more colossal heads: that of Hercules is much restored, but that of Hera (late 2nd century or early 1st century BC) is a beautiful work. The sarcophagus fragment (3rd century AD) shows the myth of Phaedra and Hippolytus. When Phaedra, Theseus' second wife, falls in love with her stepson Hippolytus, Theseus kills his son and Phaedra, in desperation, takes her own life. The story is the subject of a famous tragedy by Euripides.

Rooms 25: The *Child with a Goose* is from the Hadrianic period.

Room 26 (Sala della Duchessa): This room, with decorative frescoes, is named after Lucrezia Lante, who married into the Altemps family. The statue of the kneeling *Aphrodite at her Bath* dates from the 1st century BC (the head and arms restored). The group of *Eros and Psyche* was commissioned by Cardinal Ludovisi in the 17th century, reusing various antique fragments.

Room 27: The frieze is by Francesco Allegrini to a design by Antonio Tempesta. The striking red marble relief of the mask of Dionysus, which dates from the time of Hadrian, was used as a wall fountain, hence the two round holes. The two colossal busts and sarcophagus fragment with the *Judgement of Paris* also date from the same period.

Room 28: The pretty frescoes date from 1590. A beautiful marble circular base is displayed, with delicate reliefs of winged dancers from the Augustan period.

Room 29 (Painted Loggia): The charming frescoed decoration, with a pergola and numerous putti with garlands, and an elaborate fountain, dates from 1595. Twelve busts, nine of them of emperors, are displayed here.

Room 30 (Sala Grande del Galata): This room, with a fireplace by Martino Longhi the Elder, takes its name from the dramatic figure of the nude ***Galatian Committing Suicide***, a Roman copy from the time of Julius Caesar (46–44 BC) of an original Greek bronze. It formed part of the same group as the famous *Dying Gaul*, now in the Capitoline Museums. Other fine sculpture here includes a high relief with a head of Mars (2nd century AD; the bust was added in the 16th century) and a splendid huge sarcophagus showing a battle between Romans and barbarians, in excellent condition. It was found in 1621 near the Porta Tiburtina and dates from the 3rd century AD. The fragment of a female head, that of the dead Amazon Erinnyes, dates from the 2nd century AD.

Room 31 (Chiesa di Sant'Aniceto):

This contains the relics of one of the first popes, Anicetus. Its fine decorations in stucco, marble intarsia and fresco survive from the first years of the 17th century, when it was built by Giovanni Angelo Altemps, whose father Roberto had been beheaded (on a trumped up charge of adultery) by order of Pope Sixtus V. The iconography of the frescoes, the most important of which are by Pomarancio, reflect the determination of the family to reinstate the name of Roberto, by emphasising the cult of clemency and making parallels with Anicetus (such as inventing the saint's martyrdom also by decapitation). There are several small chapels and a sacristy, all dating from the early 17th century, adjoining the church.

Room 32: The very fine sarcophagus has battle scenes in high and low relief (AD 170–80). Also here is a statue of a seated man in a toga, signed in Greek (1st century BC); although the head is ancient, it is not the original. The two reliefs date from the 2nd century AD.

Room 33: The sculptural group of a satyr and nymph is a Roman copy of a Greek original (the head of the satyr, added in the 17th century, is attributed to Bernini). The other group, of Pan and Daphnis, dates from the 1st century AD. Also here are statues of two Muses, Urania and Calliope.

At the foot of the stairs (**34**) is the *Dadoforo*, or Torch-bearer, which was created *ex novo* by Algardi from an original antique torso.

Egyptian collection

This group of rooms is entered from Room 20 (and is sometimes kept closed).

Room 35: The splendid bull (the god Apis), made in Egypt, probably from diorite, in the 2nd century BC, was brought to Rome during the Empire and dug up in 1886 on the Esquiline hill.

Room 36 (Sala del Clero Isiaco): The ruined head of Isis (with the attributes of Demeter added) is displayed in the centre, surrounded by heads of priests of the cult of Isis.

Room 37 (right): Black sculptures (in basalt, black granite and diorite) brought from Egypt to decorate the Isaeum Campense (*see p. 181*). This area of the palace became the private residence of the martial poet Gabriele d'Annunzio after his marriage to the Altemps heir, Maria Hardouin di Galles, in 1883.

Room 38 (Sala delle Dei Madri): The marble statue of Isis (with the attributes of Demeter) dates from the 2nd century AD. The head with bas-reliefs of sphinxes and griffins, thought to belong to a statue of Artemis, was found in 2009 during work on Rome's Metro at the foot of the hill of Testaccio near the Tiber, where the ancient Roman port used to be. The room retains its pretty 18th-century decorations.

Room 39 (Sala di Serapide): Here are two small busts of Egyptian divinities, one in antique red marble and the other in alabaster (2nd century AD) and a headless statue of Serapis enthroned with his three-headed dog. Septimius Severus is also shown in the guise of Serapis. It has been suggested that the portrait of a Roman with the attributes of a pharaoh could represent the son of Caesar and Cleopatra.

Room 40 (Sala Mattei): Sculptures from the Mattei collection include numerous antique heads and busts. The sarcophagus front (AD 180), thought to illustrate the Rape of the Sabines (the horses are particularly fine), was reused in the 7th or 8th century, as the medieval carving beneath reveals. The capital which is exhibited on a column of rare coral-coloured breccia marble was carved in the 4th century AD with kneeling female figures, and may come from the Circus of Maxentius.

Appartamento della Stufa

This was once the private apartment of Roberto Altemps and his wife, Cornelia Orsini. Here are displayed the most recent finds in Rome or donations to the state collections.

Room 41: The black-figure krater dates from the 6th century BC and the red-figure kylix from the 4th century BC. Amongst the sculptures, found in excavations as recent as 2011, are fragments in porous limestone, and a head of Germanicus, member of the Julio-Claudian dynasty, who died young and was celebrated for his military victories as well as his moral integrity.

In the small **Room 42** there is a beautiful Roman sarcophagus decorated with pairs of griffins, and a head of Aphrodite, both dating from the 2nd century AD. In **Room 43** the 16th-century heating system (the eponymous '*stufa*') has been exposed beneath the floor and there are traces on the walls of the painted decoration carried out at the same time.

In the **corridor (44)** are eight detached fresco panels from the Pallavicini Rospigliosi collection dating from the 3rd century AD (including a fascinating depiction of a man in a cloak). There are more displays from the **Gorga collection (3;** *see p. 191*). More rooms around the courtyard in this wing of the palace are to be opened.

SANTA MARIA DELLA PACE

In a piazza just west of Piazza Navona is the beautiful church of Santa Maria della Pace (*map p. 654, B2; open Mon, Wed, Sat 9–11.45*). Via della Pace, in front of the church, is a typical old Roman street with *sanpietrini* cobble-stones and rust-coloured houses.

There seems to have been a circular votive chapel here with a fresco of the Madonna (now inside on the high altar), much venerated in the 15th century after a drunken soldier struck it and blood miraculously spurted from its breast. Sixtus IV had the church

SANTA MARIA DELLA PACE

rebuilt in 1480–4, probably by Baccio Pontelli, and renamed it Santa Maria della Pace as a sign of the truce when he pardoned Florence and Lorenzo the Magnificent for their bloody recriminations against the Church, the result of the revenge the Medici took on all those who had been implicated in the Pazzi Conspiracy against them. The pope also advocated peace in Europe, preoccupied as he was with the threat from the Turks (who in 1480 had actually landed in Otranto in southern Italy).

EXTERIOR OF SANTA MARIA DELLA PACE

In 1656 the façade and beautiful semicircular porch with Tuscan columns was erected by Pietro da Cortona (*see p. 341*) for Alexander VII. The aedicule façade with its concave portico clearly inspired Bernini's design for Sant'Andrea al Quirinale. The aedicule itself, with a segmented pediment enclosed within a triangular pediment, seems to borrow from the interior of Michelangelo's Medici Chapel in Florence. The design is deliberately theatrical, even to the 'stage-wings' which accommodate the split in the street on either side of the church. Unfortunately, Pietro da Cortona's design for a delightful little piazza and surrounding area was never completed.

On either side of the entrance are plaques recording the levels of the Tiber floodwaters in 1530 and 1598.

THE INTERIOR

The wealthy Chigi family of Siena provided Rome with two great patrons of the arts: the papal banker Agostino Chigi, and his great-nephew Fabio, who later became Pope Alexander VII. Agostino Chigi commissioned Raphael to decorate the sumptuous Villa Farnesina and to create the famous Chigi Chapel in Santa Maria del Popolo. Around the same time (c. 1514), for the same patron, Raphael decorated the **Chigi Chapel** here, the first chapel on the right as you enter. The splendid frescoes above the arch, against a dark ground, show the Cumaean, Persian, Phrygian and Tiburtine Sibyls, to whom the future is being revealed by angels. Their varying reactions of awe and wonder are beautifully conveyed in look and gesture. Although probably the least-known works by this great painter in the city, they are amongst his most remarkable. Above them are four Prophets (Daniel, David, Jonah and Hosea), by Raphael's pupil Timoteo Viti. On the altar is a fine bronze of the *Deposition* by Cosimo Fancelli.

In the **Ponzetti Chapel** opposite is a delightful fresco by Baldassare Peruzzi, who was born in Siena but was clearly influenced by Raphael when he came to work in Rome (and he collaborated with him in the Vatican Stanze). This work, *The Virgin, St Bridget and St Catherine*, with the donor Cardinal Ferdinando Ponzetti, has echoes of the artist's Sienese background. Peruzzi also painted the small frescoes of Old Testament subjects in the apse vault and the rather mannered *Presentation in the Temple* in the sanctuary. He was also an important architect (he built the Villa Farnesina) and took over responsibility from Raphael for the work on rebuilding St Peter's. At the sides of the chapel are the exquisite little tombs of the Ponzetti family (1505 and 1509), with delicately carved decoration and four busts in roundels: the two on the right are Beatrice and Lavinia, sisters who died of the plague when young children. Cardinal Ferdinando himself, a former physician-turned-prelate, died after being brutally mistreated during the Sack of Rome in 1527. He had been Innocent VIII's doctor. According to Gregorovius (*History of the City of Rome in the Middle Ages*; 1900–1), the old man was first robbed, then 'with his hands bound behind his back was dragged through Rome. Four months later he died in misery in his empty house'.

The **second south chapel** was designed for Angelo Cesi by Antonio da Sangallo the Younger, and has very elaborate marble decoration by Simone Mosca (1540–2). The Cesi tombs and sculptures are by Vincenzo de' Rossi. The frescoes of nudes in the window lunette above are by Rosso Fiorentino (the only work in Rome by this Florentine Mannerist). The **second north chapel** has a much-darkened altarpiece of the *Madonna and Saints* by Marcello Venusti, whose friend Michelangelo may have supplied the design. The marble decoration comes from the Temple of Jupiter on the Capitoline hill.

The nave opens out into an **octagon**, well lit by the lantern above. The cupola was probably designed by Antonio da Sangallo the Younger, with stuccoes by Pietro da Cortona. Above the **high altar** (by Carlo Maderno) is the miraculous image of the *Madonna della Pace* (*see above*), and here there are paintings of the *Nativity* and *Annunciation* by Passignano. In the chapels here are a *Baptism of Christ* by Orazio Gentileschi, and an *Adoration of the Shepherds* by Sermoneta. In the chapel with a 15th–16th-century Cross, the gilded marble reredos of 1490 commemorates Innocent VIII.

THE CLOISTERS

The cloisters, where exhibitions are now held, were commissioned in 1504 by Cardinal Oliviero Carafa and are among Donato Bramante's finest works in Rome. They have an Ionic pilastered arcade with a Corinthian trabeate loggia above—the columns of the loggia rise from the centres of the arches in arcade.

A WALK THROUGH THE OLD STREETS NEAR PIAZZA NAVONA

This walk explores narrow streets typical of old Rome, passing interesting palaces as well as two important churches in the peaceful district around Piazza Navona.

PIAZZA PASQUINO, A FEW STEPS OUT OF the southwest end of Piazza Navona, is in fact just a busy little open space where several narrow roads converge and cars are always parked, so the worn, mutilated statue on one corner is easy to miss. But ever since it was placed here in 1501 this has been one of the best-loved statues of the Romans, always known as '**Pasquino**'. Apparently named after a tailor who lived in the vicinity, it is a fragment of a marble group thought to represent Menelaus with the body of

Patroclus, a copy of a Hellenistic work of the Pergamene school which may once have decorated the Stadium of Domitian (whose outline Piazza Navona follows). When it was in a much better state, Bernini admired it as the finest Classical work he had seen. It is the most famous of Rome's 'talking' statues, and slogans ridiculing contemporary Italian politicians are still often attached to it, although they are now sometimes rather too long and complicated and have lost a little of their sense of fun and irony.

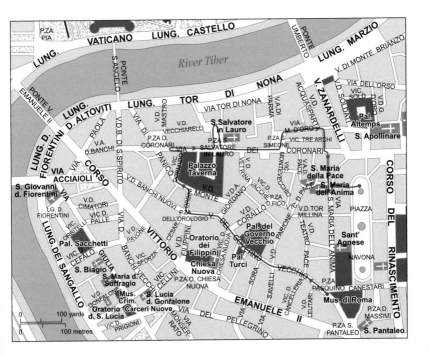

ROME'S 'TALKING' STATUES

The tailor Pasquino is thought to have originated the custom of attaching witty or caustic comments on topical subjects to the pedestal of this statue, a means of public satire which thus came to be known as a *pasquinade*. This effective (and anonymous) way of getting at the city governors, and in particular of criticising the papacy, was much in vogue in the 17th century before the days of the free press. Many printing houses and bookshops opened in the vicinity of the statue of Pasquino.

Pasquino was just one of the 'talking' statues in the city: labels were attached to various others so that they could carry on 'conversations'. Madama Lucrezia, a colossal antique bust now in Piazza San Marco, conversed with the statue of a river-god called Marforio, which is now in the courtyard of Palazzo Nuovo on the Capitoline hill. Other statues included 'Abbot Luigi', a statue of a Roman in a toga, which is still outside the church of Sant'Andrea della Valle; and the Facchino, the bust of a 16th-century water vendor in Via Lata. The only other 'talking' statue which survived as such up until a few years ago was Babuino, a very damaged Roman figure of a reclining Silenus, in Via del Babuino. Stendhal noted in 1816: 'What the people of Rome desire above all else is a chance to show their strong contempt for the powers that control their destiny, and to laugh at their expense: hence the dialogues between "Pasquino" and "Marforio".' In 2014 and 2015, during the *'Mafia Capitale'* scandal concerning links to organised crime among Roman public officials, Pasquino became extremely loquacious.

With your back to Pasquino, the narrow **Via del Governo Vecchio**, an ancient winding papal thoroughfare with many traces of the early Renaissance, leads straight ahead. It now has a bustling atmosphere, with numerous small cafés and restaurants and a miscellany of shops selling all kinds of merchandise from wine to old clothes, and there is even a motorbike repair garage along its way. The palace at no. 104, built for the old Confraternity of the Stigmata of St Francis and now in very poor condition, has numerous roundels with portrait heads in profile, tied to the façade with ribbons.

The street is named after **Palazzo del Governo Vecchio**, the palace at no. 39, built in 1473 by Cardinal Stefano Nardini, who was made Governor of Rome by Paul II. When the residence of the Governor of Rome was moved in the 18th century to Palazzo Madama, this palace was referred to as the 'old' palace of the Governor. It has a splendid Renaissance portal, but appears to have been abandoned. Opposite is the beautiful little **Palazzo Turci** (no. 123). Its perfect proportions and lovely architectural details make it clear to see why it was once attributed to Bramante. It stands on its own between two narrow streets and has arched doorways and five storeys of round-arched windows with carved stone frames. It has lovely brickwork and a handsome inscription recording its first owner, Pietro Turci, and the date 1500.

Beyond, on the left corner of Via della Chiesa Nuova, is a grand 18th-century tabernacle with a modern request by a local inhabitant not to throw rubbish beneath the framed image of the Madonna. A plaque above records the fact that Pope Clement X widened the street here for the Holy Year of 1675.

Beyond the pretty little Caffè Novecento (at no. 12; a bistro and tearoom which has delicious snacks, open until 9pm) is **Piazza dell'Orologio**, with its two grand palaces: it is overlooked on the left by a façade of the Palazzo dei Filippini (*see p. 217*), with its clock-tower by Borromini. Another elaborate tabernacle surrounded by angels on the corner faces a palace with a grand portal decorated with a scallop shell and griffins. Via degli Orsini, with a handsome palace (in the courtyard of which you can see a wall fountain), leads up to the huge 18th-century **Palazzo Taverna** with a very impressive entrance archway, beyond which rises a delightful monumental fountain by Antonio Casoni (1618) in a green topiary niche in the court. Much of the 1996 film based on Henry James' *The Portrait*

of a Lady was set here. The palace stands on **Monte Giordano**, a tiny, apparently artificial, hillock that was already inhabited in the 12th century. It takes its name from Giordano Orsini, whose legendary fortress stood here in the 13th century. Dante mentions the 'Monte' (*Inferno, XXVIII, 12*) in his description of the pilgrims crossing the Ponte Sant'Angelo on the occasion of the Jubilee of 1300 (in fact as you continue along Via del Panico, the bridge and one of Bernini's angels come into view). The Orsini continued to own the castle until 1688, and the buildings, still crowded together, betray their medieval origins.

Take Vicolo Domizio now (right), which skirts the palace (passing a huge workshop where replicas of Classical marbles are made) and descends to **Via dei Coronari**, a beautiful, straight Renaissance street on the line of the Roman Via Recta. It is still famous for its antique shops, many of which sell works in marble. The little house at no. 122–3 to the left, once the home of a certain Giuseppe Lezzani, is one of several places in the city where Raphael is believed to have stayed. Going back right, carved into the lintel of no. 148, is the inscription TUA PUTA QUE TU TE FACIS ('Consider what you do to be yours'). This was once the home of the papal breviator Prospero Mochi.

Walking east, you soon come to a piazza with the huge church of **San Salvatore in Lauro**, with a rather heavy Palladian interior, the best work of the Bolognese architect Mascherino (1594). The second north chapel contains relics of Padre Pio of Pietrelcina (canonised in 2002), including his gloves, stole and tunic. Images of this immensely popular figure can be seen today in almost every church in Italy; he is famed for his stigmata and also for his experience of transverberation, a phenomenon known to St Teresa of Avila and described by St John of the Cross as the puncturing of the soul by a seraph, using a fiery dart. Bernini's celebrated *Ecstasy of St Teresa* shows precisely this moment (*see p. 321*). Pio's elaborate burial place in Pietrelcina (San Giovanni Rotondo), with his golden tomb, has become one of the great pilgrimage destinations in the Christian world.

To the left of the church, at no. 15, is the entrance to the fine Renaissance cloister, now the premises of the Confraternità dei Piceni, founded in 1633 by prelates from the Marche.

In a picturesque alleyway on the other side of Via dei Coronari, below a flight of steps which leads up to the red-curtained door of a little theatre, Pizza del Teatro, with a few tables outside, serves especially good (but not particularly cheap) pizzas and they also run an ice cream shop and *pasticceria* next door (*Via dei Coronari 65*). The ices are homemade with the organic ingredients displayed in the shop window. There is a particularly welcoming shop at no. 195 (Lisa Corti), selling colourful household products and clothes made in fabrics designed in Italy but made in India by artisans using traditional techniques.

Via dei Coronari runs through **Piazzetta di San Simeone**, with its fountain. On the square stands Palazzo Lancellotti, with an imposing portal, begun by Francesco da Volterra and finished by Carlo Maderno. On the lower corner of Vicolo di San Simeone there is a lovely old marble column with a stone bench and the palace here has remains

of beautiful graffiti decoration. Next to it, Palazzo Milesi (no. 7) has a frescoed façade by Polidoro da Caravaggio, a very rare survival of such decoration in Rome. Opposite, no. 21 is another good palace, where the Accademia dei Lincei was founded in 1603 (its seat is now in Palazzo Corsini). Galileo was a Lincean. Just beyond, on the corner of **Via della Maschera d'Oro**, is a plain little house, apparently dating from the 15th century, with an old Doric column embedded into its masonry. It belonged to a certain 'Fiammetta', known to have been the mistress of Cesare Borgia. From here you can return to Via dei Coronari along the Vicolo di San Trifone, which crosses the medieval Vicolo dei Tre Archi and then continues as a very narrow dark lane.

Just before the end of Via dei Coronari, Vicolo delle Volpe leads right with a good view of a tower crowned with a green and yellow steeple. This belongs to the German church of **Santa Maria dell'Anima** (*open 7.30–1 & 2–6 except Sat morning; if the main door is closed, entrance is through a pretty little courtyard behind the church at Vicolo della Pace 20*), rebuilt in 1500–23 on the site of an oratory erected here by a German member of the papal guard next to a hospice he founded for Germans in the city. The façade may have been designed by Giuliano da Sangallo. In the triangular tympanum above the central door is a cast of the Virgin attributed to Andrea Sansovino, a copy of a highly venerated *Madonna between Two Souls in Purgatory*, which was formerly in the church and was the origin of its name (the original is kept in the sacristy). The interior has an unusual plan, derived from late Gothic German churches. The paintings in the vault and on the walls are by Ludovico Seitz (1875–82), who also designed the stained glass window over the central door.

In the first two chapels on either side of the nave are two paintings (1617–18) by Carlo Saraceni, a Venetian painter who worked most of his life in Rome and has evident elements of the Caravaggesque style. They portray episodes from the life of two northern European saints: on the left is St Lambert, martyred at the altar of his church at Liège, a very dramatic scene beautifully painted; on the right is St Benno, Bishop of Meissen who, as a supporter of Pope Gregory VII against the Emperor Henry IV, threw the keys of Meissen Cathedral into the Elbe to prevent the emperor from entering the church. Here he is shown with the fisherman who returned the keys to him, having found them in a fish caught in the river. The second south chapel has two funerary monuments with half-bust portraits of the deceased kneeling at their prie-dieux by Ercole Ferrata, a skilled follower of both Bernini and Algardi (there are clear echoes of the Fonseca monument in San Lorenzo in Lucina). The sculpture of the *Pietà* in the fourth chapel is, in turn, clearly based on Michelangelo's famous group in St Peter's: it is by the Florentine artist Lorenzetto (who executed Raphael's tomb in the Pantheon). On two of the nave pillars are little funeraray monuments with charming pairs of putti, typical works by François Duquesnoy.

In the sanctuary, over the high altar, is a *Holy Family with Saints* (1524) by Giulio Romano, one of his best

altarpieces in Rome. He was Raphael's favoured pupil and collaborated with him at the Vatican, but is above all famous for his work as architect and decorator in Mantua. On the right is the magnificent tomb of Hadrian VI (d. 1523). Born in Utrecht, he was a learned professor who, after his unexpected election, tried to reform the Church in answer to Luther's criticisms. He lacked support in his short papacy of under two years and could do little to resolve the problems of the Church. The tomb, which was designed by Baldassare Peruzzi, has sculptures by Michelangelo Senese and Niccolò Tribolo. The inscription on it reads 'How important, even for the best of men, are the times in which he finds himself'. He was the last non-Italian pope until Pope John Paul II.

The fourth chapel on the north side contains frescoes and an altarpiece of the *Deposition* by Francesco Salviati, amongst the last works (c. 1560) by this very able Florentine painter who also worked extensively in Rome. The head of Christ is bent dramatically in true Mannerist style.

The short street in front of the church leads back into Piazza Navona, where you can sit and enjoy a coffee (even though you will pay a lot extra for your magnificent surroundings). But if you are particularly hungry, your best bet is to cross Piazza Navona into the (unattractive) Corso Rinascimento, where at no. 89 the **Pasticceria Cinque Lune** produces excellent traditional Roman cakes using light flaky pastry and ingredients such as honey and cherries.

Caravaggio in Rome

Although paintings by Caravaggio are to be found all over the city, those in two churches just a few steps apart near Piazza Navona are among his finest.

C aravaggio's works were largely ignored in the 18th century, when the French school was in vogue and he was considered too realistic and 'modern'. Nineteenth-century travellers to the city rarely mention him, but he was 'rediscovered' in the 1950s, after an exhibition in Milan and the publication of numerous studies of his paintings. His works are now considered amongst the great 'sights' of Rome. San Luigi dei Francesi usually has many visitors (it now has a loud-speaker asking them to be quiet); Sant'Agostino is usually a little more peaceful.

SAN LUIGI DEI FRANCESI

Map p. 654, B2. Open 10–12.30 & 3–6.45. Closed Thur afternoon.

This is the French national church in Rome (1518–89). The façade, attributed to Giacomo della Porta, has two superimposed orders of equal height. The interior was heavily encrusted with marble and decorated with white and gilded stucco to a design by Antoine Dérizet (1756–64). The **Contarelli Chapel** (the fifth in the north aisle; *coin light*) contains three famous and very well-preserved paintings of scenes from the life of St Matthew by Caravaggio, painted for this chapel in 1597–1603. This was Caravaggio's first ever public commission, executed for the heirs of Cardinal Matthieu Cointrel. The apostle Matthew was chosen as the subject clearly because he was Cointrel's titular saint. The *Calling of St Matthew* is a beautifully balanced Classical composition. It was painted to face the canvas of *St Matthew's Martyrdom*. The altarpiece of *St Matthew and the Angel* shows the angel seeming to fall right out of the sky (which was to be a recurrent theme in Caravaggio's later works). The colour red, always greatly favoured by Caravaggio, is much in evidence and Caravaggio's contemporaries would have been astonished to see the Biblical figures dressed in contemporary clothes. These paintings are considered by many scholars to be his masterpiece, dating from his early Classical and luminous period, devoid of the intense, sometimes overpowering, drama of his later works. They were painted at a time when Caravaggio was beginning to be sought-after as an artist: at the same time as this he worked on his paintings of St Peter and St Paul for Santa Maria del Popolo. The vault of this Contarelli Chapel has late Mannerist frescoes by Cavaliere d'Arpino, who was Caravaggio's master.

CARAVAGGIO

Michelangelo Merisi da Caravaggio (1571–1610) was always known simply as Caravaggio, since it was thought he had been born in the town of the same name near Bergamo in Lombardy, although he may in fact have been born in Milan. He was the most important painter in Italy in the 17th century and made Rome the most influential centre of art in the country during his lifetime. He also had a profound influence on a large school of painters who came to be known as the *Caravaggeschi*, and the great number of copies of his works which exist demonstrate how much he was appreciated for his novel ideas. His works are characterised by a striking use of light and shadow, and for their dramatic realism and intensity of imagery. He was able to reduce images to the essentials, making use of brightly illuminated colours. He produced superb still-lifes and genre scenes, and (mostly after 1601) numerous paintings of religious subjects.

Caravaggio came to Rome around 1592, and established himself rapidly as an artist of note. He had a violent temperament and, in 1606, after a quarrel with his opponent in a ball game, murdered him. He was condemned to death and forced to flee Rome. He went in disguise to Naples before setting sail for Malta, where he became a Knight of Malta but was caught and imprisoned for a time. He escaped to Sicily in 1608. He still managed to paint, however, and several of his masterpieces of this period are preserved on both islands. Believing he would be able to obtain the pope's pardon he decided to return to Rome, but died on the way back, not yet 40 years old, probably of malaria contracted on the beach near Porto Ercole.

Among Caravaggio's patrons were Vincenzo Giustiniani and Cardinal Scipione Borghese (a number of masterpieces painted for the latter still hang in the Galleria Borghese). As well as his paintings in the two churches described here, and in Santa Maria del Popolo, his other masterpieces in Rome are now preserved in the Galleria Doria Pamphilj, the Pinacoteca Capitolina and the Galleria Corsini. Apart from his numerous Italian followers, the influence of his style can be seen in other great painters such as Velázquez and Rembrandt.

On the first pillar in the north aisle is a monument to the French 17th-century painter Claude Lorrain, who worked in Rome, by another, less well-known French artist, François Lemoyne, who was in Rome in 1723. Against the first pillar in the south aisle is a monument to the French who fell in the Siege of Rome in 1849 (*see p. 28*). The **second south chapel** was frescoed c. 1614 with scenes from the life of St Cecilia (damaged by restoration), by the Bolognese painter Domenichino, who spent most of his life in Rome where he was much influenced by Annibale Carracci—these are among his best-known early works. The altarpiece is a copy by Guido Reni of Raphael's famous *Ecstasy of St Cecilia* now in the Pinacoteca in Bologna.

The decorations in the **fourth south chapel** celebrate the conversion to Catholicism of Clovis, King of the Franks, who was baptised at Rheims by St Remigius in 496. They date from the 16th century and are Mannerist works by Jacopino del Conte, Pellegrino Tibaldi and Girolamo Sermoneta. The **high altarpiece** is an *Assumption of the Virgin* by Francesco Bassano.

PALAZZO GIUSTINIANI

Nearly opposite the church is the orange Palazzo Giustiniani, designed by Girolamo Fontana; the main doorway is by Borromini. The palace was acquired in 1590 by the wealthy banker Vincenzo Giustiniani, Caravaggio's patron, who owned 13 of his works, including the first version of *St Matthew and the Angel* painted for the Contarelli Chapel in San Luigi dei Francesi but which was rejected (it was subsequently taken to Berlin where it perished in the Second World War). Giustiniani also kept his important collection of antique sculpture here, but it was sadly dispersed in the early 19th century. The palace is now the official residence of the President of the Italian Senate.

SANT'AGOSTINO

Map p. 654, B1. Open 7–12 & 4–7.

The church of Sant'Agostino was built for Cardinal d'Estouteville by Giacomo da Pietrasanta (1479–83). The severely plain façade is one of the earliest of the Renaissance. The church is dedicated to St Augustine, author of the *Confessions*, whose mother, St Monica, is buried here. The interior was renovated by Luigi Vanvitelli (1750).

In the first north chapel is the ***Madonna di Loreto***, or *Madonna dei Pellegrini* (*coin-operated light on the left*), commissioned for this altar from Caravaggio in 1604 by Ermete Cavalletti. It is one of the most beautiful Caravaggio paintings in the city: the graceful figure of the Madonna appears at the door of her house to show the blessing Child to two kneeling peasants who have come on a pilgrimage. According to legend, in 1294 the *Santa Casa*, or House of the Virgin, was miraculously transported by angels from Nazareth to near Rijeka in Croatia, and from there across the Adriatic to a laurel wood in the Marche. This place became known as Loreto (from the word for a laurel grove) and is still one of the great pilgrimage shrines of the Catholic world. As in many of Caravaggio's works, the iconography is unusual: in most other paintings of this subject the house itself is shown being transported through the sky. Here instead the focus is on the human element, and there is a powerful sense of the burden Mary bore and of the sorrows she was to endure. The Child by his size seems about four years old, and must be heavy for her to carry. This literal burden suggests the metaphorical one.

Pietro Gagliardi frescoed the vault and the five prophets on the nave pilasters in 1855 to accompany the splendid ***Prophet Isaiah* by Raphael**, frescoed on the third pillar on the north side. This was commissioned by the Humanist scholar Giovanni

Goritz in 1512 for his funerary monument, and shows how much the painter was influenced by Michelangelo's frescoes in the Sistine Chapel. It was restored by Daniele da Volterra. Beneath it is a lovely *Madonna and Child with St Anne*, sculpted from a single block of marble by Andrea Sansovino.

At the west end is the so-called **Madonna del Parto** by Andrea's pupil Jacopo Sansovino (1521), a greatly venerated statue and the object of innumerable votive offerings from expectant mothers. The two 17th-century angels holding stoups are by Antonio Raggi.

In the south aisle, the first chapel contains small **paintings by Marcello Venusti**. He became a close friend of Michelangelo's and helped look after the great artist in his old age in Rome. Michelangelo admired Venusti's skills as a painter and was pleased to have him make copies from his works or use his designs. He became godfather to his first son, named Michelangelo. Today altarpieces by Venusti can be seen in many Roman churches, as well as in the Galleria Doria Pamphilj. He often adopted a very unusual enamel-like technique, and his painting on slate of *St Catherine*, over the altar, is particularly interesting, with delicate shades of pink and red predominant. The second chapel has the **Madonna della Rosa**, a good copy by Avanzino Nucci of the original painting by Raphael, which was stolen from Loreto and never recovered. This delightful work depicts the Madonna playing with the Child, with roses scattered on his bed. The altarpiece in the third south chapel, the *Ecstasy of St Rita*, is a 17th-century work by Giacinto Brandi (he also painted the altarpiece in the fifth north chapel). In the south transept is the **Chapel of St Augustine**, with an altarpiece of the saint between St John the Baptist and St Paul the Hermit by Guercino and side panels by his school. The chapel is decorated with 18th-century stuccoes and contains the Baroque tomb of Cardinal Renato Imperiali by Paolo Posi.

On the **high altar** (1628), below two kneeling angels designed by Bernini, is a Byzantine *Madonna* from Constantinople (sadly too small to see from a distance).

In the chapel to the left of the choir is the **tomb of St Monica**, mother of St Augustine. Monica was born in Carthage, where she lived as the long-suffering wife of a drunken, debauched husband. He was also a pagan: his wife's Christian piety both irritated him and made him slightly in awe of her. After her husband's death she followed Augustine to Italy, and it was through her that he was baptised (in Milan). She died suddenly in 387 in a hostel at Ostia, from where she was about to set sail to return to Africa with Augustine (a fragment of her tombstone is preserved in the church of Santa Aurea at Ostia Antica; *see p. 542*). Her relics were bought to this church from Ostia in 1430 and in 1455 the Humanist Maffeo Vegio commissioned the tomb with its serene effigy (attributed to Isaia da Pisa), but the rest was dismantled in an 18th-century restoration. The Roman sarcophagus is held to be the saint's original tomb. Four statues of **Doctors of the Church**, which belonged to the monument, are now in the little vestibule at the north door.

The chapel in the **north transept** has a marble group of *St Thomas Distributing Alms*, finished in the 17th century by Ercole Ferrata. The next little chapel was entirely decorated by Giovanni Lanfranco (1616–19) with a vault fresco and three paintings.

The **second north chapel** was designed by Bernini in 1645.

Sumptuous Churches of the Counter-Reformation

Three great churches of the Counter-Reformation stand on
Corso Vittorio Emanuele II, once the site of four ancient Republican temples.

The three churches of the Gesù, Sant'Andrea della Valle and the Chiesa Nuova were built in the 16th century for the most important new religious orders founded in the Counter-Reformation, and it is interesting to compare their gorgeous decorations, funded by wealthy clerics.

ROME AND THE COUNTER-REFORMATION

In 1527, when Pope Clement VII sided with Francis I of France against the Holy Roman Emperor Charles V, Charles allowed troops of mercenaries to sack Rome. For eight days the drunken soldiery ravaged a defenceless city, while the pope cowered in Castel Sant'Angelo. The cruelty and blasphemy of the rabble exceeded all bounds and the horror of the sack was interpreted as God's vengeance on the evils of the age. It made a mockery of the optimism of the High Renaissance. Rome lost its prestige as a centre of humanism and its population fell to around 30,000. This humiliation for Clement VII, as well as attacks on the papacy by Martin Luther—who had visited Rome in 1511—were the prelude to the Counter-Reformation. The Farnese pope Paul III recognised the urgency of reforming the Church and the cardinals he created were often scholars. He upheld the symbolic significance of Rome as the 'Holy City' and papal prestige was re-established when he made peace with Charles V and the Emperor entered Rome in triumph in 1536. During Paul's reign the Council of Trent was convoked (in 1545), which undertook to reform the Church and deal with the Protestant threat. Further sessions were held under his successor Paul IV, who increased the powers of the Inquisition. Gregory XIII's reign saw the restoration of numerous churches and the opening of new ones, notably the Gesù. Sixtus V did more than any of his predecessors to improve and adorn the city in celebration of the Catholic Church.

The Jesuit Order was founded by Ignatius Loyola in 1534 and, after 1540 when Paul III approved it, it became an extremely important part of the Counter-Reformation movement. In 1585 the Jesuit Collegio Romano was founded by another Spaniard, St Francis Borgia, third in succession after Ignatius Loyola as General of the Jesuits. Its pupils were to include eight popes in later centuries: Urban VIII, Innocent X, Clement IX, Clement X, Innocent XII, Clement XI, Innocent XIII and Clement XII.

THE GESÙ

Map p. 654, C2. Open 7–12.30 & 4–7.30.

The Gesù, or the Church of the Most Sacred Name of Jesus (*Santissimo Nome di Gesù*), is the principal Jesuit church in Rome and the prototype of the sumptuous style to which the order has given its name and which was important to the subsequent development of Baroque church design. It was built between 1568 and 1575 at the expense of Cardinal Alessandro Farnese. The façade is by Giacomo della Porta, who also completed the cupola, planned by Vignola. There are always worshippers here and confessions are heard throughout the day, so that the church retains an atmosphere of genuine sanctity. The singing of the *Te Deum* on 31st December is a magnificent traditional ceremony.

THE GESÙ

The heavily decorated interior by Vignola has a longitudinal plan, with an aisleless nave and lateral chapels: this design provided a huge space for the faithful to attend sermons, and gave especial prominence to the high altar. The architecture perfectly serves the ideas of the Counter-Reformation: while Protestant Europe was destroying images and stripping churches, Rome was responding with ceremony as theatre,

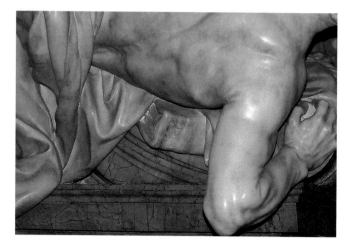

THE GESÙ
Pierre Legros' statue group of *Religion Triumphing over Heresy* shows Protestant
books being destroyed. In the detail shown here, the name of Martin Luther
can just be picked out on the book's spine.

concentrating attention to the place where the mystery of the Mass was celebrated. The idea of inserting a row of *coretti* (little niches like opera-boxes, from which spectators could enjoy the services) above the side chapels was thereafter frequently reused.

The **presbytery and high altar**, sumptuously decorated with coloured marbles, were redesigned in 1840 by Antonio Sarti when the huge altarpiece of Cardinal Roberto Bellarmine was destroyed, but his bust by Bernini was preserved and given a Neoclassical setting (in a niche left of the altar). Bellarmine was a devout Jesuit with firm ideas about the powers of rulers. He antagonised James I of England by refusing to recognise the Divine Right of Kings. In Rome he clung staunchly to the view that the pope had only 'indirect' temporal authority. In matters of dogma he was a pragmatist rather than a zealot. Knowing that the Church's position was immovable, he advised Galileo not to be too vocal in his support for Copernican theory. The two pretty little domed chapels on either side of the main apse were decorated by the Jesuit artist Giuseppe Valeriani just after the dedication of the church.

The transepts have two of the most sumptuous altars in the city. The **altar-tomb of St Ignatius**, founder of the Jesuit Order, is by the Jesuit lay brother Andrea Pozzo with the help of many assistants (1695–1700) and is resplendent with marble and gilded bronze; the columns are encrusted with lapis lazuli and bronze decorations. Above is a group of the Trinity, with a terrestrial globe also covered with lapis lazuli. In front of the altar is a magnificent balustrade, and at the sides are marble groups: *Religion Triumphing over Heresy* by Legros (right), and *Barbarians Adoring the Faith* by Jean-Baptiste Théodon (left). The chapel opposite commemorates the great

Spanish missionary **St Francis Xavier**, who was a companion of St Ignatius Loyola. It was designed by Pietro da Cortona and Carlo Fontana, and the altarpiece showing the saint's death by Carlo Maratta is based on a sketch by Pietro da Cortona. An arm of the saint is preserved in a silver gilt reliquary. It was removed from his body (which is preserved in Goa, which he evangelised) and brought to Rome in 1614.

The more sober marble decoration in the **nave** dates from 1858–61. The side chapels were decorated by some of the most important artists working in Rome at the time the church was consecrated in 1584. These include Agostino Ciampelli, Federico Zuccari (in the third south chapel, which has four carved festoons from the Baths of Trajan), Ventura Salimbeni, Francesco Bassano and Pomarancio (who frescoed two of the chapels on the north side). The elegant sacristy (now used as a chapel) by Girolamo Rainaldi also dates from this time.

On the **ceiling vault** is a superb fresco of the *Triumph of the Name of Jesus*, a remarkably original work with marvellous effects of foreshortening, the masterpiece of Baciccia (*an angled mirror on a trolley allows you to admire it without craning your neck*). Carried out in 1672–83, it marks one of the high points of Roman Baroque painting. It illustrates the Jesuit doctrine, taken from St Paul's Epistle to the Philippians: 'that at the name of Jesus every knee should bow...and that every tongue should confess that Jesus Christ is Lord.' The 'Name' is represented by a monogram rising towards a white Heaven and surrounded by a choir of angels, saints and illustrious personages (including Cardinal Roberto Bellarmine; *see above*) and St Philip Neri (*see p. 215*). Beneath the black clouds the demons can be seen tumbling about with their legs flying. Baciccia also painted the frescoes of the dome and the apse (*Worship of the Holy Lamb*) and he designed the stucco decoration, although this was executed by Antonio Raggi and Leonardo Retti. Baciccia's career centred on Rome, where he was a favourite painter in ecclesiastical circles (he painted many portraits of cardinals, some of which are now in Palazzo Corsini and the Museo di Roma) and patrician families. He was befriended by Bernini, whose portrait he painted (now in Palazzo Barberini) and he provided the altarpiece above Bernini's famous tomb effigy of Lodovica Albertoni in San Francesco a Ripa. Other altarpieces by him are to be found in several churches of Rome, but he is best remembered for this ceiling, the details and design of which can also be studied at close range in his exquisite painted sketch for it which survives in the Galleria Spada.

Entered from Piazza del Gesù 45 (*open Mon–Sat 4–6; holidays 10–12*) are the **rooms where St Ignatius lived** from 1544 to his death in 1556. There are mementoes, paintings and documents.

AREA SACRA DI LARGO ARGENTINA

Between the Gesù and Sant'Andrea della Valle, behind railings on Largo di Torre Argentina (*map p. 654, B2*), are the ruins of an impressive group of four Republican temples, identified only by letters as their dedications are still conjectural. **Temple A**, thought to have been dedicated to Juturna, is peripteral and hexastyle; most of the tufa columns and stylobate are preserved. In the Middle Ages the church of St Nicholas was built over it: its apses can still be seen. The circular **Temple B** was dedicated to Fortuna (the head of its colossal cult statue is in the Centrale Montemartini). It is the most recent temple and six of its columns survive, as well as the original flight of steps and the altar. The area just behind it is identified as the site of the murder of Caesar (*see p. 220*). Between Temple A and Temple B were the offices of the city's water distribution authority, the Statio Aquarum. **Temple C**, the oldest of the four, possibly dedicated to Feronia, an ancient Italic telluric deity, lies at a lower level; it dates from the end of the 4th or the beginning of the 3rd century BC. In the Imperial era the cella was rebuilt and the columns and podium were covered with stucco. The altar, with an inscription relating to c. 180 BC, was discovered in 1935; even this was a replacement of an older altar. **Temple D**, in travertine, is the largest; it has not been completely excavated as part of it is under Via Florida, to the south. It may have been sacred to the *lares permarini*, patron divinities of mariners.

Since 1994 the large cat colony here has been looked after by a voluntary association which has its headquarters in an underground shelter beside the temples and welcomes visitors. About 450 cats are abandoned every year in Rome and many of them find refuge here (*see romancats.com*).

SANT'ANDREA DELLA VALLE

Map p. 654, B2. Open 7–12 & 4–8.

The church of Sant'Andrea della Valle was begun in 1591 and financed by Cardinal Alfonso Gesualdo, for the Order of the Theatines, founded in 1524 by Giampietro Carafa (afterwards Paul IV). The architects included Giacomo della Porta and Pier Paolo Olivieri. Building was continued by Carlo Maderno, who crowned it with a fine dome, the highest in Rome after that of St Peter's. Maderno also designed the pretty fountain outside, decorated with an eagle and a dragon. The façade was added in 1665 by Carlo Rainaldi. Against the side wall of the church is a statue nicknamed '**Abbot Luigi**', one of Rome's 'talking' statues (*see p. 202*).

The aisleless interior has a high barrel vault and spacious apse. Inspired by the Gesù, it gives the impression of a sumptuous reception hall rather than a house of prayer.

The first south chapel, by Carlo Fontana, has green marble columns and fine 17th-century sculptures by Antonio Raggi. The design of the second, the Strozzi Chapel, shows the influence of Michelangelo and contains reproductions in bronze of his *Pietà* and also of the *Leah* and the *Rachel* from the projected tomb of Julius II (*see p. 118*). High up on the walls before the crossing are two similar monuments to two popes of the Piccolomini family—Pius II (d. 1464) and Pius III (d. 1503).

In the **dome**, high up above the crossing, is the *Glory of Paradise* (1621–7), considered one of the best works of Giovanni Lanfranco, a painter from Parma who produced a number of early Baroque works in Rome. His more famous contemporary

Domenichino added the Evangelists in the pendentives as well as the six Virtues and scenes from the life of St Andrew in the vault of the apse, but these are perhaps less inspired works. Domenichino, a leader of the Bolognese school, came to Rome in 1602, where he watched Carracci paint his great ceiling fresco in Palazzo Farnese (and was allowed to carry out some minor decorative details there). He went on to produce numerous frescoes in Roman churches, often on the vaults. Although he was a most prolific painter who also supplied altarpieces for other Roman churches and produced some fine idealised Classical landscapes, after his work in Sant'Andrea della Valle he realised that he was unable to establish himself as the pre-eminent fresco painter in the city and he left for Naples, where he spent the last ten years of his life.

The gigantic, conspicuous **frescoes above and on either side of the high altar**, showing the *Martyrdom of St Andrew*, were executed by the decorative artist Mattia Preti several decades later.

The first chapel on the north side has two frescoed lunettes and three paintings by Passignano, as well as four good late 16th–early 17th-century sculptures: on the left, *Mary Magdalene* by Cristoforo Stati and *St John the Baptist* by Pietro Bernini (Gian Lorenzo's father); and on the right, *St John the Evangelist* by Ambrogio Buonvicino and *Santa Marta* by Francesco Mochi.

CHIESA NUOVA

Map p. 654, A2. Open 7.30–12 & 4.30–7 or 7.30. On 26th May, St Philip Neri's feast day, the church is decorated with magnificent hangings.

The Chiesa Nuova, or Santa Maria in Vallicella, was built under the inspiration of St Philip Neri. Born in Florence in 1515, Neri came to Rome c. 1530, where he became known for his kindness and good works, and for his skill at attracting followers to help him in his mission of caring for pilgrims and for the sick, convalescent and mentally unwell. He was later ordained and founded the Oratorian Order. Neri was an outstanding figure of the Counter-Reformation, known affectionately as the 'Apostle of Rome'. In 1575 Gregory XIII gave him Santa Maria in Vallicella, which he proceeded to rebuild as the Chiesa Nuova, the 'new church', with the patronage of Cardinal Pier Donato Cesi and his brother Angelo. Among the architects were Martino Longhi the Elder (1575–1605) and the façade shows the influence of that of the Gesù.

The handles of the entrance doors are decorated with flaming hearts: the *cor flammigerum*, St Philip Neri's emblem. The vault, apse and dome were decorated by Pietro da Cortona (1664) and the whole church is brilliantly gilded.

(1) Nave: The ceiling fresco by Pietro da Cortona shows *St Philip's Vision of the Virgin*. It tells how in a dream St Philip saw the church roof about to fall; on waking he found it miraculously hanging in mid-air. The fresco shows the Virgin holding the splintered beams aloft.

(2) Dome and apse: The frescoes, again by Pietro da Cortona, show the *Glorification of the Trinity* (in the apse) and the *Assumption* (in the dome).

(3) Sanctuary: The three paintings here are the only works by Rubens still in a church in the city: they were commissioned by the Oratorians before the artist left Rome in 1608. Resplendent with colour, the two of *Saints Domitilla, Nereus and Achilleus* (right); and *Sts Gregory, Maurus and Papianus* (left) are more beautiful than the one over the altar itself of the *Madonna and Angels*. The central panel, painted on slate, can be moved aside to reveal the icon of *Santa Maria in Vallicella*, a miraculous image once seen to shed blood, which was placed in the church by order of St Philip Neri.

(4) Cappella Spada: This chapel, under an elaborate 18th-century cantoria, was designed by Carlo Rainaldi, with an altarpiece of the *Madonna between St Charles Borromeo and St Ignatius* by Carlo Maratta. St Charles Borromeo was a particular admirer of the Oratorians.

(5) Chapel of the Coronation: Above the altar is the *Coronation of the Virgin* by Cavaliere d'Arpino.

(6) Chapel of St Philip: St Philip Neri is buried beneath the altar of this sumptuous chapel (1600–4), whose walls are adorned with gorgeous panels in *pietre dure*. The saint's portrait in mosaic is copied from a painting by Reni. The small dark paintings depicting scenes from his life are by Pomarancio (Cristoforo Roncalli). He inherited his soubriquet from his master Niccolò Circignani. They worked together at the Vatican, and Cristoforo went on to produce rhetorical Mannerist frescoes for a number of churches in Rome. These are amongst the most successful.

(7) Chapel of the Presentation: The delightful, joyful painting of the *Presentation of the Virgin in the Temple* is by Federico Barocci, very different in spirit to works by his Roman contemporaries (note the lovely details in the foreground with a pair of doves in a basket beside a straw hat, and a ram being held back from climbing up the steps).

(8) Sacristy: The fine 17th-century sacristy has a vault fresco by Pietro da Cortona of the *Instruments of the Passion* and a statue of St Philip Neri and an angel by Algardi. Accessed from here are the **rooms of St Philip Neri**, with works by Guercino, Pietro da Cortona, Guido Reni, Garofalo and memorabilia of the saint (*usually open Tues, Thur and Sat 10–12 by appointment: oratoriopiccolo@gmail.com*).

THE ORATORY AND PALAZZO DEI FILIPPINI

In the piazza outside the Chiesa Nuova there is a charming **fountain** in the shape of a soup tureen. The **Oratory** stands to the left of the church façade and its remarkably subtle design has all the hallmarks of Borromini's authorship. Its shallow concavity has an extraordinary tense energy, as if it were bent under pressure. Elements of the

CHIESA NUOVA

1 Nave
2 Dome
3 Sanctuary
4 Cappella Spada
5 Chapel of the Coronation
6 Chapel of St Philip
7 Chapel of the Presentation
8 Sacristy

PALAZZO DEI FILIPPINI

Palazzo dei Filippini has three porticoed courtyards: the one next to the oratory (a) had the library and guest quarters; the largest one, the Cortile degli Aranci (b), still planted with orange trees, was overlooked by the living quarters. Adjoining it is the oval refectory (c), a characteristic design by Borromini. The irregular courtyard directly north of the church apse (d) opened off from the kitchen and service areas.

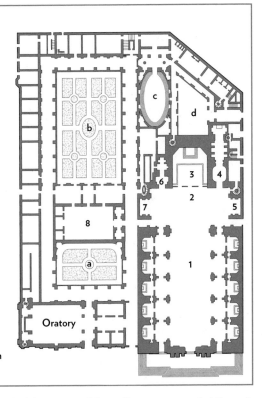

idiosyncratic window designs and of the curves of the pediments are carried through into the interior (*no access*). The congregation founded by St Philip Neri held gatherings for both lay and religious participants in which music and song played an essential part. The oratory (*oratorio*), where these concerts were performed, not only gave the Order its name but also lent its name to the concerts themselves, and thus, ultimately, to a form of musical composition.

Borromini also designed the grand adjoining **Palazzo dei Filippini**, named after the followers of St Philip. Its layout is illustrated on the plan above. Here the Oratorian fathers lived as in a monastery, and the buildings served their religious, intellectual and practical needs. The simple, rather severe façade on Via dei Filippini (where the three floors used as living quarters can be seen) is graced with a splendid clock-tower, on Piazza dell'Orologio, one of Borromini's most delightful works.

A small part of the building is still occupied by the Fathers of the Congregation but most of it is now used by libraries and learned societies (and thus is only accessible to scholars). These include the Biblioteca Vallicelliana (founded in St Philip's day and now, with some 84,000 volumes, specialising in books on the history of Rome) and (since 1922) the Archivio Capitolino (the Municipal Archives).

Around Campo dei Fiori

*Campo dei Fiori is one of the liveliest parts of the city, bustling with Romans
going about their daily business, still with some artisans' workshops and shops selling
old furniture. The narrow streets, which retain their typical cobbled surface without
pavements, surround the market place still used by many local residents.
A few metres west of Campo dei Fiori the lively atmosphere abruptly changes,
in the elegant and peaceful Piazza Farnese, created by the Farnese in front of their
splendid palace. Three other interesting palazzi are close by.*

Campo dei Fiori (*map p. 654, B2*) was once a meadow (as the name—'the field of flowers'—suggests), but it became one of the most important *piazze* in Rome in the 15th century. Since 1869 it has been a market-place, with stalls selling fruit and vegetables, fish and groceries, as well as household goods and clothing. Today the piazza is surrounded by a charming miscellany of narrow houses, with some simple cafés. The fountain in the form of a soup tureen, in pink porphyry and granite, has been here since 1898 and the flower-sellers grouped around it take advantage of its constant supply of fresh running water. From near it you can see, in the distance, the top of the spiralling Baroque campanile of Sant'Ivo.

The grimly dramatic **monument to Giordano Bruno** by Ettore Ferrari, in the centre of the square, is a constant reminder of the piazza's past, when it was occasionally used for executions. The monument marks the spot where, in 1600, the Neoplatonist thinker and philosopher Giordano Bruno was burned alive as a heretic. It was set up in 1889, after thirteen years of bitter public debate between students of Rome university, encouraged by anti-clerical supporters, and the Church. Suddenly Bruno became a symbol of the battle against ecclesiastical authority: in 1876 Garibaldi had written a letter supporting the erection of a monument and in 1878 the English poet Swinburne, a member of the international committee which promoted the same cause, published his poem 'For the Feast of Giordano Bruno: Philosopher and Martyr'. Victor Hugo and Émile Zola added their voices to the clamour for a statue. The protagonists of the campaign do not seem to have fully studied Bruno's rambling philosophical and theological writings, however, for he was by no means a proto-liberal. Born in 1545 in Nola near Naples (as 'the Nolan' he makes an appearance in James Joyce's *Finnegan's Wake*), Bruno joined the Dominicans in 1562 and was ordained a priest, but his restless spirit and speculative intellect soon brought him into conflict with authority. For 17 years he wandered around Europe, teaching the 'Art of Memory' as well as his own hermetic and esoteric doctrines. He visited Paris, Wittenberg and Prague, and spent the years 1583–5 in England, where he worked as a spy for the government, may

Limestone funerary effigy (3rd century AD) from Palmyra,
which at the time was a province of Rome.

have met Shakespeare, and was accused at Oxford of plagiarism. While staying with the Mocenigo in Venice he was betrayed by his hosts to the Inquisition. Sent under escort to Rome, he arrived there on 17th January 1593. Seven years later to the day, after a lengthy trial, Bruno was put to death. He died at the stake, steadfastly refusing to recant.

At the other end of the square (behind the statue), where there is a hodge-podge of buildings, terraces, half-destroyed houses, advertising hoardings and an old cinema, the white corner of the late 16th-century façade of the only grand palace here can be seen on the left. This is **Palazzo Pio (Righetti)**, which faces the attractive little Piazza del Biscione (note the carved lions climbing out of the first-floor windows). It was built over the ruins of the **Theatre of Pompey**, the impressive remains of which can be seen on request at the Pancrazio restaurant.

THE THEATRE OF POMPEY AND SITE OF CAESAR'S MURDER

Theatres in republican Rome were considered to be places where the public could get out of hand; to avoid such a danger it was felt best to make them temporary structures so they could easily be demolished if circumstances made it necessary. Thus it was that they were always built of wood. In 61 BC, however, Pompey decided to build a theatre in stone, surmounting the highest part of the cavea with a temple dedicated to Venus, which he hoped would ward off trouble. Huge quantities of marble were imported from Asia for the decoration. Incredibly enough, the shape of the theatre survives in the urban layout of the streets here: the semicircular auditorium can be traced today in the later buildings on Via di Grotta Pinta (reached through a dark passageway, closed at the time of writing, from Piazza del Biscione), where even a theatre still flourishes. To the east of the theatre itself there was a great rectangular quadriporticus enclosing a water garden, off which opened a building known as the Curia, since meetings of the Senate were sometimes held there. When this huge 'cultural centre' of theatre and porticus was inaugurated it was the largest enclosed space in all Rome and would have dominated the skyline of the city. Thus it was all the more significant that it was here, in the Curia building, that Pompey's famous rival Julius Caesar was murdered on 15th March 44 BC at the foot of a statue of Pompey. The podium of the Curia building has been identified in Largo di Torre Argentina (*map p. 654, B2; for more on the Area Sacra di Largo Argentina, see p. 213*).

The narrow and beautiful old **Via dei Cappellari**, which leads out of Campo dei Fiori in front of the Bruno statue, is worth exploring for its few surviving artisans' shops and pretty houses. Parallel to it is **Via del Pellegrino**, which skirts the fine side façade of the Cancelleria building (*see below*) and incorporates little shops at street level.

VIA DE' GIUBBONARI

The pedestrian Via de' Giubbonari (*map p. 654, B2–B3*) is named after the tailors who specialised in making *giubbe* (jackets and greatcoats) and who used to have their workshops here. It still has lots of clothes shops, some offering bargain prices. **Vicolo**

delle Grotte (right) has a lute-maker's workshop as well as a shop which renovates mattresses. Further on on the left is a charming little triangular space, the Largo dei Librari, squeezed into the top of which is the façade (1680, by Giuseppe Passeri, a pupil of Carlo Maratta) of **Santa Barbara dei Librari** (*open 9–12 & 4–6*). This pretty little church takes its name from the guild of booksellers who purchased the piazza in 1638, many of whom contributed to the restoration of the church over the centuries and are commemorated with memorials inside. It was built at the edge of the remains of Pompey's Theatre (*see above*) as early as the 11th century. It has a Greek-cross plan and the five altars have lovely altar fronts inlaid with *pietre dure*. The 17th-century frescoes are by the little-known Tuscan artist Luigi Garzi, who also painted several of the altarpieces. In the first chapel on the right there is a painted triptych of the *Madonna and Child between St John the Baptist and the Archangel Michael*, which even though signed by a certain 'Leonardo of Rome' and dated 1453 is also Tuscan rather than Roman in spirit. In the right transept there is a 14th-century wood Crucifix. The fine organ survives from the 17th century.

In the little piazza there is a place which for decades has sold nothing but *baccalà* (salted cod) fried in batter, a speciality much beloved of Italians (*only open from 5pm; closed on Sun*). The tiny ice cream shop here is also popular with locals.

SANTI BIAGIO E CARLO AI CATINARI

Via de' Giubbonari ends at this domed church (*map p. 654, B3; open 7.30–12 & 4.30–7*), which was built for the Barnabites in 1612–20 and given a façade in 1636 by Giovanni Battista Soria, but has been much restored. It takes its name from the basin-makers (*catini*) who used to work in the area.

The spacious interior, on a Greek-cross plan, is interesting for its 17th-century works. It was dedicated to St Charles Borromeo (the first church to be so dedicated) after a fire in the area in 1611, which had threatened to destroy some houses destined for the Barnabites, had miraculously been put out by the prayers of the local inhabitants invoking the saint, just a year after his canonisation. Borromeo was appointed bishop of Milan in 1565, and became one of the most important figures in the Counter-Reformation movement. The Barnabites were active in implementing his teachings and the church contains several pictorial representations of scenes from his life, including his miracles. The high altarpiece, a good late work by Pietro da Cortona, shows him with the plague-stricken, and his *Glory* in the apse was frescoed by Giovanni Lanfranco. The first altarpiece on the south side (the *Annunciation*) is also by Lanfranco. In the passageway between the second and third chapels is the Hamerani monument, with exquisite Neoclassical carved decoration by Luca Carimini. The third chapel, the Cappella di Santa Cecilia, beautifully lit from its little oval dome, was designed by Antonio Gherardi. In the pendentives of the dome over the crossing are the *Cardinal Virtues* by Domenichino. The altarpiece in the second north chapel, *The Death of St Anne*, is by Andrea Sacchi, a pupil of Cavaliere d'Arpino. He carried out numerous altarpieces for Roman churches but this is usually considered his best: he was also a highly skilled draughtsman and frescoist and had an important influence on Carlo Maratta, whose altarpieces can also be seen in many churches in the city.

The sacristy contains a little bronze Crucifix attributed to Alessandro Algardi and *The Mocking of Christ* by Cavaliere d'Arpino; in an adjoining room (*shown by the sacristan*) is a tondo of *St Charles at Prayer*, a fresco detached from the façade, attributed to Guido Reni, and another painting of St Charles by Andrea Commodi.

In Piazza Cairoli, opposite the church, is **Palazzo Santacroce**, a handsome building by Carlo Maderno (1602).

THE STREETS TOWARDS THE TIBER

Via dell'Arco del Monte (*map p. 654, B3*) leads south from Via de' Giubbonari, under an arch and through a piazza dominated by the imposing façade of the **Monte di Pietà**. This was designed by Ottaviano Nonni (known as Il Mascherino) and then enlarged by Carlo Maderno, but the clock (the mechanism of which is now kept in the interior court) and small marble bell-tower are attributed to Borromini. The building has a long history as a pawn shop, and the jewellery shops which line the square are a reminder of the sad fate of those who fall on hard times and are forced to sell their most treasured possessions. To comfort visitors to the pawn shop Maderno built the fine domed chapel in 1641, when the high reliefs by Domenico Guidi and Pierre Legros were made, and it was restored in 1725 when another relief was supplied by Jean-Baptiste Théodon. The building is today also partly occupied by a bank. Comfort for modern visitors is provided by the excellent pastries of Nonna Vincenza, one of a small chain of Sicilian *pasticcerie*.

Via dell'Arco del Monte skirts the flank of the building as far as the church of **Santissima Trinità dei Pellegrini** (*occasionally open 4–8*), in Via Capo di Ferro. The façade, with statues of the Evangelists, was added in 1723 by Francesco de Sanctis, although the church dates from the 17th century and the interior still contains works from that period, notably by Guido Reni (*The Trinity*), Borgognone and Cavaliere d'Arpino. In the next-door hospice (1625), the poet Goffredo Mameli (*see p. 405*) died at the age of 22 from wounds received fighting for the Roman Republic in 1849 (plaque).

On the other side of **Via Capo di Ferro**, at no. 31, four splendid Roman columns complete with their Ionic capitals supporting an ancient architrave can be seen in the masonry of a house. This is a typical example of the reuse of Classical fragments in the buildings of Rome, their solidity reinforcing masonry of many centuries later. In the other direction (southeast), Via San Paolo alla Regola leads past the church of **San Paolo alla Regola** (*open afternoons*), said to be built over a house where St Paul stayed. At the end of the south aisle is a chapel dedicated to him, which claims to occupy the site of the room where he lived and taught. Beyond the church on Via San Paolo alla Regola are the **Case di San Paolo**, a group of over-restored 13th-century houses now used as offices.

To the left is yet another church, the ancient **Santa Maria in Monticelli** (*sometimes open in the late evening*), which has a campanile and fragments of mosaic decoration (including a *Head of Christ*) from the 12th century. There is also a detached fresco of the *Flagellation* by Antonio Carracci, and a 14th-century Crucifix.

FOUR ROMAN PALACES

This section describes four palaces close together near Campo dei Fiori. Palazzo della Cancelleria and Palazzo Farnese, both built by wealthy cardinals and graced with splendid courtyards, are two of the most important Renaissance palaces in all Rome. Palazzo Spada, dating from the following century, has beautiful stucco decorations, as well as a *trompe l'oeil* perspective by Francesco Borromini in the garden. The interior contains an important gallery of 17th- and 18th-century paintings. The little early 16th-century palace which houses the Museo di Scultura Antica di Giovanni Barracco, with its collection of ancient sculpture from all over the Mediterranean world, is a particularly pleasant and peaceful place to visit.

PALAZZO DELLA CANCELLERIA

Palazzo della Cancelleria (*map p. 654, B2; courtyard open during the day*) is a masterpiece of the Renaissance with a very graceful façade. It is interesting to compare it with the Palazzo di Venezia (*see p. 139*), completed only 15 years earlier, and still obviously a fortress. Here only the accentuated corners of the building hint at defence, so it illustrates the gradual pacification of Rome at this time. The palace was built for Cardinal Raffaello Riario, probably in 1489, and the façade has a double order of pilasters and delicate patterned brickwork and marble decorations. Showing Florentine influence, it is by an unknown architect, although it is probable that Andrea Bregno was involved, and Donato Bramante may have helped at a late stage, possibly designing the beautiful courtyard. This magnificent space, always visible from the main doorway, has double *logge* with antique columns. The palace, which takes its name from the papal Chancery, still belongs to the Vatican and is used for three tribunals, including the Sacra Rota, and by the Pontificia Accademia Romana di Archeologia.

SAN LORENZO IN DAMASO

Incorporated into the palace (and so, very unusually, without a façade), this ancient basilica (*open 7.30–12 & 4.30–8*) was founded by Pope St Damasus I in the 4th century and was one of the most important and largest early Christian churches in Rome. Remains dating from the 4th and 5th centuries, as well as a cemetery in use from the 8th–15th centuries, were discovered beneath the courtyard of the palace. The church was finally demolished in the 15th century when the present building—which occupies part of the site and is contemporary with the palace—had been completed. It was entirely restored in 1868–82, and again in the 20th century after a fire.

A double atrium precedes the very wide nave which has narrow aisles, a plan which recalls the ancient basilican church. In the main apse, the *Coronation of the Virgin with Saints* by Federico Zuccari was commissioned by Cardinal Alessandro Farnese in 1568. At the end of the left aisle is a 12th-century icon of the Virgin brought here from Santa Maria di Grottapinta in 1465, and the tomb of Cardinal Ludovico Trevisan, called Mezzarota Scarampi, with his effigy: he died in 1505 but the tomb was erected some

40 years later. The inscription records the victorious battles he fought for Eugenius IV, the most famous of which was the Battle of Anghiari (1440), when the Florentines were in alliance with the papacy against Milan.

MUSEO DI SCULTURA ANTICA GIOVANNI BARRACCO

Map p. 654, B2. Open Oct–May 10–4, June–Sept 1–7. Closed Mon. Free. T: 060608, museobarracco.it.

The museum occupies the elegant Renaissance Palazzo Farnesina ai Baullari, or Piccola Farnesina (i.e. small when compared to the great Palazzo Farnese nearby).

In 1523 the French prelate Thomas Le Roy almost certainly chose Antonio da Sangallo the Younger as the architect of this palace. Le Roy, the son of a French peasant, held important posts at the pontifical court and played a significant part in the concordat of 1516 between Leo X and Francis I of France. For his services he was ennobled and permitted to augment his coat of arms with the lilies of France. This heraldic privilege is recorded in the architectural details of the palace: the three floors are divided horizontally by projecting bands displaying the Le Roy ermines and the Farnese lilies, which were substituted for the lilies of France.

The palace was built to face Vicolo dell'Aquila, to the south. The construction of Corso Vittorio Emanuele II in 1876 exposed the north side, which backed onto houses that were pulled down to make room for the new street. A fine new façade on the Corso was therefore built (1898–1901); the architect was Enrico Guj, who also modified the side of the palace facing Piazza dei Baullari and added the steps and balustrade. At this time a Roman building of the late Imperial period, with 4th-century frescoes, was discovered beneath the foundations. The little courtyard, which is thought to be by Sangallo, is decorated with columns of the three orders, Doric, Ionic and Corinthian (the *logge* on the top floor were later enclosed with glass). Some of the rooms still have their 17th-century frescoed ceilings and pretty tiled floors.

THE BARRACCO COLLECTION OF ANTIQUE SCULPTURE

The palace houses a small but choice collection of ancient sculpture displayed in just nine rooms. It was formed by the scholar and antiquarian Senator Giovanni Barracco (1829–1914) and presented by him to the city of Rome in 1902. It provides a fascinating insight into what was still to be had on the market in the late 19th century, and its interest as a private collection is what makes it so special in a city which abounds in museums of ancient sculptures. It is also particularly unusual since it includes very fine pieces of ancient sculpture from the earliest times (with examples from ancient Egypt, Babylonia and Assyria) right up to the Roman era and so provides an interesting panorama of the various civilisations which bordered the Mediterranean. The fact that it receives very few visitors makes it a delightful place to visit, even though the heavy traffic on Corso Vittorio Emanuele II disturbs the peace. Vintage photographs show how the collection was arranged in Barracco's lifetime in his residence on the Corso.

First floor

Room I: A superb group of Egyptian sculpture from the beginning of the 3rd millennium to the end of the Roman era. Two of the finest pieces are the head of Ramesses II as a young man, with a blue chaplet (1299–1233 BC) and the head of a priest wearing a diadem, once thought to be a portrait of Julius Caesar (an interesting example from Roman Egypt, in black diorite). The grey granite sphinx with the head of Hatshepsut was found in the Isaeum Campense (*see p. 181*).

Room II: Egyptian, Sumerian and Assyrian works. There is a vase used as a water-clock, with fine engraved decoration. Reliefs include a winged deity from the northwestern palace of Assurbanipal at Nimrud (883–859 BC).

Room III: Phoenician and Etruscan works are displayed here. There are three representations of the Egyptian and Phoenician god Bes, including a statue from a villa in the Alban Hills, and three antefixes in the form of female heads. The alabaster lion mask is a Phoenician work found in Sardinia.

Room IV: Works from the 6th–5th centuries BC from Cyprus include statuettes of players of musical instruments; an unusual little model of a polychrome quadriga ridden by a woman and child; and the well preserved head of a bearded priest wearing a chaplet, showing traces of colour (late 5th century).

Second floor

Room V: Greek originals of the 5th century BC. In the centre of the room is a replica of the *Westmacott Athlete* in the British Museum, after an original by Polyclitus, possibly a portrait of the celebrated boy boxer Kyniskos of Mantinea. There is a head of Marsyas, a replica of a famous statue by Myron. The head of Apollo is after an original by Pheidias which may have been the bronze statue seen by Pausanias near the Parthenon (before 450 BC). There are also excellent copies of works by Polyclitus: a statuette of Hercules, and the upper part of an Amazon, after the original in the Temple of Diana at Ephesus.

Room VI: Greek art and copies of the same (both Roman and modern).

Among the 4th-century Attic works are a beautiful votive relief to Apollo, and the superb head of *Apollo Lykeios*, the best existing replica of the statue by Praxiteles.

Rooms VII and VIII: Hellenistic sculptures include a bitch licking her wounds, perhaps a replica of the masterpiece by Lysippus, formerly in the Temple of Jupiter on the Capitoline. There is a portrait head of Alexander the Great.

Room IX: Roman and medieval art. Roman busts include two of boys (one of whom may represent Nero) which are particularly fine. The fragment of a mosaic from old St Peter's has the representation of the *Ecclesia Romana*.

PALAZZO SPADA

Map p. 654, A3–B3. Open 8.30–7.30; closed Tues. T: 06 68 32 409, galleriaborghese.it/ spada/it. Part of the palace has been the seat of the Council of State (or Supreme Court) since 1889. The State Rooms are open by appointment on the second Sun of the month.

Palazzo Spada was built for Cardinal Girolamo Capodiferro in 1548–50. The architect is thought to have been a certain Bartolomeo Baronino, who had worked as master mason on the Palazzo Farnese a few steps away, but is otherwise unknown. It may also once have been the residence of the French ambassador.

The **façade** is an outstanding example of 16th-century stucco decoration, attributed to Giulio Mazzoni or Girolamo da Carpi. The stucco niches have statues of Roman heroes and emperors (all named in the inscriptions). Between the windows on the floor above is a series of roundels with the Capodiferro emblem of a dog beside a column of flame. In the 17th century the Spada emblem (three swords) was added for the new owners on the shield high above the doorway. When Borromini restored the palace for his friend Cardinal Spada, he designed the painted niche with a statue in the narrow piazza outside to close the view from the garden entrance on Via Giulia (it has been reconstructed above an ancient sarcophagus which serves as a fountain). The **courtyard** has even more beautiful stuccoes, well worth examining in detail.

The palace was acquired in 1632 by Cardinal Bernardino Spada (1594–1661), who began his collection while in Bologna as papal legate. He commissioned his portrait (still preserved here) from each of the two greatest artists at work there, Guido Reni and Guercino. The collection, augmented by successive generations of the family, has survived almost totally intact and was acquired by the state in 1926.

BORROMINI'S PERSPECTIVE

In the little secret garden with orange trees, you can see Borromini's ingenious *trompe l'oeil* perspective, a device which makes use of the narrow area of waste space between the Spada garden and the adjoining Palazzo Massari. The dimensions of the tunnel are perspectively multiplied more than four times through the use of light and the spacing of the columns, as well as the raising of the pavement. The result gives the optical illusion of a long colonnaded walk culminating in a lifesize statue in a bower. In reality the statue is rather small and the colonnade no more than a few footsteps.

GALLERIA SPADA

The entrance is beyond the courtyard to the left, by a little spiral staircase. It is arranged in four rooms which preserve their 17th-century decoration and furnishings. The collection is particularly important for its 17th-century paintings (and Roman sculpture). The gallery retains its atmosphere of a sumptuous family residence. Numbering here corresponds with the handlists in each room (also in English).

Room I: On the end wall are the two fine **portraits of Cardinal Spada**, both of 1631: one, full-length, by Guido Reni (32), and the other, displayed close by, a

PALAZZO SPADA
View of the colonnade foreshortened by Borromini's *trompe l'oeil* perspective.

smaller painting by Guercino (35). The *St Jerome* is also by Reni.

Room II: The earliest works in the collection, mostly by artists born towards the end of the 15th century. On the entrance wall is the exquisite small *Visitation* (56) by **Andrea del Sarto**. Between the windows are two portraits of young men: one (77) by Jan van Scorel displayed beneath one by Hans Dürer (78). The very fine unfinished *Portrait of a Musician* (60) on the entrance wall is by the school of Titian. The largest painting (*Way to Calvary*) is by Marco Palmezzano. Above the paintings on the wall opposite the window are fragments of a large painted frieze by Perino del Vaga, designs for tapestries originally intended for the wall below

Michelangelo's *Last Judgement* in the Sistine Chapel (the matching frieze on the other walls was added in 1636 to complete the decoration of the room).

Room III (Galleria): In the centre of the left wall is a remarkable **sketch by Baciccia** (133) for his famous frescoed vault of the church of the Gesù. On the short end wall is a portrait of a cardinal (120) by the school of Rubens. The 17th-century works by contemporaries or near-contemporaries of Cardinal Spada include paintings by Ciro Ferri, Pietro Testa, Francesco Furini (*St Lucy*: portrayed from behind, only her shoulders and hair are visible), Nicolò Tornioli and the Flemish painters Jan Brueghel the Elder, Jacob Ferdinand Voet and Peter Snayers. There is also a 16th-century landscape by Niccolò dell'Abate and an early 18th-century historical painting by Francesco Trevisani. *The Death of Dido* (132) is by Guercino. Among the Roman sculpture are the *Seated Philosopher*, and, facing each other, two statuettes of boys, one dressed in the lion-skin of Hercules, and another in the philosopher's *pallium*.

Room IV: Here are works by the 17th-century Roman painter Michelangelo Cerquozzi, including *Masaniello's Revolt in Naples* (161). There are also works by Orazio Gentileschi and his daughter Artemisia, and Mattia Preti. The Roman bust of a boy dates from the Julio-Claudian period.

THE STATE ROOMS

The State Rooms on the first floor (*for admission, see above*) include the **General Council Chamber**, which has fine quadratura frescoes by the 17th-century Bolognese artists Agostino Mitelli and Michelangelo Colonna, with birds and figures peering into the room from around columns and window ledges. The colossal **statue of Domitian** (once taken to represent Pompey and thought to be the one at the foot of which Caesar was murdered) was presented to Cardinal Capodiferro by Julius III in 1552. The **Corridor of Stuccoes**, perhaps the best preserved room, has a delightful vault decorated by Giulio Mazzoni (1559), complemented by his ornamentation of the façade of the court seen through the windows. The **Meridiana Gallery** has a vault decorated by Giovanni Battista Ruggeri for the Spada, mapping the time at various places in the world in 1631. The eight very fine Hellenistic reliefs of mythological subjects are from the 2nd century AD. Other rooms have more interesting frescoes and stuccoes.

PALAZZO FARNESE

Map p. 654, A2. Open only by previous appointment Mon, Wed and Fri afternoons; you are required to book at least a week in advance: inventerrome.com. Original ID document required. Children under ten are not admitted. Despite this complication, the excellent guided visit, which lasts just under 1hr (in English on Wed), is exceptionally rewarding.

The beautiful Piazza Farnese was laid out in 1545 in front of Palazzo Farnese. The two huge baths of Egyptian granite were brought from the Baths of Caracalla at that time and were used by members of the Farnese family as a type of 'royal box' for the spectacles which were held here. They were adapted as fountains (using the Farnese lilies) in 1626 and the sound of water still pervades the square, which is surrounded by a group of distinguished town houses. Palazzo Farnese itself is the most magnificent Renaissance palace in Rome. It has been the seat of the French Embassy since 1874 (having first been used as such in 1635): it is in excellent condition and still preserves its exceptional atmosphere of grandeur. On the *piano nobile* is the famous Galleria with a delightful frescoed ceiling (1597–1603), the masterpiece of Annibale Carracci, which had a profound influence on later Baroque ceiling decorations.

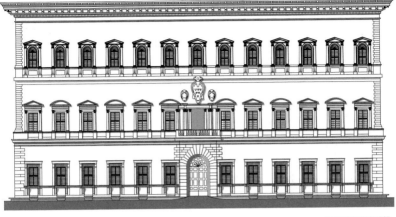

PALAZZO FARNESE

HISTORY OF THE BUILDING

Two years after he became a cardinal (aged only 23), Alessandro Farnese acquired the building on this site and appointed Antonio da Sangallo the Younger to reconstruct it and so supply the cardinal with a grand residence suitable to his rank. Work proceeded slowly over the next 40 years, but after Alessandro was finally elected Pope Paul III in 1534 (in one of the quickest conclaves in history, lasting just three days) he called in Michelangelo to complete the upper storeys and provide the cornice. After Sangallo's death in 1546, Michelangelo became the official architect and carried out alterations to Sangallo's magnificent courtyard and redesigned the garden façade before he withdrew from the building site in 1549, the year of the death of Paul III.

When Paul III's grandson, Ranuccio Farnese, took up residence here he employed Vignola to continue the building, and then his brother Cardinal Alessandro finished the wing overlooking the Tiber with the help of Giacomo della Porta. Yet another cardinal in the family, Odoardo, had the bridge (*see p. 231*) built over Via Giulia in 1603 to connect the palace to its gardens on the Tiber. The palace survives much as it was from that time, except that the two loggias on the first floor of the courtyard were enclosed in 1818.

The magnificent **Farnese collections**, begun by Paul III and continued by the brothers Alessandro and Ranuccio, were later dispersed, and when in the 18th century the palace was inherited by the Bourbons of Naples, the extremely important collection of antique sculptures (which included the huge *Farnese Bull*, found in the Baths of Caracalla in 1545, and the *Farnese Hercules*, discovered there a year later) was transferred to that city. They are now in the Museo Archeologico in Naples. On his visit to Rome in 1787 Goethe lamented this loss for his beloved Rome: 'If they could detach the Gallery with the Carracci from Palazzo Farnese and transport it, they would'.

The magnificent brick and travertine **façade**, begun by Sangallo, was completed by Michelangelo, who had the ingenious idea of crowning it with a huge cornice, or entablature, which overhangs the façade by some one and a half metres, thus hiding the roofline and providing its extremely satisfying proportions. Michelangelo also carried out the project for the central window on the *piano nobile*, with the pope's arms. During restoration work in this century, the decorative patterns in the red and yellow bricks between the windows were discovered.

THE VISIT TO THE INTERIOR

The entrance **vestibule** or portico, designed by Antonio da Sangallo, is a very fine barrel-vaulted space, lined with columns of pink granite from the Baths of Caracalla, and the vault has exquisite stuccoes decorated with the Farnese lilies and unicorns, and the wall niches have Roman busts.

The magnificent **courtyard** was begun by Sangallo, and he modelled the ground-floor arcades on those of the Theatre of Marcellus. He planned to have open loggias on the two upper floors also, but it was Michelangelo who decided to enclose two sides of the first floor with windows (surmounted by triangular pediments) between Ionic columns. He also designed the decorative frieze of festoons hung between masks and the Farnese lily, which separates this level from the upper storey, where the windows with semicircular pediments are separated instead by Corinthian pilasters. The courtyard was very skilfully altered in the 19th century when the two loggias which Michelangelo had left open on the first floor (on the entrance and garden sides) were enclosed, copying the great architect's design for the other two sides so that today you would never know this had been done so much later.

Beneath the portico are two Roman sarcophaghi, one of them of huge proportions, from the great Farnese collection of antique sculpture, left behind when almost all the rest of it was taken to Naples. Beneath the portico towards the garden there are two amusing 'trophies', created by Antonio Cipolla in around 1863 when he salvaged a few more miscellaneous antique fragments of statues and architectural elements from the collection and piled them up in an Etruscan/Roman jumble. In this romantic idea he was apparently inspired by Piranesi. In the days of the Farnese the *Farnese Bull* (*see above*) was installed in the centre of the portico so that it would have been visible from the Tiber and the garden as well as from the piazza outside the main entrance.

The garden façade by Vignola copies some of the architectural features in the courtyard, including Michelangelo's frieze of garlands. Giacomo della Porta designed the lovely loggia in the centre with its three arches on the top floor.

The piano nobile

The **grand staircase**, which survives from Sangallo's time, leads up past a landing sumptuously decorated with two fountains. Many of the walls of the *piano nobile* were repainted in a dark colour (seemingly applied with a sponge) during restorations by Balthus, who was director of the French Academy in Rome in the 1960s and 1970s.

The **Salone d'Ercole** is an extraordinary square space, 18m high. It was designed by Michelangelo by raising the ceiling to the roofline and so occupying two floors. This means it is particularly well illuminated by windows on two levels. Vignola supplied the splendid wood coffered ceiling, which helped resolve problems which arose after Michelangelo's intervention since it supports the weight of the roof and its huge cornice. Its design is reflected below in the marble and terracotta floor tiles. Vignola also designed the fireplace in coloured marbles. Above the Classical busts in roundels are two Gobelins tapestries reproducing scenes from the Raphael Rooms in the Vatican. The two reclining female statues representing *Charity* and *Abundance* were made by Guglielmo della Porta for the tomb of Paul III in St Peter's. The *Farnese Hercules* is a cast of the famous original now in Naples.

The decoration of the **Galleria**, the most famous room in the palace, was commissioned by Cardinal Odoardo Farnese in 1598–1602 from Annibale Carracci. This was where the Farnese kept many of their antique statues and Annibale decided to provide scenes on the barrel vault inspired by Ovid's *Metamorphoses*, joyously celebrating the loves of the gods. The ingenious treatment of the angles, and the impressive overall scheme centring on the *Triumph of Bacchus and Ariadne*, demonstrate the great imagination of the artist. He made much use of *trompe l'oeil*: some of the scenes are painted to look as if they were framed easel paintings hanging from the walls, and 'sculptures' in grisaille provide an architectural setting. The lower walls were decorated in 1608, when Annibale was assisted (in the frescoes above the doors and niches) by Domenichino.

A WALK ALONG VIA GIULIA: A 16TH-CENTURY STREET

From Piazza Farnese, Via del Mascherone leads down towards the Tiber, skirting the magnificent side façade of Palazzo Farnese to meet Via Giulia. This very long, straight street was laid out by Julius II (1503–13) parallel to the Tiber, and it was for a long time the most beautiful of the 16th-century streets of the city. It still has a number of fine palaces with lovely courtyards, many churches (although most of them are kept closed) and lovely street lamps. There are some antique shops and art galleries on the street, and (at no. 14) a restaurant specialising in fish and *hors d'oeuvres*: Assunta Madre, sister to one of the same name recently opened in Mayfair, London.

THE FOUNTAIN IN A PRETTY WALL niche, the eponymous ***Mascherone***, was erected by the Farnese (note the Farnese lily on the top); both the colossal mask of a girl with long hair and the porphyry basin are Roman, although the mouth was enlarged when it was adapted as a fountain. There is a view through a gate of the upper part of the rear façade of Palazzo Farnese and its garden, with palm trees and cypresses. A picturesque **arch**, usually festooned with strands of Virginia creeper and adorned with stone Farnese lilies, spans the road. This was the only arch of a viaduct planned, but never realised, by Michelangelo to connect this palace with the Villa Farnesina across the river.

The church of **Santa Maria dell'Orazione e Morte** was rebuilt in 1733–7 by Ferdinando Fuga. Skulls flank the entrance. The right-hand alms box, dating from 1694, shows Death claiming a victim and asking passers-by for alms for sufferers from malaria contracted in the Roman Campagna. Malaria

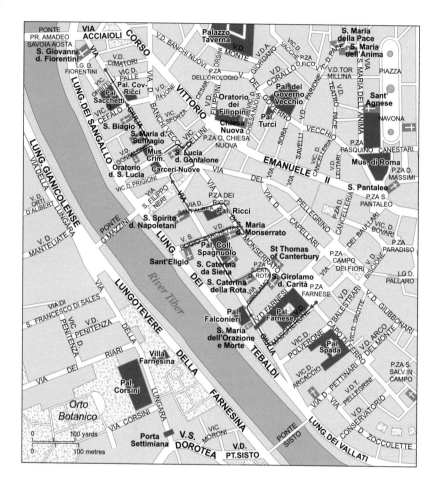

remained a serious threat up until the end of the 19th century: as late as 1883, Augustus Hare in his *Walks in Rome* was warning visitors about this mysterious and dangerous illness when from June to November certain areas of the city, including the gardens of the Villa Borghese, the Caelian and Aventine, were 'a constant prey to fever'.

Palazzo Falconieri next to the church, enlarged by Borromini (who also designed the Falconieri family crypt in

San Giovanni dei Fiorentini; *see p. 236*), is distinguished by its side pilasters: terms of female breasts topped by giant falcons' heads. It has been the seat of the Hungarian Academy since 1928. Several rooms inside have fine ceilings decorated in stucco by Borromini—alas, not on view, but the little courtyard can be seen, with its fountain grotto. Cardinal Fesch, Napoleon I's uncle, lived here in the early 19th century and amassed a splendid collection of paintings which was, however, dispersed after his death (some of it ended up in the Palais Fesch in Ajaccio, Corsica).

The narrow Via di San Girolamo della Carità leads right to Piazza Santa Caterina della Rota, where there are no fewer than three churches. **San Girolamo della Carità** (*usually only open for a service on Sun*), rebuilt in the 17th century, has a façade by Carlo Rainaldi. The Cappella Spada (first right), formerly attributed to Borromini, is now thought to be the work of Cosimo Fanzago, who worked mostly in Naples. It is delightfully decorated in precious marbles and the balustrade at its entrance is made from a single yellow marble drape held up by two putti. The chapel of St Philip Neri, to the left of the high altar, designed by Filippo Juvarra in 1710, is in a totally different style.

On Via di Monserrato is the exterior flank, built in the 19th century in Romanesque style, including an elaborate portal by Luigi Poletti, of the **church of St Thomas of Canterbury** (*entrance at no. 45; open all day on weekdays, 9–1 at weekends*), attached to the Venerable English and Welsh College. The ground on which they stand has been the property of English Catholics since 1362, when a pilgrim hospice was built here. Thomas Cromwell (Henry VIII of England's future minister and adviser) came here as a young man in 1514. Ironically it was on Cromwell's advice that St Thomas Becket's shrine in Canterbury was destroyed in 1538. The College was founded in 1579 by the Jesuits, as a seminary for the training of priests as missionaries to England. The record of visitors shows the names of Thomas Hobbes (1635), William

Harvey (1636), John Milton (1638) and John Evelyn (1644). The church was rebuilt to Virginio Vespignani's design in 1866–88, a free adaptation of a Romanesque basilica, with elaborate gilded decorations, and remains as if built yesterday. The frescoes of English martyrs in the matroneum are based on an earlier cycle, lost when the old church was destroyed, which were painted by Niccolò Circignani and included scenes of the death of Edward Campion in 1581. The beautiful tomb effigy of Cardinal Christopher Bainbridge, Bishop of York (d. 1514), borne on two Romanesque lions, is attributed to the little-known sculptor Nicola Marini. The monument to Thomas Dereham (d. 1739) is by Ferdinando Fuga, with sculptures by Filippo della Valle.

Return to Via Giulia past **Santa Caterina della Rota**. On Via Giulia there are two palaces into whose courtyards you can peer when the doors are open. The **church of Santa Caterina da Siena** (*officially open Mon–Sat 5–6.30, Sun and holidays 9.30–12*) was rebuilt by Paolo Posi in 1766. It has painted decoration by Giovanni Battista Marchetti dating from that time. The **Palazzo del Collegio Spagnuolo** next door (19th century) has a large coat of arms high up on the façade. In the courtyard are several fine tombs, notably that of Cardinal Giovanni de Mella, attributed to Andrea Bregno. In a room off the courtyard is the monument to Pedro de Foix Montoya; this incorporates a remarkable portrait bust, an early work (c. 1621) by Bernini.

The next street on the left leads toward the Tiber, passing **Sant'Eligio degli Orefici**. In 1509 Julius II gave the confraternity of Roman goldsmiths permission to erect a church dedicated to their patron saint, St Eligius. In 1514 they commissioned Raphael to design this beautiful small church, surmounted by a cupola and Greek-cross in plan, and clearly influenced by Bramante. After Raphael's death Baldassare Peruzzi finished the building, including the cupola. The façade, following Raphael's designs, was rebuilt by Flaminio Ponzio after it collapsed in 1601. The interior (*if by some great good fortune you find it open; its official times are Mon–Fri 9–1; T: 06 68 68 260, www.universitadegliorefici. it*) is particularly interesting for its architecture, but it also contains some 17th-century frescoes and a few goldsmiths' tombs (the college of gold- and silversmiths is next door).

Return to Via Giulia now and go straight across it. Via della Barchetta leads back to Via di Monserrato. On your right stands the church of **Santa Maria di Monserrato**, the Spanish national church (*open 10–1 & 3–6*). It was begun by Antonio da Sangallo the Younger (1518) but altered later, with a façade by Francesco da Volterra showing the Virgin under the sierra of Montserrat. In the interior, the first south chapel contains an altarpiece of St Diego, by Annibale Carracci, and the 19th-century tombs of the two Borgia popes, Calixtus III (d. 1458) and Alexander VI (d. 1503), as well as of the Spanish king Alfonso XIII (d. 1941). In the third north chapel is a statue of St James by Jacopo Sansovino, and two fine wall-tombs both with effigies attributed to Andrea Bregno. The first north chapel contains a group of the *Madonna and Child with St Anne* by Tommaso Boscoli (1544).

Next to the church is a house (no. 111) built in 1912, with four tiers of open loggias, inspired by St Catherine's house in Siena. On the palace opposite, a plaque records the prison here, the **Corte Savella**, from which Beatrice Cenci set out on 11th September 1599 to her death, 'an exemplary victim of injustice' (*for her story, see pp. 340–1*).

Retrace your steps and continue up Via Monserrato, which has a number of picture-framers and antique shops, and turn left into Piazza Ricci. Here the 16th-century **Palazzo Ricci** has a painted façade by Polidoro da Caravaggio, heavily restored and now badly faded, although the frieze above the ground-floor windows is still just visible. The palace takes up two sides of a charming, peaceful little piazza filled with the tables of a restaurant (Pier Luigi), which has been popular with Romans for many years.

Returning past the side of the *palazzo* to Via Giulia, you come to the church of **Spirito Santo dei Napoletani** (*only open for Mass on Sun*), begun by Il Mascherino in 1619, restored by Carlo Fontana, and again in the 19th century, when the façade was built by Antonio Cipolla. It contains paintings by Pietro Gagliardi and a *Martyrdom of St Januarius* (San Gennaro) by Luca Giordano.

The street next traverses an area demolished before 1940 for a new road which was never built; the church of San Filippo Neri was also pulled down, but its 18th-century façade by Filippo Raguzzini survives (on the right). The area is scheduled for re-development. In 2014, during work for an underground car park, remains of a stable block built here by Augustus were found.

Turn right up Vicolo del Malpasso, and to the left you will see **Vicolo**

Cellini, named after the famous sculptor Benvenuto Cellini, who had his workshop in the area. Unfortunately not a single work by this great artist can be seen in Rome today (except a pair of candlesticks in the treasury of St Peter's—and even these are not certainly his), even though he spent many years of his life here. This is partly because the size of the works of art he was producing for his wealthy Roman patrons (jewellery, tiny *objets d'art*, caskets, etc.) meant they were easily 'lost' in subsequent centuries. Even his most famous work, the salt-cellar made for Francis I of Austria, was stolen from the Kunsthistorisches Museum in Vienna in 2003 (but found three years later, buried in a forest). In his famous *Autobiography*, Cellini gives a vivid description of the 16th-century city, often boasting of his exploits, but also full of engaging minor details. For instance, early in his second period in Rome, he recounts that he used to take advantage of his days off work to go and study the ancient Roman monuments, and states that he would make copies of them 'sometimes in wax and sometimes on paper'. While enjoying the fresh air he would also take pot shots (having manufactured his own gunpowder) at the numerous 'plump' pigeons who inhabited the ruins, and so would return home with some good meat to eat. He also tells of his encounters with Lombard peasants who had come to work in the vineyards and who would often unearth ancient coins, jewellery and precious stones which Cellini would then buy from them.

Via dei Banchi Vecchi has some local shops and the church of **Santa Lucia del Gonfalone**, which was decorated in the 1860s by Cesare Mariani.

Return to Via Giulia by Via delle Carceri, named after the brick **Carceri Nuove**, on Via Giulia to your left. Built in 1655 by Antonio del Grande, this was long considered a model prison. The building, with a massive portal and barred windows on the ground floor, is now occupied by the national office set up to combat the Mafia: this notorious criminal organisation continues to blight the life of the country. In 2014 a scandal broke out in Rome after the arrest of numerous local politicians accused of links to organised crime. The **Museo Criminologico** (*open 9–1 except Sun and Mon, Tues and Thur also 2.30–6.30; T: 06 68 89 941, museocriminologico.it*) is arranged in the adjacent model prison building designed in 1827 by Giuseppe Valadier. The entrance is at Via del Gonfalone 29. It illustrates the history of criminology. Also in Via del Gonfalone is the 16th-century **Oratorio di Santa Lucia del Gonfalone**. Concerts are given here by the Coro Polifonico Romano but it is otherwise kept closed (*T: 06 68 75 952, www.oratoriogonfalone. com*). The interior has a fine pavement and a carved and gilded ceiling. It is particularly interesting for its frescoes of the Passion of Christ by painters of the late 16th-century Tuscan-Emilian school, including Federico Zuccari (*Flagellation*) and Cesare Nebbia.

Back on Via Giulia, on the left beyond the church of Santa Maria del Suffragio (by Carlo Rainaldi), are several large, rough **blocks of masonry** protruding into the street: these are all that remain of a great court of justice designed for Julius II by Bramante but never finished. Part of it can also be seen inside Hotel Indigo. Next door is the tall, narrow façade of yet another church, the small **San Biagio della Pagnotta**, used by the Armenian community. On the corner of Vicolo del Cefalo (with more huge blocks of tufa from the Court of Justice) is a very worn fountain with a cupid riding two dolphins—one of the very few Roman fountains which are now dry. It occupies a corner of **Palazzo Sacchetti**, by Antonio da Sangallo the Younger (1543), built mostly of brick, though the windows and cornice are in stone. In the garden behind towards the Tiber there is a nymphaeum built by Nanni di Baccio Bigio for Cardinal Ricci di Montepulciano, and the loggia is decorated with stuccoes, probably by Francesco Salviati.

Opposite is the 15th-century **Palazzo Covarelli Ricci** (no. 97), and the smaller palace next door (no. 93) has a pretty façade decorated with Paul III's papal arms, the Farnese lilies, two (seated) horses, lovely dragons, and a bust in a roundel. As luck would have it, just a little further up, is a simple little snack bar.

SAN GIOVANNI BATTISTA DEI FIORENTINI

Map p. 232. Open 7.30–12 & 5–7. sangiovannideifiorentini.net.

At the end of Via Giulia, with its steps invading the street, stands the church of the Florentines, dedicated to St John the Baptist. It was the Medici pope Leo X who decided that the Florentines should have a new church in Rome, and in 1513 he ordered a competition for its design. Giulio Romano, Baldassare Peruzzi and Antonio da Sangallo the Younger were among the contestants, but Jacopo Sansovino emerged the winner with his centralised plan (presumably inspired by both the Pantheon and the Florence baptistery) and he began work on it in 1519. When Antonio da Sangallo the Younger took over from Sansovino, he abandoned the original design and introduced a longitudinal plan. Work proceeded very slowly, and it is known that in 1559 Michelangelo, then aged 84, became involved and produced five different projects for a centrally-planned building. Sadly nothing came of Michelangelo's project and when Giacomo della Porta was called in some 20 years later, he reverted to Sangallo's plan.

The transept, choir and cupola were added in the early 17th century by Carlo Maderno, who is buried in the church. The façade was only finished in 1736: it is by the little-known architect Alessandro Galilei.

INTERIOR OF SAN GIOVANNI DEI FIORENTINI

A perfectly plain white barrel vault rises above the grey pilasters, arches and cornice and the simple interior is well lit by windows in the nave and side chapels. There is a Tuscan feel to the building, and it contains many paintings by artists from that region in the more heavily decorated side chapels.

In the **third south chapel** there are paintings of St Jerome: the beautiful altarpiece is by Santi di Tito; *St Jerome in his Studio* is by Lodovico Cigoli; and the painting showing St Jerome and the building of this church is by Passignano. The altarpiece in the **south transept** of *Sts Cosmas and Damian at the Stake*, by Salvator Rosa, was one of his last works. The superb nude figure fleeing the flames shows the influence of Michelangelo. The funerary busts (look upwards) are by Algardi (on the left) and Ercole Ferrata (on the right). The **Cappella della Madonna**, to the right of the sanctuary, preserves a fresco in grisaille (much restored) of the *Madonna and Child* by Filippino Lippi, held to be miraculous. Until 1640 this was in a street tabernacle in the nearby Vicolo delle Palle, where it commemorated a miracle which occurred when a man who lost at a game of bowls had in fury hit the image of the Madonna with his ball and as a result remained paralysed for 40 days.

The **chapel to the left of the sanctuary** was decorated by Giovanni Lanfranco (before his work in Sant'Andrea della Valle), with vault frescoes, two paintings (the *Prayer in the Garden* and the *Way to Calvary*) and lovely stuccoes. This was the Sacchetti Chapel, used by the family whose *palazzo* was nearby on Via Giulia. Displayed in a modern showcase is the supposed foot of Mary Magdalene (an unusual relic dating from the 15th or 16th century). The **fifth north chapel** has frescoes by Niccolò Circignani (also known as Pomarancio; his signature was found during recent restoration work) and an altarpiece of *St Francis* by Santi di Tito (or Cigoli). The **fourth north chapel** has putti on the wall tombs of the Bacelli, carved by François Duquesnoy, a Flemish sculptor who came to Rome in 1618 and who is above all remembered for his delightful chubby putti, of which these are good examples. Duquesnoy belonged to a family of sculptors (his father was the creator of the famous *Mannekenpis* fountain in Brussels). Though recognition came to him, he nevertheless suffered from bouts of insanity and his family was a troubled one (his brother was sentenced to death for committing a profane act in church).

You can go up the steps on the right of the modern high altar into the sanctuary, and then take the hidden steps behind the altar at the east end (*light on the left*) down to the oval **crypt sepulchre** (in a rather neglected state) of the Falconieri family, whose *palazzo* was also on Via Giulia. It is a fine late work by **Borromini**, who is also buried in this church (his simple oval tomb slab is under the dome, left of the high altar).

A little **museum** (*entered from the south aisle or from Via Acciaioli 2; usually open 9.30–12; closed Sun*) preserves treasures from the church. The Tuscan statuette of St John the Baptist dates from around 1495 and the oval marble relief of the *Madonna and Child with St Anne* is by Perino del Vaga. In 1612 Pietro Bernini was commissioned to carve the portrait bust of Antonio Coppola (a Florentine surgeon and benefactor of the hospital attached to the church). Most scholars agree that Pietro's son Gian Lorenzo, aged only 12 or 14, may in fact have been responsible for the carving, making this his very first autograph work. The splendid bust of Antonio Cepparelli, another benefactor of the church, is, on the other hand, a documented work by Gian Lorenzo, dating from 1622. The bell is one of the oldest in Rome (1253). You can go out onto the balcony above the organ from where there is a splendid view of the church interior.

THEATRE OF MARCELLUS
Ancient relief probably symbolising Rome: city walls and gates
encircling an eagle mounted on a club of Hercules

The Isola Tiberina & the Ghetto

The Isola Tiberina, as the only island in the Tiber, is fun to visit.
The Synagogue, facing the river, has an excellent museum illustrating the history
of the Jewish community in Rome. Behind it is the interesting area of the old Ghetto.

The Tiber or *Tevere* is the most famous of the rivers of Italy. It rises in the Tuscan Apennines, northeast of Arezzo, and flows for 418km before reaching the sea at Ostia. It is said originally to have been called *Albula* and to have received the name *Tiberis* from Tiberinus, king of Alba Longa, because he was drowned in it. Its swift waters are discoloured with yellow mud, even far from its source: hence the epithet *flavus* ('fair' or 'tawny') given to it by the Roman poets.

Over the centuries great devastation was caused by the waters of the Tiber in flood. The present embankments and the Lungotevere roads were built in the late 19th century to control the rising waters, but at the same time they irreparably altered the townscape and alienated the river from the buildings along its banks, and today the Tiber is not such a central feature of the city as other rivers which traverse the world's great capitals.

ISOLA TIBERINA

The Isola Tiberina (*map p. 654, B3*), a pretty little island in the river, is reached from the left bank by **Ponte Fabricio**, the oldest Roman bridge to have survived in the city and still in use for pedestrians. The inscription over the near arch facing the river (seen from the embankment, just to the right) records, in handsome large lettering, the name of the builder, Lucius Fabricius, thought to have been a tribune in 62 BC. The bridge is also known as the Ponte dei Quattro Capi from the two double herms of the double-headed Janus on the parapet.

Downstream from the weir (where numerous footballs are always caught), remains of the '**Ponte Rotto**' can be seen in the bed of the river (though the view is better from Ponte Palatino). This is a single arch of the Pons Aemilius, the first stone bridge over the Tiber, the piers of which were built in 179 BC, and were connected by arches in 142 BC. From the 13th century onwards it was repaired numerous times. The carved dragon is the emblem of Pope Gregory XIII, who restored it in 1573–5, but even so it collapsed in a flood in 1598 and since then has been known as the 'broken bridge'.

As you cross the bridge onto the island there is a good view of a tall medieval tower (with an ancient Roman female head set into the masonry) which was formerly part of an 11th-century fortress; the top of the Romanesque bell-tower of San Bartolomeo; the church of San Giovanni Calibita, reconstructed in 1640; and the extensive buildings of the **hospital of the Fatebenefratelli**, which occupy most of the island. Founded in 1548, it was modernised by Cesare Bazzani in 1930–4, when the lovely palms and pine trees were planted. The island is surrounded with a wide pavement of travertine (reached by steps beside the hospital on the south side). From here it is possible to walk under the Roman bridge, and at the end nearest the Ponte Rotto you can see remains of the travertine facing which decorated the island in ancient times: the stone is sculpted in the form of a ship with a (now defaced) human head carrying the serpent of Aesculapius.

The Tiber Island is thought to have been settled early in the history of Rome since it provides an easy crossing-place on the river. During a plague in 293 BC the Sibylline Books were consulted and ambassadors were sent to the famous sanctuary of Asclepios, the god of healing, at Epidaurus in Greece. They returned with his symbol, the sacred serpent, which escaped from its basket and was found on this island, so it was decided that here a temple to the god, called by the Romans Aesculapius, should be erected: the building was dedicated in 289 BC. Ever since, the island has been associated with the work of healing.

In the piazza on the site of the Temple of Aesculapius is the church of **San Bartolomeo** (*open 9.30–1.30 & 3.30–5.30, Sun 9–1; sanbartolomeo.org*), built in the 10th century in honour of St Adalbert, Bishop of Prague, and several times restored, notably by Orazio Torriani in 1624. The interior contains 14 antique columns, and an ancient sculptured well-head, probably from the original church, has been set into the chancel steps. Traditionally thought to mark the site of a spring connected to the Temple of Aesculapius, it was made from an old Roman column which was decorated with carvings in the 11th century. A huge shiny red porphyry bath from the Baths of Caracalla serves as the high altar and reliquary of St Bartholomew. In 2000 the church became a shrine to 20th-century martyrs. The Comunità di Sant'Egidio, which carries out exemplary charitable works all over the world, has had its headquarters here since 1994 (*evening prayers at 8.30*). There is a hall crypt beneath the transept. In the former convent there is a Jewish hospital, founded in 1882.

The south side of the island is joined to one of the loveliest districts of Trastevere around Piazza in Piscinula by the **Ponte Cestio**, built by Gaius Cestius or his brother Lucius in 46 BC. It was reconstructed in AD 370. A long inscription in the centre of the walkway on a large block of travertine was inscribed by Benedetto, who was a senator who ruled Rome for a brief period in the 1190s and who here records that he restored the bridge because it was in a ruined state. He appears simply to have used the huge antique block of travertine in the middle of the bridge since the matching block on the other side is unadorned. In 1892 the central arch was rebuilt to its original design and measurements.

ISOLA TIBERINA
Travertine revetment curved like the prow of a ship bears a worn carving of a figure
(part of the wavy hair and shoulder are visible) holding the staff and serpent of Aesculapius.

THE SYNAGOGUE & JEWISH MUSEUM

The monumental **Synagogue** (*map p. 654, B3*), with its conspicuous dome, was built by Vincenzo Costa and Osvaldo Armanni in 1899–1904 in a style which has been termed 'Assyrian Babylonian'. It is one of the largest synagogues in Europe. It can be visited from the excellent **Jewish Museum (Museo Ebraico)** in the basement (*entrance in Via Catalana; open Sun–Thur 10–5.15, Fri 9–2; closed Sat; ticket includes admission to the guided tour, in English every hour, of the main synagogue and the Spanish Synagogue; T: 06 68 40 061, museoebraico.roma.it*). With very good labelling, also in English, the museum recounts the history of the Jewish community in Rome, the oldest in the world outside the Holy Land.

There is a fine collection of textiles, treasures from demolished synagogues, ancient marbles (in Room IV there is a reconstructed Holy Ark in marble dating from 1523 but incorporating some ancient fragments) and documentation recording the deportation of Roman Jews in 1943, following the anti-semitic laws introduced in 1938. The **Spanish Synagogue**, still in use, is shown, as well as the magnificent main synagogue above, where services according to the Italian rite are held every day. John Paul II was the first pope recorded setting foot inside a synagogue when he made an official visit here in 1986. The Jewish community in Rome today numbers some 13,500.

A WALK AROUND THE OLD GHETTO

AT THE FOOT OF THE OLDEST BRIDGE across the Tiber, Ponte Fabricio, is **Piazza Gerusalemme**, where the church of **San Gregorio della Divina Pietà** stands near the site of a gate in the Ghetto walls. It was founded in the 12th century but rebuilt in the early 18th. Over the entrance Pius IX set up a verse in Hebrew and Latin, from the book of Isaiah, rebuking the Jews: 'I have spread out my hands all the day unto a rebellious people, which walketh in a way that was not good, after their own thoughts, a people that provoketh me to anger continually to my face.' Jews were once forced to come here to hear sermons.

The **area of the Ghetto** was bordered by the Theatre of Marcellus, the present Via Arenula and the Tiber (the ancient Circus Flaminius, built in 221 BC, used to occupy this site). From 1556 onwards, under Pope Paul IV, the Jews of Rome were segregated and lived in this area subject to various restrictions on their personal freedom (although to a lesser degree than in other European countries). Pope Paul forced them to wear distinctive yellow hats and to sell their property to Christians. The walls of the Ghetto were torn down only in 1848, and the houses demolished in 1888 before the area south of Via del Portico d'Ottavia was reconstructed around the new synagogue. At this time many of the inhabitants were forced to find new accommodation and some moved across the river to Trastevere, although many Jewish people still live in this area.

From 1645 until 1895 the Jewish cemetery was on the lower slopes of the Aventine (*see p. 259*). It moved to Campo Verano in 1934 (*map p. 649, C1*). In the park of Villa Torlonia on Via Nomentana, Jewish catacombs were discovered in 1919. In use in the 3rd and 4th centuries, they are now mostly caved in and cannot be visited.

Via del Portico d'Ottavia leads away from the Tiber, with a view right of three temple columns and the curved wall of the Theatre of Marcellus, survivals from the ancient city (*described below*), and the green hill of the Campidoglio beyond. On the wall of the little 'medieval' house here (now the headquarters of the antique monuments and archaeological excavations office of the *Comune*), a plaque commemorates the 2,091 Roman Jews who died in concentration camps in the Second World War (along with 6,000 other Italian Jews). Anti-semitic laws were enforced under the Fascist regime in 1938 and many Jews were subsequently deported to concentration camps: the little piazza has been named Largo 16 Ottobre 1943, the date on which the Jews of Rome suffered this terrible fate.

The street takes its name from the **Porticus of Octavia**, once a huge quadriporticus (c. 119m by 132m) with about 300 columns, which enclosed temples to Jupiter and Juno. Erected by Quintus Caecilius Metellus in 146 BC, it was reconstructed by Augustus in honour of his sister Octavia c. 23 BC, and restored by Septimius Severus in AD 203. According to Pliny it was filled with statues by Greek masters. The southern extremities of the area of the porticus have been exposed, and remains of columns to the west

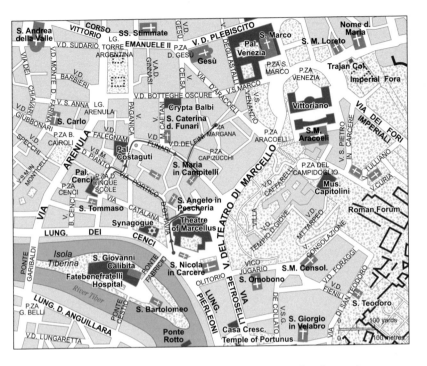

and the stylobate to the east can be seen. The entrances consisted of two propylaea with eight columns and four piers; the one on the southwest survives and serves as a monumental entrance to the church of **Sant'Angelo in Pescheria** (*closed for restoration*), founded in 755 (and rebuilt in the 16th century). Here also, from 1584 until the 19th-century papacy of Pius IX, Jews were forced to listen to a Christian sermon every Saturday. It contains a fresco of the *Madonna Enthroned with Angels* attributed to the Tuscan painter Benozzo Gozzoli or his school (north side), and, in the Chapel of St Andrew, a *Calling of St Andrew* showing the saint with his haul of fish, including squid (which he would not have found in the Sea of Galilee). The porticus was

used as a fish market (hence the name of the church, *in Pescheria*) from the 12th century up until the destruction of the Ghetto in 1888. To the right of the surviving porch (reached by an overhead walkway) is a former chapel with a relief of St Anthony over the door and an inscription identifying it as *Locus Orationis Venditorum Piscium*. The chapel is now the showroom of a shop selling magnificent porcelain.

A ramp leads down to the archaeological area (*open 9–6 or 7*) around the **Theatre of Marcellus**. This ancient Roman theatre has been partly rebuilt and partly restored. In the 16th century a palace was constructed in part of its huge cavea for the Savelli by Baldassare Peruzzi, with its façade incorporated into the curved exterior:

this shows what many ancient buildings in the city must have looked like when they were converted over the centuries for new uses. The theatre, planned by Julius Caesar, was dedicated in 13 or 11 BC by Augustus to the memory of his nephew (Octavia's son) and son-in-law, Marcellus, who had died in 23 BC at the age of 19. Restored by Vespasian and Alexander Severus, it was pillaged in the 4th century for the restoration of Ponte Cestio. It was fortified in the early Middle Ages and made into a stronghold by the Savelli and Orsini families. Renaissance architects frequently studied the theatre. When it was restored in 1932, numerous houses and shops on the site were demolished. The cavea originally had at least two tiers of 41 arches, the first with Doric and the second with Ionic engaged columns probably crowned by a Corinthian attic. Only twelve arches in each of the first two tiers survive; the upper stage has disappeared. The theatre could probably have held some 15,000 spectators.

Three tall columns still stand from the **Temple of Apollo Medicus**, built in 433 BC and restored by the consul Caius Sosius in 33 BC, and nearby are the ruins of the Temple of Bellona, built in 296 BC. There is an exit on the busy Via del Teatro di Marcello.

Via del Portico d'Ottavia continues as the **main street of the old Ghetto**. Beside the porticus, the house at no. 25 has two intricately carved ancient architraves framing the doorway and there is a stump of a column from the porticus surrounded by the tables of a *trattoria*. There are numerous kosher restaurants and shops selling kosher products and Judaica along the street and there is a Jewish school in the huge building on the left, opposite which the bar (Totò) provides a centre of local life. The bar is in part of the **House of Laurentius Manlius** (nos 2–1), which has a sarcophagus with four portrait busts of the defunct set into its wall. Manlius decorated the front with a handsome long inscription in huge lettering, dating it in the ancient Roman manner to 2,229 years after the foundation of Rome (i.e. 1476), as well as with other ancient sculptural fragments, including a relief of a lion and a gazelle. On its second façade, facing Piazza Costaguti, Manlius carved the patriotic invocation *Have Roma* ('Hail Rome!') above three of the first-floor windows. The pretty little chapel here dates from the 18th century and was another place where the Roman Church tried to convert the Jews. An excellent little **Jewish bakery**, Il Boccione (*open Sun–Thur 7–7, Fri 7–3; closed Sat*), survives on the corner here (at no. 1): it is also a centre of local life and any of the cakes and biscuits hot from the oven are worth trying. Just two old-fashioned clothes shops survive amongst the more up-to-date kosher takeaways and snack bars, and there is a 'Jewish information point' at the crossroads here. At 11 Via Santa Maria del Pianto, **Beppe** has one of the best selections of cheeses in all Rome, and you can eat here as well (*open Mon–Sat 9am–10.30pm, closed Sun; T: 06 68 19 2210, beppeeisuoiformaggi.it*).

Piazza delle Cinque Scole, which extends to the left, was laid out in the 19th century when the Ghetto was demolished, with a fountain from Piazza Giudea by Giacomo della Porta. The name of the piazza recalls the five synagogues which once occupied a building here, demolished in 1908 after a fire (although the Jews had been allowed only one synagogue in the Ghetto, they got round this restriction by creating five synagogues, one above the other, in one building). There is usually a crowd at lunchtime waiting to get a place at the simple little *trattoria* called Sora Margherita, though its prices have increased noticeably in the past few years as it has become better known.

The piazza rises up to **Monte dei Cenci**, a tiny artificial mound—probably on Roman remains—with a charming little open space on its summit overlooked by Palazzo Cenci, which belonged to the family of Beatrice Cenci, who was beheaded for parricide in 1599 (*see pp. 340–1*), and the church of San Tommaso dei Cenci, which has an ancient worn Roman altar on its exterior. The elegant old restaurant Piperno serves Jewish specialities. The last building here has a Medusa head and a fragment of a sarcophagus set into its masonry.

Return to Via del Portico d'Ottavia and take **Via della Reginella**, where the tall house at no. 27 (left), with no fewer than six floors, is typical of the crowded housing conditions, with low-ceilinged rooms, which used to exist in the old Ghetto. It ajoins the grand **Palazzo Costaguti**, with a fine cornice beneath its roof: its main portal is on Piazza Mattei (privately owned, it has painted ceilings on the *piano nobile* by Guercino). The charming **Fontana delle Tartarughe** is the work of Taddeo Landini (1584) to a design by Giacomo della Porta. One of the loveliest fountains in all Rome, it is made of grey and white marble and bronze. It was restored in 1658, perhaps by Bernini, when the tortoises were added; these

have now been replaced by copies. Via dei Funari, named after the rope-makers who used to live here, continues past the huge **Palazzo Mattei**, which comprises five palaces of the 16th–17th centuries (Carlo Maderno worked on some of the façades). Parts of the buildings, now owned by the state, are used by the Centro Italiano di Studi Americani. Through the first entrance portico (no. 19) you can look into the courtyard with its double loggia; through the next portico you can see numerous Roman statues, busts in roundels and sarcophaghi in the court, and no one seems to mind if you take the grand staircase here which leads up to the first floor loggia where there are pairs of colossal Roman busts on the terrace. The staircase itself is decorated with very fine delicate stuccoes and many more ancient Roman sarcophaghi fronts and antique reliefs, all of them still in excellent condition—one of the most curious sights in the city.

Via dei Funari crosses Via Caetani: a short way up on the right a memorial plaque and bas-relief mark the place where the body of the Italian Prime Minister Aldo Moro was abandoned by his murderers in 1978. **Santa Caterina dei Funari** (*usually closed*) was built in 1560–4 by Cardinal Federico Cesi. It has a fine façade by Guidetto Guidetti (1564) and an original campanile. The interior contains 16th-century paintings by Girolamo Muziano, Scipione Pulzone, Livio Agresti, Federico Zuccari and Marcello Venusti, and a very fine stuccoed and painted chapel by Vignola.

Just beyond (right fork), after Piazza Lovatelli, is the handsome **Piazza Campitelli**. The elegant façade of **Santa Maria in Campitelli** (*open 7am–7pm*) was erected by Carlo Rainaldi when the church was rebuilt (1662–7) in honour of a tiny, miraculous image of the Madonna, which was believed to have halted an outbreak of pestilence. The lovely, peaceful Baroque interior has an intricate perspective effect using numerous arches, columns and a heavy cornice. It is well lit by windows high up in the nave, and the good large altarpieces fit well into the architecture.

In the first south chapel is *St Michael Overcoming the Devil* by Sebastiano Conca, and in the second (designed by Carlo Rainaldi), the *Calling of the Virgin* by Luca Giordano (1685), in a lovely marble frame supported by angels and cherubs. The third chapel has reliquary busts and the cast of an altar of Apollo dedicated by Pope Gregory VII in 1073. It was the first altar of this church. In the second north chapel, the *Birth of St John the Baptist* (1692) is by Baciccia. In the first are two tombs of the Altieri family, each with a grim admonition for those who have not yet gone to the grave: NIHIL and UMBRA. Above the high altar, in a burst of Baroque golden rays, is a tiny gilt-bronze and enamel *Madonna*, (?11th century), but unfortunately too small to see with the naked eye.

In the piazza the fine 16th-century **Palazzi Albertoni and Capizucchi** (nos 2 and 3) are attributed to Giacomo della Porta, who also designed the lovely **fountain** (1589). Beneath the pretty upper marble bowl is a delicately carved Classical decoration with garlands of fruit (now very worn). On the lower travertine basin are shields with the coats of arms of local families who helped pay for the erection of the fountain, as well as the initials SPQR representing the municipality. The

deconsecrated church of **Santa Rita** by Carlo Fontana, moved here in 1937 from the foot of the Capitoline hill, below Santa Maria in Aracoeli, has an interesting oval interior, used for exhibitions.

Via Cavalletti leads out of the piazza and joins **Via de' Delfini** at the palace which houses the Polish Embassy to the Holy See, which has an ancient truncated column embedded into its masonry. A plaque set up in 2014 records that the Jesuit Order was founded here and that from 1538–41 St Ignatius Loyola was in residence. The narrow street ends in the picturesque **Piazza Margana**, where several houses are hung with old vines and one has a wisteria which climbs right up to its top floor. The restaurant and wine bar here put tables outside, and for a moment you feel you might be in Paris. The 17th-century Palazzo Maccarani-Odescalchi (no. 19), with a pretty courtyard, now serves as offices of the UN. The house at the beginning of Via Margana has an Ionic capital set into its façade and a sculptural fragment with an eagle, as well as a doorway made up from three ancient Roman friezes. This peaceful residential area, the narrow streets still with their characteristic *sanpietrini* paving, is tucked away only a few steps from the Campidoglio and very busy Piazza Venezia.

If you need to sit down for a coffee (or even a light lunch), the **Gran Caffè Roma** at 4 Piazza dell'Aracoeli is pleasant, with tables both inside and in a peaceful little side street (Via della Tribuna di Tor de' Specchi) off the busy road. Close by is a fountain which is a curious sight as it is 'overgrown' with calcium and so reduced to a trickle.

The Bocca della Verità & Ancient Velabrum

This district, between the Capitoline Hill and the Tiber, was once a marsh where legend relates that Romulus and Remus were found. A number of temples and other ancient buildings survive as well as three very early churches. Under the porch of Santa Maria in Cosmedin is the famous Bocca della Verità.

The wide **Via del Teatro di Marcello** (*map p. 654, C3*), always busy with very fast traffic, is flanked by streamlined Fascist buildings built in 1936–7 as municipal offices, angular and unadorned, mostly of brown brick with windows framed in marble (and extremely orderly roof terraces). They represent a precise period in Rome's urban architectural history when new roads were laid out on a spacious open design totally different from the appearance of the rest of the city. Parts of old Rome were often ruthlessly demolished to make way for them. Luckily the old centre avoided too much damage, especially since from 1938 urban planners concentrated their attention on creating the southern district known as EUR (*see p. 500*). On the reconstructed wall of the Theatre of Marcellus you can still see three sculpted *fasci*, which became the symbol adopted by the Fascist regime in the 1930s and which used to adorn all important buildings in Italy (*for an explanation of its origin, see p. 502*).

SAN NICOLA IN CARCERE

This church (*map p. 654, C3; open daily 7–7; underground remains open 10–6*) occupies the site of three Republican temples thought to have been dedicated to Janus, Juno Sospita and Spes. The first, to the right of the church, was Ionic hexastyle, with columns on three sides only. Its remains can be seen incorporated in the south wall of the church. Remains of the second are also incorporated. The third was on the left.

In the 11th-century the church was built, probably on the site of an older sanctuary, and it in turn was reconstructed and only consecrated in 1128. It was remodelled in 1599 by Giacomo della Porta, who designed the façade using three of the ancient Roman columns. Excavations were carried out in 1932 and again at the end of the 20th century, and the interesting ruins can be visited.

The interior has fine antique columns from the temples with diverse capitals, and a beautiful ancient urn in green porphyry beneath the high altar and baldacchino. At the end of the north aisle is an altarpiece of the *Ascension* by Lorenzo Costa (note the unusual white ground), one of the very few works in Rome by this important artist, who was born in Ferrara and worked mostly in Emilia and Mantua. The apse frescoes date from 1865. In the south aisle is a fresco fragment of the *Madonna and Child* (c. 1490) by Antoniazzo Romano detached from a lower chapel (the happy Child is particularly charming). The *Trinity* on the west wall is attributed to Guercino.

On request (*small fee*) you can take the steps down into the confessio where, on the left, a narrow iron door (*push it open*) admits to the interesting and well-labelled remains of all three temples on this site. The last one, to the north, has a particularly well preserved podium base. Also here is a little chapel with three niches containing martyrs' bones and which used to be adorned with Antoniazzo Romano's fresco (now in the south aisle of the upper church).

On the corner of Via del Teatro Marcello and Via del Ponte Rotto is the **Casa dei Crescenzi**, a quaint medieval building erected by a wealthy Roman in the 12th century, using fragments of Classical buildings or medieval copies of Roman works. Formerly a tower guarding the river, the long inscription states that it was erected by one Nicolaus, son or descendant of Crescentius and Theodora, probably members of the Alberic family, the most powerful clan in Rome at the end of the 10th century. The bricks of the lower storey are formed into half-columns, with rudimentary capitals. A fragment of the upper storey and its arcaded loggia survives. It cannot be visited since it is now used by a study centre, the Centro Studi per la Storia dell'Architettura.

PIAZZA DELLA BOCCA DELLA VERITÀ

Piazza della Bocca della Verità (*map p. 654, C3–C4*) is a busy, traffic-filled space that takes its name from the huge carved human face in the portico of the church of Santa Maria in Cosmedin, which is a well-known tourist attraction. In a little garden in the piazza are two ancient Roman temples, which have survived very well because they were transformed into churches in the early Middle Ages.

The **Temple of Portunus** is dedicated to the god of harbours. Its form is pseudoperipteral: in other words, it appears to be surrounded by a colonnade, but in fact only the front columns are disengaged; the lateral columns are embedded in the cella wall. Dating in its present form probably to the 1st century BC, the Ionic columns of the portico survive, as well as the five half columns along the cella sides, making it one of the most precious examples extant of the Graeco-Italian temples of the Republican age. In 872 it became the church of Santa Maria Egiziaca.

The charming little round **Temple of Hercules Victor** was known as the Temple of Vesta until an inscription from the base of a cult statue was found confirming its dedication to Hercules. The gilt-bronze statue of Hercules now in the Capitoline Museums (*see p. 45*) stood close to its altar (partly visible in the crypt of Santa Maria in Cosmedin; *see below*); his cult seems to have been associated with the slaying of the monster Cacus (*see p. 103*). He was also patron god of olive merchants, who frequent-

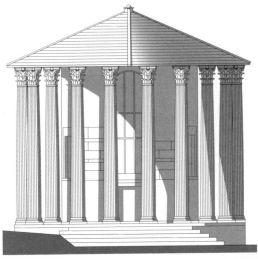

TEMPLE OF HERCULES VICTOR

ed the markets here. The temple dates from the end of the 2nd century BC and is the oldest marble edifice to survive in Rome. It is clearly modelled on Greek temples and was indeed originally constructed throughout in precious Greek Pentelic marble. An elegant colonnade of 20 fluted columns, with exquisite capitals, surrounds the cella. After severe damage in the 1st century AD the temple was restored under Tiberius and ten of the columns and capitals were replaced, using the (easily distinguishable) white Luni marble. One of the columns is missing on the north side but its base remains. The original roof and ancient entablature have not survived. In the Middle Ages the temple was adapted as a church and the cella wall replaced with brick-faced concrete.

The **fountain** is by Carlo Bizzaccheri (1717), a good work for its period though lacking strength and true style. The entrance to a side conduit of the Cloaca Maxima drain (*see p. 75*) can be seen under a square travertine lid. There are a few benches in the pleasant little garden.

SANTA MARIA IN COSMEDIN

Map p. 654, C4. Open 9.30–5; summer until 6; sung Mass in Greek and Arabic.

Santa Maria in Cosmedin is today the church of the Melkite community in Rome (Middle Eastern Catholics who use the Byzantine rite). Its rector is styled archimandrite, under the jurisdiction of the Melkite patriarch. It was for centuries known as the *Schola Graeca* since it had been assigned to Greek refugees driven from Constantinople by the Iconoclastic persecutions. Architecturally it is a fine example of a Roman medieval church, preceded by a little gabled porch and arcaded narthex, and with a fine

12th-century campanile of seven storeys. However it was somewhat over-restored in 1899 and it has lost much of its atmosphere, often being hurriedly visited by tour groups because the famous Bocca della Verità is housed under its portico.

The building stands on the site of an Imperial-era precinct perhaps connected to a *Statio Annonae* (market inspector's office) and later a Christian *diaconia* (welfare centre), erected c. 600. The Christian oratory was enlarged by Hadrian I in the 8th century into a basilican church, with a matroneum and three apses. It was at this time that it acquired the name 'in Cosmedin', from the Greek verb to adorn. Cardinal Alfano, chamberlain of Calixtus II (whose tomb is in the portico), rebuilt the church around 1123, closed the galleries, and added the schola cantorum.

THE BOCCA DELLA VERITÀ

The Bocca della Verità, the so-called 'Mouth of Truth', is a large, cracked marble disc representing a human face, the open mouth of which was believed to close on the hand of any perjurer who faced the ordeal of placing it there. It is in fact an ancient fountain-head, and was set up under the porch here in 1632. Inspired by the antics of Gregory Peck in *Roman Holiday*, visitors now flock here to have their photograph taken with their hand in the mouth, and except in low season there is always a queue of people waiting to do this. As soon as you step under the porch, you will find yourself efficiently corralled. You can choose whether to visit the church only, or whether to wait in line to photograph the Mouth (pressure of numbers behind you on busy days will allow you only a few seconds to admire it) and then go into the church from there. In fact you can see the Mouth quite well enough from outside the porch, but standing in a slow-moving queue gives you time to examine the main west doorway, the work of a certain 'Johannes' from the Veneto (11th century). The carved frame culminates in a tiny Lamb of the Resurrection at the top. Also here is the tomb of Cardinal Alfano (*see above*).

THE CHURCH

The beautiful interior, with a nave and two aisles each ending in an apse, closely follows the layout of Pope Hadrian's 8th-century basilica. The arcades are supported on antique columns with good capitals grouped in threes between piers. In the first part of the nave remains of the arcaded colonnade and side walls of the ancient Roman building and *diaconia* can be seen. High up on the walls are traces of 11th-century frescoes. But it is the enclosed choir or **schola cantorum** in the nave which is today the most interesting part of the church since the screen, paschal candelabrum, two pulpits, episcopal throne and beautiful pavement all survive intact from the time of Cardinal Alfano (1123). They are the work of the Cosmati family (*see p. 62*). The baldacchino over the high altar (an ancient Roman porphyry bath) is by Deodatus, third son of the younger Cosma (1294).

A chapel (*under restoration at the time of writing*) purports to preserve the skull of St Valentine, said to have been martyred beside the Via Flaminia in the late 3rd century.

The former **sacristy** (now, most inappropriately, a souvenir shop) contains a precious mosaic of 706 on a gold ground, a fragment of the *Adoration of the Magi* formerly in the oratory of John VII at St Peter's (rather poorly lit). The tiny **crypt** (*open on request*) was built into part of a pagan altar dedicated to Hercules, the columns of which remain.

THE ANCIENT VELABRUM

The earliest markets of the ancient city were established in the Velabrum, conveniently near the river: the Forum Holitorium, for fruit and vegetables and the Forum Boarium, for cattle. Although only a few steps from the crowded Santa Maria in Cosmedin, the little church of San Giorgio in Velabro is seldom visited, in an incredibly quiet cul-de-sac, isolated from the traffic, where you can often hear the birds sing. It is approached past the squat, four-sided **Arch of Janus** *(fenced; map p. 654, C3)* which once formed a covered passage at a crossroads *(quadrivium)* and provided shelter for the cattle-dealers of the Forum Boarium. This is particularly interesting as it is one of the very few ancient buildings still to be seen in the city which is clearly ill-proportioned. It is usually dated to the reign of Constantine, which scholars have seen as a period of decadence in the arts, when sculptural fragments from earlier centuries were often reused (as is the case here: the numerous niches would have contained statues). Steps and a walkway to the left lead to the church of San Giorgio.

SAN GIORGIO IN VELABRO

This lovely church *(map p. 654, C3; open 7.30–6.30; often used for weddings at the weekends)* is one of the most memorable medieval buildings in Rome. It is thought to have been founded in the 9th century or earlier, when it was built over an early Christian *diaconia* established here by c. 600. The campanile dates from the 12th century. The church was well restored to its medieval appearance in 1926 by Antonio Muñoz, but it was severely damaged by the Mafia in a bomb explosion in 1993, which destroyed the Ionic portico. This dated from the 9th–12th century (but was restored in the 13th century as the inscription states) and it was beautifully reconstructed from the shattered fragments so that today it is hard to tell that it is not the original.

The beautiful plain interior is basilican, with nave and aisles separated by 16 delicate ancient columns of granite and pavonazzetto. On a small scale, it has an intimate feel. The pretty lattice-work windows recall those of Santa Sabina on the Aventine. The irregular floorplan, mirrored in the wooden ceiling, is probably derived from the fact that the 9th-century building incorporated an earlier structure. The church has no paintings and its simple, bare interior is in striking contrast to the many highly decorated churches of Rome. In the apse is a fresco of *Christ with the Madonna and Sts Peter, Sebastian and George* attributed to Pietro Cavallini (c. 1296; repainted in the 16th century). A beautifully proportioned canopy dating from the 13th century protects the altar, which has a niche with some exquisite Cosmatesque decoration: through the grille you can still see the supposed skull of St George in a quaint, old-fashioned reliquary. This precious relic was brought to Rome by the Greek pope Zacharias in the 8th century and for centuries pilgrims would visit the church in order to be granted an indulgence when it was displayed (on the first Sunday of Lent). St George, martyred c. 300, is one of the most popular of all saints. Since the time of the Crusades he has always been depicted as a knight mounted on a white charger, killing a dragon. To this day worshippers push notes for the saint through the grille.

SAN TEODORO AL PALATINO
The *Dextera Dei*, the right hand of God, a common motif in Roman
early Christian mosaics from a time before God began to be represented with a human face.
It is typically shown reaching from a cloud, bearing a diadem or victory wreath, conferring
blessing and approval upon the figures depicted below.

The ornate little **Arcus Argentariorum** to the left of the church was erected by the money changers (*argentarii*) and cattle dealers of the Forum Boarium in honour of the emperor Septimius Severus, his second wife Julia Domna, and their children, Caracalla and Geta, in AD 204. The portrait and name of Geta were effaced as a mark of his disgrace after his assassination by his brother in 212.

In front of the church is an ivy-grown arch where you can see remains of the **Cloaca Maxima** (*an ancient drainage system still partly in use; see p. 75*).

SAN TEODORO AL PALATINO

From the church of San Giorgio there is a view of the Palatine hill with its massive ancient buildings. At its foot, and reached by Via dei San Teodoro, is the church of the same name, just 200m away (*map pp. 654, C3–655, D3; usually open 9.30–12.30; closed Sat; services following the Greek orthodox rite on Sun morning*). The first church was built on part of the site of the great granary warehouse known as the Horrea Agrippiana, which had been used as an early Christian *diaconia*. The present church dates from the time of Nicholas V (c. 1453) and is dedicated to St Theodore Tyro, a soldier in the Roman army who was martyred between 306 and 311 at Amasea (modern Amasya in Turkey). The famous Roman bronze *She-wolf* now in the Capitoline Museums was found beside the church.

In front of the church, steps lead down to the delightful courtyard designed by Carlo Fontana in 1642–5, planted with palms, magnolia and olive trees in pots, which surround a very worn cylindrical pagan altar. The circular interior preserves the apse of the 6th-century oratory of the diaconia with its original—though much restored—mosaic (583–90) showing *Christ Blessing* sitting on a blue celestial globe, with St Peter presenting St Theodore and St Paul with an unidentified saint (scholars have tentatively suggested that he might be Cleonicus, another martyr of Amasea). Above appears the right hand of God, holding a laurel wreath.

There are remains of the earlier Roman building and the *diaconia* beneath the foundations (*but they have been closed indefinitely*).

The Aventine Hill, Circus Maximus & Baths of Caracalla

*A secluded residential area with beautiful trees and gardens
and just a scattering of cafés and shops, the Aventine Hill is one of the
most peaceful areas of central Rome. Below it lie two magnificent survivals
from the ancient city: the huge Circus Maximus and the wonderful ruins
of the Baths of Caracalla.*

The Aventine (*map p. 654, C4 and p. 653*) is the southernmost of the Seven Hills of Rome and was not at first included within the precincts of the city, remaining outside the walls of the pomerium (*see p. 88*) throughout the Republican era. For centuries it was sparsely populated. In the Imperial era the Aventine became an aristocratic district and in the early Middle Ages it was covered with elegant mansions. Unlike much of the city, it remained remarkably unchanged throughout the 20th century. It offers fine views across the Tiber to the northwest.

Approaches to the Aventine
From Piazza della Bocca della Verità (map p. 654, C4) there is easy access on foot to the Aventine. Follow the Lungotevere Aventino along the river for a few metres as far as the Clivo di Rocca Savelli, an attractive stepped lane of sanpietrini cobbles which leads up past the wall of the 12th-century Savelli castle. Alternative approaches, Clivo dei Publicii and Via di Valle Murcia, ascend from the Circus Maximus.

SANTA SABINA

Map p. 653, A1. Open 8.15–12.30 & 3.30–6.

The church of Santa Sabina is perhaps the most beautiful basilica in Rome to have survived from the early Christian period. We know from the mosaic inscription inside that it was built during the pontificate of Celestine I by a certain Peter of Illyria (422–32), a bishop from Dalmatia. It is on the legendary site of the house of the Roman matron Sabina—who was later canonised—and near a temple of Juno.

It was restored in 824 and again in 1216: three years later Honorius III gave it to St Dominic for his new Order. It was disfigured in 1587 by Domenico Fontana (when 20 of the windows were walled up) but excellently restored by Antonio Muñoz in 1919 and 1937 (Muñoz is best remembered for the work he did on this church). Beneath the nave, remains of a small temple and an edifice of the early Imperial period with a fine marble pavement were found.

THE WEST ENTRANCE

The current entrance is through a side door on the piazza. But first go round into the **west portico**, where the original **carved wooden door of the first church** survives. Surrounded by an ancient marble doorway, the 18 panels with scriptural scenes showing parallels between the Old and New Testaments are in excellent condition. They are a precious and almost unique survival of palaeochristian art from the early 5th century. It seems that at least two woodcarvers worked on them, and Eastern influence can clearly be detected in some of the scenes, which may not be in their original order. Most are unfortunately very high up so difficult to examine (but there is a coin-operated light). The four lowest scenes, which are more or less at eye level, are as follows (from the right): Elijah in his chariot of fire ascends to Heaven while Elisha pulls at his mantle, with youths below armed with axes (the story is taken from a Palestinian legend). The next panel (*illustrated opposite*) shows Moses and the Exodus from Egypt: the three scenes show fiery serpents and the Pharoah; the Pharoah's chariot and his army drowned in the Red Sea; and (above) the head of God in a pillar of fire while an angel leads the army of Israel. The third panel shows a scene (of uncertain significance) also divided into three tiers, with figures raising their arms in acclamation. The fourth panel has more scenes from the life of Moses: when still a shepherd with his five sheep; and on Mount Horeb when he is called by God. The row of panels above these includes scenes from the life of Christ (one panel shows three miracles: the marriage at Cana; the multiplication of the loaves and fishes, and the healing of the blind man) and scenes from the Passion, including one of the oldest representations of the Crucifixion in existence.

Under the portico are some fluted columns and a worn fresco. A little round opening provides a glimpse of the oranges trees in the convent garden (*described below*).

INTERIOR OF SANTA SABINA

The beautifully-proportioned Classical interior, with its simple, clean lines, is modelled on the basilicas of Ravenna. Of its **mosaic decoration**, which formerly covered the nave walls and the conch of the apse, only one section above the west doorway remains, showing seven hexameters in Classical gold lettering on a blue ground. It praises the founder, Bishop Peter of Illyria, for his modesty and generosity and includes the name of the pope at that time (Celestine I). The two female figures at the sides personify the converted Jews (*ex-circumcisione*) and the converted pagans or Gentiles (*ex-gentibus*).

The tall, very wide nave is divided from the aisles by 24 beautiful fluted Corinthian columns from a neighbouring 2nd-century building. The spandrels of the arcades are

SANTA SABINA
Scenes of the Exodus, from the 5th-century carved west doorway.

decorated with **5th-century marble inlay** in opus sectile. Beneath a frieze of geometric shapes, and between a stylised decoration imitating a wall, there are large emblems with alternate green and porphyry roundels thought to represent the triumph of Christianity over Imperial Rome. The handsome large windows, 34 in all, have lattice-work of varied design based on original fragments. In the centre of the nave is the **tomb of Fra' Muñoz de Zamora** (a Master General of the Dominicans, d. 1300). The delightful and unusual effigy in mosaic, perhaps by Jacopo Torriti, shows him fast asleep in his cowl. Interestingly enough his name is the same as the 20th-century restorer of the church, who skilfully reconstructed the large schola cantorum from early Christian plutei, some of them fragmentary. The revetment of the apse, in grey marble with strips of porphyry, survives intact.

The apse fresco by Taddeo Zuccari which was re-painted by Vincenzo Camuccini in 1836, greatly detracts from the simple beauty of the church. The Zuccari also decorated the Chapel of St Hyacinth in the south aisle, where there is an ancient column which must predate the church. At the end of the aisle is the wall tomb of Cardinal Auxias de Podio (1485), by the school of Andrea Bregno, near a pavement tomb of a genial bishop resting his head on a comfortable cushion. The only painted altarpieces in the church are in the two side chapels: the *Madonna of the Rosary with St Dominic and St Catherine*, by Sassoferrato, is a particularly graceful work, with a wreath of roses and lilies lying at the foot of the throne.

THE DOMINICAN CONVENT

At the time of writing the convent could only be seen at 10am on the 2nd Sat of the month, on a guided tour which has to be booked in advance (*for details and updates, see circuitoaperto.it*). St Dominic's room, now a chapel, where the saint lived and had a meeting with St Francis, is shown, as well as the cloister and excavations.

GIARDINO DEGLI ARANCI

Outside Santa Sabina, in Piazza Pietro d'Illiria with its three old elm trees, there is a delightful **wall fountain** of a mascaron in the form of a gentleman with a moustache and bushy eyebrows, made less severe by the fact that his face emerges from a scallop shell. He blows water into a huge Roman bath which overflows into the basin below. A typical Roman '*nasone*' fountain provides more convenient drinking water beside it. Here is the main entrance (through a gateway removed from a Villa on the Via Flaminia) to the **Giardino degli Aranci** (also called the Parco Savello; *open 7–dusk*), a pretty walled garden planted with orange trees, and with roses in tubs, below tall umbrella pines with their typical eccentrically-shaped trunks. There are plenty of comfortable benches. The main walk of the garden is named after one of Italy's greatest actors, the much beloved Nino Manfredi (1921–2004).

The terrace has one of the best views of the entire city to the north and northwest: visible on the skyline to the right is the brick Torre delle Milizie, with the tower of Santa Maria in Cosmedin in the foreground. Next comes the tower of Palazzo Senatorio on the Capitoline hill, and the Vittoriano. In the distance you can see the bright Villa Medici, with its two towers, in the trees. Further left is the dome of Santi Ambrogio e Carlo and (nearer) the dome of the Synagogue. On the left is the Rococo spire of Sant'Ivo and the dome of Sant'Andrea della Valle. Straight ahead the dome of St Peter's is prominent, and the green hill of the Janiculum.

TURNER'S VIEW FROM THE AVENTINE

It is interesting to think that Turner must have stood near here in 1828, to make sketches for his wonderful *Rome, from Mount Aventine*, which was sold by the Earl of Rosebery in 2014 for £30.3 million. This was the highest price ever paid for a painting by Turner—and indeed more than any other pre 20th-century British work had fetched at auction.

Turner first visited Rome in 1819 and the impact of the Italian light on his work was fundamental and marked a turning point in his art. We know that he made numerous pencil sketches and some coloured *plein-air* drawings. It was on his second trip to Rome in 1828 that he painted this picture. Turner was not fully understood or appreciated in his day, and it is only since the 20th century that he has been considered perhaps the greatest British painter of all time.

Rome, from Mount Aventine is an early morning view of the Tiber as it curves downstream, featuring many of the monuments still visible today. The most obvious difference is the Tiber itself, as yet unembanked, and full of shipping activity. When the picture was first exhibited in London in 1836, Constable commented: 'Turner has outdone himself, he seems to paint with tinted steam, so evanescent and airy.'

Further along Via di Santa Sabina is another peaceful public garden (*not always open*) with orange trees, pine trees and bougainvillea. The view from the parapet is obscured by trees when they are in leaf. The garden is home to a colony of bright green monk parakeets (*Myiopsitta monachus*).

ALONG VIA DI SANTA SABINA

SANTI BONIFACIO E ALESSIO

This church (*map p. 653, A1; open 8.30–12.30 & 3.30–5 or 6*), mainly 18th century but of earlier foundation, is dedicated to St Boniface of Tarsus (said to have been martyred in Turkey in the 4th century) and St Alexis (*for his story, see below*). It is preceded by an attractive courtyard and retains a fine Romanesque **campanile** above its 18th-century façade (on the summit of which is a little Byzantine Cross from the earlier church). A Cosmati frieze with green and maroon marble inlay survives around the **main portal**, which is flanked by two statuettes of angels on pedestals attributed to the school of Arnolfo di Cambio.

In the 18th-century interior, there are strips of Cosmati pavement in the terracotta tiled floor and in the apse two exquisite little round columns entirely decorated with Cosmati inlay. In the floor of the **apse** is the pavement tomb of Lope da Olmedo (d. 1433), in his monk's habit. He was the Master General of the nearby monastery, built by the Crescentii family in the 10th century. At the west end of the north aisle, set into an altar of 1700, is part of a **wooden staircase**—one of the strangest sights in a Roman church. A legend relates that Alexis (the joint titular saint), son of a Roman senator, renounced his position on his wedding day and went out into the world as a beggar. Many years later he returned home and lived for 17 years as a servant 'below stairs' in the employ of his wealthy family, but before dying he sent the story of his life to the pope, and was thus recognised by his wife and father. In the south aisle is the severe, Rationalist tomb of the painter Antonio Mancini (d. 1930), designed by Antonio Muñoz. In the chapel to the right of the choir is a 12th/13th-century **icon of the Madonna** (its date belied by its hideous frame). The **crypt** (*kept locked*) contains relics of St Thomas à Becket.

PIAZZA DEI CAVALIERI DI MALTA

Via di Santa Sabina ends at the delightful Piazza dei Cavalieri di Malta, enclosed by walls with elaborate decorations with trophies, obelisks and emblems (including Maltese crosses) designed by Piranesi in the 18th century and today seen against a background of cypresses and palms. Piranesi also built the monumental entrance to the gardens of the Priorato di Malta, which has a famous **view of the dome of St Peter's** seen through the keyhole in the doorway. The dome appears framed by a magnificent high double hedge formed by a variety of evergreens. The gardens surround the residence of the Grand Master of the Knights of Malta, and the seat of the Order's embassies to Italy and the Vatican. The Order of Malta, the Sovereign Military Hospitaller Order of

St John of Jerusalem of Rhodes and of Malta (or Knights Hospitallers), was founded by a certain Gerard in 1113 to assist pilgrims to the Holy Land. The order was based on the island of Rhodes from 1310 to 1522, and then on Malta until 1798. Their headquarters are now in Rome, at Via Condotti 68, and the knights continue to carry out charitable work. It is the smallest sovereign entity in the world.

Not visible from the piazza is the church of **Santa Maria del Priorato** (*only open by appointment, with the garden: economato@orderofmalta.int*), a Benedictine foundation that was once incorporated in the residence of the patrician senator Alberic, who was the virtual ruler of Rome from 932–54. It passed into the hands of the Templars and from them to the Knights of Malta. The current church was built for the Knights by Piranesi in 1765. It is his only architectural work. Behind six palm trees, its remarkable façade of a single order crowned with a tympanum has rich decorative details, typical of Piranesi's imagination and quite unlike any other church façade in the city. The interior is just as interesting, with its stucco decorations and an elaborate high altar, cleverly lit, executed by Tommaso Righi. Fifteenth-century tombs are incorporated into the architecture and there is a statue of Piranesi by Giuseppe Angelini.

Also in the piazza is the late 19th-century Benedictine seminary and church of **Sant'Anselmo**, in the Lombard Romanesque style (*daily Mass with Gregorian Chant*).

PIRANESI'S ROME

Giovanni Battista Piranesi, born in Venice in 1720, first came to Rome with the Venetian ambassador Marco Foscarini in 1740. He spent most of his life here and is famous above all for the series entitled *Vedute di Roma*, 135 large-format engravings which he began around 1748. These views of Rome, as well as his engraved details of ancient monuments and his architectural *caprices*, became extremely popular with visitors on the Grand Tour and were to influence the sublime sensibilities of the Romantics. In *Le Antichità Romane*, published in 1756, he also documented the ruins of the ancient city, taking into account the discoveries the archaeologists were making at the time (a copy of it is on view at the Galleria dell'Accademia di San Luca). In 1757 Piranesi was made an honorary member of the Society of Antiquaries of London.

However it was only in the piazza and church of the Priorato that his lifelong ambition to become an architect was finally realised. He received the commission thanks to two compatriots: the Venetian pope Clement XIII (Carlo Rezzonico, 1758–69) and Monsignore Giambattista Rezzonico, Grand Master of the Knights of Malta.

SANTA PRISCA & THE NORTHERN SLOPE

The church of **Santa Prisca** (*map p. 653, A1–B1*) possibly dates from the 4th century and is said to occupy the site of the house of Prisca, an early martyr, who was a friend of

St Paul. In the interior there are pretty frescoes, all by Anastasio Fontebuoni (d. 1626), who was a pupil of the Zuccari brothers: in the nave above each column are apostles, angels and saints and at the east end is the *Martyrdom of Prisca*. The high altarpiece of *St Peter Baptising Prisca* is a good work by Passignano. Beneath the church there is a Mithraeum (*open by appointment; T: 06 39 08 071, www.santaprisca.it*) with a statue of Mithras slaying the bull and a recumbent figure of Saturn.

On the slope which leads downhill to the Circus Maximus is the **Roseto Comunale di Roma**, a rose garden with some 200 varieties of rose (*open May and June daily 8–7.30*). From 1645 until the land was expropriated in 1934, this was the Orto degli Ebrei, Rome's Jewish cemetery. Many of the Jewish remains were moved to Rome's main cemetery at Campo Verano and the rose garden was created in the 1950s. Examine the layout of the paths on a map or on Google Earth, and you will see that they are arranged in the shape of a menorah.

THE CIRCUS MAXIMUS

Only the shape survives of the Circus Maximus (Circo Massimo; *map p. 653, B1*), the largest circus of ancient Rome, but it is impressive for all that. It lies in the valley between the Palatine and the Aventine hills and is the largest uninterrupted open space in the city. Today it is an unenclosed public park, planted with a row of pines and cypresses, where Romans come to stroll, walk their dogs or jog (it is also sometimes used for political demonstrations). It has a magnificent view of the substructures of the buildings on the lower slopes of the Palatine hill.

HISTORY AND STRUCTURE OF THE CIRCUS

The circus was the first and largest in Rome. According to Livy, it dates from the time of Tarquinius Priscus (c. 600 BC), who is said to have inaugurated a display of races and boxing matches here after a victory over the Latins; but the first factual reference to it is in 329 BC. The circus was often altered and enlarged.

In the time of Julius Caesar its length was three *stadia* (1,875 Roman feet) and its width one *stadium*. The resultant oblong was rounded at one end and straight at the other. Tiers of seats were provided all round except at the short straight end; here were the *carceres*, or stalls for horses and chariots. In the centre, running lengthwise, was the *spina*, a low wall terminating at either end in a *meta*, or conical pillar, denoting the turnings of the course. The length of a race was seven circuits of the spina. Though primarily adapted for chariot races, the circus was also used for athletic contests, wild-beast fights, and (by flooding the arena) for mock sea-battles. It could accommodate from 150,000 to 385,000 spectators; its capacity varied from one reconstruction to the next. The obelisks now in Piazza del Popolo and outside St John Lateran once stood here.

The circus was destroyed by fire under Nero (AD 64) and again in the time of Domitian. A new circus was built by Trajan; Caracalla enlarged it and Constantine restored it after a partial collapse. The last games were held under the Ostrogothic king Totila in AD 549.

During the days of the ancient Empire, the Circus Maximus was the scene of a ritual procession and purification of weapons by soldiers of the Roman army, every year on 19th Oct, the feast of the Armilustrium. Tradtionally this was the day when Rome laid down its arms and called a halt to the campaigning season until the following spring. In the days of the Republic, the festival took place on the Aventine hill above the circus.

The extant remains belong to the Imperial period. Some seats and part of the substructure of the stairways can be seen at the curved east end, around the medieval Torre di Moletta near Piazza di Porta Capena, as well as the walls of some ancient taverns. In the centre of this curve was the entrance gate: here in AD 80–1 a triumphal arch was erected to commemorate Titus' conquest of Jerusalem. Part of it was discovered in 2015 but it is not at present visible. Sporadic excavations have been in progress since 1984. At the west end of the circus, on Via dell'Ara Massima di Ercole, are remains of a large Roman public building (2nd century AD) with a 3rd-century Mithraeum beneath.

On the busy modern Viale Aventino rises a huge building begun in 1938 by Mario Ridolfi (one of the most important 20th-century Italian architects) to house the Ministero per l'Africa Italiano (a Fascist ministry for the colonisation of Africa). Since 1951 it has been the seat of the **United Nations Food and Agriculture Organisation (FAO)**. Until 2005 the Stele of Axum stood here, a 4th-century monument stolen from Ethiopia by Mussolini during the Italian occupation in 1935–6. In 2005 it was air-lifted back (in three pieces) to Axum, the ancient Ethiopian capital, and re-erected in its original position.

THE LESSER AVENTINE

The wide and busy Viale Aventino separates the higher summit of the Aventine from the smaller hill known as the Piccolo Aventino, or Lesser Aventine. In Piazza Albania (*map p. 653, A2*) are extensive remains of the **Servian wall** (c. 87 BC).

SAN SABA

The first church of San Saba was founded in the 7th century by Palestinian monks escaping from the Eastern invasions. The present building (*open 8–12 & 4–7; entrance in Via di San Saba or round the corner in Piazza Bernini*), with its little porch and walled forecourt, may date from around 900, although it has been rebuilt several times and was restored in 1943. In the portico are sculptural fragments, some Oriental in character (including a knight and falcon), and a large Roman sarcophagus with figures of a bridegroom and Juno Pronuba. The portal is by Giacomo, the father of Cosma, who also probably designed the floor in the interior, where the right aisle has remains of a schola cantorum, a patchwork of Cosmatesque work. In the apse, above the bishop's throne, is a lovely Cosmatesque marble disc and a 14th-century fresco of the *Crucifixion*.

SANTA BALBINA
First-century mosaic of an amphora.

In 1463, under Cardinal Piccolomini, the *Annunciation* was painted high up on the arch over the apse (the loggia above the portico was also added at this time). On the left-hand side of the church is a short fourth aisle with remains of 13th-century frescoes of the *Virgin and Child* and stories of St Nicholas. Beneath the church were found fragments of frescoes from the 7th-century church (now exhibited in the sacristy corridor).

SANTA BALBINA

Founded in the 5th century and later rebuilt, the church (*map p. 653, B2; open Sun 10.30–11.30*) was well restored in 1930, when the transennae in the windows and the schola cantorum were installed. The wooden ceiling still bears the name of its benefactor, Cardinal Marco Barbo (1489). In the floor are numerous black-and-white mosaics (1st century AD), found in the city in 1939. The 13th-century Cosmatesque episcopal chair in the apse is in excellent condition. The apse fresco of the *Glory of Christ* is by Anastasio Fontebuoni (1623). Fresco fragments include a good *Madonna Enthroned with Four Saints* and the *Redeemer* above, attributed to the school of Pietro Cavallini. The bas-relief of the *Crucifixion* (1460) is attributed to Mino da Fiesole and Giovanni Dalmata. The tomb of Stefanus de Surdis (1303) is by Giovanni Cosmati.

THE BATHS OF CARACALLA

Map p. 653, C2. Open Tues–Sun 9–dusk, Mon 9–2. T: 06 39 96 7700, archeoroma. beniculturali.it. Combined ticket valid 7 days with the Tomb of Cecilia Metella and Villa dei Quintili on the Via Appia Antica. For the Archaeological Card and reductions for young visitors, see p. 600.

The huge Baths of Caracalla are the best-preserved and most splendid Imperial-era baths in the city. The romantic sun-baked ruins, free of modern buildings, are on a vast scale and are an architectural masterpiece of remarkably complex design. The ruins still maintain their extraordinarily romantic atmosphere, their vast walls sihouetted against the sky or glimpsed through apertures in shadow. Indeed, one cannot help thinking that they are even more impressive now in their silent ruined state than they can ever have been when they were in use. There is vegetation in some of the crevices and poppies and daisies grow in the grass under foot. The ruins are inhabited, undisturbed, by numerous seagulls, crows and pigeons. The site is surrounded by a lovely enclosed garden, planted with pines, laurels and cypresses and low box hedges (with comfortable old benches), which succeeds in isolating the spot totally from the noise of the busy roads all around it.

HISTORY OF THE BATHS

The baths were begun by Antoninus Caracalla in 212, at a time when the construction of vast concrete vaults had been perfected, allowing these to be truly monumental. It has been estimated that 9,000 workmen laboured for five years on the site. The baths opened in 217. They were fed by a branch of the Aqua Marcia, an aqueduct built specially for this purpose in 212–17, and had twelve furnaces, eight of them under the great central floor of the caldarium. After a restoration by Aurelian they remained in use until the 6th century, when the invading Goths cut the aqueducts. Roman citizens had free access to the baths, which could accommodate some 1,600 bathers at a time.

In the 16th–17th centuries, the *Belvedere Torso* (now in the Vatican Museums), the *Farnese Hercules*, *Farnese Bull* and *Farnese Flora* (all now in Naples), and many other statues were found among the ruins. The two huge bath tubs now used as fountains in Piazza Farnese and a mosaic of athletes (now in the Vatican) also came from here. Shelley composed a large part of his *Prometheus Unbound* in this romantic setting. In 1937 the first opera performance was given here and after an interruption in the 1990s the baths are now once again used for opera in summer.

The baths are built on an artificial platform and have always been above ground, though excavations in the 20th century greatly enlarged the area accessible to the public. The central core of bathing halls is surrounded by a wide enclosure dating mainly from the end of the Severan period (though the water cisterns date from Caracalla's time). Beneath ground level there is an intricate heating system and hydraulic plant, which may one day be restored and opened to the public. Of the elaborate decoration only a few architectural fragments and some floor mosaics remain, revealing the baroque taste of the 3rd century in the introduction of divinities on the fine Composite capitals. The walls were once lined with marble and stucco. There are relatively few signs, but rather too many fences.

WHAT TO SEE

The modern entrance pathway skirts the western boundary wall. On the way in you pass the remains of a **Mithraeum (A)** below ground (*no access*) and immediately afterwards a huge **exedra (B)** with an apsidal central hall (a matching exedra stood to the east). From here the entrance to the ruins of the bathing complex is to your left.

Main buildings: The main buildings of the baths (220m by 114m) were symmetrically arranged around a huge central hall. At either end of this were twin facilities for changing and exercising before immersion. The signposted route takes you into the **western palaestra (C)**, for sports and exercises. It consisted of an open courtyard with porticoes on three sides and a huge hemicycle opposite five smaller rooms. Part of the polychrome pavement survives. Behind it to the north is an **apodyterium** (dressing room) **(D)**, which is where

bathers would have gone first to change, leaving their belongings in lockers. The iron gate here is at one of the original entrances.

From the palaestra you can enter the **central hall (E)**. Opening off it to the right as you make your way down it are the scanty remains of the vast, circular **caldarium (F)**, which measured 34m across. It had high windows on two levels designed to admit the sun's rays for many hours of the day, and was covered with a dome. From here the bathers passed into the **tepidarium (G)**.

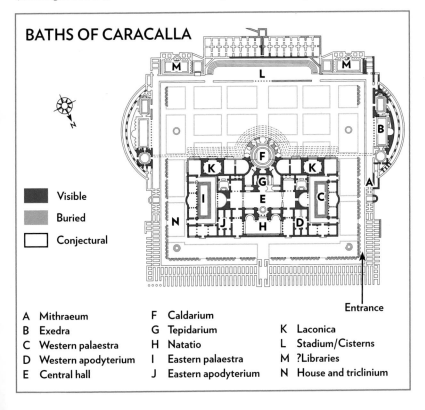

BATHS OF CARACALLA

Visible
Buried
Conjectural

A Mithraeum
B Exedra
C Western palaestra
D Western apodyterium
E Central hall
F Caldarium
G Tepidarium
H Natatio
I Eastern palaestra
J Eastern apodyterium
K Laconica
L Stadium/Cisterns
M ?Libraries
N House and triclinium

Entrance

THE ROMANS AND THEIR BATHS

The philosopher Seneca, writing in the mid-1st century AD, describes a visit to the villa of Scipio Africanus, where the bath house was a small, dark building typical of the days when it was used mainly for washing off the dust and dirt of the farm. 'Now', says Seneca, 'everyone thinks himself impoverished if his bath is not lined with contrasting marbles and the vaulted roof is not of glass. The sweat washed off in the water no longer comes from honest toil but is the result of pummelling by attendants.' Seneca may have had his own reasons for disapproval: in another account he complains of the dreadful din from the bath house under his apartment; the shrieks of the bathers, cries of pastry and sausage sellers, the grunting of the weightlifters and slapping of the masseurs.

The Roman idea of the bath originated in southern Italy, where hot springs often provided the water. Soon the hypocaust had been mastered: underground furnaces and passageways for hot air skilfully built so that the halls and pools were all heated to the required, constant temperature. In order to conserve heat, the hot rooms were often orientated towards the sun. Even so, vast quantities of wood were needed to keep the baths in full operation.

It was Agrippa who began the tradition of providing luxurious baths for the public. Those he built, in the Campus Martius (*map p. 180*), were free to enter but probably contained little other than the bathing pools themselves. Nero built new baths in the 60s AD and it is said that a next-door gymnasium gave the idea of combining bathing and exercise rooms. By the time of Trajan, the standard form of a bathing complex, with cold, warm and hot baths, swimming pools and wrestling grounds (*palaestrae*) had been perfected. The Romans were the first to give importance to the refreshing combination of exercise and cleanliness for the body.

Originally, until the 2nd century AD, men and women bathed together, but scandals led to segregation: in some cases by having separate facilities in the same building but usually by confining women to the morning and men to the rest of the day. The baths got hotter as the day went on, and some accounts recommend bathing before the rooms became too hot in late afternoon. The 2nd-century author Lucian describes the routine. The bather arrives with his attendants or slaves and goes first to the locker room to undress. He can then either take some exercise, or go straight on to be oiled. The baths were taken in a sequence of hottest (caldarium) through the tepidarium to the frigidarium. Before or after bathing there were shops to visit, libraries to browse in and plenty of spaces for socialising. Social distinctions could break down. There is a story of the emperor Hadrian visiting the baths to find there an old soldier who had served in one of his legions rubbing himself down against a column as he could not afford an attendant to scrape him. Hadrian paid for one. When his next visit was announced there were many more soldiers up against the columns. This time the emperor suggested they should scrape down each other.

C.F.

On the other side of the central hall you can see the **natatio** (swimming pool) **(H)**, which had an open-air *piscina*. This had niches on two levels for statues, and two hemicycles.

At the far end of the central hall you come out into the **eastern palaestra (I)**, where fragments of monochrome marine mosaics with dolphins, cupids and sea-horses are propped against the walls. These are from the floor of a room above, which collapsed. Also here is a fragment of entablature still *in situ* (at the top of a wall before the spring of the roof vaulting), and more fragments of the polychrome floor mosaic in peach, maroon, green and white. From here you can enter the other **apodyterium (J)** and follow a walkway above the perfectly preserved monochrome floor mosaic which has a pattern representing waves (or sails). The iron gate here is at one of the two original entrances. You then cross the natatio back into the first apodyterium.

Outer buildings: In the surrounding garden you can see the ruined caldarium and the rooms to either side of it, which may have included steam baths or **laconica (K)**. At each end of the perimeter wall were two huge exedrae, and in the middle of the south side was a shallow exedra in the form of a **stadium (L)**, with tiers of seats concealing the huge water cisterns, which held 80,000 litres each. On either side of this were two halls, probably **libraries (M)**. Excavations and restorations (including conspicuous reconstructions) have been carried out in the area of the stadium and one of the libraries. Near the eastern exedra a **house and triclinium (N)** of the time of Hadrian were discovered in recent excavations (since covered over).

AROUND PIAZZALE NUMA POMPILIO

In the middle of the road in front of the entrance to the Baths of Caracalla is the church of **Santi Nereo ed Achilleo**, important for its mosaics and Cosmati work but sadly almost never open and therefore described in the Appendix (*p. 565*). On the other side of the road is **San Sisto Vecchio**, once the residence of St Dominic (1170–1221). The campanile survives from his time (other remains of the 13th-century church are visible in the cloister). The façade and interior were designed by Filippo Raguzzini in 1725–7.

Beyond Piazzale Numa Pompilio stretches the charming, cobbled **Via di Porta San Sebastiano** (*map p. 653, C2–D3*), which envelops you at first in a rural atmosphere typical of old Rome. However, when the traffic light at its entrance changes, the cars race along it, destroying its tranquillity. The sights and monuments along its length are sporadically, intermittently or almost never open and thus are described in the Appendix. They are, a short way down on the right, the ancient church of San Cesareo (*usually open on Sun; see p. 562*); the Casina of Cardinal Bessarion (*see p. 573*); the Tomb of the Scipios (*see p. 560*) and, where the road ends, Porta San Sebastiano, the best-preserved gateway in the Aurelian Walls, which contains a museum of the history of this mighty Roman defence system (*see p. 570*). Outside the gate, the Via Appia Antica begins (*described on p. 508*).

The Caelian Hill

The Caelian Hill is a peaceful residential district with gardens of lush vegetation.
Santa Maria in Domnica on top of the hill has a very lovely 9th-century mosaic.
Santi Giovanni e Paolo covers ancient remains of houses, which you can visit.
Santo Stefano Rotondo is remarkable for its architecture.

The Caelian Hill (51m; *map p. 653*) is the most extensive of Rome's Seven Hills after the Esquiline. The name is Etruscan and during the period of the Kings the inhabitants of Alba Longa were forced to come and live here. The hill became an aristocratic district in Imperial times. Devastated by the Norman Robert Guiscard after his conquest of Sicily in 1084, it remained almost uninhabited for centuries, and even today it is sparsely populated.

Approaches to the Caelian
At the Caelian's western foot, just above the busy Via di San Gregorio, is the church
of San Gregorio Magno, from which Clivo di Scauro ascends past Santi Giovanni e
Paolo. The alternative approach to the hill is from the Colosseum up Via Claudia,
which takes you first past the churches of Santo Stefano Rotondo and Santa Maria in
Domnica.

From the Colosseum, Via Claudia ascends the hill, lined on the right by an impressive ancient brick-faced wall with niches, over 11m high, which was part of a nymphaeum built by Nero for his Domus Aurea. It is on the site of the east side of the **Temple of Divus Claudius**, built by Claudius' fourth wife, Agrippina (Nero's mother), on the emperor's death and deification in AD 54. Nero demolished part of it and used the foundations for his nymphaeum, but Vespasian rebuilt it in 69 as part of his programme of restoration to the city of land expropriated by Nero. It had impressive substructures and measured 180m by 200m. Further up Via Claudia on the left is the huge 19th-century **Ospedale del Celio**, a military hospital. In its grounds traces of Roman *insulae* and an ancient Roman *domus*, thought to be that of the Symmachi, have been found. Beyond, in the middle of the road, is an isolated tall brick ruin which was part of the acqueduct of the Aqua Claudia, which would have fed Nero's nymphaeum.

SANTO STEFANO ROTONDO

Map p. 653, C1. Entrance on Via di Santo Stefano Rotondo through a walled forecourt.
Open 10–1 & 2–5 (3–6 in summer). For updates, see www.santo-stefano-rotondo.it.

CAELIAN HILL
Mosaic on the former Trinitarian hospice for the redemption of slaves
showing Christ with two captives, one black and one white.

The church of Santo Stefano Rotondo dates from the time of Pope St Simplicius (468–83) and is one of the largest and oldest circular churches in existence. Since its restoration and the laying of a new marble floor (and the installation of unsympathetic lighting) it has lost some of its venerable atmosphere. Assigned to the Hermits of St Paul of Hungary in the mid-15th century, it is now attached to the Pontificium Collegium Germanicum et Hungaricum, a Jesuit seminary, established by Pope Gregory XIII in 1580.

The original plan of the church comprised three concentric rings, the largest 65m in diameter, intersected by the four arms of a Greek cross. It had no principal entrance or apse, and the high central drum was illuminated by windows. The design was almost certainly taken from Eastern models and the church of the Holy Sepulchre in Jerusalem, as well as from the ancient Roman circular mausoleum (of which two survive in Rome, that of Augustus and that of Hadrian). Early Christian architecture adapted this form for the circular martyrium or shrine built above the tomb of a martyr. But centrally-planned buildings disappeared from Western Christendom (apart from baptisteries) until Brunelleschi reintroduced one into Renaissance Florence in the 15th century.

The interior today

In the vestibule, above a marble double entranceway, the inscription records that in 1453 Nicholas V, pont(ifex) max(imus), restored the church, which was, he claims, in danger of collapse. The result of his interventions, with the help of Bernardo Rossellino, was to eliminate the ruins of the outer ring and three of the arms of the Greek cross, thus reducing the diameter from 65m to the present 40m.

The circular interior is still a remarkable sight, with its central ring of 22 antique granite columns well lit by windows (the two huge columns supporting three arches in the centre were added in the 12th century to stabilise the building). The spacious outer ambulatory has another ring of columns, this time of marble.

Near the entrance is the chapel of Sts Primus and Felicianus: the relics of the two martyrs were transfered here by Theodore I in the mid-7th century and the (restored) mosaic in the apse, of the two saints against a gold ground standing in a meadow of red roses on either side of a jewelled Cross, dates from his time. The next chapel is dedicated to the first king of Hungary, St Stephen. The funerary monument here commemorates Bernardino Cappella (d. 1523); it is probably by the workshop of Lorenzetto. Near the central altar is the pavement tomb of a Hungarian canon, János Lászay, who also died in 1523. There is an inscription to one Donatus O'Brienus (O'Brien), who died in 1064 and was son of the 'King of Ireland'. In the ambulatory is an antique marble chair probably once used in a Roman theatre: it was adapted as a bishop's throne.

At the height of the Counter-Reformation, on the orders of Gregory XIII, the walls were frescoed by Antonio Tempesta and Pomarancio. The scenes appear in chronological order from left of the entrance, beginning with the *Massacre of the Innocents* and the *Seven Sorrows of Mary*, continuing with the *Passion of Christ* and the martyrdom of the Apostles under Nero and Domitian. There follows a series of gruesomely vivid scenes of the martyrdom of saints over the centuries, all explained in detail in inscriptions below them (some of which are now illegible). Stendhal found the depictions of torture all too much and there was recently a proposal to have them whitewashed.

Under the church is a Mithraeum of the 2nd–3rd centuries AD (*no access at the time of writing; for information and updates, see www.santo-stefano-rotondo.it*).

THE SUMMIT OF THE HILL

On the summit of the hill, outside the church of Santa Maria in Domnica, is a copy of a little **ancient stone boat**, which Leo X had made into a fountain (with a pretty pebble-mosaic pool) when he restored the church in 1513. The original boat dated from around the 2nd century AD and was probably a votive offering from the Castra Peregrina, a barracks for soldiers from the provinces, which was on this hill.

SANTA MARIA IN DOMNICA

The church of Santa Maria in Domnica (*map p. 653, C1; open 9–12.30 & 4.30–7.30*), also called 'della Navicella' from the little boat outside, is of ancient foundation. Its title is probably a corruption of *Dominica praedia*, suggesting it was built on land formerly owned by an emperor. It was practically rebuilt in the 16th century by Leo X (when still Cardinal Giovanni de' Medici) from the designs of Andrea Sansovino, who added the graceful portico.

The lovely interior still contains 18 slender ancient granite columns with Corinthian capitals in the nave. But the chief glory of the church is the beautiful colourful **apse mosaic**, commissioned by St Paschal I (pope 817–24), in which he himself is portrayed and which is still in wonderful condition (*coin-operated light*). On the triumphal arch (flanked by two ancient porphyry columns) is Christ in a mandorla in a flowery field surrounded by two angels and all the apostles. Below are the larger figures of Moses and Elijah, also amidst flowers against a green ground. In the semi-dome, St Paschal kneels at the foot of the Madonna and Child surrounded by a throng of angels (those in the background just marked by their haloes) with a bed of red flowers at their feet. The long inscription against a blue ground relates how '*honestus*' Paschal restored this ruined building with glowing mosaics in honour of the Virgin Mary.

Just below the ceiling, a painted frieze in grisaille by Perino del Vaga from designs by Giulio Romano runs right around the entire church. There are, incredibly enough, no painted altarpieces in the church.

On the right of the church of Santa Maria in Domnica is a portal (no. 8, now the entrance to an experimental agricultural research institute) with a **mosaic tondo of Christ between two Christian slaves**, one white, the other black, both with their feet fettered (c. 1212; *illustrated on p. 267*). This was formerly the entrance to a hospice run by the Order of Trinitarians for the redemption of slaves, founded by St John of Matha (who died here in 1213). It is said that he had a vision of God holding the chains of a black and a white slave. The entrance to the Trinitarian church of **San Tommaso**

in Formis (*open only on Sun at 10.30*) is just beyond the ancient Arch of Dolabella and Silanus (AD 10), adapted later by Nero for his aqueduct to the Palatine. Here begins the very pretty **Via di San Paolo della Croce** (a lane reserved for pedestrians and once part of the ancient Clivo di Scauro), which runs between garden walls (above which can be seen orange trees) to the church of Santi Giovanni e Paolo. Alternatively you can walk to Santi Giovanni e Paolo through the Villa Celimontana park.

VILLA CELIMONTANA

The main entrance to the lovely Villa Celimontana park (*open 7–dusk; free jazz concerts on summer nights*) is to the left of Santa Maria in Domnica. These were once the gardens of the Villa Mattei, built for the wealthy art collector Ciriaco Mattei in 1582 and now home to the Società Geografica Italiana, with the best library of maps in Italy. Still today the park has some fine trees, inhabited by parrots.

Some of the ancient marble fragments which used to decorate the gardens are now in the courtyard of Palazzo Altemps (some have been replaced here by copies). From the ilex wood to the left of the villa there is a good view towards the Baths of Caracalla. The granite Roman obelisk, probably from the Temple of Isis and presented by the senate to Mattei in 1582, formed a pair with that in front of the Pantheon. It was surrounded by antique statuary and a circle of trees, only a few of which now survive. You can walk all the way though the park and leave it by a gate close to the church of Santi Giovanni e Paolo.

SANTI GIOVANNI E PAOLO

Map p. 653, C1. Open 8.30–12.30 & 4.30–7.30.

This church has had a long history. The titular saints are not the famous apostles but two obscure court officials who are said to have been martyred under Julian the Apostate. The first edifice was built above their house and an early Christian oratory. It was demolished by Robert Guiscard in 1084 and rebuilding was begun by Paschal II (1099–1118) and continued by Hadrian IV.

The handsome 12th-century Ionic **portico** has eight antique columns (closed by an iron grille in 1704). Above and behind it can be seen the early-Christian façade with its five arches and four ancient columns, which was revealed during excavations in 1949. The beautiful apse can only be seen from the Clivo di Scauro. The simple 13th-century Cosmatesque doorway is flanked by two lions, one of which is holding a rabbit in its paws (another rabbit can be seen in the talons of the eagle above).

INTERIOR OF THE CHURCH

This church, because of its position, is a popular place for weddings so that it is sometimes cluttered with celebratory paraphernalia (urns for flowers, gilt-backed chairs). The interior, with its granite piers and columns, was restored in 1718. The lovely **floor,** in opus alexandrinum, was restored in 1911; the best part of it is by the west door. Over 30 chandeliers, ingeniously hung on various levels, provide the illumination. A tomb-slab in the nave, protected by a railing, commemorates the burial place of the two martyrs to whom the church is dedicated. Their relics are preserved in a porphyry urn under the high altar. The apse has a fresco of *Paradise* by Pomarancio.

Off the south aisle is a very elaborate large 19th-century chapel around the **altar-tomb of St Paul of the Cross** (1694–1775), founder of the Passionists, whose (still very active) convent adjoins the church. In a storeroom to the left of the high altar (*shown by the very kind sacristan on request*) can be seen a remarkable **fresco of *Christ and Six Apostles***, dated 1255, by a painter of the Roman school showing the influence of Byzantine art.

THE CAMPANILE

Some travertine blocks from the Temple of Claudius (*see p. 266*) are visible in the base of the beautiful tall 12th-century campanile (45m), the first two storeys of which were begun by Paschal II and the five upper storeys completed by Hadrian IV. The Islamic ceramic plates inserted into the masonry are copies of the originals now in the antiquarium (*see overleaf*). Beyond a door beside the campanile (*readily unlocked on request*), are remains of two storeys of a huge Roman portico connected with the Temple of Claudius.

Across the road from the church, behind the arches of Roman shops dating from the 3rd century AD, are the offices of Silvio Berlusconi's TV station, Mediaset. Here a rusticated gate leads to the public park of the Villa Celimontana (*described above*).

ALONG THE CLIVO DI SCAURO

The picturesque Clivo di Scauro, the ancient Clivus Scauri, probably opened here in the 1st century BC, gently descends the hill beneath the church's medieval buttresses (which span the road) and past its fine apse, dating from 1216 and a rare example of Lombard work in Rome. The tall façade of an ancient Roman house is incorporated in the exterior wall of the church. Here is the entrance to the **Case Romane**, particularly interesting for their wall-paintings.

THE CASE ROMANE BENEATH SANTI GIOVANNI E PAOLO

Open 10–1 & 3–6. Closed Tues and Wed. T: 06 70 45 4544, caseromane.it.

According to tradition this was the site of the house where John (Giovanni) and Paul (Paolo), two court dignitaries under Constantine II, lived in the mid-4th century. They were martyred under Julian the Apostate and were buried here. Excavations began at the end of the 19th century and at least four phases of habitation have been found from the 1st–5th centuries AD, including two Roman apartment houses with shops (2nd–3rd centuries AD), a Roman *domus*, and a Christian house and an oratory founded before 410 by the senator Byzantius and his son Pammachius, a friend of St Jerome.

On the right as you enter are two rooms with explanatory panels and the little medieval **Oratory of San Salvatore**, which has 9th-century frescoes including a rare rep-

CASE ROMANE BENEATH SANTI GIOVANNI E PAOLO
Kneeling figures awaiting death with their arms bound and their eyes covered,
thought to be the earliest extant depiction of a martyrdom (4th century).

resentation of the *Crucifixion* in which the figure of Christ is robed. The other rooms are approached straight ahead from the ticket office. One of these has delightful wall paintings of youths bearing garlands and a great variety of birds beneath putti amongst vines. The rooms to the right have architectural frescoes with painted imitation marble, and figures of philosophers, goats and masks. An iron staircase leads up to the **confessio**, decorated with 4th-century frescoes of uncertain significance: on the end wall is a praying figure, perhaps one of the martyrs, between drawn curtains, at whose feet are two other figures. On the right are St Crispus, St Crispinian and St Benedicta (who tried to find the remains of the martyrs and were themselves killed), shown awaiting execution (*pictured above*). In another area below there is a **nymphaeum** with a striking fresco of Persephone and a nereid and boats manned by cupids.

The modern **antiquarium**, beautifully displayed, has ancient Roman and medieval finds, including sculptural fragments, ceramics dating from the 3rd–4th centuries AD, terracotta and glass (1st century BC–1st century AD), 12th-century Islamic ceramic plates removed from the campanile of the church in 1951, a 12th-century fresco detached in 1955 from the oratory perhaps covering an 8th-century work, roof tiles, brick stamps, architectural fragments, opus sectile decorations and amphorae.

Clivo di Scauro continues downhill towards the church of San Gregorio Magno. On the left it passes remains of the 6th-century basilican hall of the **Library of St Agapitus**, erected by that pope for his precious collection of Christian texts, on the site of his family mansion. The 17th-century portal (which provided access from the Clivo di Scauro) bears the Borghese dragons and the name of Cardinal Scipione Borghese (*see p. 363*). Through a window you can see the Roman masonry in the foundations of the oratories (*see below*), and in the little convent orchard there are walls dating from the

Republican period. In the public garden below the church there is a bronze bust of Mother Teresa of Calcutta, given to the city of Rome by the government of India.

SAN GREGORIO MAGNO

Map p. 653, B1. To visit the church (open 9–1 & 3.30–7), ring at the door ('portineria') of the Benedictine convent in the atrium. The three oratories (of greater interest) are usually opened Tues, Thur, Sat and Sun 9.30–12.30 by nuns of a missionary order who also live here. Entrance off the steps up to the church.

The church of San Gregorio Magno is a medieval building altered and restored in the 17th and 18th centuries. It is named after St Gregory the Great, one of the greatest popes in the history of the Church. The monumental staircase, church façade and lovely atrium (1633) are by Giovanni Battista Soria (a Roman architect clearly influenced by both Carlo Maderno and Pietro da Cortona) and are considered his masterpiece. The atrium is lined with tombs, including (near the entrance) that of Sir Robert Peckham (d. 1569), a self-exiled English Catholic. Nearby there is a (more elaborate) memorial to Sir Edward Carne (d. 1561), a Welsh Catholic and an envoy of Henry VIII and Mary I. Beside the convent door is a tomb (of two brothers called Bonsi) by Luigi Capponi, a little-known sculptor who carved a number of tombs in Roman churches in the last two decades of the 15th century.

ST GREGORY THE GREAT

From a wealthy patrician family, Gregory founded a monastery here on the site of his father's house and dedicated it to St Andrew. He himself was a monk here before (unwillingly) becoming pope in 590, the first monk ever to reach that position. For a long period possession of Rome had been contested between Goths and Byzantines, but Gregory succeeded in establishing control and effectively asserted the temporal power of the papacy (which was to last right up until the late 19th century). From his time onwards the history of Rome became intricately connected with that of the Church. He did much to help the citizens during outbreaks of plague, and rescued them from starvation. He revised the Roman liturgy (his letters and sermons became famous) and had a special interest in music.

St Augustine was prior in this monastery and it was here in 596 that he received Gregory's blessing before setting out with 40 other monks on his mission to convert the English to Christianity. This followed the famous incident when apparently Gregory saw some fair-haired children at a slave market in Rome, and upon hearing that they were English, declared '*non Angli sed Angeli*' ('not Angles but angels'—irreverently but wittily transposed in *1066 and All That* as 'not angels but Anglicans'.

INTERIOR OF SAN GREGORIO MAGNO

The church was rebuilt in 1725–34 by Francesco Ferrari. It preserves 16 antique columns and a restored mosaic pavement. At the end of the south aisle is the Chapel of St Gregory, with an altar-frontal carved with reliefs of scenes from his life by Luigi Capponi, and a good painting of the saint by the Emilian painter Sisto Badalocchio, one of a handful of works by him in this area. The venerable marble chair dating from the 1st century BC is known as the 'Throne of St Gregory': the bearded winged figure has a fish's tail. The altarpieces in the nave date from the 18th century, and the two small statues in the sanctuary were made in the 15th or 16th century.

THE ORATORIES

On the left of the church there is a gate (*for admission, see above*) which leads into a little garden of fruit trees, lemon trees and olives, surrounded by ancient cypresses and adjoining the convent orchard. Here are the three oratories which were part of the monastery founded by St Gregory (the rest of the complex was demolished in 1573). In the centre is the **chapel of Sant'Andrea**, preceded by a portico with four antique cipollino columns. Inside on the right is a very fine painting of the *Flagellation of St Andrew* by Domenichino, and on the left *St Andrew on the Way to his Martyrdom* by Guido Reni. On the entrance wall are depictions of St Sylvia and St Gregory by Giovanni Lanfranco. The altarpiece of the *Madonna in Glory between Sts Andrew and Gregory* is by Pomarancio.

The **chapel of Santa Barbara**, on the left, contains a statue of St Gregory by Nicolas Cordier. The 3rd-century table is believed to be the one at which St Gregory served twelve paupers daily with his own hands, among whom an angel once appeared as a thirteenth; this legend gave the alternative name to the chapel, the 'Triclinium Pauperum'. The frescoes (by Antonio Viviani) are in poor condition but include scenes of St Gregory serving the paupers (with the angel in attendance) and at a slave market in Rome. The **chapel of Santa Silvia**, on the right, is dedicated to St Sylvia, mother of Gregory. It contains her statue by Nicolas Cordier and a lovely fresco by Guido Reni (with the help of Sisto Badalocchio) showing an orchestra of angels playing a great variety of musical instruments to accompany a choir of three cherubs.

The door that leads out to the remains of the Library of St Agapitus (*see above*) is usually kept locked.

At the bottom of the hill is **Via di San Gregorio**, a busy road in the declivity between the Caelian and Palatine hills, which follows the line of the ancient Via Triumphalis (and which has an entrance to the Palatine).

San Clemente &
Santi Quattro Coronati

*These two medieval churches, still attached to religious houses and both rebuilt
by Paschal II (pope from 1099 to 1118), survive close to each other and are
particularly interesting for their very early frescoes. San Clemente also has
beautiful mosaics dating from Paschal II's time.*

The basilica of San Clemente, dedicated to St Clement, the fourth pope (90–
?99), is one of the best-preserved and oldest of Rome's medieval basilicas, dating from the 12th century. It has beautiful mosaics, a fine schola cantorum, and
also boasts one of the most important early Renaissance frescoed chapels in all Rome,
the work of Masolino. From this church you can visit the narthex, nave and aisles of
the earlier church below, with remains of ancient frescoes. This, in turn, was built on
the site of a large early Imperial building and a Roman temple and Mithraeum, the
extensive remains of all of which can still be seen. The friary houses Irish Dominicans.

*Map p. 655, E3. Open 9–12.30 & 3–6, Sun and holidays 12–6. Entrance by a side door in
Via San Giovanni in Laterano. Entrance fee for the lower church. Hideous new lights have
recently been installed. The church receives numerous visitors. basilicasanclemente.com.*

THE UPPER CHURCH

This church was begun in 1108 by Paschal II using some of the decorative marbles from
the ruins of the earlier church. The typically basilican interior is unusually light. It has
a large apse, aisles separated by two rows of seven columns, and a Cosmatesque pavement. In 1719 it was restored by Carlo Fontana's nephew, Carlo Stefano, for Clement
XI, and the walls of the nave were decorated with a cycle of paintings under the direction of Giuseppe Chiari, who also executed the *Triumph of St Clement* on the ceiling.

(A) Schola cantorum: This once
decorated the earliest church. It is
surrounded by an exquisite marble
screen marked with the well-preserved
carved monogram of John II (533–5),
reliefs, and a delicate Cosmati border
and marble inlay. It encloses two
ambones (i), a **candelabrum (ii)** and
a **reading desk (iii)**. Such enclosures
for choristers were a feature of early-
Christian basilicas and this is one of the
best preserved in all Rome. A transenna
of marble panels separates the sanctuary
from the rest of the church.

(B) Presbytery: The raised high altar is also surrounded by a transenna of marble panels, beneath a lovely baldacchino with columns of blue and white pavonazzetto marble. Against the apse wall is the bishop's throne and a simple bench for the clergy.

The **mosaics in the apse**, which were commissioned by Paschal II in the early 12th century, are especially fine (and even more rewarding with binoculars). In the centre is Christ on the Cross, flanked by the Virgin and St John. The Cross is charmingly decorated with twelve white doves which represent the Apostles. The semi-dome all around it is filled with circular vine tendrils of the Tree of Life against a gold ground inhabited by birds, stylised flowers, figures of St John the Baptist, the Doctors of the Church and other saints, and animals, so that it has the appearance of a huge illuminated manuscript. The vine springs from the foot of the Cross where there are acanthus leaves, while the rivers of Paradise flow down from it, quenching the thirst of the faithful (represented by stags) and watering the pastures of the Christian flock. Above is the Dome of Heaven and at the top the Hand of God.

In the frieze below are the Lamb of God and twelve companions in the form of sheep (an iconography typical of numerous other early mosaic cycles).

On the triumphal arch are roundels with Christ and the four symbols of the Evangelists, and below (on the right), St Peter and St Clement (with his feet on a boat), Jeremiah and, lower down, Jerusalem, and on the left, St Paul and St Lawrence (with his feet on a gridiron). Still lower down can be seen Isaiah and Bethlehem.

On the apse wall below are impressive large 14th-century frescoed figures of Christ, the Virgin and the Apostles.

To the right, at the bottom of the triumphal arch, is a lovely wall-tabernacle, probably by Arnolfo di Cambio.

(C) Chapel of St Catherine: The chapel is entirely covered with beautiful frescoes by the important Renaissance painter Masolino da Panicale. The frescoes were commissioned by Cardinal Branda Castiglione, who was bishop of the Hungarian city of Veszprém from 1412–24, as well as the titular cardinal of this church in the same period. He had already called Masolino to his home in northern Italy, Castiglione Olona, to carry out frescoes there.

Masolino collaborated with the younger artist Masaccio in the famous Brancacci Chapel in Florence, and some art historians still debate whether the two masters did not work together also on this fresco cycle, since it is known that they were both in Rome in 1428. Vasari's statement that the chapel was totally the work of Masaccio has not been accepted.

Above the entrance arch is the *Annunciation* in an open loggia (between a roundel with God the Father), and on the main wall, the *Crucifixion*. On the left wall are scenes from the life of St Catherine of Alexandria: at the top left the saint is shown, dressed in blue, in a circular temple before an idol, discussing the merits of Christianity with the emperor Maxentius. The scene next to this shows her being visited in prison by the emperor's wife, whom she converts and whom Maxentius therefore

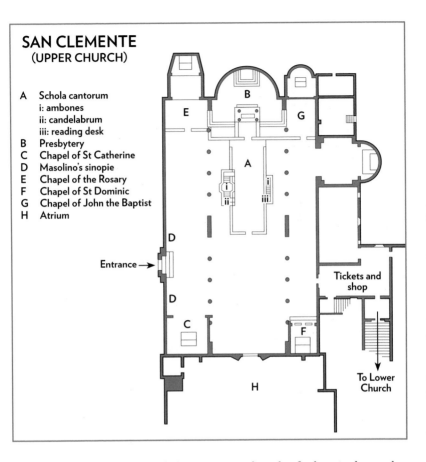

SAN CLEMENTE
(UPPER CHURCH)

A   Schola cantorum
    i: ambones
    ii: candelabrum
    iii: reading desk
B   Presbytery
C   Chapel of St Catherine
D   Masolino's sinopie
E   Chapel of the Rosary
F   Chapel of St Dominic
G   Chapel of John the Baptist
H   Atrium

Entrance →

Tickets and shop

To Lower Church

sentences to death (she is shown being beheaded outside).

The three scenes below illustrate St Catherine converting a group of Roman orators to Christianity in the magisterial presence of the emperor, who in anger has them burnt (this scene is also shown, taking place outside a window). In the centre Catherine is about to be pulled apart by two wheels (hence her attribute of the wheel and the derivation of 'Catherine wheels') but is saved by the intervention of an angel, which destroys these instruments of torture. The last scene shows her final martyrdom as she is beheaded.

On the opposite wall are scenes from the life of St Ambrose; in the archivolt, the Apostles; and in the vault, the Evangelists and Fathers of the Church. On the left entrance pier is St Christopher.

(D) Masolino's *sinopie*: These were found during restoration: one for the *Beheading of St Catherine* and one for the *Crucifixion*.

(E) Chapel of the Rosary: Sebastiano Conca painted *Our Lady of the Rosary* (outside, the tomb of Cardinal Antonio Venier, who died in 1479, incorporates two decorated columns from a 6th-century tabernacle).

(F) Chapel of St Dominic: Here are three paintings of scenes from the life of St Dominic, also attributed to Sebastiano Conca.

(G) Chapel of St John the Baptist: Here are two late 15th-century tombs of prelates: one by Luigi Capponi (that of Archbishop Giovanni Francesco Brusati) and the other (of Cardinal Bartolomeo Roverella), a simple but more beautiful tomb, by Andrea Bregno and Giovanni Dalmata.

(H) Atrium: At the west end you can walk out into the atrium. Ionic columns surround a courtyard with a little fountain, outside which is a gabled porch of four columns which survive from Paschal II's day.

THE LOWER CHURCH

Off the south aisle is the entrance to the excavations begun in 1861, a few years after remains of the ancient church below the present one had been discovered by Father Mullooly, prior of the adjoining monastery. This church was mentioned by St Jerome in 392 and was the scene of papal councils under St Zosimus in 417 and under St Symmachus in 499. Restored in the 8th and 9th centuries, it was destroyed in 1084 during the Sack of Rome by Robert Guiscard.

The stairway, which has miscellaneous fragments of sculpture, descends to the narthex. At the foot of the steps a catacomb can be seen through a grating in the floor.

Narthex: On the right wall is a remarkable fresco dating from the late 11th century of the *Legend of St Clement*, who was banished to the Crimea and there executed by drowning in the Black Sea. The scenes include the miracle of a child found alive in a church at the bottom of the sea (full of fish). Below are St Clement and the donor of the fresco.

On the other side of the nave entrance is the *Translation of St Cyril's Body from the Vatican to San Clemente* (also 11th century).

Nave: The wide nave, which has traces of its pre-Cosmatesque pavement, is obstructed by the foundation piers of the upper church and unequally divided by a supporting wall. Immediately to the left is a 9th-century fresco of the *Ascension*, with the Virgin in the centre surrounded by the Apostles, St Vitus and St Leo IV (with a square nimbus). In the corner are very worn frescoes of the *Crucifixion*, the *Marys at the Tomb*, the *Descent into Hell* and the *Marriage at Cana*.

Further along, past an embedded column with spiral fluting, on the left wall of the nave, is an 11th-century fresco of the *Story of St Alexis* (see p. 257). Above this is the lower part of a fresco of *Christ amid Angels and Saints*. Further on is the *Story of Sisinius*: the heathen Sisinius follows his Christian wife in secret, in that way hoping to capture the pope, but he is inflicted with a sudden blindness; below, Sisinius orders his servants to seize the pope, but they, also struck blind, carry off a column instead. Painted inscriptions, which are among the oldest examples of Italian writing, suggest that these scenes also refer to the building of this very church. Above is the surviving lower part of a fresco of *St Clement Enthroned with Sts Peter, Linus and Anacletus*, his predecessors on the pontifical throne.

Right aisle: Here (the second 'corridor' beyond the nave) in a niche is a 5th- or 6th-century Byzantine *Madonna* (which may originally have been a portrait of the Empress Theodora); female saints with the crown of martyrdom; and a beardless Christ. The frescoes, much damaged, probably depict the Council of Zosimus, the story of Tobias and the martyrdom of St Catherine. At the end are a sarcophagus of the 1st century AD with the story of Phaedra and Hippolytus and a Byzantine figure of Christ (7th or 8th century), almost totally obliterated.

Left aisle: Near the entrance from the narthex is a circular recess, once thought to be an early baptismal pool, but which may instead have been a bell foundry. At the end are remains of a tomb venerated as that of St Cyril, the apostle of the Slavs (869). The sound of the underground spring can be clearly heard here.

THE ROMAN IMPERIAL LEVEL

A 4th-century staircase descends to the lowest level, with a 'palazzo' and a Mithraic temple of the late 2nd or early 3rd century. Around the corner at the bottom, to the right, is the **pronaos of the temple**, with very damaged stucco ceiling ornaments; opposite is the **triclinium** with benches on either side and an altar in the centre showing Mithras, in his Phrygian cap, sacrificing a bull to Apollo, and in the niche behind is a statue of Mithras; the vault imitates the roof of a cavern, as Mithras is said to have been born in a cave (*for more on the cult of Mithras, see p. 539*). At the far end of the corridor, to the right and seen through a gate, is the presumed **Mithraic School**, with a mosaic floor and stuccoed vault, where catechumens were instructed.

From the pronaos, a door on the left leads to a **1st-century house** or 'palazzo', probably belonging to the family of Flavius Clemens, a consul and cousin of Domitian. It is possible that Pope Clement had been a freedman in the same household. A long narrow passage divides the temple area from the thick tufa wall of the building constructed, after Nero's fire, on Republican foundations. Only two sides of this building have been excavated. Immediately to the right at the bottom of a short flight of steps is a series of rooms which still have their herring-bone paving; the last two are the best-preserved, showing the original brickwork and a spring: the sound of its gushing waters pervades the whole lower building.

The second side of the building is reached by returning to the opening from the corridor; beyond a room where the spring water has been channelled away by tunnels are seven more vaulted rooms. From the last room a short flight of steps leads up to a gate beyond which can be seen a small **catacomb**, which was probably used in the 5th or 6th century (in other words, quite late), as it was within the city walls. A staircase on the right leads up to the lower church and exit.

SANTI QUATTRO CORONATI

Map p. 655, E4. Church open 9–12 & 4–5.30. Services (with sung Mass) are held frequently by the nuns. The Chapel of St Sylvester and cloister are usually open 10–11.45 & 4–5.45, holidays 9.30–10.30 & 4–5.45. However, since this is a functioning convent, the opening hours are subject to change according to the availability of the nuns.

The Gothic Hall (Aula Gotica) was at the time of writing only open twice a month by appointment on a weekday; to book, email archeocontesti@gmail.com. Explanation in situ given also in English. Donation expected. For information, T: 335 49 52 48, aulagoticasantiquattrocoronati.it.

On the feast day of the Santi Quattro, 8th Nov, a solemn Mass, at which a cardinal usually officiates, is held here and the crypt and refectory are opened.

From San Clemente, Via dei Querceti skirts the foot of the high wall of a fortified 12th-century monastery. Via dei Santi Quattro, an unexpectedly rural street on the left, continues steeply uphill. You arrive at a remarkable castellated building of the Middle Ages, enclosing a monastery of a closed order of Augustinian nuns (the Augustinians have been here since 1564) with their church dedicated to the four 'crowned' saints, martyred under Diocletian.

Beside the church and its cloister, you can also visit the very well-preserved Chapel of St Sylvester, with charming 13th-century frescoes illustrating the life of this 4th-century pope. More frescoes of the same date can now be seen on certain days of the year (*only by previous appointment*) in the Aula Gotica on the upper floor. The presence of the Augustinian nuns (and, since 1995, of another Order, the Piccole Sorelle dell'Agnello, in another part of the convent) gives these buildings a particularly sacred, peaceful feel in this secluded medieval enclave.

THE FOUR CROWNED SAINTS

To this day there is great confusion about just who the 'Santi Quattro Coronati', the titular saints of this church, actually were. It seems there were two groups of martyrs living at the time of Diocletian whose stories were both connected with the god Aesculapius, and who were all punished by drowning in lead coffins. The first group—Claudius, Nicostratus, Symphorian and Castorius—were stonemasons from Singidunum in the Roman province of Pannonia (present-day Belgrade), martyred by Diocletian because they refused to make a statue of Aesculapius. The second group were soldiers from Albano near Rome who refused to bow down before the god Aesculapius. Their relics may have been combined and bought here at some stage; what is certain is that their stories have inspired numerous works of art. They are the patron saints of woodcarvers, stonemasons and sculptors.

HISTORY OF THE BUILDING

By the mid-5th century there was a religous edifice here on this hillock of the Caelian hill. We know that both Honorius I and Hadrian I had work done on the building in the

7th and 8th centuries. But the most important work was carried out in the Carolingian period when in 847 the cardinal of the church became Pope Leo IV. His buildings, which were very extensive, were destroyed by Norman soldiers in 1084. The present church was erected on a smaller scale in 1110 by Paschal II (two years after he dedicated San Clemente). The grand cardinal's palace, which included the Chapel of St Sylvester and the Aula Gotica, dates from around 1235–47, when Cardinal Stefano Conti commissioned Roman artists and probably Giunta Pisano (who is known to have been in Rome in 1239) to decorate them with frescoes. During the papacy of Martin V, important restoration work was carried out by the Spanish cardinal Alfonso Carillo. Some of the buildings were well restored to their medieval aspect in 1914 by Antonio Muñoz.

The entrance gate passes beneath the unusual **campanile**, dating from the 9th century—this squat fortified tower is the oldest bell-tower to survive in the city. On its inner face is a handsome inscription set up by Alfonso Carillo, with his cardinal's hat and coat of arms recording his work of restoration here after the monastery had been abandoned ('*veteri prostrata ruina*') during the period that the popes were in Avignon. He goes so far as to name the very plants which used to infest the stonework before his intervention: ivy, brambles and verbena.

This small inner courtyard, which probably occupies the area of the quadriporticus of the 9th-century church and is now in rather poor condition, has a portico beneath which are 16th-century frescoes with scenes from the life of the Virgin by Livio Agresti. Beyond is the **second courtyard**, once part of the nave of the earliest (and larger) church (some of the columns have survived): the church is entered from here.

THE CHURCH

The aisled interior has a disproportionately wide apse and a matroneum, or women's gallery, and a Cosmati pavement in opus alexandrinum, all dating from the time of Paschal II. The fine wooden ceiling was installed in the 16th century. On the west wall and that of the south aisle are remains of 14th-century frescoes. There are just two side altars with paintings: the *Adoration of the Shepherds* by the 16th-century Flemish school, and *St Sebastian Tended by Holy Women* by Giovanni Baglione. The beautiful little 15th-century tabernacle with four angels is attributed to Andrea Bregno or Luigi Capponi. In the apse there are frescoes in gilded frames signed and dated by 'the Tuscan painter Giovanni da San Giovanni, 1623', depicting the history of the Santi Quattro (Giovanni here resolves the issue of their identity by illustrating both groups: the four (once five) from Serbia below, and the four from Lazio above). He also painted the splendid *Glory of All Saints* in the conch of the apse, and the *Annunciation* above a grille (once used by the nuns to attend services, unseen). At the end of the south aisle is an amusing monument to Monsignor Luigi d'Aquino (d. 1679), with his bust in a medallion and two friendly lions protecting his urn. There is a precious small portable 17th-century organ in the sanctuary (the nuns are still known for their singing and musical skills).

The 9th-century **crypt**, with the tomb of the four martyrs, is only open once a year on 8th November, the feast-day of the Santi Quattro Coronati.

THE CLOISTER

From the north aisle of the church you can enter the delightful tiny **cloister** (*ring for admission when services are not in progress; bell on right*), which survives from the early 13th century and is one of the most secluded spots in Rome. The little garden has a fountain designed by Antonio Muñoz in 1913 using a double marble basin perhaps dating from the 12th century. Excavations here in 2004 (since covered over) revealed a 5th-century baptistery with an exceptionally large font. Off the left walk is the 9th-century **Chapel of Santa Barbara**, a rare survival of early medieval architecture with fine corbels made from Roman capitals: the frescoes in the vault have almost disappeared.

THE CHAPEL OF ST SYLVESTER

Off the inner courtyard is the entrance to the Stanza del Calendario, so-named because it has remains of 13th-century frescoes of a calendar. Here is the present entrance to the Chapel of St Sylvester. (*During opening times, for which see above, ring at the old wooden bell and ask the nun beyond the grille to press the door release. When the nuns are busy or at prayer it is sometimes necessary to ring more than once; if there is no reply, wait and try again a little later. Minimum donation of one euro.*) The chapel was built in 1246 and contains a delightful and particularly well-preserved fresco cycle of the same date, illustrating legendary stories from the life of Constantine and Pope St Sylvester, decorated with colourful friezes of stylised leaves against a maroon background. The narrative begins on the entrance wall, to the right of the door:

(1) Constantine is shown enthroned but his spotty face—indicating that he has contracted leprosy—detracts from his dignity, and he is attended by a worried-looking crowd.

(2) The sick emperor dreams of St Peter and St Paul, who appear at his bedside and suggest he tries to get help from Pope Sylvester.

(3) Three mounted messengers ride towards Mt Soratte in search of the pope.

(4) The messengers climb the mountain to reach the pope's hermitage.

(5) The pope returns to Rome and shows the emperor the painted effigies of St Peter and St Paul.

(6) Constantine is baptised by the pope by total immersion (in a font rather too small for him!).

(7) Cured of leprosy, he presents his imperial tiara and parasol to the pope (emblems of his spiritual and temporal authority). This scene is a symbolic representation of the famous 'Donation of Constantine', a forged document probably from the 8th or 9th century which claimed to show that the Roman emperor had ceded dominion over all Italy to the Bishop of Rome. The popes used it to bolster their claims to temporal power during their perpetual tussles for supremacy with the Holy Roman Emperor.

(8) The pope rides off wearing the tiara, led by Constantine.

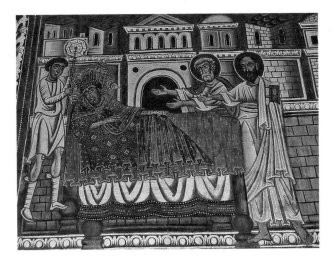

SANTI QUATTRO CORONATI
St Peter and St Paul appear in a dream to the ailing Constantine,
one of the scenes of the well-preserved fresco cycle of 1246.

(9) The pope brings back to life a wild bull (shown standing on its head).

(10) The finding of the True Cross by Constantine's mother, St Helen.

(11) Unfortunately there is almost nothing left of the last scene, which showed the pope liberating the Romans from a dragon.

Above the first scenes on the entrance wall is a fresco showing *Christ Enthroned between the Madonna and St John the Baptist*, with the twelve Apostles and two angels, just fitting into the vault above. The lovely old floor is Cosmatesque and the 16th-century frescoes in the presbytery are attributed to the Emilian artist Raffaellino da Reggio.

THE AULA GOTICA
For admission, see above. The entrance is through the convent library (where the Gothic windows have recently been exposed).
This beautiful vaulted hall has the most important secular fresco cycle to survive in Rome, discovered in 1995. Its Gothic architecture is unusual for Rome and it preserves its lovely old pavement. It was built in the 12th–13th century as a hall where the resident cardinals here could administer justice or hold banquets and receptions.

The ceiling has two cross vaults: in the first bay nearest to the entrance, an extremely interesting fresco cycle illustrates the Twelve Months and in the second bay are the personifications of Virtues and Beatitudes. All the frescoes have a wonderful emerald-green ground and the scenes are lovingly framed with friezes: some have a great variety of birds on a geometric border; others *trompe l'oeil* patterns, or dolphins with their tails entwined, or nude erotes playing with ribbons, all recalling Roman or Byzantine decorative schemes. Note the little naked figures supporting festoons of flowers and fruit; the amusing young telamones 'holding up' some of the borders; and (on the entrance wall) the pairs of fantastic little figures with curly tails, fighting each other on either side of flowerpots. This is perhaps the most important secular fresco cycle to survive in Rome.

First (south) bay: The Twelve Months are illustrated in groups of four months, all with stylised trees, on each of the three walls: January is depicted as an old man with three faces, beside sausages and hams all hanging up to be cured. In February, tree pruning is in progress, and March has the rather eccentric scene of a coy youth holding up his long leg so that a lady can remove a thorn from his foot. April is represented by shepherds tending their animals.

On the entrance wall: May has a cavalier enjoying the scent of a bunch of roses while boys with a basket are up a tree picking fruit; June shows harvesting, and July threshing on a round floor, and for August there is a seated elderly man to whom fresh figs are being offered.

On the last wall, September is represented by wine barrels being prepared; in October the grape harvest is under way; in November the fields are being ploughed; and in December the pork butchers are at work.

The lunettes above have figures representing the Liberal Arts. They are in less good condition but you can make out the female figure representing Geometry, and (on the entrance wall), Music, with an organ being operated by bellows. On the imposts of the four vaults are four male figures representing the Seasons.

Second (north) bay: In the lower register there is a series of green niches with female figures in armour, carrying smaller figures (from the Old or New Testament, or a saint) on their shoulders and trampling under their feet pairs of figures which represent the Vices. They are separated by fanciful columns topped by little figures of ladies dancing with veils. The qualities they personify (the Virtues and Beatitudes) are explained in long inscriptions. Some of them have been ruined but in the centre of the end wall there is the large figure of Solomon representing the importance of Justice (he is flanked by exotic birds).

In the lunettes of this bay are, on the left, Mithras killing the bull; on the end wall are two painted statues of Abundance (with their nicely rounded rear ends very much in evidence since their cloaks have fallen to their knees) together with baskets brimming with good things; on the right wall, the Sun (representing Christ) and the Moon (representing the Church) are drawn respectively by horses and by bulls.

St John Lateran
& its District

The basilica of St John Lateran, built by Constantine, was the first church in Rome and is still the cathedral church of the diocese. The nearby Santa Croce in Gerusalemme was by tradition founded by Constantine's mother, St Helen.

San Giovanni in Laterano (St John Lateran) and its beautiful baptistery (*map p. 655, F4*) both date from the 4th century and today are surrounded by busy roads. The palace of the popes was originally here too, and outside it the pontiffs would set up masterpieces of Classical sculpture, the first among them the equestrian statue of Marcus Aurelius (*see p. 44*), which at the time was believed to represent Constantine, the first Christian emperor and founder of St John Lateran.

Approaches to St John Lateran
On foot, the most pleasant approaches are by Via di San Giovanni in Laterano from the Colosseum, or by Via di Santo Stefano Rotondo from the Caelian hill. Otherwise, since the basilica is hemmed in by busy roads, the monuments are best reached by public transport. Bus 117 runs directly from Piazza del Popolo via Piazza Venezia and the Colosseum.

THE PIAZZE AROUND ST JOHN LATERAN

In the (recently renamed) **Piazza Giovanni Paolo II**, Sixtus V installed the splendid red granite **obelisk** facing up Via Merulana towards Santa Maria Maggiore, outside which he had erected another obelisk the previous year, 1587. The Lateran obelisk is the oldest in the city. It was erected by Thutmose IV in front of the Temple of Amun at Karnak (15th century BC) and was brought to Rome by Constantius II (357) to decorate the Circus Maximus, where it was discovered in three pieces in 1587. It is the tallest obelisk in existence (31m high, 47m with the pedestal), even though one metre had to be sawn off during its reconstruction.

The inscription on all four sides of the base records its extraordinary history: it was floated down the Nile by Constantine from Karnak to Alexandria and instead of contuining to its final destination, Constantinople, it was for some reason left abandoned in the port. Constantine's son decided it should be brought to Rome and had a ship specially built, propelled by 300 oarsmen, to bring it across the Mediterranean to Ostia and then up the Tiber to Rome

---

EGYPTIAN OBELISKS

There are 13 obelisks in Rome but only five are left in Egypt itself. These monolithic tapered shafts were constructed by the ancient Egyptians to symbolise the sun: the so-called pyramidion at the top was often plated in electrum (a gold and silver alloy) which would reflect the sun's rays, imitating the way they fall on the earth. Obelisks were often set up in pairs to decorate the entrance to temples, and were incised with inscriptions in hieroglyphs. Egypt was annexed as a Roman province in 30 BC, and its culture exerted an important influence on the Romans. A temple to Isis was erected in the city (*see p. 181*) and there was a vogue for Egyptian works of art. Many artefacts were transported to Rome, including obelisks, which were often dedicated to Apollo or the sun. Hieroglyphs continued to be used until the 4th century AD, and there are many examples of hieroglyphic renderings of Roman emperors' names.

The obelisks were reused in the 16th century in papal urban planning schemes, to decorate *piazze* and gardens and to close vistas at the end of new streets. Others were later discovered either abandoned or buried and were re-erected in the city. Bernini set one up as the crowning point of his splendid fountain in Piazza Navona and placed another, from the Temple of Isis, squarely on the back of an elephant outside the church of Santa Maria sopra Minerva. In the 18th century, the obelisks in Piazza Trinità dei Monti and Piazza del Quirinale were set up. The latter used to form a pair with that in Piazza dell'Esquilino, and they had been used by Augustus to flank the entrance to his mausoleum. The obelisk in Piazza di Montecitorio, formerly the gnomon of a huge sundial in the Campus Martius, was only rediscovered in the 18th century, when it was erected outside the Italian parliament. There are also obelisks in the Pincio gardens and the park of Villa Celimontana (the latter used to form a pair with the obelisk outside the Pantheon). Many bear Egyptian hieroglyphs (those in St Peter's Square, Piazza del Quirinale and Piazza Esquilino do not); the two in Piazza Trinità dei Monti and Piazza Navona had their hieroglyphs recut by the Romans.

The **side portico** of St John Lateran and rear flank of the Lateran Palace (with the arms of Sixtus V) are both by Domenico Fontana (16th century). Behind is the ancient bare brick exterior of the Baptistery, and closing another side of the piazza is a handsome building with a little clock-tower built in 1640 for the Ospedale del Salvatore, the first site of the hospice of San Giovanni, founded in 1348 (still the most important hospital in Rome; its modern buildings extend along Via dell'Amba Aradam). Across the busy road are tall 18th–19th-century buildings with shops and bars on their ground floors.

In front of the main façade of the Lateran Palace the piazza is named **Piazza di San Giovanni in Laterano**. By the main façade of the basilica it becomes Piazza di Porta San Giovanni (*described on p. 295*).

THE BASILICA OF ST JOHN LATERAN

Map p. 649, A3. Open daily 7–6.30; cloisters open 9–6. Entrance by the main door or (except on Sun) by the south door. NB: The basilica is non-aligned: the altar faces compass west. The description below uses liturgical north, south, east etc.

BASILICA OF ST JOHN LATERAN

The basilica of St John Lateran is the cathedral of Rome and mother church of the world (*Omnium urbis et orbis Ecclesiarum Mater et Caput*). It is on land once owned by the emperor Constantine, who in around 311 transferred it to the pope of his day so that he could build a church for the see of Rome. As the first Christian basilica to be constructed in the city, it served as a model for all subsequent churches. It still partly preserves its basilican plan from that time but it was transformed in the mid-17th century by Borromini. Numerous popes and cardinals are buried or recorded here.

HISTORY OF ST JOHN LATERAN

Constantine's property, which may once have been owned by a certain Titus Sextus Lateranus (hence the name), included the barracks built here in the 2nd century for his private horseguards, the *Equites Singulares*. The original basilica with a nave, four aisles and an apse, was probably built between 314 and 318, and was dedicated to

Christ the Saviour, a dedication later amplified by the addition of Sts John the Baptist and John the Evangelist.

Partly ruined by the Vandals, it was restored by St Leo the Great (440–61) and Hadrian I (772–95) and, after an earthquake in 896, by Sergius III (904–11). Nicholas IV (1288–92) enlarged and embellished it to such an extent that it was considered the wonder of its age; Dante described it with admiration when Boniface VIII proclaimed the first Holy Year in 1300 from the loggia on the west front.

But this magnificent building was destroyed by fire in 1308 and rebuilt by Clement V soon afterwards, at which time it was decorated by Giotto. In 1360 it burnt down again and its ruin was lamented by Petrarch. When Gregory XI (1370–8) returned to Rome from Avignon, he had it entirely rebuilt. Martin V (1417–31), who ended the Great Schism, added to its splendour, as did his later successors Sixtus V (who employed Domenico Fontana) and Clement VIII (whose architect was Giacomo della Porta).

In 1646–9, Innocent X commissioned Francesco Borromini to rebuild the church yet again, and in 1734 Clement XII added the main west façade. The ancient apse was entirely reconstructed in 1875–85 and the mosaics were reset following the original designs. The atmosphere of the basilica today is solemn and grand but it somehow fails to live up to the promise suggested by its venerable history.

THE POPES AT ST JOHN LATERAN

The popes were crowned here until 1870, when Rome became the secular capital of Italy and the popes retreated to the Vatican (*see pp. 28–9*). Under the Lateran Treaty of 11th February 1929, this basilica, with those of San Paolo fuori le Mura and Santa Maria Maggiore, was accorded the privilege of extraterritoriality. After the ratification of the treaty, the pope left the seclusion of the Vatican for the first time in almost 60 years: on 24th June 1929, Pius XI officiated at St John Lateran, and a choral Mass is held here on 24th June every year to commemorate this. The pope traditionally attends Maundy Thursday celebrations at the church, when he gives his benediction from the loggia on the south front.

EXTERIOR OF ST JOHN LATERAN

The principal façade, overlooking the vast Piazza di Porta San Giovanni, is raised above a wide pavement with low steps designed as a setting for grand ceremonies. The façade is a theatrical composition by Alessandro Galilei (1734–6), with a two-storey portico surmounted by an attic with 16 colossal statues of Christ with the Apostles and saints (often visible on the skyline of Rome). The inscription on the architrave announces that it was completed in the fifth year of the pontificate of Clement XII, to the glory of Christ the Saviour and in honour of the two St Johns.

Beneath the portico, the central portal **(1)** is perhaps today the most precious element from the past belonging to the basilica: the **bronze doors of the Curia in the Roman Forum** (*see p. 72*). In 1660 Alexander VII moved them here from ancient Rome's venerable Senate House, and through this decision may well have saved them from destruction in succeeding centuries. When he enlarged them to fit the doorway a coin from the time of Domitian was found embedded in them so they must predate AD

81. The pope felt justified in adding bronze stars to them, his Chigi family emblem. On the left under the portico is a **colossal marble statue (2)** (restored in parts), which once decorated Constantine's baths on the Quirinal and was traditionally taken to represent Constantine but is in fact a portrait of his son Constantius II.

The south façade, on Piazza Giovanni Paolo II, built by Domenico Fontana in 1586, has a portico of two tiers. Under the portico, on the left, is a **statue of Henry IV of France** by Nicolas Cordier. Henry was a Protestant by birth; the Edict of Nantes, giving freedom of worship to French Huguenots, was issued by him. Shortly after he converted to Catholicism, he made an important endowment to the chapter of St John Lateran. In gratitude this statue was erected and Henry was made an honorary canon. The title is still held by the President of France.

INTERIOR OF ST JOHN LATERAN

The interior, 130m long, still partly preserves its original 4th-century proportions, with a basilican plan with double side-aisles, but it was completely remodelled by Borromini in 1646–9. He designed the niches for statues between the massive piers, each with two *verde antico* pillars, and Alessandro Algardi and his collaborators, including Antonio Raggi, executed the scenes from the Old and New Testaments in stucco above them. Borromini also decorated the outer aisles, where he enclosed the important funerary monuments from previous centuries in elegant Baroque frames. There are no painted altarpieces.

(3) Nave: The decoration was completed in the early 18th century when Borromini's niches were filled with colossal statues of the Apostles by various artists including Camillo Rusconi and Pierre Legros. In the oval frames at the top of the walls, paintings of prophets were provided by the leading artists of the day, including Domenico Maria Muratori, Sebastiano Conca, Benedetto Luti, Francesco Trevisani and Giuseppe Chiari. Although Borromini's plan had included a new vault, it was decided to preserve the beautiful coffered ceiling (dating from 1566), and the architect also retained the 15th-century Cosmatesque pavement, restoring it where necessary.

(4) Confessio: The beautiful bronze **tomb-slab of Martin V** (d. 1431) is by the little-known Tuscan sculptor Simone Ghini. The short inscription records the length of the pope's reign and states that his time was a happy one (today visitors and worshippers throw down coins to mark their admiration). The elaborate Gothic **baldacchino** (1367) is the best-known work of another Tuscan, Giovanni di Stefano. Its frescoes may also be 14th-century Tuscan work, but they were repainted in the following century by Antoniazzo Romano. Behind the barley-twist colonnettes are two (illuminated) 19th-century gilded silver reliquaries— rather odd-looking half-figures of St Peter and St Paul—said to contain their heads. The **papal altar** beneath, reconstructed by Pius IX, encloses part of a wooden table (not visible) at which St Peter and his successors (until the 4th century) are traditionally supposed to have celebrated Mass.

South aisles: At the end of the aisles are three tombs from different periods, set into Borromini's later marble niches and interesting for their artistic value: Ranuccio Farnese, nephew of Paul III **(5)**, by Vignola (16th century); Antonio de Chaves of Portugal (1447), attributed to Isaia da Pisa **(6)**; and Casati di Giussano (1290), by the Cosmati family **(7)**. Over the window screen outside the Cappella Massimo **(8)** is a fragment of the original altar with a statuette of St James, attributed to Andrea Bregno. On the nave pier Pope Sylvester II (d. 1003) is recorded by a long medieval inscription set into yellow marble, and, above it, by a cenotaph **(9)** commissioned from the Hungarian sculptor József Damkó in 1909, in memory of this French pope who encouraged the establishment of the Church in Hungary by sending an apostolic crown to its first Christian

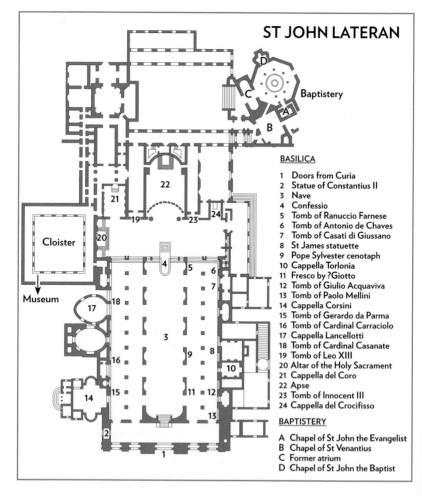

ST JOHN LATERAN

Baptistery

BASILICA

1 Doors from Curia
2 Statue of Constantius II
3 Nave
4 Confessio
5 Tomb of Ranuccio Farnese
6 Tomb of Antonio de Chaves
7 Tomb of Casati di Giussano
8 St James statuette
9 Pope Sylvester cenotaph
10 Cappella Torlonia
11 Fresco by ?Giotto
12 Tomb of Giulio Acquaviva
13 Tomb of Paolo Mellini
14 Cappella Corsini
15 Tomb of Gerardo da Parma
16 Tomb of Cardinal Carraciolo
17 Cappella Lancellotti
18 Tomb of Cardinal Casanate
19 Tomb of Leo XIII
20 Altar of the Holy Sacrament
21 Cappella del Coro
22 Apse
23 Tomb of Innocent III
24 Cappella del Crocifisso

Cloister

Museum

BAPTISTERY

A Chapel of St John the Evangelist
B Chapel of St Venantius
C Former atrium
D Chapel of St John the Baptist

king, Stephen, in 1000. Also here are the resting places of the popes Alexander III (d. 1181) and Sergius IV (d. 1013). The Cappella Torlonia **(10)**, was richly decorated by Quintiliano Raimondi (1850) and is closed by a fine iron balustrade. It has a sculptured altarpiece (*Descent from the Cross*) by Pietro Tenerani.

On the first nave pier **(11)** there is an interesting **fragment of a fresco** detached from the exterior loggia showing the elderly Boniface VIII proclaiming the Jubilee of 1300 (the first Holy Year) from the loggia of this basilica. For a long time it was considered to be by the school of Giotto, but most scholars now consider it to be by the hand of the master himself.

Opposite is the tomb **(12)** of Giulio Acquaviva (1574), made cardinal at the age of 20 by Pius V (the two female figures in relief are provocatively attractive) and **(13)** the tomb of Paolo Mellini (1527), with a very damaged fresco.

North aisles: The Cappella Corsini **(14)** is a graceful early 18th-century chapel by Alessandro Galilei, containing the tomb of the Corsini pope Clement XII (d. 1740), who commissioned the main façade of the church. The porphyry sarcophagus is from the Pantheon and the beautiful figure of *Temperance* is by Filippo della Valle. In the outer aisle are tombs of the first archpriest of the basilica, Gerardo da Parma (1061) **(15)** and, set in to a later marble niche, of Cardinal Bernardo Caracciolo (d. 1255) **(16)**. The pretty Cappella Lancellotti **(17)** is by Francesco da Volterra (1585–90), rebuilt 1675 by Giovanni Antonio de Rossi. The Baroque tomb **(18)** is that of Cardinal Girolamo Casanate (1707), who

left his famous library to the Dominican friary of Santa Maria sopra Minerva.

The transepts and apse: Both transepts were built by Giacomo della Porta during the papacy of Clement VIII (1592–1605). Above the chapels, the large frescoes, completed in 1600 under the direction of Cavaliere d'Arpino (who is buried in the church) illustrate the conversion of Constantine, his gift of the land to Pope Melchiades and the building of the first basilica. They are by Giovanni Battista Ricci, Paris Nogari, Cristoforo Roncalli, Orazio Gentileschi, Cesare Nebbia, Giovanni Baglione and Bernardo Cesari.

In the **north transept** is the tomb of Leo XIII **(19)**, by Giulio Tadolini (1907). The Altar of the Holy Sacrament **(20)**, by Pier Paolo Olivieri, dating from the time of Clement VIII, is flanked by four antique green marble columns. The four vast gilded bronze columns here are extremely rare survivals from the 2nd century AD which must once have adorned the original basilica of the time of Constantine. The Cappella del Coro **(21**; *closed*) has fine stalls of c. 1625.

The **apse (22)** was rebuilt on a larger scale by Virginio and Francesco Vespignani in 1885 when the precious apse mosaics, designed by Jacopo Torriti and Jacopo da Camerino (1288–94), were destroyed and remade. It includes representations of the Virgin with Nicholas IV and Sts Peter and Paul, and (on the right) Sts John the Baptist, John the Evangelist and Andrew. Kneeling at the feet of the Apostles in the frieze below are the tiny figures of the mosaicists Torriti and Camerino.

In the **south transept** the great organ by Luca Blasi (1598) is supported by two

HOLY YEARS AND THE PILGRIMAGE CHURCHES

Throughout the centuries, Rome and the papacy have enjoyed huge economic benefits from the number of visitors during Holy Years. The Roman Catholic Church adapted the secular Jewish idea of the Jubilee, which occurred every 50 years, as described in the book of Leviticus, when the Jews were required to free slaves and remit debts. The papacy gave the Jubilee a spiritual meaning when it allowed the remission of the temporal punishment of sins for those pilgrims who visited Rome during a specific year. In 1500 the Jubilee was renamed Holy Year.

Pope Boniface VIII proclaims the first Holy Year from the loggia of St John Lateran. Fresco attributed to Giotto.

The first Holy Year was proclaimed by Boniface VIII from the balcony of St John Lateran on 22nd February 1300. Dante, who visited Rome in that year, described the huge number of pilgrims he found in the city. In 1450 Nicholas V celebrated the Jubilee with great splendour, but that year is also remembered for the fact that hundreds of pilgrims died in a suffocating crowd on Ponte Sant'Angelo, then the only way across the Tiber to St Peter's.

In 1343 Clement VI reduced the interval between Holy Years from 100 to 33 years (the lifetime of Christ). Paul II (1464–71) brought it down to 25 years and this quarter-century interval has been maintained, with few exceptions, ever since: there were Holy Years in 1900, 1925, 1950, 1975 and 2000. In addition to the regular celebrations, a Jubilee has occasionally been proclaimed for a special reason, as in 1933, when Pius XI commemorated the 19th centenary of the Crucifixion, or in 1983–4 when John Paul II commemorated the 1,950 years since the death and resurrection of Christ. The Pauline Year was announced by Pope Benedict XVI in 2008 to celebrate 2,000 years since the birth of St Paul. Pope Francis announced the Jubilee of Mercy in 2015–16.

A Holy Year is usually inaugurated in December of the year preceding it with the opening of the Holy Door (Porta Santa) of St Peter's by the pope. He used to wield a silver hammer and a temporary wall in front of the door would fall inwards. In more recent Holy Years, the door has been unlocked beforehand and the pope has solemnly pushed it open. The Holy Doors of the three other papal basilicas (*see below*) are also opened: this is a symbolic enactment of the opening of the Gates of Heaven.

There are a number of ways to obtain a Jubilee Indulgence, though the most popular remains visiting the pilgrimage churches in Rome. There are seven of these: the four papal basilicas of St Peter's, St John Lateran, Santa Maria Maggiore and San Paolo fuori le Mura, together with San Lorenzo fuori le Mura, Santa Croce in Gerusalemme and San Sebastiano, above the catacombs of the same name on the Via Appia. Recently the popes have added other churches of their choosing in the Holy Years proclaimed by them. In 2016 Pope Francis accorded special status to Chiesa Nuova, San Salvatore in Lauro and San Giovanni Battista dei Fiorentini.

lovely ancient columns of *giallo antico*, removed from the Arch of Constantine. The monument recording Innocent III **(23)** was erected by Giuseppe Lucchetti in 1891 when Leo XIII brought the ashes of this great pope from Perugia, where he had died in 1216. In the corner of the little Cappella del Crocifisso **(24)** is a Cosmatesque kneeling statue of Boniface IX (late 14th century).

THE CLOISTER

Undoubtedly the masterpiece of Jacopo and Pietro Vassalletto (c. 1222–32), the cloister (*entrance fee*) is a magnificent example of Cosmatesque (*see p. 62*) art. The little columns, some plain and some twisted, are adorned with mosaics and have fine capitals. The frieze is exquisite. In the centre is a well-head dating from the 9th century. Many interesting fragments from the ancient basilica, including some lovely Cosmati work, are displayed around the cloister walks.

The fragmentary **altar of Mary Magdalene** incorporates an antique marble chair used up until 1559 in papal enthronement ceremonies. The beautiful **tomb of Riccardo Annibaldi**, an aristocratic papal notary, reconstructed from fragments, is the work of the Tuscan sculptor and architect Arnolfo di Cambio. The effigy is clearly derived from contemporary French tomb sculpture. Roman fragments include a funerary monument with four portrait heads of the Gavii family, all freedmen. The little **museum** displays the beautiful cope of Boniface VIII, of 13th-century English workmanship. Also here are two Florentine tapestries (1595–1608), numerous gifts, including a French cope given to Pius IX, and a model of the Column of the Immaculate Conception (1854) in Piazza di Spagna.

THE LATERAN BAPTISTERY

The Lateran Baptistery (*open 7–12.30 & 4–7; baptisms still take place here regularly; see plan on p. 290*) was built in the early 4th century, at the same time as the first basilica. It is octagonal in design, although the original baptistery, designed for total immersion and derived from Classical models, may have been circular (both the circle and the octagon—the number 8—are symbols of infinity and thus immortality). Its design was copied in many subsequent baptisteries.

The present entrance was created by Sixtus V so that it opened directly from the piazza where he had set up the obelisk (but to do this he had to demolish one of the 5th-century side chapels); it was formerly approached through the atrium on the opposite side of the building (*marked C on the plan*). In the interior are eight columns of porphyry erected by Sixtus III (the Barberini bees adorning the base of each are from the 17th-century redecoration programme by Urban VIII); they support an architrave which bears eight smaller white marble columns. In the centre is the green basalt font; deer drink from pools at either side. These are additions from 1967, recalling the silver deer from whose mouths, according to ancient sources, the baptismal waters once flowed. The harsh frescoes of scenes from the life of St John the Baptist on the drum of the cupola are modern copies of works by Andrea Sacchi.

(A) Chapel of St John the Evangelist:
Dedicated by the martyred pope St
Hilarius (461–8), as is the companion
chapel to St John the Baptist (*see below*),
its bronze doors date from 1196. The
vault has a lovely 5th-century mosaic
of the *Lamb* surrounded by symbolic
birds and flowers. The altar has
alabaster columns. On the left is a late
15th-century painting of *St Leo Praying
to St John* by Luigi Capponi.

(B) Chapel of St Venantius: Added
by Pope John IV in 640 and dedicated
to a martyr from Dalmatia, it contains
mosaics commissioned by Pope
Theodore I (642–9): in the apse, the
Head of Christ flanked by angels and
(you have to look behind the altar) the
Madonna and Saints with Pope Theodore,
and on the triumphal arch, depictions of
all the martyrs whose relics Pope John
brought from Dalmatia and (high up)
views of Jerusalem and Bethlehem and
symbols of the Evangelists.

Remains of 2nd-century Roman baths
built above a 1st-century villa, with
a mosaic pavement, can also be seen
here at both sides. The structure of the
original baptistery is visible in the walls

and beneath the apse. It is no accident
that the baptistery was sited here, where
the source of water was assured.

(C) Former atrium: This original
entrance to the baptistery was
sumptuously decorated. The door
is flanked by two splendid, huge
antique columns supporting a fine
Roman architrave. High up on the wall
opposite can be seen a fragment of the
original marble intarsia decoration. In
the north apse, now dedicated to Sts
Cyprian and Justina, two early martyrs
whose remains were buried here, is a
beautiful 5th-century mosaic with a
climbing plant on a brilliant blue ground
descending from jewelled crosses above
which are a Lamb and doves. Over the
door into the baptistery is a relief of the
Crucifixion after Andrea Bregno (1492).

(D) Chapel of St John the Baptist:
The second foundation of Pope Hilarius.
Behind a grille it preserves its original
doors (once thought to come from the
Baths of Caracalla), inscribed with the
name 'Hilarus Episcopus'. They are
famous for the musical jangling they
make when opened.

THE LATERAN PALACE

The Lateran Palace, Palazzo Lateranense, was used by the popes before the move to
Avignon in 1309. It was a residence which dated from the time of Constantine, but
which took the form of a grander Gothic palace from the 8th century onwards. This
was almost destroyed in the fire of 1308 which also devastated the basilica. On the
return from Avignon in 1377 the Holy See was transferred to the Vatican, so the palace was abandoned. In 1586 Sixtus V demolished or displaced what was left of it and
ordered his favourite architect Domenico Fontana to carry out a complete reconstruction. Only three parts of the splendid old palace have survived (now on the opposite
side of Piazza di Porta San Giovanni and all now incorporated in later buildings): the
staircase (the Scala Santa); the private chapel of the pope (the Sancta Sanctorum); and
the Triclinium of Leo III (a banqueting hall), with copies of its original mosaics.

The new 16th-century palace was intended as a summer residence for the popes, but they used the Quirinal instead. The interior was restored in 1838. Under the Lateran Treaty of 1929 the palace was recognised as an integral part of the Vatican City. It is now the seat of the Rome Vicariate and offices of the Rome diocese.

THE SCALA SANTA AND SANCTA SANCTORUM

Scala Santa open 6–1 & 3–6.30; Sancta Sanctorum open weekdays 9.30–12.40 & 3–5.10, closed Sun. Admission charge. A Passionist convent has been here since 1953. For information, T: 06 77 26 641, scalasantaroma.it.

In the 15th century the staircase from the old Lateran Palace was declared to be that from Pilate's house which Christ descended after his condemnation: a legend related how it had been brought from Jerusalem to Rome by St Helen, mother of Constantine. When Domenico Fontana built the new Lateran Palace opposite, he preserved the steps and in 1589 designed this building for them: it is officially the church of **Santissimo Salvatore della Scala Santa**, but always known as the Scala Santa (the 'Sacred Staircase'). The 28 Tyrian marble steps are protected by boards, and they are an arresting sight since worshippers ascend them in silence on their knees (although you can climb the two flights of stairs on either side on foot).

At the top is the **Sancta Sanctorum**, or chapel of St Lawrence, once the private chapel of the pope. Mentioned in the *Liber Pontificalis* in the 8th century, it was rebuilt in 1278 and contains frescoes and mosaics (barely visible above the altar) carried out for Pope Nicholas III (1277–80), restored for the first time in 1995, and it retains its beautiful Cosmatesque pavement. Protected by a silver tabernacle presented by Innocent III is the relic which gives the chapel its particular sanctity. This is an ancient painting on wood of Christ, which may date from as early as the 5th century, although it has been many times repainted and restored. It is said to have been begun by St Luke and an angel: hence its name *Acheiropoieton* ('made without hands'). The other precious relics are now in the Vatican (*see p. 473*).

Close by is the building which houses a tribune erected by Ferdinando Fuga for Benedict XIV in 1743 to house good copies of the mosaics from the **Triclinium of Leo III**, the banqueting hall of the old Lateran Palace. In the centre Christ is seen sending the Apostles to preach the gospel. On the left, Christ is depicted giving the keys to St Sylvester and the labarum (or standard of the Cross) to Constantine. On the right, St Peter is shown conferring the papal stole on Leo III and the banner of Christianity on Charlemagne.

PIAZZA DI PORTA SAN GIOVANNI

This huge space is often used for political demonstrations or concerts, and the festival of St John the Baptist is celebrated here on the night of 23rd–24th June. **Porta San Giovanni** was built in 1574 by Giacomo del Duca near an old gate in the Servian wall (*see p. 560*). This can still be seen, with its vantage-court between two fine towers, to the west of the 16th-century gateway. There is a fine stretch of the Aurelian Walls here.

THE AURELIAN WALLS

The Aurelian Walls were built by the emperors Aurelian (270–5) and Probus (276–82), and most of them survive to this day. They were raised to almost twice their height by Maxentius (306–12) and then restored by Honorius and Arcadius in AD 403.

The enceinte took in the Seven Hills, the Campus Martius, and the previously fortified area of Trastevere (*see map on p. 656*). It was about 19km round and had 18 main gates and 381 towers. The buildings of the city were contained within the walled area (just under 14 square kilometres) up until the 19th century: outside them, travellers would approach the city across many miles of desolate Campagna. The walls continued to be the defence of Rome until 1870, when the army of the Kingdom of Italy breached them with modern artillery, northwest of the Porta Pia. Many of the gates are still in use under their modern names.

Viale Carlo Felice, a busy traffic artery parallel to the walls, has public gardens down its length, laid out in 1926 by Raffaello de Vico on the site of a park created by the monks of Santa Croce, and replanted in 2000.

SANTA CROCE IN GERUSALEMME

SANTA CROCE IN GERUSALEMME

Map p. 649, B3. Open 7–12.45 & 3.30–7.30. santacroceroma.it.

The church of Santa Croce in Gerusalemme, one of the 'Seven Churches' of Rome (*see p. 292*), has been occupied by Cistercians since 1561. According to tradition, it was founded by Constantine's mother, St Helen, finder of the True Cross, hence the dedication, to the Holy Cross in Jerusalem. It was in fact probably built some time after 326, within part of the large palace erected for St Helen in the early 3rd century on the southwest extremity of the city. The principal edifice was known as the Sessorium and the church took the name of Basilica Sessoriana. Here was enshrined a relic of the True Cross, saved in Jerusalem by St Helen. The church was rebuilt in 1144 by Lucius II, who added the campanile, a simple brick structure with a statue of the Virgin in an aedicule. The present building has an impressive theatrical façade and oval vestibule, with simple conventual wings to either side—a very original design by Domenico Gregorini and Pietro Passalacqua. It dates from a reconstruction in 1743–4, as announced by the inscription across the central elevation: 'Benedict XIV Pontifex Maximus in honour of the Holy Cross in the fourth year of his pontificate'.

INTERIOR OF THE CHURCH

The interior also dates from the mid-18th century, with vault paintings of *St Helen in Glory* (over the nave) and the *Apparition of the Cross* (towards the east end) by Corrado Giaquinto, and a graceful baldacchino above the high altar where the basalt tomb encloses the remains of St Anastasius, originally a soldier of King Chosroes of Persia, who took the Holy Cross as booty from Jerusalem in the early 7th century. Impressed by the sanctity of the relic, Anastasius adopted Christianity as his religion, and was martyred at Caesarea.

Works from earlier centuries include (near the west door, to the right) the long epitaph of Benedict VII (d. 983), who is buried here, and the tomb on the east wall, behind the altar, of Cardinal Quiñones (d. 1540), by Jacopo Sansovino. The second south altarpiece, *St Bernard inducing Victor IV to humble himself before Innocent II*, is by Carlo Maratta. In the apse is a large fresco cycle of the *Invention of the Cross*, attributed to Antoniazzo Romano, pupil of Benozzo Gozzoli and the leading Roman artist of the early Renaissance, whose art never quite loses its medieval quality. The Cosmatesque pavement was restored in 1933.

A stairway at the end of the south aisle leads down to the **Chapel of St Helen**, at the level of the original Sessorium. Here, in a niche, is a statue of the saint adapted from an ancient Roman figure of Juno found at Ostia (which was copied from the Barberini statue now in the Vatican; *see p. 457*). At the foot of the statue, beneath a panel, are messages of prayer on innumerable slips of paper (soil from the Holy Land is said to have been deposited here). The striking mosaic in the vault, the original design of which was probably by Melozzo da Forlì (c. 1480), was restored by Baldassare Peruzzi and later by Francesco Zucchi. It represents Christ and the Evangelists, with Sts Peter and Paul, St Sylvester (who died here at Mass), St Helen and Cardinal Carvajal (whose titular church this was in the early 16th century). The **Chapel of St Gregory** beyond, built by the same Cardinal Carvajal in 1523, has an early 17th-century Roman bas-relief of the *Pietà*.

THE CHAPEL OF THE RELICS

At the end of the north aisle is the approach to the Chapel of the Relics, designed by Florestano di Fausto (1930), best known for his architecture in the Dodecanese, at a time when those islands were ruled by Italy. The style is stately and ponderous, the colour scheme black, white and grey. On the left as you enter is the sad little chapel of the Catholic Church's youngest mystic, Antonietta Meo, who died before her seventh birthday. The Chapel of the Relics is approached up a series of steps and platforms flanked by Stations of the Cross (in bronze; Giovanni Niccolini), between which are Latin texts from the liturgy of Good Friday. The final text, on the left, announces: 'Behold the wood of the Cross, on which the Saviour of the world hung. O come let us adore'. After this you enter the vestibule, with the findspot of the famous *Titulus Crucis* on the wall to the right. It was behind this brick that the fragment of the Titulus, or signboard of the Cross, on which was written 'Jesus of Nazareth, King of the Jews' (INRI), was discovered in the 15th century. The Titulus is now kept in the chapel proper, with all the other relics. These include three pieces of the True Cross, a nail and two thorns, all in 19th-century reliquaries. In a separate chapel is a replica of the Turin Shroud. The adjoining monastery houses the Diocesan Centre of Sindonology, dedicated to the study of this precious but controversial relic.

AROUND SANTA CROCE IN GERUSALEMME

On the right of the basilica are remains of the **Amphitheatrum Castrense** (*no admission*), a graceful brick edifice built by Elagabalus or Alexander Severus for amusements of the Imperial court. It was incorporated with the Aurelian Walls by Honorius. The wrought-iron gate, decorated with suspended chunks of coloured glass, is by Jannis Kounellis. To the left of the basilica, in the gardens of the former Caserma dei Granatieri, rises a large ruined apsidal hall known since the Renaissance as the **Temple of Venus and Cupid**. It was built in the early 4th century by Maxentius or Constantine.

In the barracks here are two military museums, and the fine **Museo Nazionale di Strumenti Musicali** (*map p. 649, C3; open 9–7, closed Mon; T: 06 70 14 796, museostrumentimusicali.it*). The attractive building of c. 1903, in the Art Nouveau style, looks north to a section of the Aurelian Walls. On its other side, near the basilica, are more Roman ruins. The museum has a representative display dating from ancient times to the 19th century, most of it collected by the tenor Evan Gorga (1865–1957), who premièred in Puccini's *La Bohème* at the Royal Theatre in Turin in 1896. He was an impulsive collector and also owned a vast collection of antiquities, part of which is displayed in Palazzo Altemps. Instruments include Roman sistra and auloi (a type of flute or pipe, originally from ancient Greece). One of the highlights is the pianoforte built by Bartolomeo Cristofori in 1722. Cristofori had invented an instrument which he called an *arpicembalo*, '*che fa il piano e il forte*' (which produces loud and soft notes) at the beginning of the century. Only three of his pianos survive (the other two are in New York and Leipzig), and this one used to be part of the collection of the early 18th-century Venetian composer Benedetto Marcello. There are curiosities such as 19th-century walking-sticks which convert into violins and flutes, a glass harmonica, and the famous Barberini Harp, a unique instrument commissioned by the Barberini

PORTA MAGGIORE
Ancient relief showing bread dough being kneaded, rolled, shaped and baked in a
brick-domed oven of a kind still in use all over Italy until the mid-20th century.
From the 1st-century BC tomb of the baker M. Vergilius Eurysaces.

family of Rome in the first years of the 17th century and decorated with splendid gild-ed carvings. Its triple row of strings enables chromatic notes to be played on it, even though it has no pedals.

To the east of the barracks, across Viale Castrense and outside the Aurelian Walls, are the well-preserved remains of the extensive **Circus Varianus**, dating from the reign of Elagabalus (218–22).

PORTA MAGGIORE

This double-arched gate in the Aurelian Walls (*map p. 649, B3*) was built by Claudius in AD 52 (the dedication survives at the top) and was formed by the archways carrying the Aqua Claudia and the Anio Novus over the Via Praenestina and the Via Labicana, the grass-grown stones of which can still be seen beneath the arches. The gate was restored by Honorius in 405 and its medieval name probably comes from its position close to Santa Maria Maggiore. On the outside of the gate is the unusual **tomb of the baker Marcus Vergilius Eurysaces**, purveyor to the state, and his wife Atistia. This pretentious monument, clad in travertine, dates from c. 30 BC. The circular openings may represent the mouths of a baker's oven; above is a frieze illustrating the stages of bread-making. From his cognomen, Eurysaces, which is of Greek origin, it is clear that the baker was not from a native Roman family. He was most likely a wealthy freed-man (the names Marcus and Vergilius were probably the names of his Roman master, which he adopted upon manumission). The funerary inscription of Atistia is now pre-served in the epigraph collection of the Museo Nazionale Romano (*see p. 318*).

Close by on Via Prenestina, diagonally opposite the Porta Maggiore (cross the tram-lines and the road), is the important **Basilica di Porta Maggiore** (*sadly closed indefi-nitely for restoration but described in the Appendix on p. 557*).

Looking up Via Giolitti from here, you can see another vestige of the ancient city, the hump-backed bulk of the **Temple of Minerva Medica** (*also described in the Appendix on p. 560*).

Santa Maria Maggiore & the Esquiline Hill

The Esquiline Hill, the highest and most extensive of the Seven Hills of Rome, is now a sprawling district crossed by busy roads. Its most visited monument is the venerable Basilica of Santa Maria Maggiore, famous for its mosaics. Two other churches close by also both have precious very early mosaics.

The Esquiline Hill had three ancient summits: the Oppian, site of the baths of Titus and Trajan and of Nero's Domus Aurea; the Cispian, now crowned by the basilica of Santa Maria Maggiore; and the Fagutalis, named from a beech grove (from *fagus*, a beech). According to Varro, the name Esquiline was derived from the word *excultus*, which referred to the ornamental groves planted by Servius Tullius. Formerly it was a place of vineyards and gardens, with a fashionable residential district between the modern Via Cavour and the slopes of the Oppian hill. Pompey lived here, in a house that after his death was occupied by Mark Antony. Maecenas, the great patron of the arts, also had a villa here; the poets Virgil and Propertius lived on the hill and Horace may have done so also.

THE BASILICA OF SANTA MARIA MAGGIORE

With its 5th-century plan and its early mosaics, Santa Maria Maggiore retains its original appearance more completely than the other three great papal basilicas (St John Lateran, St Peter's and San Paolo fuori le Mura), with whom it shares extraterritorial status. In the 16th and 17th centuries the popes added elaborate tombs and sumptuous chapels. Numerous services are held here throughout the day, and confessions are heard; it is still one of the most famous churches in Rome.

Visiting Santa Maria Maggiore
Map p. 655, E2. Open 7–7; museum open 9.30–6.30. The Loggia delle Benedizioni and the Roman house beneath the basilica are shown on guided tours throughout the day (book at the Museum). The church tends to be very crowded with tour groups; it is best to visit early. Coin-operated lights at the west end are essential for viewing the mosaics (there are separate lights for the nave mosaics and those at the east end).

BASILICA OF SANTA MARIA MAGGIORE

HISTORY OF THE BASILICA

According to a 13th-century legend, the Virgin Mary appeared on the night of 4th–5th August c. 358 to Pope Liberius (352–66) and to John, a patrician of Rome, telling them to build a church here. She told them that in the morning they would find a patch of snow (in mid-summer!) covering the exact area to be built over. The prediction fulfilled, Liberius drew up the plans and John built the church at his own expense. The original title was therefore Santa Maria della Neve ('of the Snow') and a pontifical Mass is still held here in the Borghese Chapel annually on 5th August to commemorate the miraculous snowfall. The church was afterwards called Santa Maria del Presepe, after a precious relic of the crib of the Infant Jesus, which is displayed on the high altar every year on Christmas morning, when there is a procession in its honour.

After the death of Pope Liberius, there were two contenders for the pontificate. In 366 supporters of the antipope Ursinus barricaded themselves in the church and surrendered only when the partisans of Pope Damasus I (366–84) took off the roof and pelted them with tiles. It is unlikely that anything remains of that original building. The present basilica almost certainly dates from the time of Sixtus III (432–40), who built it and dedicated it to the Virgin following the declaration of the Council of Ephesus in 431 that Mary was the Mother of God (Theotokos). This declaration gave great impetus to the westward spread from Byzantium of the cult of the Virgin.

Nicholas IV (1288–92) added the apse and transepts and completed the cycle of mosaics. Clement X (1670–6) rebuilt the apse, and in the 18th century Benedict XIV ordered Ferdinando Fuga to carry out further alterations and add the main façade.

EXTERIOR OF SANTA MARIA MAGGIORE

At the rear of the church, the **apse** is surrounded by an imposing flight of steps. This side of the building was adorned in the 16th century by Flaminio Ponzio and Domenico Fontana (and completed around 1673 by Carlo Rainaldi). The **obelisk**, nearly 15m high, was set up by Sixtus V in 1587 as part of the design to punctuate the vistas in his long, straight Strada Felice (*see p. 348*). Like its twin in Piazza del Quirinale, it once stood outside the entrance to the Mausoleum of Augustus and, as the longest inscription on its base records, it was found there in 1519 in four pieces.

Piazza Santa Maria Maggiore extends in front of the basilica, with a fluted cipollino **column** from the Basilica of Maxentius in the Forum. It was set up here in 1613 for Paul V by Carlo Maderno and crowned with a statue of the Virgin. Maderno also designed the fountain at its base, decorated with dragons and masks in travertine. The church's fine **campanile**, the highest in Rome, was given its present form in 1377 by Gregory XI, and it has restored polychrome decoration. The church **façade**, designed by Ferdinando Fuga in 1743, is approached by steps and is flanked by two grandiose wings. It masks (and protects) an older façade of the 12th century which retains its mosaics (*shown on a guided tour*). The portico is surmounted by a three-arch loggia. In the portico there is a bronze **statue of Philip IV of Spain (A)** by Bernini and his collaborator Girolamo Lucenti (1665).

THE INTERIOR

The vast, well-proportioned interior (86m long) is divided into nave and aisles by 36 columns of shining Hymettian marble and four of granite, all with Ionic capitals supporting an architrave, the whole discreetly rearranged and regularised by Fuga in the mid-18th century. Many of the architectural and sculptural works are by the four artists who also worked on the exterior: the 16th-century contemporaries Domenico Fontana and Flaminio Ponzio; Carlo Rainaldi, the most important architect at work in Rome at the end of the 17th century; and Ferdinando Fuga. The coffered ceiling, attributed to Giuliano da Sangallo, was traditionally thought to have been gilded with the first gold brought from America by Columbus, presented to the Spanish pope Alexander VI (Rodrigo Borgia) by King Ferdinand of Aragon and his wife Isabella, Queen of Castile. The Borgia emblems of rosettes and bulls are prominent.

The lovely Cosmatesque pavement dates from c. 1150. The large high altarpiece of the *Nativity*, conspicuous since it is permanently lit, is by a little-known 18th-century artist called Francesco Mancini.

The mosaics

(B) The splendid mosaics in the **nave** and over the **triumphal arch** date from the time of Sixtus III (432–40). Of exquisite workmanship in the Classical

SANTA MARIA MAGGIORE

A Statue of Philip IV of Spain
B Mosaics in the nave
C Apse
D Confessio
E Tomb of Bernini
F Tomb of Cardinal Rodriguez
G Cappella Sistina
H Borghese Chapel
I Sforza Chapel
J Cesi Chapel
K Cappella delle Reliquie
L Baptistery
M Cappella San Michele
N Tomb of Nicholas IV
O Tomb of Cardinal de Quelus
P Monument to Clement IX

Museum

Entrance

tradition, they are the most important Roman cycle of this period. The small rectangular biblical scenes high up above the nave architrave are difficult to see with the naked eye (*coin-operated light*). On the left are scenes from the lives of Abraham, Jacob and Isaac; on the right, from the lives of Moses and Joshua (restored, in part painted); over the triumphal arch the early life of Christ is illustrated.

(C) The mosaic of the **apse**, dating from the time of Nicholas IV (1288–94), is signed by Jacopo Torriti and represents the *Coronation of the Virgin*, with angels, saints, Nicholas IV, Cardinal Jacopo Colonna and others. It is the culminating point of all the mosaics in the church, commemorating the declaration at the Council of Ephesus that the Virgin was the Mother of God. The Virgin is seated on the same throne as Christ, a composition probably derived from the 12th-century mosaic in the apse of Santa Maria in Trastevere. Below, between the windows, are more mosaics by Torriti depicting the life of the Virgin, notably, in the centre, the *Dormition*. (*For the mosaics on the façade, also dating from Nicholas IV's* day, see p. 306). The four reliefs below the windows are from the old ciborium by Mino del Reame.

High altar

(D) The **confessio**, reconstructed in the 19th century by Virginio Vespignani, contains a colossal kneeling statue of Pius IX by Ignazio Jacometti. A fragment of the crib of the Infant Jesus is kept here in a reliquary adorned with swags of lilies and a figure of the Child.

The baldacchino with four porphyry columns is by Ferdinando Fuga, who designed the main façade. A porphyry sarcophagus containing the relics of St Matthew and other martyrs serves as the **high altar**.

(E) By the two sanctuary steps is the **pavement tomb of the Bernini family** with their crest, and on the step above it the name of Gian Lorenzo with the simple epitaph recording that he who was the 'glory of the arts and of this city' lies in this humble place. It is interesting to note that no important funerary monument was ever erected to Rome's greatest architect and sculptor, who himself designed some of the most sumptuous tombs in churches all over the city.

Side chapels

(F) In the chapel at the end of the south aisle is the beautiful **tomb of Cardinal Consalvo Rodriguez** (d. 1299), a masterpiece by Giovanni di Cosma, showing the influence of Arnolfo di Cambio. The mosaic of the *Madonna Enthroned with Saints* fits well with the architectonic lines of the tomb, which was completed by the beginning of the 14th century.

(G) The **Cappella Sistina**, on a domed Greek-cross plan, is a work of extraordinary magnificence executed for Sixtus V by Domenico Fontana (1585). Some of the marble panels were brought from the Septizodium on the Palatine, which had been demolished by the same pope. The chapel is a veritable church in itself, decorated with statues, stuccoes and Mannerist frescoes around the sumptuous tomb of the pontiff (and that of St Pius V on the left). The temple-like baldacchino, carried by four gilt-bronze angels by Sebastiano Torrigiani, covers the original little Cosmatesque Chapel of the Relics, redesigned by Arnolfo di Cambio (late 13th century) with figures of the crêche by his assistants (*now displayed in the Museum; see below*). The chapel is a remarkable example of competitive opulence produced by a pope who started out life as a swineherd but by the end of his pontificate had paid for this staggering profusion of statuary, marble and precious stones.

(H) A few years after the building of the Cappella Sistina, the astute diplomat Paul V decided he was not to be outdone and he commissioned the even more sumptuous **Borghese Chapel** opposite. The splendid Cappella Paolina, as it is also known, was erected for the pontiff by Flaminio Ponzio in 1611 as the pope's burial place and to give prominence (on the altar) to a famous painted image of the **Madonna and Child**, greatly venerated in past centuries as the 'Salus Populi', saviour of the Romans, and which seems to have been recorded in the city as early as the 10th century, and therefore dated to the 7th or 8th century. However some scholars now believe it was made in the 12th or even 13th century. The Madonna, with crossed hands, is in the Byzantine style and is surrounded with lapis lazuli and agate.

The best-known contemporary artists were employed to decorate the chapel, including Lodovico Cigoli, Guido Reni, Giovanni Baglione and Passignano, and the sculptors Stefano Maderno, Francesco Mochi and Nicolas Cordier. The frescoes by Cavaliere d'Arpino in the dome and upper parts of the walls are considered his masterpiece.

On the right is the tomb of Clement VIII, shown in his tiara blessing the faithful. He has gone down in history as the pope who sent Beatrice Cenci and Giordano Bruno to their deaths. On the left is Paul V, meekly kneeling and bare-headed. Another Borghese buried here, who was never known to be meek, is Pauline, sister of Napoleon Bonaparte, who married Prince Camillo Borghese in 1803.

(I) The severely beautiful and unadorned **Sforza Chapel** is reserved for prayer, but if you are discreet you can enter it (*the door is usually unlocked*) and sit in a corner to study its extraordinary architecture. Most scholars now recognise this as the work of Michelangelo, who here, at the age of 85, invented a radically new spatial concept. It was commissioned in 1562 by the pope's chamberlain Cardinal Guido Ascanio, grandson of Paul III, both as his own burial place and as the Chapel of the Sacrament. He is known to have been a great friend of Michelangelo's and it was begun just one year before Michelangelo's death, under the direction of his pupil Tiberio Calcagni (who himself died only a year after his master). The carefully planned light sources designed by Michelangelo have unfortunately been altered. We know that Borromini came here to study the complexity of the vaulting, the huge arches and the columns and capitals, and indeed its architecture points the way forward to the spirit of High Baroque. The tombs of Cardinal Guido and his brother Alessio, as well as the marble tabernacle, were designed later by Giacomo della Porta. The high altarpiece of the *Assumption* (1565) is by Girolamo Siciolante da Sermoneta.

(J) The **Cesi Chapel** dates from around 1550. In it are two family tombs by Guglielmo della Porta and an altarpiece of the *Martyrdom of St Catherine* by Sermoneta.

(K) The **Cappella delle Reliquie**, with its ten red porphyry columns and a 15th-century wooden Crucifix, is by Ferdinando Fuga.

(L) The **baptistery** is the work of Flaminio Ponzio and has a high-relief of the *Assumption* by Pietro Bernini, father of Gian Lorenzo. The Santarelli monument over the sacristy door incorporates a bust by Alessandro Algardi. On the left wall there is a bust in coloured marble of Emanuele Ne Vunda, ambassador sent by the king of Kongo to Pope Paul V in 1608 (he died here just two days after his arrival).

(M) The **Cappella San Michele** is rather inappropriately a souvenir shop: in the vault are traces of 15th-century frescoes, including two *Evangelists* by

the circle of Piero della Francesca and (above the cupboards) a *Pietà* attributed to Benozzo Gozzoli.

A column in the shape of a cannon shaft in the adjoining courtyard celebrates the conversion of Henry IV of France. Here is the entrance to the Museum (*see below*).

Tombs at the west end

(N) The **tomb of Nicholas IV**, the pope who commissioned the apse mosaics, was designed by Domenico Fontana more than three centuries after the pontiff's death.

(O) Above the Porta Santa is the tomb, in the style of the great 15th-century sculptor Giovanni Dalmata, of **Cardinal**

Philippe de Levis de Quelus and his younger brother Archbishop Eustache (1489).

(P) The **monument to Clement IX** was designed by Carlo Rainaldi, with a statue of the pope by Domenico Guidi and representations of *Faith* and *Charity* by Cosimo Fancelli and Ercole Ferrata.

THE MUSEUM, EXCAVATIONS AND LOGGIA DELLE BENEDIZIONI

The **Museum** (*open 9.30–6.30; entrance through the shop*), of relative interest, is arranged in numerous underground rooms. The most interesting contents are in the first room: the crèche figures by an assistant of Arnolfo di Cambio from the Chapel of the Relics in the Cappella Sistina in the church (*see above*). The paintings in the second room include a tondo of the *Madonna* by Beccafumi and *Christ Carrying the Cross* by Sodoma. The huge collection of Church silver and liturgical objects dates mostly from the 17th and 18th centuries, and there are lots of portraits of churchmen.

The excavations and Loggia can only be visited on a guided visit (*ask at the Museum*). Remains of an **ancient Roman house**, uncovered in 1971, are visited along modern walkways. In one room there is a collection of roof tiles with brick stamps dating from many different periods. The most interesting wall-paintings are a fragment of a large rural calendar dating from the 1st/2nd century AD, which had illustrations for each month and red panels in between, listing each day. Only the month of September survives, which shows an orchard where apples are being harvested.

From the portico of the church, stairs in the Palazzo Apostolico lead up to the open **Loggia delle Benedizioni**, where you can see the mosaics on the earlier façade of the basilica dating from the time of Nicholas IV (1294–1308). The upper part, signed by a certain Filippo Rusuti, depicts *Christ Pantocrator* with angels and saints. The four scenes below, illustrating the legend attached to the founding of the first basilica, were probably completed by his assistants. The four 18th-century statues of angels by Pietro Bracci kept here were originally over the high altar.

SANTA PRASSEDE

The church of Santa Prassede (*map p. 655, E2–F2; open 7.30–12 & 4–6.30, Sun 4–6.30*) is still enveloped on all sides by medieval and later buildings, so that the entrance is by an inconspicuous side door (the main west entrance, preceded by a medieval porch with two reversed Doric capitals, is kept locked).

The building is dedicated to Praxedes, sister of Pudentiana and daughter of a Roman senator (*see p. 310*). The two sisters are frequently depicted in the mosaics in the church. An oratory is said to have been erected here about AD 150 by St Pius I, and a church is known to have been in existence on this site at the end of the 5th century. The present building of 822 dates from the time of St Paschal I (though restored in 1450, 1564, 1832 and 1869). It was here in 118 that the Frangipani attacked Pope Gelasius II with arrows and stones, driving him to exile in France, where he died. Robert Browning's *The Bishop Orders his Tomb at Saint Praxed's Church* is set here.

The light interior is particularly inviting. St Paschal I (early 9th century) founded no fewer than three churches in Rome, which still contain the mosaics he commissioned for them (the others are Santa Maria in Domnica and Santa Cecilia in Trastevere) and which all also bear his portrait amongst the six principal figures flanking Christ. But it is here that the most extensive mosaic decoration survives from his time.

THE CHAPEL OF ST ZENO

This charming tiny chapel (*to the left as you enter*) was built by St Paschal as a mausoleum for his mother, Theodora, in 817–24. Perfectly preserved, it is the most important work of its date to have survived in Rome, and the only chapel in the city entirely covered with mosaics. The entrance is flanked by two ancient columns, supplied by Paschal, the Ionic capitals of which support a rich 1st-century architrave from a pagan temple, elaborately sculptured. Resting on this is a Roman marble urn dating from the 3rd century. Above is a **double row of mosaic busts** from the time of Paschal: in the inner row, the Virgin and Child, St Praxedes, St Pudentiana and other saints; in the outer, Christ and the Apostles, and four saints (the lowest two perhaps added in the 13th century).

The mosaics in the vaulted interior are exquisite. In the **centre of the vault** is Christ surrounded by four angels skilfully fitted into the angles of the ceiling. The mosaics show Byzantine influence, and demonstrate also how pagan symbolism became conflated with Christian. The figure of the general borne aloft on his circular shield (*clipeus*) by four winged Victories translates into Christ the victor over death portrayed in a roundel and borne aloft by angels. The **mosaics over the door** depict St Peter and St Paul upholding the throne of God; on the right St John the Evangelist, St Andrew and St James, and Christ between St Paschal and another saint (?Valentine); on the left, St Praxedes and her sister St Pudentiana together with St Agnes, and four half-length female figures including Paschal's mother Theodora (with the square nimbus indicating that she was still alive when the mosaic was executed). The **altar niche** (*permanently lit*) has a charming *Madonna and Child* (with his arms held out to us) between the sister saints Praxedes and Pudentiana. Here you can closely examine the mosaic technique.

SANTA PRASSEDE
Detail of the vault mosaics in the Chapel of St Zeno, showing angels bearing aloft a
roundel of Christ. The iconography is taken from the pagan idea of the winged
Victory bearing the shield of a military conqueror.

The pavement is perhaps the oldest known example of opus sectile. The bases of the four supporting columns also date from Paschal's time, except for the one on the right of the altar—a fine 5th-century Roman work—which he carefully reused. In a niche on the right are fragments of a column brought from Jerusalem after the Sixth Crusade (1228) and said to be that at which Christ was scourged. There are not many other relics in Rome of such doubtful authenticity still so boldly exhibited (note the charming little old-fashioned display case).

THE CHOIR

The steps are made of *rosso antico,* and on the left and right are six beautiful Roman columns of very unusual design incorporating the form of acanthus and laurel leaves. The Baroque baldacchino is by Francesco Ferrari (1730). In the **crypt** beneath are four early Christian sarcophagi, including one with the remains of Sts Praxedes and Pudentiana, and a 13th-century Cosmatesque altar with a damaged fresco above depicting the Madonna between the two sisters.

On the **choir arch** (*coin-operated light on the right of the steps*), the New Jerusalem shows the elect, preceded by angels (and on the right also St Peter and St Paul), being received at the Gates of Heaven. Heaven is charmingly depicted as a walled golden enclosure with Christ in the centre surrounded by angels, the Apostles, Elijah and Moses. Below, on either side, against a gold ground, are crowds of the faithful waving palm fronds. The **apse arch** shows the Lamb of God in a roundel with the seven golden candlesticks, the symbols of the Evangelists and 24 Elders dressed in white robes raising their crowns as a sign of glory. The **semi-dome** has Christ between St Peter, St Pudentiana and St Zeno on the right and St Paul, St Praxedes and St Paschal I on the left (with a square nimbus); below them are shown the Lamb, the flock of the Faithful and a long inscription in gold lettering stating that St Paschal I had these 'glittering enamels' made to glory the name of Praxedes together with that of the Lord. Above, on the intrados of the arch, is his monogram in gold lettering against a blue ground. The scheme of the mosaics is evidently derived from that in Santi Cosma e Damiano.

Browning in Santa Prassede

And then how I shall lie through centuries,
And hear the blessed mutter of the mass,
And see God made and eaten all day long,
And feel the steady candle-flame, and taste
Good strong thick stupefying incense-smoke!

The Bishop Orders his Tomb at Saint Praxed's Church, Rome, 15—

NAVE AND SIDE CHAPELS

Sixteen granite columns and six piers supporting an architrave made up of ancient Roman fragments line the nave. The effective 16th-century *trompe l'oeil* frescoes of angels on pedestals, which also continue round the west end of the church, are by Paris Nogari, Baldassare Croce and Agostino Ciampelli. The large porphyry disc with an inscription indicates the well where St Praxedes supposedly hid the bones of Christian martyrs. On the nave pillar outside the Chapel of St Zeno, the monument to Giovanni Battista Santoni (d. 1592) is one of the earliest works of Bernini.

At the east end of the south aisle is the tomb of Cardinal Pantaleon of Troyes (d. 1286), with Cosmatesque fragments, attributed to Arnolfo di Cambio. Behind the postcard stall outside the chapel of St Zeno is the tomb of Cardinal Alain Coëtivy (1474) by Andrea Bregno. The north aisle has late 16th-century vault frescoes by Cavaliere d'Arpino, an altarpiece of the *Way to Calvary* of the same date by Federico Zuccari (third chapel) and 17th-century paintings and frescoes by Ciro Ferri and Borgognone (second chapel).

SANTA PUDENZIANA

Santa Pudenziana (*map p. 655, E2; open 8.30–12 & 3–6*) is one of the oldest churches in Rome, thought to have been built c. 390, when the apse mosaic was made, making it the most ancient mosaic to be found in the apse of a church anywhere in the entire city. The church was built into a Roman thermal hall of the 2nd century and is dedicated to Pudentiana, sister of Praxedes (*see above*), and daughter of the Roman senator Pudens, a legendary figure who is supposed to have given hospitality to St Peter in his house on this site when the Apostle first arrived in Rome. He has been identified with the Pudens mentioned by Paul in his second Epistle to Timothy, written from Rome when the apostle exhorts Timothy to 'Do thy diligence to come before winter. Eubulus greeteth thee, and Pudens, and Linus, and Claudia, and all the brethren.' The church was rebuilt several times, notably in 1589.

The church is now well below the level of the modern street. It is little visited by tourists or worshippers, and after the crowds of Santa Maria Maggiore is a soothing relief. There is a peaceful little courtyard with benches. The façade was rebuilt and decorated in the 19th century, but the good doorway preserves an interesting medieval frieze in relief. The fine campanile probably dates from the late 12th century.

CHURCH INTERIOR

Sadly the Roman columns of the church have been partially covered by piers, and the walls are painted in a very dull brown colour. However the **apse mosaic** is extremely interesting. It shows *Christ Enthroned*, holding an open book (with the inscription *Dominus conservator ecclesiae Pudentianae*; *Lord the keeper of the church of Pudens*), between St Peter (right) and St Paul (left) and the Apostles. Two female figures representing the converted Jews and the converted pagans (or Gentiles) are placing wreaths over the heads of Peter and Paul. The Roman character of the figures is marked: the magisterial air of Christ recalls representations of Jupiter; and the Apostles, in their togas, resemble senators. Behind Christ's throne rises a hill crowned by a jewelled Cross. Around it hover four winged creatures with the head of a man/angel, a lion, a bull and an eagle, the traditional symbols of the Evangelists.

The iconography of this remarkable work has been closely studied by scholars for its significance in the early development of Christianity in Rome: it dates from the time of Theodosius, who declared 'Catholic Christianity' the state religion in 380 and banned all pagan cults. Here the bearded Christ is depicted enthroned in divine majesty, seated on a deep crimson cushion in a posture which recalls statues of Roman emperors. He is shown being acclaimed by the Apostles, who again use gestures which seem to be derived from acclamation scenes of late Roman emperors. It would appear that Imperial motifs were deliberately used in early Christian iconography to strengthen the position of the Church and make it less alien to adherents of the old Roman religion. Paul is included to bring the number of Apostles to twelve and this is one of the earliest instances in which we see him take pride of place with Peter beside Christ. He was in many ways the most important figure in early Christian Rome, and his letters were used to justify the authority the emperor might exercise over the Church. The arrangement of Christ seated in the centre of a semicircle may well reflect the way services were taken in the apsidal east ends of early Christian basilicas. The unusual arcaded portico with its golden roof tiles, which surrounds the scene, has not been satisfactorily explained, but above it the buildings (which include houses, *thermae* and a basilica) are thought to represent Jerusalem and the Holy Sepulchre in the 4th century.

In around 1588 when the church was renovated, part of the mosaic fell to the floor and the damaged parts were reconstructed in fresco. These were then remade in mosaic in 1831, so what we see today is not all the original 4th-century composition. In the 16th century the parts on the right and left were partially covered by the new apse. However we know that the original mosaic had the full figures of the seated Apostles in two rows (including two more, at each end) and that beneath Christ there was a dove, a lamb, and a mound from which flowed four rivers. Behind Christ the buildings in the background included a long portico in the centre. (*The mosaic can be viewed more closely from a balcony above on a guided tour; see below.*)

The dome above in the apse, thought to be the first elliptical dome ever built in Rome, was painted by Pomarancio. In the chapel at the end of the north aisle an altar, presented in the 19th century by Cardinal Wiseman (appointed Archbishop of Westminster by Pope Pius IX), encloses part of the legendary Communion table of St Peter; the rest of it is in St John Lateran. The Baroque Caetani Chapel, by Francesco da Volterra, was finished by Carlo Maderno.

UPPER FLOOR AND MEDIEVAL FRESCOES

It is possible to visit other parts of the church on a guided visit by appointment, only when the church itself is closed (*enquire at the door, or T: 347 14 68 745*). The frescoes in an ambulatory behind the present apse probably date from around 1130. They include the *Madonna and Child between Pudentiana and Pudens* (both in Byzantine style head-dresses and offering crowns to the Madonna), as well as damaged stories from the life of St Paul and St Cecilia. The Roman masonry of the baths, partly in *opus mixtum* (alternate rows of brick and stone) dating from 142, can be seen here, as well as beautifully constructed ancient walls in which the brick stamps survive.

The visit includes a remarkable close-up view of the apse mosaics from above the nave, and the exterior wall of the Roman baths incorporated into the structure of the church.

EXCAVATIONS BENEATH THE CHURCH

These have not yet been open to the public (*for information, see stpudenziana.org*). The masonry survives of the earliest *domus*, built in 170 BC, and of the house supposed to have been that of Pudens (AD 50), as well as of an insula on several floors built in AD 129, which later provided the foundations for the baths into which the church was built (the pools are under the present pavement).

Baths of Diocletian & Museo Nazionale Romano

The Baths of Diocletian were the largest of all the ancient Roman baths.
They could accommodate over 3,000 people and covered an area of some
380m by 370m, corresponding to that now bounded by Piazza dei Cinquecento,
Via Torino, Via XX Settembre and Via Volturno. Some of the great vaulted halls can be
visited and the state's lapidary collection is displayed on the site. Masterpieces of
sculpture and fresco are in the nearby Palazzo Massimo.

T he vast **Piazza dei Cinquecento** (*map p. 655, F1*) is by far the largest square in Rome, though it is really no more than a network of roads and is always busy with traffic. In winter hundreds of thousands of starlings come to roost here at dusk. At one end stands Stazione Termini, named after the baths (*termini*) of Diocletian. It is one of the largest railway stations in Europe. Two of Rome's Metro lines intersect here. Reconstruction of the station building began in 1938. It was opened in 1950 and modernised in 2000. A gigantic quasi-cantilever construction, sweeping upwards and outwards, serves as a portico. Near the bus ranks is a colossal statue of John Paul II (Oliviero Rainaldi, 2011), his mantle open to symbolise welcome and sanctuary. It was set up on the date of the former pope's beatification.

THE BATHS OF DIOCLETIAN
(MUSEO NAZIONALE ROMANO)

Map p. 655, E1. Open 9–7.30; closed Mon. T: 06 39 96 7700, coopculture.it or archeo-roma.beniculturali.it. Tickets are valid for three days and cover the four museums of the Museo Nazionale Romano (this one, Palazzo Massimo, Palazzo Altemps and the Crypta Balbi). The entrance is through the garden directly in front of the railway station at 79 Via Enrico de Nicola.

The Museo Nazionale Romano, the national collection of ancient Roman art, was founded here in 1889 in the halls of the ancient Baths of Diocletian, the massive brick buildings of which are conspicuous in both Piazza dei Cinquecento and Piazza della Repubblica. The collection is now spread over four different locations. Among the

BATHS OF DIOCLETIAN
Floor mosaic with twin peacocks, displayed in the former frigidarium.

ruins of the baths, the huge collection of fascinating epigraphs is beautifully arranged in modern halls, and in 2014 some of the magnificent bath buildings themselves were reopened after restoration, as well as the small cloister of the Carthusian monastery which was built into the ruins in the 16th century.

Beside the entrance, excavations are in progress of a hypogeum which is to be reconstructed. In the well-kept little garden, where lavender grows, are stelae and altars arranged according to provenance, including a group dedicated to praetorian guards found in a small cemetery near the Milvian Bridge. A huge Roman vase serves as a fountain, shaded by cypresses. There are plenty of places to sit.

Beyond the ticket check, where there are some little Roman mosaics, there is a corridor with a few Roman sculptures, mostly dating from the 2nd–3rd centuries AD (including busts, statues and sarcophagi), as well as a delicately carved funerary altar found in Via di Porta San Sebastiano (1st century AD). Off this corridor are the entrances to the Epigraph Collection (right), the Small Cloister (left) and the Great Cloister (ahead), as well as to the recently restored halls of the ancient baths.

HISTORY OF THE BATHS OF DIOCLETIAN

Begun in 299, the baths were completed in less than eight years by Diocletian and Maximian. Many of their huge walls are still visible in the streets and squares of this part of town. The baths were plundered for their building materials over the centuries, and entire new edifices were built on their site: the caldarium, which survived into the late 17th century, was partly destroyed when Piazza della Repubblica was laid out: the façade of Santa Maria degli Angeli is inserted into one of its walls and the huge church itself occupies the area of the tepidarium and the huge central hall. A Carthusian monastery with two cloisters occupied another entire wing.

The only entrance to the baths was on the northeast side, near the present Via Volturno. On the southwest side the closed exedra was flanked by two circular halls: one of these is now the church of San Bernardo alle Terme; the other was at the corner of Via Viminale and Via delle Terme. On the corner of Via Parigi, at the northwest angle of the main complex, there is a third, beautiful domed octagonal hall, hidden by a rectangular exterior: this survives intact but is not at present open to the public. In this area there would probably have been an open-air gymnasium.

RESTORED HALLS OF THE ANCIENT BATHS

Despite the many vicissitudes the baths have suffered, they still retain their architectural grandeur. Recent restorations and partial reconstructions have succeeded as far as possible in returning them to their original state.

The first room displays the **dedicatory inscription** of these baths, which survives in eight fragments, announcing their completion just eight years after they were begun in AD 299. As you can see the fragments don't match and it is presumed they come from different inscriptions set up in various halls of the baths but all with the same text. One of these, when still intact, was seen and transcribed by a pilgrim in early 9th century and is preserved in the Einsiedeln Itinerary (*see p. 145*). It speaks of the emperors Diocletian and Maximian presenting these baths to *suis romanis* ('their Romans').

The second room has a helpful **model of the baths** and a video suggesting how they might have looked in their heyday. You exit (through a 16th-century gateway moved here in 1911 from a villa in the neighbourhood) into the magnificent **Aula VIII**, which used to have a barrel vault (part of it is preserved at one end). Three ancient Roman bath tubs found in the ruins are displayed here, dating from the 2nd–3rd century AD, the largest in marble from Asia Minor with four lions' heads. Also here is a gateway which formerly led into the Carthusian monastery. The hall adjoins part of the short side of the **natatio** (frigidarium), the open-air swimming pool. You can step down onto its marble floor (the water would have been about a metre deep). The rest of the pool (really almost a small lake, open to the sky) was later occupied by the huge apse of the church of Santa Maria degli Angeli and the small cloister of the monastery. It had two apses on either side of a rectangular niche, and in the far apse a well-preserved black-and-white mosaic with a pair of peacocks in the centre is beautifully displayed on the wall.

On the other side of Aula VIII is the entrance to **Aula IX**, still open to the sky, with a collection of architectural fragments. A glass door gives access to **Aula X**, where the

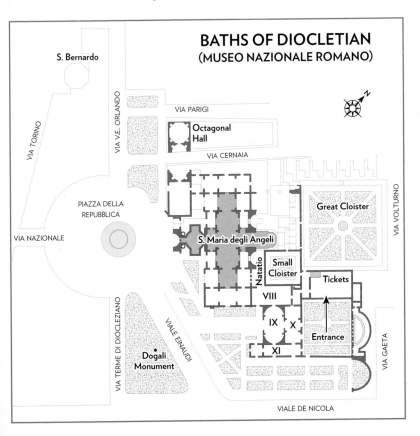

scale of the architecture can be appreciated: you can still see right up to the spring of the vaults below the modern roof. The sculpture displayed here includes a very unusual equestrian statue of a boy, in Carrara marble and alabaster, probably once part of a funerary monument of the 3rd century AD. The reconstructed tomb (named after the Platorinus family), discovered in 1880 on the right bank of the Tiber, contains niches with a great variety of cinerary urns, and two statues and a bust of a girl with long hair found in the tomb and dating from the 1st century AD. Two columbaria dating from the 2nd century AD have also been reconstructed, one with lovely paintings with figures, birds, pomegranates and peacocks, and the other with stuccoes on its vault. The sarcophaghi include one from the Via Appia with hunting scenes and another found near Via Labicana with very fine carvings of Dionysus and Ariadne. **Aula XI** (also roofed) was probably used for the storage of water since the walls had waterproof plastering up to a heigh of five metres. A number of black-and-white mosaics are displayed here, including a small one with a skeleton and the motto of the Delphic oracle: 'Know thyself'. Two more (both dating from the 3rd century AD) have representations of Hercules, and Troilus falling from his chariot during the Trojan War.

THE CLOISTERS

Return to the corridor and take the steps on the left down to the **Small Cloister**, built in the 16th century for the former Carthusian monastery. In the peaceful garden there are four little orange trees and a well. In the walks are arranged well-labelled sculptures and imperial inscriptions beside busts of emperors. Some of these were found as recently as 2011 on the outskirts of Rome.

At the end of the corridor is the **Great Cloister**, traditionally ascribed to Michelangelo, although he died the year before it was built in 1565. The arcades, 80m long on each side, are supported by 100 travertine columns, and the original pale blue colour of the plaster has been restored. The garden has palm trees and cypresses and sculptural fragments scattered among the borders. The fountain dates from 1695 and is surrounded by seven colossal animal heads (probably from the Forum of Trajan). It is shaded by four cypresses, one of which, now propped up, is centuries old. Roman sculptures—many of them damaged—are arranged in the cloister walks. They include statues, sarcophagi and altars, mostly dating from the 1st–2nd centuries AD, and all well labelled. The amusing *trompe l'oeil* of a Carthusian monk dates from the 19th century.

THE EPIGRAPH COLLECTION

The collection of about 10,000 inscriptions in Latin is one of the most important of its kind in the world. Many of the exhibits come from excavations during building work in the capital after Italian Unification, and others come from the Kircher and Gorga collections. Some of the inscriptions are from tombs along the consular roads leading out of the city, dating mostly from the end of the Republican era to the end of the 2nd century AD, and others are from Roman centres in Lazio. The present superb arrangement, which includes some 900 pieces on three floors, seeks to provide a documentation of Roman civilisation from social, political, administrative, economic and religious aspects.

BATHS OF DIOCLETIAN
Bust of Antoninus Pius as a member of the Arval Brethren,
priests of the Dea Dia, guarantor of the harvest.

Although at first sight epigraphs may seem less interesting and less easy to appreciate than, say, ancient Roman sculpture, they are fascinating documents of the ancient Roman world. This new arrangement allows the non-expert, perhaps for the first time, to appreciate their significance, although it is necessary to dedicate a lot of time to the visit in order to read the translations and history of each piece (labelled also in English). In the 18th and 19th centuries epigraphs were considered among the most important relics of the past. Travellers recorded their fascination with them and their collection and study was given first place amongst antiquarians. They seemed to go out of fashion in the 20th century, and museums hid them away in their deposits.

Round Hall: Here is a display of Archaic finds (8th–5th centuries BC). An aryballos in black terracotta (bucchero) bears a votive inscription in Etruscan. Found near Veio, it is dated to the late 7th century BC. Here too is a reproduction of the golden brooch known as the '*Fibula Praenestina*', famous in the late 20th century when most scholars decided it was a fake: if it is original, it would provide the earliest known example of a Latin inscription (early 7th century BC). Also on this wall is a display of ceramics, with inscriptions, found in a votive deposit beneath the Lapis Niger in the Roman Forum (a cast of which is exhibited here). A fragment of a cup in bucchero ware found in the Regia in the Forum bears the owner's title, Rex, thought to refer to one of the last kings of Rome. Architectural fragments of the late 7th and early 6th centuries BC from the Regia are also exhibited here. Displayed on its own is an inscription in tufa from Tivoli, which may refer to Publius Valerius, the first Republican consul of Rome (509 BC).

Other cases display finds from recent excavations on the slopes of the Palatine, some of which bear the letter V, which seems to refer to the cult of Juno Sospita (Juno the Saviour), which flourished in the 6th–5th centuries BC.

There are finds from a sanctuary in Lavinium in Lazio (*see below*), including a bronze inscription of the late 6th century BC, with a dedication to the twin heroes Castor and Pollux, the earliest reference so far found in Lazio to the Greek cult of the Dioscuri.

Main Hall: Works from the early Republican period (4th–3rd centuries BC) include black varnish ceramics with inscriptions found in the Tiber. Some of these, including ex-votos, belonged to the sanctuary of Aesculapius on the Isola Tiberina. A large marble basin with a dedication to Hercules from a sacred font dating from the 3rd century BC is the oldest known example of an inscription with metal lettering. Other finds come from Lanuvium (Lanuvio), an ancient city famous for its sanctuary of Juno Sospita, the site of which has been found near Genzano, and there are four large cippi (late 4th and early 3rd centuries BC) from Lavinium, which, according to an ancient legend, was the town founded by Aeneas after his escape from Troy, and named after his wife. Numerous ancient Roman historians, as well as Virgil, upheld this myth, and as early as 300 BC a tradition existed at Lavinium itself which attributed its foundation to the Trojan hero. A tomb sanctuary dedicated to Aeneas, in the form of a tumulus burial chamber, restored in the 4th century BC, was found nearby, and the cippi come from there.

Finds from a late 4th or early 3rd-century BC sanctuary dedicated to Demeter and Kore in Ariccia include three seated terracotta female statues and two busts of the goddesses.

In the room to the left are displayed inscriptions dating from the late Republican period (2nd–1st century BC). These include several with names of slaves, and one found recently near the Meta Sudans relating to a company of singers and actors which gave performances of Greek plays. The funerary inscriptions set up by artisans in the city include that of Atistia, the wife of the baker whose grand tomb still stands beside the Porta Maggiore (*see p. 299*). A fragment of an inscription in handsome lettering records the funerary oration of a husband to his wife, pronounced between 8 and 2 BC. A group of terracotta pots, found in Via di Porta Sebastiano, bear inscriptions with a name and date, probably referring to the cremated person to whom the small piece of bone found inside belonged.

At the end of the main hall there is a bronze dedication originally set up by a group of players of wind instruments, beneath a bronze statue of Tiberius, dating from 7 BC, which was found on the slopes of the Palatine in 1992–3. On the same site a large statue base in marble was unearthed, with handsome inscriptions ordered by the same group of musicians, relating to four statues of Augustus, Nero, Claudius and Agrippina, mother of Nero. Also here is the bronze base of the shrine of the Curiae Veteres (12 BC–AD 56), found on the northeast slopes of the Palatine.

Second floor
A very fine display of epigraphs illustrates the social structure of the Roman Empire and other aspects of Roman life. On the balcony are exhibited numerous epigraphs from a dynastic monument in the Campus Martius belonging to the *gens* Claudia. A fragment with beautiful lettering found outside Porta Pia is thought to belong to an inscription recording the historian Tacitus, who died c. AD 120. There are inscriptions relating to public officials, members of political and administrative institutions (often specifying the precise social standing of the person in question) and military dedications. Also here is a fragment of red plaster which bears graffiti made by Roman firemen. It was found in their guardroom in Trastevere (3rd century AD).

Third floor
A display of epigraphs relates to the economic life of the city during the Empire. There are also inscriptions from religious sanctuaries, including private domestic altars, official religious edicts, and very early references to the Christian religion. Remains of the fountain of Anna Perenna, a nymph connected to a spring, is beautifully displayed, together with artefacts found nearby including little lead containers used in making spells. This 'magical' spring, famous from the 4th century BC right up to the 5th century AD, was identified in 1999 in the Parioli district (Piazza Euclide).

A small room at the end has a display of fakes, and an illustration of how epigraphs were carved. The room beyond displays objects relating to Oriental cults, including a relief of Mithras, still with traces of colour and gilding, found in the Mithraeum below Santo Stefano Rotondo.

PIAZZA DELLA REPUBBLICA

This large circular piazza occupies the site of the huge exedra which closed the south-western side of the Baths of Diocletian (*see plan on p. 315*). It was laid out in 1902 by Gaetano Koch and the semicircular porticoed fronts of the *palazzi* he designed follow the line of the exedra. The abundant waters of the **Fountain of the Naiads** (1870) are supplied by the Aqua Marcia, which terminates here. This aqueduct, built from Tivoli to Rome in 144 BC, was one of the most important and longest of the Roman aqueducts. The same springs were tapped for a new aqueduct, built in part of cast-iron by a private Anglo-Italian company for the Papal States, called the Pia Marcia and inaugurated in 1870 by Pius X. On the fountain, the four groups of faintly erotic reclining nymphs, symbolising the spirits of rivers and springs, and the central Glaucus, the mythical fisherman who became a god of the sea, are by Mario Rutelli (1901–11).

In the gardens on Viale Einaudi (on the site of two of the halls of the Baths) the **Dogali Monument** by Francesco Azzurri commemorates 548 Italian soldiers ambushed at Dogali, Eritrea, in 1887. It incorporates an Egyptian obelisk found just three years earlier in the Isaeum Campense (*see p. 181*), inscribed with hieroglyphs recording the glories of Ramesses the Great or his predecessor Seti I. Its companion is in Florence. In 1936–44 it was decorated with the Lion of Judah, plundered from Addis Ababa. Second-hand book stalls line one side of the gardens.

SANTA MARIA DEGLI ANGELI

This huge church (*map p. 655, E1; open 7.30–7*) is often used for state funerals. It was Pope Pius IV who decided in 1561 that the great central hall (or Basilica) of the Baths of Diocletian should be converted into a church, and so, in the spirit of the Counter-Reformation, this pagan place (there was a tradition that some 40,000 Christians had been forced by the emperor to construct the baths) would become consecrated ground. We know that Pius commissioned Michelangelo to adapt the baths for the new church, although no plans certainly by the great architect's hand survive. It is likely that Michelangelo aimed to preserve the ancient building as far as possible, using the opportunity it afforded for a nave of vast proportions. Pius (whose second name was Angelo) is buried in a pavement tomb in the choir (there is an inscription to him on the wall, dating from 1582).

The pope also had a monastery built in the ruins and installed the Carthusians from Santa Croce in Gerusalemme. In 1749 Vanvitelli was instructed by the Carthusian fathers to alter the orientation, and so the entrance is now on the long southwest side and the nave is now a colossal transept. To compensate for the loss of length, Vanvitelli built out on the northeast side an apsidal choir, which broke into the monumental southwest wall of the natatio (frigidarium). The façade on Piazza della Repubblica, with Vanvitelli's doorway, incorporates an apsidal wall, all that is left of the caldarium.

The interior

In the disappointing interior, the circular vestibule stands on the site of the tepidarium. Here, on the right, is the tomb of Carlo Maratta (d. 1713; *see p. 167*), which he designed for himself (there is a painting by him in the church and he also produced the two *trompe l'oeil* transepts). On the left is the tomb of the Neapolitan painter Salvator Rosa (d. 1673), many of whose romantic landscapes were painted in Rome. By the entrance into the transept, on the right, stands a fine colossal statue of St Bruno, the founder of the Carthusian Order, by the celebrated French sculptor Jean-Antoine Houdon, made when he was studying at the French Academy in Rome from 1764–8.

The vast transept is nearly 100m long, 27m wide and 28m high. The eight monolithic columns of red granite, nearly 14m high and 1.5m in diameter, are Roman; the others (almost indistinguishable), in brick, were added when the building was remodelled. In the pavement is a meridian dating from 1703. The tomb of Marshal Armando Diaz (d. 1928), Italian commander-in-chief in the First World War, is by Antonio Muñoz, better known for his work as a restorer of medieval churches. In the choir (*reserved for prayer so difficult to see*) the paintings include (on the left) a *Martyrdom* by Pomarancio and a *Baptism of Christ* by Carlo Maratta.

The door to the sacristy in the left transept leads to a room with remains of the frigidarium of the Baths of Diocletian and a display explaining the history of the building. Outside there is a very good view of the huge Roman wall and here has been installed a colossal bronze statue of *Galileo Divine Man*, made in 2010 to a design by Tsung Dao Lee (who won the Nobel Prize for Physics in 1957): it was a gift from China.

PIAZZA SAN BERNARDO

The **Fontana dell'Acqua Felice** is the terminus of an aqueduct built in 1585 by Domenico Fontana for Sixtus V, bringing water all the way from Colonna in the Alban Hills. It was the first aqueduct to be built since ancient times. The fountain, also by Fontana, has an unsuccessful figure of Moses (the proportions are incorrect), and bas-reliefs of Aaron and Gideon; the four lions are copies of ancient Egyptian works removed by Gregory XVI to the Egyptian Museum he founded in the Vatican.

SANTA MARIA DELLA VITTORIA

The church of Santa Maria della Vittoria (*map p. 655, E1; open 8.30–12 & 3.30–6*) has a façade by Giovanni Battista Soria (1626). Originally dedicated to St Paul, it was renamed from an image of the Virgin (burned in 1833) that gave victory to the Catholic army over the Protestants at the Battle of the White Mountain (1620), during the Thirty Years' War (commemorated in 1885 with a fresco in the apse, the best-known work by the Bolognese artist Luigi Serra). The well-proportioned, relatively small interior by Carlo Maderno is considered one of the most complete examples of Baroque decoration in Rome. Every inch of its surface is covered with colourful glowing marbles, stucco work, sculpture or painting. There are numerous angels and cupids in white stucco in the vaults and above the side chapels. The fine organ and cantoria are by a pupil of Bernini, Mattia de' Rossi.

The church is famous for the Cornaro Chapel by Bernini (fourth north; c. 1647–50, restored 2015), where the shallow space is used to great effect. The celebrated marble group of the *Ecstasy of St Teresa* shows the saint in an almost erotic swoon before an angel beneath golden rays of celestial light (also lit, ingeniously, from a hidden side window). Teresa of Avila, a Carmelite nun who was famous for her practical reforms of the Order as well as for her mystical experiences (she was declared a Doctor of the Church in 1970), left a vivid description of her ecstasy in which the angel of the Lord pierced her heart. Bernini, a devout Catholic, portrays this divine moment in his work. Scholars usually agree with the great architect and sculptor himself in considering this to be his best work. Below is a gilt-bronze relief of the *Last Supper*. At the sides are expressive portraits by pupils and followers of Bernini of the family of Bernini's patron, Cardinal Federigo Cornaro, together with his father Doge Giovanni, and six other relations who had also been cardinals. They are shown, as if at the theatre, comfortably seated and chatting away with each other as they view the spectacle. The head of the man behind the figure reading a book on the left is said to be a portrait of Bernini himself.

The second south chapel has a *Madonna and St Francis* by Domenichino. The first north chapel has a *Martyrdom of St Andrew* by Cavaliere d'Arpino.

SANTA SUSANNA

The church of Santa Susanna (*map p. 655, E1; closed for restoration at the time of writing but usually open 9.30–11.15 & 4–5.30; santasusanna.org*) belongs to the Cistercian Order and a group of nuns live here. Benedict XV assigned the ministry to the Paulist

Fathers in 1922 and it is still the church of the American Catholic community in Rome. It may have been founded as early as the 4th century, and was restored in 795 and remodelled in the 15th and 16th centuries. It is dedicated to Susanna, a Roman martyr beheaded in a house on this site c. 295. The façade (1603) by Carlo Maderno (*see box*) is acclaimed as his masterpiece: to appreciate it, approach up Via Torino.

CARLO MADERNO AND THE FONTANA FAMILY

The architect Carlo Maderno (1556–1629) carried out numerous works in Rome's churches (including important work at St Peter's) and designed a number of palace façades (the best known of which is Palazzo Barberini) and fountains. He is also remembered for the great dome of Sant'Andrea della Valle. The façade of Santa Susanna, however, is always considered his masterpiece, and was his first important work in Rome. A distant relative of Borromini, Maderno gave the younger man work as a humble marble cutter when he first arrived in Rome, perhaps little expecting that he would become a world-famous architect.

Maderno's nephew Domenico Fontana (1543–1607) came from a successful family of architects from northern Italy. He made an extremely important contribution to the appearance of Rome when he worked for Sixtus V, carrying out his designs for roads such as the Via Sistina, and erecting ancient Egyptian obelisks to close vistas and decorate *piazze* (most famously the one in St Peter's Square). He had remarkable engineering skills also, and constructed the Acqua Felice aqueduct for the same pope. Other works for the papacy included the construction of the huge Vatican Library, the rebuilding of the Lateran Palace and the design of the Scala Santa close by. He also worked on Palazzo del Quirinale (and set up the statues of the Dioscuri in the piazza), but his greatest architectural achievement was the Cappella Sistina in Santa Maria Maggiore, again built for (and named after) his great patron Sixtus V.

Domenico's nephew Carlo (1634–1714), who succeeded Bernini as papal architect, made one of the first technical studies of St Peter's. His masterpiece is the façade of San Marcello on the Corso but he also carried out major work on the churches of Santa Maria in Trastevere, Santa Maria del Popolo, Santi Apostoli and Sant' Andrea della Valle. Some of his more unusual works in Rome include San Michele a Ripa (a hospice, church and prison), the fountain basin for the Acqua Paola, the monument to Queen Christina of Sweden in St Peter's, and the Doria Pamphilj chapel in their palace on the Corso.

The good late Mannerist interior preserves its painted decorations (frescoes and altarpieces) from the 1590s. The nave is entirely covered with frescoes by Baldassare Croce, a Bolognese artist who came to work in Rome when Ugo Boncompagni of Bologna was elected to the papacy as Gregory XIII. They depict stories from the life of the biblical Susanna on *trompe l'oeil* tapestries hung between *trompe l'oeil* Solomonic columns. The frescoes in the sanctuary are by Cesare Nebbia, and the high altarpiece is by Tommaso Laureti.

The sacristy has remains of the earlier church unearthed in 1991 beneath the pavement and (in a showcase) a remarkable painted mural dating from the end of the 8th century, one of the rare works of this period to survive in the city. This was, incredibly enough, found in some 7,000 fragments in the Roman sarcophagus still to be seen here and has been painstakingly recomposed. The *Madonna and Child* in Byzantine style is flanked by St Agatha and another female saint, probably St Susanna.

SAN BERNARDO ALLE TERME

San Bernardo (*open 6.30–12 & 4–7*), the church of the Cistercians in Rome, was built into one of the two circular halls flanking the exedra of the Baths of Diocletian in the 16th century and dedicated to the greatest saint of the Cistercian Order. The building preserves its domed Roman form (as well as four lovely columns which once decorated the baths made out of a very beautiful green marble). The eight colossal stucco statues of saints in niches by Camillo Mariani (c. 1600–5) are unusual works showing Venetian influence, which successfully fit into this setting. The two altarpieces are the best works of the early 18th-century painter Giovanni Odazzi. There is a Neoclassical monument to the sculptor Carlo Finelli (d. 1853) by Rinaldo Rinaldi, and in the Cappella di San Francesco his contemporary, the German Friedrich Overbeck, is commemorated in a tomb effigy (he has Teutonic flowing locks and is dressed in a fur-lined coat with his paintbrushes beside him). Overbeck was the most famous member of the Nazarene school of painters, founded by six students from the Vienna Academy in 1809. He moved to Rome the next year, and lived the rest of his life here (he died in 1869). The statue of St Francis is by Bernini's pupil Giacomo Fancelli.

PALAZZO MASSIMO ALLE TERME
(MUSEO NAZIONALE ROMANO)

Map p. 655, E1–F1. Open 9–7.45; closed Mon. T: 06 39 96 7700, coopculture.it or archeo-roma.beniculturali.it. Tickets are valid for three days and cover the four museums of the Museo Nazionale Romano (this one, the Baths of Diocletian, Palazzo Altemps and the Crypta Balbi). For the Archaeological Card and reductions for young visitors, see p. 600. Entrance on the south side of Piazza dei Cinquecento.

Palazzo Massimo houses the most important part of the Museo Nazionale Romano, the vast state collection of ancient Roman art. The most important archaeological finds made in Rome since 1870 have been exhibited here since 1998. The ground floor has the earliest and most famous Roman and Greek statues, masterpieces in marble and bronze; the first floor has splendid Imperial-era sculpture including many portraits; and magnificently displayed on the top floor are wall-paintings, stuccoes and mosaics (including the breathtakingly beautiful paintings from the Villa of Livia). The building was erected in 1883–7 by Camillo Pistrucci as the seat of the Jesuit Collegio Massimiliano Massimo, hence its name, Palazzo Massimo alle Terme ('by the Baths').

NB: The labelling (also in English) is excellent, but the arrangement is constantly being changed and parts of the building are often closed. The description below gives only highlights. For more on Classical sculpture, see p. 453; for more on Roman statues and portraiture, see p. 54.

GROUND FLOOR

The chronological display starts here and illustrates **Roman Republican sculpture** from the time of Sulla (138–78 BC) to Augustus (27 BC–AD 14), including many portraits and some Greek originals. One of the finest statues is the *Augustus*, found in the Via Labicana. He is portrayed as *pontifex maximus* or high priest, in a toga which also covers his head, a demonstration of his piety.

The *Daughter of Niobe* is a superb Greek original of the 5th century BC by the school of Kresilas. Made for the pediment of a Greek temple, it was part of a statuary group which illustrated the legend of Niobe, who was famous for having borne numerous children. When she dared to boast that this made her at least equal to Leto, who had had only two children (Apollo and Artemis), her own children (known as the Niobids) were all killed. The girl depicted in the statue is shown dying as she tries to extract an arrow from her back.

The headless statue of a girl in a peplos, known as the *Peplophoros*, was found in Piazza Barberini. It is also probably a Greek original of the first half of the 5th century BC. The *Pedagogue* probably portrays the attendant of one of the youngest of Niobe's children: it may be a 2nd-century AD copy of a 4th-century BC Greek original.

Two of the finest Hellensitic bronzes to have survived are also here. They were probably brought to Rome as booty from a military campaign. Both over lifesize, they were found on the Quirinal hill in 1885. The seated *Terme Boxer* is attributed to Lysippus and dated to the 3rd century BC. Copper inlay is used for the scars on his face, and his hands are bound up for the fight. The *Terme Ruler* probably dates from a century later and portrays a Macedonian prince. His pose, leaning on a lance, recalls a famous statue of Alexander the Great by Lysippus.

Neo-Attic works include *Aphrodite*, a copy of the *Aphrodite of Cnidos* by Praxiteles, signed by the Greek artist Menophantos; and a Muse who once held a tragic mask, a replica of a Hellenistic original.

FIRST FLOOR

Here are **sculptures from the Imperial era** (1st–4th centuries AD), many of them modelled on Classical Greek works. There is a marvellous display of **herms with portraits of wealthy charioteers**, found in a shrine of Hercules. **Portraits of the Flavian emperors** include three of Vespasian and two of Nerva. There is also one of the few surviving portraits of Domitian: after he was assassinated all statues and busts of him were ordered to be destroyed. The statue of Julia, Titus' daughter, has a beautiful head. The display also includes portraits of Trajan and Hadrian. A statue of Trajan shown as Hercules is exhibited next to a portrait of his wife, Plotina, found in Ostia. There is a portrait of Hadrian beside two busts—one of his wife Sabina and one of his lover Antinous.

Portraits of the Antonines include a fine statue of Antoninus Pius found in Terracina, and others of his wife and daughter. Marcus Aurelius, Lucius Verus and Commodus are also represented, including portraits found in Hadrian's Villa at Tivoli. There is a head of a young girl thought to represent Crispina, the wife of Commodus.

Sculptures found in the Imperial villas outside Rome include the headless ***Ephebus of Subiaco***, a lovely Roman copy of an original of the 4th century BC (probably of one of the Niobids) and the head of the ***Young Girl Sleeping***, possibly representing another dying Niobid. Both come from Nero's villa at Subiaco. The so-called ***Maiden of Anzio***, a masterpiece of Greek art dating from the end of the 4th century BC or beginning of the 3rd, is by a sculptor from the school of Lysippus also showing the influence of Praxiteles. It represents a young girl approaching an altar and carrying a tray with implements for a sacrifice, and was discovered in Nero's villa at Anzio in 1878. The statue of ***Apollo*** (1st century AD), modelled on a work by an unknown Attic predecessor of Praxiteles, was also found in Anzio (another statue of Apollo, found in the Tiber, is a copy of an original by the school of Pheidias, or by Kalamos). **Statues from Hadrian's Villa at Tivoli**, replicas of Hellenistic works, include a beautiful *Crouching Aphrodite* and the so-called *Dancer of Tivoli*.

The two copies of the ***Discobolos*** ('Discus-thrower') are derived from the famous statue by Myron, made in bronze c. 450 BC. It was described by Pliny the Younger, who praised it for its virtuosity in portraying the human figure in motion. It was one of the most frequently copied Greek masterpieces. The finest and best-preserved replica is the one from the Lancellotti collection displayed here, dating from the 2nd century AD and found on the Esquiline hill in 1781. It was sold to Hitler in 1938 but recovered ten years later. The other copy (without a head) was found at Castelporziano in 1906 and has been repaired.

Other statues in the collection include a marble *Hermaphroditus Asleep* (2nd century AD) and an intriguing statue of an African acrobat dating from the early Imperial period. There is also a wonderful display of the **bronzes from the huge ships built by Caligula** (AD 37–41) to transport visitors across Lake Nemi for the festival of Diana. The ships, one over 70m long, were sunk at the time of Claudius, and were salvaged in 1932 and put on display in a museum on the lakeside; when this was burnt down by German soldiers in 1944, only these bronzes survived the fire. There is an excellent film of their recovery.

The very fine **Portonaccio sarcophagus** is carved with a battle scene between Romans and barbarians, probably representing a campaign at the time of Marcus Aurelius. Another sarcophagus, from Acilia, has a finely carved procession of Roman dignitaries wearing togas celebrating the investiture of a consul. Another, dated to the 3rd century AD, which comes from the Mattei collection, is decorated with figures of the Muses holding masks. The one with a prefect and his wife holding hands and looking into each other's eyes was commissioned by the prefect in charge of the office of the *annona*, the organisation in Ostia which supplied produce to the capital. On either side are female figures personifying the port of Ostia, Abundance and Africa (from where most of the produce was shipped). A sarcophagus dating from the time of Constantine (AD 315) has Christian scenes from the Old and New Testaments.

SECOND FLOOR

Here is a superb collection of **wall-paintings, stuccoes and mosaics** which used to decorate Roman buildings from the Republican era onwards. They are excellently displayed with all the latest methods of conservation and clear lighting. One of the earliest examples is a fragment of a wall-painting with a scene from the *Odyssey*, showing Ulysses and the Sirens, found in a late Republican house on the Esquiline.

Most famous of all is the rectangular room, probably a triclinium, from the **Villa of Livia** (wife of Augustus) at Prima Porta, which has been reconstructed here. Its walls are decorated with exquisite murals of trees, an orchard with pomegranates and quinces and a flower garden. This constitutes the masterpiece of naturalistic decoration of the second style of Roman painting, which is thought to derive from Hellenistic models. Detached and restored in 1952–3, the works were saved just in time from complete decay, and are one of the most remarkable examples known of Roman art. While you stand in this room you enter into the spirit of delight felt by the Romans in the natural world and you can appreciate here perhaps more than anywhere else in Rome the freshness of their extraordinary artistic skills. A technique of perspective was used here by employing a gradation of colours, so that the trees furthest from the spectator become gradually paler adding to the sense of depth in the scene and giving us the sensation of wishing to step into the garden and so become part of it. This concept was theorised by Leonardo da Vinci in his *Trattato della Pittura*.

Magnificent **stuccoes and wall-paintings from a building of the Augustan age**, discovered in 1879 in the grounds of the Villa Farnesina, include exquisite paintings on black, red or white grounds of theatrical masks, scenes of judgement, naval battles and mythological figures. Some of them are thought to be by the hand of the landscape painter Studius. The paintings and stucco decoration from the small bedrooms are masterpieces of their kind, with friezes decorated with festoons and cupids interspersed with landscapes and mythological scenes. Geometric-patterned mosaic floors from the villa are also displayed.

Elements from other **Imperial villas** include wall paintings from a villa at Castel di Guido, thought to have belonged to Antoninus Pius. The mosaics from the villa of Septimius Severus at Baccano include four quadrangles showing charioteers holding their horses. The wall-painting of Venus, known as the ***Dea Barberini*** (early 4th century AD), was found near the baptistery of St John Lateran in the 17th century, when it was restored as the *Dea Roma*.

The last room has superb **polychrome marble intarsia panels** in opus sectile. The two panels from the basilica of Junius Bassus on the Esquiline (early 4th century AD) show a mythological scene with Hylas (son of Hercules) and the start of a chariot race. The head of the sun-god Helios-Sol (*illustrated opposite*) was found in the Mithraeum beneath Santa Prisca on the Aventine.

BASEMENT

The vaults in the basement house the **treasury**, with valuable jewellery and coins. A display illustrates an edict of Diocletian of AD 301 which attempted to combat inflation. It is known from some 132 marble fragments found all over the Empire from 1709

MUSEO NAZIONALE ROMANO (PALAZZO MASSIMO)
Marble intarsia head of the sun god (3rd century AD), found in the Mithraeum
beneath the church of Santa Prisca on the Aventine.

onwards and is of fundamental importance to scholars for the understanding of the Roman economy. There is also a fine exhibit of gold jewellery, two alabaster cinerary urns, and a sarcophagus found on the Via Cassia with the well-preserved mummy of an eight-year-old girl.

The large main hall, entered through armoured doors, houses the most important **numismatic collection** in Italy, covering all periods of its history (and including the Gnecchi collection of Roman and Byzantine coins, the Kircher collection acquired by the state in 1913, and the collection of King Vittorio Emanuele III). The superb display, divided into eleven sections, includes some 1,800 pieces. The first section is dedicated to the goddess Juno Moneta and the mint on the Capitoline hill, the Santa Marinella hoard of bronze ingots, and the earliest coined metal (4th–3rd centuries BC). The second section illustrates coins in the Republican era, and the third and fourth sections the Imperial period. Sections 5–8 cover the Goths, Byzantines, Lombards, Franks and Normans. A circular area is dedicated to pontifical coinage. Sections 9 and 10 display late medieval and Renaissance coins, and the last section has 19th-century coins up to the Unification of Italy, and those minted during the reign of Vittorio Emanuele III.

The last rooms contain some fascinating finds of great rarity, made in 2006 on the slopes of the Palatine towards the Arch of Constantine. These have been identified as parts of the **three sceptres** belonging to the emperor Maxentius (306–12). The tips of four ceremonial flagstaffs and three lances used in ceremonies connected with this emperor, also exhibited here, were found at the same time.

The Trevi Fountain
& Quirinal Hill

The Trevi Fountain is justly one of the most famous sights of Rome.
Close by rises the Quirinal hill, with the residence of the President of Italy,
which is now, together with its garden, open to visitors on most days.
Near the palace are two churches by Rome's greatest architects, Bernini and Borromini.
Palazzo Barberini contains a major national collection of paintings.

The Fontana di Trevi (*map p. 654, C1*) is not only Rome's most magnificent fountain, it is also perhaps the city's most exuberant and successful 18th-century monument, made all the more extraordinary by its confined setting in such a small square. The abundant water, which forms an essential part of the design, fills the little piazza with its sound.

The name Trevi may come from *tre vie*, referring to the three roads which converged here. Its waters are those of the Acqua Vergine Antica (*Aqua Virgo* in Latin), an aqueduct which runs almost entirely underground and was built by Agrippa from a spring some 20km east of the city to supply his public baths near the Pantheon in 19 BC. It also feeds the fountains of Piazza di Spagna, Piazza Navona and Piazza Farnese.

The original 15th-century fountain was a simple basin by Leon Battista Alberti, restored by Urban VIII, who is said to have obtained the necessary funds from a tax on wine. Bernini presented a project for a new fountain, but it was not until 1732, when Clement XII held a competition (participants included Ferdinando Fuga and Gaspare Vanvitelli), that the little-known Roman architect and poet Niccolò Salvi was given the commission. His theatrical design incorporated, as a background, the entire Neoclassical façade of Palazzo Poli, which had only just been built. The fountain was completed after Salvi's death when Pietro Bracci carved the tritons. It was beautifully restored in 2015 and provided with excellent new illumination.

DECORATION AND SYMBOLISM OF THE FOUNTAIN

The palace façade has niches containing statues symbolising Health (right) and Abundance (left). The bas-reliefs above represent the legendary virgin from which the aqueduct took its name pointing out the spring to the Roman soldiers, and Agrippa approving the plans for the aqueduct. Above are statues of the Seasons and at the summit the Corsini arms. But the most splendid figures are the central group on the enormous artificial rock, built out of tufa, where two giant tritons, one blowing a conch,

TREVI FOUNTAIN
Neptune stepping out of the Neoclassical niche
of Palazzo Poli to command the waters.

conduct the clam-shell chariot of Neptune pulled by marine horses with wings and webbed hooves, who appear to splash and gallop through the water.

There is a rooted tradition—which seems to have grown up at the end of the 19th century—that if you throw a coin over your shoulder into the fountain before you leave Rome it will bring good luck and ensure your return. The coins are collected every Monday morning when the fountain's pump has to be turned off for cleaning. The money goes to the Church organisation Caritas, which helps those in need in the city. The last scene of the film *Three Coins in the Fountain* (1954) was filmed here, and Federico Fellini's *La Dolce Vita* (1960) has a famous scene in which Anita Ekberg takes a dip in the Trevi's waters: she is rescued by Marcello Mastroianni—at the great actor's death in 1996 the fountain was temporarily silenced and draped in black. Ettore Scola in his marvellous film *C'eravamo tanto amati* (1974) includes a scene of Fellini actually filming *La Dolce Vita*, and in *Roman Holiday* (1953) Audrey Hepburn and Gregory Peck put in an appearance close to the fountain.

THE CASTELLANI JEWELLERS

To the right of the Trevi Fountain, the name of Augusto Castellani appears above the door of the grandest palace in the square (no. 86). It records the best-known member of a famous family of jewellers whose workshop here, opened in 1869, became one of the 'sights' of Rome. The family firm was founded in 1814 and by 1840 it was promoting a 'revival' style, a return to ancient designs. The Castellani became so skilled at reproducing ancient Etruscan and Roman gems that their work was often taken to be antique by the numerous famous clients who would call here: the Brownings, William Wetmore Story and Henry Layard are among those recorded in the visitors' book. The firm closed down in 1927.

Detail of a ram's head hat pin by the Castellani workshop. From the collection of the Museo Etrusco di Villa Giulia.

Augusto Castellani, who fought beside Garibaldi against the papacy, became the first director of the Musei Capitolini, and several rooms there are still named after him (they contain part of his huge collection of Etruscan finds). He also formed a remarkable collection of antique jewels and gems, much of which is preserved in the Capitoline Medal Collection, which he founded. Examples of the jewels created by his workshop can be seen there. There is also an excellent display of them in the Etruscan Museum in Villa Giulia.

SANTI VINCENZO ED ANASTASIO

Opposite the fountain this church (*open 9–8*), now used by the Bulgarian Orthodox community in Rome, was rebuilt in 1630 and given a Baroque façade by Martino Longhi the Younger. It was the parish church of the neighbouring pontifical palace of the Quirinal, and in the crypt (*no admission*) the hearts and lungs of almost all the popes from Sixtus V (d. 1590) to Leo XIII (d. 1903) are preserved. The organs are removed during the embalming process to preserve the body long enough to survive the elaborate funeral and obsequies which always follow the death of a pope.

Close by are the **Calcografia Nazionale** (with the most important collection of copperplate engravings in the world), the **Galleria dell'Accademia di San Luca**, and the **Insula del Vicus Caprarius**. These are described in the Appendix.

THE QUIRINAL HILL

The Quirinal (61m) is one of the highest of the Seven Hills of Rome. It received its name either from a temple of Quirinus, or from *Cures*, an ancient Sabine town northeast of Rome from where, according to legend, the Sabines, under their king Tatius, came to settle on the hill. 'Quirinus' was the title of Romulus after he had been deified and the festival in his honour was called the Quirinalia. In late Republican days and throughout the Empire, the hill was covered with gardens and summer villas. The huge palace which surmounts it today, built in the 16th century as the summer residence of the pope, became the official home of the President of Italy when the country became a constitutional republic after the Second World War.

PIAZZA DEL QUIRINALE

The spacious and dignified Piazza del Quirinale (*map p. 655, D2*) has a pleasant open feel to it, although you have to be careful of cars. From the balustrade there is a fine panorama across the rooftops to St Peter's in the distance. In the middle of the square is an **obelisk**, with a shaft 14.5m tall, which originally stood in front of the Mausoleum of Augustus. It was brought here by Pius VI in 1786; Pius VII added the great basin of dark grey granite, now a fountain but which until then had been used as a cattle-trough in the Roman Forum. On a high pedestal flanking the obelisk are two famous colossal groups, over 5.5m high, of **Castor and Pollux**, the Dioscuri (*see p. 82*), standing by their horses. They are Imperial-era copies of Greek originals of the 5th century BC. Found nearby in the Baths of Constantine, they were placed here by Domenico Fontana for Sixtus V (1585–90), who was responsible for the recutting of the false inscriptions on the bases, *Opus Phidiae* and *Opus Praxitelis*, which date from c. AD 450. When Master Gregory admired the statues in the late 12th century he had not heard of these two Greek sculptors and thought these were the names of two philosophers. The statues have stood somewhere in the city ever since the fall of the Empire and appear in numerous representations of Rome from medieval times onwards. They were formerly called the *Horse-tamers* and the square was known as Monte Cavallo.

Overlooking the square is a part of the **Scuderie Pontificie**, the papal stables, built in 1722 and restored in 2000 by Gae Aulenti as a superb exhibition space; and the **Palazzo della Consulta**, once the seat of the supreme court of the Papal States and since 1955 the seat of the Italian constitutional court. The façade is by Ferdinando Fuga (1739), an able architect much in favour with popes Clement XII and Benedict XIV.

PALAZZO DEL QUIRINALE

Map p. 655, D2. Open Tues, Wed, Fri, Sat, Sun 9.30–4 (last entrance at 1.30 or 2.30, depending on which tour you choose, see below), except at Christmas and in Aug. It is necessary to book a guided tour: www.coopculture.it, T: 06 39 96 7557; or at the information office at the side of the palace, 15a Salita di Montecavallo. You are required to show ID. There are two different tours: tour 1 takes in the piano nobile and the ground floor (and lasts about 1hr 20mins); tour 2 (about 2½ hrs) also includes the porcelain collection, carriage museum and the lovely gardens designed in the 16th century by Mascherino. To attend the concert given every Sun at noon in the Cappella Paolina (broadcast on the radio), book as above. For updates, see palazzo.quirinale.it.

HISTORY OF PALAZZO DEL QUIRINALE

The building was begun in 1574 by Flaminio Ponzio and Ottaviano Mascherino for Gregory XIII, and was continued by Domenico Fontana, Carlo Maderno, Bernini (who worked on the *manica lunga*, the 'long wing' in Via del Quirinale) and Ferdinando Fuga: it was not completed until the time of Clement XII (1730–40). The principal entrance is by Maderno; the tower on the left of it was added in the time of Urban VIII (early 17th century).

From 1592 the Quirinal was the summer residence of the popes, and some conclaves were held here. Sixtus V, who did more than any of his predecessors to improve and adorn the city in celebration of the Catholic Church, died here in 1590. Pius VI was forced to leave the palace as a prisoner of Napoleon and was taken to France, where he died in 1799. From its balcony Pius IX blessed Italy on his election as pope in 1846, little knowing that his pontificate would see the end of papal rule: the Italian army seized Rome in 1870. From then on the palace was the residence of the kings of Italy, and the first king, Vittorio Emanuele II, died here on 9th January 1878. In 1947, with end of the monarchy, the palace became the official residence of the President of the Republic.

THE VISIT

The collection of tapestries is one of the best in Europe. The Rococo decorations date from the 1870s and the rooms are all very grand. The Oriental vases and the Gobelins tapestries were the property of the papacy, but most of the furniture, paintings and the other tapestries belonged to the Italian royal family.

From the courtyard, where the President receives important visitors, the grand staircase leads up to the *piano nobile*. On the landing don't miss Melozzo da Forlì's magnificent fresco of ***Christ in Glory with Angels***, formerly in the church of Santi Apostoli (the Angel Musicians from this composition are now in the Vatican Pinacoteca). The **Sala dei Carozzieri** is the most beautifully decorated of all the rooms: it was built by Carlo Maderno under Paul V in 1605–12 and has a good pavement which reflects the design of the lovely ceiling. It is used for state ceremonies. The frieze illustrating the story of Moses on the upper walls, painted in 1616 by Agostino Tassi, Giovanni

Lanfranco and Carlo Saraceni, was discovered in 2006. The *grottesche* decoration in the window recesses has been uncovered. The portal of the **Cappella Paolina** has a lunette by Taddeo Landini (1578), and the angel on the tympanum to the right is by Pietro Bernini. The chapel (designed by Carlo Maderno) is the same size as the Sistine Chapel. It has fine stucco decoration by Martino Ferrabosco.

In the next series of small rooms on one side of the courtyard are paintings by Pietro da Cortona and huge tapestries of the *Washing of the Feet* and *Expulsion from the Temple*. The long **Galleria di Alessandro VII Chigi**, designed by Pietro da Cortona, is divided into three parts. The first part is decorated with truncated columns with green vegetation behind them. The fresco of *Joseph and his Brothers* is by Francesco Mola. The third part, the Sala degli Ambasciatori, has a very fine painting of the *Adoration of the Shepherds* by Carlo Maratta on the far wall (it was surrounded by four angels in the 19th century). Beneath, a grisaille painting of Cortona's façade of Santa Maria della Pace has recently been discovered. In the pavement are 1st-century BC mosaic panels of birds from Tivoli. There are frescoes by Lazzaro Baldi and Gaspard Dughet (mid-17th century).

In the **Sala di Ercole** there are three splendid large Gobelins tapestries dating from the early 18th century. The series of six paintings here is by Corrado Giaquinto. The **Sala degli Scrigni** is named after its five precious desks in ebony and ivory. The five tapestries also come from the Gobelins manufactory (1747). Ottaviano Mascherino built the pretty little **oval spiral staircase** in travertine which leads to the **loggia**, also designed by him in 1584 with its rare Classical marble columns. From here there is access to a number of rooms, including the studio used by the President of Italy.

On the last side of the courtyard, the **Sala dello Zodiaco** has tapestries of exotic animals made by the Gobelins manufactory. The small **Sala delle Fabbriche di Paolo V** has a frescoed frieze at the top of the walls, discovered in 2006, which survives from the time of Paul V (early 17th century) and includes representations of the buildings he commissioned. The **Sala degli Arazzi** has four 18th-century French tapestries made in Beauvais on designs by François Boucher (*Bacchus and Ariadne* between the windows) and three others illustrating the story of Psyche. The chandeliers come from Murano. The 19th-century **Sala degli Specchi** was decorated in Louis XV style when the Savoy rulers transformed it into a ballroom (there are pretty dancing figures on the ceiling). The **Salone delle Feste**, dating from 1873, is where new governments are sworn in.

ON VIA XXIV MAGGIO

Via XXIV Maggio (*map p. 655, D2*) was named to commemorate the day Italy declared war on Austria in 1915. On it, one opposite the other, are the entrances to two of the most attractive of Rome's princely residences. Villa Colonna is the garden annexe of Palazzo Colonna (*see p. 151*). Hidden behind a high wall opposite, on the site of the Baths of Constantine, is Palazzo Pallavicini-Rospigliosi.

PALAZZO PALLAVICINI-ROSPIGLIOSI

Built in 1613–16, probably by Carlo Maderno, the palace was purchased in 1704 by the Pallavicini-Rospigliosi family, who still live here. In the 19th century the beautiful gardens were greatly altered and diminished.

In the charming little hanging garden is the **Casino dell'Aurora Pallavicini** (*open the first day of every month except 1 Jan, 10–12 & 3–5; free; T: 06 83 46 7000, casinoaurorapallavicini.it*), designed by Giovanni Vasanzio. The fine façade is decorated with numerous good reliefs of mythological subjects from 14 Roman sarcophagi of the 2nd–3rd centuries AD. Inside is Guido Reni's celebrated ceiling fresco (1613–14) of *Aurora Scattering Flowers before the Chariot of the Sun*, which was greatly admired by travellers to Rome in the 19th century. On the walls are four frescoes of the Seasons by Paul Bril and two Triumphs by Antonio Tempesta.

The **Galleria Pallavicini** on the first floor (*open only with special permission*) contains some important paintings of the Italian and foreign schools (15th–18th centuries). The collection was founded by Nicolò Pallavicini—a friend of Rubens—and his son Cardinal Lazzaro, and includes works by Botticelli, Lorenzo Lotto, Annibale and Ludovico Carracci, Guido Reni, Guercino, Federico Barocci and Rubens (*Christ and the Apostles*).

SAN SILVESTRO AL QUIRINALE

Open 10–12; Sun 10–1. Ring at the monastery of San Vincenzo di Paola at no. 10 on the right.

This church was given a false façade in 1877: it is in fact on an upper floor and has no west door. From here the cardinals used to march in procession to shut themselves in the Quirinal when a conclave was held in summer. The interior, with a gilded and panelled ceiling, was rebuilt in 1524 on a Latin cross, when the first chapel on the north side (the pretty floor tiles are a fragment with the Medici arms left over from the loggia in the Vatican) was frescoed with fine landscapes by Polidoro da Caravaggio, who also painted the *St Catherine* and *Mary Magdalene* flanking the altar. In this work Polidoro, a little-studied painter named after his birthplace (Caravaggio) in northern Italy, anticipates the taste for landscape painting which was to develop in Rome only in the late 16th century. In the vault are later frescoes by Cavaliere d'Arpino. The second chapel has a *Nativity* by Marcello Venusti, a friend of Michelangelo and much influenced by his work (he is known for his many copies of the master's paintings and frescoes): however in this painting there are very few echoes of his friend's works.

On the south side, the second chapel has a painting of Pius V and his nephew Cardinal Alessandrino by the 17th-century Tuscan artist Giacinto Gimignani, which incorporates, in the centre, a 13th-century *Madonna and Child* by a Roman artist. The domed Bandini Chapel (the dome was rebuilt in 1823) at the end of the north transept dates from 1585, when the altarpiece of the *Ascension* was painted by Scipione Pulzone. The *tondi* in pastel shades by Domenichino, and two of the statues (the penitent Mary Magdalene, with her eyes raised to heaven, and St John the Evangelist reading a book) which are by Alessandro Algardi, probably his first Roman commission, were all added in 1628.

MICHELANGELO AND VITTORIA COLONNA

Michelangelo is known to have come to San Silvestro frequently to attend meetings held in an adjoining oratory by Vittoria Colonna, who was a poet (indeed the first Italian poetess to publish under her own name) and one of the leaders of a Church reform movement. As a member of the famous Roman noble family of Colonna (and granddaughter of Federico da Montefeltro and Battista Sforza), she married the Marquis of Pescara, Captain General of the Spanish army in Italy. After she was widowed in the early 1520s, she led a cloistered life and became an intimate friend of Michelangelo, a friendship which lasted until her death in 1547. Michelangelo made at least three 'presentation' drawings for her, including the *Christ on the Cross* now in the British Museum. A letter survives from her thanking him for this exquisite work, addressed to the 'unique master Michelangelo and my most singular friend'.

TWO CHURCHES BY BERNINI & BORROMINI

On Via del Quirinale, which skirts the long wing of the Quirinal Palace, are two important Baroque churches and two pleasant public gardens with benches, which make them good places to picnic. These two churches, within a few hundred metres of each other, provide an exceptionally interesting insight into the architectural skills of the two greatest Baroque architects of Rome: Bernini and Borromini, born within a year of each other at the very end of the 16th century. Opposite Sant'Andrea, the side portal of the Quirinal is usually open (flanked by the exceptionally tall presidential guards) so you can get a glimpse of the hedged walks in the garden beyond a palm tree.

SANT'ANDREA AL QUIRINALE
Map p. 655, D1–D2. Open 8.30–12 & 2.30–6, Sun 9–12 & 3–6; closed Mon. For updates of opening times, see santandrea.gesuiti.it.
This is often considered the most beautiful church designed by Bernini. It was commissioned by Alexander VII and the great architect received the help of his pupil Mattia de' Rossi during building work (1658–70). The **façade** is an enormous single aedicule with a convex, semicircular portico. On either side of this Bernini placed segments of wall in the form of quarter circles, thus creating a charming and intimate urban forecourt. The concave-convex-concave contour of the façade is one of the most important guiding motifs in Bernini's work, appearing again in his drawings for the eastern elevation of the Louvre and in the church of the Assumption in Ariccia. The forecourt, in the form of a half ellipse, anticipates the elliptical nave and balances the repeated aedicule and half ellipse of the altar recess. Bernini chose this form because of its symbolic meaning: by arranging the side-chapels radially he placed the emphasis not on the horizontal–vertical axis but on the oblique axiality of the St Andrew's Cross.

SANT'ANDREA AL QUIRINALE

BERNINI AND THE DECORATION OF ROME

Gian Lorenzo Bernini (1598–1680), one of the most famous architects and sculptors of all time, was born in Naples but came to Rome as a boy and remained here almost all his life, except for a short stay in France in 1665 at the invitation of Louis XIV. He began work with his father Pietro, himself an able sculptor. The boy Gian Lorenzo was considered a prodigy: in 1617 the Borghese pope Paul V ordered him to carve his bust, and the pope's nephew, Cardinal Scipione Borghese, commissioned Bernini's first important sculptures, which are still in the Galleria Borghese. He was at once recognised as the greatest artist working in Rome.

Subsequently the Barberini pope Urban VIII became his most important patron as well as a close friend, and called on Bernini to work on St Peter's. Many artists came to Rome to benefit from his guidance, and his workshop was busy carrying out the numerous commissions he received as the most celebrated sculptor and architect in Europe. After the death of Urban VIII, however, Bernini fell temporarily out of favour with the papal court, even though in the end Urban's successor Innocent X did give him the commission for his great fountain in Piazza Navona. Bernini also carried out a great deal of work for Alexander VII: besides the church of Sant'Andrea, for this Chigi pope he designed St Peter's Square, a wing of the Palazzo Quirinale, and the Chigi Chapel in Santa Maria del Popolo, as well as more work in St Peter's and the Vatican. Today his remarkable buildings, fountains, sculptures and funerary monuments can be seen all over the city, and his great urban interventions on the approach to St Peter's remain as testimony to his brilliant skills in planning spaces within the urban fabric.

The **interior of Sant'Andrea** is very fine, with columns, pilasters and frames in pink and grey marble, and gilded and stuccoed decorations. Bernini's Classical architecture is combined with his original lighting effects: each chapel is lit by windows high up behind the altars. A fisherman—another allusion to the titular saint Andrew—and numerous cherubim look down from the lantern and surmount the high altarpiece: they were executed by Bernini's assistant Antonio Raggi, who was particularly skilled in stucco-work.

The fine 17th-century altarpieces include works by Baciccia, Giacinto Brandi and Maratta, and the high altarpiece, with the *Crucifixion of St Andrew*, is by Borgognone. The sacristy (*unlocked on request*), where the pretty frescoed ceiling is part of Bernini's design, has a lavabo with two fat cherubs in a recess on the left of the altar, probably by the master himself. You can also ask to see the three rooms above, reconstructed in 1889 in memory of the Polish saint Stanislao Kostka, who died here in 1568. They contain his relics and mementoes, and a series of tempera paintings attributed to Andrea Pozzo, illustrating scenes from his life. The extraordinary statue of Kostka in a black cloak on a marble bed is by Pierre Legros.

SAN CARLO ALLE QUATTRO FONTANE

Map p. 655, D1. Open Mon–Sat 10–1, Sun 12–1. For updates to opening times, see sancarlino.eu.

This small oval church, lovingly called 'San Carlino' by the Romans, is a masterpiece by Francesco Borromini. It was his first important commission in Rome and is often considered his most innovative work. It is difficult to describe the structural richness of the façade; still more difficult to appreciate it, as the church stands right on the street in a cramped corner site, with traffic roaring mercilessly past it and the fountains (the *quattro fontane* after which it is named) at each corner of the busy crossroads. Borromini created a two-storey tripartite front with a concave-convex-concave rhythm behind the pilasters at ground level, a rhythm echoed—but not quite replicated—in the three concave bays on the upper façade. Borromini subtly combines geometric archetypes with poetic citations from nature. Thus the triangular cornice above the gable medallion becomes, on the level below, the peaked arch of two angels' wings. This peak is echoed in the interior, in the tops of the confessionals.

The interior

The interior was begun in 1638, some 30 years before the façade. The structural affinity between the two is striking—and intentional. Convex and concave surfaces alternate in a complex geometric design using triangles in a unifying scheme: the symbolism throughout is of the Holy Trinity. The intricate architecture seems almost to suggest one church inside another: there are voids where you would expect a solid wall and vice versa.

The small cloister, also designed by Borromini and entered from the church, is one of the most original architectural spaces in Rome, based on the architect's delicate sense of curved lines and ingenious designs (even every other pillar of the balustrades on the upper floor is turned upside down). Instead of reinforcing the corners of the cloister arcades with pillars or other supporting structures, Borromini left them open at ground level, raising over each a convex wall structure which anticipates the pre-stressed concrete of later centuries.

A charming little spiral staircase (again with a unique design, around a twisted central pillar) leads down to the crypt (*if closed, opened on request*), with another fantastical play of curves linked by a continuous cornice, and unusual side chapels. It is thought that Borromini intended this as the place of his own burial.

THE ARCHITECTURE OF BORROMINI

Francesco Borromini (1599–1667) was born in northern Italy, and when he first came to Rome worked as a collaborator of Carlo Maderno. He designed numerous churches as well as palaces in the city, including the Collegio di Propaganda Fide, Palazzo della Sapienza, Palazzo Barberini and Palazzo Falconieri on Via Giulia. His best-known churches, apart from San Carlo, are Sant'Agnese in Agone and the Chiesa Nuova. His work is distinguished by its geometrical complexities, the continual use of curves, and its extraordinary imaginativeness. One of his most important commissions was from Innocent X (the only pope who preferred Borromini to Bernini), when he was put in charge of major restoration work at St John Lateran and skilfully managed to retain much of the earlier building in his grand new design. He was known to have had an irascible nature, which made his relationship with his patrons difficult. His introverted temperament was in strong contrast to the ebullient nature of Bernini, and this inevitably led to antagonisms between the two—but this was later exaggerated in popular legend and in fact they both found themselves working side by side at certain times (for instance at Palazzo Barberini and at St Peter's). Borromini also left some exquisite small, delicate works which still distinguish the appearance of the city—the spiral tower of Sant'Ivo which was later copied many times, especially in German architecture; and the campanile of Sant'Andrea delle Fratte. The ingenious perspective device he designed for Cardinal Spada in the garden of his palace demonstrates his remarkable imagination. After contributing so much to the appearance of the city it is sad to think that his life ended in suicide. He is buried in the church of San Giovanni Battista dei Fiorentini.

PALAZZO BARBERINI
(GALLERIA NAZIONALE D'ARTE ANTICA)

Map p. 655, D1. Open 8.30–7; closed Mon. Entrance on Via delle Quattro Fontane (the huge stone pilasters and iron grille were added in the 19th century by Francesco Azzurri).Some rooms are often closed, especially on Sun. T: 06 48 14 591, galleriabarberini.beniculturali.it. Three-day tickets, valid also for the Palazzo Corsini (see p. 387), are available.

Palazzo Barberini, one of the grandest palaces in Rome, was begun by Carlo Maderno for the Barberini pope Urban VIII in 1624. Work was continued on the central block by Bernini, and Borromini designed the windows of the top storey, the stairs and some doorways. Until 1960 the Barberini family lived on the top floor. Pietro da Cortona (*see p. 341*) was also involved as architect, and painted the famous ceiling fresco in the huge main hall.

Urban VIII was not the saintliest of the popes, but he was a great patron of art and music. In his day he encouraged instumentalists and composers and Palazzo Barberini became a centre of opera in Rome. In 1632 and again in 1634 Stefano Landi's sacred opera *Il Sant'Alessio* was performed in this palace, whose garden was famous for its exotic plants.

The palace houses part of the Galleria Nazionale d'Arte Antica, first opened to the public in 1895 in Palazzo Corsini, where part of it is still housed. It is pre-eminent in Italian Baroque painting, although there are also some good examples from the 15th and 16th centuries and a large selection of foreign works. The arrangement is strictly chronological. The earliest works have been recently rehung and are very well labelled.

GROUND FLOOR (12TH–EARLY 16TH CENTURY WORKS)

A room with a charming painted ceiling with birds and monkeys and the Barberini bees carried aloft by cherubs has a computer display of the collection. The statue of a Gaul running is a graceful work of the 1st century AD. The first seven rooms have ceilings painted in the 1670s with episodes from Greek mythology.

Among the **earliest works** are four painted Crosses, well displayed on the pale blue walls, and the icon-like *Madonna 'advocata'*, by a Roman painter working in the second half of the 11th century. **Gold-ground works** of the 14th century include a very lovely *Madonna and Child* by Segna di Buonaventura, and S*tories of the Passion of Christ* in six panels by Giovanni Baronzio (the six smaller scenes of the same subject are by Giovanni da Rimini). There are two works by **Filippo Lippi**: the *Madonna 'di Tarquinia'* (1437), seated on a lovely marble throne, and an *Annunciation* with two donors with a pretty garden in the background and two serving women in the doorway in a great state of excitement. The angel with roses in her hair is particularly beautiful. By **Perugino** is *St Filippo Benizzi* and by **Raphael** a fresco fragment of the head of a youth. An entire room is devoted to Rome's native painter **Antoniazzo Romano**.

Works from the **Veneto, Lombardy and Emilia** include *St Jerome* by Marco Palmezzano and a *Madonna and Child* (with a bird looking out at the landscape) by Niccolò Rondinelli. There is a small male portrait attributed to Giovanni Bellini and another to Lorenzo Lotto. There are some very unusual large paintings by Pedro Fernández de Murcia, who worked in the early 16th century. The *Vision of the Blessed Amedeo de Sylva* has an extraordinary landscape.

Among the **Flemish works** are a *Mater Dolorosa* and *Pilgrims at the Tomb of St Sebastian* by Josse Lieferinxe (early 16th century) and 17th-century portraits.

The **Hall of the Columns** has a (working) fountain in a niche based on a design by Pietro da Cortona (1653), four granite columns with their capitals and bases in Greek marble, and a barrel vault decorated with birds.

FIRST FLOOR (16TH–17TH-CENTURY WORKS)

The monumental **staircase**, probably designed by Bernini, leads up to an enclosed loggia. On either side of the entrance to the gallery are two busts by Bernini: Antonio Barberini il Vecchio (whom Cosimo I of Florence had assassinated in exile for his anti-Medici activities) in his hat; c. 1625, and Urban VIII (1632).

Among the early 16th-century **Florentine works** is the beautiful *Mary Magdalene Reading* by Piero di Cosimo. She is shown at a window, on the ledge of which is placed her attribute, an oil jar. One of the most famous works in the collection is the portrait of a lady by Raphael (also attributed to his pupil Giulio Romano) which became known as *La Fornarina* when the Romantics identified the sitter with Margherita, daughter of the Sienese baker (or *fornaio*) Francesco Luti, and supposedly Raphael's mistress. The portrait has many similarities (in the sense that it appears to be the same sitter) to another superb portrait by Raphael known as *La Velata,* now in the Palatine Gallery in Palazzo Pitti in Florence. The background is very dark and one can hardly make out the beautifully rendered foliage, but the plant is a blueberry bush (a fruit sacred to Venus). There is also a portrait of Castiglione (author of *The Courtier*) by Giulio Romano and a painting of Ceres by Baldassare Peruzzi. Beccafumi's *Virgin and Child with St John the Baptist* is a superb example of his *sfumato* technique and his bold use of colour.

The great **Venetian school** is represented by **Titian**'s *Venus and Adonis*, showing the goddess attempting to stop the youth from going hunting (the sleeping Cupid is a sign to the viewer that Venus' arts are going to fail and Adonis will meet an untimely end). Other Venetian works are **Tintoretto**'s *Christ and the Woman Taken in Adultery*, and the *Mystic Marriage of St Catherine* by **Lorenzo Lotto**.

Portraits include Stefano IV Colonna in his armour (and with a purple drape), painted in 1546 by Bronzino; a portrait of Erasmus by Quinten Massys; and Henry VIII by Holbein. Other works are by Niccolò dell'Abate and Bartolomeo Veneto.

The little domed **chapel** was designed by Pietro da Cortona (*see opposite*). Its ceiling fresco of *Divine Knowledge* is by Andrea Sacchi.

The monochrome *Pietà* (derived from a work by Michelangelo) is a beautiful painting by the 'Master of the Manchester Madonna'. By **El Greco** are the *Adoration of the Shepherds* and *Baptism of Christ.* Next are displayed **landscapes** by Nicolas Poussin, Guercino and Paul Bril.

One of the most famous works in the collection is *Narcissus* by **Caravaggio**, dating from 1599. It is an extraordinarily ingenious work, the reflection of the young boy perfectly mirrored in the water. Caravaggio painted the *Judith and Holofernes* here in the same year (Judith is a portrait of the courtesan Fillide Melandroni, who was the mistress of Caravaggio's patron Vincenzo Giustiniani). The *St Francis in Meditation* is also usually attributed to him (although the painting of the same subject in the church of the Capppuccini is probably autograph). *St Francis Supported by an Angel* is by Orazio Gentileschi (although there is another painting by Caravaggio of the same subject). *St Gregory the Great* is by Jusepe de Ribera.

The **Emilian school** is represented by the celebrated *Portrait of a Lady* (or of a Sibyl) by (or attributed to) Guido Reni. This is traditionally thought to be a portrait of **Beatrice Cenci**, a young girl of 22 who was executed in 1599 for having, a year earlier, hired assassins, together with her stepmother Lucrezia and brother Jacopo, to kill her father. Although Beatrice never confessed to parricide even under torture, she was beheaded. Her father was known to have been a very violent man and was also accused of incest. Her story caught the imagination of the Romantics and in 1819 Shelley, while staying in Livorno, wrote his famous verse drama *The Cenci*. He had seen this portrait in Palazzo Colonna when he came to Rome the previous year, and Stendhal, Charles Dickens and Nathaniel Hawthorne all mention the painting, which did much to augment the aura of tragedy which surrounded the figure of Beatrice. It is interesting that her story still held so much significance that as recently as 1999 the municipality of Rome saw fit to erect a plaque to her memory on Via di Monserrato on the site of the prison of Corte Savella, where on 11th September 1599 she set out for the scaffold (*see p. 234*). The *Mary Magdalene* is also by Guido Reni. Works by Guercino include a *Flagellation*.

PIETRO DA CORTONA

Art in 17th-century Rome cannot be understood without reference to theatre: it was its nature always to be performing, dramatically illuminated and seeking to impress its audience. Pietro da Cortona (1596–1699), like the other artists of his time, was a natural figurative and spatial dramatist; and though he has neither the idiosyncrasy of Borromini's spatial imagination nor the sheer force of character of Bernini, he is a painter of impeccable technique, a magnificent decorator and a complex architect.

Pietro Berrettini, born in Cortona in Tuscany, first came to Rome as a seventeen-year-old. He set himself to study antique art and the works of Raphael. It was not long before he came to the attention of powerful and discriminating patrons: the Sacchetti family, and the pope's nephew, Francesco Barberini.

Pietro's architectural genius is best appreciated in the churches of Santi Luca e Martina (1635–50) and Santa Maria della Pace (1656/7). The former is a brilliant adaptation of a Classical central-plan design, with new and ornate elements decorating the exterior of the drum and dome. The façade of Santa Maria della Pace succeeds in creating an architectural unity far greater than the sum of its parts: its light and expansive oval portico and curved front appear like a stage set.

But Pietro is best remembered in Rome for his ceiling frescoes, especially that in Palazzo Barberini (1633–9), which is taken to be his masterpiece. The artificiality of the requirements of this commission are met with a dutiful ingenuity, down to the depiction of Divine Providence crowning, with the laurel wreath of Immortality, the heraldic arms of the Barberini—a triad of honey-bees. The prevailing obsession of 17th-century official art was with making painting an instrument of allegory. Here, for example, Pietro had to depict the triumph of Pope Urban over lust and intemperance. While this tended to reduce the artist to the level of decorator, in this ceiling each figure is a magnificent individual study, expertly conceived and executed. Though the result is overwhelming, the work is a *tour de force*, particularly in the organisation of the space and the reduction of the composition into the angles. N.McG.

The large **Salone** has a magnificent ceiling fresco by Pietro da Cortona (*see box above*). Off it is a lovely **oval hall**, with steps up to doors out into the garden. It was designed by Bernini, with four Classical statues in niches and four busts in roundels. The **Sala dei Marmi** has three sarcophagi, an extraordinary veiled statue of the Vestal Tuccia by Antonio Corradini (veiled figures were his particular speciality), and a sculpted half figure of Clement X by Bernini. The painting of the *Madonna and Child with Saints* is by Domenichino.

SECOND FLOOR (17TH–18TH-CENTURY WORKS)

The display begins with **Neapolitan works** by Mattia Preti, Salvator Rosa, Luca Giordano (portrait of a *capomastro*) and Jusepe de Ribera (*St James*). There is a *Guardian Angel* and *Male Portrait* by Pietro da Cortona and portraits of Clement IX and Gian Lorenzo Bernini by Baciccia. Paintings by **Bernini** include *David with the Head of Goliath* and a very fine portrait of Urban VIII, painted with a notable lightness of touch. Painters working in Rome in the early 18th century include Marco Benefial and **Pompeo Batoni** (*Portrait of Count Niccolò Soderini*, typical of its time). Later 18th-century works include a portrait of Sir Henry Pierce, also by Batoni, the sitter shown as a young milord with his dog and Classical bits and pieces in the background (Batoni also painted the *Hagar and the Angel* here). Neoclassical works include *Signora Carducci* by Anton Raphael Mengs and a female nude (seen from behind) by Pierre Subleyras. There are **landscapes** of Tivoli and the Alban Hills by Jakob Philipp Hackert, views of Rome by Vanvitelli, and Venetian scenes by Canaletto and Francesco Guardi.

PIAZZA BARBERINI

Piazza Barberini (*map p. 655, D1*) was transformed between the wars into one of the busiest traffic hubs in the city. In this unpleasant setting, isolated in the centre of the square, is Bernini's masterpiece, the **Fontana del Tritone** (1642–3), with four dolphins supporting a scallop shell on which is seated a triton (or merman) who blows a single jet of water through a conch shell held up in his hands. Surviving drawings by Bernini show that he made a careful study of where the water would fall, but since the water pressure is now lower, the full effect can no longer be appreciated: the spray was meant to have reached the scallop shell, and from there the water would brim over into the lowest basin. Commissioned by the Barberini pope Urban VIII, it is decorated with the beautifully-carved Barberini coat of arms with the familiar emblem of the bee.

On the north side of the square, at the beginning of Via Veneto, is the small, reconstructed **Fontana delle Api**, designed by Bernini a year later, also decorated with the Barberini bee and with an inscription on the scallop shell stating that the water is for the use of the public and their animals. The small marble basin below was designed at the beginning of the 20th century, when the fountain was moved from its original site on the corner of Via Sistina and recomposed here.

Piazza di Spagna & the Pincio

*Piazza di Spagna has for centuries been an elegant meeting place
in the heart of the city and the famous Spanish Steps provide a delightful
background to the scene, with Bernini's fountain of a sunken boat at their foot.
There are two house-museums in the square: those of the poet Keats
and of the painter Giorgio de Chirico, and both give an insight into
Roman residences of their day. Close to the top of the Spanish Steps
is the Villa Medici: its famous garden can be visited.*

Piazza di Spagna (*map p. 654, C1*), a long and irregular square, is the place which perhaps captures Rome at its most opulent, since it is in the pedestrian streets which lead from it down to the Corso—Via Condotti, Via Frattina and Via Borgognona—that the most elegant and fashionable shops are to be found, and some of the grandest old-established Roman hotels are nearby. The piazza was for centuries the focus of the artistic and literary life of Rome. Foreign travellers usually chose their lodgings in the *pensioni* and hotels in the vicinity and the English colony congregated here. John Evelyn, on his first visit to Rome in 1644, stayed near the piazza; Keats died in a house on the square; and the British Consul formerly had his office here. The Brownings' Roman residence was nearby (on the corner of Via Bocca di Leone and Vicolo del Lupo). A delightful English 'tea-room' is still open in the square, and the English church is in the neighbouring Via del Babuino. The famous Spanish Steps provide a theatrical background to the piazza, which is always filled with tourists and Romans.

ON & AROUND PIAZZA DI SPAGNA

In the centre of Piazza di Spagna is the **Fontana della Barcaccia**, a delightful fountain once thought to be the masterpiece of Pietro Bernini but now usually considered to be the work of his famous son Gian Lorenzo. The design of a leaking, half-sunk boat is well adapted to the low water-pressure of the fountain. This is one of the most 'accessible' fountains in the city, and there are almost always people sitting on its rim to refresh themselves.

The theatrical Rococo Scalinata della Trinità dei Monti, or **Spanish Steps**, were built in 1723–6 to connect the piazza with the church of the Trinità dei Monti and the Pincio. They are a masterpiece of 18th-century town planning and the best-known (and almost the only) work of Francesco de Sanctis. The monumental flight of 137 steps, interwoven with parapets and wide landings, rises between picturesque houses, some with garden terraces: it has always been a well-loved haunt of Romans and foreigners. The steps are covered with tubs of magnificent azaleas at the beginning of May. Today they provide a welcome place to linger and survey the scene.

THE KEATS-SHELLEY HOUSE

In an elegant pink 18th-century house marked with a plaque (at the foot of the steps on the right) is the apartment with a little vine-covered terrace where the poet John Keats spent the last three months of his life. It is now a museum, the Keats-Shelley House, and retains the atmosphere of that time (*entrance at no. 26 in the piazza; the museum is on the second floor; open 10–1 & 2–6; closed Sun; T: 06 67 84 235, keats-shelley-house.org. The Landmark Trust in the UK has the use of the apartment above the museum, available for short rents; www.landmarktrust.org.uk*).

KEATS AND SEVERN IN ROME

In 1820 Keats, diagnosed with tuberculosis, was told by his doctor in London that he needed to winter in Rome and when his close friend Charles Brown found he could not go with him, Keats asked Joseph Severn (whom he had first met in 1816) to accompany him on the journey. They had a terrible sea voyage to Naples, which lasted six weeks, and they were then kept in quarantine in the port aboard ship for another two weeks. The overland journey from Naples to Rome took some eight days, their carriage constantly in danger of attack from brigands. In Rome, through the English doctor there, Dr James Clark, Keats had booked rooms in this house on the Spanish Steps, which at the time was a small *pensione*. The kindly Severn, an aspiring painter, failed to realise how ill Keats was and remained optimistic that the change of air would finally help him. Keats' health was further compromised by the mistaken treatment he received from Dr Clark, who only added to the poet's sufferings (for example by putting him on a starvation diet). From Severn's letters to England we have a vivid account of the days they spent together as Keats grew steadily worse and more and more bitter, leading what he himself described as a 'posthumous life'. Severn made some sketches of Keats which are the best portraits we have of him. He died on 24th February 1821, aged 25, believing he was a great failure, and it was only some 30 years later that his poetry was re-evaluated and he was established as one of the greatest British poets of all time.

Severn stayed on in Rome in the 1820s and '30s and married Elizabeth Montgomerie (the couple had six children). He became an important figure in the group of British artists at work in the city. He then decided to return to London but late in life, with Gladstone's help, he came back to Rome as British Consul from 1860–72. He died in 1879 at the age of 85 and was buried in the Protestant Cemetery (*see p. 488*). Three years later his grave was appropriately moved next to that of Keats.

The house was purchased in 1906 by the Keats-Shelley Memorial Association and opened to the public in 1909 as a museum and library dedicated to Keats, Shelley, Byron and Leigh Hunt, all of whom spent much time in Italy. The library contains autograph letters and manuscripts and material relating to Shelley and Byron, and a painting of Shelley at the Baths of Caracalla by Severn is displayed in the *Salone*. The reliquary of Pius V was later used as a locket for the hair of John Milton and Elizabeth Barrett Browning and was owned by Leigh Hunt (see Keats's poem *Lines on Seeing a Lock of Milton's Hair*). The kitchen was in the small room opening onto a terrace on the Spanish Steps, and Severn's room now contains mementoes of Severn, Leigh Hunt, Coleridge and Wordsworth. The death mask of Keats and a sketch by Severn of the poet on his deathbed are preserved in the little room where he died. The house features in Jane Campion's 2009 film *Bright Star*, about Keats' romance with Fanny Brawne.

The house opposite, which retains its fine deep russet colour, was built by Francesco de Sanctis to form a pair with the Keats house. Here are **Babington's English Tea Rooms** (*open daily 9–8.30*), an old-fashioned café founded in 1893 by two English ladies, Anna Maria Babington and Isabel Cargill. Today it preserves its genteel atmosphere and serves pots of freshly-brewed tea, crumpets and other five o'clock delights such as cinnamon toast. Light luncheons and high tea are also served. You do pay extra for your historic surroundings, and unlike all Italian cafés there is no counter service. The **northern end of Piazza di Spagna** is particularly attractive, with its row of 18th-century houses, its five tall palm trees (one of which has recently been replanted), and a flower stall (which now also sells knick-knacks). The entrance to the metro station, one of the very few in the heart of the city, is discreetly hidden.

CASA-MUSEO DI GIORGIO DE CHIRICO

At no. 31 Piazza di Spagna, a few doors along from the Keats Museum, is the Casa Museo di Giorgio de Chirico (*open by appointment; guided tours usually at 10, 11 and 12; T: 06 67 96 546, museum@fondazionedechirico.org*). Opened to the public in 1998, the apartment on the fifth floor was the home and studio of Giorgio de Chirico, one of the most important European painters of the early 20th century, famous as the inventor of the Metaphysical style of painting before the First World War. This was characterised by a magical, enigmatic atmosphere, sometimes created by the presence of mannequins and strange objects, unusually juxtaposed in De Chirico's still lifes, and by a sense of unreal space and perspective in his deserted townscapes. De Chirico lived here from 1947 until his death in 1978 and is buried in the church of San Francesco a Ripa. His Polish wife Isabella Far (d. 1990) established a foundation dedicated to the artist in 1986. The house gives a fascinating glimpse of a Roman residence, as well as providing a clear idea of the artistic achievements of De Chirico, since the 50 works here were chosen and hung by the painter himself. His home and studio remain as they were furnished at his death. Most of the works date from the 1960s and '70s: his earliest period is less well documented. The house has three floors, two of which are open. On the main floor the living-room has some important self-portraits dating from the 1940s (and one painted in 1959), as well as portraits of his wife. The dining-room has numerous lovely still lifes, and the last room has some Metaphysical works, including, strangely enough, copies made by the artist of his earliest paintings. Above are the bedrooms and studio, which contains still life objects and terracotta models as the artist left them.

VIA CONDOTTI AND THE SOUTH END OF PIAZZA DI SPAGNA

In the fashionable Via Condotti (*map p. 654, C1*), named after the conduits of the Acqua Vergine aqueduct, is the renowned **Caffè Greco** (*open daily 9–9. T: 06 67 91 700, anticocaffegreco.eu*), founded in 1760 and a national monument since 1953. It retains its delightful interior, with numerous little sitting-rooms with small marble-topped tables. It is decorated with personal mementoes and self-portraits of some of its famous patrons, who included Goethe, Gogol, Berlioz, Stendhal, Baudelaire and Wagner.

The south end of the piazza runs into Piazza Mignanelli, where the **Column of the Immaculate Conception** (an ancient Corinthian column set up here in 1857) commemorates the establishment by Pius IX in 1854 of the dogma of the Virgin Mary's 'immaculate conception' in the womb of her mother St Anne. It was set up here outside Palazzo di Spagna, which had been the residence since 1622 of the Spanish ambassador to the Vatican, since Spain had been greatly in favour of establishing this dogma. The palace, which has a fine courtyard by Antonio del Grande (1647), gave the main piazza its name.

The **Collegio di Propaganda Fide** (which belongs to the Vatican State and has the privilege of extraterritoriality) has a recently restored eccentric façade with naturalistic details of leafy branches and trees, by the great Baroque architect Francesco Borromini. The Congregazione di Propaganda Fide was founded by Gregory XV in 1622; the college was instituted by his successor Urban VIII (hence the Barberini bees, which also decorate the exterior) for the training of missionaries (including young foreigners).

SANT'ANDREA DELLE FRATTE

The church of Sant'Andrea delle Fratte (*map p. 654, C1; open 6.30–1 & 4–7*) belonged to the Scots before the Reformation. The composer Alessandro Scarlatti was married here in 1678. The unfinished tower and refined, delightful campanile, both by Borromini, were designed to make their greatest impression when seen from Via Capo le Case (left of the church as you face it). In the second chapel on the right is the tomb of Judith Falconnet (1856), interesting because the recumbent figure is by the American artist Harriet Hosmer, who was a great friend of Elizabeth Barrett and Robert Browning. To the left of the north side door is the epitaph of an earlier female artist, Angelica Kauffmann. Kauffmann was born in Switzerland in 1741. She came to live in Rome in 1781 where she became the centre of the foreign artistic community and was greatly admired by Goethe. Wealthy and successful, she painted many portraits (works by her can be seen in the Galleria Nazionale in Palazzo Barberini). Earlier in her career she had lived in London, where she had been a founding member of the Royal Academy and a close friend of Sir Joshua Reynolds.

The cupola and apse were decorated in the 17th century by Pasquale Marini, when the three huge paintings of the *Crucifixion, Death* and *Burial of St Andrew* were hung

SANT'ANDREA DELLE FRATTE
Bernini's angel holding the Crown of Thorns, sculpted for Ponte Sant'Angelo.

here: they are by Giovanni Battista Lenardi, Lazzaro Baldi and Francesco Trevisani. By the high altar are two beautiful marble angels (holding the Crown of Thorns and the Titulus) by Bernini, sculpted for Ponte Sant'Angelo but replaced on the bridge by copies. The cloister has a pretty little garden with cypresses and citrus trees.

AT THE TOP OF THE SPANISH STEPS

On the terrace at the top of the Spanish Steps is **Piazza della Trinità dei Monti**, with its church. From the balustrade there is a fine view, with the dome of St Peter's in the distance beyond the dome of Santi Ambrogio e Carlo al Corso, and to the left the top of the Column of Marcus Aurelius. On the near right the Villa Medici can be seen. The **obelisk** here, probably brought to Rome in the 2nd or 3rd century AD, when the hieroglyphs were copied from those on the obelisk in Piazza del Popolo, formerly stood in the Gardens of Sallust (*see p. 558*). Pius VI decided to have it erected on this spot in 1788.

TRINITÀ DEI MONTI

The church of the Trinità dei Monti (*usually open 6.30am–8pm; closed Mon*) was begun in 1485, authorised by Alexander VI, for the French Order of the Minims. During the French Revolution the Minims were dispersed and the church was damaged during Napoleon's occupation of Rome. It is now in the care of another French order, the Frères et Soeurs de Jérusalem. The unusual 16th-century façade has a double staircase by Domenico Fontana and twin bell-towers probably designed by Giacomo della Porta.

The interior contains **superb works by Daniele da Volterra**, a Tuscan artist who was a close friend and follower of Michelangelo (whom he recorded in a famous portrait head; *see p. 43*). These are probably his best works. In the third south chapel (which he also designed) is a beautiful *Assumption* which includes a portrait of Michelangelo (the last figure on the right) over the altar and a *Presentation of the Virgin* on the right wall. In the second north chapel the *Descent from the Cross* is thought to have been executed from a design by Michelangelo: it is an especially fine work.

The first south chapel has an altarpiece and frescoes by Giovanni Battista Naldini. The other part of the church contains lovely frescoes by Perino del Vaga, Giulio Romano and others. In the north transept is the *Assumption and Death of the Virgin* by Taddeo Zuccari, finished by his brother Federico.

Guided tours of the convent (in French) can be arranged. The tour takes in memorabilia of San Francesco da Paola, founder of the Minims, and the refectory frescoed by Andrea Pozzo (*to book a visit, go to trinitadeimonti.net; also in French*). Excavations by the French Academy beneath the convent have revealed traces of a Roman building which seems to have had a terrace on the hillside similar in form to the Spanish Steps.

VIA SISTINA

The long, straight Via Sistina descends to Piazza Barberini and then ascends the Quirinal hill as Via delle Quattro Fontane. This handsome thoroughfare was laid out by Sixtus V as the Strada Felice, which ran up and downhill for some 3km, past Santa Maria Maggiore and out to Santa Croce in Gerusalemme, and was decorated at certain points by obelisks. Most illustrious visitors to Rome between the days of Napoleon and 1870 (when papal rule ended with the entry of the Italian army) seem to have lodged in this street. Gogol lived at no. 126; no. 48 housed in succession Piranesi, Thorvaldsen and the architect and archaeologist Luigi Canina. The top end of the street still has some old-established luxury hotels and elegant shops.

In the triangle formed between Via Sistina and Via Gregoriana is the charming and bizarre **Palazzo Zuccari**, built by the artist Federico Zuccari as his residence and studio. Sir Joshua Reynolds lived here in 1752–3 and the German archaeologist and antiquarian Winckelmann in 1755–68. In 1900 it was bought by Henriette Hertz, who left it, with her library, to the German government. Now owned by the Max Planck Institute, the Biblioteca Hertziana is one of the most famous art history libraries in the country. The entrance on Via Gregoriana has an amusing portal and two windows in the form of gaping monsters. The library also occupies the Palazzo and Villino Stroganoff, and a new building in the garden of Palazzo Zuccari, designed by Juan Navarro Baldeweg above excavations of the **Villa of Lucullus** (1st century BC).

VILLA MEDICI

Map p. 652, B3. Garden tours (which last around 90mins) by appointment, usually every day except Mon (normally at 12 in English). Consult the website for details (villamedici. it). To book, visiteguidate@villamedici.it or T: 06 67 611. On Sun there are family visits and tours of the art studios, but not in English.

Villa Medici, on the edge of the Pincian hill, has been the seat of the French Academy since 1803. It is one of the most important cultural institutes in Europe and the most beautiful villa to have preserved its garden in the centre of Rome. The garden front, which can only be seen on a guided tour, is particularly handsome and interesting for its Classical sculptures. From the centre of Rome its main façade, with its pale colour and two towers, stands out conspicuously on the skyline.

HISTORY OF THE VILLA MEDICI

The villa, built by Nanni di Baccio Bigio and Annibale Lippi for Cardinal Ricci da Montepulciano in 1564–74, was bought by Cardinal Ferdinando de' Medici in 1576. He enlarged it with the help of Bartolomeo Ammannati and the villa was soon considered one of the grandest residences in the city, important for its collection of Classical sculpture. Ferdinando had Jacopo Zucchi decorate his apartment. In 1587 he had to renounce his cardinal's hat and leave Rome for Florence to succeed his brother Francesco I as Grand Duke of Tuscany, but the villa remained in the family and Cardinal Alessandro de' Medici, who became Pope Leo XI in 1605, later lived in the palace. In the 17th century Velázquez was a tenant (his painting of the garden is now in the Prado), and Galileo was confined here by the Inquisition in 1630–3.

In 1801 the villa was bought by Napoleon and the French Academy, founded in 1666 by Louis XIV, was transferred here. Students at the École des Beaux Arts in Paris, who are aged between 20 and 35 and who win the Prix de Rome for painting, sculpture, architecture, engraving or music (or, since 1968, also for cinema, history of art, restoration, photography or stage design), are sent to study here for periods of between six months and two years at the expense of the French government. Well-known French artists and musicians who have stayed here as scholars (known as *pensionnaires*) include Berlioz, Debussy and Ingres. It is said that Berlioz composed his *Chant de Bonheur* while lying on one of the broad box hedges in the garden. Women were admitted in the early 20th century. The painter known as Balthus (Baltazar Klossowski de Rola, of Polish origin but born in Paris in 1908) was director from 1961–77. He was responsible for a number of important restoration projects, the decoration of many of the rooms and the exhibition gallery on the ground floor. In 1981–2006 excavations in front of the garden façade (since covered over) revealed a house with mosaic pavements and buildings dating from the 5th century AD.

In a group of ilexes in front of the villa is a charming fountain, with an ancient Roman red granite vase, designed in 1589 by Annibale Lippi. The lovely view, with the fountain in the foreground in a bower of trees and the rooftops beyond stretching as far as the dome of St Peter's, is familiar from many paintings, including one by Corot dated 1828. The story goes that the cannon ball was shot from Castel Sant'Angelo by Queen Christina of Sweden, when late for an appointment with the painter Charles Errard, who was staying at the French Academy here.

The 16th-century garden

The villa's splendid ivory-coloured garden façade was decorated by Ferdinando de' Medici with ancient Roman statues, medallions, columns, garlands and bas-reliefs from sarcophagi, including four delicately-carved panels dating from AD 43. Some of the reliefs are thought to have come from a Roman altar similar to the Ara Pacis. These precious pieces are the only part of the Medici collection of sculpture still preserved at the villa; others are now in Florence. The obelisk in the formal garden in front was made in 1961 by the former director of the Academy, Balthus.

In the other direction there are long, hedged walks of laurel and box, laid out symmetrically to create vistas, and numerous ilex trees and tall umbrella pines (a later addition, planted in the 18th century). Near the terrace on the Aurelian Walls is the little garden pavilion, used as a retreat by Ferdinando de' Medici. Its charming painted decoration by Jacopo Zucchi (1576–7), with a pergola inhabited by numerous birds, was only discovered in 1985. In the vestibule are *grottesche* and three interesting painted views of the villa: one showing it as it was when first built; another showing the modifications, including the garden, made by Ferdinando de' Medici some ten years later; and the third showing the original layout of the garden in three distinct parts: the labyrinth with hedges, the formal garden in front of the villa, and the ilex *bosco*.

Beyond, a former studio has been arranged as a gallery of casts of Classical masterpieces made by students of the Academy while in Rome as an obligatory part of their studies (a practice only discontinued in the 20th century). These include casts of some of the reliefs on Trajan's Column, dating back to the earliest days of the Academy in the 17th century. The blue walls are decorated with busts of ancient Romans as well as illustrious Frenchmen.

The Medici collection of ancient sculpture

The custom of decorating gardens with sculpture originated in Hellenistic times, and numerous gardens in ancient Rome were famous for their sculptures. The grand Renaissance villas continued this tradition, and Cardinal Ferdinando de' Medici's famous collection of ancient Roman statues and busts once decorated these gardens. In 1775 the masterpieces of the collection (including the so-called *Medici Venus* and the Niobe group) were transferred to the Uffizi in Florence, while the less important pieces were used to decorate the Boboli Gardens in the same city. On one of the lawns here are copies of *Niobe and her Children* (the originals came from a vineyard near the Lateran in 1583). Other copies now decorate the gardens, although the colossal statue of the *Dea Roma*, in front of the (locked) gate leading out to the Pincio, is an original Roman piece which was given to the cardinal by Pope Gregory XIII. Another original which remained in Rome is a head of Meleager, which might even be an original by Skopas (it is now in a private room of the villa).

The gently sloping **Viale della Trinità dei Monti** ends at a monument by Ercole Rosa (1883) to the brothers Enrico and Giovanni Cairoli, who died supporting Garibaldi against the papacy in 1867. From here you can take a footpath which follows a ramp up to the Pincio gardens, emerging on a terrace near the Casina Valadier.

THE PINCIO

The Pincio (*map p. 652, B2*) was laid out as a Romantic park by Giuseppe Valadier in 1809–14. Adjoining the Villa Borghese, it forms the largest public garden in the centre of Rome. Still with some magnificent trees, many of them remarkable specimens of their kind, it has broad avenues with fountains, pleasant places to sit, and over 200 busts of celebrated Italians from the days of ancient Rome to the 20th century.

HISTORY OF THE PINCIO

The Pincian Hill (46m) was anciently known as the 'Collis Hortulorum' because it was covered with the monumental gardens (*horti*) of the Roman aristocracy and emperors. In the 4th century it was owned by the Pincii family, from whom its name derives. Excavations have revealed traces of 1st-century walls.

The 18th century saw the birth of the Romantic idea of a park to be enjoyed by the whole populace. Formal French-style gardens were, at the end of the century, partly transformed into English parkland with winding paths, fake ruins and exotic vegetation. In the 19th century the Pincio was the most fashionable place for the Roman *passeggiata*, when the aristocracy came here in their carriages to hear the band play and admire the sunset. Nathaniel Hawthorne was one of many foreign visitors to observe the crowded scene: 'Here, in the sunny afternoon roll and rumble all kinds of carriages, from the cardinal's old fashioned and gorgeous purple carriage to the gay barouche of modern date.' Joseph Severn described walks here with Keats in 1820–1, during which they frequently met Pauline Borghese, Napoleon's sister.

The **Casina Valadier**, built in 1817, has a wonderful view from its terrace towards St Peter's. It became a fashionable restaurant in the early 20th century and was visited by Richard Strauss, King Farouk of Egypt, Mahatma Gandhi and Chiang Kai-shek (Mussolini was also a habitué). A grand restaurant and café reopened here in 2004.

Viale di Villa Medici leads past the monumental entrance gate to the garden of Villa Medici (from here you can glimpse the hedged vistas and the colossal Roman statue of *Dea Roma*, described above). Viale dell'Obelisco is named after the **obelisk** which was placed here in 1822: it was found in the 16th century outside the Porta Maggiore, where it may have decorated the Circus Varianus (*see p. 299*). The hieroglyphs suggest that it was originally erected by Hadrian on the tomb of his lover Antinous, who drowned in the Nile in 130. It may have been transported from Egypt by Elagabalus in the 3rd century. The avenue runs east, and across a bridge over the busy road below, it joins Viale delle Magnolie in the park of the Villa Borghese.

Piazza del Popolo

Piazza del Popolo was created in 1538 for Paul III in strict relationship to the three long straight streets which penetrate the city here as a trident. Its grand, spacious atmosphere makes it a popular venue for events and demonstrations. The church here has important works of art, including paintings by Caravaggio and sculptures by Bernini. The artists' district between the piazza and Piazza di Spagna is described in a walk.

Piazza del Popolo (*map p. 652, A2*) was designed to provide a scenic entrance to the city from Via Flaminia and the north, and numerous travellers recorded their first arrival in Rome through the monumental **Porta del Popolo**, which occupies almost the same site as the ancient Porta Flaminia. The outer face (1561) is by Nanni di Baccio Bigio, born in Florence, who had a stormy relationship with Michelangelo but who here apparently followed a design by the great architect (the side arches were opened in 1879). Queen Christina of Sweden (*see p. 401*) made a triumphant entry into Rome through this arch, dressed as an Amazon: the inner face of the gate had been redesigned in her honour by her admirer and friend Gian Lorenzo Bernini.

An **obelisk**, 24m high, rises in the centre. The obelisk's hieroglyphs celebrate the glories of the pharaohs Seti I and Ramesses II (13th–12th centuries BC). After the conquest of Egypt Augustus had the obelisk transported to Rome from Heliopolis, and it was dedicated to the Sun in the Circus Maximus. Domenico Fontana moved it here in 1589, as part of the urban plan of Sixtus V: he had already succeeded in erecting the huge obelisk in St Peter's Square for the same pope. The obelisk is surrounded by four charming fountains with lions which spout water. They had probably been projected by Domenico Fontana but were only installed by Giuseppe Valadier in 1823, when he gave the piazza its present symmetry after the return of Pius VII (*see p. 433*) from France following the fall of Napoleon. In the centre of each hemicycle at the sides of the piazza is a fountain with heroic marble groups dating from 1824: *Neptune with two Tritons* and *Rome between the Tiber and the Anio* (both by Giovanni Ceccarini), and at the ends are Neoclassical statues of the Four Seasons. Sphinxes line the walls, and against the Pincian hill are elaborate sculpted trophies and Dacian prisoners. A winding road, also designed by Valadier, ascends the hill past the abundant monumental fountain at the termination of the Acqua Vergine Nuova. It is a *mostra*, one of numerous such fountains built to display the pressure of the water on its arrival in the city (behind it a series of pipes and conduits distributes the water to various parts of town). An incongruous green gate is usually wide open here so you can go right inside the building where the sound of water envelops you as it comes cascading down the walls from a hidden source (one of the most refreshing spots in the city on a hot day).

Between the Corso and the two other streets which lead from here into the centre of Rome are a pair of decorative 17th-century Baroque churches (*not always open*), **Santa Maria dei Miracoli** and **Santa Maria in Montesanto**. The façades, designed by Carlo Rainaldi, were modified by Bernini and Carlo Fontana (1671–8).

SANTA MARIA DEL POPOLO

Map p. 652, A2. Open 7.15–12.30 & 4–7, Fri and Sat 7.30–7, Sun and holidays 7.30–1.30 & 4.30–7.30 (for updates, see santamariadelpopolo.it). The side chapels are lit by push-button lights, but for the Caravaggio chapel there is a coin-operated light.

This church, dedicated to the Virgin, was apparently built at the expense of the city (the *popolo Romano*), hence its name. Legend relates that the area had been the burial ground of the Domitia family, a member of which was the evil emperor Nero, and so it was believed to be the haunt of demons. In 1099 Pope Paschal II ceremoniously cut down a walnut tree here since it was thought to be giving shelter to these demons in the form of a group of black crows. He then founded a chapel on the site. The church was rebuilt in 1227 and again under Sixtus IV (1472–7). The simple early Renaissance façade is attributed to the architect and sculptor Andrea Bregno, who also carved a number of tombs in the church. The interior was renovated by Bernini and is a wonderful place to see works of art of all periods, including masterpieces by Bernini and Caravaggio.

High altar and apse: The triumphal arch is decorated with fine 17th-century gilded stuccoed reliefs. Over the high altar is the venerated 14th-century *Madonna del Popolo*. Behind the altar (*no access; so sadly almost impossible to see*) is the apse with its shell design, one of the earliest works in Rome by Bramante, commissioned by Julius II. Here are the two splendid tombs of Cardinal Girolamo Basso della Rovere (1507) and Cardinal Ascanio Sforza (1505), signed by Andrea Sansovino. The vault frescoes of the *Coronation of the Virgin*, as well as the Evangelists, Sibyls and Four Fathers of the Church (1508–9), are by Pinturicchio. The stained glass, also commissioned by Julius II, is by Guillaume de Marcillat.

North transept: The first chapel to the left of the choir (*coin-operated light*)

was acquired in 1600 by Monsignor Tiberio Cerasi (who worked for Pope Clement VIII), the year before his death. He commissioned Carlo Maderno to redesign it, Annibale Carracci to paint the altarpiece, and **Caravaggio** to produce two works for the side walls. Today these dramatic paintings, the *Crucifixion of St Peter* and *Conversion of St Paul*, are among the most famous in Rome. In the first, St Peter is shown already nailed to the heavy cross, but our interest is taken up more with the mechanics of just how the three executioners (only one of whose faces is partly visible) were able to elevate it, as well as the pathos involved in seeing three hale and hearty executioners inflict such cruel torture on a frail old man. Again, in the *Conversion of St Paul*, it is not the saint we are drawn to but the lovely old cart horse as he steps carefully over the prostrate figure of Saul who has 'seen the light'. After the strong naturalism of these two works, it is perhaps difficult to appreciate the altarpiece of the *Assumption*, which, although of the same date, is painted in such a different, declamatory style. Nevertheless it is a very fine work by **Annibale Carracci**, who also designed the frescoes in the barrel vault above, with attractive stuccoes.

North aisle: The third chapel has fine monuments to the Mellini family. To the right of the altar is the effigy of Cardinal Pietro Mellini (1483), his head comfortably supported by a pillow; to the left is a bust of Urbano Mellini with a moustache by **Alessandro Algardi**, who also designed the beautiful tomb of Giovanni Garzia Mellini on the left wall, with a half-figure portrait of the cardinal and restrained decoration.

The second chapel is the well-lit, octagonal **Chigi Chapel**, founded by the great papal banker Agostino Chigi (1465–1520). It is a fusion of architecture, sculpture, mosaic and painting designed by **Raphael** in 1513–16. The lovely mosaics in the dome were executed by a Venetian artist from cartoons by Raphael: God the Father, the Creator of the Firmament, is surrounded by symbols of the seven known planets, each of which is guided by an angel, as in Dante's conception. Work on the chapel was interrupted in 1520 by the deaths of both Chigi and Raphael, and it was only completed after 1652 for Cardinal Fabio Chigi (Alexander VII) by Bernini. The frescoes depicting the *Creation* and the *Fall*, between the little windows in the dome, and the four medallions of the Seasons lower down, are by Francesco

Salviati (1552–4). The altarpiece of the *Nativity of the Virgin* is by **Sebastiano del Piombo** (1530–4; *see p. 403*), a very beautiful work; the bronze bas-relief in front, *Christ and the Woman of Samaria*, by Lorenzetto, was intended for the base of the tomb of Agostino Chigi but was moved here by Bernini. By the altar are statues of the prophets *Jonah* (left), with his foot in the whale's mouth, a particularly successful work designed by Raphael and executed by Lorenzetto, and *Habakkuk* with an angel (right) by **Bernini**. By the entrance to the chapel are the prophets *Daniel* with the lion, also by Bernini, and *Elijah*, by Lorenzetto. The remarkable pyramidal form of the tombs of Agostino Chigi and of his brother Sigismondo (who died six years after Agostino in 1526), executed by Lorenzetto, was dictated by Raphael's architectural scheme and derived from ancient Roman models. They were altered in the 17th century, again by Bernini. The unfinished burial crypt below the chapel, with another pyramid would, in Raphael's original design, have been visible and illuminated from the chapel above. The lunettes above the tombs were painted by Raffaele Vanni in 1653. The marble intarsia figure of Death, with the Chigi *stemma*, in the centre of the pavement, was added by Bernini.

South aisle: Here there are frescoes by the Umbrian artist **Pinturicchio** (*see p. 61*) in the first chapel, including a delightful *Nativity* over the altar. Also here are the tombs of three cardinals by Tuscan artists: that on the right is perhaps by Antonio da Sangallo the Younger, and that on the left by Mino da Fiesole and Andrea Bregno. The second chapel was well designed, by

Carlo Fontana, using a great variety of precious marbles, to house the tombs of the Cybo family. The huge altarpiece of the *Assumption and Doctors of the Church* is by Carlo Maratta.

The third chapel has a lovely Pinturicchio altarpiece: the *Madonna and Saints*, and good frescoes in the vault lunettes as well as monochrome scenes at the bottom of the walls attributed to a collaborator.

In the fourth south chapel the beautiful bronze effigy of Cardinal Pietro Foscari (c. 1480) is attributed *in situ* to the Sienese artist Giovanni di Stefano, though some scholars ascribe it to his more famous contemporary Vecchietta.

The former Augustinian convent adjoining the church was the **residence of Martin Luther** during his mission as a priest here in 1511. It was only nine years later that Leo X issued a bull against his writings, which Luther burnt publicly in the square of Wittenberg: his subsequent excommunication marked the beginning of the German Reformation.

A WALK THROUGH THE ARTISTS' DISTRICT

Via Margutta was famous in the 17th century as the residence of numerous Dutch and Flemish painters, among them Rubens. Poussin and Claude also lived here while painting their famous Classical landscapes of the city and its surroundings. In the days of the Grand Tour, this was the area where English and German painters had their studios. In the 1820s Charles Eastlake had a splendid studio in Piazza di Spagna, and was one of a group of British artists who lived and worked in Rome. The Nelli workshop and foundry in Via del Babuino was kept busy making reproductions of great Classical sculptures in marble and bronze for the English 'milords' to take home with them. At the end of the 18th century Goethe lived close by, on the Corso. In the 19th century Rome had a huge number of artists in residence, many of them copyists who worked for months in the galleries of the city—their lives were vividly portrayed by Nathaniel Hawthorne in his *Marble Faun*. The area still has memories of its artistic heyday.

VIA DEL BABUINO, OPENED IN 1525, connects Piazza del Popolo with Piazza di Spagna and is an elegant street filled with clothing shops. The famous Flemish painter Rubens spent his last two years in Italy (1606–8) in a house here. Poussin also took lodgings in this street, in 1626. In 1625 Claude Lorrain, the other great French landscape painter, was also living in Via del Babuino.

On the right Via delle Fontanelle leads down to the Corso, where, just to the left (no. 18), is the building where Goethe stayed with his friend the painter Johann Heinrich Tischbein, during his trip to Italy in 1786–8. The **Casa di Goethe** (*open 10–6; closed Mon; T: 06 32 65 0412, casadigoethe.it*) is now a museum.

Although the house was altered in 1833, some of the rooms are probably those in which Goethe lived. The

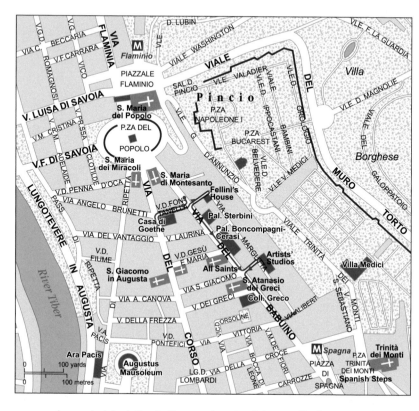

museum has material relating to the poet's travels in Italy and copies of some of his drawings, and numerous delightful informal sketches which Tischbein made of Goethe while he was staying with him here. There is also a copy (1996) of the artist's most celebrated work, his portrait of Goethe in the Roman Campagna, which was also painted here (the original is now in Frankfurt). Also on display are two paintings by Jakob Philipp Hackert, Goethe's friend, whom he met in 1787 and who accompanied him on some of his travels and taught him to draw (Goethe later wrote his biography). The colossal *Ludovisi Juno*, three times

natural size, recalls the cast Goethe had made of this work, which he particularly admired (he called it his 'first love in Rome'). Winckelmann had attributed it to a Greek master, but in fact it is now recognised as a Roman work and a portrait of Antonia, mother of the emperor Claudius, and the original is displayed in Palazzo Altemps. In the last room there is an acrylic serigraph by Andy Warhol based on Tischbein's portrait of Goethe. The apartment overlooks a charming little courtyard planted with banana trees and palms. Exhibitions are held here and there is also a library specialising in the works of Goethe, open to students.

GOETHE IN ROME

The poet Johann Wolfgang von Goethe (1749–1832) stayed in Rome from October 1786 to February 1787, and again from June 1787 to April 1788, and spent his time sightseeing and writing. His *Italian Journey* (various editions of which are preserved in the Goethe Museum), published later, in 1828, is one of the most important descriptions of Italy of its time.

When Goethe came to Italy he was already a famous literary figure in Germany—although the first part of his *Faust*, his most celebrated work, was not published until 1808—and a leading politician in Weimar. He was one of the last and most serious 'Grand Tourists': besides his attraction to Italy because of its Classical past, he was also a keen naturalist. In his *Italian Journey* he describes his progress down through Italy from Lake Garda, where he saw olive trees for the first time, and his visits to the botanical gardens of Padua and the Giusti garden in Verona. He admired the works of Palladio in Vicenza, and in Assisi was particularly impressed by the Temple of Minerva, the first complete Classical monument he had ever seen.

Goethe's circle of friends in Rome included the painter Angelica Kauffmann and Johann Winckelmann, the founding father of Classical archaeology.

Yes, I have at last arrived in this capital of the world...My desire to see Rome was so intense that I could no longer stay still and I detained myself only three hours in Florence. And here I am at last in Rome, calm, and from what I can understand, appeased for the rest of my life...I finally see all the dreams of my youth materialise: the first etchings which I remember (my father placed the ones of Rome in an ante-chamber) are now before my eyes, in fact everything I have known so long through paintings, drawings, copperplates, wood plaster and cork-cuttings, is now laid out before me; wherever I go I find an ancient knowledge of a new world. Everything is like I had imagined it, yet all is new...Wherever one goes, wherever one stops, landscapes of all varieties are disclosed: palaces and ruins, gardens and wastelands, distant or cluttered horizons, small houses, stables, triumphal arches and columns, meet in such close proximity that they could be set down in a single sheet... Goethe, *Italian Journey*, 1786

Return to Via del Babuino, and straight across it is **Via di Margutta**, where, above a large pleasant wine bar (*open every day*) with tables also outside, is the apartment building where the great film director Fellini, born in 1920, lived on the fourth floor for many years until his death in 1993. He is remembered for his numerous films, including *La Dolce Vita* (1960) and *Roma* (1972). Beside the doorway at no. 110, his name and that of his wife, the actress Giulietta Masina, are recorded simply as *Marguttiane*—residents of the street.

Back on Via del Babuino, on the left at no. 41, is the **Palazzetto Sterbini**, decorated with roundels with busts. On the same side **Palazzo Boncompagni-Cerasi** has two elaborate doorways, one with dolphins which used to surround the Babuino fountain (*see below*) and the other with dragons. Opposite is the neo-Gothic **Anglican church of All Saints** (*open mornings except Sat; T: 06 36 00 1881, allsaintsrome.org*), built in 1882 to a design by George Edmund Street, a year after the architect's death (Street also designed the other English church in Rome, now the American Episcopal church of St Paul's). The red-brick façade is typical of Street's work, and the quaint bell-tower has a travertine steeple. The pristine interior, lit by stained-glass windows, shines with various marbles. Its entirely English atmosphere is completed by the tapestry kneelers made by devoted ladies of the congregation.

The tiny short Vicolo dell'Orto di Napoli leads back to the peaceful **Via Margutta**. Many of the houses have creepers or wisteria on their façades. Dating from the 16th century, this street was famous in the 17th century as the residence of numerous Dutch and Flemish painters. Paul Bril is recorded here in 1594–5, and a census of 1634 revealed that there were 104 foreign painters (mainly French, Dutch and Flemish) in this area out of a total of 244 artists at work in the city that year. The area was favoured by foreigners since the pope had declared that all those who 'came from afar' to live in this area would be exempt from taxes.

We know that the English sculptor John Flaxman, who lived and worked in Rome from 1787 to 1794 (and ran an office of the Wedgwood ceramic manufactory which had been opened in the city), had his studio in this area, and that in 1797 it was taken over by another Neoclassical sculptor, Bertel Thorvaldsen, from Denmark, who remained in Rome for the next 40 years as Canova's main rival and was nominated president of the prestigious Accademia di San Luca. He restored a number of ancient Roman statues now in the Vatican Museums, and received the commission for the tomb of Pius VII in St Peter's on the pope's death in 1823. His famous bust of Lord Byron was used for the monument to the English Romantic poet in the Borghese Gardens, near which a piazza is named after Thorvaldsen, and where his statue of *Jason* now stands (donated to Rome by the city of Copenhagen). When Goethe's son Julius August died in Rome in 1830, Thorvaldsen was asked to carve his portrait in profile for the tomb in the Protestant cemetery (*see p. 489*).

Via Margutta is still a street of artists, with art galleries and studios with interesting courtyards and gardens facing towards the Pincio. In spring and autumn a street fair is held and paintings are for sale. In 2002 the street was 'twinned' with New York's Madison Avenue. The large building (no. 33a; mostly reconstructed in the 19th century) of **artists' studios**, set back from the road, with a garden, was where the British Academy of Arts was founded in 1821. Encouraged by Sir Thomas Lawrence, President of the Royal Academy in London, it was set up by Joseph Severn and Charles Eastlake, together with John Gibson, Richard Westmacott and Seymour Kirkup.

At no. 56 is a small luxury-class hotel, aptly named Hotel Art. The fountain a little further along, decorated with artist's tools, was set up by the municipality in 1927.

Back on Via del Babuino the church of **Sant'Atanasio dei Greci** was designed by Giacomo della Porta, who is best remembered for the work he carried out on St Peter's. It has elegant twin bell-towers, which are also a characteristic feature of the earlier church of the Trinità dei Monti at the top of the Spanish steps nearby, also probably designed by Della Porta. Erected for the Greek community in Rome, it is still in the care of the Greek Pontifical College, with Byzantine rites in Greek.

The delightful little edifice next door (no. 150) was built as an artist's studio, and is now open to the public as a café-cum-museum: **Museo Atelier Canova Tadolini** (*open daily 8am–11pm; T: 06 32 11 0702, canovatadolini.com*). This belonged to Adamo Tadolini, a pupil of Canova, who worked here in the first part of the 19th century producing numerous statues and funerary monuments in the style of his master (who also apparently used the studio in 1816–18). The studio and its contents remained in the Tadolini family—three more of whom in later generations (Scipione, Giulio and Enrico) were also sculptors—until 1967. Customers are welcome to explore the labyrinth of nooks and crannies filled to the brim with models and casts by the Tadolini, and a tiny space still arranged as a studio. Books are available for consultation, and the unusual atmosphere—when this used to be the meeting place of protagonists of the political, literary and artistic life of the city—has to some extent been retained.

Against the wall outside the studio is a very worn Roman **statue of a reclining Silenus**, which once decorated a fountain set up after 1571 by local residents by order of Pius V, in return for the pope's concession of water from the newly restored Acqua Vergine for the numerous gardens and orchards that used to exist in this district. It was one of the first fountains in the city erected by private citizens for the use of the public. It was recomposed in the street in 1957 above a small antique marble fountain basin, and until a very few years ago it was still the custom to write slogans against the governors of Rome and Italy on the wall behind. It came to be known as 'Babuino', from the word for baboon, signifying 'dolt' or 'fool', and gave its name to the street. It was one of Rome's 'talking' statues (*see p. 202*).

At no. 149 is the **Collegio Greco**, founded in 1576 for Greek clerics after the fall of Constantinople in the hope of healing the Eastern schism, and moved here when the Greek church was built (the plaque to Clement XIII records its reconstruction in 1769). Almost opposite (at no. 79) is the **house where Wagner stayed** in 1876. Next door but one (no. 89) was the **family residence of Giuseppe Valadier**, well known as the architect of nearby Piazza del Popolo and the café/restaurant on the Pincio known as the Casina Valadier. His father Luigi, a famous silversmith, had his workshop here. Both were greatly admired by their contemporaries and it is known that the pope himself, Pius VI, called on them here.

Via Alibert (on the left) was named after a theatre built here in 1718 by the French family of Alibert. It became the most famous theatre in Rome in the 18th century and stood on the corner of Via Margutta. After it was destroyed by fire in 1863 a hotel was built on the site, where Franz Liszt stayed. He was given the title of Abbé from the Church in Rome in 1865, on receiving the tonsure as a Franciscan Tertiary.

GALLERIA BORGHESE
Detail of Canova's famous and provocative portrait of Pauline, sister of Napoleon and wife to Prince Camillo Borghese (1805–8).

Villa Borghese

Villa Borghese is Rome's most famous public park, always full of Romans with their children and dogs. The Galleria Borghese is one of Rome's most visited museums, with masterpieces by Bernini and Caravaggio.

Villa Borghese (*map p. 652*) owes its origin, in the 17th century, to Cardinal Scipione Borghese, Paul V's nephew. In the 18th century Prince Marcantonio Borghese employed Jacob More from Edinburgh to design the gardens around the family villa and early in the 19th century the property was enlarged by the addition of the Giustiniani gardens. In 1902 it was bought by the state. Today it is the most extensive park in the centre of the city, with an area of 688 hectares. It is connected with the Pincio and the Villa Giulia, so that the three form one huge green area, intersected by avenues and paths, with fine trees as well as statues, fountains and terraces. It also contains the famous Galleria Borghese and provides a pleasant approach to two other important museums, just outside its northern boundary, the Galleria Nazionale d'Arte Moderna and the Museo Etrusco di Villa Giulia.

Tips for visiting

The most pleasant entrance on foot is from the Pincio gardens above Piazza di Spagna. There is another entrance, through the Porta Pinciana, at the top of Via Veneto, which is the most convenient for the Galleria Borghese. In the early 19th century a monumental entrance was built by Luigi Canina just outside Piazza del Popolo in Piazzale Flaminio. The park can also be reached from the north by the scenic flight of steps in front of the Galleria Nazionale d'Arte Moderna, on Viale delle Belle Arti, served by trams no. 3 and 19. From Piazza Venezia or the Corso, bus 160 will take you into the park through Porta Pinciana. In the park itself there are bicycles, bicycle rickshaws and segways for hire. Galleria Nazionale d'Arte Moderna has a restaurant, as does the Casa del Cinema (details are given in the text below).

GIARDINO DEL LAGO & THE CENTRE OF THE PARK

The area of the park called **Giardino del Lago**, with hedged walks and arbours, was laid out *all'inglese* in 1785 by Jacob More and Christopher Unterberger. On an island in the little lake is a Temple of Aesculapius by the Neoclassical architect Antonio Asprucci and his son Mario. Antonio Asprucci is best remembered for the garden buildings he designed in this park as well as for his work on its main building, now the Galleria Borghese. Seven statues by Vincenzo Pacetti (partly antique Roman) have been replaced by copies.

On Viale Pietro Canonica is a reconstruction of London's Globe Theatre. **Piazza di Siena** is a rustic amphitheatre with tall pines, created at the end of the 18th century by Antonio and Mario Asprucci. They also probably designed the little Tempietto di Diana.

MUSEO CANONICA

Map p. 652, C1. Open daily except Mon Oct–May 10–4, June–Sept 1–7. museocanonica.it. In 1926 La Fortezzuola, which dates from the 16th century (although the crenellations were added in the 19th century), became the studio of the sculptor and musician Pietro Canonica, who lived here until his death in 1959. A prolific sculptor, Canonica was appointed a life senator of the Italian Republic and enjoyed great success in his day, both at home and abroad. He produced portraits of many of the crowned heads of Europe. He is now perhaps mostly remembered for his funerary monuments (no fewer than 35 of which he made for the cemetery in Turin, where he was born) and for the twelve equestrian monuments for which he received commissions. He left the house and a large collection of his sculpture to the *Comune* of Rome as the Museo Canonica. The collection includes a portrait sculpture of Donna Franca Florio (1903), a bust of Princess Emily Doria Pamphilj (1901), and *Dopo il Voto* (*After the Vow*), a statue of a young nun, exhibited in Paris in 1893. There is also the model for a monument to Alexander II of Russia, which was destroyed in the Revolution of 1917; plaster casts of equestrian statues of Simón Bolívar (a statue of him by Canonica stands nearby on Piazza Thorvaldsen) and King Feysal I of Iraq (1933); and several war memorials. The gallery at the right of the entrance contains original models of portraits, notably those of Lyda Borelli (1920), Alexander II of Russia (1913), Luigi Einaudi (1948), the Duke of Portland (1896) and Margherita of Savoy (1903) and casts of portraits of the English royal family made between 1902 and 1922. The house and small studio are also open, with some fine works of art collected by Canonica, some from Palazzo Reale in Turin.

MUSEO BILOTTI, CASA DEL CINEMA AND THE ZOO

Housed in a former orangery, the **Museo Bilotti** (*map p. 652, B2; open Oct–May Tues–Fri 10–4, Sat–Sun 10–7; June–Sept Tues–Fri 1–7, Sat–Sun 10–7; museocarlobilotti.it*) has a collection of modern art donated by Carlo Bilotti (1934–2006) which includes 18 works by Giorgio de Chirico and a portrait of Bilotti and his wife by Andy Warhol.

In a house once used as a dairy, close to Porta Pinciana, is the **Casa del Cinema** (*casadelcinema.it*), an arthouse movie theatre offering exhibitions and screenings, outdoors in summer. It has a pleasant café and restaurant (**Cinecaffè Casina delle Rose**; *T: 06 42 01 6224*), with ample seating outside, very popular on sunny days.

Rome's **Zoo**, called the Bioparco (*map p. 652, C1; open 9.30–5, until 6pm in summer; www.bioparco.it*), has over 1,000 animals. Strong on bears and big cats, it also has a family of Egyptian tortoises (threatened in the wild because they are small and easily smuggled). The Museo Civico di Zoologia (*open as for the zoo but closed Mon; museodizoologia.it*) has displays devoted to biodiversity and nature conservation.

GALLERIA BORGHESE

Map p. 652, D2. NB: This is the only museum in Rome where it is obligatory to book your visit in advance (T: 06 32 810, www.galleriaborghese.it), but for all that it is still usually extremely crowded. Open daily except Mon with entrance every two hours, at 9, 11, 1, 3 and 5. You choose an available slot online and will receive printable confirmation and a booking number. There are often queues and it is worth arriving a few minutes early to give yourself time to pick up your ticket and check in your bag at the left luggage. Don't arrive too early, though, because all you will be able to do is stand in the queue waiting to be let in. Tickets are valid for two hours; during that time you can visit the rooms on your own at will. When the two hours are up, a loudspeaker announcement will be made and you will be politely but firmly ushered out. The ticket office, bookshop, café and toilets are on the lower ground floor. Sculptures are mostly on the ground floor and paintings on the upper floor. To avoid the crowds, it often makes sense to visit the upper floor first. Captioning is minimal: you need the handbills which are provided in each room.

HISTORY OF THE GALLERIA BORGHESE

The Casino Borghese was begun for the Borghese family in 1608 by Flaminio Ponzio, Paul V's architect, and continued after his death in 1613 by Giovanni Vasanzio. It was altered for Marcantonio Borghese (the father of Prince Camillo Borghese, who married Pauline Bonaparte) by Antonio Asprucci and Christopher Unterberger in 1775–90, when the splendid interior decoration was carried out. Cardinal Scipione Borghese acquired numerous works of art through the good offices of his uncle Paul V. He was also Bernini's first important patron, and the works he commissioned from him are still preserved here. He owned no fewer than twelve paintings by Caravaggio, six of which can be seen in the gallery. Later members of the family added to the collection, but much of the antique sculpture was sold in 1807 to Napoleon I by his brother-in-law Camillo Borghese and is now in the Louvre.

UPPER FLOOR: GALLERY OF PAINTINGS

Room IX (Raphael, 16th-century Florence): Some beautiful paintings by Raphael are displayed here. The famous *Entombment* (1507) was painted for the Baglioni Chapel in San Francesco al Prato in Perugia. Sixteen preparatory studies for it survive (mostly in the British Museum, London and Ashmolean Museum in Oxford). These show that the artist first decided on a Lamentation scene, but the final painting illustrates the transportation of the dead body of

Christ towards the tomb. It reveals the influence of Michelangelo, whose works Raphael had probably seen in Rome the year before he painted this. Cardinal Scipione (with the pope's blessing) boldly 'stole' it from the church in Perugia.

The famous portrait known as *Lady with a Unicorn* (in the pose of Leonardo's *Mona Lisa*) was probably painted around 1506. It has suffered from much repainting and was only attributed to Raphael in 1927. It may be

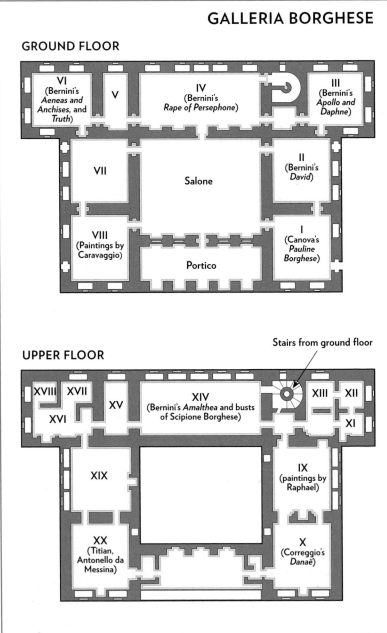

GALLERIA BORGHESE

GROUND FLOOR

VI
(Bernini's *Aeneas and Anchises*, and *Truth*)

V

IV
(Bernini's *Rape of Persephone*)

III
(Bernini's *Apollo and Daphne*)

VII

Salone

II
(Bernini's *David*)

VIII
(Paintings by Caravaggio)

Portico

I
(Canova's *Pauline Borghese*)

UPPER FLOOR

Stairs from ground floor

XVIII   XVII

XVI

XV

XIV
(Bernini's *Amalthea* and busts of Scipione Borghese)

XIII   XII

XI

XIX

IX
(paintings by Raphael)

XX
(Titian, Antonello da Messina)

X
(Correggio's *Danaë*)

that the sitter did not originally hold a miniature unicorn (a symbol of chastity) but, instead, a dog. However, the superb head of the blue-eyed lady with golden hair, and the exquisite jewel at her neck are typical of Raphael's greatest works of portraiture. The striking *Portrait of a Man* (1502) shows the influence of northern painters. The Umbrian painter Perugino is represented with a *St Sebastian*. The portrait of Pope Julius II is probably a copy of an original (now lost) by Raphael, and the *Fornarina* by Raffaellino del Colle is also a copy of a well-known work by Raphael (*see p. 340*).

Important Florentine artists represented here include Lorenzo di Credi, Botticelli (with assistants), Piero di Cosimo, Fra' Bartolomeo, Andrea del Sarto and Bronzino.

Room X (Mannerism): The Emilian school is superbly represented by *Danaë*, the work of Correggio, the only painting to be found in Rome by this artist, who spent almost all his life in his native Emilia. It formed part of his last important commission: a series of mythological paintings for the Duke of Mantua (apparently destined as a gift for the Emperor Charles V), and this is the only one of the series still in Italy. The unashamedly erotic scene shows the charming young Danaë on her bed beside the winged cupid receiving Jupiter transformed into a golden shower. The picture had numerous owners before joining this collection in 1827. Another Emilian artist, Parmigianino, painted the *Portrait of a Man* which also hangs here. The *Venus and Cupid with a Honeycomb* is by the German painter Lucas Cranach the Elder.

Room XI (16th-century Ferrara): Paintings here include Madonnas, an *Adoration of the Shepherds* by Garofalo, and a *Deposition* by Ortolano.

Room XII (16th-century Siena, Lombardy, Veneto): This room displays a *Holy Family* and *Pietà* by the Sienese artist Sodoma; *Head of a Young Man* by Beccafumi; a portrait of Mercurio Bua by Lorenzo Lotto; and an early 16th-century copy of Leonardo's *Leda and the Swan*.

Room XIII (16th-century Florence): *St Francis* and *St Stephen* are both by Francesco Francia. The *Madonna and Child with St Joseph and the Infant St John the Baptist* is by the Kress Master of Landscapes (Giovanni di Lorenzo Larciani) and *Christ at the Column* is by Lorenzo Costa.

Room XIV: Easy to miss, on a table against a wall, is **Bernini's earliest work**, dating from around 1615: the goat Amalthea with Zeus as a child and a small faun at play. It was once taken to be a Hellenistic original and may even have been made by this great Baroque sculptor as a deliberate forgery. Bernini also carved the two almost identical marble portrait **busts of Cardinal Scipione Borghese**, his patron (c. 1632); one of them was damaged while Bernini was at work on it. It has a remarkable spontaneity, as if the Cardinal were about to speak, and is one of Bernini's most famous busts, considered the first 'speaking likeness' in sculpture, as opposed to the immobile abstraction of Classical and Renaissance portraits. He made the terracotta model for the equestrian statue of Louis XIV over three decades later. He is shown in two painted self-portraits—one dating from around 1623 and the other from about ten years later. The *Portrait of a Boy* is also by him. Here also are two paintings by two important painters of the early 17th century: Guido Reni (*Moses with the Tables of the Law*) and Guercino (*Prodigal Son*).

Room XV (16th-century Ferrara, Veneto, Brescia): *Last Supper*, and *Sheep and Lamb* by Jacopo Bassano; *Sts Cosmas and Damian* by Dosso Dossi, and a beautiful painting of *Tobias and the Angel* by Giovanni Girolamo Savoldo. The black marble putto, an allegory of Sleep, is by Alessandro Algardi.

Room XVI (Florentine Mannerism): Highlights are the *Adoration of the Christ Child* by Pellegrino Tibaldi; *Nativity* by Giorgio Vasari; *Allegory of the Creation* and *Allegory of the Discovery of America* by Jacopo Zucchi.

Rooms XVII and XVIII (17th–18th centuries): The display includes Madonnas by Sassoferrato and Pompeo Batoni and a very fine *Deposition* by **Rubens**, painted during his eight-year stay in Italy around 1602. Also by Rubens is *Susanna and the Elders*.

Room XIX (17th century): Artists represented here include Domenichino, the Carracci and Lanfranco.

Room XX (16th-century Veneto): The early **masterpiece by Titian**, *Sacred and Profane Love* (1514), was painted for the wedding of Nicolò Aurelio and Laura Bagarotto and in fact depicts the bride fully dressed, beside an allegory of her eternal happiness in heaven in the form of a nude figure of Venus. The title by which the painting is now always known was only invented in the late 18th century. The two superb female figures are amongst Titian's greatest achievements. Symbolism abounds: the rabbits, the rose petals, the burning lamp.

There are three other works here by this Venetian master, all probably painted in the 1560s: *Venus Blindfolding Cupid, St Dominic* and the *Scourging of Christ*. The *Portrait of a Young Man* by **Antonello da Messina** dates from around 1475. This Sicilian artist was clearly influenced by the Flemish school of painters and he had an important influence on contemporary Venetian artists including Giovanni Bellini (here represented with a *Madonna and Child*). There are also works by other Venetian masters, including Veronese, Lorenzo Lotto and Palma Vecchio.

GROUND FLOOR: SCULPTURE BY BERNINI AND CANOVA; PAINTINGS BY CARAVAGGIO

Most of the ceilings were decorated at the time of Marcantonio Borghese (c. 1750–60). Over some of the doors are landscapes by Paul Bril from the end of the 17th century.

The Salone: In this central room you at once capture the atmosphere of the rest of the villa, where the entire ground floor is magnificently decorated.

Antique busts and sculptures are set side by side with 17th-century statues, the walls are covered with precious marbles and ancient reliefs, and the ceilings frescoed with elaborate scenes (mostly dating from the time of Marcantonio Borghese, 1750–60). Ancient Roman mosaics are often set into the floors to add to the effect of grandeur.

The ceiling of the Salone is the work of Mariano Rossi (1770s), and on the wall in front of the entrance (easy to miss since it is high above the Neoclassical decoration on the walls and a series of busts in niches) is a **high-relief of Curtius** throwing himself down into the room (the 'abyss'; *see p. 75*), a Roman work of the 2nd century AD which was reworked by Bernini's father Pietro, who set it at this bizarre angle. It is one of the strangest sights in the villa. Other ancient Roman sculpture here includes a colossal figure of a satyr and two huge heads of Hadrian and Antoninus Pius, as well as statues of Augustus and Bacchus. In front of one of the windows there is a sculpted head, a fragment of a *Pietà* group, which, when it was found in Rome in 1980, aroused much interest amongst scholars since some of them declared it to be Michelangelo's first version of the head of Christ for his famous *Rondanini Pietà*, now in Milan. However it has been largely forgotten since it is now attributed to an unknown 16th-century Roman sculptor.

Room I: The sculpture of ***Pauline Borghese*** **by Canova** is justly one of his best-known works (1805–8). Napoleon's sister, who lived in Rome as the wife of Camillo Borghese, is daringly shown half nude, justified by the fact that she is holding an apple and therefore depicted in the guise of Venus Victrix. The wooden base was designed to cover a mechanism which rotated the statue while the beholder remained still.

The *Herm of Bacchus* in bronze and precious marble is a refined work by Luigi Valadier (1773). In the 1st-century AD group of *Leda and the Swan*, Leda has the face of Antonia Minor, daughter of Mark Antony and mother of the emperor Claudius. Her features are also those of the famous Ludovisi Juno (*see p. 196*). Pietro Bracci sculpted the portrait bust of Pope Clement XII.

Room II: Bernini's statue of ***David*** was made when the sculptor was 25 (1623–4) for Cardinal Scipione. It shows the hero bracing himself in total concentration at the moment before his triumph over the giant (the face, with its determined jaw set square, is a self-portrait). David had already been a favourite subject for some of the greatest sculptors in previous centuries, and this work is in striking contrast to Donatello and Verrocchio's self-satisfied young boy murderers and Michelangelo's famous apprehensive giant. Bernini was profoundly influenced by Annibale Carracci, whose painting of *Samson in Prison* (c. 1595) hangs here. There are also paintings of the Caravaggesque school including *David with the Head of Goliath* by Battistello Caracciolo (1612). The sarcophagus with the *Labours of Hercules* on two sides dating from AD 160 was cut in half so that the two panels could be exhibited on the two facing walls of the room, a typical example of the use of ancient sculpture merely as a decorative feature in the design of an early 19th-century room.

Room III: Bernini's ***Apollo and Daphne*** (1624) was also made for the Borghese cardinal, and is perhaps the most famous piece he ever carved. The

GALLERIA BORGHESE
Pluto's bony fingers clutching at Persephone's thigh: bravura carving by Bernini.

extraordinarily difficult subject, never before attempted in sculpture, is the dramatic moment when Apollo (who has been tricked by Cupid into love through a golden arrow) reaches his beloved nymph after a long chase. Daphne, however, refuses his love as she has, instead, been 'wounded' by Cupid with a leaden arrow. She avoids capture because at the touch of Apollo her father has seen to it that she is turned into a laurel tree. The group was designed to be exhibited against a wall (therefore seen from just one stand-point, sideways on as seen today as you enter the room). From the features of the face, the distinctive hairstyle and the sandals, it is evident that the figure of Apollo is modelled on the famous *Apollo Belvedere* (now in the Vatican). Bernini's extraordinary sculptural skills are clear to see, with his almost excessive lightness of touch in the carving of Daphne, her hair flow-ing and her fingers branching into leaf while her expression vividly portrays her terror.

Circe (sometimes identified as *Melissa*) by Dosso Dossi shows the sorceress accompanied by a friendly white dog. The scene is inspired by Ariosto's *Orlando Furioso*.

Room IV: The decoration of the room is a notable example of 18th-century skill and taste in the ornamental arrangement of a great variety of precious marbles and the incorporation of bas-reliefs into the design. The busts of Roman emperors, in porphyry and alabaster, were carved in the 17th century. The **Rape of Persephone** is the last of the three early masterpieces by Bernini made for the Borghese, even earlier than the two already described. This was also designed to be seen from just one viewpoint. It shows Pluto triumphant over

Cerberus at the door of Hades, seizing Persephone in his arms as she struggles to free herself from his embrace. His right hand clasping at the flesh of her naked thigh is a masterpiece of carving. Displayed on a table at one of the short walls is a *bozzetto* in bronze of Neptune, made by Bernini for a fountain group now in the Victoria and Albert Museum, London. At the opposite end of the room is a bronze replica by Antonio Susini of the celebrated *Farnese Bull,* found in the Baths of Caracalla and taken to Naples in the 18th century.

Room V: The *Sleeping Hermaphrodite* is a replica of a famous Hellenistic prototype; above it is an alabaster vase on a red porphyry base. The 3rd–4th-century mosaic floor shows a fishing scene.

Room VI: The sculptural group of *Aeneas and Anchises* was carved by Bernini when he was only 15 years old (in 1613), with the help of his father,

Pietro. This was his first large-scale commission, and although the details of the carving reveal Bernini's precocious talent, it is a somewhat awkward, unstable group. It shows Aeneas carrying his aged father Anchises (who clutches the sacred household gods) away to safety from the burning Troy with the young Ascanius at his feet.

Also here is a late work (1645) by Bernini, a female figure representing *Truth*: it was made for the vestibule of his palace on Via del Corso and remained there until 1924. Bernini planned it as an allegory of 'Truth unveiled by Time' but he never finished it.

Room VII: Here are hung paintings by Tommaso Conca representing the gods and religions of ancient Egypt. Among the sculpture is a *Satyr on a Dolphin* (1st century AD), a copy of an original from Taranto (the head was reworked in the 16th century).

A controversial view

'How Bernini, in Rome, in the presence of the most beautiful statues of antiquity, went so far astray remains a riddle.'   *Jacob Burckhardt*

Room VIII: The *Dancing Satyr* is a 2nd-century AD copy of an original by Lysippus, discovered in 1824 at Monte Cavo and restored under the direction of Thorvaldsen. There is a *Rape of Europa* here by Cavaliere d'Arpino, the master of Caravaggio.

Six paintings by Caravaggio himself (representing just half of Scipione Borghese's original collection of works by this master) are the highlight, and

offer a superbly representative picture of the artist's skills in portraiture, religious subjects and still lifes. The *Boy Crowned with Ivy*, also called the *Sick Bacchus*, and the *Boy with a Basket of Fruit* are both early works dating from c. 1594. The former is apparently a self-portrait: although Caravaggio never painted his self-portrait as such, he often portrayed himself as a participant (especially in his religious paintings).

GALLERIA BORGHESE
Detail of the severed head of Goliath by Caravaggio, said to be a self-portrait.

The latter includes a superb still-life in the basket of fruit (familiar in several other works by Caravaggio).

The *Madonna of the Palafrenieri*, painted in 1605, was commissioned for St Peter's but was deemed unsuitable for a church and so was instead purchased by the cardinal. It shows St Anne (depicted as an elderly peasant woman) with the Madonna showing the young Christ Child (totally nude) how to crush a snake, symbolising evil. His *St Jerome*, dating from the same year, has a brilliant red cloak: the image has been reduced to its essentials by the skilled use of light.

In the *Young St John the Baptist*, it is the red cloak which is again the most striking element in the painting. This is Caravaggio's last known work, and it was sent (together with two other paintings, now lost) by the artist to Scipione Borghese to try to obtain the pope's pardon for a murder the artist had committed (*see p. 207*) and permission to return to Rome.

David with the Head of Goliath, dating from the same period, is one of several paintings by Caravaggio of this subject. It was also painted for Cardinal Scipione, and apparently includes Caravaggio's self-portrait in the head of Goliath. This also dates from the first decade of the 17th century.

GALLERIA NAZIONALE D'ARTE MODERNA

Map p. 652, B1. Open Tues–Sat 8.30–7.30; closed Mon. Sunday opening is staggered; consult website. Last tickets 45mins before closing. T: 06 32 2981, www.gnam.beniculturali. it. There is a pleasant café/restaurant, Caffè delle Arti, open daily including Mon; closes midnight Tues–Sun, 5pm on Mon (T: 06 32 65 1236, caffedelleartiroma.com).

This is the most important collection in existence of Italian modern art. The gallery was founded in 1883; this building was purpose-built for it in 1911 by Cesare Bazzani. As the collection expanded, the building was enlarged.

The arrangement is themed within a broadly chronological framework, with works dating from 1780 to the 21st century. Panels in Italian and English at the entrance to each room explain the display and its rationale. The individual works are well captioned. Helpful floorplans are available at the front desk.

LEFT WING: NEOCLASSICAL TO BELLE ÉPOQUE

The earliest part of the collection includes a work by the greatest master of this school, **Antonio Canova**: his colossal statue, three and a half metres high, of *Hercules and Lichas* (1795–1815). Hercules is shown seizing the foot and hair of the messenger Lichas in fury, about to hurl him over a cliff to his death, after the latter has delivered to him the poisoned shirt, which can be seen stuck to the hero's body. Canova told the story of some admirers of his who saw the statue in his studio and at once took it to represent the strength of the French nation in the act of overcoming the Monarchy. The sculptor ironically pointed out to them that it could just as well be taken as an allegory of the strength of the great nation in overthrowing 'licentious liberty'. *Psyche* is by another important Neoclassical sculptor, **Pietro Tenerani**.

The Venetian painter **Francesco Hayez**, who came under the protection of Canova when he arrived in Rome (and worked in the Vatican), is famous for his historical Romantic canvases. His most important painting here is the *Sicilian Vespers* (several versions of it exist), recording a famous incident of 1282 (which took place in Palermo outside a church at the hour of Vespers) which provoked a rebellion against the French and which came to symbolise the pride of the Sicilians and their struggle for freedom from foreign rule—a courageous stand particularly admired many centuries later during the Italian Risorgimento. Hayez became president of the Brera Academy in Milan.

Among the portraits in this suite of rooms is a typical likeness by **Andrea Appiani**, who worked for Napoleon in Milan. Sculptures by **Vincenzo Gemito** reveal the extent to which this artist was influenced by late Classical works.

The **Macchiaioli School** of painters, active in Tuscany before 1864, took their inspiration directly from nature, and their works are characterised by *macchie* or spots of colour. They came to be known as the Tuscan Impressionists. Giovanni Fattori is the most famous exponent of the school. Other members included Silvestro Lega, Antonio Puccinelli, Stefano Ussi, Telemaco Signorini and Vincenzo Cabianca. Their work is contrasted here with southern Italian views and *plein-air* scenes by the

Neapolitan painter **Filippo Palizzi**, for example his charming painting of two women picking oranges in Sorrento.

Palizzi was the master of another Neapolitan painter, **Domenico Morelli**, who was particularly well-known in his lifetime for his historical canvases and for his skilled use of colour. His *Tasso Reading 'Gerusalemme Liberata' to Eleonora d'Este* (1865) is exceptionally fine. He also produced religious works (an example is the slightly absurd *Temptations of St Anthony*).

Other painters of landscapes and views include **Ippolito Caffi**, famous in particular for his night scenes. There is also a particularly luminous view of the port of Genoa by him. Hung alongside are views of Rome by **Giovanni Faure** (his *Colosseum*, painted in 1835, gives a vivid impression of how suggestive the ruins were to the Grand Tourists of the day) and exquisite Neapolitan views by **Giacinto Gigante**.

The later rooms in this wing show paintings that reflect the era's growing social awareness. **Francesco Paolo Michetti** was one of the best-known artists of his day, internationally successful during his lifetime, and produced religious scenes of almost excessive fervour. His *The Votive Offering* (1883) is a supreme example.

RIGHT WING: BELLE ÉPOQUE TO 1925

As the national gallery of modern Italian art, this museum's holdings are, not surprisingly, primarily representative of native artists. This is not exclusively the case, however, and in the right-hand wing a conscious effort is made to display Italian works alongside foreign counterparts from the same date or artistic movement. **Van Gogh**'s fine painting of *The Gardener*, which is hung here together with his portrait entitled *L'Arlésienne*, are two examples. Works by other **French Impressionists**, including Cézanne, Monet and Degas, were purchased for the gallery in the 20th century in order that these artists should be represented (though none of the works is world-class). Illustrated alongside them are a number of sculptures by **Medardo Rosso**, who had a special skill in modelling wax. His original style is immediately recognisable: he seems to produce a fusion of the figure with the atmosphere in an attempt to abolish borders. Like many of his Italian contemporaries, his art also gained much from his time in Paris and he was clearly influenced by **Rodin**—two works by whom, fittingly, are displayed alongside. The male nude entitled *The Age of Bronze* (1877; the first version is in the Tate in London) caused a stir because of its anatomical accuracy: it was greeted by critics with the accusation that Rodin had made it by using a cast from a living model.

Giacomo Balla is an artist whose complex artistic development is very well traced in this museum. Today he is best known as a Futurist (*see opposite*), but we first encounter him here as a voice of a growing social conscience, with three powerful works: *The Beggar* (1902), *The Sick* (1903) and *The Madwoman* (1905).

Dreamlike works by **Gaetano Previati** illustrate the branch of Italian Symbolism that came to be known as Divisionism. One of his best works is the *Fall of the Angels* (c. 1913). The *Three Ages of Woman*, one of the most important works by the famous Viennese Secessionist **Gustav Klimt** (1905), shows how closely he studied the art of mosaic at Ravenna.

The mood changes abruptly after this, with society portraits by **Giovanni Boldini**, much of whose life was spent in Paris. Typical of his oeuvre is the dashing *Marchesa Casati with Peacock Feathers* (1911–13). Also represented is **Paolo Troubetzkoy**, a sculptor and painter who was the son of a Russian prince and an American singer and who had his more famous contemporaries sit for him. **Giuseppe de Nittis** likewise worked in the French capital (in 1874 he had participated in an exhibition of the Impressionists) and his very fine triptych of 1881 entitled *Bois de Boulogne* is hung here, brilliantly contrasted with another early work by **Giacomo Balla**, the *Villa Borghese, Parco dei Daini* (1910), which is divided into five panels and uses an almost pointilliste technique revealing the influence of photography.

Balla returns in the next room, which is devoted to Futurism (Balla was the movement's most important exponent). His *Ponte della Velocità* (*Bridge of Speed*) is a remarkable work of 1913–15. There are also works by Balla's pupil **Umberto Boccioni**.

FUTURISM

The Italian political and artistic movement known as Futurism came into being at the beginning of the 20th century in Milan and Paris and, like Cubism, was to influence all European art of its era. Most interestingly, in the visual arts, the movements that followed Futurism shared with it the idea—probably already circulating in European intellectual circles—that it is possible to paint and sculpt works of art which are not figurative, or, as they are often called, abstract (although the very first painting of this kind is generally considered to be an untitled watercolour of 1910 by Kandinsky).

The most important members of the Futurist movement, F.T. Marinetti, Giacomo Balla, Umberto Boccioni, Carlo Carrà and Gino Severini, advocated in their manifestos (the first of which was published in Paris by *Le Figaro* in 1909) a totally new way of producing art, in all fields: painting, sculpture, music, architecture, interior design, fashion, and even cooking. Futurist painters and sculptors tried to represent objects and people in movement, although in their works the subject matter (such as rain) often became merely a pretext for painting a series of oblique lines. They attempted, like the Cubists, to represent an imagined reality, in a continuous interplay between levels and lines. Their art was a celebration of technological progress (aeroplanes, cars, electric light, etc.) and showed a particular interest in speed and dynamism. Their political ideas, at first loosely anarchic and in other ways also close to Nietzsche, later developed into attitudes which in some ways anticipated those of Fascism. They were in favour of Italy's entry into the First World War, even going so far as defining war itself as the 'hygiene of the world'. Their important influence on Russian avant-garde painters such as Malevich and Goncharova is undeniable. In England the Vorticists (e.g. Wyndham Lewis and David Bomberg) and in France Duchamp and Delaunay certainly owe much to Futurism. Its influence can even be seen as late as the 1960s: for instance, Giacomo Balla's famous painting *Composizione iridescente* of 1913 (now in Birmingham, Michigan) clearly anticipates Optical Art.

The next section explores how traditional forms gave way to the avant garde: some-times retained, sometimes modified and at other times dispensed with altogether. Italian Metaphysical works by **Giorgio De Chirico** and **Morandi** are hung alongside international examples of the era by Kees van Dongen, Modigliani and Magritte. De Chirico is considered the founder of the Metaphysical school. Among some very fine works are *Self-Portrait* (1925) and *The Archaeologists* (1927). There are also paintings by his brother **Alberto Savinio** (who also painted a fine portrait of Palma Bucarelli, champion of the Italian avant garde who became director of the gallery in 1942).

From this we enter the realm of Abstraction: Mondrian, Miró, Moholy Nagy and Schwitters are here placed side by side with **Ivo Pannaggi**, whose *Architectural Function HO$_3$* (1926) was inspired by the Russian and Dutch avant garde (Malevich, Mondrian).

UPPER RIGHT WING (1926 ONWARD)

The first room in this wing displays some superb works of the Italian 'Novecento' (*see opposite*). One of the greatest works of this period is **Virgilio Guidi**'s *In the Tram*, with its rarefied atmosphere in which each figure appears isolated so that this everyday scene takes on an emblematic significance. The painting was widely acclaimed when it was exhibited at the Venice Biennale in 1924. **Antonio Donghi** was, like Guidi, born in Rome and there are similarities in his style, with its remarkable sense of immobility. One of his most significant Realist works here is entitled *The Hunter* (1929). **Felice Casorati** is known for a balanced Classical style, usually simple and severe. *Apples on the 'Gazzetta del Popolo'* (c. 1928) is a representative example. Here also is his memo-rable *Portraits* (c. 1934), a study of five members of his own family: four women of vary-ing ages, his own infant son, and a cat. **Carlo Carrà** began his career as a Futurist, but then had an important Metaphysical period and was also a theorist.

The tragic, disturbing painting entitled *Solitudine* (1925) is one of the best-known works by **Mario Sironi**. He was a painter who openly declared his sympathies with the Fascist regime. He produced Futurist and Metaphysical works before joining the 'Novecento' group. *Sailors' Brides* (1934) by **Massimo Campigli** shows eleven women on a beach looking out to sea. One shades her eyes against the light, another points to the distant, empty horizon. In the same room are works by the two friends **Emanuele Cavalli** and **Giuseppe Capogrossi**. Cavalli's lovely *The Bride* is characterised by the use of strong colours and its unique atmosphere, typical of this artist's production. He unjustly had much less success than his contemporaries and is still relatively little-known outside Italy. Capogrossi's *Thunderstorm*, showing bathers at a lido hurrying out of the water as the weather takes a turn for the worse, has extraordinary atmos-phere and is one of his most impressive works.

Capogrossi was a member of the so-called 'Scuola Romana' group of painters, more of whose works follow. The artists of the school were almost all born after 1900 and most of them worked in Rome, at least for part of their lives. They were close to part of the Novecento group and were in particular influenced by Armando Spadini, Virgilio Guidi and De Chirico. **Scipione** (whose real name was Gino Bonichi) was the Scuola's most important member. He died prematurely aged only 29 but he left some masterpieces, such as his sinister view of Piazza Navona (1930). Other artists who formed part of the school included Emanuele Cavalli, Mario Mafai and **Fausto Pirandello**, whose work takes us into the realm of Expressionism and who is well represented here. The Sicilian painter and fervent Communist **Renato Guttuso** was well known for his Realism and for a style which also owes much to Picasso.

Filippo de Pisis started out in life as a poet and after many years in Paris—where he was deeply influenced by the Impressionists—he produced numerous paintings in a light, sketchy style, favouring as subjects flowers, provincial townscapes, and still lifes with marine backgrounds (as well as nude studies of his models and partners).

THE 'NOVECENTO' ARTISTIC MOVEMENT

In 1918 Mario Broglio and Roberto Melli founded an art magazine in Rome entitled *Valori Plastici* ('Plastic Values') which, although it had ceased publication by 1921, managed to attract the attention of a number of important artists such as Giorgio Morandi, Giorgio de Chirico and Arturo Martini. Orientated towards a *richiamo all'ordine* (the Italian translation of *rappel à l'ordre*, a term coined by the French critic Maurice Raynal), and generally in opposition to the avant-garde movements of the time, it promoted the values of form while remaining interested in the development of Cubism and artists such as Picasso and Derain.

In the 1920s a group of artists was formed who first exhibited together in 1922 at the Galleria Pesaro, subsequently at the Venice Biennale of 1924, and again in 1926 and 1929 in Milan. In a sense they carried forward the ideas begun by the artists attached to *Valori Plastici* (and indeed both Morandi and De Chirico exhibited with them in 1926) but they also studied with renewed interest the great art produced in Italy in the 14th and 15th centuries, and in particular the work of Piero della Francesca, while at the same time greatly admiring Cézanne.

This artistic movement was composed not only of painters and sculptors but also of architects and musicians. The art critic and journalist Margherita Sarfatti, the theorist of the movement, apparently coined the name 'Novecento', referring to the 'nineteen hundreds'—the century in which they lived. It was ironic, but symbolic of the turbulent times of Fascism, that Sarfatti—who at one time had been Mussolini's lover—had to leave Italy in 1938 because of the anti-Jewish laws the dictator had introduced.

The most important artists of the 'Novecento' included Medardo Rosso, Giorgio Morandi, Giorgio de Chirico, Arturo Martini, Libero Andreotti, Felice Casorati, Virgilio Guidi, Gino Severini, Mario Sironi, Ardengo Soffici and Filippo de Pisis. As in other parallel artistic movements in the rest of Europe, the group included adherents of widely different political factions: some of them, led by Sironi, were considered to be artists working for the régime, and this resulted in numerous younger artists distancing themselves from the movement. Outside Italy today, the only 'Novecento' artists widely known are De Chirico and Morandi, although it is undeniable that many of the others produced works of the highest quality.

The other rooms on this floor have thematic displays by Italian and international artists, both abstract and figurative, covering a wide range of movements and media. There is a typical mobile (1958) by Alexander Calder. There are also works by Capogrossi from his later, non-figurative period. There is typical painting by Jackson Pollock and works by Alberto Giacometti, Cy Twombly, Jannis Kounellis, Daniel Buren, Michelangelo Pistoletto and Gino De Dominicis, member of the Gruppo Laboratorio 70 whose works caused an outcry when first exhibited by Palma Bucarelli in 1968. An interesting sculpture by Mario Ceroli is entitled *Last Supper* (1965), featuring twelve identical wooden template figures perched on a bench, six on each side and with a space in between: the space is for Christ, but he is not there. A separate room has works (donated by Arturo Schwarz) by Man Ray and ready-mades by Duchamp (his urinal entitled *Fountain*). Pop Art is also represented with Warhol's *Hammer and Sickle* (1977).

On the upper levels are rooms devoted to single artists: Balla, De Chirico, Guttuso and Giacomo Manzù, a sculptor who produced many works for the Church, including his well-known portraits of cardinals and bronze panels for the doors of St Peter's.

MUSEO NAZIONALE ETRUSCO DI VILLA GIULIA

Map p. 652, B1. Open Tues–Sun 8.30–7.30; last tickets 1hr before closing. T: 06 32 26 571, www.villagiulia.beniculturali.it. From Piazzale Flaminio (map p. 652, A2) take tram no. 2 to the Flaminia/Belle Arti stop, walk back on yourself and turn left up Via di Valle Giulia. Or take tram no. 19 (from San Lorenzo fuori le Mura) to Museo Villa Giulia.

Villa Giulia is a charming 16th-century suburban villa with a façade of two orders, Tuscan below and Composite above. It houses the important Museo Nazionale Etrusco di Villa Giulia, devoted mainly to pre-Roman works found in Lazio, Umbria and southern Etruria. In front of the villa, **Villa Poniatowsky**, built in the late 16th century by Vignola and altered by Giuseppe Valadier in the early 19th century, has been restored to provide more exhibition space for Etruscan finds from Umbria and Lazio.

HISTORY OF VILLA GIULIA

The villa was built in 1550–5 for Pope Julius III by Vignola, Vasari and Bartolomeo Ammannati, with some help from Michelangelo. Its correct name is Villa di Papa Giulio. In the 17th century it was used to house guests of the Vatican, including Queen Christina of Sweden (*see p. 401*) in 1665. The villa was once decorated with numerous pieces of ancient sculpture, but these were later taken to the Vatican.

The villa has housed the Etruscan Museum since 1889. In 1908 the Barberini collection was donated and later acquisitions include the Castellani and Pesciotti collections (in 1919 and 1972). Some rooms have recently undergone re-arrangement in an attempt to bring the vast collections of pots, metalwork and other grave goods to life for a lay audience. Much of the labelling is in Italian only. Nevertheless, the museum contains many extraordinary treasures and amply rewards an unhurried visit.

THE ETRUSCANS

The Etruscans have always been an intriguing people. Herodotus records a story that they were migrants to Italy from the East. It is only recently that a clear sequence has been shown from the Villanovan culture of central Italy (9th–8th centuries BC) to the fully developed Etruscan civilisation of the 7th century. The catalyst for this transformation were Greek merchants in search of mineral ores from the metal-bearing hills of western Etruria. The Greeks traded with local Villanovan chieftains, many of whom adopted Greek customs such as reclining at banquets, chariot-racing and hunting. Thus a new culture emerged, Hellenised but distinct. The Etruscans, for instance, always gave their women higher status than the Greeks did, and kept their own language (even if they borrowed Greek letters in which to write it). Greek deities were adopted into the Etruscan Pantheon but the Etruscans showed much more interest in divination, especially from a careful watching of the skies and the birds which crossed them. The style of Greek temples was adopted too, so as to have a high platform at the front of the podium for observation.

In the 7th century the Etruscans began to expand south, into Campania, to be closer to Greek trading settlements. Rome, with its access to the sea, was a natural staging post and it was under Etruscan 'kings' that it first developed into a city of temples, palaces and paved areas, with proper drainage of the lower ground. Those kings were expelled by the local aristocracy at the end of the 6th century, but Etruscan influence remained: in the Triumph, an ancient celebration of an Etruscan chieftain's victory; in chariot-racing; and in the structure of temples.

By the 6th century Etruscan supremacy, which had spread both south and north over the Apennines into the Po valley, was under threat. Fresh waves of Greek settlers and the expanding Carthaginian empire ate into its trade in the western Mediterranean. In Campania raids from the mountain peoples destroyed many Etruscan settlements. In the north the Celts were forcing their way over the Alps. In the heartland of Etruria the growing power of Rome proved too much. Although the Etruscans did have a loose confederation of some twelve cities, this did nothing to save the town of Veio (anciently Veii) when it was besieged and captured by the Romans in 396 BC. The Battle of Sentinum in Umbria in 295, in which the Romans destroyed an alliance of Etruscans and others, marked the final collapse of the civilisation. But even the Roman conquerors showed some nostalgia for what had been lost. In the words of the 1st-century BC poet Propertius:

Veii, thou hadst a royal crown of old,
And in thy forum stood a throne of gold!
Thy walls now echo but the shepherd's horn,
And o'er thine ashes waves the summer corn.
(Tr. George Dennis)

C.F.

THE VILLA AND GARDEN

The entranceway leads into an atrium with Corinthian pilasters and niches for statues. The ticket office is on the left, after which you leave the atrium and enter the semicircular portico, with Ionic columns and arches. Its delightful vaulted ceiling is painted with vine trellises, birds and putti, and the wall-panels are decorated in the Pompeian style. The courtyard is enclosed by walls with Ionic columns, niches and reliefs.

The courtyard is closed by a loggia, which preserves some of its delicate stucco ornaments by Ammannati. Curved stairways lead down from the top of the loggia to the nymphaeum, an architectural element which was frequently copied in later 16th-century Italian villas. Although it has lost much of its original decoration, the fountains are adorned with statues symbolising the Tiber and the Arno. On the lower level are a ceiling relief of the miraculous finding of the Aqua Virgo and four marble caryatids.

Formal gardens extend on either side of the courtyard. On the right is a reconstruction of the Temple of Aletrium (Alatri) by Count Adolfo Cozza (1891), according to the account of Vitruvius and the evidence of the remains in Alatri itself (southeast of Rome).

HIGHLIGHTS OF THE COLLECTION

The first rooms show finds from the **necropolis of Vulci**, one of the most important Etruscan cities of southern Etruria (now right on the border between northern Lazio and Tuscany) during the 7th–4th centuries BC. On display are some superb vases, some of them imports from Greece (Corinthian ware, Attic red- and black-figure vases) and others of local production. A superb 6th-century BC black-figure hydria showing a procession of horsemen was returned here from the Museum of Fine Arts, Boston.

A spiral staircase leads down to a reconstructed tomb from the Banditaccia necropolis in Cerveteri and the **Tomb of the Funeral Couch** from Tarquinia, its walls showing splendid painted scenes of feasting and funeral games.

Also from Cerveteri is the 7th-century BC **Tomb of the Lions**, a terracotta sarcophagus with long-fanged lions on the roof-shaped lid. One of the most famous of all Etruscan artefacts is the 6th-century BC terracotta *Sarcofago degli Sposi* from Cerveteri. The reclining figures on the lid represent a husband and wife (*a detail is illustrated on p. 377*) on a couch at a feast. This remarkable and rare sculpture shows the extraordinary skill of the Etruscan artist, evident in the expressive rendering of the features, especially the hands and feet.

Finds from Pyrgi, the Etruscan port of Cerveteri, include the pieced-together fragments of a remarkable temple relief (470–460 BC) illustrating the myth of the Seven against Thebes. In the same room are some of the terracotta antefixes that decorated the 'Twenty Cells' (small rooms thought to have housed the temple prostitutes who accounted for the enormous wealth of the sanctuary). Their iconography is unique: the devil in the form of a cockerel, interpreted as Lucifer, bringer of light, and a running sun figure. The three gold-leaf plaques also in this section date from the 5th century BC. Two of them have inscriptions in Etruscan and one in Phoenician referring to the dedication of the sanctuary to the Phoenician 'Astarte' and the Etruscan 'Uni'. They are important as they are the oldest historical inscriptions known from pre-Roman Italy.

MUSEO ETRUSCO
Painted terracotta bust of Juno (4th century BC) from Falerii.

The splendid **Cista Ficoroni** is the largest and most beautiful surviving example of the objects known as *cistae*. These were toilet boxes (or modern-day 'vanity cases') made for the mirrors, strigils, spatulae and other implements used in the care of the body, and virtually unique to Praeneste (modern Palestrina), about 40km east of Rome, which was a flourishing centre of Latin and Volscian civilisation from the 7th century BC up until the Roman era. The *cistae* are usually cylindrical, with engraved decoration in repoussé or pierced work, lids adorned with small figures, and feet and handles of cast metal. This one is named after Francesco Ficoroni, who bought it and gave it to the Kircher collection. On the body is a representation of the boxing match between Pollux and the Argonauts and Amykos, King of the Bebryces, an elaborate design pure in its lines and evidently inspired by some large Greek composition, possibly a wall-painting by Mykon for the Temple of the Dioscuri at Athens. It includes a splendid depiction of an Argonaut limbering up at a punchbag slung from a tree. The names of both the maker and the buyer of the cista are recorded in an archaic Latin inscription (*Novios Plautios med Romai fecit, dindia Macolmia fileai dedit*); it was no doubt a wedding present.

The **Castellani jewellery collection**, amassed in the 19th century by Augusto Castellani, a member of a renowned firm of goldsmiths (*see p. 330*), is one of the finest collections of antique jewellery in existence, with Minoan, Hellenistic, Roman and Oriental pieces. The collection is displayed in two parts: antique pieces on one side and on the other, copies or reworkings made by the Castellani jewellers in the 19th century.

Finds from **Capena and the Ager Faliscus** (Narce, Falerii) include a delightful 3rd-century BC plate showing a mother elephant with her calf holding onto her tail. It is thought to have been inspired by the first elephants to be seen by the Romans, which came in the triumphal procession of Marcus Curius Dentatus following his defeat of Pyrrhus of Epirus. From Falerii comes the beautiful rhyton in the shape of a dog's head by the Brygos painter (5th century BC) and finds from the Sanctuary of Apollo, including a model of a sheep's liver used for divination and a superb painted bust of Juno (4th century BC; *illustrated above*), showing the goddess as a haughty, jewel-bedecked matron.

The largest of the cities of the so-called Etruscan Confederation was probably **Veio**, only 17km from Rome, whose territory included the right bank of the Tiber and the salt-works at its mouth. It was at the height of its power between the 8th and 6th centuries BC and its position brought it into frequent conflict with Rome: it was finally captured and destroyed by the Romans in 396, after a historic siege of ten years. The most celebrated of the finds are the **statues of Hercules and Apollo** from a temple sanctuary. These colossal statues in polychrome terracotta (restored) formed part of a votive group representing the contest between Apollo and Hercules for the Ceryneian Hind in the presence of Mercury and Minerva, and are a splendid example of Etruscan sculpture of the 6th century BC. They were probably the work of Vulca, a famous sculptor who was born in Veio, and is said to have been summoned to Rome by Tarquinius Superbus to execute the statue and decorations for the Temple of Capitoline Jupiter.

VIA VENETO & THE LUDOVISI DISTRICT

Porta Pinciana (*map p. 652, C2–C3*) is a handsome fortified gateway erected by the emperor Honorius c. 403 and since enlarged. On either side can be seen a long stretch of the Aurelian Walls (272–9; *see p. 296*) with 18 turrets.

Inside Porta Pinciana, at Largo Fellini, begins the broad and tree-lined **Via Veneto**, opened in 1886 and renamed Via Vittorio Veneto after a conclusive victory by the Italian army over the Austrians in 1918. It is lined with luxury hotels, huge mansions (one of which houses the US Embassy) and elegant cafés with tables outside. The street was especially fashionable for its ambience of *la dolce vita* in the 1960s (after the success of Federico Fellini's film of that name). Fellini is recorded in a plaque set up in 1995 on the corner of Via Ludovisi.

Via Veneto runs through the aristocratic **Ludovisi district**, named after the beautiful park of the Villa Ludovisi once on this site. Cardinal Ludovico Ludovisi, nephew of Pope Gregory XV, first acquired land here in 1621, and he had bought some 19 hectares by the time of his death: the garden he laid out here was much admired by John Evelyn. He also began a collection of antique sculpture which became famous: some one hundred pieces of it were bought by the state in 1901 and are now part of the Museo Nazionale Romano (exhibited in Palazzo Altemps; *see p. 190*). The park and collection were much visited by travellers to Rome and they are mentioned by Goethe (1787), Stendhal (1828) and Henry James (1883).

The last descendant of the family, Ippolita Ludovisi (Princess of Piombino), married Gregorio Boncompagni, Duke of Sora (a descendant of Pope Gregory XIII), and in their nuptial agreement it was decided that the two surnames should be used perpetually by their heirs and descendants. By now the property included an area of some 30 hectares, from the stretch of walls between Porta Pinciana and Porta Salaria (now Piazza Fiume) down to the present Via Boncompagni and Via Ludovisi. In 1883 the Boncompagni Ludovisi were forced (by a retroactive law introduced by the Italian government) to divide their immense wealth between all their relatives and so they decided to destroy the gardens and sell off the huge property as building land. Despite an international outcry, work began in 1885 on felling the trees and laying out new roads. Most of the buildings had been constructed by 1889: one of these is now the **Museo Boncompagni Ludovisi** (*see below*). The only survival of the original villa and gardens is the **Villa Aurora** (*open by previous appointment; see p. 576*), whose luxuriant garden with tall palm trees can be seen high up above walls between Via Lombardia and Via Ludovisi.

MUSEO BONCOMPAGNI LUDOVISI PER LE ARTI DECORATIVI

Map p. 652, D3. Via Boncompagni 18. Open for guided visits Tues–Sun at 9.30, 11, 12.30, 2.30, 4 and 5.30. Visits last 1hr. Free. www.museoboncompagni.beniculturali.it.

Villa Boncompagni Ludovisi was completed by Giovanni Battista Giovenale in the early 20th century. The famous Ludovisi park (*see above*) is recorded in the charming wall decorations in one room. A satellite museum of the Galleria Nazionale d'Arte Moderna, it displays decorative arts and fashion from the Art Nouveau and Art Deco periods (1900–39). It has works by Galileo Chini (including *La Primavera*), a portrait of Princess Blancefior Boncompagni Ludovisi by Philip de László (1925), ceramics and glass by Duilio Cambellotti, *La Lionbruna*, a striking portrait in yellow of a woman in pearls by Giacomo Balla, and the elegant (often glamorous) wardrobe of Palma Bucarelli, director of the Galleria Nazionale d'Arte Moderna from 1942–75.

THE CAPPUCCINI (SANTA MARIA DELLA CONCEZIONE)

Map p. 652, C3. Church open Mon–Sat 7–1 & 3–6, Sun and holidays 9.30–12 & 3.30–6. Crypt open daily 9–7, last entry 6.30. T: 06 88 80 3695, cappucciniviaveneto.it.

This monastery church is architecturally simple and unpretentious, in accordance with Franciscan ideals and in strong contrast to the Baroque works of its time (1626). Its founder was Cardinal Antonio Barberini, brother of Urban VIII, whose burial place in the church is marked by an inscription on the pavement in front of the high altar, which reads *hic jacet pulvis, cinis et nihil* ('here lies nothing but dust and ashes'). The paintings are by important artists, all of whom produced many works for Roman churches and were born in the 1580s or 1590s: Honthorst, Domenichino, Andrea Sacchi and Pietro da Cortona. The delightful *St Michael* in the first chapel on the south side is by Guido Reni. A painting of *St Francis* (*sadly kept locked away in the monastery*) is considered by some scholars to be by Caravaggio (and by others to be a contemporary copy): the simple Franciscan life of poverty was a favourite subject for this great painter, who was out of sympathy with the pomp and excesses of the contemporary Church.

The church is visited mostly for its particularly macabre **cemetery-crypt**, where a corridor leads past five subterranean chapels which were decorated from the 17th century onwards with the bones and skeletons of over 4,000 Capuchins, arranged in patterns. It has for centuries been one of the 'sights' of Rome. There is also a museum on the Capuchin Order.

Trastevere

*Trastevere is a lively district, and today one of the most fashionable places to live
in central Rome. However, it still manages to retain something of its neighbourhood
atmosphere. Highlights for the visitor are the churches of San Crisogono, Santa Cecilia,
Santa Maria in Trastevere with their early mosaics and 13th-century works by Pietro
Cavallini; the Renaissance Villa Farnesina with frescoes by Raphael; and, in the south
of the district, San Francesco a Ripa, with a monument by Bernini.*

Trastevere (*map p. 654, A3–B4*), the area 'across the Tiber' (*trans Tiberim*) on
its right bank, lies below the Janiculum hill and the Vatican. Since Roman
times there have been numerous artisans' houses and workshops here and the
inhabitants of this essentially popular district of Rome were known for their proud
and independent character. For the visitor it is still a distinctive district of the city and
you can often see the inhabitants greeting each other or sharing time in a local café,
or passing the time of day in a neighbourhood shop. There are numerous vines and
plants outside the houses, and an increasing number of well-known restaurants and
trattorie. Trastevere is a pleasant district in which to stroll. Cars are banned from some
of the streets by the simple (but unobtrusive) method of laying large travertine blocks
at their entrances.

HISTORY OF TRASTEVERE

This was the 'Etruscan side' of the river, and only after the destruction of Veio by
Rome in 396 BC (*see p. 377*) did it come under Roman rule. In earliest Republican
days this bank of the Tiber was occupied by Lars Porsenna in his attempt to replace
the Tarquins on the Roman throne. Along the waterfront and on the higher ground
at the foot of the Janiculum, suburban villas were built by the aristocracy. One of
these next to the Villa Farnesina, dating from the Augustan age and then destroyed,
was excavated in the late 19th century and its magnficent wall-paintings are now
preserved in the Museo Nazionale Romano in Palazzo Massimo. Under the Empire
the district became densely populated by artisans and dock-workers. It was probably
not entirely enclosed by walls before the time of Aurelian (270–5).

Trastevere was home to a great number of Jews, who are recorded here as early as
the 2nd century BC, before they were confined to the Ghetto on the other side of the
river. During the Risorgimento the district was a republican stronghold.

The busy Viale di Trastevere at the foot of Ponte Garibaldi, dating from 1888 (and efficiently served by tram no. 8 from Piazza Venezia), runs down the middle of Trastevere

dividing the district into two distinct parts: that to the east is the more tranquil, while that to the west has the more important monuments and is described immediately below. A pleasant approach is by **Ponte Sisto** (*map p. 654, A3*), a footbridge over the Tiber rebuilt for Sixtus IV (1471–84), probably by Baccio Pontelli, to replace an ancient bridge. It was beautifully restored in 2000 and provided with a new brick and travertine balustrade. The untidy piazza on the Trastevere side is named after the popular local poet 'Trilussa' (Carlo Alberto Salustri, 1871–1950), who is recorded here in a monument.

THE TIBER AND TRASTEVERE

The first bridge across the Tiber was the Pons Sublicius, said to have been built by Ancus Marcius, fourth king of Rome, to connect the Janiculum hill with the centre of the city. Today its site is occupied by the Ponte Aventino, from which there is a good view of the excavations of the Roman port which lined the left bank of the Tiber (along the present Lungotevere Testaccio). In 193–174 BC a market was constructed here, backed by the Porticus Aemilia, a wharf with extensive storehouses some 500m in length.

The Roman Via Aurelia (the present Via della Lungaretta and Via della Lungarina in Trastevere) had to be raised on a viaduct in order to avoid the waters of the Tiber in flood. The inundations continued for centuries (as can be seen in the numerous plaques all over the city recording them) until 1870, when the worst flood since 1637 occurred—the waters reaching a height of over 17m. It was then that the decision was taken to construct the present embankments in travertine (and the 'Lungotevere' avenues were built), which put a stop to the floods but at the same time irreparably altered the townscape and alienated the river from the buildings along its banks.

Via del Moro leads left into one of the oldest parts of Trastevere, with a maze of winding streets. It is worth taking time to study the architecture and decorative details of the simple houses here (many of which curiously still bear plaques recording the names of their past owners). Take Vicolo de' Renzi right into a quiet little piazza with a few trees and vines. The winding Vicolo del Piede and Via della Fonte d'Olio, where many of the house-fronts are painted in deep russet colours, continue to Piazza Santa Maria in Trastevere.

PIAZZA DI SANTA MARIA IN TRASTEVERE

The delightful Piazza di Santa Maria in Trastevere (*map p. 654, A3*) is filled with the sound of water from its fountain, of Roman origin, said to be on the site of a fountain of pure oil. As the inscriptions record, it was restored over the centuries by some of the most important architects at work in the city: Donato Bramante, Giacomo della Porta, Bernini and (most recently, in 1692) by Carlo Fontana. Today it provides a centrepiece to the square as well as a nice place to sit and enjoy the scene. Palazzo di San Calisto was rebuilt in the 17th century; it is the grandest of the russet, beige and buff-brown palaces in the square, their colour characteristic of old Rome.

THE BASILICA OF SANTA MARIA IN TRASTEVERE

Map p. 654, A3. Open 7.30–9 (Aug 8–12 & 4–9). At 8.30pm every day there is a service of prayers and organ music by the Comunità di Sant'Egidio (see p. 240), when the church is usually full and wonderfully lit. The best natural light by which to see the mosaics is in the morning (if there is sun) since then they are lit from the windows on the left.

The large basilica dates mainly from the 12th century and preserves some beautiful mosaics from that period, as well as a number of other important works of art. The church was constructed by Julius I (337–52) and was probably the first church in Rome dedicated to the Virgin, following the popularity of her cult after the Council of Ephesus of 431 declared her to be the Mother of God. According to legend, a hostel for veteran soldiers existed near the site, and some sort of Christian foundation is known to have existed here under St Calixtus (217–22). The great basilica of Julius I was rebuilt in 1140 by Innocent II (he came from a well-to-do family of Trastevere) and slightly modified later.

The **façade** is unusual since it has a long mosaic panel beneath the tympanum dating from the 12th–13th centuries showing the Madonna and Child flanked by ten female figures, eight of whom are in royal regalia, while the other two are dressed more simply. They all carry lamps, two of them extinguished. The iconography of this scene is unique and its significance uncertain (the identification with the Wise and Foolish Virgins is disputed). Above rises the typical Romanesque campanile. The portico is crowned by four statues, added by Carlo Fontana in 1702 and inside, its walls are covered with an interesting lapidary collection, including Roman and medieval fragments, many of them with Christian symbols such as the dove. The three doorways incorporate Roman friezes.

Interior of Santa Maria in Trastevere

In the splendid 12th-century interior the nave and aisles are separated by vast granite columns from various ancient buildings, some with fine bases and (damaged) capitals. The gilded wooden ceiling was designed by Domenichino (1617), who painted the central *Assumption*, and the ceiling in the crossing has a high-relief of the same scene (16th century). The Cosmatesque pavement (made up from old material) and the decoration on the walls of the nave, on the triumphal arch, and the marble choir screen were executed when the church was remodelled by Pius IX in the 19th century. At this time also the baldacchino over the high altar was made by Virginio Vespignani: it fits its setting very well. Near the twisted paschal candlestick is the spot on which a miraculous fountain of oil is supposed to have flowed for a whole day in the year of Christ's Nativity.

The wonderful **mosaics of the triumphal arch and apse** (1140) are particularly fine (*coin-operated light at the foot of the sanctuary steps on the left*), with exqui-

SANTA MARIA IN TRASTEVERE
Detail of the 12th–13th-century façade mosaic. Crowned figures with burning lamps and veiled
figures with extinguished lamps make their way in procession towards the Virgin and Child.

site details including fruit and flowers on the soffit of the arch: on the arch itself,
the Cross with the symbolic Alpha and Omega between the seven candlesticks and
the Evangelical emblems; at the sides, Isaiah and Jeremiah beside two palm trees,
and above them the rare and touching symbol of the caged bird, representing Christ
imprisoned because of the sins of man ('Christus Dominus captus est in peccatis nos-
tris': *Lamentations, 4:20, Vulgate version*). In the semi-dome, Christ and the Virgin are
shown enthroned side by side beneath the Hand of God bearing a wreath and the monogram of Constantine. On the right are Sts Peter, Cornelius, Julius and Calepodius; on
the left Sts Calixtus and Lawrence, and Pope Innocent II with a model of the church.
A frieze of lambs in the apse below, reminiscent of many similar mosaic decorations,
divides the scene from the six rectangles below with more exquisite mosaics (c. 1291)
illustrating the life of Mary (from her birth to her death) by Pietro Cavallini, a painter
and mosaicist who worked almost entirely in Rome, though little of secure attribution
now survives. The best examples of his work are in Trastevere, here and in the convent of Santa Cecilia. Between late 16th-century frescoes by one of the best Florentine
Counter-Reformation artists, Agostino Ciampelli, is a mosaic rectangle (1290) with St
Peter and St Paul presenting the donor, Bertoldo Stefaneschi, to the Madonna.

To the right of the choir are the Armellini monument (1524), with sculptures by
Michelangelo Senese, and the **Chapel of the Winter Choir**, with decorations after
Domenichino's designs. The chapel was restored by Henry Stuart, Duke of York, when
he was titular cardinal of the church in 1759–61 (hence the royal arms above the gate).
Henry was the youngest son of James III, the Old Pretender, who was nominated cardinal while living at the Jacobite court in Rome: as 'Henry IX' he was the last of the
pretenders to the English throne (*see p. 158*).

The huge organ was constructed in the 16th century. To the left of the choir is the
Altemps Chapel, decorated with frescoes and stuccoes by Pasquale Cati (1588),
including a scene of the *Council of Trent*, showing serried ranks of prelates attending a session, with allegorical figures in the foreground. On the altar is a precious but

very damaged painting, the *Madonna of Clemency*, where the Virgin is shown flanked by angels, a remarkable Byzantine work thought to date from the 8th century or earlier. On the wall outside the chapel is the **tomb of Cardinal Stefaneschi** (d. 1417) signed by Magister Paulus (the serene effigy has decorative details on the vestments and the cushion); Paulus also probably carved the monument here to Cardinal Filippo d'Alençon (d. 1397), which has his effigy as well as a relief of the *Dormition of the Virgin*. In the sacristy corridor (*usually closed*) are two exquisite tiny 1st-century Roman **mosaics from Palestrina**, one of marsh birds and the other a port scene.

The last chapel in the north aisle, the **Avila Chapel**, was designed by Antonio Gherardi (1680–6), with a remarkable Baroque dome supported by angels and a very unusual altar with an odd perspective device. Between the third and second chapel is the **tomb of Innocent II** (d. 1143), erected by Pius IX in 1869.

The charming 15th-century **aumbry** at the head of the nave is by Mino del Reame.

TO PORTA SETTIMIANA

Just out of Piazza di Santa Maria in Trastevere, take the road that skirts the side of the basilica (and its garden wall, where a pine tree shades an orange tree).

In Piazza Sant'Egidio is the **Museo di Roma in Trastevere** (*map p. 654, A3; open 10–8, closed Mon; T: 06 58 97 123, museodiromaintrastevere.it*), illustrating the 19th- and early 20th-century history of this district. The contents include drawings and engravings of Roman street scenes and views by Bartolomeo Pinelli; paintings of 19th-century Rome (works by Ippolito Caffi and Gino Severini); charming life-size tableaux of Roman scenes by Orazio Amato based on paintings by Pinelli; the reconstructed studio of the poet Trilussa; and objects from the studio of the musician Maestro Alessandro Vessella (1860–1929).

The pleasant Via della Scala, with lots of small shops and cafés, passes the quaint Vicolo del Cedro. The ornate church of **Santa Maria della Scala** (1592) contains a painting of the *Beheading of St John the Baptist in Prison* by Gerrit van Honthorst (over the first altar on the right). This is a typical night scene by this painter, nicknamed *delle notti* ('of the nights'), illuminated only by torchlight. The ciborium over the high altar is by Carlo Rainaldi (1647). The **Pharmacy of Santa Maria della Scala** is the successor to one administered by the monks of a Carmelite monastery here: the old 17th-century pharmacy upstairs can be seen by appointment (*usually on Sat mornings; T: 06 58 06 233; or ring at the door on the left at the entrance to the chemist's shop*).

Via della Scala ends at **Porta Settimiana**, incorporated in the 3rd-century Aurelian Walls (*see p. 296*) and rebuilt by Alexander VI (1492–1503). Trastevere was once defended by the walls, which led away from the river here all the way up to Porta San Pancrazio on the Janiculum, where the Via Aurelia left the city. From Porta San Pancrazio the walls, still partly preserved, lead down southeast to rejoin the Tiber at Porta Portese. A branch of the ancient Via Aurelia passed through the walls at this gate, following the right bank of the Tiber towards the Vatican. Inside the gate, a restaurant with a garden now occupies a house once thought to be that of Raphael's mistress, known as 'La Fornarina' (*see p. 340*). Outside the gate begins **Via della Lungara**, the longest of all the straight streets built by the Renaissance popes. It was laid out c. 1507 by Julius II to connect Trastevere with the Borgo around St Peter's and the Vatican. It leads to Palazzo Corsini and Villa Farnesina.

PALAZZO CORSINI
(GALLERIA NAZIONALE D'ARTE ANTICA)

Map p. 654, A3. Open 8.30–7.30; closed Tues. T: 06 48 14 591, galleriacorsini.benicul-turali.it. Three-day ticket available, valid also for Palazzo Barberini. Very well labelled and handsheets available in each room.

Palazzo Corsini, the residence of the Florentine Corsini family from the 18th century up until the end of the 19th, is a grand palace with a garden of palms overlooking the Botanical Gardens. Here their library and art collection was formed and is still preserved as part of the Galleria Nazionale d'Arte Antica, which is divided between this palace and Palazzo Barberini (*see p. 338*).

The palace was built by Cardinal Domenico Riario in the early 16th century. It was rebuilt on a grand scale by Ferdinando Fuga for Cardinal Neri Maria Corsini, nephew of Clement XII (Lorenzo Corsini) in 1732–6, when the family moved from Florence to Rome. In 1800 Madame Letitia Bonaparte, Napoleon I's mother, came to live here.

The Corsini collection of paintings was founded in the 17th century by the uncle of Clement XII. Works were added by Clement himself while he was still cardinal, and then by his nephew Cardinal Neri. In 1827 their descendant Tommaso rearranged the collection and opened it to the public, but after his death the family moved back to Florence. In 1883 the palace was sold and the collection was donated to the state.

THE COLLECTION

The Corsini collection is particularly rich in 17th- and 18th-century paintings of the Roman, Neapolitan and Bolognese schools, but also has important works by Fra' Angelico, Rubens, Van Dyck, Murillo and Caravaggio. It was beautifully rehung in 2009 following the 18th-century Corsini inventories. The gallery still preserves its atmosphere of a grand private collection and is very well looked after.

Anticamera: This also serves as the ticket office. The largest painting in the room is *Christ among the Doctors* by Luca Giordano.

On the right of the door into the next room, in a special show case since its restoration in 2013, is an exquisite **triptych by Fra' Angelico**, with the *Last Judgement*, flanked by the *Ascension* and *Pentecost*, thought to have been painted by this famous Florentine artist on one of his two visits to Rome (the first in around 1445 and the second around 1450–5). The Last Judgement was a subject Fra' Angelico often painted. Above it hangs *Judith and Holofernes* by Piazzetta.

Prima Galleria: On the entrance wall is a charming small painting of a hare by Dürer's imitator and follower, Hans Hoffmann. In the centre of the wall opposite the windows is Poussin's *Triumph of Ovid*. On the table in front of the *Dream of Jacob* by Donato Creti is an elegant small bronze of the *Baptism of Christ* by Algardi. The other small bronzes in this room are by Antonio Susini (on the console table on the end wall) and (by the windows) Giovanni Battista Foggini. In the middle of the window wall (with a view of the fine palms in the garden) is Salvator Rosa's *Prometheus*, showing the eagle devouring his liver.

Galleria del Cardinale: On the wall opposite the windows: *Ecce Homo* by Guercino; *Birth of the Virgin* by Annibale Carracci; *Madonna 'della paglia'* (named after the beautifully painted straw from the manger) by Van Dyck. This was probably finished during the artist's stay in Italy. The *Archangel Gabriel* by Carlo Maratta is displayed above a *Madonna and Child* by Orazio Gentileschi (in the Corsini inventories attributed to his master and friend, Caravaggio). In the centre above the console table (on which is displayed a bronze by Algardi of the *Young Hercules with a Snake*), is a *Holy Family* by Fra' Bartolomeo. By the door, *Andromeda* by Francesco Furini and (below) a good copy of Raphael's portrait of Julius II. On the window wall are works by Carlo Dolci and battle scenes by Borgognone and Salvator Rosa, and (at the end) a copy of Titian's portrait of Philip II of Spain by an unknown Flemish painter.

Camera del Camino: Named after a fireplace no longer here. In the centre is the wonderfully preserved ***Corsini Throne***, a comfortable ancient marble 'chair' found when digging the foundations for the Corsini Chapel in St John Lateran in 1734. It has exquistite low reliefs of a wild boar hunt below a frieze of warriors and hoplites. There is a frieze of ivy tendrils and figures on the base. It is thought to be a Roman copy of an Etruscan work of the 5th century BC, perhaps made in the 1st or 2nd century BC, but it remains another of Rome's mysterious 'thrones' (*see Ludovisi Throne; p. 195*).

On the entrance wall, *Head of an Old Man* by Rubens (a study for a figure in the *Adoration of the Magi* now in the Prado), and, on the next wall, a portrait of Cardinal Alessandro Farnese in his crimson robes by Perino del Vaga, beside another *Head of a Man* by Rubens and (below) small pastels by Rosalba Carriera. On the last wall: *Christ and the Woman Taken in Adultery* by Rocco Marconi next to a portrait of a grumpy Cardinal Bernardino Clesio by Barthel Bruyn, formerly attributed to Joos van Cleve. The portrait of Wolfgang Tranvelder, in a large hat against a vivid acquamarine background, is a very fine work by Hans Maler zu Schwarz.

Camera dell'Alcova: With its two columns and ceiling decorated by the Zuccari brothers, this room survives from the 16th-century Palazzo Riario. On the table is Bernini's marble portrait of Pope Alexander VII Chigi and above it is a portrait of Queen Christina of Sweden (*see p. 401*), who is believed to have died in this room in 1689. She is here shown by the painter Justus van Egmont in the guise of the huntress Diana. Also on this wall is *St Sebastian Tended by Angels* by Rubens, who was here clearly influenced by Michelangelo's Sistine ceiling, which he saw when he first came to Rome.

Gabinetto Verde: Displays numerous portraits. On the entrance wall: Cardinal Neri Corsini by Baciccia and (below) Ferdinando de' Medici by Alessandro Allori. The *Portrait of a Man* (possibly Pietro Strozzi) is by Pier Francesco di Jacopo Foschi, and the *Portrait of a Man holding a Book* is by Franciabigio. On the wall opposite the window, Cosimo III de' Medici is by the court portrait painter Justus Suttermans. The marble bust of Pope Clement XII Corsini is by Pietro Bracci. On the next wall, the *Madonna* (with the Child fast asleep) is by Sassoferrato.

Camera Verde: On the entrance wall is a *Madonna and Child* by the 17th-century Spanish painter Murillo, one of his finest versions of a subject for which he remained famous up until the 19th century, when his works fell somewhat from favour due to their over-sweet tones. On the opposite wall, the *St George and the Dragon* in a wonderful landscape is by Francesco Francia. The *Madonna and Child with Saints*, surrounded by little scenes from the life of Christ, is a beautiful work by Giovanni da Milano, the only painting in Rome by this very skilled Lombard artist and his first known work (c. 1355). On the right of the door is a tiny *Crowning of the Virgin* by Orcagna and (on the window wall) two very small portable triptychs by Tuscan masters working in the 14th century. In front of the window is a marble *Psyche and Zephyrus* by the sculptor John Gibson, who first came to Rome in 1817 and remained here for most of his life. He worked for two years in the studio of Canova, was also influenced by Thorvaldsen and became the most important British Neoclassical sculptor.

Between the windows is hung Caravaggio's *St John the Baptist*, shown as a boy (in the Wilderness) in a splendid red cloak with a thick mop of hair covering his eyes. This saint was often painted by Caravaggio. On the table beneath it is the little '*Coppa Corsini*', a silver goblet dating from the 1st century AD illustrated with the Judgement of Orestes.

The **last room** contains the collection of paintings made on the occasion of beatifications and canonisations announced during the pontificate of the Corsini pope Clement XII (1730–40): they were commissioned to decorate the churches, including St Peter's, where the ceremonies took place.

The palace also houses the **Biblioteca Corsiniana**, founded here by the Corsini in 1754. At the time it was the most important library in Rome, together with that in the Vatican. It has been preserved intact and has a valuable collection of incunabula, manuscripts and autographs.

Here also is the **Accademia Nazionale dei Lincei**, founded by Prince Federico Cesi in 1603 for the promotion of learning, and said to be the oldest surviving institution of its kind. Galileo was a Lincean. The **Fondazione Caetani**, whose object is to promote scientific knowledge of the Muslim world, also has its seat here.

THE ORTO BOTANICO

Via Corsini (with a magnolia tree protected by a fence) leads to the Orto Botanico (*map p. 654, A3; open Mon–Sat 9–6.30; Nov–Feb 9–5.30; T: 06 49 91 7017, ortobotanicoitalia. it*). This is one of the most important botanical gardens in Italy, famous for its palms and yuccas. It covers some twelve hectares and is beautifully kept (it is a lovely place to picnic). The gardens were founded on the Janiculum in 1660 and have been on this site only since 1883, when Tommaso Corsini donated the gardens of Palazzo Corsini (*see above*) to the state.

Near the entrance are two tall cedars, beneath which are succulents. An avenue of palms leads to a fountain installed for the Palazzo Corsini by Ferdinando Fuga in 1750. A path leads uphill left to the rose garden (*entered up a flight of steps some way along the path; keep left*), specialising in species known to have been cultivated in Rome in the 17th and 18th centuries. The path continues uphill past ferns and bamboo and a rock garden. At the top of the gardens is woodland with ancient oaks and ilex. In this area of the gardens a Baroque staircase survives, and outside the fence there is a 17th-century ornamental fountain. There are several ancient plane trees here. The path continues to the edge of the gardens—from which there is view of the cupola of the Pantheon (above the trees to the left) and the little spire of Sant'Ivo—and then descends past conifers and sequoia to the foot of the monumental staircase. A signposted path leads left from here down to the Physic Garden, where raised brick beds contain some 300 medicinal plants. Near a pond with numerous aquatic species is a low greenhouse of cacti. The fine 19th-century glasshouse beyond preserves a rare collection of orchids. Near the exit is a garden of aromatic herbs, which can be identified by the blind by smell or touch.

VILLA FARNESINA

Map p. 654, A3. Open 9–2; closed Sun except 2nd Sun of the month when it is open 9–5. T: 06 68 02 7268, www.villafarnesina.it. Also open on request to groups of at least 30; for reservations, see website.

The Renaissance Villa Farnesina is one of the loveliest villas in Rome. It was built by Baldassare Peruzzi from Siena (1508–11; his most important early work) as the suburban residence of a fellow Sienese, the banker Agostino Chigi, who controlled the markets of the East and became treasurer of the Papal States in 1510. Here Chigi, known as 'the Magnificent', would entertain Pope Leo X, cardinals, ambassadors, artists and men of letters in grand style. At a celebrated banquet in a loggia overlooking the Tiber (demolished in the 19th century), as a demonstration of Chigi's extravagance, silver plates and dishes were thrown into the river after every course (it was later revealed that a net had been in position to recover them). Today the villa, in very good condition, still retains something of the sumptuous atmosphere it must have had in those days. Chigi was also a patron of Raphael, and the villa preserves delightful early 16th-century frescoes by the artist and his school.

When in 1580 Cardinal Alessandro Farnese came to live here, it received its present name. Through the Farnese it was inherited by the Bourbons of Naples in 1731, and since 1927 it has been the property of the state.

The entrance is now through the pretty **garden** with low box hedges, where citrus fruits (lemons, pink grapefriut, lime, oranges), antique roses, little medlar trees and quince trees grow. Garden benches provide very pleasant places to sit.

THE LOGGIA OF GALATEA

The painted decoration in the villa was carried out between 1510 and 1519 for Agostino Chigi by artists he called to Rome, mostly from his native Siena. The **Loggia of Galatea** has a ceiling frescoed by the architect of the villa, Peruzzi, with the constellations forming Chigi's horoscope. The lunettes, with scenes from Ovid's *Metamorphoses*, are by Sebastiano del Piombo, who came from Venice to carry out this commission for Chigi, and who was to influence Raphael (*see p. 403*). Sebastiano also painted the giant Polyphemus on the wall near Raphael's celebrated *Galatea*. The latter is a superb composition showing the sea-nymph in a deep red cloak being pulled over the sea on a scallop shell drawn by dolphins. This was Raphael's first depiction of a mythological subject and, since it interrupts the decorative sequence, it seems to have been painted just after the works here by Sebastiano. The colossal monochrome charcoal head in one of the lunettes, a striking work, is now also ascribed to Peruzzi. The other scenes were added in the 17th century by Gaspard Dughet.

THE LOGGIA OF CUPID AND PSYCHE

This festive loggia formerly opened directly onto the garden. The ceiling has famous frescoes illustrating the story of Cupid and Psyche in a beautiful painted pergola with festoons of fruit and flowers beneath a bright blue sky. The innovative decorative pro-gramme was provided by Raphael—who probably also made the preparatory cartoons, since drawings of some of the scenes survive by him—but the paintings were executed by his pupils, Giulio Romano, Francesco Penni, Giovanni da Udine and Raffaellino del Colle, in 1517. The loggia was well restored in 1693 and again in 1997. The story is taken from Apuleius' *The Golden Ass*, written in the 2nd century AD and the only Latin novel to have survived in its entirety. The young girl Psyche incites the jealousy of Venus because of her beauty: Venus therefore throws almost impossible obstacles in her way before she can finally drink the cup of immortality in order to marry Cupid.

On the short wall towards the Loggia of Galatea, the first pendentive shows *Venus and Cupid*; on the long wall, opposite the garden, is the beautiful group of the *Three Graces with Cupid*; *Venus with Juno and Ceres*; *Venus on her way to visit Jupiter* (in a chariot and accompanied by doves); *Venus talking to Jupiter* (the god has grey hair and a beard and is defended by an eagle). On the end wall is *Mercury in Flight*. On the garden wall, Psyche (always dressed in green) is shown giving a phial to Venus; also here is the *Kiss between Cupid and Jupiter*; and finally *Mercury accompanying Psyche to Olympus*. In between these pendentives are playful cupids, with birds and symbols of the gods. In the centre of the vault are two painted cloths, shown as if draped from the pergola, on which the happy end to the legend is portrayed in two scenes: the *Council of the Gods* and the *Nuptial Banquet*.

The little room at the end, approached by two doors has a beautifully painted small frieze at the top of the walls with mythological scenes by Peruzzi.

UPPER FLOOR

The **Sala delle Prospettive**, which was used as a drawing-room, has charming *trompe l'oeil* imaginary views of Rome seen between columns and mythological subjects, also by Peruzzi. On the end wall are scribblings made in 1527 during the Sack of Rome by Imperial soldiers. The frieze above has mythological scenes and on the fireplace is Vulcan's forge.

The bedroom, known as the **Sala delle Nozze di Alessandro e Rossana**, contains the *Marriage of Alexander the Great and Roxana* frescoed by another great Sienese painter, Sodoma, probably in 1517. The bedroom scene opposite the windows is particularly fine, with numerous playful cupids.

After his successful campaign in Persia, Alexander proceeded to central Asia but here met with fierce opposition. After three years of intense fighting he decided to make a gesture of reconciliation with the population of Sogdiana (a region now partly in Uzbekistan and partly in Tajikistan) by marrying Roxana, a local princess, in 327 BC. Alexander, with his flowing golden locks, approaches Roxana who sits on her bed with her eyes modestly cast down (while her three serving girls, one black in a turban, are all captivated by the hero). Numerous playful cupids accompany the scene: one is turning a somersault; another seems to be removing Roxana's sandal.

Remains of a **Roman villa** overlooking the Tiber were discovered next to Villa Farnesina in 1879 during work on the river embankment. Dating from the second half of the 1st century BC, it was one of many villas in Trastevere in this period and is thought to have been owned by Julia, Augustus' daughter. Its superb wall-paintings and stuccoes, probably the most beautiful in all Rome, are displayed in the Museo Nazionale Romano in Palazzo Massimo.

VIA DELLA LUNGARETTA & SAN CRISOGONO

Via della Lungaretta (*map p. 654, A3–B3*) is the only dead straight street of old Trastevere, since it is on the line of the ancient Roman Via Aurelia. Although barred to cars, it is always busy, and lined with numerous *trattorie* with tables outside, as well as shops. It passes Via San Gallicano, where you can see the handsome long, low façade of the huge **Hospital of San Gallicano**, its two floors divided by a balcony and incorporating a church in the centre. This remarkable utilitarian building was designed by Filippo Raguzzini in 1724. Opposite the façade of the church of Sant'Agata is the flank of San Crisogono: the main façade looks onto the busy Viale Trastevere.

SAN CRISOGONO

Map p. 654, B3. Open 7–11.30 & 4–7.30; Sun and holidays 8–1 & 4–7.30. The interesting remains of the earliest religious house and 5th-century basilica on the site are preserved below the present church and can be visited at the same times.

This church is often overlooked by visitors because of its uninviting position on the busy Viale Trastevere, but it is of great interest and has a very pleasant atmosphere. It is a church that still fully serves the local inhabitants.

Founded in the 5th century, it was rebuilt in 1129 by its titular cardinal Giovanni da Crema (or John of Crema), who is buried here. As pontifical legate he was sent all over Europe during the so-called Investiture Controversy between the papacy and the Holy Roman Emperor. The church was reconstructed by Giovanni Battista Soria in 1623 for Scipione Caffarelli Borghese, nephew of the cardinal Camillo Borghese who became Pope Paul V. It was restored in 1866. The campanile survives from 1123. The façade and portico date from the 17th century.

The church is dedicated to St Chrysogonus, who was martyred in Aquileia around 304 under the emperor Diocletian. His relics were taken from there to Zara (present-day Zadar) on the Dalmatian coast and in 1202 during the Fourth Crusade were stolen by the Venetians for the church of San Trovaso in Venice. In 1240 they were returned to Zara, and brought here at the end of the 15th or beginning of the 16th century.

The Englishman Stephen Langton (1150–1228), a theologian educated in Paris, was a titular cardinal of this church. He was nominated cardinal and Archbishop of Canterbury in 1207 by his friend Innocent III, but because of the hostility of King John was unable to take possession of that see until 1213. He then supported the feudal barons in drawing up the *Magna Carta* in 1215, which led to the first constitutional struggle in English history.

Interior of San Crisogono

The lovely plan is typical of the early Christian basilicas in Rome. Twenty-two ancient Roman columns separate the nave from the aisles: they were provided with large Ionic capitals in stucco in the 17th century. The triumphal arch is supported by two huge monolithic porphyry columns. The magnificent 13th-century **Cosmatesque pavement** is one of the most beautiful and best-preserved in Rome: when it was restored in the 17th century the Borghese crest of a dragon, in polychrome stone, was substituted for some of the porphyry discs in the paving near the sanctuary. The gilded wood ceiling was also added in the 17th century; in the centre is a copy of a painting by Guercino, *St Chrysogonus in Glory* (the original was removed in 1808).

At the beginning of the south aisle, the highly venerated ***Madonna and Child*** was painted in 1944 as a votive offering for the salvation of Rome during the Second World War (it is surrounded by ex-votos). The other paintings in this aisle, in matching frames, date from the 17th century and include two by Tuscan painters: a beautiful work by Giovanni da San Giovanni (*Three Archangels*; Gabriel is holding a lily) and a *Crucifixion* by Paolo Guidotti.

The **chapel to the right of the sanctuary** was apparently redesigned by Bernini (1677–80), although its style is unusually sober. The two Poli family monuments here have intriguing marble busts (half-figures) by Bernini's pupils (they are leaning on cushions as they look out at us). The baldacchino, by Giovanni Battista Soria, rests on four ancient columns of yellow alabaster. The high altar encloses the 12th-century **reliquary of St Chrysogonus**, seen through a glass niche. On the wall of the apse is a lovely **mosaic**, the *Madonna and Child between St James and St Chrysogonus*, placed here by Soria when it was given its square frame. Made for the church, it is usually attributed to the school of Pietro Cavallini, although some scholars believe it to be one of the earliest works in Rome by the master himself. The handsome carved wood choir stalls date from 1865.

Near the sacristy door in the north aisle are inscriptions relating to the history of the church, including one recording the work carried out by John of Crema (1129) and an exquisite little Cosmatesque wall tabernacle from the earlier church. Off the aisle is the **chapel of the Blessed Anna Maria Giannetti Taigi** (1769–1837; beatified in 1920), with mementoes of her saintly life. Born in Siena, she lived mostly in Rome where she married a butler who worked for the Chigi and had seven children. She was venerated for her great faith and prophetic vision.

Remains of the early Christian church

Beneath the present church, these excavations are entered through the sacristy in the north aisle (*small contribution for the lighting*) and approached down an iron staircase. Take care on the staircase and on the uneven ground below.

A *domus ecclesiae*, or religious house used by a very early Christian community, existed here in the 3rd century: part of its brick masonry survives. In 499 it was recorded that this had been enlarged into a basilican church (considerable remains of which can still be seen) in the early 5th century. In the 8th century Pope Gregory III added an annular crypt. Excavations were first carried out in 1908–28 and have been continued sporadically since 1993. Traces of frescoes from the 8th–10th centuries have been uncovered and are still kept *in situ*, although only fragmentary.

At the bottom of the stairs is the apse of the church and remains of the walls of the crypt built to give access to the martyrs' shrine beneath the altar. Follow the circular wall around to a little central corridor where there is a worn fresco (low down) of three saints, showing St Chrysogonus in the centre, and at the sides the two companions supposedly martyred with him, St Anastasia and a certain St Rufus. The church was orientated towards the west. A few marble steps lead up beside the south wall of the church, with traces of frescoes dating from the 6th–8th centuries (including a roundel with a pope, thought to be Sixtus II). Halfway along the wall you will notice a change in the masonry which distinguishes the earliest building (in brick) from the later basilica. There are two pagan sarcophagi here: the one beautifully carved with the Muses, found in the baptistery, might have been used as a font.

On the other side of the metal stairs is another small room, known as the Secretarium, thought to have been used for the storage of vestments. It has interesting traces of its original 6th–7th-century pavement in white marble tesserae and green serpentine marble discs. The pagan sarcophagus (3rd century) with marine scenes with tritons and nereids was found here; it was reused in the Middle Ages. More traces of frescoes dating from the 8th and 10th centuries can be seen on the north wall of the church: the best-preserved are those from a 10th-century cycle showing the life of St Benedict, with a scene of the saint in a hood healing a leper covered with spots. At the end of the north wall, another metal stairway leads up to the area of the most recent excavations.

VIALE TRASTEVERE TO PIAZZA IN PISCINULA

San Crisogono stands on the busy **Viale Trastevere**, traversed by a tram line as well as buses. Close to the Tiber is Piazza Gioacchino Belli, named after the poet (1791–1863) who wrote popular verses and satirical sonnets in the Roman dialect. The monument here (by Michele Tripisciano; 1913) shows him in a frock coat and top hat. Here is the much-restored 13th-century **Palazzetto dell'Anguillara**, with its corner tower, the last of many which once guarded the district. The picturesque courtyard is a modern reconstruction using ancient material. The building is now the **Casa di Dante**; readings from *The Divine Comedy* have been given here since 1914 (*now Nov–mid-March on Sun 11–12*). The library has the best Dante collection in Italy.

Across the Viale, **Via della Lungaretta** continues straight on past some simple local shops (including an excellent bakery and a delightful second-hand bookshop specialising in English books) to end in **Piazza in Piscinula**, where the restored medieval Casa dei Mattei has a 15th-century loggia and 14th-century cross-mullioned windows. It is worth taking time to study its exterior, since it has many ancient Roman fragments, including two columns with Ionic capitals and a relief with a leafy branch and an inscription.

On the opposite side of the piazza is the little church of **San Benedetto in Piscinula** (*open 8–12 & 4.30–7.30; Mon 7–10; sung Mass around 6.15pm*), which has a Neoclassical facade dating from 1843 and a charming miniature 11th-century campanile with a quaint tiled roof: this is the smallest in Rome and since it still has its bell dated 1069, it is also said to be the oldest. Since 2003 it has been the church of the Heralds of the Gospel, an order founded in 2001. They wear a splendid uniform. Off the vestibule, a fine doorway leads into an ancient cross-vaulted cell in which St Benedict is supposed to have lived. To the left of the entrance to the church is a detached 13th-century fresco of the saint. In the ancient interior, almost square in plan, eight antique columns with diverse capitals divide the nave from the aisles. The old pavement is Cosmatesque. Above the altar is a painting of St Benedict and a damaged fresco of the *Madonna and Child*, both dating from the 15th century.

Via in Piscinula, on the left of the church, leads into a lovely quiet enclave of Trastevere. The corner tabernacle still has its iron roof and lamp, and a grapevine forms a pergola over the street here. In the parallel **Via della Luce**, at no. 21, is the **Pasticceria Innocenti** (*open 8–8 every day; 9.30–2 on Sun*), which has preserved its old machinery and still produces good simple cakes and biscuits, and is a centre of local life. It is a very short walk from here through picturesque streets to the piazza in front of the palace-like facade of the church of Santa Cecilia.

SANTA CECILIA IN TRASTEVERE

Map p. 654, B4. Open 10–1 & 4–7. Roman remains beneath the church open 9.30–12.30 & 4–6.30. To see the very beautiful frescoes by Pietro Cavallini in the Benedictine convent you have to come here between 10 and 12.30, or on Sun between 11.15 and 12.15 (at other times enquire at the entrance to the Roman remains).

Santa Cecilia in Trastevere is an important church built on the site of the house of St Cecilia, which after her martyrdom was adapted to Christian use, probably in the 5th century. In 820 the saint's body was transferred here from the catacombs of San Callisto and a basilica was erected by Paschal I (817–24). It was radically altered from the 16th century onwards, but was partly restored to its original form in 1899–1901.

The elaborate façade was provided by Ferdinando Fuga in the early 18th century as an entrance to the atrium preceding the church, where there is a delightful fountain designed in 1929 around a large ancient Roman marble vase for ceremonial ablutions (which has been outside the basilica since the Middle Ages). The buildings on either side house convents. The slightly leaning campanile and the church portico with four antique Ionic columns bearing a frieze of 12th-century mosaic medallions (including little portraits of St Cecilia; *example illustrated below*) both date from around 1120.

THE MARTYRED ST CECILIA

Cecilia was a patrician lady of the *gens* Caecilia who converted her husband Valerian to Christianity. In 230, during the reign of Alexander Severus, she was shut up in the caldarium of her own baths here to be scalded to death. Emerging unscathed, she was beheaded in another room of her house, but the executioner did such a bad job that she lived for three days afterwards. Her body was rediscovered in 1599 and she was ceremonially re-interred in the church by Pope Clement VIII, after which she became a particularly revered Roman saint. As the reputed inventor of the organ, she is the patron saint of music: on her feast day on 22nd November churches still hold musical services in her honour.

INTERIOR OF SANTA CECILIA

The lovely interior dates from its transformation in the early 18th century into an aisled hall, when grilles were provided in the upper gallery for the nuns to attend services, and a fresco by Sebastiano Conca of the *Coronation of St Cecilia* was installed in the centre of the ceiling. In 1823 the original columns were enclosed in piers. On the

SANTA CECILIA IN TRASTEVERE
Effigy of St Cecilia by Stefano Maderno. The pose shows the saint's body as it was found
when her tomb was opened in 1599, in the presence of the sculptor.

west wall, to the right of the door, is a **monument to Cardinal Niccolò Forteguerri** (d. 1473), who assisted Pius II and Paul II in their suppression of the great feudal clans—a beautiful work attributed to Mino da Fiesole (restored in 1891). Mino, a skilled Renaissance sculptor who worked mostly in Florence, carved a number of other tombs in Roman churches. On the other side of the door is the **tomb of Cardinal Adam Easton** (d. 1398), a distinguished English churchman who was appointed cardinal in 1381, deposed by Urban VI, and reappointed by Boniface IX in 1389. It bears the arms of England.

In the south aisle, the first chapel under the organ loft contains a fresco of the *Crucifixion* (?14th century). A corridor (*access only with special permission*) has landscapes by Paul Bril and a marble figure of St Sebastian attributed to Lorenzetto. Off it is a chapel with the *Beheading of St Cecilia*, an early work by Guido Reni, who also painted the tondo of the *Mystical Marriage of St Cecilia and St Valerian* opposite.

The second chapel in the south aisle is the **Cappella dei Ponziani**, with ceiling frescoes and, on the walls, saints, all by a 15th-century painter from Viterbo called Pastura, who mostly produced frescoes close to the style of Perugino and Pinturicchio. The 18th-century **Cappella delle Reliquie** has a ceiling fresco and painting of St Cecilia, the only painted works by the architect Luigi Vanvitelli. The last chapel contains the elaborate **tomb of Cardinal Rampolla** (1929), who was responsible for the excavations beneath the church. In the chapel at the end of the aisle is a very damaged **13th-century fresco** detached from the portico showing the discovery of the body of St Cecilia, and the apparition of the saint to Paschal I.

In the sanctuary is a very fine **baldacchino** (1293), signed by Arnolfo di Cambio, with lovely marble columns and carvings. It is easy to miss this Gothic work since it is surrounded by so many carvings and decorations from later centuries. The celebrated **effigy of St Cecilia** is Stefano Maderno's masterpiece, carved when he was only 23 years old. As the inscription in the pavement states, the body of the saint is represented lying as it was found when her tomb was opened in 1599, on which occasion the sculptor was present. In beautiful, candid Parian marble, with the saint's face hidden from view by a shroud, this is one of the most dramatic statues in Rome and it is highlighted by its setting in a black marble niche.

The luminous 9th-century **mosaic in the apse** shows Christ blessing by the Greek rite, between Sts Peter, Valerian and Agatha on the right, and Sts Paul, Cecilia and Paschal (with a square nimbus indicating that he was still living at the time the mosaic was made) on the left. The two palm trees symbolise the Garden of Eden, and the phoenix sitting on one of them represents Resurrrection. Below are twelve lambs (the Apostles) emerging from the Holy cities of Bethlehem and Jerusalem, on either side of the Lamb of God in the centre. The long inscription below in nine hexameters records the finding of the relics of St Cecilia by Paschal I and the work he did to embellish the church. The mosaic decoration originally also covered the choir arch.

In the north aisle are three early 17th-century altarpieces by Giovanni Baglione.

THE ROMAN EDIFICES BENEATH THE CHURCH

The excavations have not yet been fully interpreted but are generally thought to consist of two Roman houses (possibly including the house of St Cecilia) that were probably joined together in the 4th century for Christian use. Some scholars also believe there to be remains of an early Christian basilica here. In the various rooms are mosaic pavements and Christian sarcophagi. A 2nd-century room has eight huge, round brick-lined basins let into the floor, probably used for the storage of grain. Another room, with Republican columns, contains a niche with a relief of Minerva in front of an altar. There is also a frescoed room with an ancient large font for total immersion (*not visitable at the time of writing*).

From a wrought-iron door you can look into the **crypt** of the church, which was decorated in the Byzantine style by Giovanni Battista Giovenale (1899–1901), with luminous mosaics by Giuseppe Bravi. Behind a grille are the sarcophagi of St Cecilia, St Valerian and his brother St Tiburtius, St Maximus, and the popes Lucius I and Urban I. The late 19th-century statue of St Cecilia is by Cesare Aureli.

THE FRESCOES IN THE CONVENT

NB: The 15 nuns who live here sell the delicious marmalade they make from the oranges and lemons which grow in the convent garden, as well as soap and other products made from the rosemary and lavender and plants that grow here.

The Benedictine convent is entered to the left of the façade (*for opening times, see above*). From the nuns' choir above the west end of the church you can see the remains of a splendid fresco of the ***Last Judgement*** **by Pietro Cavallini**, which used to be on the inside façade of the old church (and was formerly much more extensive). This is a famous masterpiece of medieval Roman fresco painting (c. 1293), which clearly illustrates how Italian painting began to move forward, leaving Byzantine forms behind. The subtle range of colours produces an extraordinary effect and the figures come to life as in no other pictorial representation of this date in Rome. The angels are particularly striking, with wonderfully colourful wings.

In front of the church is the picturesque **Piazza dei Mercanti**, with fine 15th-century houses, many of them covered with vines and decorated with pots of flowers and exotic tropical plants. The restaurant has old canvas shades protecting its tables outside.

Beyond can be seen the huge building of San Michele a Ripa Grande (*described below*), which stretches as far as Porta Portese. Nearby are the stables of the mounted police.

SAN FRANCESCO A RIPA

The long straight **Via di San Francesco a Ripa** begins at Piazza San Calisto (*map p. 654, A3*), a lively square not usually visited by tourists. The street has numerous local shops and gives you a glimpse of life in this area of the city.

The church of San Francesco a Ripa (*map p. 654, B4; open 7–12 & 4–7.30*) was built in 1231 to replace the old hospice of San Biagio, where St Francis stayed in 1219. In the elaborate interior, dating from different periods, the chapel in the left transept has the famous **tomb monument of the Blessed Lodovica Albertoni**, a late work by Bernini. She is shown lying on a bed in a state of mystical ecstasy, with the luxurious red marble bedcovers spilling onto the ground, splendidly lit from the window on the left. The erotic charge of the composition is somewhat lowered by the ten delightful marble cherubs' heads (each a separate portrait) daringly fixed to the frame of the painting above, a work by Baciccia. Nevertheless, the atmosphere of the chapel is decidedly sensual. In the altar below the effigy is a heart-shaped opening, behind which can be glimpsed some illuminated relics.

The other chapels on the north side have been well restored: adjoining the first is the **burial chapel of Giorgio de Chirico** (*light on left*), the well-known 20th-century painter ('*pictor optimus*'; *see p. 345*) and in the second chapel is an early *Annunciation* by Francesco Salviati. Above the sacristy, lined with 17th-century wood cupboards, is the **cell of St Francis** (*usually shown on request*), which contains relics displayed in an ingenious reliquary, and a copy of a 13th-century painting of the saint by Margaritone d'Arezzo, now in the Vatican Pinacoteca.

ISTITUTO SAN MICHELE A RIPA GRANDE

This huge building (*map p. 654, B4*), with its exceptionally long, bright orange exterior, is the seat of the Italian Cultural Ministry and of the Istituto Centrale del Restauro, as well as a study centre for the preservation of cultural property. In 1686 Monsignor Tommaso Odescalchi, nephew of Innocent XI, founded a hospice and training centre for orphans and vagabond children here. The buildings, around large courtyards, including a church on a Greek-cross plan, were all designed by Carlo Fontana. The Tiber façade was completed after Fontana's death by Nicola Michetti and the church was completed by Luigi Poletti in 1835. From the 18th century up until 1870 other buildings were used as prisons. In the past there have also been numerous artisans' workshops here, as well as a renowned tapestry manufactory.

The Janiculum Hill

*The Janiculum Hill is an area of parks and gardens with good views over Rome.
It is home to the monumental Acqua Paola fountain and to Bramante's famous
little Tempietto next to the interesting church of San Pietro in Montorio.
There are also numerous memorials of Garbaldi and the Risorgimento.*

The ridge of the Janiculum (Gianicolo; *map p. 651*), on the Tiber's right bank,
is not traditionally counted as one of the Seven Hills of Rome. It is a peaceful
area, a good place to stroll, and is adjoined by the huge public park of the Villa
Doria Pamphilj.

Approaches to the Janiculum
*The Janiculum is served by bus no. 115, which runs every 10–15mins from
Lungotevere dei Fiorentini (map p. 654, A1). On foot the prettiest approach is from
Trastevere, taking Via Garibaldi or Vicolo del Cedro behind Piazza Sant'Egidio.
Pairs of mounted police can often be seen patrolling the hill.*

The attractive Via Garibaldi (*map p. 651, D1*), lined with small trees and with raised
pavements on either side, was laid out at the end of the 19th century. It leads uphill
to the Janiculum, past little shops and restaurants. At a bend is the entrance gate (at
no. 27) to **Santa Maria dei Sette Dolori**, an Augustinian convent (*now also a hotel
as there are only three nuns left here; the church is opened on request at the hotel*). The
unfinished façade of the church (1646) was begun by Francesco Borromini in 1643. The
intricate curved design is clear in the mellow brickwork, even though its stone facing
is lacking. In the interior Borromini typically gave the church an unusual plan: oblong
with rounded ends, with two apses in the middle of the long sides and a continuous
series of pillars connected by a heavy cornice. Today it is rather dark and gloomy.

Leave Via Garibaldi at **Via di Porta San Pancrazio** (right). There is an old marble
sarcophagus which serves as a fountain, with a worn lion's head, put up here in 1627
by Urban VIII. The road continues straight uphill. On the right, by a pleasant little
locanda, a short flight of steps leads down to the former entrance gate to the **Bosco
Parrasio**, which belonged to the Academy of Arcadia, founded in 1690 to carry on the
work of the academy which Queen Christina of Sweden had set up ten years before
(*see box opposite*). It exercised a profound influence on Italian literature during the
18th century. In 1786 Goethe was admitted as a 'distinguished shepherd'. Later its
importance waned and in 1926 it was absorbed into the Accademia Letteraria Italiana.
Portraits of Arcadians can be seen at the Museo di Roma.

QUEEN CHRISTINA OF SWEDEN

Queen Christina of Sweden (1626–89) was the daughter of the 'Champion of Protestantism' King Gustavus Adolphus, whom she succeeded in 1632 at the age of six. She was crowned in 1650 and during her brief reign Stockholm became a centre of European culture: the philosopher Descartes was among numerous visitors to her court. A very clever woman who never wished to marry (rumours abounded of her sapphic inclinations), Christina abdicated in 1654 and converted to Roman Catholicism (a religion prohibited in Sweden). Pope Alexander VII received her warmly and even allowed her to stay in the Vatican on her arrival in Rome. She then moved into Palazzo Riario alla Lungara, where she was visited by the leading artists and writers of the city. In 1680 she founded an academy for literary and political discussions. However, she soon became critical of the Counter-Reformation movement and took up with a faction of cardinals who were opposed to certain aspects of the Roman Church. Despite this, she left her library to the Vatican and is buried in the crypt below St Peter's Basilica.

Via di Porta San Pancrazio continues uphill past a large school and ends at a flight of steps which lead up to emerge by the wide (open) gateway into the Passeggiata del Gianicolo and the monumental Acqua Paola, whose abundant waters fill this spot with their sound.

THE ACQUA PAOLA

This huge fountain, the terminus (or *mostra*) of the Acqua Paola (*map p. 651, D2*) was constructed in 1612 by Giovanni Fontana and Flaminio Ponzio for Paul V. As the handsome inscription in the attic states the pope restored the subterranean Aqueduct of Trajan fed by springs near Lake Bracciano about 48km northwest of Rome and by so doing brought much needed water to the district of Trastevere. In the central niche a longer inscription describes a further restoration by Alexander VIII carried out in 1690. The magnificent *mostra* incorporates ancient marble from the Forum of Nerva, and four columns from the facade of Old St Peter's. The water is collected in a large granite basin added by Carlo Fontana in 1690.

From the balustrade of the belvedere (with its travertine benches) there is a wonderful view, with the Vittoriano and Villa Medici (in trees) both prominent on the skyline. On a fine day in winter you can even see the snow-capped Apennines to the east.

Directly below the belvedere is the 18th-century Villa Giraud (Ruspoli), enlarged in 1925, and today painted in bright yellow and brown. It has been the residence of the Spanish ambassador since the end of the Second World War.

From here there is a choice of ways:
- west up to **Porta San Pancrazio and Villa Doria Pamphilj** (*p. 405*);
- north along the **Passeggiata del Gianicolo** (*p. 406*);
- downhill to **San Pietro in Montorio** (*described immediately below*).

The route to San Pietro in Montorio passes a huge monument (1941) by Giovanni Jacobucci (*open Tues–Sun 9–1*), which commemorates those who fought for the Italian Republic in 1849–70. Behind it, steps lead down to the **Mausoleo Garibaldino**, with patriotic inscriptions and a golden mosaic ceiling. Around the walls the names of all those who died fighting for the Republic are recorded. At the back is the tomb of Garibaldi's aide Goffredo Mameli (*see p. 405*).

SAN PIETRO IN MONTORIO

Map p. 651, D2. Open daily 8.30–12, also weekdays 3–6. NB: Light is very low in the church; ring at the green light on the right of the high altar for the sacristan, who will turn on the lights as you wish.

The church of San Pietro in Montorio was built on a site wrongly presumed to be the place of St Peter's crucifixion. Mentioned in the 9th century, a papal bull of Sixtus IV granted the Franciscan friary here to his Spanish confessor, the Blessed Amadeo de Silva, in 1472. The church was rebuilt in 1481 at the expense of King Ferdinand of Aragon and his wife Isabella, Queen of Castile. Philip III of Spain carried out work to shore up the hill and create the terrace in front of the church. The church is traditionally taken to be the burial place of Beatrice Cenci (*see pp. 340–1*), beheaded as a parricide at Ponte Sant' Angelo in 1599.

The fine simple travertine façade is attributed to the school of Andrea Bregno. The view from the terrace with a group of palm trees in front of the church includes the high dome of Sant'Andrea della Valle and, on the right, the hill of the Aventine with many of its churches visible on the skyline. Beside the church is the entrance to the Royal Academy of Spain, founded in 1873 in the former Franciscan convent. The apse and campanile were damaged in the siege of 1849 and you can still see a cannon ball fired by the French on a plaque set up on the exterior in 1895 as a memorial to Rome's struggle for independence (*for more on this, see p. 406*).

INTERIOR OF SAN PIETRO IN MONTORIO

The interior, on a design by Baccio Pontelli, dates from the late 15th century. The most famous work of art in the church is in the first south chapel: **Sebastiano del Piombo's** *Flagellation*, a superb fresco from designs by Michelangelo. Commissioned by the Florentine banker Pierfrancesco Borgherini in 1521, its composition skilfully fits the curved wall of the chapel, and the painted columns accentuate the motion of the torturers grouped around the central column, against which the twisted figure of Christ is superbly portrayed. The semi-nude figures are rendered with extraordinary power. St Peter and St Francis are depicted against black grounds on either side of the scene (both of them far removed from it in spirit, absorbed as they are in reading their books). Above is a *Transfiguration*, also by Sebastiano, though it lacks the force and drama of the *Flagellation* scene.

SEBASTIANO DEL PIOMBO

Sebastiano Luciani (c. 1485–1547), called 'del Piombo' because of his appointment as keeper of the papal seals, which were made of lead (*piombo*), was an artist of Venetian training and style who worked in the very different milieu of Rome and in the circles of Raphael and Michelangelo. His paintings are characterised by an innate, almost patrician, refinement and by a deeply shadowed and sensitive modelling which gives his figures a sculptural monumentality. His images are often so static that they can possess an eerie stillness. He is unquestionably a painter of great talent—talent which Vasari, perhaps exaggerating his laziness, considered to have been unfulfilled.

As a young artist Sebastiano worked with Giorgione, and the instinct for evoking mood through landscape, which he learned from his master, remained with him all his life. After his move to Rome in 1511, his contact with the work of Michelangelo soon brought out a grander and more sculptural quality. His figures become much more monumental but still retain a softness and sensuality, giving them a quality which lies somewhere between flesh and statuary. The *Flagellation* in San Pietro in Montorio shows how well Sebastiano is able to balance these two elements. In his painting technique and as a portraitist he is the equal of Raphael—who effectively blocked his progress to the most important commissions. Michelangelo befriended him and made him to all intents and purposes his deputy in Rome. In the wider context of High Renaissance art, Sebastiano treads a solitary path: his textured light and crepuscular mood was alien to the bold, classicising taste of Rome. Yet few artists succeed so well in giving a human and sensual dimension to that Classicism.   N.McG.

The **fifth south chapel** has two tombs, both with effigies and two statues above, good works by Bartolomeo Ammannati, who also designed the heavy balustrade supported by groups of over-large putti. The altarpiece by Vasari of the *Blind St Paul*, shown being given back his sight after his conversion, includes the artist's self-portrait (on the left, dressed in black). The **apse** is decorated with one of the many copies of Guido Reni's *Crucifixion of St Peter*. The original is now in the Vatican Pinacoteca. Raphael's *Transfiguration* (also in the Vatican Pinacoteca) adorned the apse from 1523 to 1797.

The **fifth north chapel** was designed by Daniele da Volterra. In the pavement in front of the chapl are the tomb slabs of two Irish noblemen: Hugh O'Neill, Earl of Tyrone ('*Hugonis principis Onelli*'), a leader in the Irish revolt supported by Spain against Elizabeth I and then James I; and the larger more elaborate slab, complete with coat of arms, of Rory O'Donnell ('*Odonallio*'), Earl of Tyrconnell, also involved in this Irish rebellion. Both fled to Rome during the so-called Flight of the Earls in 1607. O'Donnell died here in the same year; O'Neill died in 1616.

The fourth chapel, with its well-lit dome, is entirely covered with pretty stucco work attributed to Stefano Maderno: the three paintings (1617) are Flemish works, probably by Dirk van Baburen, who was influenced by Caravaggio, and his fellow countryman David de Haen. The *Descent from the Cross* over the altar is particularly

BRAMANTE'S TEMPIETTO AT SAN PIETRO IN MONTORIO

fine. The third chapel has a fresco on the altar by Antoniazzo Romano (late 15th century) of the *Madonna and Child with St Anne* (and, in the apse above, the *Redeemer Blessing*). Outside the chapel above the apse arch are the prophets David and Solomon enthroned, with pretty landscapes. The second chapel, the **Raymondi Chapel** has an altar, designed in 1647 by Bernini, showing his typical skill in dramatising the effect by hidden lighting (there is a window on the left). The unusual relief of St Francis in a swoon supported by angels was executed by his pupils Francesco Baratta and Andrea Bolgi. Near the west door (behind the font) is the tomb of Bishop Giuliano da Volterra (d. 1510), by a follower of Andrea Bregno.

THE TEMPIETTO

On the right of the church a little gate gives access to a peaceful courtyard with the famous Tempietto (*open Tues–Sat 9.30–12.30 & 2–4.30; 4–6 in summer; but you can see it even if the gate is closed*), an extremely important Renaissance work by Donato Bramante, though its date is still uncertain—either 1499–1502 or 1508–12. Erected on what was thought to be the exact site of St Peter's martyrdom, it is a miniature circular building with 16 Doric columns of granite, clearly derived from the architect's study of ancient Roman circular temples. Perfectly proportioned and raised on a moulded plinth above three circular steps, it includes numerous Classical elements— Doric columns, a frieze with triglyphs, scallop-shell niches and pilasters on the wall of the domed cella in the centre—but it has a Mannerist balcony around the top. It is particularly pleasing because of its tiny scale, which allows you to establish an intimate relationship with it. Bramante's original project envisaged it set in a circular, single-storeyed cloister, which would have made the effect even more remarkable.

In the 16th century it was Bramante who established the true Roman classicist style of architecture, and this exquisite little building at once became extremely famous and was to influence generations of architects all over the world. Wren's dome of St Paul's Cathedral in London and James Gibbs's Radcliffe Camera in Oxford are clearly derived from Bramante's classicism, even if on a much larger scale. After working in Milan in close contact with Leonardo da Vinci, Bramante came to Rome in 1499 and spent the last years of his life here. Julius II called him to work on the new St Peter's and Belvedere courtyard in the Vatican.

The upper chapel has a Cosmatesque pavement and a rather stiff statue of St Peter, attributed to Lorenzo Marrina. Exterior stairs designed by Bernini lead down to a crypt with pretty stuccoes by Giovanni Francesco Rossi. In the cloister (on the north wall) a plaque records the restoration here financed by King Juan Carlos, '*hispani catholici regis*', in 1978, three years after he became king (he abdicated in 2014).

PORTA SAN PANCRAZIO & VILLA DORIA PAMPHILJ

At the summit of the Janiculum is **Porta San Pancrazio** (*map p. 651, C2*), built in the mid-17th century by Urban VIII and rebuilt by Virginio Vespignani in 1857. Once known as the Porta Aurelia, it was the starting-point of the Via Aurelia, which ran from Rome up the Tyrrhenian coast to Pisa. Here is the **Museo della Repubblica Romana e della Memoria Garibaldina** (*open Tue–Fri 10–2, weekends 9–6; closed Mon; museodellarepubblicaromana.it*), which illustrates with mementoes the struggle to establish a Roman republic independent both of France and of the Church (*see overleaf*).

THE PARK OF VILLA DORIA PAMPHILJ

To the right of Porta San Pancrazio is the **Villa Aurelia** (*villaaurelia.it*; rebuilt after the French siege of 1849; *see overleaf*), surrounded by a lovely garden. It was acquired by the **American Academy in Rome** in 1911 (the main seat of the Academy is on the other side of the road, entered from Via Masina). The Academy supports artists, writers and scholars and has an excellent library: the premises and gardens can be visited on a tour by previous appointment (*aarome.org*).

Viale delle Mura Gianicolensi, leading south, skirts a magnificent stretch of walls. Just beyond the gate, in Via di San Pancrazio on the right, are the **ruins of the Vascello**, a Baroque villa where Goffredo Mameli, Garibaldi's aide, was fatally wounded at the age of 22 in a last sally in 1849. He was a poet and author of the Italian national anthem, which bears his name (*L'Inno di Mameli*) and which has the rousing patriotic refrain '*Fratelli d'Italia*', 'Brothers of Italy'. He is buried on this hill (*see p. 402*).

Just beyond this, at a junction between two very busy roads, is the entrance to the **Villa Pamphilj**, or Belrespiro (*open daily sunrise–sunset; villapamphili.it*), the largest park in Rome (9km in circumference). It was landscaped in 1644–52 for Prince Camillo Pamphilj, nephew of Innocent X. It is now owned partly by the state and partly by the *Comune* of Rome. Beyond a huge orange archway erected in 1859, the noise of the city is left behind as the grounds slope downhill with meadows and numerous fine trees. The views beyond take in the environs of Rome (including stretches of open countryside) as well as the city itself. The splendid umbrella pines are a special feature of the park, which also has palms and ilexes. In the park, and surrounded by a formal garden, is the **Casino del Bel Respiro**, a splendid Baroque building and the most important architectural work of Alessandro Algardi (possibly assisted by Bernini). Algardi also carved the stuccoes in 1646. It is sometimes used for receptions by the Italian state, but is not open to the public.

NB: The basilica of San Pancrazio is described in the Appendix on p. 566.

ROME AND THE RISORGIMENTO

Rome took an active part in the agitated period of the Risorgimento, the political renaissance of Italy in the 19th century, and shared with the rest of Europe the revolutionary ideals of liberty and independence. While the military leader Giuseppe Garibaldi was the most famous and charismatic supporter of the cause, Camillo Cavour was the prime mover of Italian political autonomy and a republic was proclaimed by an elected assembly in Rome under the guidance of Giuseppe Mazzini. At this point, in 1849, the pope fled to Gaeta and the French sent an army in his support. The defence of the city was entrusted to Garibaldi, who made a famous stand on the Janiculum, declaring '*Roma o Morte!*', 'Rome or Death!' The stand was unsuccessful and Rome—for a time at least—remained under papal control.

In 1867 Garibaldi made another attempt to rouse the Romans against the papal government with the help of the Cairoli brothers, who were killed in the same year when, at the battle of Mentana, the French and papal troops won a victory. In 1870 the French garrison, which had occupied Castel Sant'Angelo since 1849, finally withdrew, and a month later, on 20th September, the Italian army under Raffaello Cadorna entered Rome from the north through a breach in the walls beside Porta Pia (*map p. 648, A4*). This brought papal rule of the city to an end. The pope retreated to the safety of the Vatican and Rome was proclaimed the capital of united Italy in 1871.

There are numerous memorials to this period on the Janiculum hill, where most of the fighting took place. The fallen are commemorated in a mausoleum (*see p. 402*) and the museum at Porta San Pancrazio (*see p. 405*) illustrates the struggle.

THE PASSEGGIATA DEL GIANICOLO

Beside the Acqua Paola fountain (*described on p. 401*) is the monumental gateway, surmounted by four terracotta urns, to the Passeggiata del Gianicolo (*map p. 651, D2–C1*), a wide avenue of plane trees laid out in 1884 across the former grounds of the Villa Corsini. At Piazzale del Gianicolo there is a panoramic terrace with busts of Risorgimento heroes decorating the garden behind. The huge 7m-high **equestrian statue of Garibaldi** here, by Emilio Gallori, was erected in 1895 on the site of the hero's exploits of 1849. Around the base are four bronze groups: in front, *The Charge of Manara's Bersaglieri* (Rome, 1849); behind, *The Battle of Calatafimi* (Sicily, 1860); at the sides, *Europe* and *America*. Every day a cannon is wheeled out of the storeroom below the terrace by a small group of soldiers who fire a blank shot at 12 noon (you can watch the ceremony from the terrace). The report is heard all over the city and Romans are particularly fond of this tradition: it marks the time of day and reminds them that it is nearly time for lunch. A salvo of 21 shots is fired from here when a new President is sworn in.

The Passeggiata continues downhill past more busts. On the right is the lovely **Villa Lante** (now the Finnish Embassy), with a splendid loggia, built by Giulio Romano in 1518–27: it was much influenced by Raphael's Villa Madama. On the left is the bronze **equestrian statue of Anita Garibaldi**, Garibaldi's wife, by Mario Rutelli, presented by the Brazilian government in 1935 to honour her Brazilian origins and incorporating her tomb. From this point there is an especially fine view of Rome, even better (because it is clear of trees) than that from Piazzale del Gianicolo above. The avenue continues downhill past a **memorial tower** by Manfredo Manfredi, presented to Rome in 1911 by Italian residents of Argentina.

SANT'ONOFRIO

Map p. 650, C3. Open Mon–Fri 7.30–1.30, or by appointment, T: 06 68 64 498.
The church of Sant'Onofrio was founded by Blessed Nicolò da Forca Palena in 1419 and restored by Pius IX in 1857. A graceful L-shaped Renaissance portico connects the church and friary: in the lunettes beneath it are three frescoes from the life of St Jerome (his baptism, chastisement for reading Cicero and temptation) by Domenichino. By the friary entrance is the tomb of the founder.

The dark church interior is paved almost entirely with tombstones. The first chapel on the left contains a monument (1857) by Giuseppe de Fabris to Tasso (*see below*). The third chapel has the tombstone of Giuseppe Mezzofanti (d. 1849), titular cardinal of the church, who could speak over 50 languages. In the pretty apse over the main altar are repainted frescoes by the school of Pinturicchio. The fresco of *St Anne Teaching the Virgin to Read*, on the right above the monument to Giovanni Sacco (d. 1505), is by a pupil of Andrea Bregno. The second chapel on the right contains a *Madonna di Loreto* attributed to Annibale Carracci or his school; in the vault pendentives above the altar in the first chapel is an *Annunciation* by Antoniazzo Romano.

The friary is now occupied by American Friars of the Atonement. The epic poet Torquato Tasso (1544–95) spent his last days here. The Museo Tassiano (*open only by appointment; T: 06 68 77 341*) contains the poet's death mask, mementoes, manuscripts and editions and translations of his works. The French writer Chateaubriand made arrangements to be buried here also, in what he termed '*un des plus beaux sites de la terre*', should he be fortunate enough (his own phrase) to die in Rome. A plaque outside the church commemorates this fact. Chateaubriand died in Paris in 1848. Nevertheless, his burial site is far from prosaic. He lies on an island near his native Saint-Malo, accessible only at low tide.

From here the Salita di Sant'Onofrio descends to the Tiber near the Vatican.

CASTEL SANT'ANGELO
The marble angel with copper wings by Raffaello da Montelupo which stood on the top terrace of the castle until the mid-18th century.

Castel Sant'Angelo & the Borgo

Castel Sant'Angelo, which dominates the Tiber, was originally the mausoleum of the emperor Hadrian. It is now a museum. The small area known as the Borgo, with some old streets close to St Peter's, was part of Vatican territory up until 1586.

The famous **Ponte Sant'Angelo** (*map p. 654, A1*), a footbridge over the Tiber, stands on ancient foundations: in origin it is the Pons Aelius, built by Hadrian (Aelius Hadrianus) in AD 134 as a grand approach to his circular mausoleum, which still dominates the other side of the river and is known today as Castel Sant'Angelo. The three central arches of the bridge belong to the original structure; the end arches were given their current form in 1892–4 during the construction of the Tiber embankments. At the bridgehead furthest from the castle are statues of *St Paul* (right) by Paolo Taccone and *St Peter* (left) by Lorenzetto. They were set up by Clement VII in 1534. On the parapets is the graceful series of ten angel sculptures designed by Bernini and executed in 1668–71, mainly by his pupils, including Ercole Ferrata, Pietro Paolo Naldini, Cosimo Fancelli and Antonio Raggi. They were conceived as a theatrical Via Dolorosa, leading towards St Peter's: each angel holds one of the Instruments of the Passion, which are as follows: the Column of the Flagellation and Scourge; the Sudarium and Crown of Thorns; the Nails and Garments and dice; the Cross and Titulus; the Lance that pierced Christ's side and the Vinegar sponge. Two of the angels (the one with the Titulus and the one holding the Crown of Thorns) are copies. The originals, executed in part by Bernini himself, are now in the church of Sant'Andrea delle Fratte (*see p. 347*).

CASTEL SANT'ANGELO

Map p. 654, A1. Open daily except Mon 9–7.30; last tickets 1hr before closing. T: 06 32810 or 06 68 96 003, castelsantangelo.com. Free first Sun of the month. The works of art are frequently rearranged. Audio guides are available. The prisons, Passetto and Bathroom of Clement VII are only shown by appointment. Requests must be made in writing: ssp-sae-rm.castelsantangelo@beniculturali.it. There is a café on the upper terrace. The lift is reserved for staff and the disabled.

The enormous Castel Sant'Angelo was begun by Hadrian as a mausoleum for himself and his family. Since then it has served successively as fortress, prison, barracks and museum. The round tower up until the first string course, built of great stone blocks, is from Hadrian's time; it would originally have been faced with marble. The upper levels are additions of the Renaissance and later. The central tower once formed the base of a statue of the apotheothised emperor, now replaced by a bronze angel.

Today the castle is open as a museum: the interior spiral ramp leading to Hadrian's burial chamber is superbly preserved and the upper rooms and courtyards are well worth a visit, fascinating for the picture they give of the artistic taste of the Renaissance popes. The main entrance is directly in front of Ponte Sant'Angelo.

HISTORY OF CASTEL SANT'ANGELO

Hadrian began his mausoleum c. 128. It was completed in 139, a year after his death, by his successor Antoninus Pius. Rising to a height of nearly 50m, it consisted of a base 89m square on which stood a circular structure supporting a central round tower 64m in diameter, of peperino and travertine overlaid with marble. The top was adorned with statues, lost in the 6th century when they were hurled as missiles against the besieging Ostrogoths. Within the tower was an earthen tumulus planted with cypress trees, on whose summit stood an altar bearing a bronze quadriga driven by Hadrian, represented as the Sun, ruler of the world. Inside the building, a spiral ramp (still extant) led to a straight passageway ending in the cella, in which was the Imperial tomb. Hadrian, his wife Sabina and his adopted son Aelius Caesar were buried in the mausoleum, as were succeeding emperors until Septimius Severus. Marble plaques recording their names once adorned the outside of the structure, but these were removed by Gregory XIII and used as revetment for his Cappella Gregoriana in St Peter's Basilica (*see p. 431*).

In the Middle Ages the mausoleum was gradually transformed into a castle. Theodoric (474–526) used it as a prison and for a time it became known as the Carceri Theodorici. According to legend, while crossing the Pons Aelius at the head of a procession to pray for the cessation of the plague of 590, St Gregory the Great saw an angel sheathing his sword on the top of the fortress. The vision accurately announced the end of the plague and from then onwards the castle bore its present name.

In the following centuries the possession of Castel Sant'Angelo was contested between popes and antipopes, the imperial forces and the Roman barons. In 1084 Gregory VII was rescued from Henry IV's siege by Robert Guiscard. By the late 12th century the castle was established as papal property. It was from here that Cola di Rienzo (*see p. 36*) fled to Bohemia on 15th December 1347, at the end of his first period of dictatorship. When in 1378 Gregory XI was persuaded by St Catherine of Siena to return to Rome from Avignon, the castle was severely damaged by citizens of Rome resentful of the interference of the papacy in city government.

In the reign of Boniface IX rebuilding began. Alexander VI had Antonio da Sangallo the Elder complete the four bastions of the square inner ward, which had been begun by Nicholas V. After these improvements it was estimated that the castle could withstand a three-year siege. Julius II built the south loggia, facing the river. When Clement VII and some 1,000 followers (including 13 cardinals and 18 bishops) took

CASTEL SANT'ANGELO
Detail of the Library frieze of frolicking mermaids and mermen. Part of the decorations
carried out for Paul III by Luzio Luzi and his assistants.

refuge here in 1527 from the troops of Charles V (*see p. 23*), Benvenuto Cellini took part in its defence (in his *Autobiography* he gives a colourful description of his own valour contrasted with the behaviour of the sculptor Raffaello da Montelupo, who, he says, cowered terrified in a corner). Paul III built the north loggia and decorated the interior with frescoes. The outer ward, with its defensive ditch, was added by Pius IV. Urban VIII provided the castle with cannon made of bronze taken from the ceiling of the Pantheon portico, and he employed Bernini to remodel the outer defences.

From 1849 to 1870 the castle was occupied by French troops. Under the Italian government it was used as a barracks and as a prison until 1901, when the work of restoration was begun. In 1933–4 the castle was adapted for use as a museum.

MUSEO NAZIONALE DI CASTEL SANT'ANGELO

Beyond the entrance a cobbled way leads between the foot of Hadrian's splendid round tower and the medieval castle walls. At the time of writing, the ticket office was to the left, down this path. Just beyond it, you pass some colossal ancient heads set into the wall. One is of Antinous, the young favourite of Hadrian, probably one of the statues flung from the attic storey against the Ostrogoths in 537.

THE MAUSOLEUM

A modern iron walkway leads down to an underground vestibule. In the back wall is a tall **niche**, which would once have been filled with a statue of Hadrian (possibly an acrolith; what may have been its head is now in the Vatican; *see p. 456*). To the left is a conjectural model of the mausoleum as it might have appeared when first built. To your right a **ramped corridor**, 125.5m long, winds gently upwards to the sepulchral cella. The ramp is in a remarkable state of preservation and the floor has traces of the original tiny white mosaic tesserae. Along it are four vents, one of which is illuminated.

At the end of the ramp on the right is the **shaft of a lift** traditionally said to have been built for the portly Leo X. Here the Staircase of Alexander VI cuts diametrically across the circular building. By means of a bridge built in 1822 by Giuseppe Valadier in place of a drawbridge, the staircase passes above the **sepulchral cella**, of which only the travertine wall-blocks survive. The sarcophagi containing the imperial ashes were kept here. Hadrian's was taken for use as the tomb of the Holy Roman Emperor Otto II (*but see p. 428*). A plaque inscribed with Hadrian's famous poem to his own soul has been set up here. In later centuries the room was used as a prison. Inmates, it is said, were left to starve to death.

SECOND FLOOR

At a landing lit by a round window, the Staircase of Alexander VI originally turned to the right. Paul III closed this section and opened another stair to the left, by Antonio da Sangallo the Younger, to give access to the **Courtyard of the Angel (1)**, named after the marble statue of an angel by Raffaello da Montelupo, which used to stand on the terrace at the top of the castle. At the far end of the court is the **Staircase of Urban VIII (2)** (note the finial decorated with Barberini bees). At the base of the stairs on the left is **Michelangelo's window aedicule (3)** on the Chapel of Leo X, built c. 1514. This was his first architectural work. The round niche above it is by Raffaello da Montelupo.

The **Hall of Apollo (4)** is named after the 16th-century mythological *grottesche* on the ceiling, attributed to Luzio Luzi. The renderings of songbirds—sparrows, goldfinches, wagtails—are particularly successful. A grille in the floor looks down into the lift shaft: you can see the winch mechanism. The **Chapel of Leo X (5)** is dedicated to Cosmas and Damian, patron saints of the Medici family. On the other side of the Hall of Apollo are two **rooms of Clement VII (6)**, with the Medici coat of arms. The central room is the **Hall of Justice (7)**.

The large **Courtyard of Alexander VI (8)** has a fine marble well-head. Theatrical performances were given here in the time of Leo X and Pius IV. Off the courtyard on the right (*but both only open for guided tours; see above*) are the charming **Bathroom of Clement VII (9**; *reached up a small staircase*), decorated with stuccoes and frescoes attributed to Giovanni da Udine, and (*below, reached by another staircase*) the historical **prisons (10)**. In the second cell from the right, Benvenuto Cellini was imprisoned during the first period of his captivity. Here also were two large oil stores, with a capacity of c. 22,000 litres. The oil served not only as food, but also as a defence, since boiling oil could be poured on attackers. There were grain silos here too, later used as prison cells. Numerous bones found under the floors indicate that prisoners were buried where they died. Cellini is said to have passed his second period of captivity in the last cell.

UPPER FLOORS

From the Courtyard of Alexander VI, two stairways lead up to the semicircular **Walkway of Pius IV**, a terrace with a splendid view, and where a series of small rooms

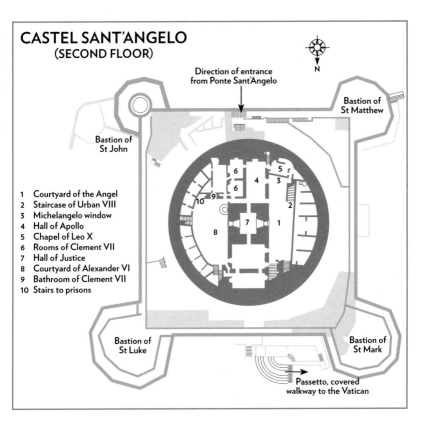

CASTEL SANT'ANGELO
(SECOND FLOOR)

Direction of entrance
from Ponte Sant'Angelo

N

Bastion of
St Matthew

Bastion of
St John

1 Courtyard of the Angel
2 Staircase of Urban VIII
3 Michelangelo window
4 Hall of Apollo
5 Chapel of Leo X
6 Rooms of Clement VII
7 Hall of Justice
8 Courtyard of Alexander VI
9 Bathroom of Clement VII
10 Stairs to prisons

Bastion of
St Luke

Bastion of
St Mark

Passetto, covered
walkway to the Vatican

was used originally as quarters for the household of the papal court and later as political and military prison cells. Here, as everywhere in Castel Sant'Angelo, the lintels are carved with papal names. To the left is the **Loggia of Paul III**, built by Antonio da Sangallo the Younger and decorated with stuccoes and Mannerist grotesques in 1543–8. Beyond the charming little café, four rooms display part of the **Museum of Arms and Armour**, which has material from the 15th–20th centuries.

The columned **Loggia of Julius II**, designed by Giuliano da Sangallo, faces Ponte Sant'Angelo. The ceiling is decorated with *grottesche* and mottoes suitable to this warrior pope, such as *Pacis filia religio est* (Religion is the daughter of Peace). A short staircase leads from here to the papal apartments, decorated for Paul III in 1542–9. The large **Sala Paolina** is very lavish. On the right as you enter is an amusing *trompe l'oeil* fresco of a courtier entering the room through a painted door. After this, everything is splendour. There are stuccoes by Girolamo da Sermoneta and Baccio da Montelupo. The ceiling bears the motto *Festina lente* (favourite adage of the emperor Augustus) and another, in Greek (*Dikis Krinon*; 'Lily of Justice'), referring to Pope Paul, who was a member of the Farnese family, whose emblem is a lily. Here the pagan (temporal) meets the Christian (spiritual). The patrons of the building are represented on the two short walls: the emperor for whom it served as a mausoleum, Hadrian, on the entrance wall (by Perino del Vaga and Girolamo da Sermoneta) and the Archangel Michael by Pellegrino Tibaldi on the far wall. Inscriptions explicitly inform us that Paul III has turned a pagan shrine into a godly abode. To the left of St Michael, a female figure holds a three-faced head surmounted by a triangle, symbolising the Holy Trinity. Below St Michael, two baboons are seen feasting on grapes. In the centre of the floor is the coat of arms of Innocent XIII, who restored the room in the 18th century.

The **Sala del Perseo** (right) takes its name from the beautiful frieze of Perseus by Perino del Vaga and his *bottega*. The carved wooden ceiling, with a central figure of Perseus, dates from the 16th century. Paintings include *St Jerome* by Lorenzo Lotto (1509) and *Girl with a Unicorn* attribtued to Luca Longhi. The **Sala di Amore e Psiche** has another frieze by Perino del Vaga and his *bottega*, illustrating the story of Cupid and Psyche in 17 episodes. It has a fine carved and gilt 15th-century ceiling, a large 16th-century canopied bed, a clavichord, and other furniture. The paintings include *Christ Carrying the Cross* by Sebastiano del Piombo.

From the Sala Paolina a corridor (left) frescoed in the Pompeian style by Perino del Vaga and his *bottega* leads to the **Library**, with a stucco frieze of pagan sacrifices, Classical gods and Farnese emblems, and above it a painted frieze of cavorting mermaids and mermen. These decorations are by Luzio Luzi and assistants. Luzi also provided the frieze of Dionysian revels in the **Hadrianaeum** and the decorations in the **Room of Festoons** beyond it. A door opposite the Library fireplace (the chimneypiece is by Raffaello da Montelupo) leads to the central **Room of the Treasury**, where the walnut cupboards were used for the archives inaugurated by Paul III. In the centre are some large chests in which Julius II, Leo X and Sixtus V kept the Vatican treasury.

Stairs continue up to the terrace at the top of the castle, scene of the last act of Puccini's opera *Tosca*. Above the terrace towers the huge **bronze Angel** (4m high, by Peter Anton Verschaffelt; 1747), shown in the act of sheathing his sword. This commemorates the vision of Gregory the Great after which the castle is named (*see p. 410*). The bell behind the Angel, known as the **Campana della Misericordia**, used to announce the execution of capital sentences. The view from the terrace is superb.

THE RAMPARTS

The ramparts are traversed by open walkways which connect the four bastions of the inner ward. The bastions are dedicated to the Evangelists, and each is marked by a small marble plaque. Beyond the Bastion of St Mark is the beginning of the covered way (Passetto del Borgo) that connects the castle with the Vatican (*only shown by appointment*). Adjacent to the Bastion of St Luke, behind a sentry box, is the Chapel of the Crucifix (or of Clement XII), in which condemned criminals attended Mass before execution. In niches beside the steps leading down to ground level are two ancient busts. One, very mutilated, is said to be of Julius Caesar. The other is of Hadrian, though it has only been here since 1788. The original head of Hadrian that was found here, a very fine one, is now in the Vatican (*see p. 456 and illustration on p. 54*).

A WALK THROUGH THE BORGO

The Borgo, a district on the right bank of the Tiber, has been associated with the Roman Church since the first shrine of St Peter was built here on the site of the apostle's tomb. It was the stronghold of the papacy from 850 until 1586, when it was formally incorporated in the city of Rome. Five streets in the district still have the prefix 'Borgo'.

HISTORY OF THE BORGO

The Borgo was known in ancient Rome as 'Ager Vaticanus'. It was chosen by Caligula for his circus, which was enlarged by Nero. The site of the Circus of Nero, just south of the basilica of St Peter, has been identified in excavations. In the adjoining gardens many Christians were martyred under Nero in AD 65, including St Peter, who was buried in a pagan cemetery nearby. Over his grave the first church of St Peter's was built (c. AD 90) to commemorate his martyrdom. Also within the Ager Vaticanus, Hadrian began his mausoleum (now Castel Sant'Angelo) in AD 128.

Inscriptions found on the temples of Cybele and Mithras suggest that paganism retained its hold in Rome with great tenacity until the late 4th century. Despite this, churches, chapels and convents were built round the first church of St Peter, and the district attracted Saxon, Frankish and Lombard pilgrims. Around this time it came to be called the *borgo* ('borough'), a name of Germanic origin from *borgus*, meaning a small fortified settlement. In 850 Leo IV (847–55) surrounded the Borgo with walls 12m high, fortified with circular towers, to protect it from the incursions of the Saracens: hence the name *Civitas Leonina* or Leonine City. Remnants of the wall survive to the west of St Peter's. The Leonine City became the papal citadel: within its walls John VIII was besieged in 878 by the Duke of Spoleto; in 896 Arnulph of Carinthia attacked it and Formosus crowned him emperor. Gregory VII took refuge in Castel Sant'Angelo from the Holy Roman Emperor Henry IV.

During the 'Babylonian captivity' (1309–78), when the papacy was in Avignon (*see p. 178*), the Borgo fell into ruin, but when the popes returned they chose the Vatican as their residence instead of the Lateran. Eugenius IV and Sixtus IV in the 15th century, and Julius II and Leo X in the early 16th, were active in developing and embellishing the Borgo. The original area was enlarged to the north of Borgo Angelico. After the Sack of Rome in 1527, however, the Borgo became one of the poorest and least populated districts of Rome, and in 1586 Sixtus V relinquished the papal claim to the area, so that it was united to the city.

BEGIN ON PONTE SANT'ANGELO (*see p. 409*), the famous Tiber crossing. The bridge is almost always crowded: and it must ever have been thus, since a bridge here has always provided the main pedestrian access to St Peter's. During the Holy Year of 1450, a shying mule caused pandemonium here and hundreds of pilgrims were crushed to death.

Once across the bridge, turn left, first looking up to see the **defaced arms of Alexander VI** on the Bastion of St Matthew, the first bastion left of the

Castel Sant'Angelo entrance. This is not the only defaced escutcheon on the fortress; but it is an appropriate one to see, for it was to the fastness of this castle, in 1494, that Rodrigo Borgia, Pope Alexander VI, fled from the Vatican, along the Passetto (*see below*), on learning that French troops were advancing towards Rome. The pope won his victory against France, but his days in Castel Sant'Angelo were not over: in 1495 his son Giovanni's murdered body was washed up by the Tiber. In an access of grief, the pope shut himself up in the castle. Legend tells how a later pope, who was very fond of emblazoning his family emblem all over Rome, had the Borgia crest disfigured deliberately. This was Urban VIII, of the Barberini family, whose symbol (the bee) is prominent on many of the city's monuments. He may have done so, but it is more likely that this Borgia crest was vandalised during another French invasion: that of Napoleon's men in the 18th century.

From Castel Sant'Angelo, thread your way past vendors' stalls to a park on your right, which has good views of the castle and its moat and from where you can also closely approach the brick arches of the **Passetto del Borgo**, which heads straight for the Bastion of St Mark, tracing the very line of Pope Alexander's flight. The Passetto or Corridoio is a raised covered way connecting Castel Sant'Angelo with the Vatican. It was built in 1277–80 by Nicholas III above Leo IV's 9th-century defensive wall. It was reconstructed by Alexander VI and was again used in 1527 when Clement VII took refuge in the castle from the troops of Charles V.

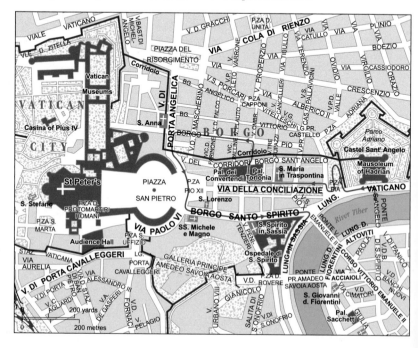

Come out of the park again and cross the busy Largo Giovanni XXIII, named after St John XXIII, 'Papa Giovanni', one of the best-loved popes in history, very different in character from the Borgia pope (he was canonised in 2014). Once across the lights, you enter the broad, austere **Via della Conciliazione**, which leads towards St Peter's. The approach to the great basilica was transformed by this wide, straight thoroughfare, typical of Fascist urban planning, which was completed in 1937 to celebrate the accord reached between Mussolini's government and the papacy (*see pp. 29–30*). Its construction involved the destruction of two ancient streets of the Leonine City, and it totally altered the impact of Bernini's colonnade in a way which the great architect never intended.

The avenue passes the Carmelite church of **Santa Maria in Traspontina** (1566–87). Its third north chapel has an altarpiece of St Peter and St Paul being flogged by Giovanni Battista Ricci (1619).

Continue along Via della Conciliazione and as you go, keep looking up the streets to the right to see the Passetto keeping pace with you. A short way further on, **Palazzo Torlonia** (no. 30) is a delightful reproduction of the Palazzo della Cancelleria (*see p. 223*), built by Andrea Bregno in 1495–1504 for Cardinal Adriano Castellesi. The cardinal gave the palace to the English king Henry VII, and Henry VIII then donated it to his papal legate, Cardinal Campeggio. The Torlonia themselves were a self-made family of merchants and bankers, staunchly loyal to the papacy. In 1870 the head of the clan is said to have altered the colours of his livery because it bore too much resemblance to that of the Italian king.

On the corner of Via dell'Erba is **Palazzo dei Convertendi**, built in the second half of the 17th century and re-erected in its present position in 1937 when Via della Conciliazione was constructed. It is thought to occupy the site of a house built by Bramante for Raphael, who died in it in 1520.

Turn up Via dell'Erba. Parallel to Via della Conciliazione is Borgo Sant'Angelo, which is skirted by the wall that supports the Passetto. The arch which pierces the wall is decorated with the coat of arms of the Medici, the family of the other pope who fled along this raised corridor: Clement VII. Go through the arch and up to **Borgo Pio**, the prettiest street to have survived in the Borgo. Partly closed to traffic, it is a local shopping street and has several *pizzerie*, bars and hotels, as well as shops selling sacred and secular souvenirs and clerical garb. It leads you up to an eagle-guarded gateway to the Vatican City. To the left of the gate are the barracks of the Swiss Guard, and to the right of it **Sant'Anna dei Palafrenieri**, the parish church of the Vatican City, built in 1573 by the Papal Grooms (Palafrenieri della Corte Papale) to the designs of Vignola.

Turn left up Via di Porta Angelica. Suddenly you are in **St Peter's Square**, where the crowds, the hubbub and the queues are possibly much the same as in the days of the medieval pilgrims. To end the walk here and visit St Peter's, see overleaf. Otherwise cross the square towards Borgo Santo Spirito. Here a flight of steps leads up to the church of **Santi Michele e Magno** (*open Wed and Sat 10–1, Tues and Fri 3–6 but not in Lent, Sun at 10am*), founded in the 8th century and retaining a 13th-century campanile. Inside is the tomb of the painter Raphael Mengs (d. 1779). The Dutch Kerk van de Friezen (Church of the Frisians) holds Mass here on Sun.

Go up **Borgo Santo Spirito**. Devoid of shops and restaurants, it is by far the most tranquil of the streets here. On the left is a small brick church, **San Lorenzo in Piscibus**, completely enclosed by buildings.

On the corner of Via dei Penitenzieri (named after the Penitentiaries, who hear confessions in St Peter's) is **Santo Spirito in Sassia** (*open 7–12 & 3–7.30*), a church founded in 726 for Saxon pilgrims by Ine, King of Wessex, who died in Rome in the same year. It is known that this was the place where English clerics and visitors stayed when they came to Rome in the Middle Ages. The church was rebuilt in 1540 by Antonio da Sangallo the Younger: the design of the façade was probably his, but the work itself was done in 1585 by Ottaviano Mascherino. The campanile, entirely Tuscan in character and attributed to Baccio Pontelli (who also carried out the design for the Sistine Chapel), is one of the most graceful in Rome. In the interior the wooden ceiling dates from 1534–49. On the west wall are two interesting paintings in elaborate frames: the *Visitation* by Francesco Salviati, and the *Conversion of Saul*, attributed to a certain Marco da Siena. On the south side, the first chapel contains the *Pentecost* by Jacopo Zucchi; and the second chapel the *Assumption* by Livio Agresti. The interesting little porch in front of the side door, with two pairs of columns, has 16th-century frescoes and a pretty ceiling. It supports the organ of 1546–52. The huge apse was covered with frescoes by Jacopo and Francesco Zucchi in 1583. On the north side, the third

chapel has a 16th-century Crucifix and frescoed decorations in ancient Roman style imitating precious marbles with figures in grisaille. On the second altar, the *Coronation of the Virgin* is by Cesare Nebbia. It was from the ramparts near here that Benvenuto Cellini, according to his own statement, shot the Constable de Bourbon in 1527.

Adjoining the church are the buildings of the huge **Ospedale di Santo Spirito**, founded by Innocent III c. 1198 as a hospital for foundlings and the sick and as a hostel, and rebuilt for Sixtus IV c. 1473–8. The first building, the Palazzo del Commendatore (the house of the director of the hospital), with a spacious courtyard, dates from c. 1567. The arches of the portico further on were blocked by Benedict XIV. Beyond its portal, behind a wrought-iron screen, is a wooden turning wheel of the kind that religious houses used for the anonymous receipt of unwanted babies. At the time of writing the entire complex was undergoing extensive restoration (*for updates and information, see santospiritoinsassia.it*).

The hospital contains two institutions devoted to the history of medicine, the Lancisiana Library, founded 1711, and the Historical Medical Academy. At no. 3 Lungotevere in Sassia, entered down steps and under a brick porch, is the **Museo Storico Nazionale dell'Arte Sanitaria** (*open Mon, Wed, Fri 10–12; T: 06 68 33 262, www.accademiartesanitaria.it*), which illustrates the history of medicine. It includes anatomical drawings by Paolo Mascagni (1752–1815), the collection of the surgeon Giuseppe Flajani (1741–1808), sad little skeletons of hydrocephalic children, and reconstructions of a 17th-century pharmacy and of an alchemist's laboratory.

St Peter's Basilica

St Peter's Square is the masterpiece of Gian Lorenzo Bernini.
As one of the most superb conceptions of its kind in civic architecture,
it makes a fitting approach to the world's greatest Roman Catholic basilica.

S t Peter's Basilica (*map p. 650, B2–C2*) stands on land now part of the independent Vatican State, the residence of the pope, usually called the Vatican City, on the right bank of the Tiber. It is the composite work of some of the greatest artists ever to work in Rome and a masterpiece of the Italian High Renaissance, crowned by Michelangelo's splendid dome.

NB: As well as being one of the chief pilgrimage destinations in the Christian world, St Peter's is also one of Rome's top tourist sites. Large numbers of tour groups visit the basilica and its piazza: the crowds can be overwhelming; and if you are concerned about not losing your place in the queue for the security check you will find it hard to drink everything in, much less appreciate the finer details. Late afternoons and very early mornings are the quietest times. Be aware, though, that in the early morning most of the altars in St Peter's will be in use and many parts of the basilica will consequently be viewable only from a distance. However, early morning and during the last Mass of the day are the only times to experience the great church as a place of solemn sanctity.

THE ARCHITECTURE OF ST PETER'S SQUARE

Partly enclosed by two semicircular **colonnades**, the magnificent piazza, laid out by Gian Lorenzo Bernini in 1656–67, has the form of an ellipse adjoining an open trapezium. Each colonnade (they were splendidly restored in 2014) has a quadruple row of Doric columns, forming three parallel covered walks. There are in all 284 columns and 88 pilasters. On the entablature of the colonnade stand 96 statues of saints and martyrs, with 44 further statues above the rectilinear forecourt. At the end of the forecourt, at the top of a triple flight of steps, rises the basilica itself, with the buildings of the Vatican Palace towering above it on the right.

In the middle of the piazza, on a tall plinth, is an **obelisk** devoid of hieroglyphs, 25.5m high. It was brought from Alexandria (where it had been set up by the emperor Augustus) in AD 37, and it is thought that Caligula placed it in his circus, later called the Circus of Nero. In 1586 Sixtus V ordered its removal to this site and put Domenico Fontana in charge of operations. No fewer than 900 men, 150 horses and 47 cranes were required. In the 18th century the delightful story was invented that the pope forbade the spectators, on pain of death, to speak while the obelisk was being raised into position. A sailor called Bresca, seeing that the tension on the ropes had not been correctly assessed and that they were giving way under the strain, flouted the order, and shouted '*Acqua alle funi!*' ('Wet the ropes!'). The pope is said to have rewarded him by granting his family the privilege of supplying St Peter's with palms for Palm Sunday.

Round the foot of the obelisk is a plan of a mariner's compass, giving the names of the winds. The obelisk was surmounted by a globe until 1586, when it was replaced by a cross. The globe is now in the Capitoline Museums.

The two abundant **fountains** are supplied by the Acqua Paola. The one on the right was designed by Carlo Maderno (1614): a similar fountain had existed here since 1490. It was moved to its present site and slightly modified by Bernini in 1667, when the second fountain was begun. Between the obelisk and each fountain is a **porphyry disc** from which you have the illusion that each of the colonnades has only a single row of columns.

ST PETER'S BASILICA

St Peter's, or the Basilica di San Pietro in Vaticano, on a vast scale, is probably the world's most imposing church. It is built on the site of a basilica begun by Constantine, the first Christian emperor, in turn above the spot where the apostle Peter was buried after his martyrdom close by. This splendid edifice was famous throughout Europe, and in the mid-15th century it was decided to rebuild it on an even grander scale: this herculean task, carried out by a succession of leading architects, was only completed in the early 17th century. Despite its importance, St Peter's does not have cathedral status, nor is it the mother church of the Catholic faith (that position is held by St John Lateran).

Because of the security check, it is no longer possible to ascend the great triple staircase to the basilica portico. The entrance is on the right-hand side, past a colossal statue of St Paul (by Adamo Tadolini), set up by Pius IX. A companion statue of St Peter (by Giuseppe de Fabris) stands on the other side; you will go past it on your way out.

Opening times
The basilica is open Oct–March 7–6.30; April–Sept 7–7. The entrance (and security check) is under the right-hand portico (and the exit on the left). There can be long queues except early in the morning and late in the afternoon. The treasury is open 8–7; Oct–March 8–6.30. The dome (see p. 437) can be climbed Oct–March 8–5, April–Sept 8–6 (ticket reqired), although it is sometimes closed. The Vatican Grottoes (Tombs of the Popes; see p. 431) are open 9–5, Oct–March 9–4, except when the pope is in the basilica. The necropolis and tomb of St Peter can only be seen on group tours (see p. 437). Hours are always subject to change; for updates, check the vatican.va website (under 'Basilicas and Papal Chapels').

Dress
You are not allowed inside St Peter's or the Vatican City wearing shorts or mini-skirts, or with bare shoulders.

Services

Sung Mass in Latin is held on Sun at 10.30 and at 5pm on weekdays. Mass in Italian is held frequently throughout the day. Check vatican.va for times ('Basilicas and Papal Chapels' > 'St Peter' > 'Vita Liturgica').

Papal audiences

If the pope is in Rome, general audiences take place on Wed mornings in the New Audience Hall, or in the piazza. The New Audience Hall is reached under the colonnade to the left of the façade of St Peter's. A special section is set aside for newly-married couples. Audiences are also sometimes held in St Peter's. For information on how to apply, see vatican.va (under 'Prefecture of the Papal Household'). Tickets are free.

On Sundays at noon, the pope appears at his window, marked by the red Vatican banner, overlooking St Peter's Square to say the Angelus with the people.

Vatican Information Office and Post Office

In St Peter's Square, to the left of the basilica façade (closed Wed, when papal audiences are held in the piazza). Tickets for the Vatican Museums and Vatican Garden tours can be booked here. The Post Office sells Vatican postage stamps.

THE OLD ST PETER'S

According to the *Liber Pontificalis*, it was Pope St Anacletus who founded St Peter's, around AD 90. It is now thought, however, that there was a confusion of names and that St Anicetus (155–66) was probably the founder, building an oratory over the tomb of St Peter, close to the Circus of Nero near which he had been martyred. At the request of Pope St Sylvester I, the emperor Constantine began a basilica on the site of this oratory c. 319–22. The basilica, consecrated on 18th November 326, was 120m long and 65m wide (about half the size of the present edifice). In front was a great quadrangular colonnaded portico. The nave and double aisles were divided by 86 marble columns, some of which were said to have been taken from the Septizodium on the Palatine (if so, this was long before the demolition of that building by Sixtus V). The basilica contained numerous monuments to popes and emperors, was decorated with frescoes and mosaics, and was visited by pilgrims from all over Europe. Charlemagne was crowned Holy Roman Emperor here by Leo III in 800. Its façade is shown in Raphael's fresco of the *Incendio di Borgo* in the Raphael Rooms in the Vatican (*see p. 465*).

BUILDING THE NEW ST PETER'S

By the mid-15th century the old basilica was showing signs of collapse and Nicholas V, recognising its importance to the prestige of the Roman Catholic faith, decided that its structure needed attention. As a young man Nicholas had worked as a tutor to two of the great families of Florence (the Strozzi and the Albizzi). He had become imbued with the spirit of humanism and the Renaissance, and it seems that he desired a basilica that would reflect these values. He did not receive unanimous support for this plan but persevered nonetheless, entrusting the work to three Florentines: Bernardo Rossellino, Leon Battista Alberti and Giuliano da Sangallo; but on Nicholas's death in

ST PETER'S BASILICA

1455, building work came to a halt. It was Julius II who decided on a complete reconstruction, and employed for the purpose Donato Bramante, from Urbino, who started work in 1506. The old basilica still existed in its dilapidated state while work on the new basilica went on all around it, but eventually most of the old church was dismantled. Much was destroyed which could have been preserved: only a few monuments and architectural features survived the final demolition and Bramante was nicknamed 'Bramante Ruinante'. His new basilica was on a Greek-cross plan surmounted by a gigantic central dome and flanked by four smaller cupolas. At the same time Bramante was working on other commissions, including the Belvedere courtyard in the Vatican and the sanctuary of Santa Maria del Popolo, in which members of Pope Julius' family (the Della Rovere) are buried. Bramante also introduced the pope to a young artist (likewise a native of Urbino) by the name of Raphael. Entranced by the young man's talent, the pontiff ordered all other artists to cease work in the Vatican Palace and placed Raphael in sole charge of the painting. Pope Julius had a bellicose nature but he was a great lover of art. It is to him also that we owe the involvement of Michelangelo, whom he commissioned to decorate the ceiling of the chapel which his uncle Sixtus IV had built, and to sculpt his tomb, the story of which is told on p. 118.

The two geniuses did not work harmoniously together. Raphael, handsome and popular, and Michelangelo, saturnine and suspicious, had little in common. Nevertheless, while Bramante lived, building work on the basilica went on. By the time of his death in 1514, the four central piers and the arches of the dome had been completed.

Julius II had died in 1513. His successor, Leo X, was a Medici from Florence. To continue the building he looked to the brilliant Raphael, who shared the commission with two Florentines, Fra' Giocondo (d. 1515) and Giuliano da Sangallo (d. 1516). The design was now changed from a Greek to a Latin cross. On Raphael's early death in 1520, Baldassare Peruzzi, who had collaborated with Raphael on the Vatican *Stanze*, was appointed Chief Architect. He reverted to Bramante's Greek cross.

But the basilica was not completed in Leo's reign, nor in that of his immediate successors. Hadrian VI was an austere theologian who regarded art as hostile to the Church; Clement VII was too overwhelmed by political disturbances brought about by the Reformation and culminating in the Sack of Rome (1527; *see p. 23*). Under Paul III, however, the work received fresh impetus, first from Antonio da Sangallo the Younger, who readopted the Latin-cross plan, and then, after Sangallo's death in 1546, by Michelangelo. At last, at the age of 71, the artist who had worked so long at the Vatican and for so many masters, was summoned by Paul III and given his chance to bring the project to fruition. Michelangelo immediately reverted to the original Greek-cross plan, and developed Bramante's idea with even greater audacity. He took as his model Brunelleschi's dome of Florence cathedral, replaced Bramante's piers with new, stronger ones, and completed the dome as far as the drum. His plan for the central façade was derived from the Pantheon. Confirmed in his appointment by Paul III's successors, he continued to direct the work until his death in 1564.

After Michelangelo came Vignola and Pirro Ligorio, who were followed by Giacomo della Porta (assisted by Carlo Fontana). Della Porta completed Michelangelo's dome in 1590, adding the vault and lantern and the two smaller domes. Clement VIII covered the vault with strips of lead reinforced with bronze ribs. In 1605 Paul V demolished what was still left of the old basilica, pulled down the incomplete façade of the new one, and directed Carlo Maderno to lengthen the nave outwards. Thus, after many vicissitudes, the basilica was completed on a Latin-cross plan. The present façade and portico are Maderno's work; the façade has been criticised for concealing the impact of the dome.

On 18th November 1626, the 1300th anniversary of the original consecration, Urban VIII consecrated the new church. Bernini, who succeeded Maderno in 1629 and was commissioned to decorate the interior, wanted to erect two bell-towers by the façade, but the one that he completed began to crack on its sinking foundations and was pulled down. Alexander VII retained Bernini as architect of St Peter's, and under him the piazza was begun in 1656. The sacristy was built in the 18th century.

In 1940 the ancient cemetery in which St Peter was buried after his crucifixion was discovered beneath the Vatican Grottoes, and on 23rd December 1950 Pope Pius XII announced that the tomb of St Peter had been conclusively identified.

EXTERIOR OF ST PETER'S

It requires dedication to concentrate on the exterior of St Peter's. As soon as you are released from the queue and security check, it is tempting to plunge straight inside. But restraint brings its reward: there is much to see and enjoy, despite the ropes and the guards directing you one way or another.

Begin on the exterior terrace by looking upwards at the long polychrome façade. Eight columns and four pilasters support the entablature. A dedicatory inscription on the frieze records its erection in 1612, during the pontificate of the Borghese pope Paul V. The attic, almost without ornament, is surmounted by a balustrade on which are statues of Christ, St John the Baptist and eleven of the Apostles (St Peter's statue is inside) and, near the ends, two clocks by Giuseppe Valadier. Under the left-hand clock are the six bells of the basilica, electrically operated since 1931. The oldest bell dates from 1288; the largest (1786) is 7.5m in circumference and weighs 9.75 tonnes. Above the doors and extending beyond them on either side is a row of large windows with balconies. The central balcony is that from which the senior cardinal-deacon proclaims the newly elected pope and from which the new pope gives his blessing. Below the balcony is a relief, by Ambrogio Buonvicino, of *Christ Handing the Keys to St Peter*.

THE PORTICO

The portico (*see plan overleaf*) is prolonged by vestibules at both ends connecting with the covered colonnades of the piazza. The pavement was designed by Bernini. The magnificent stuccoes of the **vault**, by Martino Ferrabosco, include the arms of Paul V; in the lunettes below it are 32 statues of canonised popes. Of the five entrances to the church, that on the extreme right is the **Porta Santa (a)**, which is sealed from the inside and opened only in Holy Years (*see box on p. 292*). The panels on the door are by Vico Consorti (1950). The door on the right of the central door (now used as the main entrance) is by Venanzio Crocetti (1968). The **bronze central door from Old St Peter's (b)** was decorated by Filarete in the 1430s with reliefs of Christ, the Virgin, St Peter and St Paul and their martyrdoms, on a commission from Eugenius IV. After 1439 he added the four small narrow panels depicting events in the life of Eugenius, including the Council of Florence, at which he had attempted to heal the rift between the churches of East and West. Around them is a frieze of Classical and mythological subjects, animals, fruits and portraits of emperors. The door to the left **(c)** is by Giacomo Manzù (1963), the most important of numerous commissions he received from the Church, and has sculptures depicting the deaths of religious figures and abstract themes of death; the door on the extreme left is by Luciano Minguzzi (1977).

ST PETER'S BASILICA

Crucifixion of St Peter, detail of the central basilica door by Filarete (1430s). The building in the foreground is Castel Sant'Angelo. On the far left sits a personification of Rome holding an effigy of the god Mars. The martyrdom is shown taking place beyond the Tiber (in Filarete's day the site was believed to have been the Janiculum). Nero watches the scene from an Imperial loggia.

ST PETER'S BASILICA

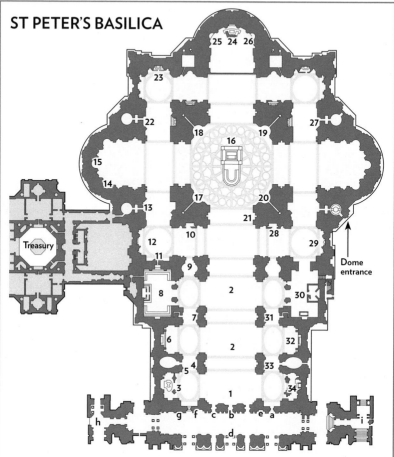

In the tympanum above the central entrance (look backwards, against the light) is the ***Navicella*** **(d)**, a mosaic representing Christ walking on the waters. Commissioned by Boniface VIII's nephew, Cardinal Stefaneschi, in 1297 and executed by Giotto for the quadrangular courtyard of Old St Peter's, this huge mosaic was designed to be seen by pilgrims as they left the church: it symbolised the role of the Church through Christ of bringing help to those in trouble. It has frequently been moved, and has suffered from resetting and restoration; it is now virtually a copy of the original.

High up on the wall between the doors are **three framed inscriptions**: the bull of Boniface VIII **(e)**, right of the entrance, proclaims the first Jubilee or Holy Year (1300). To the left of the Manzù door is the Latin epitaph of Hadrian I **(f)** (772–95), attributed to Charlemagne. The inscription on the far left **(g)** commemorates the donation by Gregory II of certain olive trees to provide oil for the lamps over the tomb of St Peter.

At the far ends of the portico are two **equestrian statues**, not at present accessible (nor even barely visible), but all the same, because of their symbolic weight, it is important to know that they exist. At the left end, by Agostino Cornacchini, is Charlemagne **(h)**, the first Holy Roman Emperor, who received his crown here in 800; on the right, by Bernini, is Constantine **(i)**, the first Christian emperor and builder of the original basilica on this site.

INTERIOR OF THE BASILICA

The interior of the basilica is extraordinary: vast and monumental, with towering empty spaces overhead and teeming humanity below, giving it the air of a busy railway station concourse. The space is immense: 186m long and 137m wide across the transepts, though the effect is disguised somewhat by the symmetry of the proportions. The gilded coffered ceiling was designed by Bramante. The coloured marble of the walls and pavement is the work of Giacomo della Porta and Bernini. The sumptuous revetment follows the same pattern throughout: a dove holding an olive branch, above which appear putti carrying aloft the papal insignia. Uniformed vergers (sometimes rather gruff) operate a system of mobile barriers on rubber castors. They roll these soundlessly around to barricade different parts of the basilica at different times, and to prevent tourists from entering chapels reserved for prayer. What you manage to see will depend entirely on the configuration of these barriers at the time of your visit.

The first part of the nave is Carlo Maderno's extension, which transformed the plan of the church from a Greek to a Latin cross. The **round slab of porphyry (1)** let into the pavement in front of the central door is that on which the emperors used to kneel for their coronation in front of the altar of the old basilica. All the way up the centre of the nave, a **succession of metal inscriptions (2)** (enclosed by barriers) indicates the lengths of the principal churches of the Catholic World. The nave is separated from the aisles by colossal piers, each decorated with two fluted Corinthian pilasters, supporting great arches. In the niches between the pilasters, both here and in the transepts, are statues of the founders of the religious orders. Over the spaces between the piers are elliptical cupolas, three on either side, decorated with elaborate mosaics.

NORTH SIDE

The side chapel in the northwest corner is the **Baptistery (3)**. The font consists of an upturned porphyry sarcophagus lid, which scholars think may well be that which once covered the remains of Hadrian in Castel Sant'Angelo. It was first recycled as the tomb of the Holy Roman Emperor Otto II, who died in Rome in 983. Beyond is Canova's splendid **monument to the last Stuarts (4)**, fashioned to look like a tomb, with busts of the Old and Young Pretenders and of Henry, Cardinal York above the carved entrance, which is flanked by grieving angels. King George IV contributed to the expense of the monument, which was erected in 1819 directly above the Stuarts' resting place in the crypt below (*see p. 435*). Opposite is the **monument to Clementina Sobieska (5)** (d. 1735), wife of James Stuart, the Old Pretender (she is here styled 'Queen of Great Britain, France and Ireland'; *for more on the Jacobites in Italy, see p. 158*).

The **Chapel of the Presentation of the Virgin (6)** preserves the body of St Pius X under the altar. On the left is a monument to Benedict XV by Pietro Canonica and Luca Beltrami (1928). The beautiful bronze **monument to Pope Innocent VIII (7)** is by Antonio Pollaiolo, the only funerary monument from the old basilica to have been re-erected in the new (although the composition was altered somewhat).

The **Cappella del Coro (8)** (*usually closed*) preserves relics of St John Chrysostom in an ancient granite basin. From here you pass between two large papal monuments, to **Leo XI and Innocent XI (9)**. The former is a very fine work by Alessandro Algardi. The body of the beatified Innocent XI is preserved beneath a nearby altar, above which is a **mosaic of the *Transfiguration* (10)**, a copy (enlarged four times) of Raphael's famous painting in the Vatican Pinacoteca (*see p. 445*).

Canova's influence can be seen in the **monument to Pius VII (11)** (d. 1823) by Bertel Thorvaldsen. The **Cappella Clementina (12)** is named after Clement VIII, who ordered Giacomo della Porta to decorate it for the Holy Year of 1600. The cupola has mosaics after Pomarancio, and beneath the altar is the tomb of one of the most important of all the popes, St Gregory the Great (d. 604; *see p. 273*).

High up above the Treasury entrance is the **monument to Pius VIII (13)**. (*The Treasury itself is described on p. 434.*) Beyond, in the north transept, is the **Altar of the Crucifixion of St Peter (14)**. The altarpiece is an 18th-century mosaic copy of Guido Reni's *Crucifixion* painted for San Paolo alle Tre Fontane (where there is also a copy). The original work is now in the Vatican Pinacoteca. The influence of Caravaggio in the composition of the scene is clear. Beneath the **Altar of St Joseph (15)** is a lead urn containing the relics of the apostles Simon and Jude.

THE HIGH ALTAR AND DOME

The work of Bernini for this majestic church, which begins with the approach to it in the piazza outside, culminates in the grandiose baldacchino **(16)** and tribune against the east wall. The great **baldacchino**, unveiled on 28th June 1633 by Urban VIII, rises over the high altar. To understand the concept of this solemn edifice, one must remember that this church was originally conceived on a central plan: its entire focus was intended to be this altar, which rises over the burial place of St Peter. The baldacchino is a colossal Baroque structure, a combination of architecture and decorative sculpture, cast from bronze taken from the Pantheon. Four gilt-bronze Solomonic columns rise from their marble plinths, which are decorated with the Barberini bees, Urban VIII's family emblem. The columns resemble in design the *Colonna Santa* (*see p. 436*) but are decorated with figures of genii and laurel branches. They support a canopy from which hang festoons and tassels (with more Barberini bees) and on which angels by Duquesnoy alternate with putti. From the four corners of the canopy ascend ornamental scrolls, which support the globe and Cross. Inside the top of the canopy, the Holy Spirit is represented as a dove in an aureole.

The **high altar**, at which only the pope may celebrate, is formed of a block of Greek marble found in the Forum of Nerva and consecrated by Clement VIII on 26th June 1594. It covers the altar of Calixtus II (d. 1123), which in turn encloses an altar of Gregory the Great (d. 604). In front of the altar is the **confessio**, built by Maderno and encircled by perpetually burning lamps. The urn and the mosaic in a niche of Christ Blessing mark the position of the grave of St Peter, which is in the necropolis directly below this spot.

THE CENTRAL DOME

The great dome of St Peter's is an architectural masterpiece. It was designed by Michelangelo, although built by him only as far as the drum: the cupola itself was executed by Giacomo della Porta following his design. Simple and dignified and flooded with light, it rises immediately above the site of St Peter's tomb. In the pendentives are huge mosaics of the Evangelists: the pen held by St Mark is 1.5m long. On the frieze below the drum is inscribed in letters nearly 2m high: *Tu es Petrus et super hanc petram aedificabo ecclesiam meam et tibi dabo claves regni caelorum* ('Thou art Peter, and upon this rock I will build my church; and I will give unto thee the keys of the kingdom of heaven'). The dome is divided into 16 compartments by ribs ornamented with stucco; in these compartments are six bands of mosaic by Cavaliere d'Arpino, representing saints, angels and the company of Heaven; in the lantern above is the Redeemer.

Four pentagonal piers support the arches on which the cupola drum rests. The piers are decorated with balconies and niches designed by Bernini. Each balcony niche has two Solomonic columns taken from the saint's shrine in the old basilica (another of these, the *Colonna Santa*, is in the Treasury; *see p. 436*). The main niches below are filled with colossal statues that give each of the piers its name: **St Andrew (17)** by François Duquesnoy; **St Veronica (18)** by Francesco Mochi; **St Helen (19)** by Andrea Bolgi; and **St Longinus (20)** by Bernini. Below the balcony consoles are reliefs referring to the *Reliquie Maggiori*; these precious relics, which are displayed in Holy Week, are preserved in the podium of the pier of St Veronica. They are the lance of St Longinus, the Roman soldier who pierced the side of Christ on the Cross, acquired by Innocent VIII from the Ottoman sultan Beyazit II; a piece of the True Cross preserved by St Helen; and the cloth of St Veronica with the miraculous image of Christ's face. The head of St Andrew, St Peter's brother, was presented to Pius II in 1462 by Thomas Palaeologus, despot of the Morea (the Peloponnese), who had saved it from the Turks during their invasion of Greece in 1460. At the end of the 20th century it was returned to the Greek Orthodox Church at Patras.

Under a canopy against the pier of St Longinus is the famous **bronze statue of St Peter (21)**, seated on a marble throne. It was once believed to date from the 5th or 6th century, but since its restoration in 1990 is considered to be the work of Arnolfo di Cambio (c. 1296). The extended foot of the statue has been worn smooth by the touch of worshippers. The statue is robed on high festivals.

EAST END

NB: This part of the basilica is always roped off and can only be viewed from a distance.

The **monument to Alexander VII (22)** shows the Chigi pope (d. 1667) kneeling above two allegorical figures of *Charity* and *Truth*, all in white marble, while over the little door is a huge carved shroud beneath which the macabre figure of Death appears holding up an hour-glass. This was Bernini's last work for the basilica. The **Cappella della Colonna (23)** was decorated in 1757 with figures of angels carrying garlands and with symbols of the Virgin. Above the tomb of St Leo the Great (d. 461) is a splendid relief by Alessandro Algardi (1653) representing *Leo Arresting the Progress of Attila with the help of St Peter and St Paul*. On the altar to the left is an ancient and greatly venerated representation of the Virgin, painted on a column from the old basilica.

At the far east end, two porphyry steps from the old basilica lead to the tribune, the most conspicuous object in which is the **Cathedra of St Peter (24)**, an ambitious and theatrical composition by Bernini (1665). This enormous gilt-bronze throne is supported by statues of four Fathers of the Church: St Augustine and St Ambrose of the Latin Church (in mitres), and St Athanasius and St John Chrysostom of the Greek Church (bare-headed). It encloses an ancient wooden chair inlaid with ivory, said to have been the episcopal chair of St Peter. A circle of flying angels surrounds a great halo of gilt stucco in the centre of which, providing the focal point of the whole church, is the Dove, set in the window above the throne.

The **tomb of Paul III (25)**, the great Farnese pope (d. 1549), is a magnificent creation by Guglielmo della Porta, later re-erected by Bernini. Della Porta began work on it just before the pope's death in 1549 and continued until he himself died in 1577. The present tomb comprises less than half the monument as planned. The figures of *Justice* (left) and *Prudence* (right) are both signed. Guglielmo's son Teodoro had to make imitation-marble clothes out of metal for the nude figure of Justice.

On the other side of the tribune is the **tomb of Urban VIII (26)**, Bernini's fine monument to the pope who consecrated this basilica, with statues of the pontiff and allegorical figures of *Charity* and *Justice*. The design of the tomb is clearly influenced by the Medici tombs in Florence by Michelangelo. The unusual curved lid of the sarcophagus is the same; the allegorical figures pose on top of it while an effigy of the deceased sits above. The use of different materials in the sculpture gives an effective colour to the monument. The **tomb of Clement XIII (27)** is by Canova. Unveiled in 1792, it consolidated the young sculptor's reputation.

SOUTH SIDE

The embalmed body of the fondly-remembered **St John XXIII (28)** (d. 1963, canonised in 2014) lies in a glass casket (the face is covered with a wax mask). The **Cappella**

Gregoriana (29) was built for Gregory XIII. The marble was taken from the Tiber-facing side of Castel Sant'Angelo. The chapel is dedicated to the *Madonna del Soccorso*, an ancient painting on part of a marble column from the old basilica, placed here in 1578. It contains the tomb of Gregory XVI (d. 1846) by Luigi Amici. The adjacent **Chapel of the Holy Sacrament (30)** is reserved for prayer. Its iron grille was designed by Francesco Borromini. Over the altar is a gilt-bronze ciborium by Bernini, modelled on Bramante's Tempietto (*see p. 404*). Behind is a painting of the *Trinity* by Pietro da Cortona.

In the south aisle is Bernini's **monument to Matilda of Tuscany (31)** (d. 1115), whose remains were brought here from Mantua in 1635. Diagonally opposite, under the altar of the Chapel of St Sebastian (*reserved for prayer*), is the much-venerated tomb of **St John Paul II (32)** (*see overleaf*). Against the first south pier is Carlo Fontana's 1689 **monument to Queen Christina of Sweden (33)** (*see p. 401*). In the side chapel beyond, a small crowd is almost always standing in admiration of **Michelangelo's *Pietà* (34)**.

MICHELANGELO'S *PIETÀ*

This exquisite work is the most famous sculpture in the basilica, made by Michelangelo in 1499 (when he was just 24) for the French ambassador Cardinal Jean de Bilhères de Lagraulas. It is perhaps the most moving of all the artist's sculptures and is the only one inscribed with his name (on the ribbon falling from the Virgin's left shoulder). Vasari recounts that Michelangelo, overhearing some Lombards praise it as the work of a sculptor from their native Milan, came with his chisel at dead of night to leave his name upon it. To understand the reasons why Michelangelo decided to represent the Madonna younger than her Son, it is perhaps enough to read the famous opening verse in the last Canto of Dante's *Paradiso*: '*Vergine madre, figlia del tuo figlio...*' ('Virgin mother, daughter of your son...'). The voluminous folds of the Virgin's drapery skilfully obscure the fact that her lap is vast, in order to allow it to support the body of Christ. If she were to stand to her feet, she would be a giantess. Since 1972, when a mentally unstable Hungarian geologist attacked the sculpture with his hammer and chopped off the Virgin's nose, the *Pietà* has been housed behind bullet-proof perspex. Sadly this lovely work can only now be admired from a very circumspect distance.

THE VATICAN GROTTOES (CRYPT)

Open 9–4 or 5. The entrance at the time of writing was beneath the Pier of St Andrew.
In the space (3m high) between the level of the existing basilica and that of the old one, the Renaissance architects built the so-called Sacred Grottoes and placed in them various monuments and architectural fragments from the former church. They have also been used for the burial of numerous popes.

Around the shrine at the heart of the crypt, which covers the tomb of St Peter, are the radially-arranged New Grottoes (*closed at the time of writing*). The area of the so-called Old Grottoes has the form of a nave with aisles (corresponding to Maderno's nave but extending beyond it). Piped devotional music and recorded admonitions to observe silence set the tone for the whole experience. The tombs are all well labelled.

IMPORTANT POPES IN ROMAN HISTORY

Julius II (Giuliano della Rovere; 1503–13)
Born into a branch of the Della Rovere family in 1443, Julius was a nephew of Sixtus IV. Ruthless and implacable, he led his armies into battle dressed in full armour, and was known as '*il Terrible*'; but he was a great lover of antiquity and patron of the arts, and he employed both Raphael and Michelangelo. When the grandiose funerary monument planned for him by the latter came to nothing (*see p. 118*), Julius was buried simply beneath the pavement of St Peter's.

Leo X (Giovanni de' Medici; 1513–21)
The second son of Lorenzo the Magnificent, Giovanni de' Medici was created cardinal when only 13. The celebrated portrait by Raphael (of whom Leo was an enthusiastic patron) shows him fat and worried-looking. Leo perspired a good deal and during ecclesiastical functions was always wiping his face and hands, to the distress of bystanders. He had a beautiful white elephant called Hanno, who wore four red slippers exactly like Leo's, and genuflected in the pope's presence. Leo's bull *Exsurge Domine* of 1520 condemned 41 errors of Martin Luther. His tomb is in Santa Maria sopra Minerva.

Clement VII (Giulio de' Medici; 1523–34)
The bastard nephew of Lorenzo the Magnificent, Giulio de' Medici was declared legitimate and created cardinal in 1513. He had a squint in his left eye. According to Benvenuto Cellini he had excellent taste—the beautiful but faded portrait by Sebastiano del Piombo (Capodimonte, Naples) makes him look vain and supercilious. Clement's bitter relations with the Emperor Charles V led to the disastrous Sack of Rome in 1527 (*see p. 23*). Trapped for seven months in Castel Sant'Angelo, he grew a beard as a sign of mourning. Henry VIII's request for a divorce from Catherine of Aragon fell on deaf papal ears. Clement is buried in Santa Maria sopra Minerva.

Paul III (Alessandro Farnese; 1534–49)
As cardinal, Alessandro Farnese fathered four children, but he put away his mistress long before his election as pope. He loved masked balls, fireworks, clowns and dwarfs, and in 1536 he revived the carnival, when enormous floats were dragged through the streets of Rome by teams of buffalo. Yet he was a great reformer, and as well as his human children he begot a number of religious orders: the Barnabites, the Theatines, the Capuchins and most importantly the Society of Jesus or Jesuits (in 1540). From Michelangelo Paul commissioned the *Last Judgement* and the new layout of the Capitoline Hill. He is buried in St Peter's in a beautiful tomb by Guglielmo della Porta.

Urban VIII (Maffeo Barberini; 1623–44)
Authoritarian, highly conscious of his own position, and a terrible nepotist, Urban was also learned and artistic. He wrote Latin verses—and indeed spoilt many hymns

in the Breviary by rewriting them in a 'correct' but bloodless classical style. He was unpopular, and there was unseemly rejoicing when he died; but he gave Rome the art and architecture of Bernini, the young sculptor whom he made architect of the new St Peter's. The basilica was consecrated in 1626, and Bernini's great bronze baldachin was completed in 1634. Urban lies buried close beside it, in a tomb and funerary monument designed by his brilliant protégé.

Innocent X (Giovan Battista Pamphilj; 1644–55)
Innocent was elected in 1644 after a stormy conclave, and was consecrated on 4th October at a particularly splendid ceremony, when for the first time the dome of the basilica was lit up by flaming torches. Velázquez's celebrated portrait in the Palazzo Doria Pamphilj has caught for us his famously ugly features and disturbing, implacable gaze. His life was blameless, but he was irresolute and suspicious. Innocent died in January 1655 after a long agony; no one wanted to pay for his burial, but a funerary monument was eventually set up in the church of Sant'Agnese on Piazza Navona, which has a façade by his favourite architect, Borromini.

Pius VII (Luigi Barnaba Chiaramonti; 1800–23)
Elected in March 1800, Pius was constrained by political and military events to sign a concordat with Bonaparte in 1801. In 1804 he went to Paris to officiate at the emperor's coronation; he was rudely treated, and Napoleon placed the crown on his own head. In 1809 Pius was arrested by the French and interned. In 1814, after Bonaparte's fall, he returned to Rome amidst general rejoicing. Pius was magnanimous towards Napoleon's family. His likeness by Thomas Lawrence is one of the greatest of all papal portraits. Pius died after falling and breaking a leg: the dying pope was not told about the disastrous fire at the Basilica of San Paolo fuori le Mura, his favourite Roman church. His tomb is in St Peter's.

John Paul II (Karol Józef Wojtyła; 1978–2005)
As a child in Wadowice, the future pope John Paul II was known as Lolek. He worked in a quarry and at the Solvay chemical factory before joining an underground seminary in 1942; he studied at the Angelicum in Rome but had some difficulties with his degrees (poverty, Communist interference). In 1967 Paul VI made him Cardinal-Priest of San Cesareo in Palatio (*see p. 562*). His election to the papacy caused general astonishment. Not only was he the first non-Italian pope for 455 years, but he came from the Eastern European, Soviet bloc. He brought to the Vatican his love of sports (which he saw as a means of emancipation for the poor), especially skiing. As pope, John Paul travelled a good deal, made 104 foreign journeys and visited 317 of Rome's 333 parishes. He canonised 482 saints, created 232 cardinals, appointed more than half of the world's 4,000 bishops. His funeral in April 2005 was watched on TV by thousands of millions. He was himself canonised in 2014.

M.R.

Major memorials in the crypt are marked on the plan opposite. In the corridor with the tomb of Calixtus III (with a good relief of the *Risen Christ*) are preserved some column stumps from the Old St Peter's.

THE ENGLISH POPE

Only one Englishman has ever been elected pope, Nicholas Breakspear. Born at Abbot's Langley near St Albans in Hertfordshire, he reigned from 1154 to 1159 as Pope Hadrian IV. His tomb is a 3rd-century sarcophagus of red Egyptian porphyry, carved with a festoon, two rosettes, an ox's skull, and two Medusa heads. When this tomb was opened in 1606, Hadrian was found to be of below-average height; he was wearing Turkish slippers and a ring with an enormous emerald.

M.R.

THE TREASURY

The Treasury or Museo Storico Artistico (*open 8–6.30 or 7; entry fee*) is entered under the monument to Pius VIII (*no. 13 on the plan on p. 426*). On the vestibule wall is a large stone slab with the names of all the popes buried in the basilica. The treasury contents were plundered in 846 by the Saracens, and again during the Sack of Rome by Imperial troops in 1527, and it was impoverished by the Treaty of Tolentino (1797), which Pius VI was forced to conclude with Napoleon, assigning many precious artworks to France. It still, however, contains objects of great value and interest. Highlights include the exquisite **Vatican Cross**. This is the most ancient possession of the Treasury, dating from the 6th century, and was the gift of the emperor Justinian II. It is made of bronze and set with jewels.

The ancient **Cathedra of St Peter**, which Bernini incorporated in the decoration of the tribune of the basilica, can be seen here in a copy made in 1974.

Occupying almost all the central space in a further room, the huge **monument to Sixtus IV** (recently restored) is a masterpiece in bronze by Antonio Pollaiolo (1493). This pope is remembered as the builder of the Sistine Chapel (which is named after him), and for opening the Vatican Library to the public for the first time. He also donated some important Classical bronzes to the city of Rome. He is shown recumbent but slightly raised up, as if awake and keenly aware of the nubilely beautiful Liberal Arts cavorting round his bed.

Also displayed is the **garb for the bronze statue of St Peter** in the basilica (*no. 21 on the plan on p. 426*), which on high festivals is arrayed in full pontificals. Photographs show what the statue looks like with them on.

The Treasury also preserves a clay model of an **angel by Bernini** (1673), used as a model for one of the angels flanking the ciborium in the Chapel of the Holy Sacrament (*no. 30 on the plan*). The **ciborium from the old St Peter's** made by Donatello is also kept here. Dating from c. 1432, this beautiful work encloses a painting of the *Madonna della Febbre* (protectress of victims of malaria—once rife in the Roman Campagna). The **gilt-bronze cock** (9th century) stood on top of the campanile of the old basilica (it evokes the cock which crowed when Peter denied Christ).

The superbly-carved **sarcophagus of Junius Bassus**, prefect of Rome in 359, was found near St Peter's in 1505. It is an extremely important example of early Christian

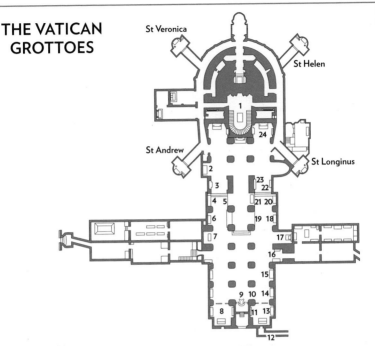

THE VATICAN GROTTOES

St Veronica

St Helen

St Andrew

St Longinus

1 Behind glass and flanked by two lions and two angels, a mosaic marks the tomb of St Peter, directly below the confessio in the church above. The Tropaion of Gaius (*see p. 437*) is behind on a lower level with the foundation of the altar of Calixtus II enclosing that of Gregory I, where the rear wall was breached during the excavations for St Peter's tomb. Beyond this point lie the New Grottoes (*no admission*), whose centre is immediately below the high altar of St Peter's. The four radial extensions reach to points below the four piers of St Longinus, St Helen, St Veronica and St Andrew.

2 Pius XI (d. 1939)
3 Cardinal Merry de Val
4 Tomb of the last Stuarts: 'James III', Bonnie Prince Charlie and Cardinal York
4 Cardinal Tedeschini
6 Innocent XIII (d. 1724)
7 Urban VI (d. 1389)
8 Julius III, Gregory V, Hadrian IV, Emperor Otto II
9 Pius VI. A very fine kneeling statue by Canova. The actual tomb of the pontiff is at the other end of the aisle (no. 24).

10 Innocent VII
11 Nicholas III (d. 1280)
12 Calixtus III (d. 1458)
13 Boniface VIII (d. 1303)
14 Nicholas V (d, 1455)
15 Paul II (d. 1471). The tomb (unfinished) is the work of Mino da Fiesole, Giovanni Dalmata and others. Giovanni Dalmata had worked on Palazzo di Venezia for this same (Venetian) pope.
16 At the beginning of a corridor are four beautiful mosaics from the old basilica.
17 Paul VI (d. 1978) lies under a very simple slab. The relief of the *Madonna* is attributed to Isaia da Pisa.
18 Marcellus II (d. 1555). The pontiff lies in an antique sarcophagus. He was the last pope to take his own baptismal name as his regnal title. Palestrina's *Missa Papae Marcelli* was written for him.
19 John Paul I (d. 1978)
20 Innocent IX (d. 1591)
21 Benedict XV (d. 1922)
22 Queen Christina of Sweden (*see p. 401*)
23 Queen Charlotte of Cyprus (d. 1487)
24 Pius VI (d. 1799)

art (Junius Bassus is thought to have adopted the new religion shortly before his death). Its scenes from the Old and New Testaments are explained in labels *in situ*. Among the collection of Church plate are two candlesticks traditionally attributed to Benvenuto Cellini.

The ***Colonna Santa***, displayed on the way out, is a 4th-century Byzantine spiral column, one of twelve from the old basilica. Eight decorate the balconies of the piers of the great dome, but the remaining three are lost. The column once claimed to be that against which Christ leaned when speaking with the doctors in the Temple of Jerusalem.

ROME AS A CENTRE OF PILGRIMAGE

As the burial place of St Peter, Rome has always been considered a holy city—a second Jerusalem. A huge quantity of relics, endowed by popular belief with miraculous powers, were brought to the city from the East and in the Middle Ages pilgrims from all over Europe travelled to see them. The medieval route from Northern Europe to Rome was one of the three main pilgrimage roads in medieval Europe (the other two led to Santiago de Compostela and Jerusalem). By 1024 it had assumed its current name, the Francigena, because it originated in Frankish territory. The Anglo-Saxon churchman Sigeric travelled along it in 990 to receive the pallium, the symbol of his investiture as Archbishop of Canterbury, from the hands of the pope. His return journey, with its 79 stopping-places, is described in a manuscript which survives in the British Library.

The journey from England to Rome was usually made in spring and took about ten weeks. Most pilgrims probably covered the entire distance on foot carrying a staff, although prelates such as Sigeric would have travelled on horseback. The road was rough and paved only in places, and was not suitable for wheeled vehicles, but this overland route was considered safer and easier than the trip by sea. Numerous *ospedali* grew up along the way to offer help and accommodation to travellers. Apart from pilgrims, the road was used by merchants and traders, and goods as well as works of art were transported along it. Its importance diminished after the 13th century, when other routes were opened over the Alps. Gradually, Rome became more and more organised for the reception of pilgrims: the hospital and hostel of Santo Spirito in the Borgo, for example (*see p. 418*), was built for them in the 12th century.

Rome was especially busy in Holy Years (*see p. 292*), when the pope gave a full pardon to confessed communicants who visited the two major basilicas of St Peter's and San Paolo fuori le Mura 15 times (for foreigners) or 30 times (for Romans), or every day for three weeks. Visits to St John Lateran and Santa Maria Maggiore were later added. In 1500 San Lorenzo fuori le Mura, Santa Croce in Gerusalemme and San Sebastiano were added to the four major basilicas to establish the Seven Churches of Rome, which were the most important places pilgrims were required to visit. In 1600 it is estimated that some 1,200,000 visitors came to Rome. Today that figure is hazarded at around ten million, with more even than that during the Extraordinary Jubilee of Mercy of 2015–16.

THE DOME OF ST PETER'S

Open 8–5 or 6. Entry fee. You can choose to take the lift to roof level and climb the rest of the way (320 steps) or go the whole way on foot (551 steps). The elevator option costs slightly more.

Outside the basilica, at the right end of the portico, is the entrance to the dome (clearly signed). From the level of the roof, where the lift stops, there is a close-up view of the spring of the dome, with the Cross 92m above. The two side cupolas, by Giacomo della Porta, are purely decorative and have no opening into the interior of the church. On the roof are buildings once used by the *sanpietrini*, the workmen permanently employed on the fabric of the basilica. Two stairways lead to a curving corridor from which you can enter the first circular gallery around the interior of the drum of the dome: 53m above the ground and 67m below the top of the dome. From here there is an impressive view of the pavement far below and of the dome interior; the decorative details and mosaics are on a vast scale.

Signs indicate the way, up a spiral staircase with lancet windows and a curving narrow stair between the two shells of the dome. The first big window has a view south, with the roof of the huge Audience Hall (1971) directly below. Iron stairs continue up to the tiny marble stairs which emerge on the loggia around the pretty lantern. There is a splendid view of the Vatican City and gardens, and beyond, on a clear day, of the whole of Rome and of the Campagna from the Apennines and the Alban Hills to the sea. A copper ball 2.5m in diameter is surmounted by the Cross, 132.5m above the ground. Another staircase leads down and out onto the roof, beside the huge statues on the façade, with a view of St Peter's Square.

THE NECROPOLIS AND TOMB OF ST PETER

Admission is by previous appointment only. Visitors must be over 15. Guided tours lasting approx. 90mins are given to groups of a maximum of twelve people. To book, email scavi@fsp.va or Fax: 06 69 87 3017. To apply in person, go to the Ufficio Scavi (left of the basilica), which is open Mon–Fri 9–6, Sat 9–5. NB: There is no way of booking a specific time and the processing of applications can be slow. But a virtual tour (in Italian) is available at www.vatican.va/various/basiliche/necropoli/scavi_italian.html.

In 1940 a double row of mausolea was discovered, dating from the 1st century AD, running from east to west below the level of the old basilica. The extreme west series of these is on higher ground and adjoins a graveyard which is immediately beneath the high altar of the present church. Constantine significantly chose to erect his basilica above this necropolis, presumably knowing that it contained the tomb of St Peter. This was a most difficult undertaking because of the slope of the hill; he had to level the terrain and make use of supporting foundation walls.

A baldacchino in the presbytery covered the Tropaion of Gaius, a funerary monument in the form of a small aedicule or niche, mentioned in documents dating from around 200 and probably built some decades before by Pope Anicetus. This monument was discovered during excavations in the 20th century. It backs onto a supporting wall plastered with red, dating from the same period. An empty space beneath it is believed to be the tomb of St Peter. This was probably a mound of earth covered by brick slabs, and it shows signs of the interference which history records. That this was a most revered grave is evident from the number of other burials which crowd in on it, without cutting across the tomb. In front of the red wall, on which a Greek inscription (ΠΕΤΡ) is taken to name the saint, is a later wall, scratched with the names of pilgrims invoking the aid of Peter. Bones, obviously displaced, of an elderly and powerfully-built man, were found in 1965 beneath this second graffiti wall and declared by Paul VI to be those of St Peter. The site of the Circus of Nero, the most likely place of St Peter's martyrdom, lay along the south flank of the basilica and extended as far as the present Piazza del Sant'Uffizio. The necropolis was in use until Constantine's reign.

MAUSOLEA IN THE NECROPOLIS

The necropolis takes the form of a long corridor in brick and tufa, off which open individual mausolea, some of them very fine, with wall-paintings, mosaics, niches for cinerary urns and tombs and arcosolia. **Mausoleum F**, of the Tullii and Caetenni, has holes in the mosaic floor through which libations would have been poured at feasts to honour the dead. Particularly fine is **Mausoleum H**, of the Valerii, with well-preserved stuccoes and portrait busts, and a moving death mask of a child with its eyes closed, its long eyelashes particularly carefully rendered. **Mauseoleum I** has a beautiful wall-painting of a peacock, which to the early Christians was a symbol of immortality. On the floor is a monochrome mosaic of Mercury leading the chariot of Pluto, interpreted as an image of victory over death. Many of the burials here were pagan; the only purely Christian mausoleum is **Mausoleum M**, which has yielded the most ancient mosaics yet discovered on a Christian subject. Here, on the vault, richly decorated with a vine pattern, is Christ as Sol Novus, the new Sun or new Apollo. He is shown beardless, dressed in Roman garb and driving a chariot, with a globe in his left hand and brilliant rays emanating from his head. The iconography is clearly derived from images of pagan sun-worship, which seems to have been sanctioned in Rome from the 1st or 2nd century. On the walls are the sinopie remains of mosaics which have become detached from the surface (on the left, Jonah, and ahead, fishermen; both of these with symbolism of purely Christian derivation). **Mausoleum U** has wall-paintings personifying Lucifer and Vesper, the morning and evening stars, allegories of the trajectory of human life. At the far end of the corridor is the site of the **Tropaion of Gaius**; you can see where the rear wall was breached during the excavations for St Peter's tomb. Here also is the **wall plastered in red**, marking the site of the Apostle's resting place.

The Vatican Museums

*The Vatican Museums contain some of the world's greatest
art treasures, and are unique in their scope, quality and abundance.*

The museums of the Vatican include the largest collection in existence of ancient Greek and Roman sculpture, a picture gallery with some very fine works, Egyptian and Etruscan museums, collections of tapestries and early Christian art. All this is housed in the Vatican Palace, which is a work of art in itself for its magnificently decorated halls and chapels, most famous of which are the Sistine Chapel frescoed by Michelangelo and the *Stanze* decorated by Raphael.

Not surprisingly, the museums are apt to get very crowded and visiting them can be something of an ordeal. It is worth it when you get there, but to some extent you have to steel yourself. Be prepared for a long trek to the entrance on Viale Vaticano (*map p. 650, B1*); for queues and crowds; for a lot of walking up and down stairs and along museum corridors; and for not particularly welcoming staff.

Visitor information
The museums website (museivaticani.va) should be your first port of call. This is the only way to get quick, up-to-date information on opening times and prices, both of which are apt to change. The museums are also closed on certain Church holidays, which are different from year to year. You can buy tickets online (see below) or book a guided tour (guided tours of the gardens are also available). By doing either of these, you won't have to queue at the entrance. If you don't book online, aim to visit in the afternoon, around 4pm. This means that you will have to rush around the collection somewhat, but the lines at the entrance will be much shorter.

Opening times
Official opening times at the time of writing were as follows: Mon–Sat 9–6, last tickets at 4pm. Closed Sun except the last Sun of every month, when the museums are open free of charge from 9–2, last tickets 12.30. Closed New Year's Day, 6 Jan, 11 Feb, 19 March, Easter Sun and Mon, 1 May, 29 June, 15 Aug, 8 Dec, Christmas Day and Boxing Day, and whenever special reasons make it necessary.

Tickets
All the museums are covered by one ticket, but only for a single visit. The admission fee is quite hefty. Buying tickets online (from museivaticani.va) is a way of avoiding the queue at the entrance, although it is more expensive (you pay an extra

reservation fee on top). You can buy tickets online up to 60 days before you plan to visit. Print off the confirmation and exchange it for your ticket when you get there. Instructions are on the confirmation sheet. You can also book a visit with a tour guide and arrange to see parts of the palace not normally on show. To book an evening private view, email visitespeciali.musei@scv.va.

Approaches

The only access to the museums is from the north, on Viale Vaticano (map p. 650, B1). Buses to Piazza del Risorgimento include no. 23 from the Lungotevere at Trastevere and no. 81 from Via del Teatro di Marcello. Metro A from Termini Station and Piazza di Spagna to Ottaviano-San Pietro or the next stop Cipro-Musei Vaticani, both north of Piazza del Risorgimento. From St Peter's it is a long, uninteresting walk (head north through Bernini's colonnade) along via di Porta Angelica skirting the high wall of the Vatican City all the way.

Planning your visit

The volume of visitors to the Vatican Museums can seriously impede enjoyment, especially because of the number of groups, which have their own momentum and make it difficult for individual visitors to see things. The museum guards are not always very helpful, and when there is a shortage of custodians the less 'popular' sections are often closed.

Almost six million people a year visit the Vatican, and the Sistine Chapel is the exclusive goal of almost all the tour groups. This presents obvious problems: how to protect the masterpieces and how to prevent the visitor experience from deteriorating even further. The Sistine Chapel recently received LED lighting and a new air conditioning system—and the idea of putting a cap on the number of visitors to the Chapel has once again been mooted.

There have been recent attempts to improve labelling, but it is still minimal and at times non-existent. The description that follows is thus very long; even so, it only attempts to highlight the most important works. Good audio guides are available, but they must be returned to a designated place at the exit, which means you cannot make use of the earlier exit from the Sistine Chapel, which leads directly to the portico of St Peter's. At the time of writing this was usually only open to tour groups but if you are on your own you can very often linger around one of these and go out with them, thus avoiding the long trek back from Viale Vaticano. If you do exit here, you will miss the Museum of Christian Art and the Vatican Library.

TOUR OF THE MUSEUMS

From the ticket offices a steep escalator or gradually sloping helicoidal ramp (take your pick) leads up to the roofed Cortile delle Corazze. On the terrace leading off it, the first great piece of ancient sculpture is exhibited. This is the **base of the Column**

VATICAN MUSEUMS
Base of the Column of Antoninus Pius, showing the apotheosis of the emperor and his wife.

of Antoninus Pius (A), found in 1703 near Montecitorio. A monolithic block of Greek marble, it has a high-relief showing the apotheosis of Antoninus and his wife Faustina, who are being conducted toward celestial reward by a winged genius personifying Rome (AD 138–61). From this terrace (good views of St Peter's and the Vatican Gardens) you have a choice: visit the Pinacoteca and other museums in the modern wing (*described below*); or embark on the long route towards the Sistine Chapel (*description begins on p. 468*). If the weather is fine, you can descend the steps to the café and have a pleasant drink and snack at one of the outdoor tables, either before or at the end of your visit (you will return here to exit the museums).

HISTORY OF THE VATICAN PALACE AND ITS COLLECTIONS
In the days of Pope St Symmachus (498–514), a house was built beside the first basilica of St Peter. This house was not the residence of the popes (at that date they lived in the Lateran Palace) but it was used on state occasions and for the accommodation of foreign sovereigns. Charlemagne stayed here on the occasion of his coronation in 800, for example, and Otto II in 980. By the 12th century it had fallen into disrepair. Eugenius III (1145–53) was the first of numerous popes to restore and enlarge it. In 1208 Innocent III built a fortified residence here, which was added to by his successors. For much of the 14th century the popes had their seat in Avignon. When Gregory XI returned to Rome in 1378, he found the Lateran uninhabitable and so took up residence in the Vatican. The first Vatican conclave was held on his death in the same year.

Nicholas V, at the same time as he instigated the embellishment of St Peter's (*see p. 421*), transformed the old fortified house into a palace, which he built round the Cortile del Pappagallo. In 1473 Sixtus IV added the Sistine Chapel. The Borgia pope Alexander

VI decorated a suite of rooms on the first floor. Around this time too, another nucleus began to form on the north summit of the Vatican hill, where Innocent VIII had built a pavilion known as the Belvedere. On his accession to the pontificate in 1503, Julius II began to form his famous collection of Classical sculpture and installed it in what is now the octagonal courtyard of the Belvedere. He then commissioned Donato Bramante to unite the Belvedere with the palace of Nicholas V by means of long corridors, thus creating the great Cortile del Belvedere.

Leo X decorated the east side of the palace with open galleries, one of which became known as the Loggia of Raphael. Paul III employed Antonio da Sangallo the Younger to build the Cappella Paolina and the Sala Regia. Sixtus V assigned to Domenico Fontana the construction of the block overlooking St Peter's Square and of the great library, which was built at right angles to the long corridors and thus divided the Cortile del Belvedere in two. Bernini's Scala Regia was begun under Urban VIII and completed under Alexander VII.

The Museum of Pagan Antiquities was founded by Clement XIII. Clement XIV converted the Cortile del Belvedere into a museum which his successor Pius VI enlarged; hence its name, Pio-Clementino. Pius VI was also the founder of the Pinacoteca. Pius VII Chiaramonti founded the sculpture gallery which bears his name and added the New Wing, parallel to the library, thus dividing the Cortile del Belvedere into three: the courtyard nearest the pontifical palace retains the old name. Gregory XVI was responsible for the Etruscan and Egyptian Museums. Pius IX restored the Borgia Rooms.

Under Pius XI the new picture gallery was built, dating from 1932. A building was constructed in 1970 by Paul VI to house the former Lateran museums, the Gregorian Museum of Pagan Antiquities and the Pio Christian Museum; in 1973 the Ethnological Missionary Museum was opened beneath it. An extensive series of galleries in and around the Borgia Rooms was opened in 1973 as a Museum of Modern Religious Art. A grand new entrance of no great architectural distinction (by Lucio Passarelli) was opened in 2000 on Viale Vaticano. Major restorations in many of the museums were underway at the time of writing.

THE PINACOTECA

The Vatican Picture Gallery (Pinacoteca Vaticana) owes its origin to Pius VI, but under the Treaty of Tolentino (1797) he was forced to surrender the best works to Napoleon. Of these, 77 were recovered in 1815. The present building, by Luca Beltrami, was opened in 1932. The collection is devoted mostly to Italian painters and the arrangement is chronological and by schools. *NB: The Pinacoteca was under restoration at the time of writing: some works might be rearranged.*

Room I: The oldest picture in the gallery is a very interesting *Last Judgement*, signed by 'Nicolaus' and 'Iohannes', painters at work in Rome in the late 11th century. There are also 14th- century works by painters from Venice, Bologna, the Marche and Tuscany and a 13th-century portrait of St Francis by Margaritone d'Arezzo.

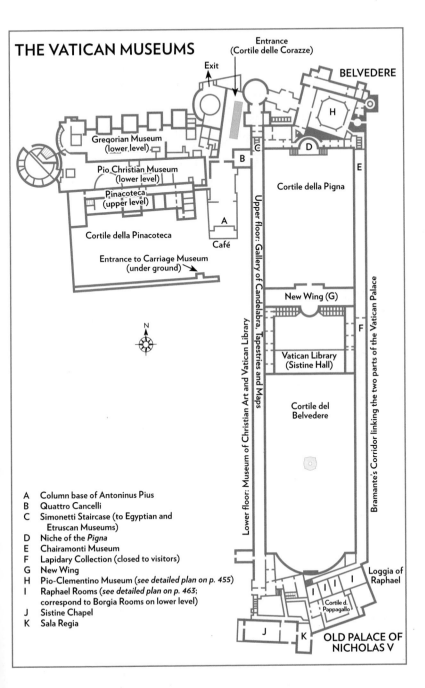

THE VATICAN MUSEUMS

Entrance (Cortile delle Corazze)

Exit

BELVEDERE

Gregorian Museum (lower level)

Pio Christian Museum (lower level)

Pinacoteca (upper level)

Cortile della Pinacoteca

Café

Entrance to Carriage Museum (under ground)

N

Upper floor: Gallery of Candelabra, Tapestries and Maps

Lower floor: Museum of Christian Art and Vatican Library

Cortile della Pigna

New Wing (G)

Vatican Library (Sistine Hall)

Cortile del Belvedere

Bramante's Corridor linking the two parts of the Vatican Palace

Loggia of Raphael

Cortile d. Pappagallo

OLD PALACE OF NICHOLAS V

A   Column base of Antoninus Pius
B   Quattro Cancelli
C   Simonetti Staircase (to Egyptian and Etruscan Museums)
D   Niche of the *Pigna*
E   Chairamonti Museum
F   Lapidary Collection (*closed to visitors*)
G   New Wing
H   Pio-Clementino Museum (*see detailed plan on p. 455*)
I   Raphael Rooms (*see detailed plan on p. 463; correspond to Borgia Rooms on lower level*)
J   Sistine Chapel
K   Sala Regia

Room II: The **Stefaneschi Altarpiece** is one of the most important works in the collection, commissioned from Giotto for the confessio of Old St Peter's by Cardinal Jacopo Stefaneschi. The cardinal belonged to a patrician Roman family and was known as a patron of the arts (he also commissioned the huge *Navicella* mosaic from Giotto for the atrium of the old basilica; *see p. 427*). The polyptych is painted on both sides so that it could be seen by the congregation as well as by the prelates celebrating the service: On one side, the central panel depicts *St Peter Enthroned*, with St George presenting Stefaneschi to St Peter (Stefaneschi is kneeling and offers up an image of the altarpiece itself to Peter). Pope Celestine V is also shown kneeling, making a gift of a codex to Peter (sometimes identified with the *St George Codex*, which is still preserved in the Vatican Library). The side panels show Sts James, Paul, Andrew and John the Evangelist. On the other side the central panel shows *Christ Enthroned*, surrounded by angels, with the donor Stefaneschi kneeling at the foot of the throne, with his cardinal's hat at his feet. On either side are the *Crucifixion of St Peter* and the *Martyrdom of St Paul*. The scene showing St Peter is very striking, showing the cross placed between two elongated structures. The one on the right, crowned by a tree, represents Castel Sant'Angelo. The pyramid is an old Roman tomb, which in Giotto's day still stood in the Borgo, at the beginning of the present Via della Conciliazione.

Around the walls are some exquisite small paintings by **Sienese and Florentine painters** of the 14th and 15th centuries. The Sienese school is represented by some of its greatest masters—Pietro Lorenzetti, Simone Martini, Sano di Pietro, Sassetta and Giovanni di Paolo. There are also panels with stories from the lives of St Benedict and St Nicholas of Bari by Lorenzo Monaco and Gentile da Fabriano, the main exponents of the International Gothic style, both born around 1370.

Room III: Works here are by 15th-century Florentine masters. The two beautiful **panels by Fra' Angelico**, with three scenes each from the life of St Nicholas, were part of a polyptych painted for the Dominicans of Perugia around 1437. One panel shows the birth of the saint, his calling to the Church as he stands listening to a sermon with a group of women seated on the grass in front of a pink church, and the famous scene of his giving a bag of gold to three poor girls. The other panel shows him meeting a messenger from the emperor and his rescue of a galleon from shipwreck. Fra' Angelico frescoed a chapel in the Vatican for Nicholas V (*see p. 466*) some ten years after he painted these scenes. The great artist died in Rome and is buried in Santa Maria sopra Minerva; *see p. 178*).

Benozzo Gozzoli, who collaborated with Fra' Angelico, is represented with a painting of *St Thomas Receiving the Virgin's Girdle*. There is also a *Crucifixion* and *Transition of the Virgin* by Masolino, and a large triptych of the *Coronation of the Virgin* by Filippo Lippi.

Room IV: Here are some of the most important works of **Melozzo da Forlì**, who was a follower of Piero della Francesca and had a lasting influence on the course of painting in the late 15th century in Rome and central

Italy. In 1480 he painted a splendid large fresco of *Christ in Glory* for the apse of Santi Apostoli in Rome. This was detached and the central part is now in the Quirinal (*see p. 332*), but its eight delightful Angel Musicians, some cherubs and the heads of four apostles are displayed here. A few years earlier Melozzo was commissioned to paint another fresco for the Vatican Library: this has also been detached (and transferred to canvas) and is preserved here. It shows Sixtus IV conferring on the humanist Platina the librarianship of the Vatican in the presence of Giuliano della Rovere (afterwards Julius II), his brother Giovanni, and Girolamo and Raffaele Riario.

There are also works by Marco Palmezzano, a collaborator of Melozzo, including a beautiful *Madonna and Saints*.

Room VI: Beyond Room V, a narrow gallery with more 15th-century works, is a room of fine polyptychs by the late 15th-century **Venetian school**, including the brothers Carlo and Vittorio Crivelli, and Antonio and Bartolomeo Vivarini, whose magnificent *Pesaro Polyptych* (1464) shows St Anthony Abbot (in relief) beneath Christ in Pietà surrounded by eight other saints. Also here are two polyptychs by the Umbrian painter (L'Alunno).

Room VII: This room has works by the **Umbrian school**. Perugino is well represented.

Room VIII: This, the largest room in the gallery, is devoted to **Raphael**. It contains three of his most famous paintings, as well as two exquisite predellas and a set of tapestries made from his original cartoons. The lovely ***Coronation of the Virgin*** was his first large composition, painted in Perugia in 1503 when he was just 20 years old. It shows the Apostles looking up from the empty tomb to a celestial scene of the Virgin receiving a crown from Christ. The predella is exhibited in front in a showcase, with scenes of the *Annunciation*, *Adoration of the Magi* and *Presentation in the Temple*.

The magnificent ***Madonna of Foligno*** is a mature work painted about 1511. It was a votive offering by Sigismondo Conti in gratitude for his escape when a cannon ball fell on his house during the siege of Foligno. He is shown with St Jerome, and in the background is Foligno during the battle. The painting was kept in the convent of Sant'Anna in Foligno (Umbria) from 1565 until it was stolen by Napoleon in 1797.

The ***Transfiguration*** is Raphael's last work: the superb scene is shown above the dramatic episode of the healing of the young man possessed by a devil. It was commissioned in 1517 by Cardinal Giuliano de' Medici for the cathedral of Narbonne, but in 1523 it was placed in the apse of San Pietro in Montorio. It was taken to France in 1797 and only restored to Rome after the fall of Napoleon. It is not known how much of the painting had been finished by the time of Raphael's death in 1520, and although the composition is Raphael's, it seems likely that it was executed by his pupils Giulio Romano and Francesco Penni.

The celebrated **'Acts of the Apostles' tapestries**, displayed around the walls behind protective glass, were intended for the lower portion of the Sistine

Chapel walls. They were commissioned by Leo X and woven in Brussels by Pieter van Aelst from cartoons drawn by Raphael in 1515–16. Seven of the cartoons (the other three have been lost) are in the Victoria and Albert Museum, London, though some scholars believe that these seven, which were bought in 1630 by Charles I of England, are 17th-century copies and that all the originals have been lost. Other tapestries from the same cartoons are in Hampton Court Palace near London, in the Palazzo Ducale at Mantua, and in the Palazzo Apostolico at Loreto. The tapestries displayed here belong to the so-called 'Old School' series (ten of the 'New School' series are in the Gallery of Tapestries; see p. 459). They have decorative side panels of *grottesche* and scenes along the base, imitating bas-relief, of episodes from the life of Leo X. The subjects of the main panels themselves are scenes from the lives of the apostles Peter, Paul, Stephen and Barnabas. When the tapestries were unveiled in 1519 they received rapturous acclamation. Art historians have tended to rate them very highly; historians of the art of textile weaving are more ambivalent. Some contend that Raphael's designs show scant understanding of what can and cannot be done on a loom. Also displayed here is a 16th-century Flemish tapestry of the *Last Supper*, derived from Leonardo's famous fresco in Milan.

Room IX: One of the least famous but most memorable works by **Leonardo da Vinci**—his *St Jerome*—is hung here. An early work, dating from around 1480, it was probably painted in Florence, but was left unfinished. It shows the aged penitent saint, the pose and head owing much to Hellenistic sculpture, with his lion with its magnificent tail lightly sketched at his feet, in a shadowy 'desert'. As can be seen here, Leonardo's method of painting was to leave the foreground to the last. Since the discovery in 1991 of an inventory of the possessions of Leonardo's helper and pupil Salaì, we know that he inherited this work along with the *Mona Lisa* and other paintings at Leonardo's death in France, and that he brought them all back with him to Milan. The *St Jerome* is next heard of in Rome, in the possession of the painter Angelica Kauffmann. It subsequently passed into the collection of Napoleon's uncle Cardinal Fesch and was acquired by Pius IX in the mid-19th century.

Another remarkable work here is **Giovanni Bellini's** *Pietà*, once the cimasa of a monumental altarpiece of the *Coronation of the Virgin* painted for the church of San Francesco in Pesaro (where its original frame is still preserved). Scholars have recently suggested that the subject is the 'embalming' of the body of Christ.

There is also a portrait of Bramante, architect of much of the Vatican and St Peter's, and the man who introduced Raphael to Rome.

Room X: Venetian works include two paintings by Titian: the *Madonna of San Niccolò de'Frari*, and *Doge Niccolò Marcello*. The *Madonna of Monteluce* is by Raphael's pupils Giulio Romano and Francesco Penni. In composition it owes much to Raphael's *Coronation* (in fact it is Raphael's design, but the commission passed to his pupils after his death). There is also a wonderful *St Helen* by Veronese, showing the mother of Constantine richly attired, enveloped in a dream of the Cross of Christ, which she will soon unearth in Jerusalem.

Room XI: An important group of works by **Federico Barocci** (born in the Marche but at work in Rome between 1561 and 1563) include a *Rest on the Flight into Egypt*, *Annunciation* and the *Blessed Michelina*. The *Stoning of St Stephen* is by Vasari, whose famous patron Cosimo I is depicted in the marble bas-relief by Perino del Vaga in the centre of the room.

Room XII: The powerful and almost too dramatic *Descent from the Cross* (1602) by **Caravaggio**, which was copied by Rubens, is displayed here along with works by his contemporaries Guido Reni, Domenichino and Guercino, all protagonists of the **Bolognese school** who also worked in Rome. Guercino's works include the *Incredulity of St Thomas*, *St Margaret of Cortona* and *Mary Magdalene*. The *Communion of St Jerome*, signed and dated 1614 by Domenichino, was his first important work (there is a copy of it in mosaic in St Peter's). The ***Crucifixion of St Peter* by Guido Reni**, painted in 1604–5 for the church of San Paolo alle Tre Fontane, shows the influence of Caravaggio's painting of the same subject in Santa Maria del Popolo. Other works by this artist include *St Matthew*, showing the elderly Evangelist busily writing as an angel dictates, and a very fine *Virgin in Glory with Saints*. The *Martyrdom of St Processus and St Martinian* is by the French painter Valentin, who arrived in Rome around 1612 and was much admired by his contemporaries. He was to influence Nicolas Poussin, whose *Martyrdom of St Erasmus* is also hung here. The *Vision of St Romuald* (1631) is one of the most important works by Andrea Sacchi.

Room XIII: The fine painting of *St Francis Xavier* was painted by Van Dyck for the church of Gesù c. 1622. Other artists represented here include Orazio Gentileschi and Pietro da Cortona.

Room XIV: 17th–18th-century Flemish, Dutch, German and French painters.

Room XV: The splendid portrait of Clement IX is by Carlo Maratta. Other papal likenesses include Gregory XII, an idealised portrait of the pope who abdicated in 1415, by Muziano; Pius VI by Pompeo Batoni (known for his numerous portraits painted in the days of the Grand Tour); and Benedict XIV by Giuseppe Maria Crespi (painted while still a cardinal—the papal robes were added afterwards). There is also a portrait of George IV of England by Sir Thomas Lawrence (donated by the sitter to Pius VII).

Room XVI: An eccentric collection of works by the Austrian artist Wenzel Peter range from scenes of savage beasts to Adam and Eve in a pastoral idyll where the wolf dwells with the lamb.

Room XVII: Clay models by Bernini, including a *bozzetto* for the tabernacle of the Holy Sacrament in St Peter's and heads of Fathers of the Church and angels. The small inscription of 1638 commemorates the construction of one of the bell-towers of St Peter's, which was later demolished.

Room XVIII: A fine collection of 16th–17th-century Russian and Greek icons.

GREGORIAN MUSEUM OF PAGAN ANTIQUITIES, PIO CHRISTIAN MUSEUM, PHILATELIC MUSEUM, ETHNOLOGICAL MISSIONARY MUSEUM, CARRIAGE MUSEUM

All these superb and important collections are open in theory, but in practice they are often kept closed, and if you particularly want to see one or more of them, it is best to make an appointment. The first four are housed in a modern wing opened in 1970, when the collections formerly kept in the Lateran Palace were moved here.

The **Gregorian Museum of Pagan Antiquities** (Museo Gregoriano Profano) was founded by Gregory XVI (1831–46) to house the overflow of the Vatican Museums and the yields of excavations at Rome, Ostia, Veio and Cerveteri. It was enriched by further excavations up to 1870, and at the end of the 19th century by a collection of pagan inscriptions. It contains superb examples of Classical sculpture, including original Greek works, Roman copies of Greek works and Roman originals, including mosaics and sarcophaghi. There is also a good lapidary collection from the Jewish catacombs.

The **Pio Christian Museum** was founded by Pius IX in 1854 with objects found mainly in the catacombs, including a valuable collection of Christian sarcophagi of the 2nd–5th centuries, important for the study of early Christian iconography, and the largest and finest collection of Christian inscriptions in existence.

The **Philatelic and Numismatic Museum** contains examples of the stamps and coins issued by the Vatican since it became a sovereign state in 1929.

The **Ethnological Missionary Museum** was established by Pius XI in 1927 as a development of the Vatican Missionary Exhibition of 1924–6.

The **Carriage Museum**, in a long subterranean chamber dating from the 1960s, has a small display of papal conveyances, both horse-drawn coaches and limousines.

THE MAIN COLLECTIONS

From the atrium known as Quattro Cancelli (**B** on the plan on p. 443) you are directed up the grand, Neoclassical Simonetti Staircase to the Egyptian Museum. However, if the weather is fine and the door is open, you can cut across the Cortile della Pigna to the Chiaramonti Museum and New Wing. The end of the Egyptian Collection also brings you out by these, but if you don't want to skip the Egyptian Collection, visit it now.

EGYPTIAN MUSEUM

The Egyptian Museum was founded by Gregory XVI in 1839 and was arranged by Father Luigi Maria Ungarelli, one of the first Italian Egyptologists, to continue the research of Jean-François Champollion (1790–1832), the founder of modern Egyptology. The rooms were decorated in the Egyptian style in the 19th century by Giuseppe de Fabris. The collection is beautifully arranged and well labelled.

Highlights include the splendid **sculptures from the Serapeum of Hadrian's Villa at Tivoli**, which he built after his journey to Egypt in 130–1. There is a statue of the god Serapis, a colossal bust of Isis and a superb likeness of Antinous in the guise of Osiris. The colossal grey marble statue in the next room personifies the Nile (1st century AD); there are also two statues of Hapy (one headless), the god representing the Nile in flood; and the headless baboon (representing the god Thoth) that once stood in a sanctuary near the Pantheon (*see p. 181*).

In the Hemicycle, which follows the shape of the niche of the Pigna (**D** on the plan on p. 443), is a **sandstone head of Mentuhotep II** (reigned 2010–1998 BC). This is remarkable as the oldest portrait in the museum. The statues in black granite (1391–1353 BC) represent the lion-headed goddess Sekhmet. The colossal statue of Queen Tuya, mother of Ramesses II, was brought to Rome by Caligula. Ptolemy II Philadelphus (3rd century BC) and his wife Arsinoë are also represented in colossal granite statues. The black bust of Serapis dates from the 2nd century AD.

The display also includes limestone funerary reliefs from Palmyra in Syria (2nd–3rd century AD), finds from Syria and Palestine from the Neolithic to the Roman period and cylinder seals from Mesopotamia. The final section has exquisite bas-reliefs from Nimrud and Nineveh (9th–7th centuries BC).

CORTILE DELLA PIGNA

From the Egyptian Museum stairs go down to the Chiaramonti Museum (*described below*) and a door leads into the large Cortile della Pigna, one of the three sections into which the Cortile del Belvedere was divided. At the north end is a niche **(D)** where Paul V (1605–21) placed the **colossal bronze pine cone** (*pigna*), over 4m high, found near the Pantheon. There are tiny perforations in the cone's scales; it originally formed the centrepiece of a fountain beside the Temple of Isis and gave its name to that district of the city, the Rione della Pigna. It was made by a certain Cincius Salvius in the 1st century AD. In the Middle Ages it was in the portico of Old St Peter's, together with the two gilt-bronze peacocks (those here are copies; the originals are in the New Wing). The pine cone was seen in the portico by Dante and is mentioned in his *Inferno* (*XXXI, 53*).

Also here are seated black granite statues of the goddess Sekhmet and, in the courtyard below, two lions, once part of a monument to Nectanebo I (30th Dynasty), removed by Gregory XVI from the Fontana dell'Acqua Felice on the Quirinal. A sculpture entitled *Sphere within Sphere* by Arnaldo Pomodoro (1990) stands in the centre of the courtyard. There are at least seven other versions of it around the world. In 1981 a building was constructed deep beneath this courtyard to house the Secret Archives of the Vatican Library.

CHIARAMONTI MUSEUM

The splendid Chiaramonti Museum **(E)** is named after Barnaba Chiaramonti (Pope Pius VII), for whom it was arranged by Antonio Canova. At first glance all one is aware of are serried ranks of ancient sculptures, extending almost as far as the eye can see. On closer inspection, many of the works reveal themselves to be exceptionally fine. It is well worth taking a moment to familiarise yourself with the confusing labelling, and spending time here. This is a superb collection.

The exhibits are divided into 59 sections, numbered on little lecterns with Roman numerals. Odd numbers are on the left, even on the right. Within each section, each item is assigned an Arabic numeral, which appears on the artefact itself. The labelling is not exhaustive: only the best items are listed. A few highlights are given below:

On the right, in Section X (no. 26), is the **monument of Nonnius Zethus** and his family (1st century AD), which consists of a square marble block with eight conical cavities for the remains of family members. The reliefs of a mill being turned by a donkey and of baking implements probably indicated the man's trade. Just to the left of it, in Section XII (no. 4), there is a **relief from a 3rd-century sarcophagus** with a mule in blinkers turning a wine press.

In section XI (no. 12; on the left) is an expressive portrait head of **Cicero**. Also in Section XI is a **sarcophagus with a reclining figure** of the deceased woman holding an apple, as if commending herself to Venus, while two cupids guard her rest, one holding a garland, the other with his quiver firmly shut. Further down there is a good head of **Pompey** (XV; 14; left).

On the right, in Section XVI, the **Head of Athena** (no. 4) is a copy of a 5th-century original; the eyes are restorations but they indicate the skill with which Greek artists caught human expression. The whites of the eyes were probably of ivory, the pupils of semi-precious stone, and the lashes and brows of bronze.

In Section XXI is an ***Eros*** (no. 1) of the Lysippus type.

Imperial portraits on the left-hand side include a **colossal head of Augustus** (Section XXIX; 2). **Tiberius** is represented in the same section with both a portrait head (no. 5) and a statue (no. 4). Also on this side are many fine **portrait busts of ladies**, fascinating for the details of the changing fashions in hairstyles.

The very fine **statuette of Ulysses** (no. 18 in Section XLIII on the left) was part of a group showing Ulysses offering wine to Polyphemus (copy of a 3rd-century original). Another colossal head, this time of **Trajan**, is in Section XLV (no. 3).

The sculpture representing the **personification of Winter** in Section LVIII (at the far end on the right; no. 8) has a female figure wrapped in a cloak holding a pine branch in her left hand; she is reclining near a stream where cupids are catching waterfowl. This is a Hellenistic-Roman work of the 2nd century AD; its companion piece, the **personification of Autumn** (a female figure surrounded by cupids gathering grapes), is displayed opposite.

At the end of the Chiaramonti Museum is a closed gate, beyond which is the **Gallery of Inscriptions** (Galleria Lapidaria; **F**), open only to scholars. It occupies all the remaining part of Bramante's long east corridor. The collection was founded by Clement XIV and reorganised and classified by the epigraphist Monsignor Gaetano Marini (1742–1817). It contains over 5,000 pagan and Christian inscriptions from cemeteries and catacombs. On the right a door leads into the New Wing.

THE NEW WING

The New Wing (Braccio Nuovo; **G**) is an extension of the Chiaramonti sculpture gallery. It contains some of the most valuable pieces in the Vatican, many of them Roman copies of Greek or Hellenistic originals. The impressive hall, 70m long, was constructed by Raffaele Stern (1817–22) for Pius VII. The floor is inlaid with mosaics of the 2nd century AD. Restoration was taking place at the time of writing and the museum was inaccessible. The description below gives some highlights.

The collection possesses a **caryatid** (no. 5), a copy of one of the 5th-century BC caryatids from the Erechtheion in Athens, and a head of a Dacian (no. 9) from the Forum of Trajan (2nd century AD). Perhaps the most famous of all the works, however, is the ***Augustus of Prima Porta*** (no. 14), found in 1863 in the empress Livia's villa at Prima Porta, 12km north of Rome. The statue, in fine Parian marble, celebrates the emperor as a general and orator. He held a bronze sceptre or lance in his left hand; his raised right hand shows that he is about to address his troops. The head is full of character and the majestic pose suggests the influence of Greek athletic statues of the 5th century BC. Augustus was always depicted as a young man, although he died at the age of 76. His cuirass, intricately carved, is decorated with scenes that date the statue: the central scene depicts the restoration by the Parthians in 20 BC of the eagles lost by Crassus at Carrhae in northern Mesopotamia in 53 BC. The small cupid riding a dolphin, placed as a support for the right leg, is an allusion to Venus, the goddess from whom Augustus' family, the Julii, claimed descent. The statue is probably a replica of a bronze original.

THE COLOUR OF ANCIENT MARBLE STATUES

In 1814, very soon after Winckelmann had declared that a carved figure becomes more beautiful the whiter it is, studies proved that Pheidias' famous statue of Zeus at Olympia had originally been coloured. As exhibitions in Berlin and Chicago at the end of the 19th century showed, ancient Greek and Roman sculptures were normally painted to intensify their effect and highlight their meaning, and also to provide greater legibility from afar. When the *Augustus of Prima Porta* was discovered in 1863, it still bore traces of colour: these were recuperated after restoration work and scholars have since been able to deduce what the great work may once have looked like. It seems that the emperor's cloak was a rich purple, and the reliefs on his breastplate were picked out mostly in purple and bright blue.

Studies are still being carried out to reconstruct the appearance of polychrome statues—it is difficult for us today to imagine these when we are so familiar with abstract and idealised pure white Classical works. However, just as over the centuries from the Etruscans onwards, terracotta ornaments and friezes on temples were often enriched by colour, so marble statues were painted and often also gilded. Thus they were made to fit their settings, where frequently the walls against which they stood were also brightly decorated. Statues were often also adorned with jewellery.

The **bust of Julius Caesar** (30) is one of the best examples of a posthumous portrait to have survived, dating from the time of Augustus. The two restored **gilt-bronze peacocks** (30c–d) probably once stood at one of the entrance gates to Hadrian's Mausoleum: the bird was the emblem of Hadrian's *gens*, the Aelia. For the ancient Romans it was a symbol of the sun and thus life. Hadrian promoted the cult of the sun-god: later this was to translate into Christian iconography, where the peacock became a symbol of immortality. There are also six **tombstones found near the Mausoleum of Augustus** (30a, b, e–h); five of them belong to the Julian family and the sixth to that of Vespasian.

The very fine **statue of Demosthenes** (64) is a replica of an original by Polyeuctus of Athens set up in 280 BC to the memory of Demosthenes, the orator and statesman. The hands were originally joined, with the fingers crossed. The mouth plainly suggests the stutter from which the great Athenian suffered.

The ***Wounded Amazon*** (67) is a copy of a work by Kresilas. The arms and feet were restored by Bertel Thorvaldsen in the early 19th century.

The statue of a **goddess of the Borghese Hera type** (76) is a copy of a 5th-century original attributed to Alcamenes, a contemporary of Pheidias.

The huge **sculpture of the Nile** (106) is a fine Hellenistic work, found in 1513 near the Temple of Isis with a statue of the Tiber (now in the Louvre). The river-god reclines beside a sphinx and holds a horn of plenty. The 16 children who frolic over him are supposed to symbolise the 16 cubits which the Nile rises when in flood.

The statue of Julia, daughter of Titus (108), is displayed near the famous ***Giustiniani Athena*** (111), after a Greek original of the 4th century BC. It portrays the goddess's twofold function as the divinity of the intellect and of arms.

It was not uncommon for a Roman sculptor, when copying a Greek model, to place a contemporary portrait head on his copy. The statue of a man in a toga (114) was given a portrait head of Claudius, just as the body of a victorious athlete (120; probably a copy of a work by Myron) was given the head of Lucius Verus, to rather comic effect.

The ***Resting Satyr*** (117) is one of several replicas of the famous statue by Praxiteles (there is another in the Capitoline Museums). The ***Doryphoros*** is a copy of the famous bronze by Polyclitus.

It is now necessary to return through the Chiaramonti Museum to the staircase up past the exit from the Egyptian Museum. From here, continue up the stairs to the top.

PIO-CLEMENTINO MUSEUM

The Pio-Clementino Museum **(H)**, a wonderful collection of Greek and Roman sculptures, was founded in the 18th century by Pius VI and is named after him and his predecessor, Clement XIV. The Belvedere Pavilion was adapted for it by Michelangelo Simonetti. It includes many works collected by the Renaissance popes, in particular Julius II, as well as acquisitions made in the late 18th and early 19th centuries.

ROMAN COPIES OF GREEK STATUARY

The civilising artistic influence of Greece on the martial culture of the ancient Romans is nowhere more apparent than in the field of sculpture. Museums all over Rome and the former Roman world are full of copies (usually in marble) of Greek originals (usually bronzes which have not survived) from the great age of Classical sculpture, the 5th–4th centuries BC. Among the myriad examples on display, many sculptures or sculptural groups appear again and again. Sometimes they are images of gods or goddesses. Equally often the subject matter is secular: images of heroes, orators, athletes or animals. Some of the greatest Greek sculptors and their most admired works, copies of which can be seen in the Vatican sculpture collections and elsewhere in Rome, include the following:

Polyclitus (5th century BC): His best known written work was the *Canon*, a study of human proportions and how they present an ideal of beauty. Fragments of the text survive. His sculptural work which best exemplifies this ideal is the *Doryphoros* (*Spear-bearer; see opposite*). Others are the *Diadoumenos* (an athlete crowning himself with a wreath) and the *Wounded Amazon*.

Pheidias (5th century BC): Pheidias made some famous temple sculptures, notably the chryselephantine statue of Zeus at Olympia (one of the Seven Wonders of the World) and two of Athena for the Athens Acropolis: *Athena Promachos*, the warrior goddess, and *Athena Parthenos*, the virgin.

Myron (5th century BC): A sculptor particularly known for his bronzes of athletes, of which the most celebrated is the *Discobolos* (*Discus-thrower*).

Kresilas (5th century BC): Pliny writes of a contest held between leading artists (among them Pheidias, Polyclitus and Kresilas) to sculpt an Amazon for the Temple of Artemis at Ephesus. The prize was awarded to Polyclitus. 'Wounded Amazons' now abound in the world's museums, in various versions, copies of the works by all the competition entrants. An example of the Kresilas type is held by the Pio-Clementino Museum here in the Vatican.

Lysippus (4th century BC): Alexander the Great was his patron, and Lysippus sculpted his portrait. Other famous works include the *Eros* (shown stringing his bow) and the *Apoxyomenos* (an athlete scraping himself with a strigil; *see overleaf*).

Praxiteles (4th century BC): Praxiteles' *Aphrodite of Cnidos*, which shows the goddess nude, about to take a bath, was the prototype for the *Capitoline Venus* (*see p. 52*), the *Venus* at Hadrian's Villa (*see p. 556*), the *Venus* in the Vatican collections (Mask Room; *see p. 456*) and the *Medici Venus* in Florence. The courtesan Phryne, mistress of the sculptor and famed for the beauty of her breasts, is said to have modelled for the original. The statue type known as the *Resting Satyr* is also from a Praxitelean work, as is the *Apollo Sauroctonos* (*Lizard-slayer*).

Skopas (4th century BC): Skopas made a famous statue of Pothos, son of Aphrodite (example in the Centrale Montemartini), and another of Meleager.

The contents of these sculpture galleries are mainly Greek and Roman originals, or Roman copies of Greek originals executed in the 1st and 2nd centuries AD. Later restorers often made additions in marble, stone or plaster and also, in some cases, put heads on statues to which they do not belong. It was Paul IV, in the 16th century, who decided that the nudity of each male sculpture should be covered with a fig leaf.

(1) Square Vestibule: This space at the top of the stairs has the handsome peperino sarcophagus of Lucius Cornelius Scipio Barbatus, from the Tomb of the Scipios (*see p. 560*); the sarcophagus is in the form of a Doric altar but the general character is Etruscan. The inscription, in Saturnine verse, is said to be by the great Roman poet Quintus Ennius. Above are two inscriptions, also from the Tomb of the Scipios, to the son of Scipio Barbatus, who conquered Corsica in 259 BC.

(2) Cabinet of the *Apoxyomenos*: Here stands the famous copy of Lysippus' masterpiece of an athlete. His arms are missing but he would have been cleaning himelf with a strigil. The statue was found in Vicolo dell'Atleta in Trastevere in 1844. On the walls are inscriptions: those on the left in Archaic Latin are from the Tomb of the Scipios, and those on the right include one of Lucius Mummius Achaicus, the conqueror of Corinth (146 BC).

OCTAGONAL COURTYARD OF THE BELVEDERE

This open court was where Julius II placed the first Classical sculptures which formed the nucleus of the great Vatican collections, including the *Belvedere Torso* (*see p. 456*). When Pius VI had the museum enlarged in 1775, Simonetti made the courtyard into an octagon by forming the recesses (*gabinetti*) in the four corners. Today, when not too crowded, it is a pleasant place to sit and get a breath of fresh air.

(3) Gabinetto dell'Apollo: Here is the famous ***Apollo Belvedere***, a 2nd-century Roman copy of a bronze original of the 4th century BC. The slender, elegant figure of the young god is stepping forward to see the effect of the arrow that he has just shot. The statue was brought to the Vatican in 1503 and became a centre of attention during the Grand Tour. Byron admired it enormously and even modelled his own appearance upon it.

Under the adjoining colonnade, behind a grey granite basin found in the Mausoleum of Hadrian, is a relief of a procession from the Ara Pacis (*see p. 167*), but nearly all the heads are restorations.

(4) Gabinetto del Laocoönte: This recess contains the famous ***Laocoön*** group, in Greek marble, showing the priest of Troy and his two sons in the coils of serpents, a vivid and striking illustration of the story related by Virgil in the *Aeneid*. Laocoön, priest of Apollo, warned his fellow Trojans against the trickery of the Greeks and entreated them not to admit the wooden horse into the city. In punishment Apollo or Athena sent serpents to crush him and his sons to death. The violent realism of the conception as well as the extreme skill and accurate detail with which the agonised contortions of the bodies are rendered are typical of late Hellenistic

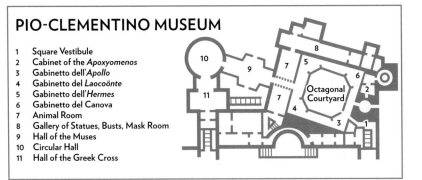

PIO-CLEMENTINO MUSEUM

1 Square Vestibule
2 Cabinet of the *Apoxyomenos*
3 Gabinetto dell'*Apollo*
4 Gabinetto del *Laocoönte*
5 Gabinetto dell'*Hermes*
6 Gabinetto del Canova
7 Animal Room
8 Gallery of Statues, Busts, Mask Room
9 Hall of the Muses
10 Circular Hall
11 Hall of the Greek Cross

sculpture. It is ascribed to the Rhodian sculptors Agesander, Polydorus and Athenodorus (c. 50 BC). It was found on the Esquiline hill in 1506 and was at once recognised as that described by Pliny, though it is not carved from a single block, as he states, but from at least three pieces. It was purchased by Julius II and brought to the Vatican, where it was greatly admired by the artists of the time: it has been suggested that one of the nudes in Michelangelo's *Doni Tondo* (now in the Uffizi) may be a copy from the Laocoön. One of the best-known Classical sculptures, it influenced other Renaissance and Baroque artists and was particularly admired in the 19th century. Byron, in *Childe Harold*, describes 'Laocoön's torture dignifying pain'.

(5) Gabinetto dell'Hermes: Named after the statue thought to represent Hermes Psychopompos, the conductor of souls to the Underworld, a copy of an original by Praxiteles. In the portico beyond (in a niche) is a sarcophagus with a *Battle of the Amazons*, with Achilles and Penthesileia grouped in the centre (3rd century AD) and *Venus Felix and Cupid*: the body is copied from the

Cnidian *Aphrodite* in the Mask Room; the inscription states that the group was dedicated to Venus Felix by Sallustia and Helpis. It has stood in this courtyard since Julius II began the collection here.

(6) Gabinetto del Canova: Here are three Neoclassical statues by Canova: Perseus (inspired by the *Apollo Belvedere*) and Creugas and Damoxenes (both boxers), put here to replace Classical masterpieces taken to Paris by Napoleon.

(7) Animal Room (entered by the door flanked by two hounds): Most of the animal statues (*usually roped off, but still visible*) are by Francesco Antonio Franzoni, who made them for this room for Pius VI. Some are entirely Franzoni's work; others were made up from ancient fragments. The Roman pieces include, in the section on the left, a sow with a litter of twelve, perhaps of the Augustan period, and, under the far window, the colossal head of a camel (a fountain-head), a copy of a Hellenistic original of the 2nd century BC. In the niche at the end, *Meleager with his Dog and the head of a Boar* is a very fine copy of a 4th-century original by Skopas. In the section on the right is *Mithras Slaying the Bull* (2nd century AD) and, on the wall behind it, two beautiful mosaics of animals from Hadrian's Villa at Tivoli (2nd century AD). The mosaics in the pavement date from the same period.

(8) Gallery of Statues, Gallery of Busts, Mask Room: These three rooms, beyond the Animal Room, are usually only shown on guided tours. They contain copies of Greek and Hellenistic originals, including the Vatican version of the *Aphrodite of Cnidos* (*see box on p. 453*).

(9) Hall of the Muses: This is an octagon with a vestibule at either end, built in 1782 by Simonetti; the paintings are by Tommaso Conca. In the vestibule are herms, including one of Sophocles (left), and reliefs. Above on the right is the *Pyrrhic Dance*, a 4th-century Attic work; on the left is the *Birth of Bacchus*, showing the god emerging from the thigh of Zeus. Around the walls of the octagon, statues of **Apollo and the Muses** alternate with more herms. The Apollo (of the Kitharoidos type, gowned and with his lyre) and seven of the Muses were found in a villa near Tivoli and date from the 2nd century AD (though many of the heads do not belong). The herms (also with mismatching heads) and stelae include portraits of Homer, Socrates, Plato, Euripides, Epicurus and Demosthenes.

In the centre is the famous ***Belvedere Torso***, bearing the signature of Apollonius, an Athenian sculptor of the 1st century BC. The figure is sitting on a hide laid over the ground. There have been various identifications of the statue, including Hercules, Polyphemus, Prometheus, Marsyas and Philoctetes, but recent studies have suggested that it may represent Ajax meditating suicide (in his right hand he probably held a sword with which he was about to kill himself). Found in the Campo dei Fiori at the time of Julius II, the torso was formerly exhibited in the Belvedere, where it was greatly admired by Michelangelo and Raphael. It was frequently drawn by Renaissance artists, and in the 16th and 17th centuries it was copied in small bronzes.

(10) Circular Hall: This domed hall was also designed by Simonetti (c. 1782) and modelled on the Pantheon. In the pavement is a very well preserved polychrome mosaic from Otricoli (in Umbria), representing a battle between Greeks and centaurs, with tritons and nereids in the outer circle. The huge monolithic **porphyry basin** was found in the Domus Aurea. Around the walls are displayed important colossal busts and statues (described from right of the entrance): ***Jupiter of Otricoli***, a colossal head of majestic beauty, attributed to Bryaxis (4th century BC); the ***Braschi Antinous***, showing Hadrian's favourite as Bacchus/Osiris. The headdress (incorrectly restored in the early 19th century by Thorvaldsen) would have had the cobra (uraeus) and lotus in the centre; bust of **Faustina the Elder** (d. 141), wife of Antoninus Pius; a beautiful statue of a **female divinity**, perhaps Demeter, wearing the peplos, after a Greek original of the late 5th century BC; **head of Hadrian**, from his mausoleum (Castel Sant'Angelo; *see p. 411*); **Hercules**, a colossal statue in gilded bronze, an early Imperial copy of a work of the school of Skopas; bust of

Antinous; Juno (the ***Barberini Hera***), a Roman copy of a cult image in the manner of the late 5th century; head of a **marine divinity** (from Pozzuoli), believed to personify the Gulf of Baiae, an interesting example of the fusion of marine elements and human features; **Galba**, after a seated statue representing Jupiter; **bust of Serapis**, after a work by Bryaxis; **Claudius as Jupiter**; a **head of Claudius** (reworked from a likeness of his predecessor Caligula: the label explains this very well); ***Juno Sospita*** from Lanuvium, dating from the Antonine period; **head of Plotina** (d. 129), wife of Trajan; **head of a lady** from the family of Septimius Severus; **Genius of Augustus**.

(11) Hall of the Greek Cross: This is another Neoclassical room by Simonetti, dominated by two magnificent **porphyry sarcophagi**: that on the left, decorated with Roman horsemen, barbarian prisoners and fallen soldiers, belonged to St Helen, mother of Constantine, and that on the right to Constantia, Constantine's daughter. It is decorated with vine-branches, putti and Christian symbols of grapes, peacocks and sheep. It was moved here in 1791 from Santa Costanza (*see p. 485*). In the centre is a mosaic pavement with a shield decorated with the head of Minerva and surrounded by the phases of the moon. Between two granite sphinxes is another exquisite mosaic representing a basket of flowers.

From here you can sometimes go straight on into the Gallery of Candelabra, the beginning of the long walk to the Raphael Rooms and Sistine Chapel. However, barricades often force you up to the Etruscan Museum first. Its rooms are usually almost deserted, and its collection is exceptionally rich.

ETRUSCAN MUSEUM

One of the most important collections of its kind in existence, this was founded in 1837 by Gregory XVI. Many of the objects come from southern Etruria (north Lazio), but there are also outstanding examples of Greek and Roman art and a notable collection of Greek vases. In 1989 the Giacinto Guglielmi collection of finds from Vulci was acquired. The exhibits are well labelled. Highlights include (in Room II) the splendid **finds from the Regolini-Galassi Tomb**, found in a necropolis south of Cerveteri in 1836 and named after its discoverers. Three important people were buried here in 650 BC, including a princess called Larthia, a warrior of high rank, and a priest-king who was cremated. Their funeral equipment includes gold jewellery (a superb gold clasp with decorations in relief, necklaces and bracelets); ivories; cups; plates; silver ornaments of Graeco-Oriental provenance; a bronze libation bowl with six handles in the shape of animals; and a reconstructed throne. A beautiful cremation urn; a series of pottery statuettes; a bronze incense-burner in the shape of a wagon; a bronze stand with figures in relief; two five-handled jars; silverware including a drinking cup and jug; and small dishes of Eastern origin were also found in this tomb. The biga has been reconstructed, as well as a funeral carriage with a bronze bed and funeral couch.

In the centre of Room III is the ***Mars of Todi***, a very fine bronze statue of a man in armour dating from the beginning of the 4th century BC, but inspired by Greek art of the 5th century BC. In Room IV are sarcophagi: a limestone sarcophagus with a polychrome relief of a procession, from a tomb at Cerveteri (late 5th or early 4th century BC), with an effigy of the deceased holding a paten on the lid; and a **sarcophagus from Tuscania** of the 4th century BC with an effigy of a man with an enormous stomach: it is known that the Romans considered the Etruscans to be luxurious people, their habits a far cry from lean Roman austerity.

On the upper level are **works in terracotta**, including some striking portrait heads (the bust of a middle-aged woman from the 3rd century BC is particularly remarkable) and some magnificent items of **gold jewellery**, displayed chronologically from the 7th century BC. Most are from Vulci and include a necklace with pomegranate drops.

Room IX displays the **Guglielmi Collection**, half of which, from Vulci, was donated to the Vatican in 1937. The other half was purchased from the Guglielmi in 1988. It is especially important for its Attic black- and red-figure vases, a number of them attributed pieces displayed in the central cases. It also has Villanovan objects, bronzes and fine stamnoi, bucchero vases and Corinthian ware.

Further on are alabaster and limestone **funerary urns**, and a particularly fine terracotta one with the *Dying Adonis* on the lid (3rd century BC, from Tuscania). The hero is shown naked except for his boots. The fatal gash on his thigh is prominent.

From the next room a glass door leads to the spiral **Bramante Staircase** (*shown on guided tours*). The design is masterly; at each turn the order changes, starting with Tuscan at the bottom and ending with Corinthian at the top.

The last rooms display a valuable collection of **Greek, Italic and Etruscan vases**. Most of them come from the tombs of Southern Etruria, discovered during excavations in the first half of the 19th century. From the end of the 7th century to the late 5th century BC many Greek vases were imported. By the middle of the 4th century BC the Greek imports were largely replaced by the products of Magna Graecia (southern Italy). There are two particularly fine pieces here, found at Cerveteri, attributed to the Attic painter Douris (5th century BC). One is a kylix showing Jason swallowed by a dragon. On the other a woman tends a man with a hangover and on the underside is a symposium scene with the guests playing the drinking game known as *kottabos*.

The **Room of the Biga**, the last room of the collection, is shown on guided tours. It was designed to house the magnificent Biga, or two-horse chariot, reconstructed in 1788 by Francesco Antonio Franzoni from ancient fragments: only the body of the chariot and part of the offside horse are original. The chair was used as an episcopal throne in the church of San Marco during the Middle Ages. The bas-reliefs suggest that it was a votive chariot dedicated to Ceres and that it dates from the 1st century AD.

THE 'SISTINE ROUTE'

The 'Sistine Route' is an itinerary imposed by the Vatican authorities to regulate the flow of people to the Sistine Chapel. It is long and tiring, but when the museums are not too crowded, you can usually take your time over things and even back-track if you need to. The description below follows the itinerary imposed at the time of writing, down the very long west corridor. There are plans on pp. 443, 455 and 463 to help you orientate yourself. The corridor is divided into three sections, named as follows according to their exhibits:

GALLERY OF THE CANDELABRA

The gallery takes its name from the pairs of marble candelabra, of the Roman Imperial period, placed on either side of the arches which divide it into six sections. The ceiling has late 19th-century frescoes by Ludovico Seitz and others. In the pavement are marbles from the warehouses of ancient Rome. The display is of ancient Greek and Roman (mostly 2nd- and 3rd-century) statues, reliefs, sarcophagi and candelabra, as well as a few small mosaics and fresco fragments. Some of the most interesting pieces are in the last three sections.

Section IV has two sarcophaghi dating from the 2nd century AD, one (30; right) with Dionysus and Ariadne and Dionysiac scenes, and the other (85; left) showing the slaughter of the Niobids (*for the story, see p. 324*). The statue of a fisherman (38; right) is a realistic work of the school of Pergamon dating from the 3rd century BC. The *Boy Strangling a Goose* (66; left), of the same date, is a replica of a famous Hellenistic work in bronze by Boethus, which is meant perhaps as a parody of the Labours of Hercules.

Section V contains a fine statue of a girl running in a race during a Peloponnesian religious festival (right), a Roman copy of a Greek bronze original of the 5th century BC, deliberately archaising in style. In the last section are more Roman copies of Greek works, including a statuette of a Persian in battle, modelled on a bronze from the series of statues given by Attalus I of Pergamon to the Athenians and placed on the Acropolis.

GALLERY OF TAPESTRIES

Hung here is a series of splendid tapestries of scenes from the life of Christ, executed from cartoons by pupils of Raphael (some of which were copied from his drawings) after the great artist's death. Woven in Brussels in the 16th century, they are known as the 'New School' tapestries (as opposed to the 'Old School' series displayed in the Pinacoteca; *see pp. 445–6*). On the opposite walls are tapestries illustrating the life of Urban VIII, the most important product of the Barberini workshop, active in Rome in 1627–83. In the last part of this gallery is a Flemish tapestry of 1594 showing the death of Julius Caesar, and beautiful tapestries from the late 15th century including one illustrating the Creed.

GALLERY OF MAPS

This gallery was superbly decorated at the time of Gregory XIII with numerous maps and plans painted in 1580–2 by Egnazio Danti, the celebrated Dominican cosmographer, mathematician, architect and painter. Danti sat on the pope's commission, set up in 1577, to reform the calendar—until that time the calendar in use had been that introduced by Julius Caesar. Gregory XIII's new calendar, adopted in Italy in 1582, corrected an error by eliminating ten days. This new system of calculating the passage of time was not accepted in England until 1752.

The maps are extremely important to our knowledge of 16th-century Italy. They represent the Italian peninsula, the Italian regions and the neighbouring islands, the most important ports, and the papal territory of Avignon. It is the largest decorative scheme of its kind: it was intended to be seen from the far door, since the regions of northern Italy are at the southern entrance.

Taking the central axis of the gallery as the Apennine range, the west wall (overlooking the Vatican Gardens) represents the Adriatic and Alpine regions, and the opposite wall the Ligurian and Tyrrhenian side of Italy. Each map is labelled in Latin at the top. By the far door is Venice, and two general maps showing the country under the Roman Empire (labelled 'Italia Antiqua') and in the 16th century (labelled 'Italia Nova'). The paintings were restored several times up until the 17th century. The ceiling was decorated at the same time with stuccoes and frescoes illustrating the importance of history and geography to the Church, by a group of painters including Cesare Nebbia, under the direction of Girolamo Muziano.

THE APPROACH TO THE RAPHAEL ROOMS

French and Brussles tapestries are exhibited in the **Gallery of Pius V**. After this, the long gallery ends, and the route turns left into the **Sobieski Room**, named after John Sobieski (John III of Poland), who liberated Vienna from a siege by the Turks in 1683. An enormous painting on the left wall, carried out for the bicentenary in 1883, depicts the battle. The frescoes in the **Hall of the Immaculate Conception**, by Francesco Podesti, were painted to celebrate the definition and proclamation of the dogma of the Immaculate Conception of the Virgin pronounced by Pius IX on 8th December 1854. The floors of both rooms are inlaid with polychrome Roman mosaics from Ostia.

THE RAPHAEL ROOMS

The Raphael Rooms (Stanze di Raffaello; *plan overleaf*) were originally built by Nicholas V as papal audience chambers, a library and a hall for the papal tribunal. When Julius II moved into the apartment (not wanting to occupy that of his infamous predecessor, Rodrigo Borgia), he employed a group of great artists to continue its decoration, including Luca Signorelli, Perugino, Sodoma, Bramantino, Baldassare Peruzzi, Lorenzo Lotto and the Flemish painter Jan Ruysch. But when in 1508, on Bramante's suggestion, the pope called Raphael from Urbino, Pope Julius was so pleased with his work that he dismissed all the other painters, ordered their works to be destroyed, and commissioned Raphael to decorate the whole of this part of the Vatican.

Raphael began work in the Stanza della Segnatura (iii), with the frescoes of *Astronomy, Apollo, Adam and Eve* and the *Judgement of Solomon*, which were probably his trial works, and then carried out the other frescoes in this room. After this the chronological order is: Stanza d'Eliodoro (ii), Stanza dell'Incendio (iv) and the Stanza di Costantino (i), decorated by the master's pupils after his death. The decoration spans the reigns of four popes, three of whom—Julius II, Leo X and Clement VII—influenced its design.

RAPHAEL IN ROME

The *Stanze* are Raphael's masterpiece: they show the extraordinary development of his art during the years between his coming to Rome in 1508 and his death at the age of 37 in 1520. Rome was of the first importance during the High Renaissance, and when Raphael arrived he found the court of Julius II a stimulating intellectual centre. The Curia included many celebrated savants, humanists and men of letters, and a crowd of artists, led by Bramante and Michelangelo, were at work in the city. In this highly cultured environment Raphael, who had great powers of assimilation, acquired an entirely new manner of painting.

Raphael painted a famous portrait of Julius II (now in the National Gallery in London) two years before the pope's death in 1513. The new Medici pope, Leo X, appointed Raphael head of the building works in St Peter's in 1514, and commissioned him to decorate the Vatican Loggia. In 1518 Raphael also painted Leo X, with two cardinals: this portrait is in the Uffizi. Leo appointed him commissioner of antiquities to ensure that everything possible was done to preserve the ancient buildings of Rome. Raphael left the huge altarpiece of the *Transfiguration*, now in the Vatican Pinacoteca, incomplete at his death and it was displayed above his coffin at his funeral in 1520. He left his own self-portrait (*illustrated above*) in his great *School of Athens*, in the Stanza della Segnatura here. He is buried in the Pantheon.

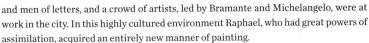

Room i (Sala di Costantino): This room was mainly painted for Clement VII (1523–34), after Raphael's death, by Giulio Romano with the assistance of Francesco Penni and Raffaellino del Colle. Its theme is the triumph of Christianity over paganism. On the wall to the right of the window, *Constantine Addressing his Soldiers* and *The Vision of the Cross* are by Giulio Romano, perhaps from Raphael's design; to the right of this are *St Clement with Temperance and Meekness*; to the left, *St Peter with The Church and Eternity*.

Facing the window is the *Victory of Constantine over Maxentius near the Milvian Bridge*, for which Raphael had made some sketches. The reddish tint which suffuses the picture is characteristic of Giulio Romano. To the right are *St Urban with Justice and Charity*; to the left, *St Sylvester with Faith and Religion*.

To the right of this is the *Baptism of Constantine by St Sylvester* (a portrait of Clement VII) by Francesco Penni; at the sides to the right are *St Leo with Innocence and Truth*, and to the left *St Damasus with Prudence and Peace*.

On the window wall, *Constantine's Donation of Rome to Sylvester* is by Raffaellino del Colle (*for the Donation of Constantine, see p. 282*). On the right are a pope (thought to be Gregory VII) and *Fortitude*; and to the left *St Sylvester* and *Courage*. Below are other scenes from the life of Constantine. On the ceiling is the *Triumph of Christianity*, interesting for its unusual iconography, by Tommaso Laureti. In the floor is a 2nd-century mosaic of the Seasons.

Room ii (Stanza d'Eliodoro): This is the second of the rooms frescoed by Raphael, begun in 1512 for Julius II and completed two years later for Leo X. Restoration work was completed here in 2013. The overall theme is the triumph of the Church over its adversaries. The popes are shown here in the guise of great men of the past. The work that gives the room its name is the *Expulsion of Heliodorus from the Temple at Jerusalem* (right of the window), an allusion to Julius II's success in freeing the States of the Church from foreign powers. The scene illustrates a story in the Apocrypha (*Maccabees II: 3*): King Seleucus sends his treasurer Heliodorus to Jerusalem to steal the Temple treasure, but the crime is avenged by a horseman assisted by two angels with whips. In the middle of the crowd on the left is Julius II, carried on the *sedia gestatoria* (the front bearer is a portrait of the engraver Marcantonio Raimondi). In the centre of the composition, under the vault of the Temple, the high priest Onias renders thanks to God before the Ark of the Covenant.

The *Miracle of Bolsena* represents a famous event which took place at Bolsena in 1263. A Bohemian priest who had doubts about the doctrine of Transubstantiation was convinced when he saw blood drop from the Host onto the altar cloth (the stained corporal is preserved in the cathedral at Orvieto). Julius II, on his first expedition against Bologna in 1506, had stopped at Orvieto to pay homage to the relic. He is shown kneeling opposite the priest in place of Urban IV, the contemporary pope. The warm colours, and especially the harmony of reds in the composition, show how much Raphael was influenced by Venetian painters (Sebastiano del Piombo and Lorenzo Lotto arrived in Rome at this time).

On the window wall is the *Liberation of St Peter*, alluding to the captivity of Leo X after the battle of Ravenna. Three night scenes, with remarkable light effects, illustrate three different episodes: in the middle, the interior of the prison is seen through a high barred window, with St Peter waking up as the Angel frees him from his chains; on the left are the guards outside the prison; and on the right St Peter escaping with the Angel.

To the left of the window is *Leo I Repulsing Attila*, a subject originally selected by Julius II and taken up again by Leo X, when considerable changes were made in the design. It was executed partly by Raphael's assistants. The scene representing the banks of the Mincio, where the historic event took place, was replaced by the environs of Rome, and the figure of the pope, on a white mule, was brought from the back of the picture into the foreground in order to accentuate the allusion to the Battle of Ravenna on 11th April 1512, at which Leo X, then a cardinal, had been present and which resulted in the expulsion of the French from Italy. Attila, mounted on a white horse, with his Huns behind him, are struck with terror by a vision of St Peter and St Paul.

The decoration of the lower part of the walls is attributed to Perino del Vaga. The ceiling paintings of *God Appearing to Noah*, *Jacob's Dream*, *The Burning Bush* and *Abraham's Sacrifice* are generally attributed to Peruzzi.

Room iii (Stanza della Segnatura): The Stanza della Segnatura, where the

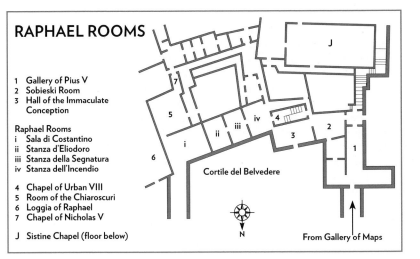

RAPHAEL ROOMS

1   Gallery of Pius V
2   Sobieski Room
3   Hall of the Immaculate
    Conception

Raphael Rooms
i   Sala di Costantino
ii   Stanza d'Eliodoro
iii Stanza della Segnatura
iv   Stanza dell'Incendio

4   Chapel of Urban VIII
5   Room of the Chiaroscuri
6   Loggia of Raphael
7   Chapel of Nicholas V

J   Sistine Chapel (floor below)

Cortile del Belvedere

N

From Gallery of Maps

pope signed bulls and briefs, has the most beautiful and harmonious frescoes in the series, painted entirely by Raphael in 1508–11, for Julius II. The theme of the works is philosophical truth, wisdom and beauty, as epitomised, by inference, by the Church, though the Renaissance blend of Christian and pagan makes some of the works at first seem profane.

On the wall nearest the Courtyard of the Belvedere is the famous **Parnassus** scene. Apollo is playing the violin in the shade of laurels, surrounded by the nine Muses and the great poets. Calliope (muse of epic poetry) is seated on the left, and behind her are Melpomene (tragedy), Terpsichore (dancing) and Polyhymnia (sacred poetry); on the right, also seated, is Erato (love poetry), and behind her are Clio (history), Thalia (comedy), Euterpe (music) and Urania (astronomy). In the group of poets on the left is the figure of the blind Homer, between Dante and Virgil; lower are Alcaeus, Corinna, Petrarch and Anacreon, with the voluptuous

form of Sappho seated beside them. In the group on the right are Ariosto (?), Ovid, Tibullus and Propertius, and, lower, Jacopo Sannazaro, Horace and the seated Pindar. Below the picture are two monochrome scenes: that on the left is thought to show Alexander placing Homer's poems in the tomb of Achilles (or, possibly, the discovery of a sarcophagus containing Greek and Latin manuscripts on the Janiculum in 181 BC). The subject of the scene on the right is either Augustus preventing Virgil's friends from burning the *Aeneid*, or Roman consuls ordering the burning of Greek works considered harmful to the Roman religion. Below these again is some very fine painted intarsia work by Fra' Giovanni da Verona.

On the long wall to the right of this is the splendid **School of Athens**, symbolising the triumph of Philosophy. The setting is a portico, representing the Palace of Science, a magnificent example of Renaissance architecture. At the sides are statues of Apollo and Minerva. On the steps the greatest philosophers and scholars of all ages are gathered round the two supreme masters, Plato and Aristotle. The figure of Plato—probably intended as a portrait of Leonardo da Vinci—points towards heaven, symbolising his system of speculative philosophy, while Aristotle's calm gesture indicates the vast field of nature as the realm of scientific research.

At the top of the steps, on Plato's side, is the bald head and characteristic profile of Socrates; near him, in conversation, are Aeschines, Alcibiades (represented as a young warrior), Xenophon and others. The beckoning figure next to Xenophon is probably Chrysippus. At the foot of the steps on the left is Zeno, an old man with a beard, seen in profile; near him Epicurus, crowned with vine-leaves, is reading a book; in the foreground Pythagoras is writing out his harmonic tables, with Averroës, in a turban, and Empedocles looking over his shoulder. The seated figure of Heraclitus, isolated in the centre foreground, was not part of the original composition; obviously inspired by the Sistine Chapel frescoes (where the first section of the vault was uncovered in 1510), it has been suggested that it was intended as a portrait of Michelangelo.

On the right, around Aristotle, are the students of the exact sciences; standing at the foot of the steps—holding a globe and, because of a confusion with the Egyptian kings of the same name, wearing a crown—is Ptolemy, with his back to the spectator. Opposite him is Zoroaster, holding a sphere. On the extreme right of the composition, Raphael has introduced a portrait of himself, in the guise of the painter Apelles, the artist from the island of Kos who, according to Pliny,

'surpassed all the painters that preceded him and all who were to come after'. To the left Archimedes or Euclid (with the features of Bramante), surrounded by his disciples, bends over a blackboard on which he is tracing figures with a compass. The solitary figure sprawling on the steps in the centre, with a blue tunic, is Diogenes. The monochromes beneath, by Perino del Vaga, represent *Philosophy*, *Astrologers in Conference* and the *Siege of Syracuse* with the death of Archimedes.

On the other long wall is the famous **Disputa** (or *Disputation on the Holy Sacrament*), representing a discussion on the Eucharist and intended as a glorification of Catholicism. It forms a pendant to the *Triumph of Philosophy* opposite. Given an extremely difficult subject, Raphael divided the composition into two zones, making the relatively limited space appear far larger than it is. In the celestial zone Christ appears between the Virgin and St John the Baptist; above is God the Father surrounded by angels; beneath, the Holy Dove between four angels holding the book of the Gospels; on the left are St Peter, Adam, St John the Evangelist, David, St Lawrence, and Jeremiah (?); on the right, St Paul, Abraham, St James, Moses, St Stephen and Judas Maccabaeus. In the middle of the terrestrial zone is a monstrance with the Host on an altar. On the right are St Augustine and St Ambrose, and on the left St Gregory and St Jerome; they are surrounded by an assembly of Doctors of the Church, popes, cardinals, dignitaries and the faithful. Certain figures are thought to be portraits: of the British medieval theologian Duns Scotus, St Dominic, St Francis, St Thomas Aquinas and St Nicholas. On the right is the profile of Dante crowned with laurel, and, beyond him (just visible at the back of the figures in a black hat), is Savonarola, the learned theologian and inflammatory preacher who had been excommunicated by Pope Alexander VI and executed for heresy and treason in Florence in 1498. On the extreme left are Fra' Angelico, in the black Dominican habit, and, in the foreground, Bramante. Beneath the picture are three monochrome paintings by Perino del Vaga: *A Pagan Sacrifice*, *St Augustine and the Child on the Seashore*, and the *Cumaean Sibyl showing the Virgin to Augustus*.

On the fourth wall, above the window, are three of the four Cardinal Virtues—Fortitude, Temperance and Prudence. On the left of the window, *Justinian Publishing the Pandects* represents Civil Law, and on the right, Gregory IX (in the likeness of Julius II) is shown handing the Decretals to a jurist (1227), to represent Canon Law. The prelates around the pope are portraits of Raphael's contemporaries: on the left, in front, is Giovanni de' Medici, afterwards Leo X, then Cardinal Antonio del Monte, Alessandro Farnese (Paul III), and others. Beneath both are works by Perino del Vaga: *Solon Haranguing the Athenians* and *Moses Bringing the Israelites the Tablets of Stone*. The ceiling was also painted by Raphael: above the *Disputa* is the figure of *Theology*; above the *Parnassus*, *Poetry*; above the *School of Athens*, *Philosophy*; and above the window wall, *Justice*. In the pendentives are *Adam and Eve*, *Apollo and Marsyas*, *Astronomy* and the *Judgement of Solomon*. The small central octagon is attributed to Bramantino. The floor, in opus alexandrinum, shows the name of Julius II.

Room iv (Stanza dell'Incendio):
The Stanza dell'Incendio was frescoed in 1514–17 for Leo X, and the scheme aims to glorify him and his pontificate by showing him acting out the notable deeds of earlier popes who shared his regnal name. Thus facing the window is the *Incendio di Borgo*, illustrating the fire that broke out in Rome in 847 and which was miraculously extinguished when Leo IV made the sign of the Cross from the loggia of St Peter's. This was probably intended as an allusion to the achievement of Leo X in restoring peace to Italy. In the background, flames threaten the façade of the basilica; on the right, the pope leaves the Vatican. On the left is a scene of the burning of Troy, with Aeneas carrying his father Anchises, followed by his wife and son. The frescoes on all four walls were designed by Raphael, though he entrusted much of the execution to his pupils Giulio Romano, Francesco Penni, and perhaps Perino del Vaga.

To the right of the *Incendio* is the *Coronation of Charlemagne*, who was crowned Holy Roman Emperor by Pope Leo III in 800: since Leo and Charlemagne have the features of Leo X and Francis I of France, the fresco is taken as a reference to the meeting of the later pope and king at Bologna in 1516, when they drew up a famous alliance and the pope's role as peacemaker between Christian rulers was confirmed.

On the opposite wall is the *Victory of Leo IV over the Saracens at Ostia* (849), an allusion to the crusade against the Turks proclaimed by Leo X. The window wall depicts the *Oath of Leo III*, made in St Peter's on 23rd December 800. On this occasion the pope cleared himself of the false charges, including perjury and adultery, that had been brought against him. This alludes to the Lateran Council of 1516, where Leo X promulgated the dogma that the pope is answerable to God alone for his deeds.

On the ceiling is the *Glorification of the Trinity* by Perugino, Raphael's master, the only work not destroyed when Raphael took over the decoration of the Stanze.

THE EXIT TO THE BORGIA ROOMS

There are two possible ways to leave the Raphael Rooms, and one of them is often closed for one reason or another. Signs will direct you which to use. The description below describes both possiblities.

If you exit from the Sala di Costantino, you will pass through the **Room of the Chiaroscuri (5)**, which has a magnificent carved and gilded ceiling with the Medici arms. The monochrome frescoes were restored in 1560 by Taddeo and Federico Zuccari. The famous **Loggia of Raphael (6)** is always closed to the public, but you can see a small part of it from the window of the Room of the Chiaroscuri. The long gallery of 13 bays was begun by Bramante about 1513 and completed after his death by Raphael and his pupils. The vault of each bay has four little paintings of Old Testament scenes. The *grottesche* of the borders are thought to have been inspired by those in the Domus Aurea (*see p. 115*), which were discovered in the 15th century and known to Raphael. The designs were carried out by Giulio Romano, Giovanni da Udine, Francesco Penni, Perino del Vaga, Polidoro da Caravaggio and others. Controversial restoration work was carried out on the paintings in 1978.

The little adjoining **Chapel of Nicholas V (7)** (*usually shown only on guided tours*) is entirely decorated with lovely frescoes by Fra' Angelico, painted between 1448 and 1450. These represent scenes from the lives of the deacon saints Stephen (upper section) and Lawrence (lower section); especially fine is the painting of *St Stephen Preaching*. On the ceiling are shown the four Evangelists and on the pilasters the Doctors of the Church.

If you exit from the Stanza dell'Incendio, you will go through the **Chapel of Urban VIII (4)**, its ceiling richly decorated by Pietro da Cortona. Outside the chapel, a stairway leads down to the Borgia Rooms and Sistine Chapel.

THE BORGIA ROOMS AND GALLERY OF MODERN RELIGIOUS ART

The Borgia Rooms are named after Pope Alexander VI (Rodrigo Borgia), who adapted this suite in the palace of Nicholas V for his personal use and had it decorated with frescoes by Pinturicchio and his school (1492–5). The *grottesche* are inspired by the decorations discovered in the Domus Aurea at this time. After the death of Alexander VI and the disgrace of the Borgia family, the apartment was abandoned, and it was not until 1889 that Leo XIII had the rooms restored by Ludovico Seitz and opened them to the public. The collection of modern relgious art, inaugurated by Paul VI in 1973, is now displayed here and in some 50 rooms on the level below.

Room 1 (Room of the Sibyls): Each of the lunettes (attributed to a pupil of Pinturicchio, probably Pastura) has a sibyl accompanied by a prophet. The juxtaposition illustrates an ancient belief that the sibyls foretold the coming of the Messiah (it is for the same reason that sibyls are featured in the Sistine ceiling). Cesare Borgia was imprisoned here by Julius II in 1503, in the very room where he had had his cousin Alfonso of Aragon murdered in 1500.

Room 3 (Room of the Creed): The room takes its name from the scrolls held by the Twelve Apostles in the lunettes, on which the sentences of the Creed are written. The frescoes are attributed to Pier Matteo d'Amelia, a successor of Pinturicchio.

Room 4 (Room of the Liberal Arts): The Trivium (grammar, dialectic, rhetoric) and the Quadrivium (geometry, arithmetic, astronomy, music) which are symbolised here were the basis of medieval learning. The paintings are attributed to Pastura. The *Arch of Justice*, in the middle, was painted in the 16th century. The ceiling is decorated with squares and *grottesche* alternating with the Borgia bull. The fine chimneypiece is by or after Jacopo Sansovino.

Room 5 (Room of the Saints): The frescoes on the walls and vault are Pinturicchio's masterpiece. The room is divided by an arch into two cross-vaulted areas forming six lunettes. On the ceiling is the *Legend of Isis and Osiris and the Bull Apis* (a reference to the Borgia arms), with reliefs in gilded stucco. Entrance wall, the *Visitation*; *St Paul the Hermit and St Anthony Abbot in the Desert*, on the right. The end wall shows the *Disputation between St Catherine of Alexandria and the Emperor Maximian*; the figure of the saint was once thought to be a portrait of Alexander VI's daughter Lucrezia Borgia, or his mistress Giulia Farnese. The figure behind the throne is a self-portrait by Pinturicchio and in the background is the Arch of Constantine. The window wall shows the *Martyrdom of St Sebastian*, with a view of the Colosseum; and the exit wall, *Susanna and the Elders* and the *Legend of St Barbara*.

Room 6 (Room of the Mysteries of the Faith): The mysteries, by Pinturicchio and assistants, are the *Annunciation, Nativity, Adoration of the Magi, Resurrection* (the kneeling pontiff is Alexander VI; the central soldier may be Cesare), *Ascension, Pentecost* and *Assumption of the Virgin*.

Room 7 (Room of the Popes): Formerly decorated with portraits of popes. The frescoes and stucco decoration of the splendid vaulted ceiling were commissioned by Leo X from Perino del Vaga and Giovanni da Udine.

The collection of modern religious art continues now on the floor below. It is mainly made up of donated works. Artists known for their religious output, such as Giacomo Manzù and Georges Rouault appear alongside others whose oeuvre is mainly secular. Artists represented here include Rodin, Matisse, Chagall, Morandi, Fernando Botero (his charming *A Trip to the Ecumenical Council* of 1972) and Francis Bacon (*Study for Velazquez Pope II*, 1961).

THE SISTINE CHAPEL

The Sistine Chapel **(J)** is one of the most magnificently decorated spaces in the world and represents the largest single concentration of Renaissance wall-paintings executed in pure fresco. It is no surprise, therefore, that it is crowded at all times. A new system of air conditioning will go some way to preserving the magnificent works from the effects of the multitudes of visitors, but Vatican authorities were, at the time of writing, considering imposing restrictions on the numbers admitted at any one time.

The painted decoration follows a complex programme illustrating Christian cosmology, and designed to reinforce the origins of papal authority. The chapel is the place where the cardinals gather to elect each pope in secret conclave: they deliberate their decision in the presence of a pictorial map of the whole of spiritual history. When the chapel is crowded, it is unfortunately extremely difficult to appreciate the decorative scheme and its significance.

The chapel building

The chapel takes its name from Pope Sixtus IV, who commissioned its construction in 1475 to provide a new and grander place for papal ceremony and for the convocation of the conclave which elected a new pope. The design, to plans drawn up by Baccio Pontelli, is bare of architectural interest, with little natural illumination and a height which is disproportionate to its breadth. The ratios represented by its dimensions (40.5m by 13.2m, by 20.7m high) are those given for Solomon's temple (*I Kings 6:2*). It may also be significant that its appearance and dimensions recall the ancient Curia in the Roman Forum: this was the council chamber of the senators of ancient Rome, and Sixtus may have wished his chapel to be seen as a direct successor to it as the papal curia of the new Christian Empire which had replaced the former pagan one. Contemporary with the chapel's construction is the decorated floor—a fine example of opus alexandrinum. The choir loft and the delicate, carved marble transenna which divides the chapel are the work principally of Mino da Fiesole.

The scheme of the decorations

The Renaissance Christian mind divided human existence into three epochs: *ante legem* (from the Creation up until the Law of Moses); *sub lege* (under the law of Moses) and *sub gratia* (the time 'of Grace' or Redemption following the teachings of Jesus Christ). The first of these periods is elaborated on the ceiling, in Michelangelo's images of the Creation and the life of Noah; the second in scenes from the life of Moses, painted three decades earlier on the south wall; while the third is illustrated on the north wall, in scenes from the life of Christ. The culmination of this sequence is a depiction of the triumphal Second Coming on the Day of Judgement, painted by Michelangelo above the altar between 1536 and 1541. In the areas in between are images of those who bore witness: the Old Testament prophets and the pagan sibyls (interpreted as having foretold the redemption of mankind through a saviour); the ancestors of Jesus of Nazareth in the lunettes; and the apostolic succession of the popes in the spaces between the windows. Larger than almost any figure and directly above the altar, is the

THE SISTINE CHAPEL

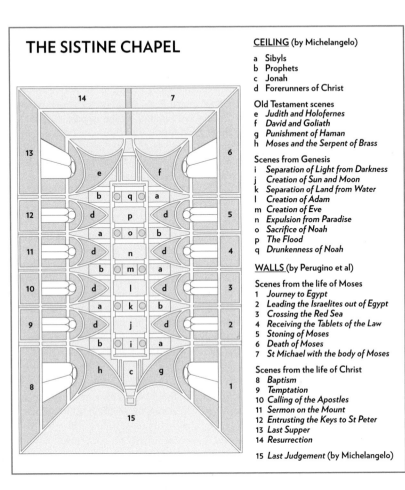

CEILING (by Michelangelo)

a Sibyls
b Prophets
c Jonah
d Forerunners of Christ

Old Testament scenes
e *Judith and Holofernes*
f *David and Goliath*
g *Punishment of Haman*
h *Moses and the Serpent of Brass*

Scenes from Genesis
i *Separation of Light from Darkness*
j *Creation of Sun and Moon*
k *Separation of Land from Water*
l *Creation of Adam*
m *Creation of Eve*
n *Expulsion from Paradise*
o *Sacrifice of Noah*
p *The Flood*
q *Drunkenness of Noah*

WALLS (by Perugino et al)

Scenes from the life of Moses
1 *Journey to Egypt*
2 *Leading the Israelites out of Egypt*
3 *Crossing the Red Sea*
4 *Receiving the Tablets of the Law*
5 *Stoning of Moses*
6 *Death of Moses*
7 *St Michael with the body of Moses*

Scenes from the life of Christ
8 *Baptism*
9 *Temptation*
10 *Calling of the Apostles*
11 *Sermon on the Mount*
12 *Entrusting the Keys to St Peter*
13 *Last Supper*
14 *Resurrection*

15 *Last Judgement* (by Michelangelo)

unusual Jonah, whose return to the world after three days in the whale's belly prefigured the Resurrection of Christ. The Evangelists and Apostles are absent from much of the plan, although the tapestries which were to have hung along the walls at the lowest level, where the *trompe l'oeil* drapery is now, and which were executed to designs by Raphael (*see p. 445*), related scenes from the lives of St Peter and St Paul.

The paintings on the side walls

Pope Sixtus commissioned the greatest artists of his age to decorate his new chapel, under the general superintendence of Perugino, one of the finest masters of painting technique then alive. The wall-paintings, executed between 1481 and 1483 by Perugino (assisted by Pinturicchio), Botticelli, Cosimo Rosselli (assisted by Piero di Cosimo), Domenico Ghirlandaio and Luca Signorelli, line the two long sides of the chapel and part of the wall at the opposite end from the altar. They depict scenes from the life of Moses on the south wall (liturgical north) and pendant scenes from the life and teachings of Christ on the north wall (liturgical south). The aim was to underline papal authority by showing Moses and Christ as the eternal lawgivers, and St Peter being entrusted with the continuation of that authority in what is the most strikingly beautiful fresco of the whole series, *Christ giving Peter the Keys of Heaven*, painted by Perugino. The classically-inspired octagonal building in the background of this scene is an exquisite premonition of the highest ideals of the new architecture of the Renaissance. The chapel ceiling at this time was a simple, solid blue colour, studded with gold stars, and the altar (west) wall was decorated with two further (now lost) frescoes by Perugino, of the *Finding of Moses* and the *Nativity of Christ*.

The Sistine Ceiling

Michelangelo was 33 years old in 1508 when he received the commission from Pope Julius II to paint the chapel's ceiling, an area of over 500 square metres. He had done little painting in his life before this date, and it had anyway been in the very different medium of egg-tempera on panel. He repeatedly protested his unsuitability and unwillingness to execute the work: this was to no avail in the face of the pope's inflexible intentions. From the beginning, the project was beset with difficulties: the problem of painting on a curved horizontal surface over 20m above the viewing level; a cramped and insecure painting platform; insufficient illumination; and assistants whom Michelangelo considered a hindrance. He early on dispensed with all help, continuing the enormous project alone: he also designed an entirely new kind of scaffolding, creating a fixed, arched platform which spanned the whole width of the chapel and kept him at a constant distance of about two metres from the surface which he was painting in the standing position. This meant that he could execute the frescoes in successive bands across the ceiling, repeatedly removing the scaffolding bridge and re-immuring it (just above the third moulded cornice) in preparation for the next band. In this way, he worked from the east end, where his figures are noticeably too small, towards the altar end, where he appears to acquire confidence and soon masters the issue of scale. It should not be forgotten that Michelangelo worked constantly in very poor light, and without the possibility of seeing how his painting might appear from 20m below, because his scaffolding blocked his view of the work in progress when he descended to the floor. By the time he could see what he had done, it was too late to alter anything because the scaffolding was gone. He also had to contend with the impatience of Julius II and the discomfort of his working conditions, which he described with grim humour in a sonnet in 1510. He concludes by protesting that his art 'was dead' and that he 'was no painter': his face was like a floor mosaic from the dripping paint and his spine 'doubled back like a drawn bow'.

The subject matter chosen for the ceiling paintings concentrates on the early chapters of Genesis. The exact programme would have been given to Michelangelo, probably by Egidius of Viterbo, who was charged with formulating and refining Church doctrine; but the artist's own genius emerges in the extraordinary handling of the subject matter. He encapsulates elusive concepts in simple and unforgettable images, and brilliantly articulates the huge expanse with the indispensable aid of a fictional architectural framework which both separates and unites the individual elements of the design. Clear primary colour is used in the main narrative scenes, while neutral tints define the architectural framework and its imaginary 'sculptural' decoration. Many of the nude male figures of this were inspired by the late Hellenistic *Belvedere Torso*, which was a centrepiece of Julius' collection of antiquities and is still to be seen here in the Vatican (*see p. 456*). Indeed, Michelangelo paints like a sculptor: close examination of the surface of his frescoes reveals how he often used his brush with rapid hatching strokes, as though it were his chisel working on stone. The celebrated scene of the *Creation of Adam* is perhaps the greatest piece of sculpture ever created in paint. The reposed and idealised figure of Adam is based on the pose of the ancient Roman river-god; but in the hands of Michelangelo it goes far beyond its ancient prototype to become a celebration of solitary and uncorrupted humanity, marvellously balanced by the large area of void before him. His dignified repose contrasts, too, with the concentrated dynamism in the features of the Almighty who reaches out towards him.

Michelangelo's frescoes were restored (not uncontroversially) in 1984–93. A system of LED lighting, designed to improve colour perception and enhance the effects of contrast, was installed in 2014.

The *Last Judgement*

A changed world and a more pensive Michelangelo (now 61 years old) produced the *Last Judgement* (1536–41) on the wall above the altar. In the interval between the two painting campaigns, the Sack of Rome of 1527 (*see p. 23*) had irrevocably altered the Church's perception of itself and had left its scars upon the imagination of its artists—in particular one as devout as Michelangelo, who in any case was now facing the decay of his own life and the destiny of his soul. In his *Last Judgement*, however, there is no hint either of simplistic gloom or grating optimism. Where other artists had evoked contrasts of light and impenetrable dark, Michelangelo sets the whole against a unifying, unearthly, intense lapis blue: the huge empty spaces in the composition become thereby as eloquent as the groups of floating figures which they balance. Where many earlier painters had particularised the Judgement Day, dwelling upon the multifarious punishments of the wicked, Michelangelo has unified the event into a vast, single, cyclical motion, with the blessed rising to the left of the altar and the damned falling to the right. Everything else in the chapel has a linear direction: this alone is circular in sweep, radiating out from the magnificent gestures of Christ's arms. The beardless, youthful Christ, like a dynamised Apollo irrupting into the viewer's space, is in deliberate contrast to the reposed Adam at the centre of the ceiling.

The eye is drawn into the movement of the whole piece, passing from the central focus of Christ to the figure of his Mother beside him, turning away and partly drawing her veil in demure fear. Above, groups of angels and nude figures expand the scene outwards as they carry away the Cross and the column of the Flagellation to either side: there is a masterful audacity to some of these swirling figures, which are perceived from often bizarre angles as they somersault in the sky with a momentary glance towards us, which manifests itself in no more than a pair of eyes and nostrils emerging from beneath the bulk of a twisting abdomen. In the depths of Hades below, a few flourishing brush-strokes give form to a lurking soul, who, anxious of his fate, peers from partial darkness into the Eternal Future: the crazed glances, the floating figures, and the rapid and confident adumbrations of the master's technique, all seem to prefigure Goya's caricature by nearly 300 years. This is high bravura painting: urgent, restless, sometimes even playful, but a world away from the poise and balance of the earlier Michelangelo above.

The original nudity of the figures inevitably caused offence to some, and many of them were covered by Daniele da Volterra, at the request of Pope Pius IV, in 1565. (These draperies have—with the exception of the figure of St Catherine which has been repainted in fresco—been added to the surface in a soluble tempera, which could in theory be removed: papal policy is currently to leave them in place.) Even while work was in progress on the painting the pope's master of ceremonies, Biagio da Cesena—according to Giorgio Vasari—was constantly chiding Michelangelo about the issue of nudity, irritating him to the point that he procured his revenge by painting Biagio prominently above the entrance-door to the right of the altar, as the figure of Minos with ass's ears on his head and a serpent wound around his body, poised with jaws open to detach his genitals. Michelangelo's other personalisation in this great work is on a more sombre note. The gigantic figure of St Bartholomew (below and to the viewer's right of Christ) holds up, as was traditional, the attribute of his martyrdom: the knife with which he was flayed and the flayed skin itself. The tousled hair and broken nose scarcely visible on the face in the limp, hanging skin is a self-portrait of the artist. That so tortured an image should have suggested itself to Michelangelo as the way to sign his last great essay in painting speaks eloquently of his state of mind in these later years. He obdurately believed he was condemned to perdition.

SALA REGIA

Through the main door of the Sistine Chapel the sumptuous Sala Regia can sometimes be seen (*although closed to the public*). It was begun by Antonio da Sangallo the Younger in 1540 for Paul III for the reception of ambassadors, and was used as a dormitory during conclaves. It contains stucco decoration by Perino del Vaga and Daniele da Volterra, and frescoes by Giorgio Vasari, Salviati and the Zuccari. The first official meeting between the Pope and the Archbishop of Canterbury since the Reformation took place here in 1966. The Cappella Paolina (*also closed to the public*), by Antonio da Sangallo the Younger, has two remarkable frescoes by Michelangelo—the *Conversion of St Paul* and *Crucifixion of St Peter*—painted in 1542–5 and 1546–50.

NB: At the time of writing an exit reserved for tour groups was by the Scala Regia (usually open every day except Wed), a magnificent staircase by Bernini, which descends past his equestrian statue of Constantine to the portico of St Peter's. If you do not wish to continue the tour of the museums (and do not have an audio guide), you are sometimes able to attach yourself to a group and leave with them. Otherwise the exit is by a small door in the north wall of the nave, which leads to the Museum of Christian Art at the beginning of the lower floor of Bramante's long west corridor.

THE ROUTE TO THE EXIT

MUSEUM OF CHRISTIAN ART

The Museum of Christian Art was founded by Benedict XIV in 1756 and enlarged in the 19th century, partly by the acquisitions of Pius IX but mainly by finds made during excavations in the catacombs by Giovanni Battista de Rossi and his successors.

Leading off a room with vestments is the **Chapel of St Pius V**, decorated by Jacopo Zucchi to designs by Vasari. In the wall case is part of the treasury of the Sancta Sanctorum (*see p. 295*).

The **Room of the Addresses** (*degli Indirizzi*) was so called because in the time of Pius XI the addresses or congratulatory documents sent to Leo XIII and Pius X were kept here. A splendid collection of liturgical objects is displayed here. In the cases opposite the window is a wonderful collection of ivories including the Rambona Diptych (c. 900; with Christian scenes and the representation of the Roman wolf in the bottom of the left-hand panel) and precious book covers. There is also a collection of Limoges enamels and silver dating from the 14th–17th centuries.

The **Room of the Aldobrandini Wedding** on the left is named after a Roman fresco of a marriage scene, a masterpiece of Augustan art, which combines realism and symbolism and was inspired by a Greek model of the 4th or 3rd century BC. It was found on the Esquiline in 1605 and acquired by Cardinal Pietro Aldobrandini. The room also has other ancient frescoes from Ostia and other sites. The ceiling was frescoed by Guido Reni with scenes from the story of Samson.

The **Room of the Papyri** is named after a collection of 6th–9th-century papyri from Ravenna (now replaced by facsimiles). The frescoes are by Raphael Mengs and his assistant Christopher Unterberger. In the cases are *bozzetti* by Bernini. The room beyond displays early **Christian antiquities from the catacombs** of St Calixtus, Domitilla and St Sebastian, and other Roman cemeteries. These include a collection of glass, some of the finer specimens gilded, and engraved 4th-century glass from Ostia. Many of the lamps (1st–4th centuries) have symbols of the Good Shepherd, the fish, the peacock, and the monogram of Christ. Fabrics include 11th–13th-century Church embroideries.

VATICAN LIBRARY

The Vatican Library (Biblioteca Apostolica Vaticana; *only open to scholars*) was founded by Nicholas V with a nucleus of some 350 volumes, which he increased to 1,200. Sixtus IV brought the total to 3,650. The library was pillaged in the Sack of 1527. Towards the end of the 16th century Sixtus V commissioned Domenico Fontana to build the great Sistine Hall to accommodate its collection. Later popes adapted numerous rooms in Bramante's west corridor to house the steadily increasing number of gifts, bequests and purchases. Among the most important acquisitions were the Biblioteca Palatina of Heidelberg (1623), the Biblioteca Urbinas founded by Federico, Duke of Urbino (1657), Queen Christina of Sweden's library (1690), the Biblioteca Ottoboniana, formerly the property of Alexander VIII Ottoboni, bought in 1748, the Jesuit Library

(1922), the Biblioteca Chigiana (1923) and the Biblioteca Ferraioli (1929). There are now about 60,000 manuscripts, 7,000 incunabula and 1,000,000 other printed books. Leo XIII added a reference library; Pius X reorganised the manuscripts and provided a study room; and Pius XI carried out further reorganisation. The route to the exit along Bramante's long west corridor takes you through the following rooms:

Gallery of Urban VIII: Two seated Roman statues flank the entrance. Astronomical instruments are shown here.

Sistine Rooms: These two rooms form part of the Library of Sixtus V. In the first are frescoes of St Peter's as Michelangelo may have planned it and of the erection of the obelisk in St Peter's Square. Here too is a press designed by Bramante for sealing papal bulls. Over the doors of the second room are depictions of *Sixtus V proclaiming St Bonaventura a Doctor of the Church* in the church of the Santi Apostoli (Melozzo's frescoes are seen in their original place on the wall of the apse; *see p. 156*), and of the *Canonisation of San Diego* in old St Peter's.

Sistine Hall: Named after its founder Sixtus V, this was built in 1587–9 by Domenico Fontana across the great Cortile del Belvedere, cutting it in two. The hall is decorated with themes glorifying literature and the pontificate of Sixtus V, with interesting views of Rome. In the vestibule, above the doors, are paintings of the Lateran Palace, before and after its reconstruction by Domenico Fontana.

The Pauline Rooms: These two rooms were added by Paul V, and decorated in the Mannerist style in 1610–11.

The Alexandrine Room: This was adapted in 1690 by Alexander VIII and decorated with scenes from the life of Pius VI.

The Clementine Gallery: The gallery was added by Clement XII in 1732. In 1818, under Pius VII, it was decorated with paintings of scenes from the life of that pope. Exhibits from numerous excavations are displayed here.

A modern staircase leads down from the last room (where Mithraic divinities flank the far door) and you are obliged to use it. This means that the main hall of the **Museum of Pagan Antiquities** of the library (Museo Profano della Biblioteca) beyond, can only be viewed from a distance. It can also be seen from the side through a glass door in the Quattro Cancelli. It contains a collection begun by Clement XIII in 1767, with additions from excavations in 1809–15. It was completed in the time of Pius VI and decorated by Luigi Valadier, with ceiling paintings symbolising Time. In the niches on either side of the entrance wall are a head of Augustus (one of the best portraits of this emperor) and a bronze head of Nero. In the cupboards (usually kept closed) are carved Roman ivory, busts in semi-precious stones, a mosaic from Hadrian's Villa, Roman and Etruscan bronzes and the head and arm of a chryselephantine statue of Minerva, claimed to be a 5th-century BC Greek original.

THE VATICAN CITY & GARDENS

The Vatican City (*map p. 650*), surrounded by a high wall, comprises an area of 44 hectares (less than half a square kilometre) and has a population of just over 800. It is, in size, the smallest independent state in existence. It has its own postal service, its own radio station (which was prominent in the Second World War) and, since 1983, its own television channel. Its newspaper, the *Osservatore Romano*, has a worldwide circulation. Policing is carried out by the 130-strong Gendarme Corps and by the pontifical Swiss Guard, founded in 1506, who wear a picturesque striped uniform. Until 2002, when it adopted the euro, it also had its own currency. Like all other countries in the Eurozone, the Vatican has its own specially-designed coins. It has its own internet top-level domain: .va.

There are three entrances to the Vatican City. They are not open to the general public and are protected by members of the Swiss Guard. The Portone di Bronzo, in the colonnade to the right of St Peter's, is the official entrance to the Holy See. The Arco delle Campane, to the left of St Peter's, is the entrance for cars; it is also used for access to the Audience Hall, and for the organised tours of the gardens and city and of the necropolis below St Peter's. It is protected by a sentry of the Swiss Guard, armed with a rifle instead of the halberd carried by the guard at the Portone di Bronzo. The Cancello di Sant'Anna, in Via di Porta Angelica, is used for the various offices of the Vatican State, including the Vatican Printing Press and the Vatican newspaper, *Osservatore Romano*.

HISTORY OF THE VATICAN CITY

The temporal power of the popes ended with the breach of Porta Pia and the entrance of Italian troops into Rome on 20th September 1870, signifying the unification of Italy. Until that time much of central Italy had been controlled by the papacy: the States of the Church had extended for 44,547 square kilometres. On the same day an agreement was made with the papacy that the Leonine City was excluded from the jurisdiction of Italian troops, and this led the way to the creation of the Vatican State by the Lateran Treaty (or Concordat), signed on 11th February 1929, which defined the limits of the Vatican City. The Treaty also granted the privilege of extraterritoriality to the basilicas of St John Lateran (with the Lateran Palace), Santa Maria Maggiore and San Paolo fuori le Mura, and to certain other buildings, including the Palazzo della Cancelleria and the pope's villa at Castel Gandolfo. Special clauses in the treaty provided for access to St Peter's and the Vatican Museums. Under the treaty, Italy accepted canon law on marriage and divorce and made religious teaching compulsory in secondary as well as primary schools. Italy also agreed to make a payment in final settlement of the claims by the Holy See for the loss of papal property taken over by the Italian government. After the signing of the Treaty the pope came out of the Vatican for the first time since 1870. (A new Concordat—which made religious instruction in schools optional, and contained modifications regarding marriage—was signed between the Italian government and the Vatican in 1984.)

Arranging a visit

Visits are by guided tour only, daily except Wed and Sun. The tour (on foot) lasts about 2hrs and by open-top bus, about 40mins. It takes in the gardens and you can see the exteriors of some the buildings (the Vatican Palace itself is never open to the public). To book, ask at the Vatican Museums, at the Tourist Office in St Peter's Square, or send an email to: tours.musei@scv.va. T: 06 69 88 4676 or T: 06 69 88 3145.

TOUR OF THE VATICAN CITY

Just inside the Arco delle Campane is **Piazza dei Protomartiri Romani** (*map p. 650, C2*), the site of the martyrdom of the early Christians near the Circus of Nero. On the left is the **Camposanto Teutonico**, dating from the 8th century, and probably the oldest medieval cemetery; it is still reserved for the Germans and Dutch. Adjacent is the Collegio Teutonico. Beyond, against the wall of the city, is the **Audience Hall** by Pier Luigi Nervi (1971). Designed in the shape of a shell (a shape which allows the whole audience a view of the pope), it has a capacity of over 10,000 both seated and standing. The large **Domus Sanctae Marthae**, built in 1996, is the Vatican's guesthouse. It is here that the cardinals stay when in conclave to elect a new pope. On his election in 2013, Pope Francis chose to have his residence here, instead of in the Papal Apartments in the Vatican Palace.

THE POPE AND THE HIERARCHY OF THE VATICAN STATE

The Vatican is a sovereign state, ruled by the pope as absolute monarch. The pope is also the Bishop of Rome, successor to St Peter, and, as such, the head of the Roman Catholic Church and the Vicar of Christ. He enjoys the *primatus jurisdictionis*, that is, supreme jurisdictional power over the whole Church; he is head of the legislature, executive and judiciary, and he nominates the General Council and the Governor of the Vatican. He is assisted by the Sacred College of Cardinals and by the Roman Curia.

The Sacred College of Cardinals was limited by Sixtus V to 70 members, but after the consistory of March 1962 the number was increased to 87. At present there is no limit to the number of cardinals that can be appointed. The College consists of three orders: cardinal bishops (whose dioceses are the suburbicarian sees of Ostia, Velletri, Porto and Santa Rufina, Albano, Frascati and Palestrina), cardinal priests, and cardinal deacons. At the time of writing the majority of cardinals were from Italy, followed by the United States and then Spain. Cardinals retain their positions for life; only those under the age of 80 may vote for a new pope.

The Roman Curia comprises the nine Sacred Congregations, which deal with the central administration of the Church, the three Tribunals, and the five Offices, which include that of the Cardinal Secretary of State, who represents the Vatican in international relations. The population of the Vatican state includes about 450 citizens, all of whom are cardinals and clergy who work for the Holy See, and some 300 permanent or temporary non-citizen residents.

Behind (east of) the Audience Hall is the **Palazzo del Sant'Uffizio**, where the Holy Office or tribunal, commonly known as the Inquisition, was established in 1542 by Paul III to investigate charges of heresy, unbelief and other offences against the Catholic religion. The preparation of the Index of Prohibited Books was originally entrusted to the Congregation of the Holy Office. In 1571 Pius V established a special Congregation of the Index, which survived until its suppression by Benedict XV in 1917, when these duties were resumed by the Holy Office. The tribunal was formally abolished by the Roman Assembly in February 1849, but it was re-established by Pius IX a few months later. The secret archives of the Inquisition were opened to students for the first time in 1998, covering the period from its inception to the first years of the 20th century.

Opposite the majestic west (liturgical east) end of St Peter's is the little church of **Santo Stefano degli Abissini**, founded in the 5th century. In 1479 Sixtus IV conceded it to Coptic monks; it was rebuilt by Clement XI. A road ascends past the **Governorate Palace**, built in 1931 as the seat of the Vatican's civic administration. The flowers in the bed in front of it are arranged to form the coat of arms of the incumbent pope. To the south is the little-used Vatican railway station. Further uphill is the **Palazzo Etiopico**, founded by Pius XI for seminarians from Ethiopia. Futher west, past exotic vegetation, is the **old Vatican radio station**, designed by Guglielmo Marconi and inaugurated in 1931. Since 1957 Vatican Radio has transmitted from a station at Santa Maria di Galeria, 25km outside Rome. At the western extremity of the city is a stretch of the wall built by Nicholas V on the site of the ancient walls put up by Leo IV. At the angle of the walls is the **Tower of St John**, once an observatory but now used to accommodate distinguished visitors to the Holy See. The papal helipad lies beyond.

At the highest point of the gardens (71m) is a reproduction of the **Grotto of Lourdes**, to which pilgrims come in a candlelit procession every May. It was presented by French Catholics to Leo XIII in 1902. Following the line of the Leonine Walls, you come to the little monastery of the **Mater Ecclesiae**, founded by John Paul II and chosen by Benedict XVI as his place of retirement after his resignation in 2013. Close by is the **Fontana dell'Aquilone**, designed for Pope Paul V Borghese by Giovanni Vasanzio (the Dutch artist Jan van Santen, who was born in Utrecht and began life as a cabinet maker, but Italianised his name when he came to live in Rome). The triton is by Stefano Maderno.

Closer to the huge bulk of the Vatican Museums is the **Casina of Pius IV**, consisting of two small garden buildings by Pirro Ligorio (1558–62), which are a masterpiece of Mannerist architecture and were decorated by various artists including Santi di Tito, Federico Zuccari, Federico Barocci and Durante Alberti. Once used as a summer residence and hunting lodge, they are now the seat of the Pontifical Academy of Sciences.

One of the few non-clerical buildings in the gardens is the pretty little **Head Gardener's lodge**.

Outside the Ancient Walls

Outside Rome's city walls to the east and north stand two pilgrimage basilicas: San Lorenzo and Sant'Agnese fuori le Mura. In the garden of the latter is the important mausoleum of Santa Costanza. The Catacombs of Santa Priscilla are also in this area.

The huge **Piazzale San Lorenzo** (*map p. 649, C1*) a busy traffic hub and bus and tram terminus, is traversed by Via Tiburtina, on the site of the ancient Roman road to Tibur (modern Tivoli). On the site of the Campo Verano, once the estate of the emperor Lucius Verus, is the huge municipal cemetery known as **Cimitero del Verano**. It was designed by Giuseppe Valadier in 1807–12, with a chapel and quadri-porticus added in 1852 by Virginio Vespignani. The four colossal allegorical figures at the entrance date from 1878. The cemetery has numerous family burial chapels erected in the early years of the 20th century (including that of Ettore Ximenes) and a First World War cemetery by Raffaele de Vico (1928).

Here too stands perhaps the loveliest Early Christian basilica in Rome: San Lorenzo fuori le Mura, one of the seven pilgrimage churches. It has remarkable architectural features, including two storeys of ancient columns in the chancel and superb Cosmati work. Although the part of town in which it stands is noisy and fraught, the basilica is a haven of calm spirituality.

SAN LORENZO FUORI LE MURA

Map p. 649, C1. Bus 71 from Via San Claudio (map p. 654, C1) or 3 from the Colosseum. Open 8–12 & 4–6.30. It is best to visit in the afternoon since funerals are often held in the morning.

The basilica is dedicated to St Lawrence, thought to have been a deacon under Pope Sixtus II and martyred in 258. Despite the tradition that he was roasted alive on a gridiron (and the numerous paintings and sculptures which show the scene; in the gardens of Piazzale del Verano here, the granite column bears a 19th-century statue of the saint with his gridiron), he was probably in fact beheaded. He was buried here and has always been venerated as one of the most important early Roman martyrs. By the 4th century he was considered one of the patron saints of the city, together with St Peter and St Paul, and tradition holds that Constantine ordered a cemetery basilica to be built here in his honour. In 579 Pope Pelagius II built a new church to enclose

SAN LORENZO FUORI LE MURA

Detail from an ancient sarcophagus. The bride and groom are depicted in the act of the *dextrarum iunctio*, the joining of hands before witnesses. Behind the couple stands the goddess Juno Pronuba, resting her hands on their shoulders to symbolise their union. Below their hands is a damaged figure of Hymen, the god of marriage, with his flaming torch.

the relics of St Lawrence, alongside this basilica, which was radically altered in 1216 when Honorius III demolished the apse and built another church onto it, placing the entrance at the opposite end. This explains the curious architectural features of the basilica today. Restoration was carried out in 1864–70 by Virginio Vespignani.

San Lorenzo was the only church in Rome to suffer serious damage during the Second World War, when it was partly destroyed by Allied bombs (the target was meant to have been Tiburtina railway station close by): the façade and the south wall were carefully rebuilt in 1949.

EXTERIOR OF SAN LORENZO FUORI LE MURA

On the right of the church behind two umbrella pines is the **friary**, owned by Franciscan Capuchins since 1857, with a façade of four wide arches supported by ancient columns and a charming gallery above. The simple Romanesque **campanile**, not particularly tall, dates from the 12th century.

The church is entered through a very beautiful (reconstructed) 13th-century **narthex** with six antique Ionic columns, a delicate Cosmatesque frieze, and, above, a tiny intricately carved marble frieze with lions' heads. These are thought to be the work of the Vassalletto family (*see p. 498*). Under the porch are three Roman sarcophagi (the huge one with wine-harvest scenes and putti playing amongst the vines is particularly delightful). The conspicuous monument (1954) commemorating the statesman Alcide de Gasperi, the Christian Democrat who dominated Italian politics between 1943 and 1953, is by Giacomo Manzù. The 13th-century fresco cycle (restored in the 19th century and again after war damage) depict the lives of St Lawrence and St Stephen.

THE INTERIOR

The lovely light, basilican interior, with a raised chancel and no transept, retains the aspect given to it in the 13th century. Twenty-two Ionic columns of granite support an architrave, and the floor is paved with a 12th-century Cosmatesque mosaic. The beautiful Cosmatesque ambo in the nave has exquisite carvings and marble inlay, and incorporates a paschal candlestick with a twisted stem.

The **confessio** preserves the relics of St Lawrence and two companions; and you can go down to process all the way around the relic chest. Steps lead up to the beautiful **raised chancel**, where the baldacchino is signed by Giovanni, Pietro, Angelo and Sasso, sons of a master mason called Paolo (1147). It has porphyry columns with exquisitely carved bases, surrounded by a miniature Cosmati pavement (the upper part was restored in the 19th century).

Here the chancel incorporates the remains of the 6th-century church: the Corinthian columns with magnificent huge capitals support an entablature charmingly constructed out of miscellaneous antique fragments mostly dating from the 1st century AD and, above, there is a delicate arcaded gallery with smaller columns and windows with transennae. The two antique capitals at the west end of the chancel are decorated with trophies and winged Victories. From here you can look back to see the inner face of what was once the **triumphal arch** (from when the church faced the other way), which bears a remarkable 6th-century mosaic (reset during the Byzantine revival) of Christ seated on a globe flanked by St Peter, St Paul, St Stephen, St Lawrence, St Hippolytus and Pope Pelagius II offering a model of the church. Beneath the two latticed windows are representations of Bethlehem and Jerusalem. On the arch is a beautiful mosaic inscription against a blue ground dedicated to St Lawrence. On the soffit is a ribbon charmingly twined around fruit and flowers. The chancel also has two long marble benches with a lion's head at each end. In the apse is the handsome 13th-century **episcopal throne**, flanked by a magnificent Cosmati screen of the same date, very well preserved.

The lower level has some remains of the earliest basilica, including some of the original pillars. In what would have been its narthex is the **mausoleum of Pius IX** (d. 1878, beatified in 2000), rebuilt by Raffaele Cattaneo in 1881 and decorated with mosaics by Ludovico Seitz. The pope has been given a silver mask and is wrapped in red fur-lined vestments. The marble slab on which St Lawrence's body is said to have been placed after his martyrdom is also on display here.

On the west wall of the church is the **tomb of Cardinal Fieschi**, a large Roman sarcophagus with a splendid relief of a marriage scene, converted to its present use in 1256; it was rebuilt from the original fragments after the war (*see illustration on p. 479*).

THE CLOISTER

The charming cloister (*entered through the sacristy*), which dates from 1187–91, has two storeys of little columns and the walks are covered with carved fragments, both ancient and Early Christian, and inscriptions from the Catacombs of St Cyriaca (*no longer open to the public*). A shattered shell from the bomb attacks of 1943 is also preserved here (and in the corridor you can see photographs of the war damage).

VIA NOMENTANA

At the beginning of the wide Via Nomentana, which runs northeast on the line of the ancient consular road, stands **Porta Pia** (*map p. 648, A4*). This was Michelangelo's last architectural work, commissioned by Pius IV in 1561 (the exterior face was added in 1868 by Virginio Vespignani). It is famous in Italian history since it was here that Italian troops under General Raffaele Cadorna entered Rome on 20th September 1870, and so brought to an end the temporal reign of the popes. The breach was a few steps to the left of the gate, in Corso d'Italia, where there are commemorative inscriptions.

Via Nomentana continues due north, traversing an elegant residential district of palaces and suburban villas, many with beautiful gardens laid out in the late 19th and early 20th centuries. The most important of them is Villa Torlonia.

MUSEI DI VILLA TORLONIA

Map p. 648, B3. Via Nomentana 70. Express bus no. 60 from Piazza Venezia and Via Nazionale to the Villa Torlonia stop on Via Nomentana. Open Tues–Sun 9–7. You can visit the park, the Casina delle Civette and the Casino Nobile (two separate tickets). You have to make an appointment to see the theatre (T: 06 44 04 768 or 060608, teatrodivillatorlonia.it) and to visit the bunker (sotterraneidiroma.it). There is a café in the orangery.

When Prince Giovanni Torlonia bought the villa in 1806, he had Giuseppe Valadier renovate it and add the garden buildings. Today the well-kept park of some 16 hectares is decorated with 19th-century obelisks, lakes, a theatre, an orangery and a Moorish conservatory. At the entrance is a magnificent grove of palm trees. In 1925 the villa itself (called the Casino Nobile) was given to Mussolini and he and his family lived here until 1943. From June 1944 until 1947 it was occupied by the Allied command. The property was expropriated by the Comune di Roma in 1977.

The first floor of the **Casino Nobile**, interesting for its 19th-century decorations, has frescoes by Francesco Coghetti, a stucco frieze by Bertel Thorvaldsen and works by Francesco Podesti. On the top floor there is a collection of paintings and sculpture by artists of the 20th-century Scuola Romana, including Cavalli, Donghi, Cagli, Capogrossi and Ziveri. As the war grew close, Mussolini had an **anti air-raid bunker** constructed in the garden, nearly seven metres below ground.

A path leads to the delightful little Art Nouveau **Casina delle Civette** ('House of the Owls'), the most interesting building in the park. Part of it was built in the form of a Swiss chalet by Giuseppe Jappelli in 1840, and it was rebuilt as a charming folly by Vincenzo Fasolo in 1916–21. It has gabled majolica roofs, antique fragments, unusual windows and, inside, attractive panelling, stuccoes and tiled floors. It is especially interesting for its stained glass, made in 1908–30 by Duilio Cambellotti and Paolo Paschetto.

The largest building in the park is the **Theatre**, dating from 1840–70 and recently restored. The **Casino dei Principi**, close to Via Nomentana, is used for exhibitions.

On the other side of Via Nomentana is the **Villa Paganini**, which has early 20th-century mansions in its park, recently restored.

SANT'AGNESE FUORI LE MURA AND SANTA COSTANZA

Map p. 648, C2. Express bus no. 60 from Piazza Venezia and Via Nazionale to the XXI Aprile stop on Via Nomentana.

The basilica of Sant'Agnese fuori le Mura is in an important group of early Christian buildings. According to tradition, St Agnes, having refused the advances of a praetor's son, was exposed in the Stadium of Domitian (today's Piazza Navona), where her nakedness was covered by the miraculous growth of her hair. She was then condemned to be burned at the stake but the flames did not touch her. Finally she was beheaded by Diocletian. The pallium, the stole worn by the pope and by metropolitan archbishops, is made of the wool of lambs blessed annually on the morning of her festival, 21st January, at around 10.30. The saint's name is close to the Latin *agnus*, or lamb.

HISTORY OF THE BUILDINGS

At some time between 337 and 350 Constantia, the elder daughter of the emperor Constantine, built a cemetery basilica on her estate, next to the tomb where the martyred St Agnes had been buried in 304. To this basilica she then joined a circular mausoleum for herself, so that the intercessions of pilgrims at the martyr's shrine might also benefit her own soul. That mausoleum was subsequently converted into a church and has thus survived (*described below*). The cemetery basilica fell into ruin and its site was abandoned when in 625–38 Pope Honorius I constructed a basilica directly above the saint's tomb and adjoining catacombs. Pope Honorius was a great embellisher of the burial places of saints. During his pontificate he built the basilica of San Pancrazio and enlarged the basilica of San Paolo fuori le Mura.

SANT'AGNESE FUORI LE MURA

Open 7.30–12 & 4–7.30. Entrance either through the garden on Via Sant'Agnese or through the gate of the convent of the Canonici Lateranensi at Via Nomentana 349.

Honorius' 7th-century basilica was restored in 1479 by Giuliano della Rovere (later Pope Julius II), again by Cardinal Varallo after the sack of 1527, and by Pius IX in 1856. Nevertheless, it retains many original features. The side entrance take you down a broad **staircase** of 45 white marble steps (1590); the walls on either side are covered with inscriptions from the catacombs, including St Damasus' 4th-century record in ten lines of the martyrdom of St Agnes (at the bottom, on the right of the glass door).

In the interior of the church (best light in the afternoon), the nave and aisles are separated by 14 ancient **Roman columns**, placed in pairs close together, so the arches are unusually tall. At the back of the church there is a **narthex** for catechumens, and the columns here and those that follow in the nave are of plain grey breccia. The beginning of the chancel is marked by a pair of fluted columns. Those alongside the chancel itself are of a rich red marble. Their capitals are different too, with smooth-leaved foliage. A **matroneum**, with smaller columns and a marble screen, was built over the aisles and the west end in 620 (this is earliest such feature to survive in a Roman basilica). The carved and gilded wood ceiling dates from 1606 (restored in 1855).

The glory of the church is its **apse**, which preserves its 7th-century revetment of grey marble divided by narrow strips of porphyry, and a marble synthronon. An antique alabaster torso was turned into a **statue of St Agnes** holding a lamb, with bronze additions dating from 1605 (Nicolas Cordier). Due to its modern base and illumination it is easy to overlook it. The beautiful **apse mosaic**, from the time of Pope Honorius I (625–38), shows three solitary figures against a gold ground: St Agnes flanked by popes Honorius (holding a model of the basilica) and Symmachus (identified by some scholars as Gregory the Great). Above St Agnes the Hand of God reaches down from beyond a starry firmament to confer on her a celestial diadem.

The **baldacchino** above the high altar dates from the time of Paul V. Just outside the enclosed chancel is a fine **candlestick**, thought to be a neo-Attic work of the 2nd century, carved with acanthus leaves and sporting rams' heads and sphinxes. Just inside the chancel is an ancient episcopal throne in the same marble as the apse. You can descend to the crypt to see the reliquary urn.

In the second south chapel, over a Cosmati altar, is a fine relief of *St Stephen and St Lawrence* by Andrea Bregno (1490), and a bust of Christ, probably the work of Nicolas Cordier after a lost work by Michelangelo. The third south chapel, painted with poorly-preserved *trompe l'oeil* drapery, is the **Chapel of St Emerentiana**, the foster-sister of Agnes, who was stoned to death beside her sister's tomb. Paintings (1892, Eugenio Cisterna) show her stoning and burial, and a sweetly sentimental altarpiece shows her holding her stones in her hand. The second north chapel has a good 15th-century fresco of the *Madonna and Child.*

THE CATACOMBS

Open Tues–Sat 9–12 & 3–7 except Nov. Visits are by guided tour. T: 06 86 10 840, santagnese.com. For a general history and description of Roman catacombs, see pp. 516–7.
The Catacombs of Sant'Agnese (entered from the basilica narthex), consisting of 6km on three levels, part of one of which is open to the public, are the best-preserved and among the most interesting in Rome. They were in use for about 100 years from the second half of the 3rd to the second half of the 4th centuries, and continued into later centuries as a place of pilgrimage, before falling into disuse and oblivion. They were rediscovered in 1865–6. The guided tour normally takes about 30mins (*for opening times and how to book, see above*). The catacombs contain no paintings but the loculi and arcosolia are of considerable interest, as are the numerous inscriptions. Many of these contain symbols only (the Chi Rho, the anchor, the dove). A terracotta plaque showing a ham and the word '*Perna*' is shown, as having marked the burial place of a butcher. Many of the loculi are intact, closed by marble or terracotta slabs. A chapel was built where the body of St Agnes was found, and a silver coffer bearing the Borghese arms was provided in 1615 by Pope Paul V. This is also shown. It contains the relics of the saint, except for the head, which is in Sant'Agnese in Agone in Piazza Navona.

SANTA COSTANZA

From Sant'Agnese a path leads around a playground to the exquisite, peaceful mausoleum of Constantia (*open 9–12 & 3–6; coin-operated light*), known since the 9th century as the church of Santa Costanza. It was built by Constantia as a mausoleum for herself and her sister Helena, daughters of the emperor Constantine. Both sisters were buried here.

Before you enter the mausoleum, look to your right. In a grassy area with a few umbrella pines, behind a modern fence, you can see the remains of the original **cemetery basilica**, to which this mausoleum was attached by a capsule-shaped vestibule (its curved ends survive to right and left of the gate).

The **mausoleum** is annular in plan. Originally it would have had a further exterior colonnaded hall. The beautifully-preserved interior consists of an outer ambulatory separated from the central space by 24 **paired granite columns**. The inner column of each pair is slightly larger, with exquisitely carved composite capitals from the 1st century AD. The outer columns are smaller, also surmounted by composite capitals, but of later date (3rd century) and lesser quality. There are twelve large windows with restored transennae beneath the dome. The pavement is in terracotta except between

SANTA COSTANZA
Detail of the 4th-century mosaics above and to the side of
Constantia's tomb: fruitful branches, birds and amphorae.

the columns, where it is marble. The walls, now of bare brick, have lost their revetment.

On the barrel vaulting of the ambulatory are remarkable **mosaics** (4th century), executed for a Christian purpose though pagan in character, designed in pairs on a white ground. They were restored by Vincenzo Camuccini in 1834–40. Those flanking the entrance have a geometric design, and the next pair has a circular motif with animals and figures. Scenes of the wine harvest and vine tendrils with grapes follow, and the fourth pair has roundels with a leaf design, busts and figures. In the square niche opposite the entrance is a **cast of Constantia's sarcophagus**. The original magnificent porphyry tomb chest was removed to the Vatican in 1791 (*see p. 457*); Helena's sarcophagus was removed in 1606 and has not survived. Above the tomb to either side, the mosaics are of leaves, fruits, branches, amphorae and exotic birds. Over the sarcophagus only a fragment remains of a mosaic with a star design.

The mosaics of the dome were replaced by frescoes in 1620, but from early drawings we know that they represented a Paradise scene. The two **side niches** also have fine mosaics (5th or 7th century): on the left is a scene of the *Traditio Legem*, where Christ presents the scroll of the Law to St Peter, with St Paul on Christ's other side. On the right we see the *Traditio Clavium*, with Christ presenting the keys of Heaven to St Peter.

THE CATACOMBS OF PRISCILLA

Map p. 647. Open Tues–Sun 9–12 & 2–5; closed Mon and for a period during the summer. T: 06 86 20 6272, catacombepriscilla.com. You can ring ahead to book a time and specify the language you need. The excellent tour lasts about half an hour, is easy under foot and well lit. Entrance at no. 430 Via Salaria. To get there, take bus no. 92 from Termini Station or no. 63 from Piazza Venezia (nearest stop, Via di Priscilla). For a general history and description of Roman catacombs, see pp. 516–7.

A good place to have something to eat or drink in this residential part of town is Pistacchio in Piazza Acilia, a Sicilian café, snack bar and pizzeria.

The Catacombs of Priscilla, discovered in 1578 and now attached to a convent of Benedictine nuns, are among the most important in Rome. They extend for some 13km and it is estimated that there must have been about 40,000 burials here, including those of many popes between 309 and 555. They are on three levels, but only the uppermost (and oldest) level, dating from the 2nd century AD, is accessible. All along the walls are loculi, many of them of children, some still closed with their terracotta or marble slab. Many inscriptions and fragments of inscriptions survive. The main features shown on the tour are as follows (the order will depend on how many tours are in the catacombs at the same time):

Cubiculum of the Velata: This has well-preserved late 3rd-century paintings, including a woman in prayer wearing a veil, representing the deceased between scenes of her marriage and her motherhood. In the pretty vault is the *Good Shepherd* (with a goat on his shoulders), surrounded by sheep, trees, peacocks and doves. In the side lunettes are scenes from the Old Testament (*Shadrach, Meshach and Abednego in the Fiery Furnace* and the *Sacrifice of Abraham*). Above the entrance is a depiction of *Jonah and the Whale*.

The Virgin and Child: In an area presumed to be near a martyr's tomb, there is (on the roof) a remarkable fragment of stucco decoration combined with painting, in a vault dating from AD 220. The Good Shepherd is depicted flanked by two sheep amongst graceful trees. The figures of the Virgin and Child are the oldest known representations of this subject: next to the Virgin stands a prophet (identified as Balaam) pointing up to a star.

Cryptoporticus and Greek Chapel: The cryptoporticus, with cross-vaulting, was part of a villa of Priscilla's family, the Acilii, which probably stood above the cemetery and later became a funerary chapel named after the Greek inscriptions found here. It has superbly-preserved 3rd-century decorations in stucco and fresco, as well as dado panels in imitation marble. On the apse arch, against a bright red ground, is a scene of the breaking of bread, and there are also depictions of biblical stories (the *Three Wise Men, Susanna and the Elders*). From the other side of the chapel, through the window, can be seen a scene of *Moses Striking the Rock* as well as a pagan bust representing Summer.

You can sometimes ask to see the **Basilica di San Silvestro**, which adjoins the catacombs. It dates from the 4th centry but was reconstructed in the 19th century and restored in 2013. Part of the church is used as a museum of pagan marble fragments and sarcophagi, found in a cemetery on the Via Salaria.

Along the Via Ostiense

*Porta San Paolo, the south gate in Rome's city walls, is named after St Paul, who
was martyred at Tre Fontane and lies buried under the great basilica of San Paolo
fuori le Mura. All these sights are covered in this chapter, along with the pretty little
Protestant Cemetery beside the southern walls and Centrale Montemartini,
the superb satellite branch of the Capitoline Museums.*

The well-preserved **Porta San Paolo** (*map p. 653, A3*) was the Porta Ostiensis
of ancient Rome; its inner side is original, with two arches from the time of
Aurelian. The outer face, rebuilt by Honorius in 402, has been restored. The
gate houses the **Museo della Via Ostiense** (*open Tues–Sat 9–1.30; T: 06 57 43 193*),
which illustrates the history of the road which linked Rome to the coast at Ostia. The
collection is very modest (it includes milestones and reliefs; many are only casts),
but it provides good context for a trip to the ruins of Ostia. In the first room there is
a splendid oil painting showing the ancient Via Ostiensis leaving Rome at Porta San
Paolo and winding past temples and necropoleis to the salt flats of the coast. Towers
mark the river mouth and the ports of Claudius and Trajan are clearly marked. To the
southeast stretches the pine forest of Castel Porziano. A map in the next room shows
the end of the road in the other direction, reaching Rome at the Forum Boarium cattle
market (*see p. 251*). At the end of the corridor, in the east tower, is a model of the ports of
Claudius and Trajan and casts of those emperors' busts. At the top of the gatehouse you
can get out onto the ramparts, from where there is a fine view of the Pyramid of Cestius.

Getting there
*Metro line B to Piramide for Porta San Paolo and the Centrale Montemartini and
to San Paolo for the basilica of San Paolo fuori le Mura. Bus 23 goes from Piazza
Monte Savello (map p. 654, C3) to Piazzale Ostiense and continues to Ostiense-
Garbatella for the Centrale Montemartini and to Ostiense-San Paolo for San Paolo
fuori le Mura. Bus 792 links Ostiense-Garbatella and Ostiense-San Paolo with the
Baths of Caracalla and Piazza San Giovanni in Laterano.*

THE PYRAMID OF CESTIUS
*Visits by guided tour on Sat. Booking required. See archeoroma.beniculturali.it or T: 06
39 96 7700 (individuals) or 06 39 96 7450 and 06 57 43 193 (groups).*
Beside Porta San Paolo stands the recently restored Pyramid of Gaius Cestius. Cestius
was praetor, tribune of the plebs, and member of the college of Roman priests called
the *Septemviri Epulones*, who organised public banquets at important festivals. He

died in 12 BC and this is his tomb: a tall pyramid of brick faced with grey marble, 27m high with a base 22m square. An inscription records that it was built in less than 330 days. It was included in the Aurelian Walls in the 3rd century and remains one of the best-preserved monuments of ancient Rome (there were a number of similar pyramids in the ancient city, of which this is the sole survivor). At the heart of the pyramid is the barrel-vaulted sepulchral chamber, robbed of its contents in the Middle Ages. The walls are painted in a sober Pompeian style.

The pyramid overlooks the Protestant Cemetery (*see below*). On the wall next to it is a plaque commemorating the liberation of Rome on 4th June 1944 by the US and Canadian 1st Special Service forces.

THE PROTESTANT CEMETERY

Map p. 653, A3. Open Mon–Sat 9–5, Sun and holidays 9–1. Last entry 30mins before closing. Donation requested. T: 06 57 41 900, cemeteryrome.it. Entrance at no. 6 Via Caio Cestio.

The so-called Protestant Cemetery (officially the Cimitero Acattolico per gli Stranieri al Testaccio) is famous as the burial place of John Keats. In a romantic setting with tall cypresses and pine trees, the cemetery is beautifully kept and inhabited by numerous friendly cats. Formerly reserved for Protestant or Orthodox foreigners—mostly British and German—the cemetery has been open to all non-Catholics since 1953. Since the earliest recorded grave dating from 1738, some 4,000 people have been buried here. The Catholic Church once stipulated that burials had to take place after dark, and up until 1870 papal censorship was exercised on the tomb decorations and epitaphs: expressions of hope for salvation were not permitted, as no salvation was deemed possible for those outside the true Church.

Straight in front of you as you enter is the New Cemetery. To the left, beyond a wall, is the Old Cemetery. It has far fewer graves, as burials were soon forbidden here on the grounds that too many tombs would obscure the view of the Pyramid. The view of it is indeed splendid. When Shelley saw the cemetery he wrote: 'It might make one in love with death to think that one should be buried in so sweet a place.' His ashes were interred here in 1822.

Graves in the Old Cemetery: One of the most impressive tombs here is that of **Lady Elisa Temple**, the American wife of an English baronet. It features a relief of a mourning father and children bidding farewell to the deceased as she turns away, a shade, to the Underworld.

In the far left-hand corner is the grave of 'A Young English Poet', **John Keats** (1796–1821), who wrote his own epitaph: 'Here lies one whose name was writ in water'. Keats spent the last three months of his life in Rome (*see p. 344*), where he died from turberculosis, tended by his friend **Joseph Severn** (1793–1879), who is buried next to him. Severn returned to Rome as British Consul in 1860–72 and died here at the age of 85. Between the two graves is the little tombstone of Severn's son Arthur, 'accidentally killed' before his first birthday.

PROTESTANT CEMETERY
The tomb of Lady Elisa Temple (1809).

Graves in the New Cemetery: In use from 1822 onwards, this is crowded with gravestones. On the highest ground, at the base of a tower in the walls, lie the ashes of **Percy Bysshe Shelley** (1792–1822), the *cor cordium* ('heart of all hearts'), brought here by his friend Edward Trelawny. Shelley lived in Italy after 1818: in 1822 he and his wife Mary moved to Lerici in Liguria, and he was drowned at the age of 30 when his boat sank off Viareggio. When the body was washed ashore some time afterwards, it was cremated, following the quarantine rules of the time, but Trelawny seized the heart and buried it here. The epitaph on the gravestone is from 'Ariel's Song' in *The Tempest* (Shelley's boat was called the *Ariel*). When **Trelawny** died in 1881 at the age of 88 he was buried nearby, under a plain tomb slab.

In the row in front is the grave of the American sculptor and poet **William Wetmore Story** (1819–95) and his wife, decorated with a sculpture by him entitled the *Angel of Grief*. Next to it lies **J. Addington Symonds** (1840–93), historian of the Renaissance. The tomb of **Rosa Bathurst**, by Richard Westmacott Jr., has fine Neoclassical reliefs. Rosa's brief life (she drowned in the Tiber aged 16), her beauty ('the loveliest flower ever cropt') and the mysterious, never solved disappearance of her diplomat father while on a mission to Vienna some years before, all caused her fame among Rome's foreign residents to outlast her death by many decades.

Near the next tower in the walls, but on lower ground between two tall pine trees, is the tomb of Julius August, the only **son of Goethe**, who died in Rome in 1830: his profile in relief is by Bertel Thorvaldsen: the tombstone does not

CENTRALE MONTEMARTINI
Marble *Aphrodite* in front of the cast-iron extraction pump.

name him; he goes down to posterity as 'Goethe Filius'. Two rows below it is the tomb of the great British Neoclassical sculptor **John Gibson** (d. 1866), who lived most of his life in Rome where he had been a pupil of Canova.

At the far end of the cemetery is the grave of **Antonio Gramsci** (1891–1937), one of the founders of Italian Communism, who was imprisoned by the Fascist regime from 1926 until his death.

Nearby, beautifully-sited along the line of the city wall, is the **Rome Commonwealth Military Cemetery**, where 426 members of the three armed services are buried (*Via Nicola Zabaglia 50; usually open until 3pm on weekdays; for up-to-date information, see cwgc.org*).

MONTE TESTACCIO

Immediately west of the Military Cemetery is Monte Testaccio (Monte dei Cocci), an isolated mound 54m high and some 1000m round. It is entirely composed of pot-sherds (*testae*) dumped here from the Augustan period up to the middle of the 3rd century AD, from the neighbouring storehouses of the Republican port which lined the Tiber between Ponte Testaccio and Ponte Sublicio (now Ponte Aventino). Among the finds here was a hoard of amphorae used to import oil from Spain, with official marks scratched on them, which are of fundamental importance to our knowledge of the economic history of the late Republic and early Empire. Jousts and tournaments were held in this part of the city during the Middle Ages. The district of Testaccio, near the 'ex-Mattatoio', a huge building of 1888–9 which used to be a slaughterhouse, is now renowned for its restaurants and bars of all categories.

CENTRALE MONTEMARTINI

Map p. 647. Via Ostiense 106. Open Tues–Sun 9–7. T: 060608, centralemontemartini. org. Combined ticket (the Capitoline Card, valid one week) available with the Capitoline Museums. For public transport, see p. 487.

On the west side of Via Ostiense (on the right as you go down it), more or less oppo-site the Mercati Generali—the old wholesale food markets of Rome—and set back from the road (not well signposted), is the Centrale Montemartini, with a superb display of Roman Classical statues from the Capitoline Museums. The building occupies the **site of the Chapel of the Separation** where, according to an apocryphal tradition, St Peter and St Paul bade a last farewell to each other before their separate martyrdoms. A relief of the two saints embracing has been set up on the wall.

The entrance is through the yard at the side. The first thing that you see after the tick-et office and coat check is a **statue of Aphrodite** in Pentelic marble, a copy of a 5th-cen-tury BC work by Callimachus. She stands in front of a massive cast-iron extraction pump emblazoned with the name of the manufacturer, Franco Tosi. This sets the tone for the whole museum. All the works are beautifully displayed and labelled (also in English). This is one of the most original and enjoyable museums anywhere in the world.

> ## HISTORY OF THE MUSEUM
> Built in 1912, this was the first public electrical plant to be opened in Rome, and was named after its designer, Giovanni Montemartini. Operated by diesel and steam, it provided enough power to illuminate half the streets and *piazze* of the city. It continued to function throughout the Second World War and only fell into disuse in 1963. It was restored by the Rome water and electricity board (ACEA) in 1990 as a superb exhibition space and is also of the greatest interest as a monument of industrial archaeology. Since 1997 some 400 Classical sculptures formerly kept in the Capitoline Museums have been exhibited here.

Ground floor

Among the many Republican-era portrait heads displayed here is an early bust of Augustus (27–20 BC) found in Via del Mare and another of Julius Caesar. The most famous exhibit is the ***Barberini Togatus***, a statue of a man in a toga carrying two busts, one of his father and one of his grandfather. In the last room is a fragment of a bed with very delicate inlaid decorations in bone, from Greece (late 1st century BC), and exquisite small mosaics of fish from Via San Lorenzo in Panisperna, dating from the same century. There is a case of finds from a *domus* unearthed in Via del Babuino.

Upper floor

Sala Macchine (Engine Room): Here there is a superb display of Roman sculpture inspired by Greek masterpieces (*see p. 453*). The colossal **statue of Athena**, found in Via del Corso, derives from a Greek original by Kresilas of 430 BC (the head is a cast from a statue in the Louvre). The statues in the centre of the room include a **draped figure of Apollo** (originally playing the lyre) and *Aphrodite* from a Greek original by Praxiteles. The **two grey statues** nearby are particularly interesting: that of a praying female figure has been identified as Agrippina the Younger, wife of Claudius. It is made out of basanite, a precious stone from the Egyptian desert, and was unearthed on the Caelian hill: the original head was recently found in Copenhagen.

In the corridors behind the huge generator are reliefs from the time of Claudius, a pastoral scene with two cows, and **Imperial portraits**, including Tiberius, Claudius, Domitian and (window wall) Septimius Severus and Caracalla. Also facing the window is a head of Antinous, the young favourite of Hadrian who mysteriously drowned in the Nile at the age of 19.

Raised up at the back of the hall is the reconstructed **pediment from the Temple of Apollo Sosianus**, dedicated to Apollo Medicus in 433 BC and restored by the consul Sosius in 33 BC (three columns of it still stand near the Theatre of Marcellus; *see p. 243*). The nine pediment fragments, thought to date from 450–425 BC, show a battle between Greeks and Amazons. Behind the pediment are more fragments from the temple including a frieze with a triumphal procession. In front of the temple pediment are sculptures from other such pediments, including a colossal figure of Jupiter and a female figure, both also found near the Theatre of Marcellus and thought to date from the Augustan era.

By the door into the Boiler Room are fragments of a colossal **acrolithic statue of Fortuna** from her temple in Largo Argentina (*see p. 214*). The earlobes are pierced for earrings. It must have been some 8m high and is attributed to a Greek artist working in Rome in 101 BC.

Sala delle Caldaie (Boiler Room):

Here are finds from the *horti*, the gardens of the villas of Rome's wealthiest citizens, areas which were built over at the end of the 19th or early 20th centuries. The beautiful **statue of a Muse**—possibly Polyhymnia—shown leaning on a pillar of rock was found near the Variani Gardens. Close to the wall are statues found in the Gardens of Licinius (*see p. 560*), including a charming **seated figure of a girl**, a Hadrianic copy of a Hellenistic work. Near the machines at the far end are two **statues of Pothos**, son of Aphrodite, symbol of physical yearning. At the side of the machines are **funerary monuments** (some from the nearby Ostiense necropolis), including the memorable 1st-century AD grave marker of the shoemaker Gaius Julius Helius, balding and bare-chested, his trade denoted by two cobbler's lasts (one with a sandal on it). His name denotes his descent from freedmen or clients of the family of Julius Caesar.

Stairs lead up to a balcony with a good view of the 4th-century AD **mosaic with hunting scenes**: one part shows a wild boar hunt, the other shows animals being herded into a cage, prior to shipment to the amphitheatre.

SAN PAOLO FUORI LE MURA

Map p. 647. Open 7–6.30. Cloisters open 8–6.15 (entry fee). T: 06 69 88 0800, basilicasanpaolo.org. For public transport, see p. 487.

San Paolo fuori le Mura, 2km from Porta San Paolo, is the largest church in Rome after St Peter's. It is one of the four great papal basilicas of Rome and as such has the privilege of extraterritoriality. The church commemorates the martyrdom of St Paul, whose remains are preserved under the altar. In 2009 forensic analysts joined voices with tradition in their opinion that these remains were indeed the bones of the Apostle.

HISTORY OF THE BASILICA

According to Christian tradition, a Roman matron called Lucina buried the body of St Paul in a vineyard on the site of this basilica. A small shrine existed here when, in 384, a large basilica was begun by Valentinian II and Theodosius the Great at the request of Pope Damasus. It was enlarged by Theodosius' son, Honorius, and decorated with mosaics at the expense of Galla Placidia, Honorius' sister. After the additions made by Leo III (pope 795–816), it became the largest and most beautiful church in Rome. In the 9th century it was pillaged by the Saracens and John VIII (872–82) enclosed it in a fortified village known as Giovannipolis. It was restored c. 1070 by Abbot Hildebrand,

BASILICA OF SAN PAOLO FUORI LE MURA

later Gregory VII. The façade, overlooking the Tiber, was preceded by a colonnaded quadriporticus. Before the Reformation, the king of England was an *ex officio* canon of San Paolo and the abbot, in return, was decorated with the Order of the Garter. This great basilica was almost entirely destroyed by fire on the night of 15th–16th July 1823.

Leo XII ordered the reconstruction, which was directed by Pasquale Belli, Pietro Bosio and Pietro Camporese, and afterwards by Luigi Poletti. The decision was taken to use new materials instead of repairing the damaged structure, although in plan and dimensions, if not in spirit, the new basilica follows the old one almost exactly. The transept was consecrated by Gregory XVI in 1840 and the complete church by Pius IX in 1854. In 1891 an explosion in a neighbouring fort broke most of the stained glass, which was replaced by sheets of alabaster. The church is attached to a Benedictine abbey. In 2008–9 the Vatican celebrated the Pauline Year, a celebration of the two thousandth anniversary of the Apostle's birth, and an eternal flame was lit. Later in that year, after forensic analysis of the remains beneath the altar confirmed their authenticity, Pope Benedict XVI was able to proclaim this site to be without doubt the resting place of St Paul. The tomb is greatly venerated.

EXTERIOR OF THE BASILICA

The Romanesque campanile was pulled down to make way for a bell-tower by Luigi Poletti: it looks like a lighthouse and consists of a square base surmounted by an octagon and then a cylinder, with columns rising through the Orders. Poletti was also responsible for the north portico, which incorporates twelve Hymettian marble columns from the old basilica. On one of the nearest columns, beneath the frieze, is a 4th-century inscription of Pope Siricius. The main façade (west end) is preceded by a great quadriporticus with 146 enormous monolithic granite columns, added by Guglielmo Calderini between 1892 and 1928. The elaborate frescoes on the façade date from 1885. The central bronze doors **(1)** are by Antonio Maraini (1928–30). To the right is the Porta Santa **(2)**, which is only opened in Holy Years.

ST PAUL THE APOSTLE IN ROME

As a Pharisee, Paul's Hebrew name was Saul, and he apparently earned a living as a tent-maker. While on a journey to Damascus, on a mission to persecute the Christians, he had a dramatic conversion—vividly portrayed in Caravaggio's famous painting in the church of Santa Maria del Popolo. A Roman citizen by birth, he appealed to Caesar after he was arrested in Jerusalem for his Christian beliefs c. AD 60, and was allowed to be tried in Rome. He travelled here as a prisoner by boat via Crete, Malta (where he was shipwrecked) and Sicily (as described in Acts). This was the fourth and last of the long journeys he made during his lifetime (the first three were made as a missionary).

Paul was met on the Via Appia outside Rome by Roman friends and lived for two years under house arrest before his martyrdom, at about the same time as St Peter was crucified. It is thought there must have been contact between St Peter and St Paul (an oratory, now demolished but marked by a plaque outside the Centrale Montemartini, is supposed to mark the site where they took their final leave of each other; *see p. 491*). Paul is thought to have been imprisoned in the Tullianum (*see p. 63*) and to have been beheaded on the site of the abbey of the Tre Fontane (*see p. 498*).

Although he was little known outside the Christian world in his lifetime, and numerous legends grew up around his name, St Paul is well known to us through his remarkable letters. As he says in his Epistle to the Galatians: 'The gospel of the uncircumcised was committed to me.' He recognised the importance of also preaching to the gentiles and it is generally acknowledged that it was Paul who succeeded in transforming Christianity into a universal religion. Although a Christian community already existed in Rome, it was as a result of Paul's preaching that the new cult took a firm hold in the city. He is now honoured with St Peter as joint patron saint of Rome: their annual festival is held on 29th June.

INTERIOR OF THE BASILICA

The nave and transept form a tau, or Egyptian cross, 132m by 65m; the height is 30m. The highly polished marble, alabaster, malachite, lapis and porphyry give an impression of Neoclassical splendour.

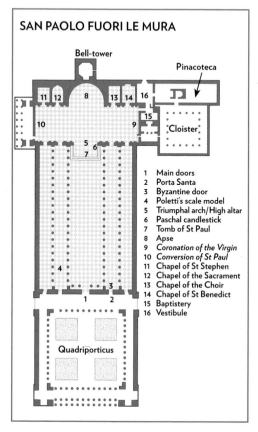

SAN PAOLO FUORI LE MURA

Bell-tower

Pinacoteca

Cloister

1 Main doors
2 Porta Santa
3 Byzantine door
4 Poletti's scale model
5 Triumphal arch/High altar
6 Paschal candlestick
7 Tomb of St Paul
8 Apse
9 *Coronation of the Virgin*
10 *Conversion of St Paul*
11 Chapel of St Stephen
12 Chapel of the Sacrament
13 Chapel of the Choir
14 Chapel of St Benedict
15 Baptistery
16 Vestibule

Quadriporticus

to Francis. At the time of writing there were still roundels left for 16 more popes. In the outermost aisles are niches with statues of the Apostles. The six huge alabaster columns beside the entrance doors were presented by Mohammed Ali of Egypt.

On the inner side of the Porta Santa is the splendid **Byzantine door (3)** of the old basilica. It was made at Constantinople by Stavrakios in 1070 and has 54 panels inlaid with silver (*panel showing the execution of St Paul illustrated above*). Also in the nave is Poletti's 1844 **wooden scale model** of the basilica **(4)**.

At the foot of the sanctuary steps are two 19th-century statues of St Peter and St Paul. The **triumphal arch (5)**, a relic of the old basilica, is supported by two colossal granite columns. Its much-restored mosaics represent a grim-faced Christ blessing in the Greek manner, with angels, symbols of the Evangelists, the Elders of the Apocalypse, and St Peter and St Paul. On the other face of the arch are the remains of early mosaics by Pietro Cavallini. Over the **high altar**, supported by ancient porphyry columns, is a splendid ciborium signed by Arnolfo di Cambio (1285), the first such canopy to use figural sculpture. The huge 12th-century **paschal candlestick (6)** is an exquisite work by Nicolò di Angelo and Pietro Vassalletto. Around the base, the Whore of Babylon is seen mounted on a monstrous creature. Passion scenes surround the stem above.

Nave and aisles: The nave, with double aisles separated from one another by 80 columns of Montorfano granite, is the new part of the basilica. In the centre of the ceiling, which is richly decorated with stuccoes in white and gold, are the arms of Pius IX. The paintings between the clerestory windows, executed in the mid-19th century and depicting scenes from the life of St Paul, are by Pietro Gagliardi, Francesco Podesti, Guglielmo de Sanctis, Francesco Coghetti and Cesare Mariani; under these (and in the aisles), forming a frieze, are the portraits in mosaic of all the popes from St Peter

Confessio: The **tomb of St Paul (7)** is beneath the altar, viewed from the confessio, with chains in a casket similar to that of St Peter (*see p. 119*). On the top is the figure of St Paul between two Roman soldiers. Part of the side of the saint's sarcophagus can be seen behind a grille. The Pauline Flame burns beside the sarcophagus niche.

East end: The magnificent ceiling of the transept is decorated with the arms of Pius VII, Leo XII, Pius VIII and Gregory XVI, as well as with those of the basilica, an arm holding a sword. The walls are covered with rare marbles. The Corinthian pilasters are made up of fragments of the old columns.

The great mosaic of the **apse (8)** was executed c. 1220 by Venetian craftsmen sent by Doge Pietro Ziani at the request of Pope Honorius III. Although it was heavily restored after damage in the fire of 1823, it is a very beautiful work showing a mild-faced Christ blessing in the Greek manner, with St Peter, St Andrew, St Paul and St Luke; at the feet of Christ is a tiny Pope Honorius III; below this, a gem-studded Cross on the altar, with angels and apostles. On the outer face of the arch are the Virgin and Child with St John blessing Pope John XXII.

At both ends of the transept are altars of malachite and lapis lazuli, presented by Nicholas I of Russia: the mosaic at the south end **(9)** is a copy from the *Coronation of the Virgin* by Giulio Romano, and at the opposite end (north) is the *Conversion of St Paul* **(10)** by Vincenzo Camuccini.

The **Chapel of St Stephen (11)** has a statue of the saint by Rinaldo Rinaldi, and paintings of the *Expulsion by the Sanhedrin* by Francesco Coghetti and the *Stoning of St Stephen* by Francesco Podesti. The **Chapel of the Blessed Sacrament (12)**, by Carlo Maderno, was the only chapel saved in the fire. On the altar is a 14th-century Crucifix said to be miraculous. Also here is a wooden statue of St Paul which pilgrims used to take shavings from as relics. In this chapel, in 1541, St Ignatius Loyola and the first Jesuits took the corporate oaths that formally established their society as a religious order.

The **Chapel of the Choir**, or of St Lawrence **(13)**, has 19th-century choir stalls inlaid with images of Benedictine saints. The **Chapel of St Benedict (14)** is a sumptuous work by Luigi Poletti, fashioned like the cella of an ancient temple; the twelve fluted columns are from Veio.

Baptistery and vestibule: The **baptistery (15)** was designed by Arnaldo Foschini on a Greek-cross plan in 1930. Leading off it is the **vestibule (16)**, which precedes the east door of the church. It contains a colossal statue of Gregory XVI by Rinaldo Rinaldi, and 13th-century mosaics from the old basilica. Also here is a bust of the architect of the new basilica, Poletti.

THE CLOISTERS AND PINACOTECA

The **cloisters** of the Benedictine abbey are remarkably similar in atmosphere and design to those of St John Lateran. The walks have coupled colonnettes of different forms decorated with Cosmati mosaics. Between them sit tiny couchant animals, almost all of which have lost their heads. Many are gone altogether. In the centre is a rose garden. The cloisters were begun under Abbot Pietro da Capua (1193–1208) and finished after 1228, and are the work—at least in part—of the Vassalletto family, Roman sculptors who were active in the 12th and 13th centuries and who also worked on the cloister of St John Lateran, hence the similarity. Pietro, who is known to have been at work between 1154 and 1186, was its best-known member. Along the walls are placed numerous lapidary fragments, both Christian and pagan. In the walk to the right of the entrance is an inscription ('*Hoc specus excepit...*') purporting to record the spot where Nero hid before his eventual suicide, the house of a freedman between Via Nomentana and Via Salaria. It is probably a 17th-century forgery. Also in this walk is a large sarcophagus which retains its lid and very worn reliefs depicting the story of Apollo and Marsyas.

Off the cloister is the **Chapel of the Relics** (which proudly displays the staff of St Peter and the right arm of St Anne, mother of the Virgin) and the **Pinacoteca**, which has works by Antoniazzo Romano (*Madonna and Child with Saints*) and Bramantino (*Flagellation*) as well as ecclesiastical vestments and Church silver.

Near the basilica shop and café are **excavations of the Borgo di San Paolo**, the suburb that surrounded the basilica and which included religious houses, pilgrims' hostels and attendant shops and service buildings. Tickets are available at the entrance to the cloister. Excavations have uncovered remains spanning the 6th to the 17th centuries.

NECROPOLI OSTIENSE

At the edge of the park just north of San Paolo fuori le Mura is a small burial ground known as the Necropoli Ostiense, which contains pagan and Christian tombs (*map p. 647; Via Ostiense 190; admission by appointment, T: 060608*). The site, seen through railings, extended over a wide area and spans the modern road. It was in use from late Republican times (2nd century BC) to the 4th century AD.

ABBAZIA DELLE TRE FONTANE

Map p. 647. Bus 716 from Teatro di Marcello (get off at the Tintoretto-Ballarin stop, from where it is a short walk up Via Laurentina) or bus 671 between Terme di Caracalla and Laurentina-Tre Fontane. Alternatively, take Metro line B to Laurentina, from where it is 10–15min walk. NB: Follow brown signs to 'Abbazia delle Tre Fontane', not to 'Santuario delle Tre Fontane'. Opening times for the individual churches are given below but they are subject to variation. Check for updates on www.abbaziatrefontane.it.

Cocooned in a remarkably placid grove of trees, though very close to the hectic Via Laurentina, the Abbazia delle Tre Fontane ('Abbey of the Three Fountains') was built on the traditional site of the martyrdom of St Paul, whose severed head, bouncing three times, is supposed to have caused three fountains to spring up. A monastic community from Asia Minor was established here by 641. St Bernard, the greatest of all Cistercian saints, is believed to have stayed here on his visit to Rome in 1138–40. Three churches were built, but the locality was afterwards abandoned as malarial. In 1868 it was acquired by the Trappists (a branch of the Cistercians dedicated to the strict observance of the Order of St Benedict), who drained the ground and planted large groves of eucalyptus.

THE APPROACH TO TRE FONTANE

From Via Laurentina you pass through a gateway onto a drive lined with ilex trees. On your right is a large **statue of St Benedict** with the exhortation *Ausculta O Fili / Obedientia Sine Mora / Ora et Labora* ('Hearken, my son! Unhesitating obedience! Work and pray!'). Shortly after this you come to a courtyard with a bookshop and the **Bottega dei Trappisti** (*labottegadeitrappisti.it*), which sells snacks, coffee, liqueurs and Trappist beer of the abbey's own production. Labelled 'Tre Fontane', it is flavoured with eucalyptus leaves and is very refreshing. At the end of the courtyard is a medieval **fortified gate** with a frescoed vault (remnants of the Evangelists). Beyond is a small garden, filled with the sound of birdsong, another shop, and two of the three churches.

Santi Vincenzo e Anastasio (*open 6.30–12.30 & 3–8.45*): The church was founded by Pope Honorius I (625) as part of his plan to build churches on the site of important martyrdoms. It was rebuilt by Honorius III (1221) and restored by the Trappists. House martins nest in the rafters of the porch. The plain, spacious brick interior preserves its marble windows. In the nave are poorly restored frescoes of the Apostles (16th century).

Santa Maria Scala Coeli (*open 8–1 & 3–6*): This is an old church with an octagonal interior, rebuilt by Giacomo della Porta (1582). The design can best be appreciated from the outside. It owes its name to the legend that St Bernard, while celebrating Mass, saw in a vision the soul for which he was praying ascend by a ladder from purgatory to heaven. The vault is painted blue and spangled with stars. The mosaics in the main apse, of saints with Clement VIII and his nephew Cardinal Pietro Aldobrandini, are by Francesco Zucchi from designs by Giovanni de' Vecchi. Stairs take you down to the crypt, where the Cosmatesque altar that was the scene of St Bernard's miracle is preserved. To right and left are windows behind which is a relic of the prison where St Paul was held prior to his decapitation. You exit the crypt from the other side, continuing the Early Christian tradition of processing around a holy site.

San Paolo alle Tre Fontane (*open 9–12 & 4–6*): Between the two churches described above, an ilex-lined avenue (with eucalyptus trees behind them on the right) leads to San Paolo alle Tre Fontane, a 5th-century foundation rebuilt by Della Porta in 1599 (it has a good façade). Inside to the right is the pillar which is supposed to have served as St Paul's execution block. Beside it, in a line along the wall opposite the entrance, enclosed in marble tabernacles, are the three springs which miraculously flowed when the saint's head was cut off. In the centre of the floor is a Roman mosaic pavement of the *Four Seasons* from Ostia.

Twentieth-Century & Contemporary Rome

The most interesting piece of 20th-century urban planning is EUR, built in the austere,
monumental Fascist style, and which survives today as a distinctive district.
In more recent years there have been a number of important contributions to
museum design as well as a new group of concert halls designed by Renzo Piano.

The walls built by the emperor Aurelian in the 3rd century AD to defend ancient Rome, which had over one million inhabitants, still defined the urban limits of the city in the late 19th century. It was only in the 1940s that the population began to equal (and then quickly supersede) that of ancient Rome. By the 1950s there were some 2.1 million inhabitants, and by 1981 around 3 million. The metropolitan area of the city continued to expand and the population at present is around 4 million.

Most of the residents, including immigrants from Europe, Asia, America and Africa, inhabit the suburbs which have been spreading into the Roman Campagna in a more or less uncontrolled way since the 1960s. In 2000 an urban plan for Rome was approved by the city council, the first in 38 years, but how to deal with the disastrous living conditions in some of Rome's suburbs has become the most pressing issue to be faced by local government. Today the historic centre suffers from depopulation (it is estimated that there are now only some 150,00 residents) and many of the buildings are used as offices or for tourist rentals. The problem of Rome's traffic is still unresolved: there are 978 vehicles for every 1,000 inhabitants (as against 398 per 1,000 in London).

EUR

The monumental white marble buildings of the Esposizione Universale di Roma (always abbreviated to EUR and pronounced 'eh-oor'; *map p. 647*) are spaciously laid out in a setting which recalls the Metaphysical paintings of Giorgio de Chirico. An extremely interesting example of Fascist town planning, it was built on land well outside the historic centre and, even though residential buildings have gradually covered the space between it and the centre of Rome, it still remains entirely detached from the urban context of the ancient city. Today it is a strange place to visit: it is unusual to meet anyone on foot and all the streets—and even the pavements—seem to be occupied by the cars of the people who come to work in the offices, ministries and museums here. It is rare to experience such an empty, show-town sort of feel anywhere else in Italy. But the centre of EUR is worth visiting for its townscape as well as its huge museums, which are extremely interesting not only for their content but also for their design and arrangement, often dating back to the days of Fascism. These, too, tend to be deserted, except when visited by school parties.

Getting to EUR

EUR is about 6km from the Porta Ardeatina in the Aurelian Walls, and approached along Via Cristoforo Colombo, which passes straight through the middle of the site as a ten-lane highway. Easily reached in 12mins from Termini and Colosseo stations by Metro line B, on which it is the penultimate station, it is also reached by numerous buses, including no. 30 from Largo Argentina and no. 714 from Termini.

HISTORY OF EUR

EUR was begun in 1938 to the designs of Marcello Piacentini, a prolific architect whose later monumental and triumphalist style was particularly attractive to Fascism: he was adopted as official architect of the regime. EUR was an ambitious project intended to symbolise the achievements of Fascism and it included vast buildings designed as museums to glorify Italy's past and present civilisation. It was to have opened for the 1942 World Expo, but this was cancelled because of the war, and so not all the buildings were completed. From 1952 onwards some new ones were added, and government offices and public institutions were moved to the site, which was also developed as a residential district. In 1999 *Titus*, starring Anthony Hopkins and based on Shakespeare's play *Titus Andronicus*, was filmed here. Fellini greatly appreciated the 'artificiality' of EUR as a stage set and used it in some scenes of *La Dolce Vita*.

THE LAYOUT OF EUR

The broad highway from the centre of Rome, Via Cristoforo Colombo, is lined with umbrella pines right up to the entrance to EUR at the **Piazza delle Nazioni Unite**. This is flanked by twin palaces whose façades form two grand hemicycles. The main road continues across **Viale della Civiltà del Lavoro**, which was designed to provide vistas in either direction to two of the most important buildings in EUR. On the left the view is closed by the linear **Palazzo dei Congressi**, designed by Adalberto Libera (1938–54), which has paintings in the atrium by Gino Severini. On the right is the building which symbolises EUR, always called the 'Square Colosseum' since it is a cube consisting of tiers of arches on all four sides. It was built as the Palazzo della Civiltà Italiana in 1938–43 by Giovanni Guerrini, Ernesto Bruno La Padula and Mario Romano, but was renamed **Palazzo della Civiltà del Lavoro**. There are statues symbolising the arts beneath the lowest arches.

The centre of EUR is the vast **Piazza Marconi**. In it stands a stele of Carrara marble, 45m high, by Arturo Dazzi (1938–59), dedicated to Marconi. It has become a well-known landmark. Via Colombo ends at a lake roughly 1km long divided into three basins, its sides planted with a thousand cherry trees from Japan. This area is perhaps the most successfully planned in the complex. Bridges lead to the **Palazzo dello Sport**, designed by Pier Luigi Nervi and Marcello Piacentini for the 1960 Olympics and an outstanding work of modern architecture. Constructed of prefabricated concrete, it is covered by a fine rib-vaulted dome 100m in diameter, and seats 15,000 spectators.

Also on the western border of EUR is the huge, centrally-planned church of **Santi Pietro e Paolo**, with a dome 28m in diameter, conspicuous from many miles away. It was begun in 1938 by Arnaldo Foschini and others but only finished in 1955.

THE INFLUENCE OF FASCISM ON THE URBAN CONTEXT OF ROME

After the First World War the movement known as *Fascismo* rapidly developed. It was the creation of Benito Mussolini, whose politics had always been Socialist. He organised the 'March on Rome' on 28th October 1922, after which King Vittorio Emanuele III invited him to form a government. Mussolini idolised the Classical Roman period, attempting to imitate it through building programmes which introduced a triumphalist, rhetorical style, as well as through colonial ambition, a bid to create a new 'Empire'. Some of the planning projects were disastrous: the Capitoline hill was hemmed in by two broad thoroughfares, Via dei Fori Imperiali and Via del Teatro di Marcello, both opened in 1933. Beyond the Tiber, the old medieval district of the Borgo was transformed by the building of Via della Conciliazione (1937), which irrevocably altered the dramatic effect of Bernini's piazza in front of St Peter's. However, in the last few decades scholars have been paying more attention to the Fascist style. In its best incarnations it produced some superb examples of Rationalist Modernism and stylised Classicism, making it more than just a symptom of Mussolini's *folie de grandeur*.

The symbol of Fascism were the *fasces lictoriae*, which existed in Etruscan and Roman iconography as an emblem of authority: these were bundles (*fasces*) of elm branches tied together which would be carried by the officials ('lictors') who preceded magistrates when they appeared in public. They symbolised the power created by union. In 1926 the '*fascio*' became the official symbol of the regime (and as such was protected against vandalism by stringent laws). After the fall of Mussolini and his death at the hands of partisans in 1945, these symbols were deliberately expunged from public places in an attempt to blot out the memory of the Fascist dictatorship. Very few escaped destruction; although in the Capitoline Museums, in the little cabinet where the *Capitoline Venus* is exhibited, if you look back up above the door, you can still see one painted there, and another survives in sculpted form, overlooked and thus reprieved, on the side of the Theatre of Marcellus along Via del Teatro di Marcello.

The foundation stone of a huge new congress hall on a plot of land which has never been built on, between Via Cristoforo Colombo, Viale Europa, Viale Asia and Viale Shakespeare, was laid in 2007. Designed by Massimiliano Fuksas, it will include an auditorium (the **Nuvola**) as well as a hotel. But serious administrative problems have arisen and doubts have been raised by the architect himself whether it will ever be finished.

THE MUSEUMS OF EUR

MUSEO NAZIONALE DELLE ARTI E DELLE TRADIZIONI POPOLARI

Northeast side of Piazza Marconi. Open Tues–Sun 8.30–7.30; closed Mon. T: 06 59 26 148, idea.mat.beniculturali.it.

The collection provides an extraordinarily complete picture of traditional Italian life up to the Second World War. On the ground floor are exhibits relating to transport, and on the stair landing is a gondola of 1882. The sections on the upper floor include furniture from rural houses, toys, Neapolitan crib figures, carnival and theatrical costumes, musical instruments used during local festivals, and puppets. The great hall, with frescoes of 1941–2 (including one by Emanuele Cavalli), exhibits arts and crafts, with reconstructions of artisans' workshops. There are also sections illustrating agricultural life and seafaring.

MUSEO NAZIONALE PREISTORICO ED ETNOGRAFICO LUIGI PIGORINI

Southeast side of Piazza Marconi. Open Mon–Sat 9–6; Sun and holidays 9–1.30. Free entry on first Sun of the month. T: 06 54 9521, pigorini.beniculturali.it.

This is one of the most important museums of its kind in the world. It originated with the collection formed in the late 17th century by Father Anastasius Kircher in the Collegio dei Gesuiti. From 1871 onwards it was greatly enlarged by Luigi Pigorini, its first director, and in 1876 it became the Museo Preistorico del Nuovo Regno d'Italia. After 1913 the proto-historic objects went to Villa Giulia; Classical and Christian antiquities to the Museo Nazionale Romano; and medieval exhibits to Palazzo di Venezia. Between 1962 and 1977 the prehistoric and ethnographic collections were arranged here. In the entrance hall, with its monumental staircase, is displayed a Neolithic canoe found in Lake Bracciano.

Ethnographic collection: On the first floor there is a very fine modern display of material from the Americas, Africa and Oceania. There is a pre-Columbian collection from Mexico and the Andes, artefacts made by the Inuits of the Arctic Circle, and Asian exhibits.

Prehistory: The rooms on the second floor are arranged geographically within Italy to show how civilisation developed regionally through the Stone, Bronze and Iron Ages. Material from all parts of the peninsula gives a full picture of the commercial and artistic influences of the East and of the countries bordering the Aegean. Labelling is very informative. The most interesting exhibits include material from cemeteries in Lazio; finds of the Italian School in Crete; curious Sardinian statuettes of priests and warriors in bronze; a tomb from Golasecca, representative of the western civilisation of northern Italy. The objects found in the cemeteries of western and southern Etruria (including Vetulonia, Tarquinia, Vulci and Veio) are particularly interesting; among them are well-tombs (10th–8th centuries BC) with ossuaries resembling those of Villanova, closed with a flat lid or shaped like a house, and trench-tombs (8th–7th centuries BC) showing the influence of Greek commerce, especially on pottery.

MUSEO NAZIONALE DELL'ALTO MEDIOEVO

Same building as previous museum. Open Tues–Sun 9–2. T: 06 54 22 8199.

A disappointingly small collection, made in 1967, of Italian material from the fall of the Roman Empire to the 10th century. The exhibits include Byzantine jewellery found on the Palatine; 8th–9th-century pottery from the Roman Forum; 7th-century jewellery from tombs in central Italy; mosaics; and Coptic fabrics of the 5th–8th centuries.

The last room is entirely filled with very fine **opus sectile from Ostia Antica**, found outside the Porta Marina in 1959. In 2007 it was decided to make use of the high exhibition space here to reconstruct this magnificent panelled room (which had been in store for many years), even though it dates from a period outside the museum's scope. This is one of the most important discoveries ever made of late antique Roman art (AD 388). Most of the panels have exquisite geometric designs but two of them have a lion and a tiger attacking a deer. There are also smaller panels with male figures, one of whom appears to represent Christ blessing (with a halo), although this has also been interpreted as a Neoplatonic philosopher divinely inspired, or a portrait of Homer. The beautiful inlaid floor is also preserved, as well as fragments of the green mosaic ceiling.

MUSEO DELLA CIVILTÀ ROMANA

Closed at the time of writing. For updates, see en.museociviltaromana.it.

From Piazza Marconi, go through the colonnade and follow the wide Viale della Civiltà Romana, whose vista is closed by the colonnade of the museum of the same name. This is one of the most interesting buildings in EUR. It has two wings, without windows, connected by a very high double Doric colonnade. It was purpose-built by Pietro Aschieri, Domenico Bernardini, Cesare Pascoletti and Gino Peressutti from 1939 to 1952, funded by the FIAT organisation (the piazza here is named after its famous president, Giovanni Agnelli). There are two monumental twin entrances in each wing, approached by huge narrow colonnades of seven columns each: that on the right provides access to the museum. Since 2004 a planetarium and museum of astronomy has also been housed here (*shows at 9.30, 11 and 12.30; more frequently at weekends*).

A curiosity of the museum is the fact that there is not a single original exhibit: it consists entirely of plaster casts or replicas. It was created to house the didactic material produced for exhibitions held in 1911 and 1937 to illustrate the history of ancient Rome and the influence of Roman civilisation throughout the world. The casts of famous statues and monuments, and reconstructions of buildings, are displayed in no fewer than 59 rooms of monumental proportions (but now rather shabby). Those on the right of the ticket office each illustrate a specific period of the history of the Empire, in chronological sequence: the origins of the city; the conquest of the Mediterranean; Julius Caesar; Augustus; the Roman emperors; Christianity; the Roman army.

The halls on the left of the ticket office each take a theme from the life of the ancient Romans (such as art, economics, hunting and fishing, agriculture, industry and crafts). The most interesting gallery (LI), beneath the colonnade which connects the two wings of the building, exhibits (at eye-level) a complete set of **casts from Trajan's Column**, made in 1860 and extremely important for our knowledge of the details of the original carving, which since then have been eroded by the polluted air of central Rome. Here you can study each scene with ease and 'read' the entire column, from the relief on the lowest drum to that on the summit. In the far wing there are halls dedicated to medicine, science, music, libraries, Roman law and education. There follows a huge room (XXXVI–XXXVIII) where you can look down on a fascinating large-scale model (1:250) of the ancient city as it was in the 4th century.

On the west side of Piazza Marconi, the Palazzi dell'Esposizioni are twin edifices with symmetrical fronts close to a skyscraper known as the Grattacielo Italia (1959–60). Further south, entered from Viale Europa (no. 190), is the **Museo Storico della Poste e delle Telecomunicazioni** (*open by appointment, weekdays 9–1; T: 06 54 44 2045*). The postal display begins with a casket of 1300 used by the Pontifical Post Office of Urbino and 17th-century letter boxes, including a *bocca di leone*, and there is a fine copy on tile of the *Tabula Peutingeriana*, an ancient map of the principal roads and cities of the Roman Empire. Later postal history—pioneer air-mail flights, Ethiopian military cancellers, etc—is well chosen. The electronic calculator invented by Enrico Fermi, made in 1956, is also displayed here. The history of telegraph and telephone is copiously illustrated by original appliances, including apparatus used by Marconi in his 1901 experiments between Cornwall and Newfoundland.

OTHER BUILDINGS FROM THE FASCIST ERA

In the northern district of Monte Mario, the **Foro Italico** (*map p. 647*) is an ambitious sports centre built in 1928–31 by the former Accademia Fascista della Farnesina, and is one of the most impressive building projects carried out by Mussolini in imitation of ancient Roman Imperial architecture. Designed by Enrico del Debbio and finished by Luigi Moretti in 1936, it was altered during work on preparations for the 1990 World Cup. Facing the entrance is Ponte Duca d'Aosta (1939). A marble monolith, 17m high, inscribed 'Mussolini Dux', rises at the entrance in front of an imposing avenue paved with marble inlaid with mosaics designed by Gino Severini, Angelo Canevari and others. On either side of the avenue are marble blocks, with inscriptions recording events in the history of Italy. The avenue ends in a piazza, beyond which is the **Stadio Olimpico**, finished for the Olympic Games in 1960, with accommodation for 100,000. It was reconstructed for the 1990 World Cup with little respect for the setting. To the right is the **Stadio dei Marmi**, with 60 colossal statues of athletes. There are open-air and enclosed swimming pools, the latter with mosaics by Giulio Rossi and Angelo Canevari. Another building has more mosaics by Gino Severini. There are also lawn tennis and basketball courts, running tracks, gymnasia and fencing halls.

The **Città Universitaria**, east of Termini station (*map p. 649, B1–C1*), is a very interesting example of Fascist architecture, designed partly by Marcello Piacentini.

In the southern area of the city is **Cinecittà** (*Via Tuscolana 1055, metro line A*). First opened in 1937, it soon became the centre of the Italian film industry. It was probably the only film studio in the world which provided facilities for complete motion picture production. After the Second World War it was used by Visconti, De Sica and Rossellini, and soon attracted international film directors and stars from Hollywood. In the 1950s and early '60s, 'epics' such as *Quo Vadis?* and *Cleopatra*, using some of the largest sets ever constructed, were made at Cinecittà. Antonioni and Pasolini worked here, but it is above all associated with the name of Federico Fellini (d. 1993), who created the grandiose sets for many of his films here. In 2014 it was turned into a 'theme park' named Cinecittà World.

THE LATER TWENTIETH CENTURY

The huge **Stadio Flaminio** football stadium (*map p. 647*), in reinforced concrete, is by Pier Luigi and Antonio Nervi (1959). A little further north, the **Palazzetto dello Sport** is an adventurous and striking construction also by Pier Luigi Nervi (together with Annibale Vitellozzi), designed for the Olympic Games in 1960. Beyond is the Villaggio Olimpico, built to accommodate athletes in 1960 and now a residential district. Earlier in the same decade **Ponte Flaminio** was built over the Tiber, as a monumental entrance to the city from the north. Nervi also designed the **Audience Hall in the Vatican** in 1971 (*see p. 476*). The same year Sir Basil Spence opened the new **British Embassy** just inside Porta Pia (*map p. 648, A4*) on Via XX Settembre, a conspicuous building surrounded by water on the site of a Torlonia villa which had been blown up in a terrorist attack by the Zionist organisation Irgun in 1946.

Rome's **mosque**, built in 1984–93 on the northern edge of Villa Ada (*map p. 647*), was designed by Paolo Portoghesi, Vittorio Gigliotti and Sami Mousawi. It can hold up to 3,000 people and is the largest in Europe.

BUILDINGS FROM AFTER 2000

The Auditorium in the **Parco della Musica** (*map p. 647*) is the seat of the orchestra of the renowned Accademia Nazionale di Santa Cecilia, and concerts are held here throughout the year: it has been acclaimed as one of the best-designed musical venues in Europe (*entrance at Via P. de Coubertin 15; the concert halls can be visited when not in use, on guided tours daily 11–8. T: 06 80 24 1281, auditorium.com. Bus 53 from Piazza San Silvestro in about 40mins, or no. 910 from Termini station. For performances, bus M direct from Termini station every 15mins from 5pm until the end of the last concert*). Designed by Renzo Piano (the acoustics are excellent due to the copious use of wood) there are three concert halls (the largest with 2,700 seats) around an open-air theatre which also serves as a piazza, surrounded by a hanging garden and park. During construction work, ancient Roman remains were (rather inevitably) found here and have been carefully incorporated between two of the halls. Overlooking the excavations is a small museum (*open 11–6*) with models and finds (well labelled also in English) explaining the various levels, from the earliest, dating from c. 530 BC, when there was a farm on the land, to the most recent, a villa built by a wealthy Roman in AD 150. There is also a museum of musical instruments (*open 11–6 except Wed*). The large café and bookshop contribute to the very pleasant atmosphere.

MAXXI, the Museo d'Arte Contemporanea del XXI Secolo (*entrance on Via Guido Reni; open Tues–Fri and Sun 11–7, Sat 11–10; T: 06 32 01 954, fondazionemaxxi.it*), was inaugurated in 2010. It has a permanent collection of 21st-century art, 20th- and 21st-century Italian architectural archives and hosts exhibitions and performing arts events in a very unusual building designed by the Baghdad-born London-based architect Zaha M. Hadid. It is the first national museum dedicated to contemporary art in Italy. It cost three times the original estimate to build and there are fears that it may prove very costly to run. With inclined and curving walls, its declared intent is not to provide white walls on which to hang paintings, and it has been noted that there appears to be a lack of space even though it covers some 27,000 square metres. There has already been lively debate about its utility: according to one prominent Italian art critic it actually 'rejects' (other) works of art.

At the time of writing plans had been put forward for three tall towers by Daniel Libeskind in a business park at Tor di Valle on the southwestern outskirts.

CONTEMPORARY DESIGN IN EXHIBITION SPACES

Some of the most interesting contemporary architecture in Rome can be seen in its museums. The **Hall of Marcus Aurelius** (by Carlo Aymonino) and adjoining galleries in the Capitoline Museums are exceptionally fine. These museums also have a superb satellite museum space in the **Centrale Montemartini**, a former electrical plant brilliantly adapted in 1997 to display part of the Classical sculpture collection. Strangely enough, it has received relatively little acclaim and the name of the architect is not even recorded. Since 2006 the **Ara Pacis** has been successfully housed in a light and airy pavilion by Richard Meier.

Amongst the many newly-arranged museums in Rome, perhaps the most successful has been **Palazzo Altemps**, where important sculptures from the collections of the Museo Nazionale Romano were installed in an excellent spacious arrangement at the end of the 20th century. A few years ago a fine new museum was created in the **Markets of Trajan**, with all the latest methods of display (though again it has gone virtually unnoticed by the press). An ambitious project was carried out in the **Vatican** in the Jubilee Year of 2000 to create a new entrance to the museums: the resulting vast halls and escalators are grand and spacious, but seem to do nothing to ameliorate the notoriously crowded atmosphere.

New exhibition spaces in the centre of Rome include the magnificent **Scuderie**, the papal stables on the Quirinal hill, adapted by Gae Aulenti in 2000 to provide a venue for major temporary exhibitions. Nearby in Via Nazionale is the monumental **Palazzo delle Esposizioni**, designed in 1880–3 by Pio Piacentini in Neoclassical style for the first International Exhibition in Italy. It was radically restored at the end of the 20th century, and again in 2007 as another exhibition centre, extremely well illuminated.

PARCO DEGLI ACQUEDOTTI
View of the Aqua Claudia.

The Via Appia Antica & The Catacombs

The Via Appia Antica, an ancient Roman road leading southeastwards out of the city, is lined with ancient funerary monuments and early Christian and Jewish catacombs. It begins on the outskirts of the historic centre and is reached by (rather infrequent) public transport: you should allow the best part of a day to do it justice. Parts of the countryside on either side still give a feel of what it must have been like to approach the city from the desolate Roman Campagna in past centuries. Since 1997 the road and the countryside close to it have been protected as a regional park, which covers some 3,500 hectares (larger than the historic centre of Rome itself).

When to go
Sunday is a good day to go because the Via Appia is closed to all through traffic. One drawback, though, is that several of the restaurants along the road are closed.

Information
The information office of the Parco Regionale Appia Antica is at no. 60, close to the beginning of the road. Open daily (closes 1–2 Mon–Sat). T: 06 51 35 316, parcoappi-aantica.it. Helpful staff, leaflets and maps, and bicycles for hire. The stylised sketch map entitled La Via Appia Antica is useful for identifying the tombs. Casale Vigna Cardinali information office on Largo Tacchi Venturi (off Via Latina) at the north edge of Parco della Caffarella is open Fri–Mon.

How to get there
On foot: *Except on a Sunday, when the Appia is officially closed to private cars, it is unpleasant to tackle the first part of the road on foot, since it is very narrow and filled with fast and noisy traffic. The early stretch of the road is, in any case, without distinction, although the information office is located here. Beyond the Catacombs of San Sebastiano (see map on p. 512) the road becomes much quieter and you can enjoy a walk through the countryside on the ancient paving stones.*
By public transport: *The Via Appia is served by bus 118, which you can catch in the centre of the city at Piazza Venezia, Via dei Fori Imperiali, the Colosseum and Baths of Caracalla. It stops at several places on the Via Appia: Domine Quo Vadis, the turnings for Parco della Caffarella and Catacombs of San Callisto, and San Sebastiano. From there it follows the Via Appia Pignatelli. If you get off it at the corner of Via Erode Attico, it is a short walk from there back down to the remotest*

and most beautiful part of the ancient road. However, it is not a very frequent service and it is not really feasible to use it as a hop-on-hop-off solution. Bus 660 runs every 20–30mins between the Via Appia Antica (the stop is near the Bar Appia Antica beyond the Tomb of Cecilia Metella on the corner of Via Cecilia Metella) and the Appia Nuova (via Via Cecilia Metella), where it stops at the Metro stations of Arco di Travertino and Colli Albani on line A (for Termini Station and Piazza di Spagna).

For the Villa dei Quintili, you can take Metro line A to Cinecittà and then bus 654 down to Via Appia Nuova.

The Parco della Caffarella can also be approached from Via Latina, about 300m from the Metro line A station of Colli Albani.

For the Fosse Ardeatine, take bus 218 from Porta San Giovanni (map p. 649, A3).

By bicycle: *Bikes can be hired from the information offices at Via Appia Antica 60 and Largo Tacchi Venturi and from the snack bar on the corner of Via Cecilia Metella.*

FOOD AND DRINK ON THE VIA APPIA

There are a number of restaurants and a few cafés along the Via Appia Antica, and since you are likely to spend the whole day here, many of them have been listed below (in the order in which you will pass them on your way out of Rome).

€ **La Botticella da Franca**. *No. 28, T: 06 51 36 792; closed weekends*. Inside an ancient Roman building, this is a very simple place where you will usually also find Romans enjoying a meal.

€ **Priscilla**. *No. 68, T: 06 51 36 379; closed Sun*. A very small typical *trattoria*.

€ **Bar L'Incontro**. *No. 64; closed Sun*. A place for a very simple snack.

€€ **Hostaria Antica Roma**. *No. 87, T: 06 51 32 888; closed Mon*. Worth visiting since it is inside the ancient **Columbarium of the Freedmen of Augustus**, where some 3,000 inscriptions were found. A farmhouse was built beside it, but the columbarium still stands (it is now an outdoor dining area) and preserves its rows of niches which contained urns for ashes. Inside the restaurant is a copy of a drawing by Piranesi (1747) of the interior of the columbarium when it was used as a barn and wine cellar. The food is perfectly adequate and the water they serve is Egeria (from the nearby spring; *see p. 516*).

€€ **Cecilia Metella**. *No. 125, T: 51 36 743; closed Mon*. This is one of the best places on the Via Appia for a reasonably priced good meal.

€€€ **L'Archeologia**. *No. 139, T: 06 788 0494; closed Tues*. With a large garden but on a busy crossroads, this has for long been one of the best-known places to eat here, with a very good wine list.

€ **Garden Ristò**. *No. 172, T: 06 78 34 8607; closed Mon*. Regional cuisine and pizza in the evenings.

€ **Appia Antica Caffè**. *No. 175; closed Mon*. Has a few tables outside. Serves snacks and sandwiches.

€ **Alessandrini**. *No. 198, T: 06 78 03 922; closed Sun and Mon*. A pleasant little *trattoria*. This is a sound choice and in a convenient position on Via Cecilia Metella.

Places to **picnic** include the garden of Capo di Bove (*no. 222; there are also toilets and a café here*) or in the peaceful stretch of the road beyond Vicolo di Tor Carbone. Other good places are the Parco della Caffarella and the Circus of Maxentius.

HISTORY OF THE VIA APPIA

Called by Statius *regina viarum* (the queen of roads), the Via Appia was the most important of the consular Roman highways. It was built by the censor Appius Claudius in 312 BC as far as Capua, and later extended to Beneventum (Benevento) and Brundusium (Brindisi). In 37 BC Horace, Virgil and Maecenas travelled the 375km to Brindisi in 15 days. It originally began at Porta Capena, a gate in the Servian Wall near the Circus Maximus (*map p. 653, B1*), but after Aurelian built his walls across it about 1.5km outside the Servian circle, this first stretch of the road was enclosed within the city limits and became known as its 'urban section'. For the first few kilometres the road served as a patrician cemetery and was lined on either side by a series of family graves. Some of the tombs, often in the form of a tower, temple or tumulus, can still be seen, although often only their concrete cores survive. The solid bases were sometimes used in the Middle Ages as the foundations of watch-towers and small forts. The Via Appia was also used by the early Christians for their underground cemeteries, or catacombs, the most important of which are open to the public. When the road was reopened in 1852, many monuments were re-erected by Luigi Canina.

Although the road survives as far as the twelfth Roman milestone (over 16km) and its junction with the modern Via Appia Nuova, little or no attempt was made to preserve it in the 20th century, despite the fact that it was declared a public park in 1965. The ancient paving was almost totally covered with asphalt up to the third milestone, the monuments were vandalised, and part of the historic area bordering the road was even occupied by luxurious private villas in the 1940s and 1950s. A final blow came when the motorway circling Rome was allowed to cut the historic old road in half at the seventh milestone.

Largely thanks to the conservationist Antonio Cederna, the area became a regional park in 1997. In 1999–2000 the circular motorway was diverted into a tunnel (1.5km) beneath the ancient road (an extremely rare instance in Italy of money being spent on improving the scenery rather than facilitating traffic flow). With special funds received during the Jubilee Year, important restoration was carried out on the ancient paving and sidewalks as far as the seventh milestone. More work began on the stretch between San Sebastiano and the tomb of Cecilia Metella in 2015. However, there is concern about the future of the area: pressure to keep the road open to traffic is still vigorously asserted.

SECTIONS OF THE VIA APPIA

- **Porta San Sebastiano to Domine Quo Vadis** (*described on p. 514*): This initial stretch is traffic-ridden and unpleasant to explore on foot except on Sundays, when the road is officially closed to traffic. The Tomb of Priscilla is here.
- **Parco della Caffarella** (*described on p. 515*): A detour from the Via Appia into a peaceful park with some interesting monuments.

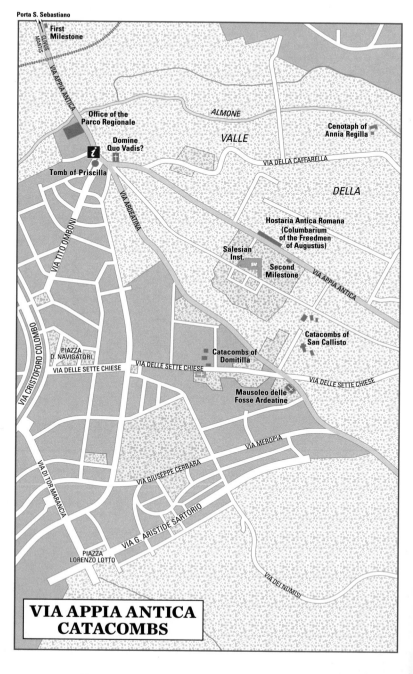

VIA APPIA ANTICA CATACOMBS

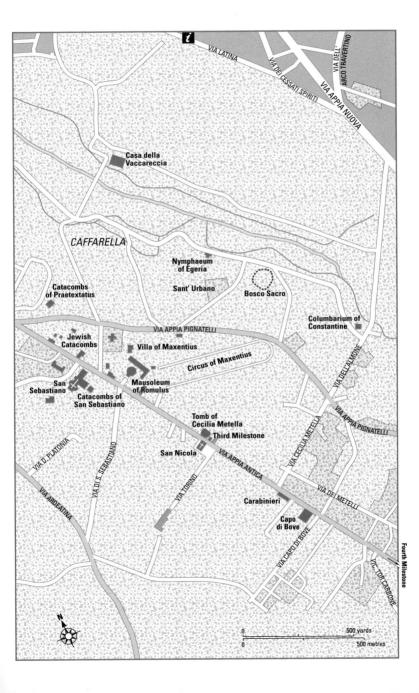

- **The catacombs** (*described on p. 516*): Those of San Callisto and San Sebastiano are right on the Via Appia. The Catacombs of Domitilla are some way off it, reached along Via delle Sette Chiese.
- **Villa of Maxentius to Capo di Bove** (*described on p. 521*): A very attractive section of the road, peaceful and with the original paving in many parts. It includes the Tomb of Cecilia Metella.
- **Tombs at the Fourth and Fifth Milestones** (*described on p. 523*): Many remains of ancient tombs line this part of the road, which is peaceful and closed to cars.
- **The Villa of the Quintilii and last stretch of the Via Appia** (*described on p. 525*): Ask at the information office if the Via Appia entrance to the villa is open. If it is not, it must be accessed from Via Appia Nova.

PORTA SAN SEBASTIANO TO DOMINE QUO VADIS

The initial section of the Via Appia, the ancient Clivus Martis, descends gently from Porta San Sebastiano. About 120m from the gate is the site of the first milestone, marked by a column and an inscription (the original milestone is now on the Capitoline hill; *see p. 37*). The Via Appia passes under a flyover bearing a fast new road, where excavations have revealed ancient Roman remains, and then under the Rome–Civitavecchia railway. It crosses the Almone (or Marrana della Caffarella), a brook where the priests of Cybele, the *Magna Mater*, used to perform the annual ceremony of washing the image of the goddess. At no. 42 is the seat of the Parco Regionale dell'Appia Antica, housed in a former paper mill. (The information office is further on, at no. 60.)

DOMINE QUO VADIS
On the left of the road, situated on a busy bend, is the little church of Domine Quo Vadis (*officially open 8–6 but often closed except for Mass*). This stands on the spot where—according to tradition—St Peter, fleeing the city, met an apparition of Jesus which shamed him into returning to Rome and martyrdom: the story was the subject of a novel by the Polish writer and Nobel prizewinner Henryk Sienkiewicz (1896). A monument to him was erected inside the church by Polish residents in Italy in 1977. The church preserves a copy of the stone which claimed to have been imprinted by the feet of Christ when he met the fleeing Peter.

TOMB OF PRISCILLA
Opposite and partly hidden by two farmhouses are the remains of the tall cylindrical core of the Tomb of Priscilla (*T: 06 51 26 314 to arrange a visit*), the young wife of a freedman of Domitian, Titus Flavius Abascantus. Her elaborate funeral in the 1st century AD (in which the body was embalmed and wrapped in purple) was described by the poet Statius. On a monumental scale, with each of the four outer walls measuring some 20m, it had niches containing statues of the deceased in the guise of goddesses and heroines from mythology. A fortified tower was built on the site in the Middle

Ages, and up until the 1960s the cool inner chamber was used for maturing the sheep's cheeses made by the local farmers. The sepulchre was restored in 2003.

At this point the Via Ardeatina branches off to the right to the Fosse Ardeatine, 1km away (*see p. 562*). The Via Appia continues left (go this way for the Parco della Caffarella). The peaceful central road (open to walkers) leads through olive groves to the catacombs of San Callisto (*see p. 517*).

PARCO DELLA CAFFARELLA

About 100m from the church of Domine Quo Vadis is a turning to the left, onto Via della Caffarella, which ends at a gate into an area of some 400 hectares of country-side and farmland, protected since 2000, when the *Comune* of Rome bought about half the land (the other half belongs to the Vatican). This is probably the area clos-est to the centre of the city where you can still see a landscape reminiscent of the famous *Campagna Romana*, the undulating plain around Rome between the sea and the Sabine and Praenestine foothills. It was characterised by its wide, open landscape of pastureland, green for most of the year, with a few wooded areas and others cov-ered with typical low vegetation known as the *macchia mediterranea*. This landscape was praised and described by visitors, writers and artists up until the end of the 19th century, when it was gradually engulfed by new suburbs. In Roman times the wealthy Athenian Herodes Atticus, patron of the arts and tutor to Marcus Aurelius in the 2nd century AD, and famous above all for his numerous buildings in Greece, had his villa here, known as the 'Triopio'. It had come to him in the dowry of his aristocratic Roman wife, Annia Regilla (*see below*).

MONUMENTS AND REMAINS IN THE PARCO DELLA CAFFARELLA
After the first few hundred metres, you enter a well-preserved green valley from which there is a view back across fields to the Porta San Sebastiano and the dome of St Peter's in the far distance. In the other direction, on a clear day, the Alban Hills and the Terminello mountains can be seen. This district has been used as farmland since the days of the ancient Romans, and flocks of sheep still graze here. Less than a kilometre along the lane is a path to the left which leads to a medieval mill near the Almone brook beside the **Cenotaph of Annia Regilla** (*open weekends 10–4, until 6pm in summer; closed Jan, July and Aug*), wife of Herodes Atticus. This sumptuous edifice is in the form of a temple built on two storeys and was once preceded by a pronaos. The brick exterior is well preserved, with pilasters with Corinthian capitals, a horizontal frieze, rectangular windows with lintels, and the pediment. Inside, although the floor which divided the two storeys has collapsed, traces of the decoration in stucco and fresco sur-vive. Herodes Atticus erected it here after his wife died in mysterious circumstances in Greece, kicked to death while in the advanced stages of pregnancy. Regilla's brother maintained that her husband was the culprit, an accusation he strenuously denied.

Beyond, the lane passes a tumbledown medieval farm known as the **Casale della Vaccareccia**, still operating, where *ricotta* sheep's cheese is made. After passing a number of water channels (and a view left of a rockface with grottoes, used as huts by shepherds up until the early 20th century), you come to the **Nymphaeum of Egeria**, a picturesque and romantic monumental fountain. The huge vault survives above a niche and Roman masonry in opus mixtum. It is still fed by a branch of the Almone, although the water channel dates from the 19th century. It was once identified with the spring where Numa Pompilius is said to have consorted with the nymph Egeria, but is in fact a summer banqueting grotto constructed by Herodes Atticus.

A lane leads up to a little hillock where three ancient ilexes mark the site of the **Bosco Sacro**, the 'sacred wood' planted by order of Herodes Atticus. A charming tradition has developed whereby an acorn from one of the three ancient trees is planted for every child born in the local area. The church of **Sant'Urbano** has been the object of a legal battle for some decades. It was originally a temple, converted into a church in the 9th or 10th century and restored in 1634, when four fluted columns from the pronaos were incorporated into the wall. Inside are remains of stucco ornamentation and extremely interesting frescoes (1011) by a certain Bonizzo: over the door is the *Crucifixion*; on the end wall, *Christ Blessing*, with saints and angels; on the other walls, *Life of Jesus* and the *Lives of St Cecilia and her Companions*, and *Life of Pope St Urban I*.

Close to Via dell'Almone is the so-called **Columbarium of Constantine**, a 2nd-century temple tomb. Its situation so close to the Almone meant that it was converted into a mill in the Middle Ages.

THE CATACOMBS

Unlike the ancient Romans, who often cremated their dead, the early Christians always practised inhumation, since the body was expected to rise again. Because of this, they needed spacious burial grounds and so began to use the catacombs as subterranean cemeteries. The catacombs were often situated on property donated by a wealthy individual, after whom the cemetery was named (Domitilla, Agnese, Priscilla, Commodilla). Easily quarried in the soft tufa, the catacombs provided space for the tombs of thousands of Christians and many Jews. They were in use from the 1st to the early 5th centuries. Many martyrs were buried here and the early Christians chose to be buried close to them. Later they became places of pilgrimage until the martyrs' relics were transferred to churches, when Christianity became the official religion. The catacombs were pillaged by the Goths (537) and the Lombards (755), and by the 9th century they were abandoned. They received their name *ad catacumbas* (literally, 'by the caves') from the stone quarries on the site of the cemetery of St Sebastian.

In the 16th century the archaeologist Antonio Bosio explored the catacombs and his remarkable study of them was published posthumously in 1632. They were not systematically explored again until 1850, when Giovanni Battista de Rossi carried out excavations, at first at San Callisto. Once opened to the public, the catacombs became one of the most famous sights of Rome, when visits by candlelight fired the romantic imagination of 19th-century travellers. The once-popular belief that they were used as hiding places by the early Christians has been disproved.

THE CATACOMBS AS CEMETERIES

The catacombs are a system of tunnels, the shallowest at 7–8m beneath the surface, while the deepest are some 22m below ground level, often arranged on as many as five levels, and sometimes extending for several kilometres. Burials within them are of two main types: loculi (shelves in the rock, cut in tiers) and arcosolia (a sarcophagus set into a niche with an arch above it). There are also larger *cubicula*, family 'chapels', containing multiple burials of either type. The body was dusted with quicklime to dry it, wrapped in a sheet, and placed in the tomb. The loculus was then closed with a slab of marble or terracotta, sometimes inscribed (if the family was literate) with the date or the words '*in pace*'. The earliest inscriptions are Greek; later they are in Latin. Inscriptions typically begin with the words ENΘΑΔΕ ΚΕΙΤΑΙ ('here lies'). Next to the burials, hollow niches were often scooped out where offerings could be deposited or where small items would be left for identification. The tombs were sometimes decorated with paintings. Terracotta lamps were hung above them to provide illumination in the tunnels.

Most of the tombs were rifled at some time in the search for treasure and relics, but the inscriptions and paintings which survive are of the greatest interest. The symbols most commonly seen are the fish (from the Greek word *ichthys* formed of the initial letters of Jesus Christ God's Son Saviour); the dove (the Christian soul flying towards Heaven); the anchor (hope); an olive branch (peace); and a palm branch (victory and martyrdom). Allusions to the Church appear in the female figure praying (*Orans*, with arms uplifted) and in the vine. Amongst the allegorical and biblical representations, the most frequent is that of the Good Shepherd.

Burials typically attached themselves to those of a saint or martyr. Visitors to the catacombs would touch these tombs with cloths and so make relics by contact.

NB: The catacombs tend to be very crowded with tour groups. Because of the different levels and uneven ground in the dark corridors, they are not easy places for the elderly or those with difficulty walking. Some of them close for certain periods in winter, so it is always advisable to telephone or check the website (if there is one) before planning a visit.

THE CATACOMBS OF SAN CALLISTO

Open 9–12 & 2–5; closed Wed and in Feb. T: 06 51 30 151, catacombe.roma.it. Entrance about every half hour. Visits are by guided tour (30mins).

These, the first official cemetery of the early Christian community, are usually considered the most important of the Roman catacombs. They were named after St Calixtus (San Callisto), who was appointed to look after the cemetery by Pope St Zephyrinus (199–217), and who enlarged them when he himself became pope in 217. They were the official burial place of the bishops of Rome. First investigated in 1850 by Giovanni Battista de Rossi, they have still not been fully explored.

The visit

The **Oratory of St Sixtus and St Cecilia** is a small basilica with three apses, where the dead were brought before burial. Here are inscriptions and sculptural fragments from the tombs, and a bust of De Rossi. Pope St Zephyrinus is generally believed to have been buried in the central apse.

The catacombs, excavated on five levels, are reached by an ancient staircase. The tour usually remains on the second level, from which several staircases can be seen descending to other levels. The remarkable **papal crypt** preserves the tombs with original Greek inscriptions of the martyred popes St Pontianus (230–5), St Anterus (236), St Fabian (236–50), St Lucius I (253–4; martyred under Valerian), St Stephen I (254–7), St Dionysius (259–68) and St Felix I (269–74). In honour of the martyred popes, Pope St Damasus I (366–84) set up the metrical inscription seen at the end of the crypt.

In the adjoining crypt is the **Cubiculum of St Cecilia**, where the body of the saint was supposedly buried after her martyrdom at her house in Trastevere in 230. It is thought that in 820 it was moved by Paschal I to the church built on the site of her house (*see p. 391*). A copy of Stefano Maderno's statue of the saint in the church has been placed here. On the walls are very worn 7th–8th-century frescoes of the head of Christ, St Urban and other saints. Beyond the crypt, a 3rd-century passage leads down a short flight of stairs, with Christian symbols carved on stone slabs, to the **Cubicula of the Sacraments**, with symbolic frescoes. In the first cubicle are frescoes of the *Raising of Lazarus* and, opposite, the *Miracle of the Loaves and Fishes*. On the end wall is a fine double sarcophagus, with a lid in the form of a roof. The other cubicles have similar frescoes, several depicting the story of Jonah. Further on is the **Crypt of St Eusebius**, martyred in 310. In the adjoining cubicles are the sepulchral inscriptions of Pope St Caius (283–96) and two sarcophagi with mummified bodies.

The Tomb of Pope St Cornelius (251–3), with a contemporary Latin inscription containing the word 'martyr' and fine 6th-century Byzantine paintings, and the adjoining Crypt of Lucina, the oldest part of the cemetery, were closed at the time of writing.

THE CATACOMBS OF SAN SEBASTIANO

Usually open Mon–Sat 10–4. Closed Sun and mid-Nov–mid-Jan. T: 06 78 50 350. Tours last approx 30mins; the order of the visit is sometimes changed. The best approach from San Callisto is to continue along the drive through the estate (ignoring the path signposted for the Via Appia), taking the exit which is very close to the small piazza on the Via Appia in which, on the left, is a column set up by Pius IX in 1852 to commemorate his restoration of the ancient road. Here is the entrance to the catacombs and basilica.

The basilica was originally dedicated to St Peter and St Paul and called the 'Basilica Apostolorum'. It was built in the first half of the 4th century over the cemetery into which the bodies of the Apostles had been temporarily moved from their tombs in St Peter's and San Paolo fuori le Mura; this is said to have occurred in 258 during the persecution of Valerian. An apsidal cubiculum with interesting graffiti has been found in part of the catacombs, indicating that this was the temporary grave of St Peter. At a later date St Sebastian, who was martyred under Diocletian in 288, was buried here. After the 9th century the association with the Apostles was forgotten and the church

BASILICA OF SAN SEBASTIANO

was named after St Sebastian. From the 3rd to the 9th centuries this was the most venerated area of subterranean Rome.

These catacombs have two special claims to fame: they are the only ones that have always been known and visited (even though this means they have as a consequence also been damaged over the centuries), and they were originally the only underground burial place to receive the name of catacombs, *ad catacumbas*, since they were built in an abandoned stone quarry here.

The visit

Steep stairs lead down to the catacombs, excavated on four levels. The tour usually begins in the corridors of the first level just below ground, where the Chapel of Symbols has carved Christian motifs. Steps lead up to the restored **Crypt of St Sebastian**, which contains a copy of a bust of St Sebastian attributed to Bernini. Here you can see a 4th-century staircase which used to provide access to the church. You now descend to the second level below ground to the area below the basilica—the walls of which can be seen—known as the **Piazzuola**, which has three pagan tombs of the early 2nd century, extremely interesting for their architecture and elaborate decoration. They each have a façade with a terracotta tympanum. The first, on the right, has a fresco above the tympanum of a pastoral scene and a banquet. The marble inscription names this as the sepulchre of Marcus Clodius Hermes. Inside is a vault fresco with a Gorgon's head, and decorative frescoes on the walls include a beautiful composition with a vase of fruit and flowers flanked by two birds. The floor preserves a mosaic. The centre tomb has a magnificent stucco vault, very well preserved, dating from the early 2nd century, terminating in a shell design decorated with lotus and acanthus leaves and a peacock. It is believed both pagan and Christian burials took place in this composite tomb on several levels. The tomb to the left has a well-preserved stucco vault which descends to a lunette finely decorated with a grape and vine design. The cubicles here are also decorated with stucco.

A steep staircase ascends to the ***Triclia***, a room reserved for the funerary banquets held in honour of the Apostles Peter and Paul. There is a bench around the wall, and remains of red-painted decorations and fragments of pictures. The walls are covered in tesserae scratched with graffiti invoking the Apostles, including one dating from 260.

The basilica

The basilica, one of the traditional seven pilgrimage churches of Rome (*see p. 292*), is usually shown at the end of the tour. It originally had a nave and two aisles; the aisles were walled up in the 13th century. In 1612 it was rebuilt for Cardinal Scipione Borghese by Flaminio Ponzio; the façade has a portico with Ionic columns taken from the earlier 15th-century portico. The beautiful 17th-century wooden ceiling is by Giovanni Vasanzio. On the north side is the **Chapel of St Sebastian**, with his relics and a very fine recumbent statue of the saint by Antonio Giorgetti, from a design by Bernini. Immediately opposite is the apsidal **Chapel of the Relics**, containing an arrow of St Sebastian in a casket and the original stone which was once believed to bear the imprint of Christ's feet. A copy is in the church of Domine Quo Vadis (*see p. 514*). Also on the south side is a huge **bust of the Saviour**, made by Bernini in 1678. The **Cappella Albani**, built as a sepulchral chapel for Clement XI, is by Carlo Fontana. On the high altar are four columns of *verde antico*. On the third north altar, *St Francis of Assisi* is attributed to Girolamo Muziano.

CATACOMBS OF DOMITILLA

Open daily except Tues 9–12 & 2–5. Closed mid-Dec–mid-Jan. T: 06 51 10 342, domitilla. info. Entrance at no. 282 Via delle Sette Chiese.

The Catacombs of Domitilla, or Catacombs of Sts Nereus and Achilleus, are among the most extensive in Rome and may be the most ancient Christian cemetery in existence. They contain more than 900 inscriptions. Flavia Domitilla (of the *gens* Flavia, the family of Domitian) and her two Christian servants, Nereus and Achilleus, were buried here, as well as St Petronilla, another Christian patrician, perhaps the adopted daughter of St Peter.

At the foot of the entrance stairway is the aisled **Basilica of Sts Nereus and Achilleus**, built in 390–5 over the tombs of the martyred saints. There are traces of a schola cantorum, and ancient columns probably from a pagan temple. The area below floor level has sarcophagi and tombs. By the altar is a rare small column, with scenes of the martyrdom of St Achilleus carved in relief. The adjoining **Chapel of St Petronilla** (shown during the tour of the catacombs), with a fresco of the saint, contained her sarcophagus until the 8th century, when it was removed to St Peter's.

The **catacombs** are excavated on two levels. The Cemetery of the Flavians (the family of Domitilla) had a separate entrance on the old Via Ardeatina. At this entrance is a vaulted vestibule probably designed as a meeting-place for the service of Intercession for the Dead, with a bench along the wall and a well for water. A long tunnel slopes down from here, with niches on either side decorated with 2nd-century frescoes of flowers and genii. From the original entrance a tunnel leads to another hypogeum, with four large niches decorated with 2nd-century paintings (including *Daniel in the Lions' Den*). At the foot of a staircase is another ancient area; here is a cubicle with paintings of winged genii and the earliest known representation of the *Good Shepherd* (2nd century). On the upper level is the Cubiculum of Ampliatus, with paintings in the Classical style. Other areas contain more painted scenes including the *Madonna and Child with Four Magi, Christ and the Apostles*, and a scene of a cornmarket.

CATACOMBS OPEN BY ARRANGEMENT

The Pontificia Commissione di Archeologia Sacra (*www.archeologiasacra.net, pcas@arcasacra.va*) looks after the following, and should be contacted to arrange a visit:
Catacombs of Praetextatus (*Via Appia Pignatelli 11*).
Hypogeum of Vibia (*Via Appia Antica 101*). Has pagan paintings of the 3rd century.
Catacombs of Commodilla (*Via delle Sette Chiese 42*).

The **Vigna Randanini Jewish catacombs** (*Via Appia Pignatelli 4/Via Appia Antica 119; T: 06 68 80 6897 or 060608*), excavated in 1857, have tombs and loculi dating from the 3rd–6th centuries. The symbols include the cornucopia (plenty), the palm-leaf (victory) and the seven-branched candlestick, and the epitaphs are mostly in Greek.

VILLA OF MAXENTIUS TO CAPO DI BOVE

As the Via Appia leaves the area of the catacombs, it becomes more attractive and interesting for its ancient remains. After Via di San Sebastiano diverges right, the motor traffic along the road finally greatly diminishes.

VILLA OF MAXENTIUS

Open Tues–Sun 10–4 or Tues–Sat 9–1 in low season; check times on parcoappiaantica. it. Free. T: 06 78 01 324.

On the left of the road, in a hollow at no. 153, are the extensive ruins of the Villa of Maxentius. Built in 309 by the emperor Maxentius, it included a palace, a circus and a mausoleum built in honour of his son Romulus (d. 307).

The **Circus of Maxentius** is the best-preserved of the Roman circuses, and one of the most romantic sites of ancient Rome. It has a good view of the Tomb of Cecilia Metella. The circus was excavated by Antonio Nibby in 1825 for the Torlonia family, and restored in the 1960s and '70s. The stadium (c. 513m by 91m) was probably capable of holding some 10,000 spectators. The main entrance was on the west side with the twelve *carceres* or stalls for the chariots and *quadrigae* and, on either side, two square towers with curved façades. Two arches, one of which has been restored, connected the towers to the long sides of the circus and provided side entrances. In the construction of the tiers of seats, amphorae were used to lighten the vaults, and these can still clearly be seen. In the centre of the left side is the conspicuous emperor's box, which was connected by a portico to his palace on the hill behind. At the far end was a triumphal arch where a fragment of a dedicatory inscription to Romulus, son of Maxentius, was found, thus identifying the circus with Maxentius (it had previously been attributed to Caracalla). In the centre is the round *meta* and the *spina*, the low wall which divided the area longitudinally and where the obelisk of Domitian, now in Piazza Navona, originally stood. The course was seven laps around the spina. This and the *carceres* were both placed slightly obliquely to equalise, as far as possible, the chances of all competitors, although it is likely that the circus was never actually used, since Maxentius fell from power in 312.

Fenced off on the hillside to the left are the overgrown remains of the **palace**, which include fragments of baths, a basilica and a cryptoporticus.

MAUSOLEUM OF ROMULUS

The conspicuous high wall near the west end of the circus belongs to the quadriporticus around the Mausoleum of Romulus, which faces the Via Appia. Some of the pilasters survive, as well as much of the outer wall. In the centre is the circular tomb, in front of which is a rectangular pronaos lying beneath a farmhouse built by the Torlonia family. The entrance is through the house and into the pronaos, beyond which is the mausoleum itself, with niches in the outer wall for sarcophagi and a huge pilaster in the centre, also decorated with niches. The upper floor, probably intended to be domed, was never completed.

THE TOMB OF CECILIA METELLA

Open Tues–Sun 9–1 hour before sunset. T: 06 39 96 7700. For the Archaeological Card, see p. 600.

The Tomb of Cecilia Metella, a massive circular tower built in the Augustan period, was the burial place of Cecilia, daughter of Quintus Metellus Creticus (conqueror of Crete) and wife of Marcus Licinius Crassus, one of Caesar's generals in Gaul. A hundred Roman feet (29.5m) in diameter, on a square base, and extremely well preserved, this is the most famous landmark on the Appia, and numerous drawings of it were made over the centuries. Much of the marble facing is still intact, as is also part of the elegant frieze surrounding the upper part, with garlands of fruit and bucrania (hence the name *Capo di Bove*, meaning 'ox-head', given to the adjacent ground) on either side of a very worn relief representing a soldier with Gallic shields and a prisoner from Gaul kneeling at his feet. Just below it is a large inscription to the deceased.

In 1303 the Caetani transformed the tomb into a crenellated tower to serve as the keep of their large castle, which extended as far as the present Via Cecilia Metella, on both sides of the Appia. The original road entrance was closed up in the 19th century and ancient inscriptions and sculptural fragments were exhibited on the brick wall. Above can be seen the Caetani coat of arms. Beneath the two-light windows the (very worn) third milestone of the Via Appia survives. The enceinte also included the Gothic **church of San Nicola** opposite the mausoleum, now roofless. In 1306 the castle passed to the Savelli family and from them to the Colonna and the Orsini.

Interior of the tomb

A low corridor leads into the sepulchral chamber, now open to the sky and inhabited by pigeons. Its construction technique is particularly interesting, using small flat bricks. It was built on a lava flow from the Alban Hills: the volcanic rock can be seen at the bottom of a flight of steps leading from the courtyard. Several of the castle rooms can also be seen: in the largest one, still roofless, Antonio Muñoz arranged a little museum of sculptures from the Via Appia when he carried out excavations and restored the monument in the early 20th century. His arrangement was retained when the building was restored in 2000, and the fragments include statues, capitals, friezes, urns and reliefs. Ceramic shards found on the site are exhibited in a little adjoining room, and more sculptures are arranged beside the ticket office.

CAPO DI BOVE

Where the old paving begins, about 100m beyond the Tomb of Cecilia Metella, cars are (officially) banned. Where Via Cecilia Metella joins the Appia there is a snack bar, police station and *trattoria* (and the terminus of bus 660). Further on, at no. 222, is the entrance to Capo di Bove (*open daily 10–4; Sun 10–6 in summer*), a villa which houses the archives of Antonio Cederna, the conservationist who did so much to preserve the Appia Antica. In the garden are excavations of baths dating from the 2nd century AD, some of which have mosaic floors. They were part of the huge property of Herodes Atticus (*see p. 515*) and in the floor of the frigidarium a marble slab was found inscribed in Greek: 'The light of the house'. This almost certainly refers to Herodes Atticus' wife Annia Regilla, as an inscription with the same wording, and also mentioning her by name, was found near Athens. Behind the excavations stretches a peaceful little garden with a café and another house whose rooms are used for exhibitions.

TOMBS AT THE FOURTH & FIFTH MILESTONES

The section of road between the third and eleventh milestones, excavated in 1850–9, is the best-preserved stretch of all. It was 4.2m wide (to allow two carts to pass each other) and the surface is now either covered with the massive polygonal blocks of grey basaltic lava from the Alban Hills, known as *basolato*, or by *sanpietrini* blocks.

On either side were *crepidines*, sidewalks for pedestrians, and beyond these there are now low dry-stone walls. For ten Roman miles or more it was bordered with tombs: the picturesque remains of some of these were recovered and others reconstructed in the 19th century by Antonio Canova and Luigi Canina. Some of the original sculptures have been removed to the Museo Nazionale Romano and replaced by casts.

The area of tombs begins at a prominent memorial on the right with a marble relief of a nude hero. The site of the fourth milestone is here. On a brick pillar on the left are fragments of a **tomb of a memorial to Marcus Servilius**. An inscription records that this was a gift made in 1808 by Canova, who, contrary to the general practice of his time, felt that objects found during excavations should be left *in situ*. The sporadic remains you see today give little idea of the dense thicket of memorials that would once have crowded the road on both sides, clamouring for the attention of living passers-by, the best form of immortality an ancient Roman could hope for.

On the right, in the Proprietà Lugari near a clump of huge umbrella pines, is a superb **monument in the form of a small temple**—supposed to be that of St Urban—surrounded by the ruins of what was probably a villa. Opposite it is the **Round Tomb**, a square base surmounted by a circular cella with four *loculi*, and next to it, the **Tomb of the Children of the Freedman Sextus Pompeius Justus** (with inscriptions and other fragments, partly replaced by casts). Beyond this, set back from the road, are the ruins of the so-called **Temple of Jupiter**, square with apsidal niches.

The interesting tombs now continue on the right, with the **Doric Tomb** in the form of an altar, and next to it the **Tomb of Hilarius Fuscus**, its relief of five busts replaced by a cast. A memorial with remains of an **eipgraph to Tiberius Claudius Secundinus** is followed by the remains of a columbarium and then the **Tomb of Quintus Apuleius Pamphilius**, with architectural fragments. Beyond the substantial remains of a sepulchre in the form of a temple is the **Tomb of the Rabirii**, where the three busts have been replaced by casts. Further on on the same side is the **Tomb of the Festoons** (from the worn frieze of putti and garlands) and the **Tomb of the Frontispiece**, with a relief of four busts of the deceased (casts).

The Appia now crosses Via Erode Attico and Via Tor Carbone. The lines of tombs continue on the other side, where the Via Appia is particularly well preserved. On the right is the brick and concrete core of a high tower with, at its base, a slab recording **three Jewish freedmen**. Beyond it is a round mausoleum (converted into a tower in the Middle Ages), and on the left two sepulchres in the form of temples (with the Villa Dino between them). At a point marked by a group of gigantic pines, near the fifth milestone, the road bends, probably to avoid some earlier tumuli, one of which on the right—now surmounted by a tower—is called the **Tumulus of the Curiatii.** There was a popular legend recorded by Livy that in this vicinity the Curiatii, three brothers from the Alban Hills, engaged the Horatii, three brothers from Rome, in mortal combat, and this was traditionally believed to be the burial place of the three Curiatii. Further on, on the right, surrounded by pines, is the so-called **Tumulus of the Horatii**, twin mounds, perhaps the burial place of two of the Horatii, or part of a monument erected here in the Augustan era to commemorate the Curiatii and Horatii. In the field to the right of the first mound are the remains of an *ustrinum* or cremation place, which may

VIA APPIA

Cast of the busts of the Tomb of Hilarius Fuscus (left), displayed *in situ* on the Via Appia; and (right) the original relief, now preserved in the Museo Nazionale Romano in the Baths of Diocletian.

have been connected with the famous battle. Opposite the second of the graves of the Horatii, an inscription of the 1st century BC marks the **tomb of Marcus Caecilius**, in whose family grave was buried Pomponius Atticus, the friend of Cicero, thought to be the first owner of the Villa of the Quintilii.

Opposite the Tumulus of the Curiatii, a farm track leads off the Via Appia to the left. On the corner on the left are the remains of a huge pyramidal mausoleum. This may have belonged to a member of the Quintili family, the remains of whose vast nymphaeum can be seen stretching off to the left, along with the other magnificent and picturesque ruins of their great villa.

THE VILLA OF THE QUINTILII

Open Tues–Sun 9–sunset. Although the villa's nymphaeum is right on the Via Appia Antica, the entrance here is often closed (it is officially only open on Sundays in April–Oct). Check with the information office before you visit (T: 06 51 35 316). If closed, the entrance is at Via Appia Nuova 1092. To get there on foot from the Via Appia Antica, take the farm track mentioned above. For public transport, see pp. 509–10. From the end of the track, on Via Appia Nuova, you will also start to see signs to the Parco degli Acquedotti, which is described on p. 528. For the Archaeological Card, see p. 600.

Part of the site of the huge Roman residence called the Villa dei Quintili, between the Via Appia Antica and the Via Appia Nuova, is enclosed in a park of some 24 hectares. The villa, the earliest parts of which date from the time of Hadrian, belonged to the wealthy and cultivated Quintilius brothers, consuls under Antoninus Pius (AD 151), who wrote a treatise on agriculture. They were put to death by Commodus for the sake of their possessions, including this villa. The emperor enlarged the property and it was kept in repair by his successors up until the 4th century.

As late as the 15th century the area was known as 'Statuario', referring to the numerous ancient Roman statues and sculptures which were found here. In the 17th and 18th centuries it was called 'Roma Vecchia', as the ruins were so extensive as to suggest a small town. In 1797 the property was purchased by the Torlonia family and in 1828–9 Antonio Nibby carried out excavations. Many of the finds are kept in properties still belonging to the Torlonia (*see pp. 481–2 and p. 571*). The Vatican also carried out excavations here and some of the sculptures are now in the Vatican Museums; others found their way to the Louvre and the Hermitage. In the early 20th century Thomas Ashby, director of the British School at Rome from 1906–25, carried out a systematic study of the villa. Excavations were renewed from 1998 and are still in progress.

THE ANTIQUARIUM

This is arranged in the stable block of a former farmhouse near the road. It contains finds from excavations carried out in 1929 on private property in the area between the Via Appia Pignatelli and Via Appia Nuova, as well as those in 1997–9 in the area of the villa itself. In the centre of the room is a large seated statue of Zeus dating from the 2nd century AD. In the middle of the right wall is a herm, thought to represent Dionysus (2nd century AD) and, on the opposite wall, another herm unearthed in a room near the frigidarium of the villa's baths in 1998. A group of statues mostly related to Oriental cults was found in 1929, dumped together ready for use in a medieval lime kiln. There are also two statuettes of Hercules, a relief with a Greek inscription to Astarte, and an alabaster slab reused in the Christian period. Brick stamps found in the villa, some of which are exhibited here, date from AD 123 up until the early 3rd century. The capital decorated with fantastic animals (3rd century AD) is very unusual. The rare seated statue of *Zeus Bronton*, representing the God of rain and thunder, is derived from similar cult statues in Asia Minor. Also preserved here are architectural elements, a fragment of a fresco with flowers, and opus sectile work in marble.

THE VILLA

The impressive buildings of the villa can be seen along a ridge formed by an ancient lava flow from the Alban Hills. Near the path are the ruins of the **baths**, most conspicuous among which is the rectangular caldarium, its walls still standing with four huge arched windows on two levels overlooking the valley. Low steps surround the rectangular pool, which used to be filled with hot water. Beside it are the ruins of the tepidarium. The best preserved of the thermal buildings is the frigidarium, a little to the east, which also retains its walls and its splendid pavement of polychrome marble in opus sectile (2nd century AD). The two cipollino columns were recently returned here (they were removed many years ago and later found their way to the Baths of Diocletian).

In front of the baths was an oval edifice built in the 2nd–3rd century AD (its shape can be seen clearly in the ground). This is usually called the **Maritime Theatre** because of its similarity to a building at Hadrian's Villa in Tivoli, but its precise function is unknown; it may have been a small amphitheatre or simply a garden for taking

VIA APPIA
Inscription commemorating Baricha, Zabda and Achiba,
Jewish freedmen of a certain Lucius Valerius.

the air. The **residential area** was further east, on the edge of the hill. Near the reception rooms was a large open courtyard paved with white marble. The service areas and private quarters are marked by a high arch. There is another small thermal complex to the south, on the line of an aqueduct which descended past several cisterns from the nymphaeum at the top of the hill on the Via Appia Antica at the original entrance to the villa. The nymphaeum was enclosed in a castle in the 15th century. Also in this area there was a garden, a hippodrome and a stadium.

THE LAST STRETCH OF THE VIA APPIA

The Via Appia Antica now becomes more deserted and the monuments are more widely scattered. Some way beyond the nymphaeum of the Villa dei Quintili rises the **Casal Rotondo**, a large round tomb on a square base, with an incongruous modern house and an olive garden and pine tree on the summit. This was the largest tomb on the Via Appia and dates from the Republican period; it was enlarged in early Imperial times. It was once thought to have been erected to the memory of Marcus Valerius Messalla Corvinus, conqueror of Aquitaine, superintendent of aqueducts and poet, by his son Valerius Maximus Cotta. The stylobate is 120 Roman feet (c. 36m) in diameter. Attached to a wall here, erected by Canina, are numerous architectural fragments and inscriptions now known not to belong to this tomb. They refer to another monument, commemorating members of the Aurelii Cottae, of the family of the mother of Julius Caesar.

From here there you can explore the Appia on foot for another mile or so. On the left, just beyond the crossroads, where the Rome–Naples railway passes diagonally below the road, was the site of the sixth milestone. On the right is a tomb with reliefs of griffins and a columbarium. Opposite another columbarium, on the right of the road, is a tomb with four busts (casts). Some way further on on the left, about 1km from the Casal Rotondo, is the **Torre Selce**, the 'Flint Tower', a pyramidal tumulus surmounted by a medieval tower. Beyond inscriptions of Marcus Julius Pietas Epelides and Caius Atilius Eudos, a jeweller, the road swerves a little and begins to descend. On the right is a monument with a headless statue of the deceased in a toga, and on the left can be seen the arches of an aqueduct which formerly brought water from a sulphur spring near Ciampino to the Villa of the Quintilii. A column marks the seventh milestone.

The Via Appia Antica continues now for four kilometres (as far as its junction with the Appia Nuova). Beyond the site (on the right) of the Torre Rossa or Torre Appia, a 12th–13th-century structure on a Roman base, which collapsed after a violent storm in 1985, the road passes ruins of a sepulchral chamber (or possibly a sanctuary) and **stumps of columns in peperino** from a Roman porticus. Once known as the Pillars of Hercules, these may have belonged to a temple to Silvanus. The eighth milestone was just beyond. Further along, beyond the Torraccio del Palombaro (preserved through having been turned into a church in the 10th century), a path on the right leads to **La Giostra**, a little hill upon which the ruins are thought to be those of a 4th-century Roman fortified outpost. At the ninth milestone is what is left of the **Villa of Gallienus**, with a fine circular ruin regarded as the mausoleum of that emperor. The road crosses the Rome–Terracina railway and, a little beyond the site of the twelfth milestone, joins the busy Via Appia Nuova.

PARCO DEGLI ACQUEDOTTI

If you are approaching from the Via Appia, take the track across farmland just before the Villa dei Quintili nymphaeum, cross the Via Appia Nuova and follow the signs along a narrow road which takes you under two railway bridges and past the golf course. By public transport from the centre of Rome, take Metro line A to Subaugusta.

The Parco degli Acquedotti, a beautiful protected area of some 15 hectares, is traversed by seven aqueducts. Majestic long stretches of several survive above ground in open countryside. On a clear day there is a distant view of the dome of St Peter's.

The aqueducts are supplied from springs in the upper valley of the Aniene beyond Tivoli and in the Alban Hills. The oldest aqueduct in the area of the park is the Anio Vetus (3rd century BC), but it is not visible here as it is almost totally underground. The most conspicuous aqueduct is the graceful **Aqua Claudia**, long stretches of which survive, carried on high arches. There are also lower arches belonging to the **Acqua Felice**, which is here covered by a vault. It feeds a pond in the little public park here.

THE TOMBE LATINE
Via Arco di Travertino 151 (near the Arco di Travertino metro stop). Visits only by appointment. T: 06 39 96 7700, www.coopculture.it.
The Area delle Tombe Latine is a group of tombs dating from the 1st and 2nd centuries. Most of them are square and brick-built, with recesses on the outside and interior chambers with stucco ornament. The so-called **Tomb of the Valerii** (AD 160) is a sub-

terranean chamber decorated with fine reliefs of nymphs, sea-monsters and nereids in stucco on a white ground. The **Tomb of the Pancratii**, of the same date, has landscape paintings, coloured stuccoes and bas-reliefs of the *Judgement of Paris*, *Admetus and Alcestis*, *Priam and Achilles*, and *Hercules playing a lyre*, with Bacchus and Minerva.

THE AQUEDUCTS OF ROME

Although a high proportion of the spring water brought to ancient Rome was channelled underground, stretches of aqueduct were also built, and their magnificent arches crossing the Campagna used to be one of the most romantic sights for travellers approaching the city. Like roads and bridges all over the Empire, some aqueducts still survive to demonstrate the skill of the Roman engineers.

The first aqueduct of all, the Aqua Appia, was built c. 312 BC by Appius Claudius, the censor who also gave his name to the Via Appia. Some 16km in length, it entered Rome at the present Porta Maggiore, at a time when the city had around 200,000 inhabitants. Ten more aqueducts were constructed during the Republic and Empire. The Anio Vetus, the oldest aqueduct in the Parco degli Acquedotti, was built, mostly underground, between 272 and 269 BC, and supplies water from the valley of the Aniene, some 64km east of Rome. The Aqua Marcia, begun in 44 BC, stretched from near Tivoli to the Capitoline, a distance of some 91km. It ran underground until it emerged in the present area of the park (where it merges with the Aqua Tepula and Aqua Julia, both from the Alban Hills). The Aqua Claudia was begun by Caligula in AD 38 and completed by Claudius in AD 42. The Anio Novus, completed in 52, was the longest and highest of all the aqueducts (95km; some of its arches were 28m tall). The last aqueduct of ancient Roman times was built by Alexander Severus c. AD 226.

A fascinating account of the waters of Rome, written in AD 97 by Sextus Julius Frontinus, head of the city's water works during the reigns of Nerva and Trajan, was discovered in the 15th century. Frontinus helped to reorganise the supply, bringing water for the first time to the poorer districts of Rome. Many of the aqueducts leaked and frequently needed repair, but by AD 52, when nine aqueducts were in use, they were sufficient to supply nearly 1,000 litres a day for each of Rome's estimated one million inhabitants. No other city at any time has been supplied with so much water (the present supply is around 500 litres per family).

The aqueducts were cut by the Goths in 537, and it was only in the 16th century that attention was again paid to Rome's water supply, from then onwards under the care of the popes. The Aqua Virgo was restored by Pius V in 1570; Sixtus V built the new Acqua Felice in 1585; and Paul V restored the Aqua Traiana in 1611, calling it the Acqua Paola. These papal aqueducts are still functioning, but the water supply has had to be greatly increased. The Acqua Vergine Nuova dates from 1937, and the Peschiera-Capore aqueduct was constructed between 1938 and 1980. It uses springs near Rieti and supplies more water than all the other aqueducts put together. It claims to be the largest aqueduct in the world using only spring water.

OSTIA ANTICA
Via di Diana.

Ostia Antica

*The excavations of the ancient port city of Ostia are one of
the most interesting and beautiful sights near Rome. Guided tours can also
be taken of the ancient port installations of Claudius and Trajan.*

The ruins of Ostia, in a lovely park of umbrella pines and cypresses, give a remarkable idea of the commercial and domestic life of the Empire in the late 1st–4th centuries AD. The excavations cover about two-thirds of the area of the city at its greatest extent. Many of the less frequented ruins are delightfully overgrown with grasses and wild flowers.

HISTORY OF OSTIA ANTICA

Ostia was probably the first colony of Rome, perhaps founded around 335 BC. Its earliest industry was the extraction of salt from the surrounding marshes but it soon developed into the port of Rome, and shortly before the First Punic War (264 BC) it also became a naval base. The link between the port and the capital was the Via Ostiense: carrying as it did all Rome's overseas imports and exports, it must have been one of the busiest roads in the ancient world.

One of Ostia's main functions was the organisation of the *annona*, the supply of produce—mainly grain—to the capital. In charge of this was the *quaestor ostiensis*, who had to live at Ostia. He was appointed by lot and his office, according to Cicero, was burdensome and unpopular. By 44 BC the quaestor was replaced by the *procuratores annonae*, answerable to the *praefectus annonae* in Rome.

By the 1st century AD, the city had outgrown its harbour. A new port, Portus, planned by Augustus, was built by Claudius to the northwest (*see p. 544*). Ostia developed into a residential town, though it was still used by passenger boats—in 387 St Augustine was about to embark for Africa with his mother, St Monica, when she was taken ill and died in a hostel in the city. In the following centuries, Ostia's decline was accelerated by loss of trade and by the increase of malaria. Its monuments were looted—items from the ruins have been found as far afield as Pisa, Orvieto, Amalfi and Salerno. An attempt to revive the city was made by Gregory IV, when he founded the *borgo* of Ostia Antica. By 1756, however, the city which at the height of its prosperity had a population of some 80,000, had 156 inhabitants. Augustus Hare, writing in 1878, speaks of a single human habitation breaking the utter solitude.

Opening times and getting there

Site open Tues–Sun 8.30–sunset. The nuseum (within the park) opens at 9.30. Free on the first Sun of the month. There is a bookshop and cafeteria. T: 06 56 35 0215, ostiaantica.beniculturali.it. To book a visit to the houses with painted decorations (Sun mornings), T: 06 56 35 8044. For guided tours, T: 06 56 35 2830.

Access is by suburban train (normal transport ticket valid) from Stazione Ostiense, outside Porta San Paolo (map p. 653, A3). Trains run approx. every 15mins. Get off at Ostia Antica (journey time 30mins). The ruins are a short walk from the station, across the footbridge.

The entrance to the excavations opens onto a street lined on both sides by tombs, including terracotta and carved stone sarcophagi. This was the landward approach to the city. The entrance was through the **Porta Romana**, a gate in the walls of the Republican period. Its bases remain, and some fragments of marble facing of the Imperial era have been found and placed on the inside of it. The gate opens onto **Piazzale della Vittoria (1)**, dominated by a cast of the winged statue of Minerva Victoria, dating from the reign of Domitian and inspired by a Hellenistic original, that probably decorated the gate (original in the museum). On the right are the remains of warehouses and of the **Baths of the Charioteers (2)** ('Cisiarii'), with a well-preserved black and white mosaic with marine motifs and depictions of chariots and wagons.

ALONG THE UPPER DECUMANUS MAXIMUS

The decumanus maximus, the main east–west street of Ostia, runs through the city for over a kilometre. On the right, a flight of steps leads to a platform on the second storey of the **Baths of Neptune (3)**. You can look down at the tepidarium and caldarium, remains of columns, and the floor of the large entrance hall with a beautiful mosaic of Neptune driving four sea-horses and surrounded by tritons, nereids and dolphins.

Beyond the baths, on the corner of Via della Fontana, is a **tavern (4)** which was owned by a certain Fortunatus, who wooed customers through the (now broken) inscription in the mosaic pavement: *Dicit Fortunatus: vinum cratera quod sitis bibe* ('Fortunatus says: drink wine from the bowl to quench your thirst'). Through the tavern you get to **Via della Fontana**, one of the best-preserved streets in Ostia. Here are examples of typical apartment houses, with ground-floor shops and living quarters over them. About halfway along on the right is the old covered fountain from which the street takes its name. Just beyond it, a right turn leads to the **Firemen's Barracks (5)** (Caserma dei Vigili), built in the 2nd century AD. It once had a large arcaded central courtyard. On the left are the remains of an Augusteum, or shrine for the cult of the emperors, with a mosaic of the sacrifice of a bull. Two huge curved water cisterns survive at the other end of the yard. Behind the right-hand one are remains of a latrine.

THE THEATRE AND PIAZZALE DELLE CORPORAZIONI

Ostia's **theatre (6)** (still used for performances in summer) was built by Agrippa and enlarged by Septimius Severus in the 2nd century. It has two tiers of seats (originally there were three) divided by stairways into five sections or *cunei*. It could accommodate 2,700 spectators. A tufa wall with some marble fragments and three marble masks survive from the stage, behind which some cipollino columns that once decorated the third tier of the auditorium have been set up.

Behind the theatre extends the spacious **Piazzale delle Corporazioni (7)** (Square of the Guilds). Around its perimeter were 70 offices of commercial associations ranging from workers' guilds to representatives of foreign tradesmen, from all over the ancient world. Their trademarks are preserved in the mosaic floors and are fascinating for the information they give on where the traders were from: e.g. Carthage (KARTHAG), Alexandria (XANDRAN) and Cagliari (KARALITANI) and what their trade was (e.g. grain or ivory, the latter illustrated by an elephant). Those of the guilds indicate their business, such as ship repair, salvage crews, dockers or customs and excise officials. In the middle of the square are the remains of a small temple known as the Temple of Ceres, and the bases of statues erected to the leading citizens of Ostia.

VIA DEI MOLINI AND VIA DI DIANA

Further along the decumanus, at the junction with Via dei Molini, stood the **Porta Orientale**, the east gate of the original *castrum*. Diagonally opposite it the ruins of huge **horrea (8)**, large warehouses for the storage of grain, can be seen on the right of the decumanus. They had multiple small rooms, some of them arranged around a central courtyard. Opposite them, across Via dei Molini, are the remains of **mills and bakeries (9)** (some rooms still preserve the stone kneading basins). Grain would have been fed into these from the warehouses across the street.

Running perpendicular to the west of Via dei Molini is Via di Diana, another fine street, which takes its name from a house called the **Casa di Diana (10)**. It has a characteristic layout: shops on the ground floor and steep stairways leading to apartments above. Those on the second floor had projecting balconies. The house is entered through a vaulted corridor. A room on the left has fragments of restored frescoes. The small inner courtyard has a fountain and a relief of Diana. At the back are two rooms converted into a Mithraeum (*for the cult of Mithras, see p. 539*).

Further along Via di Diana on the left is the remarkable **thermopolium (11)** or snack bar. Outside the entrance door, under the alcove, are three brick-topped benches where one can imagine customers sitting in the shade with their jugs of wine. Just inside the door is a marble counter on which is a small stone basin. Inside is another counter for the display of food; above are wall-paintings of fruit and vegetables. On the rear wall is a marble panel which once had hooks for hats and coats. To the right is a latrine. At the rear is a delightful outdoor courtyard and fountain.

Opposite the thermopolium, on the corner of Via di Diana and Via dei Dipinti, is a 2nd-century apartment block, originally of four storeys, enclosing a garden and known as the **Caseggiato dei Dipinti (12)** (*it can be seen on guided tours; see opposite*). The ground floor (entered around the corner from Via dei Dipinti) has traces of 'architectural' wall-paintings in many of its rooms. In a hall behind, a substantial piece of fine polychrome mosaic flooring has been set up. In the adjacent garden of the **Caseggiato dei Doli (13)** are numerous *dolia*, large terracotta jars for the storage of corn and oil, sunk into the ground. At the end of the street is the museum, which contains the principal finds from the excavations.

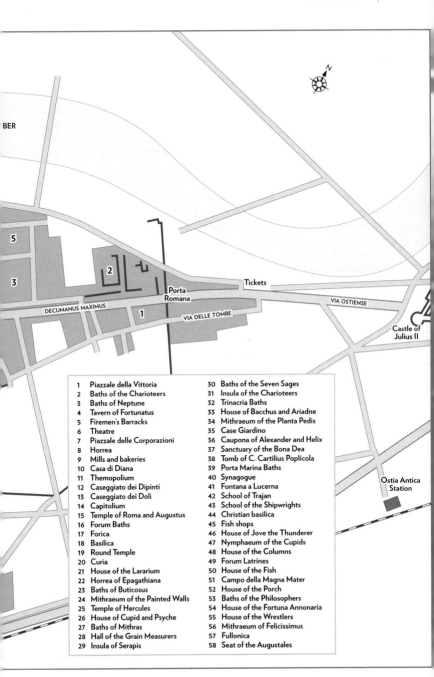

BER

Tickets

Porta
Romana

DECUMANUS MAXIMUS

VIA DELLE TOMBE

VIA OSTIENSE

Castle of
Julius II

Ostia Antica
Station

1	Piazzale della Vittoria	30	Baths of the Seven Sages
2	Baths of the Charioteers	31	Insula of the Charioteers
3	Baths of Neptune	32	Trinacria Baths
4	Tavern of Fortunatus	33	House of Bacchus and Ariadne
5	Firemen's Barracks	34	Mithraeum of the Planta Pedis
6	Theatre	35	Case Giardino
7	Piazzale delle Corporazioni	36	Caupona of Alexander and Helix
8	Horrea	37	Sanctuary of the Bona Dea
9	Mills and bakeries	38	Tomb of C. Cartilius Poplicola
10	Casa di Diana	39	Porta Marina Baths
11	Themopolium	40	Synagogue
12	Caseggiato dei Dipinti	41	Fontana a Lucerna
13	Caseggiato dei Doli	42	School of Trajan
14	Capitolium	43	School of the Shipwrights
15	Temple of Roma and Augustus	44	Christian basilica
16	Forum Baths	45	Fish shops
17	Forica	46	House of Jove the Thunderer
18	Basilica	47	Nymphaeum of the Cupids
19	Round Temple	48	House of the Columns
20	Curia	49	Forum Latrines
21	House of the Lararium	50	House of the Fish
22	Horrea of Epagathiana	51	Campo della Magna Mater
23	Baths of Buticosus	52	House of the Porch
24	Mithraeum of the Painted Walls	53	Baths of the Philosophers
25	Temple of Hercules	54	House of the Fortuna Annonaria
26	House of Cupid and Psyche	55	House of the Wrestlers
27	Baths of Mithras	56	Mithraeum of Felicissimus
28	Hall of the Grain Measurers	57	Fullonica
29	Insula of Serapis	58	Seat of the Augustales

THE DOMESTIC ARCHITECTURE OF OSTIA

The ruins of Ostia Antica give a vivid idea of the living conditions and types of housing occupied by Romans of all classes.

A typical Ostian *insula*, or apartment block, of the tenement type and urban in character, had four storeys and reached a height of 15m, the maximum permitted by Roman law. It was built of brick, probably not covered with stucco, and had little ornamentation, although sometimes bricks of contrasting colours were used. The entranceways had pilasters or engaged columns supporting a simple pediment. Some buildings had shops on the ground floor, either opening directly onto the street or under arcades, above which were residential apartments or sets of rooms, accessed by steep stairways, many of which survive. There were numerous rooms or apartments, each with its own window. The arches over the windows were often painted in vermilion. Mica or selenite was used instead of glass.

From the time of Hadrian comes the large residential enclave known as the Case Giardino, a self-contained housing development. Single-storey houses of the *domus* type were built for the richer inhabitants. Surviving examples date mostly from the 3rd and 4th centuries, when Ostia had ceased to be a commercial port and was enjoying a new lease of life as a residential town by the sea. These houses were decorated with wall-paintings and mosaic floors. Many had elaborate nymphaea, water grottoes perhaps used for summer dining, with statues in niches and softly burbling fountains.

MUSEO OSTIENSE

The museum (*opens at 9.30; the cafeteria and bookshop are behind it*) is housed in a building dating from 1500, originally used by officials from the salt works; it was given its Neoclassical façade in 1864. It displays finds from the excavations. Two rooms are devoted to the Oriental cults that flourished in Ostia. Chief among the exhibits is the **statue of Mithras slaying the bull**, from the Baths of Mithras (*see p. 538*), signed by Criton of Athens (1st century BC). Other important finds include **sculpture inspired by Greek art**, notably a statue of Diana dressed for the hunt, from the House of the Fortuna Annonaria, and two versions of *Eros Stringing his Bow*, modelled on an original by Lysippus (there is another version in the Capitoline Museums). They were found in the Nymphaeum of the Cupids. The *Cupid and Psyche* is a copy of a Hellenistic original; once again, a more famous version exists in the Capitoline Museums.

Roman sculpture ranges from the 1st century BC to the mid-2nd century AD. The headless male statue from the Temple of Hercules, nude except for the drapery over the left arm, is signed with the name of the donor, Cartilius Poplicola, whose sarcophagus is near Porta Marina (*see p. 540*). It is regarded as the best extant copy of the type known as the *Hero in Repose*. Also here are **imperial portraits** of Augustus, Trajan (from the School of Trajan), Hadrian, and Sabina his wife, the latter a particularly poignant statue of the solemn-faced empress as Venus Genetrix. Sabina was unloved by Hadrian and their marriage produced no children.

AROUND THE FORUM

The forum of an ancient Roman town stood at the point where the decumanus maximus crossed the cardo maximus. In Ostia the wide space once occupied by the forum is surrounded by noble ruins. At its north end rises the **Capitolium (14)**, once the city's most important temple, dedicated to the Capitioline Triad (Jupiter, Juno and Minerva) and reached by a wide flight of steps. Dating from the first half of the 2nd century, it had a porch of six fluted white marble columns. In the cella are niches and a plinth for the cult statues. During the early Middle Ages the temple was stripped of nearly all its marble revetment, but a magnificent slab of African marble is still in place on the threshold and a few surviving marble fragments have been placed to the east behind a colonnade, which defined the sacred area.

At the opposite end of the forum are the remains of the 1st-century **Temple of Roma and Augustus (15)**. Like the Capitolium it had six fluted marble columns across the front, but two side staircases. The cult statue of Roma showed her as Victory, dressed as an Amazon. Fragments of the pediment have been placed on a modern wall to the east. Behind this wall stretch the **Forum Baths (16)**, built in the 2nd century and restored in the 4th, when they were decorated with mosaics and cipollino columns; some of the columns have been re-erected. The frigidarium survives, together with a series of rooms warmed by hot air. Off the north side is the town **forica (17)** (public lavatory), its 22 seats extremely well preserved.

On the west side of the forum are the scant remains of the **Basilica (18)**. The side facing the forum had a portico of marble arches with a decorated frieze. Fragments of this and of the columns survive. Next to it are the ruins of the Tempio Rotondo or **Round Temple (19)**, dating from the 3rd century and probably an Augusteum, dedicated to the worship of the emperors. The peristyle was paved with mosaics and surrounded by marble-faced niches. It was reached by a flight of steps, which have been preserved: these led to the pronaos, which comprised a portico with brick piers faced with marble and with cipollino columns. In the cella are seven niches, three rectangular and four circular. Between the niches are column bases; to the right are the remains of a spiral staircase that led to the dome.

Opposite the Basilica, on the other side of the decumanus maximus, are the scant vestiges of the **Curia (20)**, or senate house. Next to it is the **House of the Lararium (21)**, named from the pretty niche, with inlaid red and yellow brick, that would once have contained images of the household gods.

Just beyond the forum to the west was the **Porta Occidentale**, the west gate of the original *castrum*. Square blocks of opus quadratum, remains of the ancient town walls, can be seen in Via degli Horrea Epagathiana, the road which leads right (north). Just beyond the traces of wall are the **Horrea Epagathiana et Epaphroditiana (22)**, warehouses in a remarkable state of preservation, including the bolt-holes in the doorways. They were built by two Eastern freedmen, Epagathus and Epaphroditus, whose names are preserved on a marble plaque above the entrance, a brick portal with two engaged columns supporting a pediment.

Opposite the horrea are the ruins of the **Baths of Buticosus (23)**, with a mosaic of the eponymous Buticosus, a bath attendant, naked and carrying a bucket. Traces of the hollow bricks that once lined the walls to allow hot air to circulate can still be seen and there is a fine mosaic of marine creatures, tritons and nereids in the caldarium. From here you can explore the ruins of Via della Foce, the Street of the River Mouth.

VIA DELLA FOCE

Off to the left of Via della Foce, a path leads to the **Mithraeum of the Painted Walls (24)**, built in the 2nd century into a house of the Republican period. In the rear wall is an altar on which the cult image of Mithras would have stood. On the north wall (hardly visible) are paintings of initiation rites. Further up Via della Foce to the right is a sacred area of three Republican temples. The central and largest is the hexastyle **Temple of Hercules (25)**, probably of the 1st century BC. The pronaos, which was paved in black and white chequered mosaic, is reached by a flight of nine steps as wide as the façade. The statue of the nude hero in repose, inscribed on the base with the name of the donor, Cartilius Poplicola, is a copy of the original now in the museum. To the left as you descend the steps is the base of a tetrastyle temple of the same date, its dedication unknown. Between the Temple of Hercules and Via della Foce is the **Temple of the Round Altar**, named after the circular marble altar with winged cupids found there. It was built in the early Republican era and rebuilt under the Empire.

Behind the sacred area is a street leading to the **House of Cupid and Psyche (26)**, an elegant *domus* from the 4th century: someone once lived a very gracious life here. In the centre is an atrium, with four rooms opening off to the left. One has a pavement of coloured marbles and a pretty fluted pedestal on which was found the marble *Cupid and Psyche* now in the museum. Opposite is a nymphaeum (sections of its lead pipe still survive) in a courtyard with columns and brick arches. At the far end is a large room gorgeously paved with opus sectile and preserving some marble wall cladding.

Further along Via della Foce is Via delle Terme di Mitra to the right. The **Baths of Mithras (27)** date from the time of Hadrian, though modified in later centuries. They had elaborate systems for heating and for pumping water. In the basement (entered from the back) is a long, narrow Mithraeum, in which was found the *Mithras Slaying the Bull* now in the museum (*copy in situ*).

On the left side of the main street are three blocks of small apartment houses; then follows a complex of two apartment blocks with baths between them. On the right is the **Hall of the Mensores (28)** (Grain Measurers), with a fine mosaic floor. Opposite, the **Insula of Serapis (29)** is named after a headless stucco figure of Serapis, an Egypto-Graeco-Roman grain deity, in an aedicule in the courtyard. The cavernous **Baths of the Seven Sages (30)** were so called from a satirical painting of the Seven Sages (statesmen and lawgivers of ancient Greece) found in one of the rooms, formerly a tavern. The baths have a round central frigidarium that was once domed and is paved with a beautiful mosaic with hunting scenes, including a bear, a lion and a tiger. In the next room, with a marble plunge pool, is a painting of *Venus Anadyomene* (Venus 'arisen from the sea'). A covered passage leads to the extensive and well-preserved **Insula**

of the Charioteers (31) ('Aurighi'), an apartment block which takes its name from two small paintings of rival charioteers in the arcade. It still has remains of its upper storey and the view of it from the top of the street is extremely picturesque.

THE CULT OF MITHRAS

The cult of Mithras was one of the most popular foreign cults to spread in the Roman Empire in the 2nd and 3rd centuries AD. Its origins were in Persia, where worship of the god is said to have been founded by the sage Zoroaster. Mithras was associated with the sun and with cattle-herding or stealing, and the most common representation of him, found in reliefs or statues in all Mithraic temples, shows him astride a large bull which he is stabbing in the neck.

There is a great deal of unresolved debate over how and why Mithraism spread from Persia, and the extent to which the Romans developed the cult for their own ends. In the Western Empire, Mithraism was especially popular among soldiers, slaves and ex-slaves. Women seem to have been excluded. Members met in small groups, up to 35, in sanctuaries which were designed to resemble caves, the traditional haunt of the god. At the eastern end there would be a relief or statue of Mithras, surrounded by symbols of constellations and two deities carrying torches. This was the 'light' end of the sanctuary, which contrasted with the 'dark' western end and made the point that this was a saviour god who brought the initiate from darkness into light. During ceremonies the initiates would recline on platforms along the side walls of the sanctuary and enjoy a ritual meal. Some 400 sanctuaries are known, a high proportion of them in Rome (35) and Ostia (15), which shows that the cult must have been very popular here. They are also found in army camps along the northern border of the Empire from Britain to the Danube.

In the Roman Empire the most important feature of Mithraism was its series of graded initiations, each of them associated with a planet. The highest grade was the 'Father'. Inscriptions show that there might be one or two 'Fathers' in each group and its status was such that it could be recorded on an initiate's tombstone. It has been

suggested that the disciplined ascent through the grades appealed especially to soldiers because the rise within the cult mirrored their ascent through the ranks to officer; and to slaves hoping to make a similar transition into freedom. C.F.

The seven grades of Mithraism, depicted by their symbols, at the Mithraeum of Felicissimus:

1) Raven: beaker and caduceus. Planet: Mercury;
2) Bridegroom: lamp (obliterated) and tiara. Planet: Venus;
3) Soldier: helmet, spear, leather pouch. Planet: Mars;
4) Lion: thunderbolts, sistrum, fire-shovel. Planet: Jupiter;
5) Persian: scythe, moon and star, dagger. Planet: Moon;
6) Heliodromos: torch, whip, crown with rays. Planet: Sun;
7) Father: Phrygian head-dress, sickle, staff. Planet: Saturn.

In Ostia, as elsewhere in the later Roman world, a variety of religious cults was permitted.
As well as temples dedicated to the deities of the Roman pantheon, there was a popular cult of the
emperors and a large number of cults from the East. There was also a Jewish community.
The mosaics above are, from left to right: emblem of Priapus from the House of Jove the Thunderer;
Solomon's Knot from the ruins of the synagogue; Christian symbols from the House of the Fish.

Further along Via della Foce, the **Trinacria Baths (32)**, from the time of Hadrian, preserve installations for heating and conducting the water as well as good mosaics. One is of a female head crowned with the three-legged emblem of Sicily, the trinacria. Another, in one of the warm rooms, baldly announces, '*Statio cunnulingiorum*', leaving a vivid picture of the goings-on in a Roman bath.

Via Serapeo is named after its Serapeum, whose priests perhaps lived in the adjoining **House of Bacchus and Ariadne (33)**, which has an exceptionally fine mosaic floor. At the other end of the street is the **Mithraeum of the Planta Pedis (34)**, its entrance decorated with a mosaic footprint.

From here you can make your way across the Cardo degli Aurighi and into the huge Case Giardino complex, and so on to explore the lower decumanus maximus.

THE LOWER DECUMANUS MAXIMUS

The **Case Giardino (35)**, at the lower end of the decumanus, is a huge domestic housing complex built during the time of Hadrian (2nd century). This is, in effect, a Roman housing estate—and a very comfortable one. Some of houses have fine painted decorations (*visitable on guided tours; see p. 532*). Two central blocks of apartments occupy the middle of the garden estate, with more housing enclosing it on all four sides. The complex was provided with its own fountains, three on the southeast and three on the northwest side (still well preserved).

The **Porta Marina** (Sea Gate) was an opening in the walls built by Sulla, remains of which can be seen. Just inside the gate is a tavern (probably of ill-repute), the **Caupona of Alexander and Helix (36)**, with a mosaic of two boxers bearing those names. The extension of the decumanus maximus beyond the gate, built in the time of Augustus, ran through an earlier cemetery. On this section on the left stood the **Sanctuary of the Bona Dea (37)**, a small tetrastyle temple dedicated to a goddess worshipped exclusively by women; the four column bases survive. Further on, a turning to the left (Via di Cartilio Poplicola) leads past the **tomb of C. Cartilius Poplicola (38)**, a prominent citizen of the 1st century BC. The surviving fragment of its decorative frieze shows a trireme with the helmeted head of a goddess. This and another tomb close by attest to the existence of a cemetery in the Republican era. The road ends at the **Porta Marina Baths (39)**, where a mosaic shows an athlete with a ball remarkably similar to a modern soccer ball.

Further out, between the sea and the ancient Via Severiana (on the southwest side of this street), is the most ancient **synagogue (40)** known from monumental remains. It was in continuous use from the 1st–5th centuries AD. Ritual carvings and poorly-preserved mosaics have been found; several Ionic columns have been re-erected.

From here you can either walk across the fields to the lower cardo maximus (*see below*), or return to Porta Marina for the lower decumanus maximus, which returns past the charming **Fontana a Lucerna (41)**. Beyond is the **School of Trajan (42)**, where a statue of the emperor was found. At the back of the complex is a marble-clad four-seater latrine. On the other side of the decumanus is the **School of the Shipwrights (43)**, with a temple. The arcade of the courtyard in front of the temple was evidently a marble store: unused and partly finished columns, bases and capitals have been found in it. The store appears to have belonged to Volusianus, a senator of the 4th century, as his name is carved on some of the column shafts. Adjoining is the **Christian basilica (44)**, an unpretentious structure with two aisles divided by columns and ending in apses. At the end of the street on the right are two **fish shops (45)** with superbly-preserved marble counters and a tank open onto the decumanus. Behind them is the macellum, or market-place.

THE LOWER CARDO MAXIMUS

Via del Tempio Rotondo leads to the south continuation of the cardo maximus. The area is rather overgrown but has some points of interest. On the right is the **House of Jove the Thunderer (46)** ('Giove Fulminatore'), a house of the Republican period remodelled in the 4th century, with a striking phallic 'doormat' mosaic. Symbols of Priapus were often put in entrances to ward off intruders. Further down on the same side is the well-preserved **Nymphaeum of the Cupids (47)**, in which were found the two copies of the *Eros* of Lysippus. The next building is the **House of the Columns (48)**. In the centre of the courtyard is a stone basin with back-to-back niches and short white marble columns; beyond is the large tablinum with its entrance between two columns. Opposite are the remains of the **Forum Latrines (49)**, occupying a triangular site. On the sidestreet to the right is the **House of the Fish (50)**, evidently a Christian house (the mosaic of a chalice and fish pictured opposite is here).

Further up the cardo, to the left, a ramp leads to the triangular **Campo della Magna Mater (51)**, once an important sacred area. At the far end is the base of the hexastyle Temple of Cybele. On the near left-hand corner, the Sanctuary of Attis has an apse flanked by telamones in the shape of fauns.

Opposite the ramp, from the cardo maximus, the **Semita dei Cippi** ('Alley of the Tombstones'; a couple survive) leads north. On the right you will pass, in succession: the **House of the Porch (52)** ('Domus del Protiro'), with a fine doorway and beyond it, a splendid nymphaeum (you can go down the steps to inspect it from underground); the **Baths of the Philosophers (53)**; and, on the corner, the **House of the Fortuna Annonaria (54)**, which has a tranquil garden, remains of an elaborate nymphaeum and an under-stair latrine still with its marble seat.

Soon after the **House of the Wrestlers (55)**, named from the mosaic which shows two pugilists, one having vanquished the other, turn right for the **Mithraeum of Felicissimus (56)**, with a mosaic pavement showing the grades of the Mithraic cult (*see box on p. 539*). Heading back towards the decumanus maximus, you pass a large **dyer's workshop (57)** (*fullonica*) with huge vats. Next to it is the **Seat of the Augustales (58)**, the headquarters of the priests of the imperial cult.

The exit is back along the decumanus maximus, in the same place as the entrance.

MEDIEVAL OSTIA

The medieval *borgo* of Ostia Antica, a fortified village whose walls are still standing, was founded by Gregory IV in 830 and given the name of Gregoriopolis. The walls enclose a tiny picturesque hamlet of russet-coloured houses beside the castle, bishop's palace and church. It is a superb example of a Renaissance fortified enclave.

The **castle** (*open for guided tours only on Sun at 11 or 12, and Thur at 11; free; closed at the time of writing; for updates, see ostiaantica.beniculturali.it*), built in 1483–6 by Baccio Pontelli for Julius II while he was still a cardinal, is a magnificent example of military architecture of its period. Key features include a remarkable spiral stone staircase used by the guards, an old oven, a bath house, and a corridor with casemates (cannon emplacements). A spiral ramp (designed for use by horses) leads up to the residential area, with traces of frescoes by the school of Baldassare Peruzzi. From the battlements and terrace there are views towards Fiumicino and the present site of the Tiber (which formerly flowed beneath the castle walls). An old fortified tower which predates the castle can be seen from here, and the site of a drawbridge which connected it to the main building.

The **church of Santa Aurea**, by Baccio Pontelli or Meo del Caprina, contains the body of the martyred St Aurea (d. 268) and, in a side chapel, a fragment of the gravestone of St Augustine's mother, St Monica (*see p. 209*), who died at Ostia in 387. The **Episcopio**, the bishop's palace, has fine monochrome frescoes on the first floor attributed to Baldassare Peruzzi (1508–13), inspired by Trajan's Column.

THE ARCHAEOLOGICAL AREA OF FIUMICINO

North of Ostia, between the Tiber and the coast, is a rectangle of marshy ground known as the Isola Sacra, the 'holy island'. It was made into an island by the cutting of the Fossa Traiana canal from the Port of Trajan (*see below*) to the sea. At its northwestern edge, a necropolis has been excavated, the Necropoli di Porto. Just beyond this, close to Fiumicino airport, are the remains of the harbours built by Claudius and Trajan. Public access to most of the area is restricted. Visiting is difficult without your own transport, and requires some determination. The main points of interest are outlined here.

NB: For all the sites mentioned below, the website is archeoroma.beniculturali.it. It is worth checking the information given here before you attempt to visit, as work is in progress and access details are subject to change.

NECROPOLI DI PORTO

On Via Monte Spinoncia/Via Pal Piccolo (parallel to the main airport highway). Visits by appointment on Thur, Sat and the first Sun of the month in the morning; third Sun of the month in the afternoon. T: 06 65 83 888 to book.

This was the necropolis of Portus, the settlement that grew up around the port of Claudius and the later port of Trajan. Only part of the site has been excavated as much of it is under cultivation, but some of the tombs have been restored. The tombs, which date from the 1st–4th centuries AD, flank the ancient road from Ostia to Portus, the Via Flavia Severiana.

Most of the burials are of merchants, artisans, craftsmen and sailors; there are no elaborate mausolea. The tombs, which have been preserved by the sand that covered them for centuries, are arranged in groups. They have—or had—barrel vaults of brick and masonry faced with stucco; some of them had gable roofs. Internally they are decorated with stuccoes, paintings and mosaics. Sarcophagi and urns in columbaria have been found, often in the same tomb, evidence of the simultaneous practices of burial and cremation. Nearly every tomb has a name inscribed over the door. The tombs of the wealthier citizens have sepulchral chambers with fanlights. Outside, by the door, are couches for funeral feasts. Terracotta reliefs have representations of the daily activities of the deceased.

Some of the tombs are like old-fashioned round-topped travelling trunks, and recall similar examples in North Africa. The poorest citizens buried their dead in the ground and marked the place with amphorae through which they poured libations; or they set up large tiles to form a peaked roof over the remains.

THE PORTS OF CLAUDIUS AND TRAJAN

Open by appointment from 9.30–1 on the first Sat and last Sun of the month. T: 06 65 29 192, archeoroma.beniculturali.it. Visitors are asked to congregate outside the Museo delle Navi at Via Alessandro Guidoni 35, from where it is a short drive (you need your own transport) to the site of the Port of Trajan (Via Portuense 2360, just under the airport highway flyover). The tour lasts approx. 3hrs.

The meeting point for the tour, at Via Alessandro Guidoni 35, almost within the confines of Fiumicino airport, is on the site once occupied by the **Port of Claudius**. The foundations of the north mole are still visible. The **Museo delle Navi Romane**, a purpose-built museum (*closed at the time of writing*) houses the remains of five Roman boats found at the entrance to the port. They include four flat-bottomed cargo ships or barges (*naves caudicariae*) which used to carry goods upstream to Rome (AD 300–400) and a fishing boat (1st century AD).

HISTORY OF THE PORTS

When the harbour of Ostia, already inadequate for its trade, began to silt up, Augustus planned a larger seaport. In AD 42 Claudius began operations. The work was completed in 54 by Nero, who issued commemorative coins stamped *Portus Augusti*. With an area of some 80 hectares and a wharf frontage of 800m, it was the most important commercial port in the Mediterranean, and was connected to the Tiber by a canal. Part of the site is now covered by the airport buildings and by the grassy fields near the museum, in which fragments of the quays and wharves can be seen. Still extant is part of the quay incorporating the form of Caligula's ship (104m by 20m), which brought from Egypt the obelisk now in St Peter's Square. The ship was sunk and used as the base of a huge four-storey lighthouse.

Even this harbour soon silted up, however. Moreover, it was in a very exposed site, right on the sea, vulnerable to storms. In AD 62 one such storm wrecked 200 ships as they lay at anchor. In 103 Trajan constructed an artificial hexagonal basin, the Port of Trajan, further inland to the south and better protected. It was connected to the Port of Claudius by a series of docks. Today most overseas traffic still reaches Rome here: the airport of Fiumicino could not have been constructed in a more appropriate spot.

TOUR OF THE PORTS

Via Portuensis was the ancient road which followed the right bank of the Tiber from Rome to the ports laid out by Claudius and Trajan. The sea has retreated some three or so kilometres west since then, and most of the area has dried out or been drained, but some of the old contours remain.

The tour begins in the Claudian area of the site, where **granaries** still retain parts of their old flooring, built up on brick stilts known as *suspensurae*, a device designed to minimise damp. From here visitors are taken along a short **colonnaded street**, with a double enfilade of chubby travertine columns, to see the site of the **Darsena**, Trajan's inner harbour. Today it is only a reed-filled marsh, but at one side the stone harbour wall can be seen. Analysis of the **warehouses** here has shown that those used for marble, the heaviest item to move, were—perfectly logically—placed closest to the dock. On the further side were warehouses that had possibly held grain, or some other commodity sensitive to damp, since the walls are coated in pozzolana, a waterproof cement made from a mixture of lime and volcanic ash.

The **channel** that once linked the old Port of Claudius with the hexagonal Port of Trajan is now completely grass-grown but still very flat and broad: it was wide enough for several ships to pass along it at once. At its far end, past more warehouses, is a narrower path, another former water channel linking the harbour complex with the Fossa Traiana, the canal that Trajan dug to link his port to the Tiber (it is now the Canale di Fiumicino and is still navigable).

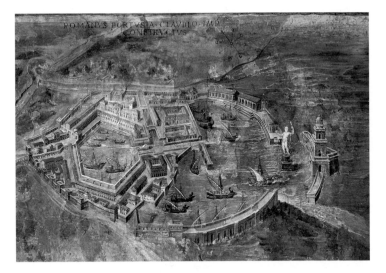

Depiction of the ports in the Gallery of Maps in the Vatican. The Port of Claudius is near the water, with its two curved moles jutting out to sea and the gigantic lighthouse between them. The hexagonal Port of Trajan lies further inland. The Fossa Traiana canal connects the sea and the Tiber.

The huge **hexagonal basin** (650m across), constructed with travertine blocks, is perfectly preserved. Part of it is flanked by warehouses of the Severan period, probably built during the reign of Antoninus Pius. There is a viewing platform but sadly the view from the ground is nothing compared to the sight of it that you have from the air, when flying to or from Fiumicino. This huge six-sided harbour has always been full of water. In the Middle Ages it was stocked with fish. It has been suggested that the hexagonal shape was chosen by Apollodorus of Damascus, the architect who designed the Markets of Trajan in the Imperial Fora, because the ripples caused by ships moving into it would create 'echo-waves' from the sides, which would meet the outgoing wave and effectively cancel it out.

Also shown are the ruins of the 4th–5th-century **Basilica of St Hippolytus**, patron saint of Portus in the early Christian era.

PORTO

The village of Porto, 2km from the airport on Via Portuense, takes its name from the ancient city of Portus, which grew up around the ports of Claudius and Trajan. Excavations of the area (the Portus Project) are currently underway. In 2009 a British team discovered the remains of an amphitheatre-shaped building and a fine marble head of a bearded man in a cap, conjecturally identified as Ulysses. For pictures and more information, see www.portusproject.org.

Tivoli & Hadrian's Villa

The busy little town of Tivoli, 31km east of Rome, is well worth visiting to see the lovely gardens of Villa d'Este and the magnificent ruins of Hadrian's Villa, one of the most important archaeological sites in all Italy.

Roman Tibur was built on the lower slopes of the Sabine Hills at the end of the valley of the Aniene river, which narrows at this point into a gorge and forms spectacular cascades. The location was cool and pleasant and by the end of the 1st century BC numerous wealthy Romans were coming to live or spend the summer here: Cassius, Sallust and Maecenas all had sumptuous villas in the town or nearby; Augustus and the poets Catullus, Propertius and Horace were frequent visitors. Trajan also favoured Tibur, but it reached its greatest fame when Hadrian chose it as his residence and built his remarkable villa on the outskirts, whose ruins still baffle scholars and archaeologists. Tibur was sacred to the cult of the Sibyl Albunea. The waters of the Aniene were carried to Rome by two aqueducts, the Anio Vetus and Anio Novus. Water is still the reason to visit Tivoli town, for the magnificent gardens of Villa d'Este with their abundant and ingenious fountains, and for the waterfalls that tumble down the dramatic cliff below the remains of the Sibyl's temple.

Getting there
There is no quick and easy way to get from Rome to Tivoli. It is possible to make the trip by taxi (but agree the fare first; it should cost a little but not excessively more than the fixed fare to Fiumicino). By public transport the trip is long and somewhat laborious, as follows:

Rome to Hadrian's Villa: *Metro line B to Ponte Mammolo (penultimate stop), from where you take the bus marked 'Tivoli' (run by COTRAL; ticket office one level down from where the bus leaves, or from the bar, also on the lower level). Ask the driver to let you off at the request stop called Villa Adriana (journey time c. 50mins, depending on the traffic). From here it is about 15mins' walk to the villa entrance: follow the brown signs.*

Rome to Tivoli: *Either take the bus as above and stay on it to Tivoli town centre, or take a train from Tiburtina station. Trains run c. every hour, and take about an hour. To get to Tivoli centre from the station, walk across the wooden bridge over the river.*

Between Tivoli and Hadrian's Villa: *The villa is about 5km from the town. The two are linked by bus no. 4 (run by CAT; services c. every 20mins), which runs from the villa into Tivoli (Piazza Garibaldi, right in the centre) and from Tivoli to the*

VILLA D'ESTE
Water spout, Viale delle Cento Fontane.

villa. Tickets from kiosks and tobacconists, and at Hadrian's Villa, from the ticket office. You can also call a taxi (T: 0774 317071 or 0774 334233).

Where to eat
The Hotel Adriano, just beside the entrance to Hadrian's Villa, is convenient for lunch (T: 0774 382235, hoteladriano.it). In Tivoli itself is the famous Ristorante Sibilla, perched above the Aniene valley. It has been a popular place to sit and admire the view since the mid-18th century (Via della Sibilla 50, T: 0774 335281, ristorantesibilla.com; closed Mon).

MAJOR SIGHTS OF TIVOLI TOWN

The road from Rome enters town from the southwest and ends at Largo Nazioni Unite/Piazza Garibaldi, a busy traffic hub (if you are coming by bus, this is where it will drop you). Above the bus stop rises a narrow triangular square (more an area of busy roads with trees between them) with an information kiosk where you can get a map of the town. At the top of the square is the imposing **Rocca Pia** (*closed to the public*), a castle built by Pius II (1458–64) to dominate the inhabitants. In the castle grounds are the remains of a 2nd-century Roman amphitheatre (its stone was used to build the castle).

Standing with the castle behind you, at the bottom end of the square, across the main road on the left, is the **Giardino Garibaldi**, with a splendid view of the open country below: almost due west is Rome, and to the southwest the Roman Campagna extends to the sea. At the right-hand end of these gardens is the open Piazza Garibaldi, diagonally across which to the right is the entrance to Villa d'Este.

VILLA D'ESTE

Open Tues–Sun 8.30–dusk. The water organ plays every two hours (at the time of writing at 10.30, 12.30, 2.30, 4.30, and also at 6.30 in summer). Pleasant café with tables outside overlooking the Fontana di Roma. T: 0774 332920, villadestetivoli.info.

The villa, formerly a Benedictine monastery, was appropriated as a residence for the governor of Tivoli. When the cultivated Cardinal Ippolito II d'Este, son of Lucrezia Borgia and friend of Ariosto, Tasso, Cellini and the musician Palestrina, became governor in 1550, he commissioned Pirro Ligorio to transform the monastery into a grand villa with elaborate gardens, in which water features played a prominent part. An underground conduit was constructed from the Aniene, to increase the water supply. The work was still incomplete by the time of the cardinal's death in 1572, and it was continued by his successor Cardinal Luigi d'Este, who employed Flaminio Ponzio after 1585.

Additions and restorations were carried out in the 17th century, in part by Bernini. In the 19th century the villa and gardens were neglected and all the Roman statues were sold. From 1865 to 1886, the year of his death, Franz Liszt lived in an apartment on the top floor: it is here that he composed his 'Les Jeux d'Eau à la Villa d'Este'. The villa passed to the Italian government in 1918. In 2000 the gardens and villa were restored.

THE GARDENS

The famous gardens, laid out on a series of terraces below the villa, are filled with the sound of water. The original vegetation included plane trees and elms. Evergreens were introduced in the 17th century, and sequoia and cedars were planted in the 19th. Near the top of the gardens, on the side overlooking the valley, is the elaborate **Fontana di Roma**, designed by Pirro Ligorio and executed by Curzio Maccarone. This has numerous fountains and sculptures including a model of the Tiber with an islet (representing the Isola Tiberina) in the form of a boat, on which is an obelisk, a seated statue of *Rome*, the wolf suckling Romulus and Remus, and miniature reproductions of the principal buildings of the ancient city. From here the **Viale delle Cento Fontane** leads right across the garden, parallel to the villa. It is skirted by a long narrow basin lined with a hundred jets of water, one of the most delightful features of the whole garden. Halfway along, look up to see the **Fontana del Bicchierone**, in the shape of a huge goblet, added in 1661 by Bernini. Below is the **Fontana dei Draghi** by Pirro Ligorio. This was probably intended as a homage to Gregory XIII (it reproduces the dragons in his coat of arms), who was a guest at the villa in 1572.

On the level below is the monumental **Fontana dell'Organo**, built around a water-operated organ (1568) in the centre of the niche (later protected by a little temple). On the other side of the gardens is the bizarre **Fontana della Civetta**, which once used water power to produce birdsong which was interrupted and silenced by the screech of an owl. It was begun in 1565 by Giovanni del Duca and finished by Raffaello Sangallo in 1569. The central huge **Fishponds** create beautiful and picturesque reflections. At the bottom of the gardens is a fountain in the form of the **Diana of Ephesus**.

TEMPLE OF THE SIBYL AND VILLA GREGORIANA

The Ristorante Sibilla occupies a site on the edge of what was the acropolis of ancient Tibur. In its garden (*also accessible from the side, without going through the restaurant*) are the remains of two ancient temples, one round and one square, perched on the cliff edge with dramatic views of the Aniene waterfalls. The older temple is the square one, c. 150 BC, built entirely of blocks of travertine. Its original dedication is unknown. The circular temple, which has a concrete core clad in travertine, was built about half a century later. Ten of its original 18 Corinthian columns survive, as well as some of the entablature. Known as the **Temple of the Sibyl** or Temple of Vesta, it was a favourite subject for artists in the 18th and 19th centuries, and inspired many a folly in English landscaped gardens of that time, as well as Sir John Soane's 'Tivoli Corner' section of the Bank of England building in London. It was originally assumed to have been dedicated to Vesta, or to the prophetess Albunea, whose cult developed here, this latter theory partly supported by Horace's description of the 'house of resounding Albunea' (*Ode VII, To Munatius Plancus*). Scholars now think that the temple may instead have been dedicated to Hercules, like the little circular temple in Rome's Forum Boarium (*see p. 251*).

Entered from just beside the temples is the park of the **Villa Gregoriana** (*open Tues–Sun 10–4; in April–mid-Oct until 6.30; closed Mon and open only by appointment in mid-Dec–Feb; T: 0774 332650*). Maintained by FAI, the Italian environment trust, it provides spectacular views of the waterfalls on the other side of the valley.

HADRIAN'S VILLA

The Villa of Hadrian, about 5km southwest of Tivoli (*Largo Marguerite Yourcenar 1; open daily 9–dusk; T: 0774 530203, villaadriana.beniculturali.it; for directions, see p. 546*) was the largest and richest imperial villa in the Roman Empire. Hadrian became emperor on the death of Trajan in 117, and began the villa the following year, completing it ten years later. It is known that he prided himself on his abilities as an architect, and it is assumed that this remarkably original complex was designed at least in part by him. He seems to have used it as a residence, particularly in the summer.

HISTORY OF HADRIAN'S VILLA

Hadrian elected to build his magnificent estate on low-lying land some way distant of the resort town of Tibur. The land was owned by his wife, the empress Sabina, which may have influenced his choice, though it has also been suggested that he wished to keep himself apart from his courtiers, many of whom owned villas in the hills nearby.

A villa had existed on this site since the 1st century BC and some of its structures were retained in Hadrian's complex. Most of the Hadrianic buildings, however, were entirely new, inspired by monuments and landscapes which the emperor had seen during his travels. He recreated the Canopus of the Nile Delta, for example; the Vale of Tempe in Thessaly and the *Aphrodite* of Cnidos in Asia Minor. Hadrian's successors enlarged the villa, but Constantine is supposed to have stolen some elements to decorate Byzantium. In the Middle Ages the site was plundered, and it later became a quarry for builders and lime-burners.

The first excavations were ordered by Pope Alexander VI and Cardinal Alessandro Farnese. After taking up residence in Tivoli in 1550, Cardinal Ippolito II d'Este employed Pirro Ligorio to continue excavations, and he took many of the finds to decorate his villa. Piranesi drew a plan of the site, and made engravings of the buildings and sculptures (now in the Calcografia Nazionale in Rome; *see p. 568*). In 1870 the Italian government acquired most of the site and systematic excavations were begun (still far from complete). The works of art discovered in the villa (more than 260) are scattered in museums all over Europe as well as in Rome.

LAYOUT OF THE VILLA

The complex occupies 120 hectares (of which 40 can be visited), with living quarters, meeting halls, dining rooms, libraries and a theatre, as well as functional rooms (baths, storage rooms and lodgings for the praetorian guards and servants) interspersed with gardens, open vistas and shaded walks. Identifications should however be treated with caution. Excavations and restorations are still in progress and the function of many of the buildings is still only conjectural. New theories are being advanced as excavations continue; scholars are forced to admit that they still know very little about how this extraordinary complex was actually used.

From the ticket entrance, a tarmac drive leads uphill to a wide car park, where a small building houses a very useful scale model of the villa. The entrance to the ruins is just beyond, through the massive north wall of the Pecile.

(1) Pecile: The Pecile was traditionally thought to have been inspired by the Stoa Poikile ('Painted Porch') in the Athens agora, famous for its paintings and for its association with the Stoic philosophers. Hadrian's version is a rectangular peristyle (232m by 97m) with the ends slightly curved, similar to a Greek gymnasium. The roofed colonnades provided a shaded or sheltered place for exercise: they were used for walking after meals, as an aid to digestion. The central pool has been restored.

(2) Philosophers' Hall: At the northeast angle of the Pecile, a few steps lead up to the so-called Philosophers' Hall, with an apse with seven niches for statues, perhaps of philosophers or of members of the imperial family. This is thought to have been a large throne room or auditorium, where the emperor held audiences and met in council with court dignitaries (though this function has also been ascribed to the Hall of the Doric Pilasters; *see below*).

(3) Maritime Theatre: This interesting circular building was almost certainly a private retreat for the emperor, where he could be totally isolated. A circular moat (3.5m broad), lined with Luni marble, encloses an island on which stands a building complex of intricate design, a symmetrical interplay of curved and straight lines, forming a series of rooms used as living quarters and baths. It could only be reached by two small wooden (removable) bridges. It is thought that Hadrian was directly involved in the design of this space.

(4) Heliocaminus Baths: Once assumed to have been a sun room, hence the name, this is now identified as part of the villa's earliest suite of baths (AD 118–25). They face southwest, to maximise the amount of sun they catch, and their roofs were carefully planned so as not to cast the hot rooms in shadow.

(5) Library Court: The buildings here are some of the earliest, retained from the first Republican villa. The courtyard itself is now a secluded olive plantation, as yet unexcavated. Off it to the north are remains of two rooms once identified as libraries but now thought to have belonged to a nymphaeum. The cryptoporticus on the opposite side was used by Hadrian as a substructure for his Great Peristyle

(6) Hospitalia: This interesting set of rooms closes the Library Court to the northeast. The Hospitalia was a residential wing, probably used by high-ranking staff. Five small cubicula are arranged on either side of a wide corridor. Rectangular alcoves indicate space for the beds (three in each room). Lighting was provided by the high openings. The rooms are decorated with well-preserved black and white mosaics, both geometric and floral. The simpler patterns are in the alcoves where the beds would have been. Although very well preserved, the materials used are not as fine as in other areas of the villa, which is why scholars believe this would have been a guest house or even the quarters of the imperial guard. At the end of the corridor is a hall, perhaps used as a shrine to the imperial cult.

Triclinium and Belvedere: From the Hospitalia, steps lead down to a **triclinium (7)**, with some capitals with a lotus motif and a mosaic floor. To the right is a long corridor with oblique openings in the vault, to allow the light of midday to enter. This leads to the **Belvedere (8)**, which overlooks a valley with a stream, which is thought to have been landscaped by Hadrian to recreate the Vale of Tempe in Thessaly, famed for its beauty.

(9) Great Peristyle: This huge area comprises the first phase of Hadrian's rebuilding. A central peristyle overlooking the Library Court was surrounded by living and reception rooms, including a private library, a nymphaeum, a summer triclinium and a basilican hall divided internally by colonnades, possibly used for meetings.

(10) Hall of the Doric Pilasters: This once magnificent space was in fact not a hall at all, but a peristyle court surrounded on four sides by a covered colonnade. This was supported by fluted Doric pillars with a fine Greek-style entablature. The function of the space is uncertain.

Some scholars have suggested that it was a throne room or that it was used for important gatherings and consultations.

(11) Piazza d'Oro: This is perhaps the most extraordinary area of the villa, a vast space once occupied by a colonnaded courtyard. It was named 'Piazza d'Oro' because excavations here yielded such rich finds. Remains of its highly original entrance vestibule, octagonal with alternating curved and straight sides, survive. It was flanked by richly decorated exedrae. The colonnade around the central court was formed of alternate columns of cipollino and granite in two rows. The east side would have commanded lovely views of the 'Vale of Tempe'. At the far end are remains of an elaborate nymphaeum, probably used for banquets—yet another space tentatively identified as a summer triclinium.

(12) Firemen's Barracks: These were almost certainly not barracks but a large storehouse and staff quarters, with internal rooms on two floors linked by a balcony overlooking a central courtyard. At the back are the ruins of a guardhouse and communal latrines.

(13) Peschiera: This large tank, once filled with water, was probably not a fishpond as its name suggests but an ornamental pool attached to Hadrian's living quarters. It had a portico of fluted Composite columns and today commands views of Tivoli on the hill beyond. It leads into a series of rooms considered to be at the residential heart of the villa. The upper floors were supplied with heating systems and thus could be used in winter. A one-person latrine, built into a wall niche, survives.

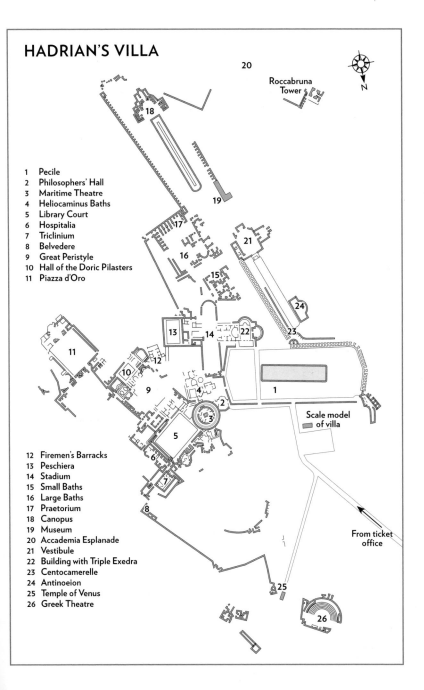

HADRIAN'S VILLA

20

Roccabruna Tower

N

1 Pecile
2 Philosophers' Hall
3 Maritime Theatre
4 Heliocaminus Baths
5 Library Court
6 Hospitalia
7 Triclinium
8 Belvedere
9 Great Peristyle
10 Hall of the Doric Pilasters
11 Piazza d'Oro

12 Firemen's Barracks
13 Peschiera
14 Stadium
15 Small Baths
16 Large Baths
17 Praetorium
18 Canopus
19 Museum
20 Accademia Esplanade
21 Vestibule
22 Building with Triple Exedra
23 Centocamerelle
24 Antinoeion
25 Temple of Venus
26 Greek Theatre

Scale model of villa

From ticket office

THE EMPEROR HADRIAN

Hadrian (ruled 117–38) remains one of the most intriguing of all the Roman emperors, a man of immense culture and intellectual sophistication, a trained soldier with realistic and far-seeing strategies for the Empire, but ultimately unfathomable as a personality, even by his intimates.

Hadrian's origins were Spanish and he rose through the imperial system as the protégé of the highly successful emperor Trajan (another Spaniard), whose great-niece Sabina he married. On Trajan's death in Cilicia in 117 Hadrian announced that he was the emperor's designated successor and quickly seized control. Back in Rome, the senators were shocked—but Hadrian had legions and they did not.

The reign began with some important decisions. Hadrian had noted how Trajan's conquests in the East had left him vulnerable to unrest and rebellion in the provinces behind him. The Empire was simply too big and further expansion could not be risked. Its frontiers needed to be consolidated and made permanent. Hadrian's Wall in northern Britain (AD 121) is a symbol of this fresh approach. The new policy left the legions with a diminished role but Hadrian was a stickler for keeping them in good training and this paid off when barbarian raids on the frontiers began again later in the century. Within the Empire a major Jewish revolt led by the 'messiah' Bar Kokhba was crushed with much brutality in 135.

No emperor travelled more than Hadrian and he was lavish in his patronage of cities he visited. The Greek world was always his favourite, and he created a festival of the ancient Greek cities that met in the enormous Temple of Zeus that he completed in Athens. He presided as *Panhellenios*, leader of 'all the Hellenes'.

Hadrian's marriage was loveless, but he had a favourite, the handsome youth Antinous, whose relationship with his master echoed those between older men and boys in Classical Athens. In 130 Antinous drowned in the Nile. It might have been suicide under the pressures of the emperor's attention, or possibly an accident. Whatever the truth, Hadrian was hysterical in his grief. He founded a city in the boy's memory and ordered that Antinous be deified. Statues of the beautiful boy-god were set up throughout the Empire.

Despite his initial unpopularity in Rome, Hadrian did not neglect the city. He built an enormous temple to Venus and Roma close to the Forum (*see p. 86*), and rebuilt the Pantheon, the temple to all the gods. Then he began his mausoleum in the fields north of the Tiber, where his remains were buried in 138. It survives today as the Castel Sant'Angelo (*see p. 408*).

A fascinating personal detail about Hadrian has come from an examination of his ears, which are always sculpted with creases (*see bust on p. 54*). These have been linked to signs of coronary artery disease and suggest that this may have been the cause of his death. As he faltered he appointed an excellent successor in the shape of Antoninus Pius, whose reign (138–61) is often seen as marking the most stable period in the entire history of the Empire. C.F.

(14) Stadium: The imperial residence commands a very fine view of the Stadium, a part of the villa named from its shape, though probably not a stadium at all, but instead a rectangular area of garden, with flowerbeds and pools.

The Baths: The so-called **Small Baths (15)** were luxuriously appointed and highly original in design, with an interplay of curved and flat walls. They may have been reserved for the emperor, though there is no consensus among scholars as to why two sets of baths were constructed so close together. The **Large Baths (16)**, on a more traditional design, include well-preserved remains of the large apsidal frigidarium with, beyond it, a circular hall identified conjecturally as a laconicum or sauna.

(17) Praetorium: Once believed to have been the quarters of the imperial guard, this is now thought more likely to have accommodated slaves or stores. It functions partly as a substructure to support the hillside behind it.

(18) Canopus: The celebrated Canopus was designed to imitate the canal which linked the city of Alexandria to Canopus on the Nile Delta, site of a sanctuary of Serapis. Reproductions of statues found on the site have been set up around the edge of the pool, between marble columns surmounted by an epistyle arched over alternate pillars. Along the west side are reproductions of colossal caryatids and telamones (the originals were found in the pool in the 1950s). At the south end is the so-called **Serapeum**, a monumental triclinium with a segmental semi-dome, formerly covered with mosaics, above a semicircular banquet-ing table (reconstructed) from which the diners had a scenic view of the Canopus. The nocturnal dinners held here were much talked-about. Segmental domes were a famous feature of Hadrian's Villa: the gifted architect of Hadrian's predecessor Trajan, Apollodorus of Damascus, scornfully likened them to pumpkins.

The Canopus may have been built by Hadrian in honour of Antinous (*see p. 554*). Many sculptures found at the site (including the *Antinous as Osiris*) are in the Capitoline and Vatican museums. Others are kept in the museum here.

(19) Museum: Open only for exhibitions—a pity as there are some fine objects here, all of them finds from excavations. The statues include the *Venus* from the Temple of Venus, and from the Canopus two *Wounded Amazons*, one a mutilated copy of a Polyclitan original, the other a fine replica of the famous original by Pheidias (*see p. 453*); *Hermes* (known as *Ares*) from a mid-5th-century original; a crocodile and the four marble Caryatids (modelled on the 5th-century originals on the Erechtheion at Athens).

(20) Accademia Esplanade: The area is so called because it may have been inspired by the grove of the Academy in Athens. It is reached by the path that leads past the museum. It consisted of a complex of buildings which some scholars identify as a secondary palace or as Hadrian's 'secret garden'. The group included a circular hall, known as the **Temple of Apollo**, and the remains of three rooms with delicate stucco ornamentation. Further southeast are the ruins of an odeion, with the imperial box in the centre of the cavea. To the east a path descends to a hollow (150m long),

HADRIAN'S VILLA
Cast of the Roman copy of the *Aphrodite of Cnidos* by Praxiteles, in the ruins of the Temple of Venus.

hewn in the tufa, which leads to a semi-circular vestibule (once perhaps guarded by an image of Cerberus). This was the **'Entrance to Hades'**, represented by a quadrangle of four subterranean corridors. Smaller tunnels connected it with other parts of the villa. At the far end of the esplanade (now an olive grove) are the remains of the **Roccabruna Tower**, perhaps used as a belvedere.

(21) Vestibule: This part of villa remains unexplained. It has been suggested that it was a palaestra, or possibly a lararium.

(22) Building with Triple Exedra: A (?)banqueting hall with three exedrae is closed on its fourth side by a garden surrounded by porticoes and with a large fountain.

(23) Centocamerelle: Multiple small rooms on several floors occupy the substructres of the Pecile. The rooms did not interconnect but were linked by external balconies. Those on the upper floors were probably used as staff quarters while stables might have occupied the ground floor.

(24) Atinoeion: The remains of an Egyptian-style shrine planned by Hadrian in memory of Antinous were unearthed in 2002–5.

(25) Temple of Venus and Greek Theatre: The path that leads towards the exit passes the small **Temple of Venus**, modelled on the temple at Cnidos on the coast of modern Turkey. Venus was a goddess particularly venerated by Hadrian. The original of the Cnidian-type *Venus* is in the site museum; a copy has been placed *in situ*. Just before the exit are the remains of the **Greek Theatre (26)**.

Appendix

These buildings and monuments (listed alphabetically in categories) are described in brief since they are either not open regularly, are difficult of access, or are outside the areas covered in the guide. If the monument itself is not marked on the maps in this guide, the street name will be. Some of the monuments can be visited by appointment (contact details are given).

ARCHAEOLOGICAL REMAINS

Aqueduct of Nero

Map p. 649, B3. Via Statilia.
A fine series of arches survives of the extension to the Aqua Claudia built by Nero to provide water for his constructions on the Palatine and Oppian hills. Some arches of the Aqua Claudia, restored to carry the Aqua Marcia (1923), can also be seen here.

Arch of Gallienus

Map p. 649, A2. Via di San Vito.
This is the central arch of a triple gate, on the site of the Porta Esquilina of the Servian Wall. It was erected in the time of Augustus and then in AD 262 rededicated (by the city prefect Aurelius Victor) in honour of the emperor Gallienus and his learned consort Cornelia Salonina. Gallienus and Cornelia were both murdered six years later.

Auditorium of Maecenas

Map p. 649, A2. Largo Leopardi. 060608.it.
Despite its name, this is thought to have been a nymphaeum in the Gardens of Maecenas, built in the Augustan period. The unusual apse has tiered seats in a semicircle. Although restored, the traces of red landscape paintings in the apse and wall niches have all but disappeared.

The building is adjoined by a stump of the Servian Wall. Benches in the public square outside have mosaic copies of motifs from the surviving paintings, e.g. birds in flight.

Basilica di Porta Maggiore

Map p. 649, B2. On Via Prenestina, diagonally opposite Porta Maggiore (cross the tramlines and the road). Closed indefinitely for restoration; see archeoroma.beniculturali.it.
This is a remarkable and very well preserved building of the 1st century AD which was unearthed under the railway in 1917. It has the rudimentary form of a cult building, with a central porch, an apse at the east end, a nave and two arched aisles with no clerestory. The ceiling and walls are covered with stuccoes representing landscapes, mythological subjects, and scenes of early childhood; the painting in the apse is thought to depict the suicide of Sappho. This has led some scholars to suggest that the basilica may have been used by a mystical sect, perhaps the Pythagoreans. Others believe it was a funerary hall. Research continues.

Baths of Trajan

Map p. 655, E3. Via delle Terme di Traiano (Parco di Colle Oppio).

These baths were built over Nero's Domus Aurea on the Oppian hill. Traces of them can be seen in the park. Beneath a building thought to have been a library (*not yet open to the public*) a fascinating Roman fresco of a city was discovered in 1998 and two mosaics of satyrs gathering grapes and poets or philosophers received by the Muses. A reservoir which supplied water to the baths called the **Sette Sale** (*entrance at Via Terme di Traiano 2; for admission, see sovraintendenzaroma.it*) also survives: this is a remarkable large vaulted building divided into nine compartments for the collecting tanks. The famous sculpture of the *Laocoön*, now in the Vatican museums (*see p. 454*), was discovered in 1506 in a vineyard nearby.

Castro Pretorio

Map p. 648, A4. Viale Castro Pretorio.
This huge site was the barracks of the Praetorian Guard. The *Praetoriae Cohortes*, or emperor's personal bodyguard, originally nine or ten cohorts (9,000–10,000 men), were instituted by Augustus and concentrated into a permanent camp here by Sejanus, minister of Tiberius, in AD 23; some portions of his building survive. In later Imperial times the Praetorian Guard acquired undue influence in the conduct of affairs of state. Many an emperor had to bribe them on his accession with a 'donative'. On one occasion, after the death of Pertinax in 193, they put up the Roman Empire itself for sale by auction; it was bought by Didius Julianus, who enjoyed his purchase for 66 days. Centuries later the Castro Pretorio passed into the hands of the Jesuits, who renamed it Macao after their most successful foreign mission. The site is now partly occupied by the Biblioteca Nazionale, but the Italian Army's logistics division is here, proud to be on the oldest barracks in the world still in military use.

Columbarium of Pomponius Hylas

Map p. 653, D3. Via di Porta Latina (Parco degli Scipioni). Admission by prior arrangement for groups only (max. 7); T: 060608.
This is an extremely well-preserved underground sepulchre. The steep original staircase, with a small mosaic inscription giving the name of the founder and his wife, Pomponia Vitalis, leads down to the 1st-century burial chamber, which preserves its niches and funerary urns as well as stucco and painting decoration.

Roman Fire Station

Map p. 654, B3. Via della VII Coorte 9.
The remains of this fire station or guardroom were discovered during excavations in 1865–6. At the time of Augustus the fire brigade in Rome was organised into seven detachments to protect the city. Interesting graffiti referring to reigning emperors, from Septimius Severus to Gordian III, and a bath or nymphaeum survive. Remains of the exterior can be seen in Via di Monte Fiore.

Gardens of Sallust

Map p. 652, D3. Piazza Sallustio.
The *Horti Sallustiani*, laid out in 40 BC and once owned by Julius Caesar, received their name from the historian Gaius Sallustius Crispus, who lavished the wealth he had accumulated during his African governorship on embellishing them. All that remains of them today are fragments of a villa which once stood in their midst. Here, too, can be seen the foundations of the Trinità dei Monti obelisk, showing where it stood in the Middle Ages.

Insula del Vicus Caprarius

Vicolo del Puttarello 25, east of Piazza Trevi (map p. 654, C1). Open Wed–Fri 11–5.30, weekends 11–7. For information,

see romasotterranea.it/insula-del-vicus-caprarius.html.
During restoration work on a cinema in the 1990s, excavations brought to light Roman houses of the Imperial era under the present commercial premises. The building occupied the site between Via di San Vincenzo (the ancient Vicus Caprarius) and Via del Lavatore. An *insula,* with its walls still some 8m high, was converted into a residence in the 4th century. A large water cistern was also found, probably connected to the Aqua Virgo, and later medieval constructions. The finds on display include 16 amphorae (thought to have been used to store oil).

Ipogeo degli Aureli

Map p. 649, B3. Near Via Luzzatti.
This early Christian tomb, which belonged to the freedmen of the *gens* Aurelia, has mosaics and well-preserved wall-paintings (AD 200–50), suggesting a mixture of Christian and gnostic beliefs. It was discovered in 1919.

Ponte Milvio

Map p. 647. Via Flaminia.
This was the Ponte Molle (*Pons Milvius*), built by the censor Marcus Aemilius Scaurus in 109 BC, which once carried the Via Flaminia over the Tiber (it is now used only by pedestrians). It was here that Cicero captured the emissaries of the Allobroges in 63 BC during the Catiline conspiracy; but it is most famous as the scene of the battle between Constantine and his co-emperor Maxentius on 28th October 312. Before the battle Constantine is said to have had a vision of the Cross when he successfully ambushed Maxentius here and drove them backwards to drown in the Tiber, he ascribed his victory to Christ. This has therefore always been considered one of the decisive battles in European history.

The bridge was remodelled in the 15th century by Nicholas V, who added the watchtowers, and it was restored in 1805 by Pius VII, who commissioned Giuseppe Valadier to erect the triumphal arch at the entrance. Blown up in 1849 by Garibaldi to arrest the advance of the French, it was again restored in 1850 by Pius IX.

The 2006 film of the novel *Ho voglia di te* sparked a worldwide craze for attaching padlocks to bridges. In 2012 the Roman authorities had the clotted mass of locks removed from the parapets here.

Porta Tiburtina

Map p. 649, B2. Viale di Porta Tiburtina.
A gate in the Aurelian Walls built by Augustus and restored by Honorius in 403. The triple attic carried the waters of the Aquae Marcia, Tepula and Julia (*see p. 529*). There are more remains of ancient aqueducts nearby in Piazza Guglielmo Pepe and Piazzale Sisto V, where an arch was built out of a section of the Aurelian Walls by Pius V and Sixtus V at the end of the 16th century to carry the waters of the Acqua Felice.

Septizodium

This was one of the most famous buildings on the Palatine (*its position is marked on the plan on p. 97*). Its immense three-tiered façade, some 90m long, was divided vertically into seven zones (hence its name), the number corresponding either to that of the known planets or to the days of the week. Built by Septimius Severus in AD 203, this monumental building, richly-decorated with statues, was intended to impress visitors to Rome arriving by the Via Appia. During a conclave in 1241, at a time of a crisis between the papacy and the Holy Roman Emperor Frederick II, Matteo Orsini, a Roman baron who had taken control of the government of the city, imprisoned twelve cardinals here. He forced them to elect Pope Celestine IV, but the new pope died, as did three of the cardinals as a result of their confinement. The Septizodium was often drawn by Renaissance artists, but was finally deemed in danger of collapse and demolished by Domenico Fontana, by order of Sixtus VI, in 1588–9. The huge quantity of columns, blocks of marble and travertine was reused in various buildings in the city. Sixtus had Carlo Maderno insert some of the exquisite marble panels into his sumptuous funerary chapel in Santa Maria Maggiore, where they can still be seen, wonderfully preserved (*see p. 304*). Recent excavations have revealed the building's unusual plan.

Servian Wall

The best-preserved fragment of the Servian Wall, with its massive blocks of tufa, can be seen in front of Termini station (*map p. 655, F1*). It was traditionally attributed to Servius Tullius, sixth king of Rome, but probably dates from about 378 BC, although sections of an earlier earthen bank (*agger*), which may be the work of Servius, have been identified. It was some 11km long with twelve gates (*see map on p. 656*). Only a few other fragments remain of this very ancient wall: in the garden of the Acquario Romano in Via Rattazzi (*map p. 649, A1*); one of its gates, the Porta Esquilina, on the site of the Arch of Gallienus and more nearby outside the Auditorium of Maecenas (*map p. 649, A2*). There are more extensive remains of it much further south (dating from a repair in around 87 BC) in Piazza Albania off Viale Aventino (*map p. 653, A2*). The Porta Celimontana in these walls survives in part close to Porta San Giovanni near St John Lateran.

Temple of Minerva Medica

Map p. 649, B2. Via Giolitti.
This large, ten-sided domed hall is a remarkable survival from the 4th century. It was probably the nymphaeum of the Gardens of Licinius but was given its present name after the discovery inside it of a statue of Minerva with a serpent, which probably occupied one of the nine niches in its walls. The cupola, which collapsed in 1828, served as a model for many later buildings. The hall is now surrounded by ugly buildings but it is conspicuous on the approach to Rome by train, just before you reach Termini station.

Tomb of the Scipios

Map p. 653, D3. Via di Porta San Sebastiano 9. Admission by prior arrangement for groups only (max. 12); T: 060608.
The tomb, one of the first to be built on the Via Appia, was discovered in 1780. It was built for Lucius Cornelius Scipio Barbatus, consul in 298 BC, and great-grandfather of Scipio Africanus. Many other members of the *gens* Cornelia were buried here, up until the mid-2nd century BC (the sarcophagus of Scipio Barbatus and the funerary inscriptions found here are now in the Vatican; *see p. 454*). Beside the tomb, an open gate leads into a peaceful little public park called the Parco degli Scipioni (in which is the Columbarium of Pomponius Hylas; *see p. 558*).

Trophies of Marius

Map p. 649, A2. Piazza Vittorio Emanuele II.
Despite the name, these are in fact the impressive ruins of a fountain dating from the time of Alexander Severus, and formerly the terminus of an aqueduct (either the Aqua Claudia or the Anio Novus). The so-called Trophies of Marius themselves were removed from here to the balustrade of Piazza del Campidoglio in the 16th century. Also in the piazza (protected by a fence) is the curious **Porta Magica** or Porta Ermetica, with an alchemist's prescription

for making gold, dating from 1680. This was moved here in the 20th century from the villa of Massimiliano Palombara. The huge piazza itself, its porticoes laid out in 1871 by Gaetano Koch, is planted with palms and plane trees, cedars and oleanders. The gardens have been redesigned in recent years (but are very poorly kept). Up until 2001 there was a daily food market in the piazza, noted for its abundance of North African, Middle Eastern and Chinese products, but this has been moved to a covered building (a former barracks) nearby (*open in the mornings*). However, the area, with its crowded streets, is still full of multi-ethnic shops and restaurants.

CHURCHES AND MAUSOLEA

Most of the churches listed below are closed, or only open for a single weekly service (usually on Sun). Otherwise opening times are given.

Sant'Agata dei Goti

Map p. 655, D2. Via Mazzarino. Admission sometimes granted on request at no. 16.
Built by an Arian community of Goths in 462–70, its Byzantine plan remains, with antique columns and decorative capitals with pulvins, despite heavy-handed restoration in the 20th century. In the apse is a well-preserved 12th–13th-century Cosmatesque tabernacle. The long inscription in Greek on the west wall marks the burial place of Janus Lascaris (1445–1535), a scholar who worked for Lorenzo the Magnificent in Florence, in the courts of France, and for Leo X in Rome. The picturesque 17th-century court is hung with ivy. The original fabric of the building can be seen on leaving the church by the south door.

Sant'Anastasia

Map p. 654, C4. Via di San Teodoro.
Founded in 492 and restored several times. The Classical façade is by the little-known architect Luigi Arrigucci. Inside, under the high altar, is a recumbent statue of St Anastasia, begun by the minor artist Francesco Aprile and finished by the better-known Ercole Ferrata. Beneath the church are remains of an Imperial-era Roman building.

Sant'Andrea in Via Flaminia

Just beyond map p. 652, A1. Via Flaminia and Viale Tiziano.
A graceful little circular church by Vignola (1550–5), erected by Julius III to commemorate his deliverance from Charles V's soldiers while he was a cardinal.

Sant'Antonio Abate

Map p. 655, F2. Via Carlo Alberto.
The doorway is attributed to the Vassalletto family (1262–6), but the interior was redesigned around 1730. The liturgy of the services follows the Russian Byzantine rite.

Sant'Antonio dei Portoghesi

Map p. 654, B1. Via dei Portoghesi.
Dating from the 17th century, the ornate façade behind a pretty balustrade preserves a delightful 15th-century doorway and tower. The good Baroque interior has a painting of the *Madonna and Saints* by Antoniazzo Romano over the first north altar.

Santa Bibiana

Map p. 649, B2. Via Giovanni Giolitti.
A 5th-century church rebuilt by Bernini in 1625—his first architectural work—when the remains of St Bibiana (Vivian) were found here. It contains Bernini's expressive statue

of the saint (in an aedicule above the altar), which was his first commission for a church sculpture. The sensual figure of the martyr, eyes raised to heaven, has the characteristics which were to become typical of the highly-charged religious fervour of the Counter-Reformation. Eight of the church's columns are from pagan temples, including, to the left of the entrance, that at which St Bibiana was supposedly flogged to death. On the architrave (on the left) are frescoes by Pietro da Cortona, early works in the same spirit as Bernini's statue (those on the right are by his contemporary Agostino Ciampelli).

Santa Caterina da Siena (a Magnanapoli)

Map p. 655, D2. Largo Magnanapoli.
Approached by a double staircase, the façade was designed by Giovanni Battista Soria in 1641. The 17th-century high altarpiece of the *Ecstasy of St Teresa* is by Melchiorre Caffà.

San Cesareo

Map p. 653, C2. Via di Porta San Sebastiano. Open Sat 10–4, Sun 10–12; closed Aug.
The church, properly San Cesareo in Palatio, was rebuilt at the end of the 16th century, with a façade attributed to Giacomo della Porta. Inside is some fine Cosmati work (similar to that in Santi Nereo ed Achilleo; *see p. 565*), including the high altar, the bishop's throne, the transennae, the candelabrum, the ambo and the altar fronts. The two angels beneath the high altar are probably from a 15th-century tomb. The beautiful wooden ceiling, gilded on a blue ground, bears the arms of the Aldobrandini pope Clement VIII, who restored the church in 1600. The apse mosaic of the *Eternal Father* was designed by Cavaliere d'Arpino, who also painted the frescoes. The baldacchino is from the time of Clement VIII. Below the church (*see 060608.it*) is a large black-and-white mosaic of the 2nd

century AD. The fantastic sea-monsters, animals and figures may have decorated the floor of Roman baths. When the future Pope John Paul II was first made a cardinal, this was his titular church.

Cristo Re

Map p. 647. Viale Giuseppe Mazzini.
Built in 1930 by Marcello Piacentini, with a sculpture by Arturo Martini over the central door. It contains frescoes by Achille Funi.

Santi Domenico e Sisto

Map p. 655, D2. Via Panisperna. Admission sometimes granted on request at the college next door (bell by the gate).
The tall façade is preceded by a theatrical staircase (1654) by Vincenzo della Greca. Inside is a huge fresco (1674–5) by the Bolognese painter Domenico Canuti, a sculptured *Noli me Tangere* by Antonio Raggi, and a *Madonna and Child* thought to be an early work by Antoniazzo Romano.

Sant'Eusebio

Map p. 649, A2. Piazza Vittorio Emanuele II.
Founded in the 4th century on the site of the house of a certain Eusebius, believed to have been a parish priest who was imprisoned for his beliefs. The cover of his tomb, carved in the 15th century, is preserved in the sacristy. The church was rebuilt twice in the 18th century, when Raphael Mengs provided the ceiling painting of the *Triumph of St Eusebius*. There are finely carved 16th-century stalls in the apse. Today, there is a mosque next door.

Fosse Ardeatine

Map p. 512. Via Ardeatina. Open Mon–Fri 8.15–3, Sat–Sun until 4.30. Open longer on 24th March. See 060608.it.
The Mausoleo delle Fosse Ardeatine is built on the site of a reprisal killing during

the German occupation of Rome. On 24th March 1944, after the killing on the previous day of 32 German soldiers by the resistance movement in Via Rasella, the Germans shot 335 Italians. The victims, who had no connection with the incident, included priests, professionals, about a hundred Jews, a dozen foreigners, and a boy of 14. The Germans then buried the bodies under an avalanche of sand created by exploding mines. Local inhabitants helped a legal and medical team to exhume and identify the bodies after the German retreat. The scene of the massacre, below a huge tufa cliff, now has cave chapels. The victims, now reinterred, are commemorated by a huge single concrete slab placed over their mass grave, with a group of standing figures, in stone, by Francesco Coccia (1950).

Gesù e Maria

Map p. 652, B3. Corso, opposite S. Giacomo in Augusta.
This small church was designed inside and out by Girolamo Rainaldi around 1675.

San Giacomo in Augusta

Map p. 652, B3. Corso.
The façade is by Carlo Maderno. The church is also known as San Giacomo degli Incurabili from the adjoining hospital, but its present name refers to the proximity of the Mausoleum of Augustus.

San Gioacchino

Map p. 650, D1. Via Pompeo Magno.
Erected by Raffaele Inganni in 1890, with bronze capitals and an aluminium cupola painted inside to represent a star-strewn sky.

San Giovanni Battista dei Genovesi

Map p. 654, B4. Via Anicia.
The church is attached to a remarkable 15th-century cloister which has an arcaded

lower gallery and a trabeated upper storey, which surrounds a beautiful garden of orange trees. There is also a lovely walled garden.

San Giovanni Decollato

Map p. 654, C3. Via San Giovanni Decollato.
The interior has fine stucco and fresco decoration dating from 1580–90. The altarpiece of the *Beheading of St John* is by Giorgio Vasari. An oratory preserves remarkable frescoes by the 16th-century Roman Mannerists, including Jacopino del Conte, Francesco Salviati and Pirro Ligorio. There is also a 16th-century cloister.

San Giovanni in Oleo

Map p. 653, D3. Via di Porta Latina. Access on request at the church of San Giovanni a Porta Latina.
This little octagonal chapel traditionally marks the spot where St John the Evangelist stepped unharmed from a cauldron of boiling oil. Rebuilt in the early 16th century during the reign of Julius II, it has an interesting design, formerly attributed to Bramante, but now usually thought to be by Antonio da Sangallo the Younger or Baldassare Peruzzi. It was restored in 1658 by Francesco Borromini, who added the frieze. The interior contains stuccoes and paintings by Lazzaro Baldi.

San Giovanni a Porta Latina

Map p. 653, D2. Porta Latina. Usually open 7.30–12.30 & 3–6. T: 06 70 47 5938, sangiovanniaportalatina.it.
Preceded by a narthex of four Roman columns and with a beautiful 12th-century campanile, this church was founded in the 5th century, rebuilt by Hadrian I in 772 and restored several times since, but the interior retains its beautiful 11th-century basilican form. The apse has three lovely windows

of selenite, a fine marble pavement in opus sectile and restored 12th-century frescoes.

San Girolamo degli Schiavoni

Map p. 652, A3. Largo degli Schiavoni.
The name 'Schiavoni' refers to the Serbs who came to live in this district as refugees after the battle of Kosovo polje in 1389. The church was rebuilt in 1587.

Sant'Isidoro

Map p. 652, C3. Via degli Artisti.
Built by Antonio Casoni (1620), with a pink façade by Carlo Bizzaccheri (1704), it was attached to a college for Irish students founded by Luke Wadding (1588–1657), a distinguished Irish Franciscan who instigated the Irish rebellion of 1641 against the confiscation of Ulster. His tomb is in the church, which contains several works by Carlo Maratta and a chapel designed by Bernini with sculptures attributed to his son Paolo.

San Lorenzo in Panisperna

Map p. 655, E2. Via Panisperna.
On the traditional site of the martyrdom of St Lawrence (depicted in a vast late 16th-century fresco by Pasquale Cati in the interior), although not his burial place (which is San Lorenzo fuori le Mura). The building is surrounded by a delightful court of old houses.

Madonna dei Monti

Map p. 655, D2–D3. Via dei Serpenti.
A fine church by Giacomo della Porta, who also designed the fountain nearby. The interior contains 17th-century stuccoes (by Ambrogio Buonvicino) and frescoes, including those in the first south chapel by Giovanni da San Giovanni. The third chapel on this side has an altarpiece of *Christ Carrying the Cross* by Paris Nogari, dating

from around the time when the dome was decorated (in 1599–1600) by Cesare Nebbia and Orazio Gentileschi. The prolific Nebbia also painted the altarpieces in two chapels on the north side, where an *Adoration of the Shepherds* by his master Girolamo Muziano is also hung. The *Annunciation* is by their contemporary Durante Alberti.

Santa Maria della Consolazione

Map p. 654, C3. Piazza della Consolazione. Open 6–12 & 3.30–6.
The façade is by Martino Longhi the Elder (1583–1606); the upper part was added in the same style in the 19th century. In the first chapel to the right are frescoes by Taddeo Zuccari (1556) of the life of Christ (including a very fine *Flagellation*) and the *Crucifixion*. In the sanctuary, the *Birth of the Virgin* and the *Assumption* are by Pomarancio, and over the altar is the *Madonna della Consolazione*, a 14th-century fresco repainted by Antoniazzo Romano. In the first chapel on the left is a marble relief of the *Marriage of St Catherine* by Raffaello da Montelupo (1530).

Santa Maria dell'Orto

Map p. 654, B4. Via Anicia.
The unusual façade is crowned with obelisks and is attributed to Vignola. The ornate interior contains 17th- and 18th-century works.

Santa Maria in Trivio

Map p. 654, C1. Via dei Crociferi.
A plaque on the exterior records the foundation of a hospice on this site by Belisarius during the Gothic conquest in 537. The church was rebuilt in 1594, with a good Baroque front, completed in 1670.

San Martino ai Monti

Map p. 655, E3. Via delle Sette Sale, by its junction with Viale del Monte Oppio.

The earliest church on this site was founded by St Sylvester, who became pope in 314, the year after Constantine's famous Edict of Milan when Christians throughout the Empire were granted freedom of worship. In the same pope's reign the decisions of the Council of Nicaea in 325, which recognised that Christ and God were of the same substance, were proclaimed in this church in the presence of Constantine, and the heretical books of Arius, Sabellius and Victorinus were burnt. When St Symmachus rebuilt the church around 500 he dedicated it to St Sylvester and St Martin, and it was again rebuilt in the 9th century. The interior, with a broad nave divided from the aisles by 24 ancient Corinthian columns which support an architrave, and its presbytery raised above the crypt, was given its present appearance around 1650 by Filippo Gagliardi. Gagliardi also painted the views of the interiors of St John Lateran and St Peter's in the left aisle, interesting since they record those basilicas before their reconstruction. Of the same date are the frescoes of the life of Elijah and landscapes of the Roman Campagna by Gaspard Dughet in the lower side aisles. The church belongs to the Carmelites, and sometimes on request you can visit a private chapel of the 3rd century, with traces of frescoes and mosaics, incorporated in eight large halls of a Roman building beneath the church.

Santi Marcellino e Pietro ad Duas Lauros (Mausoleum of St Helen)

Via Casilina 641 (some 5km southeast of Santa Croce in Gerusalemme; map p. 647). Open at weekends; santimarcellinoepietro.it.
The catacombs of Santi Marcellino e Pietro, recently reopened next to a church rebuilt in 1922, were in use at the time of Diocletian, and have numerous paintings. They are beside the ruins of the **Mausoleum of**

Helen, mother of Constantine, built by the emperor in 330 on land owned by his mother. It is circular outside and octagonal, with niches, within and has terracotta amphorae in the vaulting to lighten the load. St Helen's magnificent porphyry sarcophagus is preserved in the Vatican.

Santi Nereo ed Achilleo

Map p. 653, C2. Viale delle Terme di Caracalla. Only open when weddings are taking place, sometimes on Sun; for information, T: 06 68 75 289.
This church stands on the site of the 4th-century Oratory of the Fasciola, named from the bandage which is supposed to have fallen from the wounds of St Peter after his escape from the Tullianum (Carcer). In 524 the oratory was enlarged into a church by Pope John I, when he brought here the bodies of Nereus and Achilleus, the Christian servants of Flavia Domitilla, niece of the emperor Domitian, who had been martyred at Terracina. The church was enlarged by Leo III c. 800 and again by Pope Sixtus IV (1471–84), and was rebuilt in 1597 by Cardinal Baronius, who was a member of the recently-founded Oratorian order (*see p. 215*).

The beautiful interior preserves almost totally intact its exquisite 13th-century Cosmati work on the high altar (which covers the body of St Domitilla) and the choir screen. The mosaic on the choir arch survives from the time of Leo III (815–16): the very unusual iconographical scheme shows the *Transfiguration*, with Christ in a white tunic bordered with red and gold, in the act of blessing, flanked by Moses and Elijah. The three prostrate apostles (Peter, James and John) cover their faces with their robes to protect them from the light shining forth from Christ. On either side of this scene is an *Annunciation* (left) and Mary as the Mother of God (right), shown spinning wool with the Christ Child on her lap, still accompanied by the Archangel. The back of the bishop's throne in the apse, resting on two very docile lions, is entirely covered with carved letters which reproduce a fragment of St Gregory the Great's 28th homily (relating to the importance of founding churches dedicated to saints only in places where there was a known connection with the saint), which he delivered from this very throne when it stood in the first church dedicated to Sts Nereus and Achilleus in Via Ardeatina. The amusing fresco in the apse, commissioned by Cardinal Baronius, shows St Gregory addressing the prelates and cardinals (some of whom have trouble hearing the pope). Above is a beautiful curved marble cornice, carved with masks, which probably once adorned the Baths of Caracalla. The frescoes of martyrdoms in the nave and aisles are by Pomarancio. The ancient ambo and the 15th-century candelabrum come from other churches.

San Nicola da Tolentino

Map p. 655, D1. Salita di San Nicola da Tolentino (off Via Barberini).
Rebuilt in 1620 by Carlo Buti and finished by Martino Longhi the Younger and Giovanni Maria Baratta, who built the façade in 1670. The high altar is by Alessandro Algardi. It contains a chapel thought to be the last work of Pietro da Cortona (1668), with sculptures by Ercole Ferrata, Cosimo Fancelli and Antonio Raggi.

Sant'Omobono

Map p. 654, C3. Vico Jugario. Open only on the first Sun of the month at 11.
Vico Jugario is built on the site of the ancient road that connected the Forum Holitorium, the vegetable market near the Tiber, with the Roman Forum. The church, with a 16th-century façade, contains a 17th-century lunette showing God as divine tailor putting a fur coat on Adam. Excavations (visible through the railings) around the church have revealed traces of habitation on seven different levels, the oldest dating from c. 1500 BC. The most conspicuous remains mostly date from after 213 BC. The material found on the site is displayed in the Capitoline Museums (*see p. 46*).

San Pancrazio

Map p. 651, B3. Via di San Pancrazio. Open 9–12 & 5–7; Sun 8–1 & 5–8.
This was the site of the tomb of St Pancras who, according to tradition, was martyred under Diocletian in 304. A Christian cemetery and 5th-century oratory existed here, and the present large basilica was built by Honorius I in 630 and remodelled in the 17th century. The Baroque interior incorporates the apse of the 7th-century church. The side altars are in *trompe l'oeil* with altarpieces in stucco relief. There is even an amusing *trompe l'oeil* ambo and pulpit. The reliquary head of St Pancras is kept in a niche in the south aisle, the supposed spot of his martyrdom. The 4th-century catacombs of San Pancrazio (*closed at the time of writing*) contain Oriental inscriptions. They are entered from inside the church, down a narrow stair through a trap door.

San Pantaleo

Map p. 654, B2. Corso Vittorio Emanuele II.
Founded in 1216, it retains its 17th-century interior by Giovanni Antonio de Rossi with a vault fresco by Filippo Gherardi. The façade was added by Giuseppe Valadier in 1806.

St Paul's

Map p. 655, E1. Via Napoli, corner of Via Nazionale.

This is the American Episcopal church, called 'within the walls' to differentiate it from the papal basilica of San Paolo fuori le Mura ('without the walls'). It was built by the British architect George Edmund Street in 1872–6. The conspicuous red-and-white exterior, in travertine and red brick, is in a Romanesque style (the mosaics are by George Breck, former director of the American Academy in Rome). In the interior are very fine mosaics by Edward Burne-Jones, a friend of Street, who had made close studies of 15th-century Italian art. They were made by a Murano firm and were begun in 1885 (and completed after Burne-Jones's death by Thomas Matthews Rooke in 1907). On the first arch is the *Annunciation*, and then on the choir arch the *Tree of Life*. In the choir itself is *Christ in Glory and the Holy Jerusalem*. The figures in Earthly Paradise in the lower register include portraits of the artist himself together with J.P. Morgan (who had funded the work in part), Archbishop Tait, General Grant, Garibaldi and Abraham Lincoln. On both walls of the nave are ceramic tiles designed by William Morris, who together with Burne-Jones was the most important member of the second generation of pre-Raphaelites. The stained-glass windows are by the English firm of Clayton and Bell.

San Rocco

Map p. 654, B1. Via di Ripetta.
The Neoclassical façade is by Giuseppe Valadier (1834). In the sacristy is a lovely painting of the *Madonna with St Anthony Abbot and St Roch*, with plague victims, an early work by Baciccia. The high altarpiece of *St Roch in Glory* is by Giacinto Brandi.

Sacro Cuore Immacolato di Maria

Map p. 647. Piazza Euclide.
A huge church by Armando Brasini (1923) in the centre of the Parioli residential district.

San Salvatore in Onda

Map p. 654, A3. Via dei Pettinari.
A little church built at the end of the 11th century but transformed in the 17th. The interesting crypt was built over a Roman building of the 2nd century AD.

Santissime Stimmate

Map p. 654, B2. Via dei Cestari.
Rebuilt at the beginning of the 18th century by Giovanni Battista Contini, it contains paintings by Francesco Trevisani, including the high altarpiece *St Francis Receiving the Stigmata* (1714).

Chiesa del Sudario

Map p. 654, B2. Off Largo Torre Argentina.
A small church built in 1604 with a façade by Carlo Rainaldi, decorated with late 19th-century works by Cesare Maccari. This was the court church of the Royal House of Savoy from 1871 to 1946.

San Vitale

Map p. 655, D2. Via Nazionale.
Now well below the level of the road, this little church was dedicated in 416 but has been restored several times. It has a fine portico with old columns and 17th-century doors. In the interior is a carved wood ceiling, and the walls are decorated with effective 17th-century *trompe l'oeil* frescoes with landscapes by Cavaliere d'Arpino, Dughet and Andrea Pozzo.

Santi Vito e Modesto

Map p. 655, F2. Via San Vito.
Founded in the 4th century but restored in the 20th century, it contains late 15th-century frescoes by Antoniazzo Romano. Excavations have revealed traces of the Servian Wall and a Roman aqueduct.

MUSEUMS

Antiquario Comunale

Map p. 655, D4. Viale del Parco del Celio.
Closed indefinitely.
This extremely important archaeological collection, with some 60,000 works, was founded in 1885 for objects unearthed during excavations in Rome, and illustrates the everyday life of the city from earliest times to the end of the Empire. In 2014 it was announced that the material is being studied and catalogued by a group of institutions outside Italy in the hope that it will one day be exhibited.

Calcografia Nazionale

Map p. 654, C1. Via della Stamperia. Open 9–1 except Sun.
This, the most important collection of copperplate engravings in the world, was formed in 1738 by Clement XII and moved to this building by Luigi Valadier in 1837. It contains almost all the engravings of Giovanni Battista Piranesi (1,432 plates) and examples of the work of Marcantonio Raimondi, Bartolomeo Pinelli and many others among a total of more than 19,600 plates. Exhibitions are often held; any items not on display can be seen on request, and copies purchased. The institute also owns Palazzo Poli next door.

Galleria dell'Accademia di San Luca

Map p. 654, C1. Via della Stamperia. Open Mon–Sat 10–7. T: 06 679 8850, www. accademiadisanluca.eu/it.
This academy was founded in 1577 and incorporated the Università dei Pittori (Painters' University), inaugurated in the previous century, whose members used to meet in the little church of San Luca. Federico Zuccari gave the academy its first statutes, and it soon became famous for its teaching and for its prize competitions. Numerous foreign artists who came to work in Rome also joined the academy. Since 1934 it has been in Palazzo Carpegna. The eclectic gallery on the upper floor contains gifts and bequests from its members, together with donations from other sources. It is arranged by themes: drawings, sculptures, landscapes and portraits. It includes a portrait (of Ippolito Rimanaldo) attributed to Titian; *Mary Magdalene* by Anton Raphael Mengs; a *Madonna and Child with Angels* by Van Dyck; a plaster sculpture of the *Three Graces* by Bertel Thorvaldsen; a delightful putto, a precious fragment of a fresco by Raphael (1512); 18th-century terracotta reliefs by Richard Westmacott (who was in Rome studying under Canova); two notable self-portraits by Federico Zuccari and Elisabeth Vigée le Brun; and landscapes by Salvator Rosa and Paul Bril. Piranesi is recorded in a bust by Joseph Nollekens and by an album of his drawings '*Le Antichità Romane*'.

Galleria d'Arte Moderna di Roma Capitale

Map p. 655, D1. Via Francesco Crispi 24. Open Tues–Sun 10–6.
Arranged in the former Carmelite convent of San Giuseppe, with a pleasant cloister with four young orange trees. On the ground floor are sculptures by the important Neapolitan artist Vincenzo Gemito, whose graphic work is also well represented in the gallery. The floors above are used for temporary exhibitions of 20th-century art. The permanent collection includes works by some of the best 20th-century Italian artists: Scipione, De Chirico, Felice Casorati, Donghi, Emanuele Cavalli, Mario Sironi, Filippo De Pisis, Carlo Carrà, Gino Severini, Giorgio Morandi, Alberto Savinio. Among

the earliest works are paintings by Aristide Sartorio and a bronze, *Conca dei Bufali,* by Duilio Cambellotti.

Museo dell'Arma del Genio

Map p. 647. Lungotevere della Vittoria 31. Closed at the time of writing; see 060608.it or www.iscag.it.
Documents Italian military transport, bridge-building and communications, and contains models of historical fortifications and armoury from Roman times to the present day, and a military aircraft of 1909.

Museo d'Arte Contemporanea di Roma (MACRO)

Map p. 648, A3. Via Nizza 138 (corner of Via Reggio Emilia). Open 11–7; closed Mon.
Housed in a very fine old brewery building, erected in 1901–14 by Gustavo Giovannoni, in a mixture of Art Nouveau and Rational styles, and in use up until 1971. It was then restored and the exhibition space was enlarged by Odile Decq in 2010 for the collection of Italian art dating from 1946 onwards. There are pleasant terraces and a café and restaurant.

Museo Astronomico e Copernicano

Map p. 647. Villa Mario Mellini (Monte Mario). Closed for restoration; see 060608.it.
Founded in 1873, it contains mementoes of Copernicus, astrolabes, sextants, quadrants and telescopes, and a large collection of globes. It is part of the Astronomical and Meteorological Observatory.

Museo Hendrik Christian Andersen

Map p. 652, A2. 20 Via Pasquale Stanislao Mancini. Open Tues–Sun 9–7.30.
This was the home and studio of the sculptor and painter Hendrik Andersen, who was born in Norway in 1872 and whose family emigrated to America. Andersen came to Rome in 1894 and remained here until his death in 1940. In 1899 he met Henry James, who admired his work, and an interesting collection of letters from the writer to him survives. The Bostonian writer Olivia Cushing, his sister-in-law, inspired his work which was to have decorated a 'world city' under the auspices of the World Conscience Society, founded by Andersen in 1913. The house and studio, owned by the state since 1978 and opened in 1999 as a satellite museum of the Galleria Nazionale d'Arte Moderna, remains as Andersen built it in 1925, together with his monumental sculptures displayed in a gallery and studio on the ground floor.

Museo Mario Praz

Map p. 654, B1. Via Giuseppe Zanardelli. Open on the hour 9–1 and on the half-hour 2.30–6.30; closed Mon morning. A maximum of ten visitors are accompanied and lent a handsheet (in Italian only). The tour lasts about 30–40mins. There are no labels; museopraz.beniculturali.it.
Housed on the top floor of Palazzo Primoli (there is a lift), this was the residence of the art historian and man of letters Mario Praz from 1969 until his death in 1982.

Although he was a Shakespeare scholar and wrote books on Charles Lamb and Lord Byron, Praz is perhaps best remembered for his *History of Interior Decoration* (1945). The apartment is filled with his remarkable collection of decorative arts, paintings, sculpture, drawings, miniatures, fans, wax portraits, porcelain and furniture, particularly representative of the Neoclassical period (late 18th and early 19th centuries), which up until his time had been out of vogue and largely ignored by scholars.

The nine rooms here, crowded with possessions and rather gloomy in atmosphere, give a clear idea of Praz's taste.

Praz formed his collection while living in the more spacious Palazzo Ricci on Via Giulia, described in his autobiographical book *La Casa della Vita* (published in 1958; translated into English as *The House of Life* in 1964). The works of art include a marble statue of *Cupid* attributed to Adamo Tadolini, a portrait of Foscolo by François-Xavier Fabre (the French artist lived for many years in Rome), and early 19th-century watercolours of period interiors.

Museo delle Mura

Map p. 653, D3. Porta di San Sebastiano. Open Tues–Sun 9–2. T: 060608, museodellemuraroma.it.

This museum dedicated to the history of the Aurelian Walls is fittingly arranged in the largest and best-preserved gateway in those walls, in rooms above the gate and in its two towers. The terrace at the top of the gate, from which there is a fine view of woods in both directions, is also open, but the ramparts along the inner face of the walls, traversing nine defensive towers, have been closed for restoration. This was the Porta Appia of ancient Rome, and was rebuilt in the 5th century by Honorius and restored by Belisarius, the 6th-century Byzantine general. The inside arch, on the left, has a carving of St George. The two medieval towers at the sides rest on basements of marble blocks. It was at the Porta San Sebastiano that the senate and people of Rome received the last triumphal procession to enter the city by the Via Appia, that of Marcantonio Colonna II after the victory of Lepanto in 1571. Just inside the gateway is the so-called triumphal Arch of Drusus, in fact the arch that carried the aqueduct for the Baths of Caracalla over the Via Appia. Only the central of three openings survives; it is decorated on its outer façade with two Composite columns of *giallo antico*.

Museo Napoleonico

Map p. 654, B1. Via Giuseppe Zanardelli. Open Tues–Sun 10–6.

On the ground floor of Palazzo Primoli, this was created and presented to the city of Rome in 1927 by Count Giuseppe Primoli (1851–1927), a descendant of Napoleon I who frequented the court of Napoleon III. This interesting collection illustrates the various periods of Napoleonic rule in Italy, but is particularly important as a record of the prolonged stays in Italy of Napoleon's numerous brothers and sisters and their descendants, and it documents the history of the Roman branch of the Bonaparte family. Although Napoleon Bonaparte never came to Rome himself (his trip, planned in 1812, failed to take place), he led some brilliant military campaigns in northern Italy, and in 1798 French troops entered the city and remained here for a year. Rome was again occupied in 1808–9.

The 16th-century palace was acquired by the Primoli family in 1820–8 and reconstructed in 1901 by Raffaello Ojetti, who added the monumental entrance on Via Zanardelli and a new façade overlooking the Tiber. The interior arrangement has been left more or less as it was in Giuseppe Primoli's time (the majolica floors were made in Naples in the early 19th century).

Museo Nazionale d'Arte Orientale

Map p. 655, F3. Largo Brancaccio (Via Merulana). Open Tues, Wed, Fri 9–2; Thur, Sat, Sun 9–7.30; closed Mon.

Housed in Palazzo Brancaccio, which was built for Mary Elizabeth Bradhurst Field by Gaetano Koch in 1879 and enlarged by Luca Carimini. The interior has decorations in the neo-Baroque style by Francesco Gai. Founded in 1957, this is the most important collection of Oriental art in Italy.

Museo di Roma

Map p. 654, B2. Via di San Pantaleo 10. Open Tues–Sun 10–7; museodiroma.it.

Housed in the huge Palazzo Braschi, which was built after 1792 by Cosimo Morelli, the museum was founded in 1930 to illustrate the history and life of Rome from the Middle Ages to the present day, but most of the exhibits relate to the period between the 17th and 19th centuries.

At the foot of the staircase is a colossal sculptural group of the *Baptism of Christ* by Francesco Mochi. The magnificent staircase (1791–1804), by Cosimo Morelli, incorporates 18 antique columns of red granite. The ancient Roman statues decorating it are the only works from the huge Braschi collection to have survived. The fine Neoclassical stuccoes are by Luigi Acquisti (perhaps on a design by Valadier).

First floor: Rooms 1 and 2 are devoted to Pius VI, who commissioned Palazzo Braschi and died in exile in 1799. Room 3 has busts of popes and cardinals including works by Filippo della Valle and François Duquesnoy. Room 4 contains 17th-century portraits and scenes of tournaments in Rome. Room 8 has 18th-century views of celebrations in Piazza del Popolo. In Room 9 are paintings of 18th- and 19th-century Rome by Ippolito Caffi and Gaspar van Wittel. The windows in Rooms 10 and 11 have splendid views over Piazza Navona. The tapestries of garden scenes date from the early 18th century. There is also a painted self-portrait by Canova (c. 1799) and a plaster model for a colossal self-portrait bust in marble he made for his own tomb (1811–12). The portrait of John Staples (1773) is by Pompeo Batoni. In Room 12 is a very fine ceiling fresco of the fable of Psyche by Cigoli (1610–13), detached from Palazzo Borghese on the Quirinal hill.

Second floor: Remnants of collections once owned by the great patrician families of Rome are arranged on this floor. There are busts of the Barberini by Francesco Mochi, and the pretty '*alcova*' from a demolished Torlonia palace. The last room has a fine collection of 19th-century photos. There are long-term plans to open more rooms to exhibit the rest of the collection.

The **Gabinetto Comunale delle Stampe e Archivio Fotografico** is housed in the same building (*admission by appointment*).

Museo Storico dei Bersaglieri

Map p. 648, A4. Porta Pia. Open Mon–Fri 9–3; May–Sept also weekends 9–2; bersaglieri.net.

Documents the wars of independence, the African campaign, and the First World War.

Museo Torlonia

Once housed in the Palazzo Torlonia in Via Corsini in Trastevere, this was founded by Gian Raimondo Torlonia (1754–1829) with sculptures from other Roman collections, to which he later added the yields from excavations on the family estates, including Cerveteri, Vulci and Porto. Considered the most important private collection of ancient sculpture in existence, there are over 620 pieces of sculpture, including a few Greek originals. After years of closure 'for restoration', in the 1970s the interior of the museum was converted into flats and the works put in store. In 1977 the palace and collection were officially sequestered, and interminable procedures were instigated by the state in an attempt to acquire the collection. The museum has never been reopened. (*For further information apply to the Amministrazione Torlonia, Via della Conciliazione 30.*) The most important works include the *Giustiniani Hestia*, a splendid statue of Vesta attributed to Kalamis (5th century BC), and a bas-relief of *Hercules Liberating Theseus and Pirithous*, by the school of Pheidias (4th century BC). There are numerous Roman copies of works by Greek sculptors, notably Cephisodotus, Polyclitus, Praxiteles and Lysippus. Of the Roman originals, perhaps the most striking is a portrait statue of Lucilla, daughter of Marcus Aurelius. The Roman iconographic collection contains over one hundred busts of the Imperial era. The valuable Etruscan paintings (4th century BC) are from Vulci. There is also a very fine collection of sarcophagi.

Museo Teatrale

Map p. 654, B2. Via del Sudario 44. Open Tues and Thur 9.15–6.30. T: 06 68 19 471. For tours, email visite.burcardo@siae.it. Housed in the delightful little Palazzetto del Burcardo, which was built in 1503 for Strasbourg-born Bishop Hans Burckardt (or Burckhardt), who came to live in

Rome in 1479. He called the house the Torre Argentina, from the Latin name for Strasbourg (*Argentoratum*), which in turn became the name of the piazza and theatre (the back doors of which open onto the courtyard). Burckardt wrote a remarkable account of the papal court under Innocent VIII and Alexander VI. The well displayed museum illustrates the history of theatre with statuettes of characters from the *commedia dell'arte*, puppets, costumes, autograph texts, prints, drawings and paintings. On the first floor you can see frescoes which survive from Burckardt's time. The building also houses a library of some 40,000 volumes, the earliest of which date from the 16th century, including nearly all the editions of Carlo Goldoni's works, as well as a photographic archive, and is the seat of the Italian Authors and Publishers Society.

PALACES, VILLAS AND ACADEMIC INSTITUTIONS

Acquario Romano

Map p. 655, F2. Piazza Manfredo Fanti 47. This circular edifice was built in 1887 as an aquarium by Ettore Bernich and it is surrounded by a garden with remains of the Servian Wall. The remarkable interior in Pompeian style with its cast iron columns has been carefully restored as the Casa dell'Architettura, used as a space for exhibitions and conferences connected to architecture.

Banca d'Italia

Map p. 655, D2. Via Nazionale. A huge Neoclassical building by Gaetano Koch (1886–1904), behind a row of palm trees and colossal lamp-posts. It is the headquarters of the Bank of Italy.

Biblioteca Angelica

Map p. 654, B1 (beside the church of Sant'Agostino). Open Tues–Thur 10–6, Mon and Fri 10–4, Sat 9–1; T: 06 68 40 801, bibliotecaangelica.beniculturali.it. Visitors must be over 16.

The Biblioteca Angelica was the first public library to be founded in Rome, in 1614 by the Augustinian scholar Angelo Rocca. When the erudite Gabriel Naudé (who was to become librarian to Richelieu and Mazarin in Paris) spent the 1630s in Rome, he recorded that this was one of only three libraries in all Europe which were freely open (the other two were the Bodleian in Oxford and that of Cardinal Borromeo in Palazzo dell'Ambrosiana in Milan). A new wing was added by Borromini in 1659.

British School at Rome

Map p. 652, B1. Via Antonio Gramsci.
Established in 1901 as a School of
Archaeology. After the 1911 International
Exhibition of Fine Arts in Rome, the site,
where the British Pavilion once stood,
was offered to the School by the *Comune*
of Rome. The pavilion, designed by Sir
Edwin Lutyens, with a façade based on
the west front of St Paul's Cathedral, was
reproduced in permanent materials. In 1912
the school widened its scope to the study of
the fine arts, literature and history of Italy.
Scholarships are awarded, and an annual
exhibition of the artists' work is held in June.
The researches of the School are published
annually in *The Papers of the British School*.

House Cardinal Bessarion

*Map p. 653, C2. Via di Porta San Sebastiano
8. Visits for groups only (max. 15) by prior
arrangement; T: 060608.*
The house and garden are a delightful
example of a 15th-century summer home,
with frescoes and wall-paintings of garlands
and ribbons which cast painted shadows,
and overall patterns of acanthus leaves and
pomegranates. It is thought to have been
owned by Bessarion (*see p. 155*).

Casa dei Cavalieri di Rodi

*Map p. 655, D2. Piazza del Grillo 1;
sovraintendenzaroma.it. Open only by
appointment; T: 060608.*
The house was built over a Roman edifice
at the end of the 12th century, and restored
in 1467–70 by Cardinal Marco Barbo,
nephew of Paul II. It has a well-preserved
colonnaded atrium dating from the time
of Augustus; the roof is a Renaissance
addition. It is now used as a chapel by the
Knights of St John (*open for services on Sun
at 10.30*). At the top of a flight of restored
Roman stairs is a fine Renaissance hall, off

which are several contemporary rooms; one
of these, the Sala del Balconcino, contains
part of the attic storey of the portico of the
Forum of Augustus, with caryatids. Stairs
lead up to a loggia with restored frescoes
and fine views over the Imperial Fora.

Collegio Romano

Map p. 654, C2. Piazza del Collegio Romano.
A large building erected in 1585 by order of
Gregory XIII for the Jesuits. The architect
was probably the Jesuit Giuseppe Valeriani.
The Jesuit library founded here formed
the nucleus of the Biblioteca Nazionale
Centrale Vittorio Emanuele. The Salone
della Crociera, with its original bookcases,
has been used to house part of the library
of the Istituto Nazionale di Archeologia e
Storia dell'Arte in Palazzo di Venezia.

Galleria Sciarra

*Map p. 654, C2. Piazza del Oratorio (north of
Via dell'Umiltà).*
Commissioned in 1888, this huge arcade
was designed by Giulio De Angelis, and
totally covered with painted decoration by
Giuseppe Cellini celebrating the virtues of
the women of the time.

Hostaria dell' Orso

Map p. 654, B1. Via dei Soldati.
This is a medieval building which was
altered around 1460. It first became a hotel
in the 16th century and Rabelais, Montaigne
and Goethe were among its later patrons.
Today it houses a restaurant, club and piano
bar (*hdo.it*).

Palazzina of Pius IV

Map p. 652, A1. Viale delle Belle Arti.
An elegant little house probably designed
by Pirro Ligorio in 1562, which incorporates
a fountain of the Acqua Vergine erected by
Bartolomeo Ammannati at the same time.

Palazzo Borghese

Map p. 654, B1. Via Borghese. Headquarters of the Circolo della Caccia, a club founded in 1869 and only open to members.

Called from its shape the 'harpsichord of Rome', it was begun (c. 1560) perhaps by Vignola, and completed by Flaminio Ponzio, who designed the beautiful terrace on the Tiber front. It was acquired by Cardinal Camillo Borghese, who became Pope Paul V in 1605, and was renowned for its splendour. For nearly two centuries it contained the paintings from the Galleria Borghese; they were restored to their former residence in 1891. The pretty courtyard has long lines of twin columns on two storeys, and colossal statues representing Ceres and the empresses Sabina and Julia Domna; a garden beyond contains fountains and Roman sculpture.

Palazzo Capranica

Map p. 654, B2. Piazza Capranica.
Built by Cardinal Domenico Capranica (c. 1450), this is partly Gothic and partly Renaissance in style. The tower has a delightful loggia.

Palazzo di Giustizia

Map p. 654, A1. Piazza dei Tribunali..
This colossal Palace of Justice is an over-ornate building in solid travertine begun in 1888 and opened in 1910. Its foundations were never sufficient to support its weight and for decades it was in danger of collapse, provoking inevitable gibes from the Romans who enjoyed pointing out the mismatch between the structure of the building and its ostensible purpose. It has always been known as the 'Palazzaccio'. The quadriga is, however, a good work added by Ettore Ximenes in 1926. After lengthy restoration it has been able to house the Supreme Court, and there is now a whole new area of law courts near Piazzale Clodio at the foot of Monte Mario.

Palazzo Massimo alle Colonne

Map p. 654, B2. Corso Vittorio Emanuele II 141.

Built by Baldassare Peruzzi (1532–6), this is skilfully set in a narrow, irregular site, and the convex façade follows the line of the cavea of the Odeon of Domitian, which stood here. The beautiful portico is decorated with stuccoes. The palace has two courtyards: one a charming Renaissance work with a frescoed loggia and a Baroque fountain, and the second (in very poor repair) with 17th-century decorations. In the interior a fresco has been uncovered which may be the work of Giulio Romano.

In Piazza dei Massimi, behind the palace (reached from Corso Rinascimento) is the Palazzetto Massimi, called the Palazzo Istoriato because it has remains of a painted façade by the school of Daniele da Volterra (1523). Here Pannartz and Sweynheim transferred their press from Subiaco in 1467 and issued the first books printed in Rome. The marble cipollino column set up in the piazza belonged to the Odeon of Domitian.

Palazzo Pamphilj

Map p. 654, B2. Piazza Navona. The seat of the Brazilian Embassy; closed to the public.
Also called Palazzo Doria, this palace was started by Girolamo Rainaldi and completed by Borromini for Innocent X in the mid-17th century. The interior is of the greatest interest for its architecture and painted decorations. The state rooms overlooking the piazza, decorated between 1634 and 1671, include the Sala Palestrina, a magnificent example of Borromini's secular architecture, using the minimum of surface decoration, adorned with busts by Algardi. It has had an interesting history as a music

room since the days of Benedetto Pamphilj (1653–1730), who was a patron of the arts and who wrote librettos for cantatas by Handel and Scarlatti, whose compositions were performed here under the direction of Arcangelo Corelli, whose own *Concerti Grossi* were premiered in the palace. The long gallery, also designed by Borromini, has a splendid fresco of the *Story of Aeneas* by Pietro da Cortona, who also frescoed the ceiling of the charming papal bedroom. The palace was later occupied by Innocent X's sister-in-law Olimpia Maidalchini, an ambitious woman who came to dominate the affairs of the pope.

Tormarancia Estate

Via G. Aristide Sartorio (map p. 512). To book a visit, T: 06 51 35 316. For information, see parcoappiaantica.it.
This is an area of Roman Campagna now part of the Appia Antica regional park but still mostly privately owned and not open regularly to the public. Plans to build a new residential district here have been kept at bay through the campaigning of conservationists.

The University (La Sapienza)

Map p. 649, B1. Piazzale Aldo Moro.
The Città Universitaria is an interesting example of Fascist architecture. The faculty buildings and chapel were designed on a monumental scale by Marcello Piacentini and completed in 1935, in which year the seat of the University of Rome was transferred here from Palazzo della Sapienza. Numerous other buildings were built (some by Giovanni Michelucci, the Tuscan Rationalist architect) as the university expanded. The entrance is near a bronze statue of Minerva by Arturo Martini. In the Rector's Palace there is a fresco by Mario Sironi, an artist of the 'Novecento' (*see p. 375*).

The University Library was founded by Alexander VII and now has more than a million volumes. The scientific study collections are open by appointment (*www.uniroma1.it under 'musei'*). These consist of some 19 museums, among the most important of which are the Museo delle Origini (founded in 1942), which illustrates the prehistory of Italy; the Museo dell'Arte Classica, which has more than 1,000 casts of Greek and Hellenistic statuary; the Botanical Institute, which has an important herbarium; and the Museo della Matematica, a museum which illustrates the history of mathematics.

Two other universities have been opened in Rome: Roma 2 (**Tor Vergata**) in 1982 on the Via Casilina, south of Rome; and **Roma 3** on the Via Ostiense, towards EUR, in 1992.

The **Policlinico** (*map p. 648, B4*) is a large teaching hospital, designed by Giulio Podesti in 1893.

Vignola

Map p. 653, B1. Piazza di Porta Capena.
A charming little 16th-century palace moved here from near Via Santa Balbina in 1911 and reconstructed using the original masonry.

Villa Ada

Map p. 648, A1. Via Panama (off Via Salaria).
The huge Villa Ada, formerly Savoia, with a walled garden, was once the private residence of Vittorio Emanuele III and is now the Egyptian Embassy. Part of the grounds are open as a public park.

Villa Aldobrandini

Map p. 655, D2. Via Nazionale.
Built in the 16th century for the Duke of Urbino, the villa was acquired by Clement VIII (Ippolito Aldobrandini) and given by him to his nephews. It became a famous meeting-place for the Roman aristocracy

during the Napoleonic era. Now owned by the state, it contains an international law library. The splendid Roman fresco known as the *Aldobrandini Marriage* (*see p. 473*) was kept in one of the garden pavilions here until 1838. Part of the garden—with some fine palm trees—is now a little public park, entered from Via Mazzarino, where steps lead up past impressive 2nd-century ruins.

Villa Aurora (Casino Boncompagni)

Map p. 652, C3. Via Lombardia 46. Only open by previous appointment; T: 06 48 3942 Mon, Wed, Fri morning, or email ttl@glgnet.it.
This is the only surviving part of the famous park of the Villa Ludovisi (*see p. 380*) and is still owned by the Boncompagni. The first Roman scene in Henry James's novel *Roderick Hudson* takes place in the gardens here, which still have some magnificent trees. The 16th-century garden-house, enlarged in the 19th century, contains a hall with *grottesche* and a room with a ceiling-painting of Aurora in her chariot, considered one of Guercino's best works (1621). Beyond it can be seen a living room and an enclosed loggia decorated with antique reliefs.

A spiral staircase leads up to a hall with a ceiling painting of *Fame*, also by Guercino (and Agostino Tassi). A small room here was used by Caravaggio's patron Cardinal del Monte as an alchemist's study and distillery after he purchased the villa in 1595. The following year he apparently commissioned the artist to paint the ceiling with a celestial globe with zodiacal signs surrounded by Pluto (with his three-headed dog Cerberus), Neptune (with a sea-horse) and Jupiter (with an eagle). After its restoration in 1990 this very unusual work, painted in extraordinarily daring perspective, has almost unanimously been attributed to Caravaggio, and it is thought that he included his own self-portrait in the three gods.

Villa Glori

Map p. 647. Viale dei Parioli.
Laid out in 1923–4 by Raffaello de Vico as a memorial park to commemorate the brothers Enrico and Giovanni Cairoli, who were killed in 1867 during Garibaldi's attempt to liberate Rome from papal rule. The park is planted with cypresses, oaks, elms, maples and horse chestnuts. A clump of oak trees commemorates heroes of the First World War. There is a fine view of the Tiber valley. Beyond is the mineral spring called Acqua Acetosa; the well-head (1661) is probably by Andrea Sacchi.

Villa Madama

Map p. 647. Via di Villa Madama (Monte Mario). Used by the Italian government as accommodation for prominent visitors, it is rarely open to the public.
This lovely suburban villa was designed by Raphael and begun for Cardinal Giulio de' Medici (later Clement VII) by Giulio Romano. It was modelled on the well-documented villa built by Pliny. It was altered by Antonio da Sangallo the Younger. Later it came into the possession of Madama Margaret of Parma and was afterwards owned by the kings of Naples. The beautiful loggia, decorated with stucco reliefs by Giovanni da Udine and paintings by Giulio Romano (1520–25) after Raphael's designs, rivals and even excels the famous loggia of the Vatican. In one of the rooms is a frieze of cupids by Giulio Romano. The attractive hanging garden, replanted in the mid 20th century, served as a model for many Italian gardens. It is on the east slope of Monte Mario, the ancient Clivus Cinnoe and medieval Monte Malo, which takes its present name from the Villa Mario Mellini built on the summit (139m), now part of the Observatory (*see p. 469*).

Villa Paolina

Map p. 652, D3. Via XX Settembre (just inside Porta Pia).

The home of Pauline Bonaparte from 1816 to 1824, once famous for its garden. It is now the seat of the French Embassy to the Vatican.

Villa Sciarra

Map p. 651, D3. Via Calandrelli. Park open 7–dusk.

The villa was purchased in 1902 by George Washington Wurts, an American diplomat from Philadelphia. During his residence here he and his wife Henrietta Tower were the centre of the American expatriate community. They laid out the gardens, which have wonderful wisteria. Some of their art collection, including precious paintings, early wooden sculpture and silver, was left to the Museo di Palazzo Venezia, where it forms part of the permanent display.

Villa Torlonia

Map p. 648, A3. Via Salaria 92. Permission to visit the collection is rarely granted, although you are asked to apply in writing to the Amministrazione Torlonia: amministrazione@srdps.191.it; Fax: 06 68 19 9934.

The villa, formerly Villa Albani, in a large park of umbrella pines, is privately owned by the Torlonia. It was built in 1760 by Carlo Marchionni for Cardinal Alessandro Albani, whose valuable collection of Classical sculpture was arranged here in 1765 by Johann Winckelmann, the German archaeologist who had become superintendent of Roman antiquities in 1763. By order of Napoleon, 294 pieces of the villa's original collection were taken to Paris; after Waterloo nearly all of them were sold at Munich instead of being returned. The rest of the collection continued to increase, and in 1852 it passed into the possession of the Chigi. In 1866 it was bought, with the villa, by Princess Alessandra Torlonia.

The Casino, surrounded by a formal garden, has a hemicycle with 40 Doric columns. In the portico are niches with busts of Roman emperors. Beyond an atrium with caryatids, the first gallery has a collection of herms. The staircase, with Roman reliefs, leads up to the Oval Hall with a statue of an *Athlete*, signed by Stephanos (1st century BC). In the Great Hall the fine ceiling painting of *Parnassus* is by Raphael Mengs. Here is displayed the *Albani Pallas*, a statue of the Attic school. In the right wing are paintings by L'Alunno, Perugino, Giovanni Paolo Pannini, Gerrit van Honthorst, Pompeo Batoni, Van Dyck, Taddeo Zuccari, Tintoretto, Jusepe de Ribera and Guercino.

The left wing has a beautiful relief of Antinous from Hadrian's Villa, the only piece brought back from Paris in 1815; the so-called *Leucothea* relief from the beginning of the 5th-century BC; a splendid 5th century relief of a battle scene, showing the influence of Pheidias; the *Apollo Sauroctonos*, an ancient copy after Praxiteles; a bust of Quintus Hortensius; and the *Apotheosis of Hercules*, in the style of the *Tabula Iliaca* in the Capitoline Museums. The so-called *Aesop* is a naturalistic nude statue of a hunchback, possibly a portrait of a court dwarf of the time of Hadrian. The paintings include sketches by Giulio Romano for the story of Psyche in Palazzo Te in Mantua, and works by Borgognone, Luca Giordano and Gaspare Vanvitelli. On the ground floor is the Stanza della Colonna, a room with twelve fine columns—one fluted, in alabaster—in which is displayed a sarcophagus with a scene of the marriage of Peleus and Thetis, considered by Winckelmann to be one of the finest in existence. The Kaffeehaus contains Roman mosaics.

PRACTICAL
INFORMATION

Planning Your Trip

WHEN TO GO

Rome's climate is usually very pleasant except in the height of summer and periodically in the winter. The best months to visit are November or March; if possible, avoid the busiest periods—Easter, May, June, September, October and Christmas. July and August have become less crowded in recent years, but the summer can be uncomfortably hot.

USEFUL WEBSITES

The **municipality website** lists hotels and opening times for sights and monuments: *turismoroma.it*. For the **Roma Pass:** *romapass.it*. **Public transport:** *atac.roma.it* or *muoversiaroma.it*. **Airports:** *adr.it*. **Vatican:** *vatican.va*.

DISABLED TRAVELLERS

All new public buildings are obliged to provide access and facilities for the disabled. Airports and railway stations offer assistance and certain trains can transport wheelchairs. Check the municipality website (*060608.it*) for hotels, museums and galleries accessible to the disabled. Although most city buses take wheelchairs, the historic centre of Rome remains difficult to traverse in a wheelchair. For access, *T: 800 154451*.

TOURIST OFFICES

The municipal tourist office (*T: 060608, 060608.it*) runs a number of information points in green kiosks (known as PIT, *Punti di Informazione Turistica*). In the city centre, these are usually open daily 9.30–7: **Via del Corso** (Via Marco Minghetti; *map p. 654, C2*); the **Imperial Fora** (*map pp. 654, C2–655, D2*); **Castel Sant'Angelo** (*map p. 650, D2*); **Via Nazionale** (Palazzo delle Esposizioni; *map p. 655, D2*); **Piazza delle Cinque Lune** (*map p. 654, B1*); **Ghetto**, Via Santa Maria del Pianto, off Via Portico d'Ottavia (*map p. 654, B3*); **Piazza San Pietro** (*map p. 650, C2*); and at the railway stations and airports.

THE ROMA PASS

There are two versions of this discount card: for 48hrs or three days. It gives you free entrance to a museum of your choice (two museums with the three-day card) and considerable reductions at many others, as well as free transport around the city. It can be purchased directly at museums, tourist information points, airports and railway stations.

Getting Around

TO AND FROM THE AIRPORT

Fiumicino (also called Leonardo da Vinci; *adr.it*), 26km southwest of Rome, is the main airport. Non-stop trains run from Stazione Termini every half hour from about 7am–9.15pm (30mins) and underground trains every 15mins from Stazione Roma Tiburtina via Ostiense and Trastevere from about 5am–11pm (41mins). There are also night bus services to/from Stazione Tiburtina.

Ciampino (*adr.it*), 13km southeast of Rome, is used mainly for domestic flights and by low-cost airlines. It can be reached by underground Line A from Stazione Termini to Anagnina station, and from there by COTRAL airport bus from 6am–10pm (every 30mins).

If you arrive late at night it is best to take a taxi. Official Rome taxis (*see opposite*) wait at taxi ranks at the airports. There are fixed tariffs to the centre of town.

BY TRAIN

Stazione Termini (*map p. 655, F1*) is Rome's main station. It has left-luggage facilities and a supermarket open 24hrs. **Stazione Roma Tiburtina** (*map p. 647*) is used by some trains. Both stations are on the Metro.

BY BUS AND TRAM

Rome is served by a fairly efficient bus and tram service. City buses are run by ATAC (*atac.roma.it*). Their website has a journey planner and they have an information kiosk on Piazza dei Cinquecento in front of Stazione Termini. The website *muoversiaroma.it* also has a good journey planner and an app, useful if you have roaming.

Tickets must be bought in advance either at tobacconists, bars and newspaper kiosks, or at ATAC booths and from the automatic machines at many bus stops and metro stations. They are valid for 75mins on any number of lines and for one journey on the Metro. They have to be stamped on board the vehicle. Those found travelling without a valid ticket are liable to a heavy fine.

It is often worth purchasing a one-day ticket, a BIG (*biglietto giornaliero*) which expires at midnight on the day it was purchased. Three- and seven-day tickets are also available. They must be stamped just once.

Express bus no. 60 provides a fast service between Piazza della Repubblica (*map p. 655, E1*), Piazza Venezia (*map p. 654, C2*), the Colosseum (*map p. 655, E3*) and Porta San Paolo (Piramide; *map p. 653, A3*). A good bus for St Peter's and the Vatican is no. 64 from Stazione Termini (*map p. 655, F1*) via Piazza Venezia. Transport advice for sights well beyond the city centre is given in the text of this guide.

There are usually no bus or underground services in Rome on 1 May or on the afternoon of Christmas Day, and services are limited on other holidays. Night bus services operate from ten past midnight to 5.30am; the numbers on these routes are followed by 'N'. Because of one-way streets, return journeys do not always follow the same route as the outward journey.

The few tramlines which survive are slow but in some cases charmingly old-fashioned. A new line (no. 8) runs to Trastevere from Piazza Venezia.

BY METRO

There are two lines in Rome's underground (*metropolitana*), mainly serving the outskirts. A third line was partially opened in 2014. The service begins at 5.30am and ends at 11.30pm; on Sat the last train is at half past midnight. Platforms are indicated with the name of the end stop on the line: you need to know these in order to work out where to go.

Line A runs from Battistini in the western suburbs to Anagnina in the east. The Ottaviano-San Pietro stop is useful for the Vatican. Stops in the centre of Rome are Flaminio (Piazza del Popolo), Piazza di Spagna, Piazza Barberini, Piazza della Repubblica, Stazione Termini and San Giovanni (St John Lateran). It terminates beyond Cinecittà at Anagnina (for Ciampino airport). It runs underground for the whole of its 14km length except for the bridge across the Tiber.

Line B runs from Laurentina in the south to Rebibbia or Conca d'Oro in the north (the line splits). If you need the Tiburtina or Ponte Mammolo stop, make sure you are on a Rebibbia train. It intersects with Line A at Termini and then has stations at Via Cavour, the Colosseum, Circus Maximus, Piramide (for Centrale Montemartini), Basilica San Paolo (for San Paolo fuori le Mura) and EUR. The last stop, Laurentina, is useful for Tre Fontane.

Line C was partially opened in 2014 connecting the eastern outskirts of the city on Via Casilina (Pantano) with Centocelle. After that it was under construction at the time of writing, with planned stops at San Giovanni, Fori Imperiali, Piazza Venezia, Chiesa Nuova and Ottaviano-San Pietro. As was to be expected, progress has been hampered by archaeological finds (a book has even been published recording all the ancient remains unearthed during work on the line).

BY TAXI

Taxis (white in colour) are provided with an identification name and number, the emblem of the municipality of Rome, and a meter; you should always make sure the latter is operational before hiring a taxi. The fare includes service, so tipping is not necessary. Licensed taxis are hired from ranks; there are no cruising taxis, and it is never advisable to accept rides from non-authorised taxis at the airports or railway stations. There are additional charges for travel at night (10pm–7am), on Sun and for each piece of luggage.

To call a taxi, *T: 060609* or *6645*: you will be given the approximate arrival time and the number of the taxi.

There are fixed tariffs to and from the airports. These are posted clearly on the exterior of all official taxi doors.

Accommodation

R ome offers a wide range of accommodation, from luxurious hotels to family-run B&Bs and monasteries and convents. The following is a small selection, listed by area. Prices are as follows, for a double room per night in high season:

€€€€   (over €400)
€€€   (€200–€400)
€€   (€100–€200)
€   (around €100)

BLUE GUIDES RECOMMENDED

Hotels and restaurants that are particularly good choices in their category—in terms of excellence, location, charm, value for money or the quality of the experience they provide—carry the Blue Guides Recommended sign: ◼. All these establishments have been visited and selected by our authors, editors or contributors as places they have particularly enjoyed and would be happy to recommend to others. To keep our entries up to date, reader feedback is essential: please do not hesitate to contact us (*blueguides.com*) with any views, corrections or suggestions.

PANTHEON, PIAZZA NAVONA AND CAMPO DEI FIORI

€€€€ **Grand Hotel de la Minerve**. The building has been a hotel since the late 18th century and its old-fashioned feel has been retained. There is a quiet interior courtyard and the comfortable rooms have close carpeting. The ground-floor restaurant moves up to the lovely roof terrace in summer. *Piazza della Minerva 69. T: 06 69 5201, grandhoteldelaminerve.it. 135 rooms. Map p. 654, B2.*

€€€ **Abruzzi**. Small, old-established hotel in front of the Pantheon. Modern décor and air conditioning. Quiet: only two rooms actually overlook the busy piazza. Helpful staff.

Piazza della Rotonda 69. T: 06 67 92 021, hotelabruzzi.it. 26 rooms. Map p. 654, B2.

€€€ **Raphael**. ◼ An independent hotel run by the son of the founder and a long-standing favourite, also with Italian guests. Tucked away just outside Piazza Navona, it is totally covered with wisteria. Some of the rooms are a bit small but the more expensive ones have their own terraces. Those on the third floor were redesigned by Richard Meier. The rooms at the front can be noisy at weekends when the restaurant in the piazza below is full. The hotel has its own restaurant on a charming little roof terrace with views of the tower of Sant'Ivo and of the dome of the Pantheon. *Largo Febo 2. T: 06 68 2831, raphaelhotel.com. 55 rooms. Map p. 654, B2.*

€€€ **Santa Chiara**. ■ This hotel, just two steps away from the Pantheon, has been run by the same family for over a century and has a devoted clientèle. Courteous staff and an atmosphere of quiet efficiency. It is worth asking for a room on the fourth floor since some (such as 407) have little terraces. If you require total silence, ask for a room on the inner courtyard. Some of the rooms have been modernised while others are still quite old-fashioned. Breakfast is served from 7am onwards. There is a very spacious ground floor with lots of comfortable places to sit (and a tiny patio with a couple of tables outside). *Via di Santa Chiara 21. T: 06 68 72 979, albergosantachiara.com. 90 rooms. Map p. 654, B2.*

€€–€€€ **Del Senato**. Delightful old-established hotel in an attractive 19th-century building overlooking the Pantheon. You need to book well in advance. The rooms mostly have parquet floors and are handsomely furnished. Some have wonderful views of the Pantheon. Those on the back are quieter. Roof terrace in summer. *Piazza della Rotonda 73. T: 06 67 84 343, albergodelsenato.it. 57 rooms. Map p. 654, B2.*

€€ **Campo dei Fiori**. Just out of Campo dei Fiori, the rooms on the first five floors are very small with close carpeting, some quieter than others. The best are the three with parquet floors on the top (sixth) floor, two of which have a terrace. The lovely small roof terrace has a superb view of all Rome's greatest monuments. However, the staff could be friendlier. *Via del Biscione 6. T: 06 68 80 6865, hotelcampodefiori.com. 27 rooms. Map p. 654, B2.*

€€ **Relais Teatro Argentina**. ■ In a quiet street just off Largo Torre Argentina, on the second floor, a delightful guesthouse with spacious rooms excellently decorated and furnished, with red walls and pretty wall paper in the bedrooms. Breakfast is served in your room. Very helpful English-speaking young owner. There is a tiny terrace on an inner courtyard. Two of the rooms have three beds; families can be comfortably accommodated. *Via del Sudario 35. T: 06 98 93 1617, relaisteatroargentina.com. 6 rooms. Map p. 654, B2.*

€ **Albergo del Sole**. Reputed to be on the site of the oldest hotel in the city, although its appearance today doesn't suggest this. But it is still something of an institution and very reasonably priced. One of the very few hotels in the city which still has some rooms without bathrooms and which does not provide breakfast. There is a labyrinth of corridors and back stairs, with four little terraces and gardens connected with iron steps. The rooms on the top floor with a terrace are the most pleasant, while others (considerably cheaper) are pretty basic. If you coincide with a group booking, the hotel can be noisy. It has its own garage. *Via del Biscione 76. T: 06 68 80 6873, www. solealbiscione.it. 65 rooms. Map p. 654, B2.*

€€ **Teatro di Pompeo**. ■ In a quiet small square close to Campo dei Fiori, this tranquil hotel in an old house sits on the remains of Pompey's theatre, whose original 55 BC structure is still partly visible in the lounge and breakfast room. All the attractive rooms feature old wood-beamed ceilings and tiled floors. They are on three floors, some on the front and others on the courtyard, but all of them quiet. Cordial staff. *Largo del Pallaro 8. T: 06 68 72 812, hotelteatrodipompeo.it. 13 rooms. Map p. 654, B2.*

FORUM, COLOSSEUM, CAELIAN

€€€€ **Forum**. Old-established hotel overlooking the Imperial Fora and just a few steps from the entrance to the Roman Forum, but yet surprisingly peaceful. Many of the rooms and the rooftop terrace (with restaurant and bar) offer some of the best views in the city onto the ruins of ancient Rome. The décor is slightly dated but it has a quiet and distinguished atmosphere with cordial staff. Parking available. *Via Tor de' Conti 25. T: 06 67 92 446, hotelforum.com. 78 rooms. Map p. 655, D3.*

€€€ **Residenza Torre Colonna**. Just five rooms (one on each floor) in a converted 13th-century tower, once the family home of the couple who run it. The iron bedsteads and other furnishings are made by the owner. All rooms have ethernet and well-equipped bathrooms. Breakfast is served on the top floor, below the plant-filled roof terrace with hot tub. *Via delle Tre Cannelle 18 (corner of Via IV Novembre). T: 06 83 60 0192, torrecolonna.it. Map p. 655, D2.*

€ **Domus Caracalla**. ■ A small B&B in a quiet road on the Caelian hill, on the top floor of a large residential block of apartments. You are given your own key. Just six rooms, some of them family rooms, and one with a kitchen, very well designed with pretty floors and good bathrooms. All have little terraces where you can sit outside. Very pleasant and efficient staff who serve you breakfast in your room. This is an unusual place to stay but you couldn't make a better choice if you are on a budget and wish to be on this side of Rome. The hotel is well served by buses to Piazza Venezia and to Termini Station. *Via Sant'Erasmo 11. T: 06 70 80 053, domuscaracalla.com. Map p. 653, C1.*

CORSO AND SPANISH STEPS

€€€€ **D'Inghilterra**. ■ In a quiet cul-de-sac surrounded by Rome's fashionable shopping streets a few steps from Piazza di Spagna and a brisk seven-minute walk from Piazza Venezia, this is one of the best-known old-established hotels in the city, with a long-standing returning clientèle as well as a distinguished historic guest list. The rooms overlook Via Borgognone or an interior court, and those on the fourth floor have been modernised. Some can be rather small (specify if you want space); only one room (suite no. 676) has a terrace. The Caffè Romano restaurant, where breakfast is served (also open to the public for lunch and dinner), has a few tables outside. The English-style bar, low-ceilinged and snug, is famous for its Bloody Marys. *Via Bocca di Leone 14. T: 06 87 50 3987, niquesahotels. com. 97 rooms. Map p. 654, C1.*

€€€€ **Grand Hotel Plaza**. Opposite the church of Santi Ambrogio e Carlo on the short stretch of the Corso which is closed to traffic, so very quiet. First opened around 1865, this is a magnificent example of faded splendour with expansive ground-floor reception rooms including a huge ballroom. There is a huge marble lion clambering down the splendid Art Nouveau staircase with its stained glass windows, and even the lift is a period piece. The bedrooms are a little dingy and the staff sometimes offhand. *Via del Corso 126. T: 06 69 92 1111, grandhotelplaza.com. 200 rooms. Map p. 654, C1.*

€€€€ **Hassler Roma**. ■ In a wonderful position at the top of the Spanish Steps, this is one of the most famous independent luxury hotels in Rome. Huge reception rooms on the ground floor include one with a grand piano. Professional service in great style. In the small palm court at the back, breakfast is served in good weather and there is a bar. Many of the rooms have private terraces or balconies and there is a terrace open to guests on the seventh floor. The magnificent penthouse suite has its own huge private roof terrace, totally secluded. The panoramic restaurant Imàgo (*T: 06 69 93 4726*), at the level of the roof of the Trinità dei Monti church, is open in the evenings and is run by a Neapolitan chef. For the hotel's annexe, see below. *Piazza Trinità dei Monti 6. T: 06 69 9340, hotelhasslerroma. com. 95 rooms. Map p. 652, B3.*

€€€ **Il Palazzetto**. Delightful annexe of the Hassler with elegant rooms overlooking the Spanish Steps. It is considerably cheaper and has its own restaurant (closed Mon) and wine bar. *Vicolo del Bottino 8. T: 06 699 34 1000, hotelhasslerroma.com/en/ il-palazzetto. 4 rooms. Map p. 652, B3.*

€€ **Intercontinental De La Ville Roma**. Next door to the Hassler, in a good position at the top of the Spanish Steps. Part of the Intercontinental group. Some of the rooms, with fitted carpets, are rather small. There is a restaurant, breakfast is served on the second floor, and the pleasant roof terrace has fine views. It has a quiet atmosphere although it does take groups. There is a

small garage nearby (book a space ahead of arrival). *Via Sistina 69. T: 06 67 331, ihg.com. 192 rooms. Map p. 652, C3.*

€€ **Internazionale**. A pleasant hotel in a superb location. The rooms are particularly spacious (those on the back are very quiet) and five have balconies. The breakfast room has delightful old-fashioned décor and the pretty terrace has a view of St Peter's. Well run, with very helpful staff. Garage. No groups. *Via Sistina 79. T: 06 699 41 823, hotelinternazionale.com. Map p. 652, C3.*

€€ **Gregoriana**. A small hotel on one of the quietest streets in this very central area. There are 16 smallish rooms on three floors, with rather eccentric furnishings and wood floors. The top floor has very comfortable, but more expensive, suites (including no. 3 with a large terrace). Good bathrooms. Breakfast room in the basement. No groups. The staff could be more friendly. *Via Gregoriana 18. T: 06 67 94 269, hotelgregoriana.it. Map p. 652, B3.*

€€ **Scalinata di Spagna**. In a perfect position beside the Spanish Steps. Some rooms are a bit small but pleasantly furnished. The three rooms on the first floor have their own terraces; the largest is no. 6. Breakfast is served on the first floor next to a charming terrace where you can sit in warm weather. The hotel is quiet (no groups) and friendly, with cordial young staff. Special last-minute rates usually available. *Piazza Trinità dei Monti 17. T: 06 45 68 6150, hotelscalinata.com. 16 rooms. Map p. 652, B3.*

TRASTEVERE

€€€ **Buonanotte Garibaldi**. ■ A beautiful garden court with orange trees and magnolia, reminiscent of Spain or

Morocco, provides the special feature of this delightful B&B run by the artist Luisa Longo, who lives here. There are just three rooms (the Rome room on the first floor has a lovely large terrace), all furnished in a crisp modern style with fabrics hand-painted by Luisa, whose atelier is off the courtyard. She offers guests tea and home-made biscuits in her spacious living room, as well as a superb breakfast with home-made jam (and bacon and eggs if you so wish) in the elegant dining room. Special offers can sometimes be arranged. *Via Garibaldi 83. T: 06 58 33 0733, buonanottegaribaldi.com. 3 rooms. Map p. 654, A3.*

€€€ **Donna Camilla Savelli**. This occupies three floors of the former convent of Santa Maria dei Sette Dolori, with its church by Borromini. There is a large garden in the old cloister and plenty of places to sit and relax, although large conferences and events are also held here. Run by the Alpitour group. *Via Garibaldi 27. T: 06 58 88 61, hoteldonnacamillasavelli.com. 77 rooms. Map p. 654, A3.*

€€ **Guesthouse Arco de' Tolomei**. ■ Comfortable B&B in the wing of the delightful house where the owners live. It is on a tiny hillock in a very short back street, rarely used by cars, which leads out of Piazza in Piscinula and through the arch from which the street is named. The rooms are delightfully furnished and the three on the upper floor have their own terraces. Guests are encouraged to use the books and guides as well as the computer. The simple sound of life in the street below is exceptional in any city today. Breakfast is served in the family dining room and the owners are always available (together with their very friendly staff) to help you plan your day. It is a true delight to set off each morning from here to explore the city across the Roman footbridge on the Tiber island, and all the great monuments are within walking distance. There is a garage nearby in Via Anicia. Minimum stay 2 nights. *Via Arco de' Tolomei 27. T: 06 58 32 0819, bbarcodeitolomei.com. 6 rooms. Map p. 654, B3.*

€€ **Hotel Santa Maria**. ■ A very unusual hotel, opened in 2000 in an area once a convent and later a repair yard for carriages. The rooms are arranged around two large garden courts planted with orange trees and the porticoes recall the convent cloister. The atmosphere suggests you are in the countryside rather than a large city, and you are encouraged to borrow a bicycle (free of charge). The rooms, plainly furnished with tiled floors, are particularly suitable for families as some of them can sleep four or more. Breakfast is served across the courtyard in a pleasant room beyond a bar where a free buffet is prepared with snacks between 5.30 and 7 (you buy your own drinks). Very pleasant staff. If you give advance warning you can park inside (just two spaces) or at the garage next door. Residenza Santa Maria (*see below*) is under the same management. *Vicolo del Piede 2 (corner of Via della Pelliccia). T: 06 58 94 626, hotelsantamariatrastevere.it. 18 rooms. Map p. 654, A3.*

€€ **Residenza Santa Maria**. ■ A sister hotel of the Hotel Santa Maria, in a charming little building with a tiny inner courtyard with comfortable chairs. The rooms (some of which can sleep families) are well designed and furnished (the paintings are copies of works by the artist Antonio Donghi, grandfather of the manager). Breakfast is served downstairs in a remarkable barrel-vaulted room which was once a Roman cistern, appropriately decorated with ancient marbles. *Via dell'Arco di San Calisto 20. T: 06 58 33 5103,* *residenzasantamariatrastevere.it. 6 rooms. Map p. 654, A3.*

€ Casa di Santa Francesca Romana a Ponte Rotto. A simple hotel in the house where St Francesca Romana lived and died (in 1440), in one of the quietest parts of Trastevere, near the church of Santa Cecilia. Although a religious institution, there is no curfew. It has tables in a pretty courtyard. The rooms are basically furnished with tiled floors, and some of them can sleep families of three or four. *Via dei Vascellari 61. T: 06 58 12 125, sfromana.it. 37 rooms. Map p. 654, B4.*

TERMINI STATION AND SANTA MARIA MAGGIORE

€€€€ St Regis Grand. When it opened in 1894, this was the first hotel in Rome to have electric light and a bathroom for every room. Afternoon tea is still served in winter in the magnificent *Salone*, which retains its Art Nouveau decorations. Even though the rest of the hotel has been discreetly modernised, the atmosphere remains elegantly old-fashioned. With its marble baths and Murano chandeliers, it still recalls a day when no expense was spared to decorate top-class hotels. Most of the rooms, which are heavily furnished, have close carpeting. Professional service is provided by the cordial staff. On the ground floor is the Vivendo restaurant. Part of the Starwood hotel group, it is very convenient for the station but otherwise the position is not today very attractive. *Via Vittorio Emanuele Orlando 3. T: 06 47 091, stregisrome.com. 161 rooms. Map p. 655, E1.*

€ Hotel Giuliana. Run by an English lady and her daughter, on the first floor of a large *palazzo* with a spacious staircase and old-fashioned lift. It is extremely handy for the railway station, but ask for a room on Via Cesare Balbo, which overlooks a street market (held in the mornings); those on Via Depretis are noisy. Rooms are simply furnished with cool tiled floors and there is a tiny bar and breakfast area. *Via Agostino Depretis 70. T: 06 48 80 795, hotelgiuliana. com. 11 rooms. Map p. 655, E2.*

AVENTINE

€€ Aventino San Anselmo Hotels. This is a group of three hotels all close together in the exceptionally peaceful residential area of the Aventine. They are ideal places to stay if you have a car as you can park on the street outside. They are all in pleasant villas built in the early 20th century, surrounded by gardens. The **Hotel Sant'Anselmo** (*Piazza Sant'Anselmo*) has 34 cheerful Venetian-style rooms, nine of which have balconies, and is marginally more expensive than the **Villa San Pio** (*Via Santa Melania 19*), which is really three distinct villas, with 78 rooms in all. The most reasonably priced (and the smallest) is the **Aventino Hotel** (*Via San Domenico 10*) with 21 rooms. *Piazza Sant'Anselmo 2. T: 06 57 0057, www. aventinohotels.com. Map p. 653, A1.*

€€ Domus Aventina. Modernised ex-convent. The spacious rooms, some with balconies, face onto a courtyard and the wall of Santa Prisca. Reasonably priced. *Via di Santa Prisca 11b. T: 06 57 46 135, hoteldomusaventina.com. 26 rooms. Map p. 653, A1–B1.*

VIA VENETO

€€€€ **Eden**. Owned by Dorchester Hotels, this is another of Rome's famous luxury-class hotels, just off the Via Veneto. Very elegant with all the comforts and services you would expect. Its roof restaurant, La Terrazza, is listed on p. 594. *Via Ludovisi 49. T: 06 47 8121, dorchestercollection.com. Map p. 652, C3.*

€€€€ **Westin Excelsior**. Across Via Boncompagni from the American Embassy, opened in 1906, this is still one of Rome's most famous hotels. Owned by Starwood Hotels, it has a luxurious atmosphere, and an indoor swimming pool and fitness centre. The Doney restaurant is on the ground floor.

Via Veneto 125. T: 06 47 081, westinrome. com. 287 rooms. Map p. 652, C3.

€€€ **Victoria**. Just off the top end of Via Veneto, this is a Swiss-run hotel which offers excellent value: spacious, spotless rooms mostly with parquet floors, and good bathrooms. Friendly and efficient staff. In good weather a restaurant operates on the small roof terrace (there is a view over the Borghese Gardens, although you do hear the traffic up here). There is another restaurant on the ground floor. Both have reasonably-priced set menus. *Via Campania 41. T: 06 42 3701, hotelvictoriaroma.com. 111 rooms. Map p. 652, C3.*

VATICAN

€€ **Hotel Bramante**. In an old building with a charming old entrance door, just off the pleasant Borgo Pio, this is a beautifully decorated hotel with a welcoming atmosphere. Tiled floors and beamed ceilings. Very convenient for St Peter's and the Vatican but well away from the crowds. *Vicolo delle Palline 24. T: 06 68 80 6426, hotelbramante.com. 16 rooms. Map p. 650, C2.*

€€ **Sant'Anna**. In a delightful quiet pedestrian street with local shops, very

close to St Peter's, this is a small hotel decorated in Art Deco style. The ample rooms on the top floor have small terraces. Parking. You can sit out in the charming tiny garden court. *Borgo Pio 134. T: 06 68 80 1602, hotelsantanna.com. 20 rooms. Map p. 650, C2.*

€€ **Angelina's Bed and Breakfast**. Close to Castel Sant'Angelo, with five 'suites' furnished with eccentric modern taste. *Via Cicerone 28 (corner of Piazza Cavour), T: 06 32 27 691, angelinashome.com. Map 650, D1.*

MONASTERY ACCOMMODATION

Monasteries and convents are an excellent option for good-value accommodation, particularly as some of the buildings are located in central positions that rival many hotels. Each property is individually run and all offer clean, basic accommodation, many with private bathrooms. **Monastery Stays** (*monasterystays.com*) offers an online booking service, which lets you choose a location and view its facilities before making a reservation. It is best to book well in advance, especially over Easter and during the summer. Note that most of the institutions have a curfew, around 10.30 or 11pm.

Rome Food & Drink

You can eat extremely well in Rome, in the simplest places as well as in the most sophisticated. Basic Roman cuisine has surprisingly few typical dishes: short pasta is often served in a spicy sauce (*alla matriciana* or *amatriciana*) made from bacon, tomato, *pecorino* cheese and chili; *spaghetti alla carbonara* has beaten egg, bacon, *pecorino* cheese and black pepper; and other homemade types of fresh spaghetti include *bucatini* and *tonnarelli*, often served with *cacio* cheese and black pepper, or with walnuts. *Fettuccine* are ribbon noodles usually served with a meat sauce or porcini mushrooms. Another typical first course is *gnocchi di patate*, small potato dumplings served in a meat and tomato sauce. A traditional Roman soup is *stracciatella*, a meat broth with parmesan and a beaten egg.

Second courses include *abbacchio arrosto* or *al forno* (roast suckling lamb), *saltimbocca alla romana* (veal escalope with ham and sage), *coda alla vaccinara* (oxtail stewed in a tomato and celery sauce), and *ossobuco al tegame* (stewed shin of veal).

Vegetables are usually very good and an important part of the Roman cuisine are artichokes (*carciofi*), cooked in a great variety of ways. They are always young and small so they can be eaten whole. If served *alla giudia* they are deep fried, whereas *alla Romana* means they will be stuffed with wild mint and garlic and then stewed in olive oil and water. Courgettes (*zucchini*) are sometimes served *ripieni* (stuffed) or grilled or fried. Their flowers (*fiori di zucca*) can be stuffed with mozzarella cheese and salted anchovies, dipped in batter and fried. Particularly good green vegetables served lightly cooked sometimes with garlic, and dressed just with olive oil can usually be ordered, such as *cicoria* (chicory) and *broccoletti* or *broccoletti di rapa* (broccoli and rape). *Misticanza* is a rich green salad with a great variety of wild lettuce and herbs. *Puntarelle* are sprouting chicory tips, usually served with an anchovy sauce.

You are certain to find some of the above in the simpler and cheaper places. In the more expensive restaurants the menu is usually much more sophisticated. Rome is well supplied with good fresh fish. You can also eat very good pizza here: Rome is considered second only to Naples for this national dish (typically eaten in the evening).

Even at the simplest places it is always wise to reserve a table, as restaurants can get very crowded and the Romans themselves particularly enjoy eating out. Nearly everywhere has seating outside (especially since the ban on smoking indoors), even if this means only one or two tables on the street. It is quite acceptable nowadays to order just one course. Prices include service, unless otherwise stated on the menu (if in doubt, check with the waiter), but most Italians usually leave the change from their payment or a few euro on the table in gratitude for a good meal.

Wines from all over Italy are freely available. The white house wine will be from the nearby Alban Hills and Frascati; in the simpler places it will be served to you in a carafe.

Some museums and exhibition venues now have good restaurants and/or cafés, notably the Galleria Nazionale d'Arte Moderna, the Capitoline Museums, Palazzo delle Esposizioni and the Auditorium concert hall in the Parco della Musica.

Romans who dine out often, and those who expect a culinary experience when choosing a restuarant, will tell you that nowadays you have to move out of the historic centre to find good places. They maintain that the old Roman *trattorie* now cater exclusively to the (uncomplaining) tourist. While this is true to a certain extent (particularly in the historic centre), there are still many professionally-run restaurants, not solely geared to visitors, where you can get a very good, reasonably-priced meal made with fresh seasonal ingredients. If you are happy to keep slightly later hours, eating dinner at around 9pm for example, you will find plenty of Romans in the restaurants with you. A number of places where you can eat well have opened outside the centre, especially in the Ostiense area beyond Testaccio. Some are listed here, although we have mainly selected places in the historic centre since this is the area where visitors are likely to be.

A selection of restaurants—grouped according to location and divided into four categories according to price per person for dinner, with wine—is given below. Blue Guides recommended (*see p. 582*) restaurants are marked ▬.

€€€€ over €125
€€€   €80–€125
€€   €30–€80
€   under €30

PANTHEON, PIAZZA NAVONA, CAMPO DEI FIORI, CORSO

€€€€ **Il Convivio Troiani.** ▬ Hidden away in a lane only wide enough to be used as a park for motorbikes, just behind Palazzo Altemps. Very professionally run, it serves extremely imaginative dishes in an intimate atmosphere. *Hors d'oeuvres* include prawns with goat's cheese strudel and smoked aubergine purée. The pasta is homemade and served with fish, game and duck sauces. Meat or fish dishes provide the main courses, which usually include lamb, pigeon and rabbit. The desserts are magnificent, with chocolate or fruit as the main ingredient and featuring sorbets, mousses and water ices. There is an excellent '*menù degustazione*'—a many-course set tasting menu. Dinner only Mon–Sat. Closed Sun. *Vicolo dei Soldati 31. T: 06 68 69 432, ilconviviotroiani.it. Map p. 654, B1.*

€€€€ **La Rosetta.** ▬ A famous restaurant widely held to be the top fish restaurant in Rome. It has a few tables outside on the street. The menu is very short but each dish is prepared with great care to accentuate the flavour of wonderfully fresh fish and seafood. Oysters are often available as an *hors d'oeuvre*, and clams feature in the pasta dishes. Excellent list of wines and champagne. There is an affordably-priced set menu. Lunch and dinner daily. *Via della Rosetta 8. T: 06 68 61 002, larosetta.com. Map p. 654, B2.*

€€€–€€ Fortunato al Pantheon. An efficiently run old-style Roman restaurant with particularly high-quality food. Frequented by politicians and businessmen. Seasonal fare and good fish. Lunch and dinner daily. *Via del Pantheon 55. T: 06 67 92 788, ristorantefortunato.it. Map p. 654, B2.*

€€ Ditirambo. A simple, cosy place with two small rooms and seating outside in fine weather. It serves rather unusual dishes, made from carefully-sourced Italian ingredients, which make a change from standard Rome fare. There is a good wine list with some interesting dessert wines. Closed Mon lunch. *Piazza della Cancelleria 74–75. T: 06 68 71 626, ristoranteditirambo. it. Map p. 654, B2.*

€€ L'Eau Vive. In a 15th-century palace, this is run by French nuns (for charity) so you will find only traditional French cuisine here—and you will not be disappointed. Lunch and dinner Mon–Sat. Closed Sun. *Via Monterone 85. T: 06 68 80 1095, restaurant-eauvive.it. Map p. 654, B2.*

€€ Maccheroni. Off Via delle Coppelle, between Piazza Navona and the Corso. A popular, lively place which cleverly mixes tradition and trend. Old-look décor and an open kitchen. Filling Roman pasta staples such as *amatriciana* and *cacio e pepe*. There is a very good little market in the piazza where local produce is sold in the mornings. Lunch and dinner daily. *Piazza delle Coppelle 44. T: 06 68 30 7895, ristorantemaccheroni.com. Map p. 654, B1.*

€€ Pesci Fritti. Good fish, try the *carbonara di spigola*. Lunch and dinner Tues–Sun. *Via di Grotta Pinta 8 (the curving street just west of Via dei Chiavari). T: 06 68 80 6170. Map p. 654, B2.*

€€ Renato e Luisa. In a narrow alley off Largo Arenula, a small *trattoria* which serves good pasta and often has seafood. Excellent desserts. Frequented by Italian families, it has a particularly jolly atmosphere. Closed Mon. *Via dei Barbieri 25. T: 06 68 69 660, renatoeluisa.it. Map p 654, B2.*

€€ Settimio. At the far end of this old road, with an unassuming entrance, this has a limited menu of typical Roman dishes (*stracciatella, bollito di manzo, involtini*) but remains in the very best tradition of serious cuisine served in a basic but very pleasant setting. The Cesanese del Piglio is an excellent wine from Lazio. Closed Wed. *Via del Pellegrino 117. T: 06 68 80 1978. Map p. 654, A2.*

€€–€ L'Hosteria de Memmo 'i Santori'. Reliable food (a seafood *hors d'oeuvre* that is a meal in itself; good *saltimbocca*) and a lively atmosphere. Very close to Palazzo Altemps. *Via dei Soldati 22–23. T: 06 68 13 5277, osteriadememmo.it. Closed Sun. Map p. 654, B1.*

€ La Montecarlo. A good place to eat a pizza or simple meal, at crowded old-fashioned tables, in a narrow lane off Corso Vittorio Emanuele II. It has a bustling atmosphere without any pretension (paper tablecloths and tin plates), typical of Rome, and it can be difficult to find a table if you don't come early. Good simple local dishes, as well as pizzas. It is well worth accepting whatever fried *hors d'oeuvre* is offered.

Ideal for a good quick meal, but you have to be in the right mood to deal with the off-hand, almost too casual attitude of the army of young male waiters. There are a few tables in the alleyway outside, but it is a shame not to savour the special atmosphere inside. No credit cards. Lunch and dinner Tues–Sun. *Vicolo Savelli 12. T: 06 68 61 877, lamontecarlo.it. Map p. 654, A2.*

€ **La Quercia.** A *trattoria* with tables outside in the piazza beside Palazzo Spada. Very pleasant atmosphere with kind staff serving basic Roman fare. Lunch and dinner daily. *Piazza della Quercia 23. T: 06 68 30 0932, osterialaquercia.com. Map p. 654, B3.*

€ **La Sagrestia.** A rather anonymous place with a very extensive menu—which might put you off, but the cooking is sound and the pizzas excellent. It is frequented by Romans who want a good but not grand meal. Lunch and dinner Thur–Tues. *Via del Seminario 89, T: 06 67 97 581. Map p. 654, B2–C2.*

€ **Roscioli.** Excellent for a plate of pasta at lunch time at the back of this old-established grocery. Very wide selection of cheeses and wines. Lunch and dinner Mon–Sat. *Via dei Chiavari 34 and Via dei Giubbonari 21. T: 06 68 75 287, salumeriaroscioli.com. Map p. 654, B3.*

NEAR THE COLOSSEUM

€–€€ **Caffè Propaganda.** Reminiscent of a Paris bistro, this prides itself on being both a café and a restaurant, so you can have a cup of tea and a cake, a cocktail or glass of wine (with homemade crisps), or a full meal. Excellent for lunch. It has become very popular in the evenings, when it stays open until 2am. Imaginative menu and pleasant décor. Lunch and dinner Tues–Sun. *Via Claudia 15. T: 06 94 53 4255, caffepropaganda.it. Map p. 655, E4.*

€ **Morgana.** A *trattoria* serving genuine Roman food, including traditional dishes such as tripe and snails. Lunch and dinner Thur–Tues. *Via Mecenate 19/21 (in front of the Teatro Brancaccio). T: 06 48 73 122, trattoriamorgana.com. Map p. 655, F3.*

THE GHETTO

€€–€€€ **Evangelista.** Just outside the area of the Ghetto, across Via Arenula. A pleasant place with a few tables also outside in a patio. It has recently become renowned for its artichokes, especially *carciofi al mattone*. Delicious desserts. Good wine list. Dinner only, Mon–Sat. *Via delle Zoccolette 11. T: 06 68 75 810, ristorantevangelista.com. Map p. 654, B3.*

€€ **Piperno.** Traditional Roman cooking (much use is made of offal) and Roman Jewish dishes too, including the delicious fried artichokes. Refreshing house Frascati. On the top of the tiny peaceful hillock of Monte dei Cenci. Old-fashioned formal atmosphere (gentlemen tend to wear ties, even at lunchtime). Its reputation has, however, diminished in recent years. Lunch Tues–Sun, dinner Tues–Sat. *Monte dei Cenci 9. T: 06 68 80 6629, ristorantepiperno. it. Map p. 654, B3.*

€–€€ **Nonna Betta.** Despite the competition from other restaurants close by, this kosher restaurant is now said to be one of the best in the Ghetto. It also has a good value set menu. Naturally the *carciofi alla giudia* are a speciality. Lunch and dinner Wed–Mon, closed Tues. *Via del Portico d'Ottavia 16. T: 06 68 80 6263, nonnabetta.it. Map p. 654, B3.*

TRASTEVERE

€€€ **La Gensola**. Although the address suggests a piazza, this is in fact on the corner of Via della Gensola, two steps out of Piazza in Piscinula. Run by Irene and Claudio, it serves excellent fish. Lunch and dinner daily. *Piazza della Gensola 15. T: 06 58 16 312, osterialagensola.it. Map p. 654, B3.*

€€€–€ **Checco er Carettiere**. This has been one of the best-known restaurants in Trastevere for many years (although some feel it has rather had its day). The menu usually includes *coda alla vaccinara*, but you can also order a simple grilled fish. Homemade desserts. Lunch and dinner daily. *Via Benedetta 10. T: 06 58 17 018, checcoercarettiere.it. Map p. 654, A3.*

€€ **Il Ciak**. This is a place where you can enjoy Tuscan food, and many locals suggest it is the best place in the city for steak. Dinner nightly. *Vicolo del Cinque 21. T: 06 58 94 774, ristoranteilciak.com. Map p. 654, A3.*

€€ **Le Mani in Pasta**. In a peaceful area of Trastevere, this is a well-run restaurant with good food, particularly strong on meat dishes (but also fish when available). Lunch and dinner Tues–Sun. *Via dei Genovesi 37, T: 06 58 16 017, lemaniinpasta.net. Map p. 654, B4.*

€€ **Roma Sparita**. With tables outside in this beautiful quiet piazza. A large busy restuarant, also a pizzeria. Try the *tagliolini a cacio e pepe*. Lunch and dinner Tues–Sat. Low season closed all day Mon and Sun eve; high season closed all day Sun and Mon lunch. *Piazza Santa Cecilia 24. T: 06 58 00 757, romasparita.com. Map p. 654, B4.*

€€ **Spirito DiVino**. Special care is taken to ensure the quality of the ingredients used to produce interesting dishes. Service can be a little overdone. Dinner Mon–Sat. The *hors d'oeuvres* and first courses are particularly good. *Via dei Genovesi 31. T: 06 58 96 689, ristorantespiritodivino.com. Map p. 654, B4.*

€€–€ **Enoteca Ferrara**. ■ This justly popular place comes alive in the early evening as a wine bar (*see p. 597*), but there is a restaurant too, where the chef Maria shows her skill in bringing Roman tradition up to date. Ingredients are always fresh and seasonal. Dinner daily (best to book), also open for lunch on Sun. Closed Sun in Aug. *Piazza Trilussa 41. T: 06 58 33 3920, enotecaferrara.it. Map p. 654, A3.*

€ **Ai Marmi**. Large, very popular pizzeria. There is no name outside; the Romans irreverently call it the '*obitorio*', or morgue, because of its marble table tops. The busy atmosphere is typical of old Rome, and you are not expected to linger over your meal. The thin pizzas are amongst the best you can find in a city renowned for this Italian speciality, but they are so thin they can sometimes be served rather over-cooked with a charred underside. You can also eat typical Roman dishes here, including excellent fried *baccalà* (salt cod). Dinner only Thur–Tues. *Viale Trastevere 53. T: 06 58 00 919. Map p. 654, B4.*

€ **Antico Carlone**. In a quiet back street off Via della Lungaretta, where you can also sit outside, this is a good place to come for a filling pasta dish: *gnocchi* (potato dumplings); *pappardelle a fiori di zucca* (short pasta with courgette flowers; *fettuccine asparagi e funghi* (home-made pasta with asparagus and mushrooms; *tonnarelli alle noci* or *al cacio e pepe* (fresh noodles similar to spaghetti with a walnut or cheese and black pepper sauce). If you still have room for a second course, these usually include roast lamb and veal (*saltimbocca alla romana*), but you get the impression that the chef's attention is mainly concentrated on the first courses. Very pleasant staff and relaxed atmosphere (although it has now been discovered by tourist groups). Good value. Lunch and dinner Tues–Sun. *Via della Luce 5. T: 06 58 00 039. Map p. 654, B3.*

€ **Fish Market**. You choose the fish you wish to have cooked and mark it on the menu, and then pay before you sit down at your table where you are served with a drink and your fish is then delivered to you. The staff are all cooks rather than waiters. The quality of the fish is excellent (caught daily off the coast of southern Lazio) and prices are very reasonable. Delightful atmosphere. Dinner nightly, lunch weekends. *Vicolo della Luce 3/5. T: 366 9144 157 (no reservations), fishmarket-roma.com. Map p. 654, B3.*

€ **Trattoria da Teo**. Run by Teo and Tiziana. Many diners who used to frequent Trattoria da Enzo in Via dei Vascellari now come here. Excellent food and reasonable prices. Very pleasant seating in the quiet little piazza. *Piazza dei Ponziani 7 (at the end of Via dei Vascellari). T: 06 58 18 355, trattoriadateo.it. Map p. 654, B4.*

NEAR PIAZZA DEL POPOLO

€€€ **Dal Bolognese**. ◼ In a wonderful position, with elegant clientèle and professional service. As the name suggests, the cuisine is from Bologna, with excellent fresh pasta and classic dishes. Lunch and dinner Tues–Sun. *Piazza del Popolo 1/2. T: 06 36 11 426, dalbolognese.it. Map p. 652, A2.*

€€€–€€ **Nino**. Venerable old Roman institution, in business since 1934, and still with an air of a more elegant age, with watiers in white jackets and bow ties. Tuscan specialities such as *fagioli al fiasco*. *Via Borgognona 11. T: 06 67 86 752, ristorantenino.it. Map p. 652, B3.*

€€ **Settimio all'Arancio**. An offshoot of the well-established Settimio near Campo dei Fiori, this has a similar menu. A good choice. Lunch and dinner Mon–Sat. *Via dell'Arancio 50. T: 06 68 76 119, settimioallarancio.it. Map p. 654, B1.*

€ **Matricianella**. A simple restaurant with tables outside in this quiet little side street. Basic Roman cuisine, with particularly good fried vegetables. Lunch and dinner Mon–Sat. *Via del Leone 4, T: 06 68 32 100, matricianella.it. Map p. 654, B1.*

VIA VENETO, VILLA BORGHESE, PIAZZA FIUME, PORTA PIA

€€€€ **La Terrazza dell'Hotel Eden**. On the top floor of the well-known hotel and famous first and foremost for its stunning view. The menu features modern interpretations of Italian classics, beautifully presented. However its culinary reputation has waned somewhat in recent years. Breakfast, lunch and dinner daily. *Via Ludovisi 49. T: 06 47 8121, dorchestercollection.com/en/rome/ la-terrazza-delleden. Map p. 652, C3.*

€€€ **Marzapane**. Opened in 2013 by a young Spanish chef and winner of many plaudits. The 'concept' is described as 'a tale of taste'. Sophisticated dishes combining unexpected ingredients. Just a few tables, and undoubtedly a culinary experience. Not far from the Galleria Borghese. Lunch and dinner Thur–Tues. *Via Velletri 39. T: 06 64 78 1692, marzapaneroma.com. Map p. 652, D2.*

€€ **Le Colline Emiliane**. ■ A very pleasant, old-fashioned restaurant where it is unusual to find a non-Italian. It has a discreetly simple interior which seems to have survived from the days when there were many fewer restaurants in the city. The service is impeccable and you are treated with great respect whether you choose to have a long drawn-out meal or just a quick plate of pasta with salad. If you order the excellent pumpkin ravioli you are asked if you would like them normal or on the sweet side. Lunch Tues–Sun, dinner Tues–Sat. *Via degli Avignonesi 22. T: 06 48 17 538. Map p. 655, D1.*

€€–€ **Trimani**. This is one of the oldest wine shops in Rome, with a friendly wine bar round the corner. The menu includes a few hot dishes, such as soups, quiches, grilled beef and seasonal vegetables, as well as a tempting selection of cheeses, smoked fish and cured pork. Good desserts. Lunch and dinner Mon–Sat. *Via Cernaia 37b. T: 06 44 69 630, trimani.com. Map p. 655, F1.*

€ **Cantina Cantarini**. A dependable, down-to-earth *trattoria* in a rather anonymous position. Excellently cooked ingredients which include fish Thur evening and on Fri and Sat. Lunch and dinner Mon–Sat. *Piazza Sallustio 12. T: 06 47 43 341, ristorantecantinacantarini.it. Map p. 652, D3.*

NEAR SANTA MARIA MAGGIORE

€€€€ **Agata e Romeo**. The location is somewhat out of the way, but this is considered by many gourmets to be the best place in Rome for fish. Lunch Tues–Fri, dinner Mon–Sat. *Via Carlo Alberto 45. T: 06 44 66 115, agataeromeo.it. Map p. 655, F2.*

PRATI AND MONTE MARIO

€€€€ **La Pergola**. In the Hotel Cavalieri Waldorf Astoria, on the slopes of Monte Mario (*map p. 647*), which can only be reached by car or taxi. In the last few years the Pergola has become famous since it has been repeatedly acclaimed by restaurant critics as the best in Rome (and among the top ten in the country). Impeccable service and elegant décor. Dinner only, Tues–Sat. *Via Cadiolo 101. T: 06 35 09 2152, romecavalieri.com/lapergola.php.*

€ **Trattoria Ai Villini**. Run by the second generation of the family who founded it, serving all the Roman specialities you would expect such as *spaghetti all'amatriciana* and *rigatoni alla carbonara*, with, as they say, '*nessun fronzolo*' (no frills). Very good value and a long way from the tourist trail. A few steps from the Lepanto Metro station, almost due north of Castel Sant'Angelo. Lunch Thur–Tues, dinner daily except Wed and Sun. *Via Marcantonio Colonna 48 (just above Via Pompeo Magno). T: 06 32 16 766, trattoriaaivillini.it. Map p. 650, D1.*

TESTACCIO, PIRAMIDE, OSTIENSE

€€€ **Checchino dal 1887**. Literally carved out of Monte Testaccio and run by the same family for over a hundred years, Checchino serves all the dishes you would expect to find in this typically Roman place. Simple décor and good wine list (also available by the glass). Lunch Tues–Sun, dinner Tues–Sat. *Via di Monte Testaccio 30. T: 06 57 43 816, checchino-dal-1887.com. Map p. 653, A3.*

€ **Eataly**. Housed in a building originally intended to be an air terminal attached to Ostiense railway station. On four floors, this is part of a chain of establishments throughout Italy (and now also in New York) which provide places of all kinds to eat, snack and shop for food products. All the produce is Italian. It has become a favourite place for family outings. Open daily 10am–midnight. *Piazzale 12 Ottobre 1492 (at the end of Via Pellegrino Matteucci; map p. 653, A3), reached by underpass from Piramide Metro station. T: 06 90 27 9201, eataly.net.*

€ **La Dogana Food**. Fixed-price Oriental buffet in a huge converted warehouse. You choose what you want and it is cooked in front of you. Try the Mongol 'soup'. You are charged extra if you leave something on your plate. Lunch and dinner daily. *Via del Porto Fluviale 67b. T: 06 57 40 260, ladoganafood.com. Map. p 653, A3.*

€ **Novecento**. Excellent pizza as well as meat dishes. A large, pleasant place with a very cheerful atmosphere. Lunch Sun–Fri, dinner nightly. *Via dei Conciatori 10 (off Via Ostiense). T: 331 323 4399, 9cento.com. Map p. 653, A3.*

€ **Pizzeria Da Remo**. Excellent very simple and good-value pizzeria. Dinner Mon–Sat. *Piazza Santa Maria Liberatrice 44. T: 06 574 6270. Just beyond map p. 653, A2.*

€ **Porto Fluviale**. In a former industrial building, this is perhaps the cheapest pizzeria in town. There is also a *trattoria*, snack bars and places to sit and read. Very popular, it stays open until 3am on Fri and Sat. Lunch and dinner nightly. *Via del Porto Fluviale 22. T: 06 57 43 199, portofluviale. com. Map p 653, A3.*

€ **Trattoria Perilli**. Well-known to Romans, this has remained something of an institution, with very traditional dishes. Excellent *pasta all'amatriciana*. Lunch and dinner Thur–Tues. *Via Marmorata 39. T: 06 57 55 100, trattoria-romana.it/da/perilli. Map p. 653, A2.*

WINE BARS

In recent years there has been a proliferation of wine bars in Rome, just as in the rest of Italy. They range from smart places with modern décor where you can have a drink and an elaborate snack at all hours of the day to crowded, jolly places where people come for a glass of wine in the early evening. A few favourites are listed below.

Cul de Sac. Near Piazza Navona. Long and narrow, warm and friendly, this claims to have been the first wine bar in Rome. Cheeses, cold meat, quiches; hearty lentil soup in wintertime. There are over 700 wine labels to choose from. It has become rather touristy but is still better value than places in Piazza Navona. Lunch and dinner daily. *Piazza Pasquino 73. T: 06 68 80 1094, enotecaculdesacroma.it. Map p. 654, B2.*

Enoteca Ferrara. ■ Popular, friendly place in Trastevere with an excellent variety of wines and superb bar snacks (you are given a plate and can serve yourself). There is also a good restaurant (*see p. 593*). Wine bar open from 6pm. *Piazza Trilussa 41. T:* *06 58 33 3920, enotecaferrara.it. Map p. 654, A3.*

G-Rough. Near Piazza Navona. Mid-century chairs and tables, palm trees, black mirrored walls, low lighting. Don't be put off by the name: this tiny space is as smooth as they come. On the ground floor of a building that houses the G-Rough luxury suites ('rough' because of the salvage architecture aesthetic). *Piazza Pasquino 69–70. T: 06 68 80 1085. Map p. 654, B2.*

Il Vinaletto. Crowded, convivial place near Via Giubbonari, where people spill out onto the streets with their glasses of wine. *Via del Monte della Farina 37. Map p. 654, B2.*

COFFEE, SNACKS AND ICE CREAM

Rome serves particularly good coffee and its cafés are open all day. Most people pop in for a coffee and a snack which they eat standing at the bar. Order what you want and pay the cashier, and then show the receipt (*scontrino*) to the barman in order to get served. In almost all bars, if you sit at a table you are charged more—at least double— and are given waiter service (you should not pay first). Well-known cafés include:

Caffè Greco on Via Condotti 86 (*map p. 654, C1*), famed for its historic guest list as much as for the pastries (*see p. 346*); and **Rosati**, at Piazza del Popolo 4 (*map p. 652, A2*).

La Casa del Caffè on Via degli Orfani and **Il Caffè** in Piazza Sant'Eustachio (both near the Pantheon; *map p. 654, B2*) serve particularly good coffee. Also in Piazza Sant'Eustachio is **Camilloni**.

Pascucci on Via di Torre Argentina (*map p. 654, B2*) is justly famous for its fresh fruit milkshakes. **Vanni**, in Via Frattina (*corner of Via Belsiana; map p. 654, C1*), has good snacks and a yoghurt bar.

Forno La Renella, at Via del Moro 15 in Trastevere (*map p. 654, A3*), is a very popular bakery with excellent bread, snacks and cakes. **Cinque Lune** at Corso Rinascimento 89 (*map p. 654, B2*) is an excellent *pasticceria* selling delicious cakes made with traditional recipes, using honey and light flaky pastry.

For ice cream, **Tre Scalini** at Piazza Navona 31 (*map p. 654, B2*) is famous. The recipe for its *tartufo*, a chocolate ice cream truffle, dates back to 1946. **Gelateria del Teatro** on Via dei Coronari (*map p. 654, A1*) has delicious homemade ice creams with fresh ingredients, including fruit in season.

General Information

BANKING SERVICES

Banks are usually open Mon–Fri 8.30–1.30, and for an hour in the afternoon, usually 2.30/3–3.30/4; closed Sat, Sun and holidays. A few banks are now open on Sat mornings, including the Banca di Roma in Piazza di Spagna and the Banca Nazionale del Lavoro at Via del Corso 266. All banks close early (about 11) on days preceding national holidays.

BOOKSHOPS

English-language books are stocked at the following shops:

The Almost Corner Bookshop. A particularly delightful old-fashioned bookshop which has for years been a gathering place for the English-speaking community in Rome. Closed Mon morning. *Via del Moro 45. T: 06 58 36 942. Map p. 654, A3.*

The Open Door Bookshop. New and used books, flexible long opening hours. *Via della Lungaretta 23. T: 06 58 96 478, books-in-italy.com. Map p. 654, B3.*

The Anglo-American Book Co. Excellent selection in all categories: fiction, non-fiction, guide books, children's, academic. Open Mon–Fri 9–1 & 2–6, Sat 9–1. Closed Sun. *Via della Vite 102. T: 06 67 95 222, aab.it. Map p. 654, C1.*

La Feltrinelli International, Open Mon–Sat 9–8, Sun 10–1.30 & 4–8. *Via Vittorio Emanuele Orlando 84/86. T: 06 48 27 878, lafeltrinelli.it. Map p. 655, E1.*

CHURCHES: OPENING TIMES AND DESCRIPTIONS

The opening times of churches vary greatly. They have been given where possible in the text but as with all opening times, are subject to change. Generally speaking churches open early (except on Sun) and almost always close around noon. Some reopen around 3, 4 or 5pm for a few hours. A few of the major churches now stay open throughout the day. Most churches ask that sightseers do not visit during a service. Mass takes place several times on Sun and during the week usually in the early morning and/or early evening. If you are wearing shorts or a mini-skirt or have bare shoulders you can be stopped from entering some churches.

The four great papal basilicas of St Peter's, St John Lateran, Santa Maria Maggiore and San Paolo fuori le Mura are all open throughout the day, usually 7am to 7pm. The choir of St Peter's sings on Sunday at High Mass at 10.30 and at vespers at 5. High Mass, with music, is celebrated in the other basilicas on Sunday at 9.30. The ringing of the evening Ave Maria or Angelus bell from many of Rome's churches still takes place every day at sunset.

Many altarpieces and frescoes are difficult to see without adequate lighting, which is sometimes provided (coin-operated; most systems take 1 euro coins). Many are not lit, however; when visiting churches it is always useful to carry a torch and a pair of binoculars.

Churches in Rome are very often not orientated, in other words the high altar does not face compass east. In the text the terms north and south refer to the liturgical north (left) and south (right) sides, taking the high altar as being at the 'east' end.

Roman Catholic services in English take place in San Silvestro in Capite (*map p. 654, C1*) and San Clemente (*map p. 655, E3*). San Clemente also offers services in Irish Gaelic. The church of Sant'Anselmo on the Aventine Hill (*map p. 653, A1*) is noted for its **Gregorian chant** at 9.30 on Sun.

Other places of worship

American Episcopal	St Paul's Within the Walls. *Via Napoli 58, T: 06 48 83 339, stpaulsrome.it. Map p. 655, E1.*
Anglican	All Saints. *Via del Babuino 153, T: 06 36 00 1881, allsaintsrome.org. Map p. 652, B3.*
Baptist	*Piazza San Lorenzo in Lucina 35, T: 06 68 76 652. Map p. 654, C1.*
Greek Orthodox	Sant'Atanasio dei Greci. *Via del Babuino. Map p. 652, B3.* San Teodoro al Palatino. *Via di San Teodoro, T: 06 67 86 624. Map p. 654, C3.*
Jewish	Synagogue. *Lungotevere dei Cenci, T: 06 68 40 061. Map p. 654, B3.*
Methodist	*Piazza Ponte Sant'Angelo. T: 06 68 68 314. Map p. 654, A1.*
Muslim	Centro di Cultura Islamica. *Via della Moschea (Parioli), T: 06 80 82 167. Map p. 647.*
Scottish Presbyterian	St Andrew's. *Via XX Settembre 7, T: 06 48 27 627, presbyterianchurchrome.org. Map p. 655, E1.*

CRIME AND PERSONAL SECURITY

As in large cities all over the world, pickpocketing is a widespread problem in Rome; it is always advisable not to carry valuables in handbags and to be particularly careful on public transport. It is a good idea to make photocopies of all important documents in case of loss. Particular care should be taken when drawing cash from an ATM.

Crime should be reported at once, theft to either the Polizia di Stato or the Carabinieri. A detailed statement has to be given in order to get an official document confirming loss or damage (*denunzia di smarrimento*), which is essential for insurance claims. Interpreters are usually provided.

Polizia di Stato foreigners' office: *T: 06 46 86 2102*
Carabinieri: *T: 112*
Municipal police: *T: 06 67 691*
Traffic police: *T: 55 441*
Railway police: *T: 06 48 19 561.*

EMERGENCY SERVICES

For all emergencies, T: 113. The switchboard will coordinate the help you need.

First aid services (*pronto soccorso*) are available at all hospitals, railway stations and airports. San Giovanni, in Piazza San Giovanni in Laterano (*map p. 655, F4*), is the central hospital for emergencies: for first aid, T: 06 77 05 5297. The American Hospital in Rome at Via Emilio Longoni 69, east of the centre off Via Prenestina (*T: 06 22 55 290*), is a private English-speaking hospital which accepts most American insurance plans. The International Medical Centre will refer callers to English-speaking doctors (*T: 06 48 82 371; nights and weekends T: 06 48 84 051*).

> **First-aid and ambulance service:** *T: 118*
> **Red Cross ambulance service:** *T: 5510*
> **Fire brigade:** *T: 115*
> **Road assistance:** *T: 116.*

ENTERTAINMENT

Up-to-date listings information in English is available at *060608.it* (or *T: 060608*); and at the websites *unospitearoma.it* and *oggiroma.it*.

Every Thursday *La Repubblica* newspaper publishes 'TrovaRoma', which gives details of the week's forthcoming events in town. Mostly in Italian but with a few pages listing the 'Best in Rome' in English.

MUSEUMS

Opening times for museums, collections and monuments are given in the text (though opening times vary and often change; you should always check online or by telephone before visiting). All museums are usually closed on the main public holidays: Easter Sunday, 29 June, 15 Aug and Christmas Day. The closing times given in the text indicate when the ticket office closes, which is usually 30–60mins before the actual closing time.

Admission costs: For state- and municipality-owned museums and monuments EU citizens between the ages of 18 and 24 are entitled to reductions (you must show proof of nationality), and all those under 18 are given free entrance. There is a student discount for the Vatican Museums.

Reductions can be had if you buy the Roma Pass (*see p. 579*). An inclusive ticket, called the Roma Archeologia Card, valid for seven days, allows entrance to Palazzo Massimo, Palazzo Altemps, Crypta Balbi, Baths of Diocletian, Colosseum, Roman Forum and Palatine, Baths of Caracalla, Villa dei Quintili and the Mausoleo di Cecilia Metella (the last two are on the Via Appia Antica).

Tickets for any of the four museums run by the Museo Nazionale Romano (Palazzo Altemps, Baths of Diocletian, Palazzo Massimo and Crypta Balbi) are valid for seven days and include entry to all four sites.

Archaeological sites are free to all on the first Sunday of the month.

Agencies for special **guided tours** include Tour in Rome (*tourinrome.com*).

La Settimana dei Musei Italiani (Museum Week) is an annual event, usually held in March or April. Entrance to most museums is free and some have longer opening hours. Some private collections and monuments not generally accessible are opened at this time.

PHARMACIES

Pharmacies or chemists (*farmacie*) are identified by their street signs, which show a luminous green cross. They are usually open Mon–Sat 9–1 and 4–7.30 or 8. Some are open 24hrs a day, including the one outside Stazione Termini on Piazza dei Cinquecento (*map p. 655, F1*). A few are open on Sun and holidays, and at night: these are listed on the door of every chemist and in the daily newspapers.

POSTAL SERVICES

If you plan to send postcards, the head post office in Rome is in Piazza San Silvestro (*map p. 654, C1*), open daily 9–6. Stamps (*francobolli*) are usually also sold at tobacconists displaying a blue 'T' sign. Mail for outside Rome should be posted into red boxes, or the blue boxes in the centre of town. The Vatican postal service is generally more efficient than the Italian and costs the same. Within the Vatican City there are post offices in Piazza San Pietro and the Vatican Museums, and there is also one in Trastevere in the courtyard of Palazzo San Calisto, Piazza San Calisto 16 (*map p. 654, A3; blue letterbox*). NB: Vatican stamps are not valid for the Italian state postal service.

PUBLIC HOLIDAYS AND ANNUAL FESTIVALS

The main holidays in Rome, when offices and shops are closed, are as follows:

1 January (New Year's Day)	1 November (All Saints' Day)
25 April (Liberation Day)	8 December (Immaculate Conception)
Easter Monday	25 December (Christmas Day)
1 May (Labour Day)	26 December (St Stephen)
15 August (Assumption)	

In addition, the festival of the patron saints of Rome, Peter and Paul, is celebrated on 29 June as a local holiday in the city. There is usually no public transport on 1 May and the afternoon of Christmas Day.

Annual festivals

5–6 January: Epiphany (*Befana*), celebrated at night in Piazza Navona;
Shrove Tuesday: Carnival is celebrated in the streets and *piazze*;
21 April: Anniversary of the birth of Rome, celebrated on the Capitoline hill;
23–24 June: Festa di San Giovanni, at night, near Porta San Giovanni (*map p. 649, B3*);
First Sunday in June: Festa della Repubblica, military parade in the Via dei Fori Imperiali;
July: Festa di Noantri, celebrations in Trastevere for several weeks.

SHOPPING

The smartest shops are in Via Frattina and Via Condotti, which lead out of Piazza di Spagna. A good and less expensive shopping area is in the area of the Pantheon and Campo Marzio. Another important shopping street in the city (if in a less attractive area) is Via Cola di Rienzo (*map p. 650, D1*) in the Prati district, between Piazza del Risorgimento and the Tiber.

There are small supermarkets all over the historic centre but you need to look out for them as they are never brashly lit or obtrusively signed. The supermarket at Termini Station is open 24hrs a day. There is a supermarket with a good deli counter and fresh bread at Via Giustiniani 18b (north of Salita de' Crescenzi) near the Pantheon (*map p. 654, B2*).

Opening hours: More and more shops in the historic centre are staying open all day now, although food shops still usually close between 1 and 5.

TELEPHONES AND THE INTERNET

Telephone numbers in Italy can have from seven to eleven numbers. All require the area code, regardless of whether you are making your call from within or outside Rome.

Italy country code	39
Rome area code	06
dialling UK from Italy	(00 44) + number
dialling US from Italy	(00 1) + number

Most hotels in Rome now offer free wifi. Your device will either connect automatically or you will be given a login name and password at reception. Many bars and cafés also offer wifi if you need to be connected and don't have roaming.

TIPPING

Most prices in hotels and restaurants include a service charge, which means that tipping is far less widespread in Italy than it is in North America, for example. Taxi journeys also officially include service, but drivers are always very grateful if you round up the fare by a euro or so. In hotels, porters who show you to your room and help with your luggage, or find you a taxi, do usually expect a couple of euro.

Glossary

Acrolith, statue where the head and undraped (visible) extremities are of stone, while the remainder is of wood; this was a style of statuary typically reserved for gods, and later for emperors

Aedicule, small niche or opening framed by two side columns and a pediment

Agnus Dei, small wax objects made from melting down the paschal candles (*qv*) used in the previous year

Ambo (pl. ambones), pulpit in a Christian basilica; two pulpits on opposite sides of a church from which the gospel and epistle were read

Amorino (pl. amorini), in art and architecture, a chubby, winged male child. A cupid (cf. putto)

Amphora, antique vase, usually of large dimensions, for oil and other liquids

Annunciation, the appearance of the Angel Gabriel to Mary to tell her that she will bear the Son of God; an image of the 'Virgin Annunciate' shows her receiving the news

Antefix, ornament placed at the lower corners of the tiled roof of a temple to conceal the space between the tiles and the cornice

Antiphonal, choir-book containing a collection of antiphons—verses sung in response by two choirs

Antis, 'in antis' describes the portico of a temple where the side walls are prolonged to end in a pilaster flush with the columns of the portico

Apodyterium, dressing-room in a Roman bath

Apostles, those who spread the Christian word, traditionally twelve in number, in other words the disciples (excluding Judas but with his replacement Matthias), and later including St Paul and his followers

Apse, vaulted semicircular end wall of the chancel of a church or of a chapel

Arca, wooden chest with a lid, for sacred or secular use. Also, monumental sarcophagus in stone, used by Christians and pagans

Archaic, period in Greek civilisation preceding the Classical era: from about 750 BC–480 BC

Architrave, the horizontal beam running above the columns in ancient architecture; the lowest part of the entablature (*qv*)

Archivolt, moulded architrave carried round an arch

Arcosolium (pl. arcosolia), a tomb where the sarcophagus or funerary bed is in a recessed niche surmounted by an arch

Aryballos (pl. aryballoi), small Greek pottery vase for oil or perfume with a globular body, narrow neck and single handle

Assumption, the ascension of the Virgin to Heaven, 'assumed' by the power of God

Atlantes (or telamones), male figures used as supporting columns (cf. caryatid)

Atrium, forecourt, usually of a Byzantine church or a classical Roman house

Attic, topmost storey of a classical building, hiding the spring of the roof; in art, it refers to a style from Attica in ancient Greece

Aumbry, a small cupboard, niche or cabinet for holy oil, often set into the walls of churches and inscribed 'O.S.' or 'Oleum Sacrum'. It is distinct from a tabernacle (*qv*), which is used for storing the elements of the Eucharist (Communion bread and wine)

Baldacchino, canopy supported by columns, usually over an altar

Barley-sugar column, a Solomonic column (*qv*)

Basilica, originally a Roman hall used for public administration; in Christian architecture, an aisled church with a clerestory and apse, and no transepts

Biga, a two-horse chariot

Black-figure ware, ancient Greek pottery style of the 7th–5th centuries BC where the figures appear black against a clay-coloured ground

Borgo, a suburb; a street leading away from the centre of a town

Bottega, the studio of an artist; the pupils who worked under his direction

Bozzetto, sketch, often used to describe a small model for a piece of sculpture

Bucchero, Etruscan black terracotta ware

Bucrania, a form of Classical decoration—heads of oxen with flower garlands

Caldarium (or calidarium), room for hot or vapour baths in a Roman bath

Campanile, bell-tower, often detached from the building to which it belongs

Camposanto, cemetery

Canephora, figure bearing a basket, often used as a caryatid

Canopic vase, Egyptian or Etruscan vase enclosing the entrails of the dead

Capitoline Triad, the three deities worshipped in the Temple of Jupiter on the Capitoline hill were Jupiter, Juno (*qv*) and Minerva, who became the three principal gods of the Roman pantheon

Carceres, openings in the barriers through which the competing chariots entered the circus; the 'traps'

Cardo, the main street of a Roman town, at right angles to the decumanus

Cartoon, from *cartone*, meaning large sheet of paper. A full-size preparatory drawing for a painting or fresco

Caryatid, female figure used as a supporting column

Catechumen, a novice preparing for baptism into the early Christian Church

Cavea, the part of a theatre or amphitheatre occupied by the row of seats

Cella, the inner sanctum of a pagan temple

Chiaroscuro, distribution of light and shade in a painting

Chi-Rho, Christian symbol formed by the superimposition of the first two letters of Christ's name in Greek, X and P

Chiton, linen tunic worn by the ancient Greeks

Chryselephantine, made of gold and ivory

Ciborium, casket or tabernacle containing the Host (Communion bread)

Cipollino, a greyish marble with streaks of white or green, from the Greek island of Euboea, highly prized by the ancient Romans

Cippus, sepulchral monument in the form of an altar

Cista, casket, usually of bronze and cylindrical in shape, to hold jewels, toilet articles, etc, and decorated with mythological subjects

Classical, in ancient Greece, the period from 480–323 BC

Clerestory, upper part of the nave of a church above the side aisles, with windows, usually a feature of Gothic architecture

Cloisonné, type of enamel decoration divided by narrow strips of metal, typical of Byzantine craftsmanship

Columbarium, a building (usually subterranean) with niches to hold urns containing the ashes of the dead

Comune, in medieval Italy, a city ruled by a government of the people. Today the word signifies the municipality

Confessio, crypt beneath the high altar and raised choir of a church, usually containing the relics of a saint

Corbel, a projecting block, usually of stone, to support an arch or beam

Corinthian, order of Classical architecture easily identified by its column capitals decorated with curling acanthus leaves

Cornice, topmost part of a temple entablature; any projecting ornamental moulding at the top of a building beneath the roof

Cosmatesque (or Cosmati), inlaid marble work using mosaic and coloured glass and stone to decorate pavements, pulpits, choir screens, columns, cloisters, etc

Cryptoporticus, vaulted subterranean corridor

Cuneus, wedge-shaped block of seats in an ancient theatre

Cyclopean, the term applied to walls of unmortared masonry, older than the Etruscan civilisation and attributed by the ancients to the giant Cyclopes

Damascened, decorated with a metalwork technique that involves inlaying patterns in gold and silver into a steel base material

Decumanus, a main east–west street of a Roman town, running parallel to its longer axis

Deposition, the taking down of Christ's body from the Cross

Diaconia, early Christian charitable institution

Dioscuri, name given to Castor and Pollux, twin sons of Zeus (*see p. 82*)

Dipteral, temple surrounded by a double peristyle

Diptych, painting or ivory tablet in two sections

Doric, one of the ancient orders of architecture, characterised by a plain capital and a stout fluted column standing directly on the platform, without a base (cf. Tuscan Doric)

Engaged columns, columns which partially retreat into the wall

Entablature, upper horizontal part of a temple above the columns, made up of an architrave, frieze and cornice

Ephebus, Greek youth under training (military or university)

Epistyle, horizontal beam resting upon columns, an architrave (*qv*)

Evangelists, the authors of the four Gospels, Matthew, Mark, Luke and John, often depicted in art through their symbols, respectively the man/angel, lion, bull and eagle

Exedra (also, properly, exhedra), recessed area projecting from a room or other space, originally with benches

Extraterritorial, refers to Vatican property outside the confines of the Vatican City

Ex-voto, tablet or small painting expressing gratitude to a saint or given in fulfilment of a vow

Flavian, of the emperors Vespasian, Titus, Domitian, Nerva and Trajan; or of the period of their rule

Forum (pl. fora), open space in an ancient town serving as a market or meeting-place

Fresco, painting executed on wet plaster. On the wall beneath is sketched the sinopia, and the cartoon is transferred onto the fresh plaster (intonaco) before the fresco is begun, either by pricking the outline with small holes over which a powder is dusted, or by means of a stylus which leaves an incised line. In recent years many frescoes have been detached from the walls on which they were executed

Frieze, strip of decoration usually along the upper part of a wall; in a temple this refers to the horizontal feature above the columns between the architrave and the cornice

Frigidarium, room for cold baths in a Roman bath

Gens, Roman clan or group of families linked by a common name

Giallo antico, red-veined yellow marble from North Africa; Numidian yellow

Giant order, column or pilaster (*qv*) with a vertical span of two or more storeys on a façade

Gigantomachia, contest between giants

Gonfalone banner of a medieval guild or commune

Graffiti, design on a wall made with an iron tool on a prepared surface, the design showing in white. Also used loosely to describe scratched designs or slogans on walls

Greek cross, cross with all four arms of equal length

Grisaille, painting in various tones of grey

Grotesque (or *grottesche*), painting or stucco decoration based on the style of the ancient Romans found during the Renaissance in the Domus Aurea (then underground, hence the name, from 'grotto'). The delicate ornamental decoration usually includes patterns of flowers, sphinxes, birds and human figures, against a light ground

Hellenistic, Greek culture of the period from the death of Alexander the Great to the victory of Rome over Antony and Cleopatra (323–30 BC). Art from this period often displays more sentiment than Classical works

Hemicycle, a semicircular structure or space

Herm (pl. hermae), quadrangular pillar decreasing in girth towards the ground, surmounted by a head

Hexastyle, of a portico, having six columns

Horreum (pl. horrea), a warehouse

Hydria, a vessel for water

Hymettian marble, marble from Mt Hymettus, near Athens

Hypogeum, subterranean excavation for the interment of the dead (usually Etruscan)

Impasto, early Etruscan ware made of inferior clay

Imperial period, period of ancient Roman history under the Roman emperors (27 BC–AD 476)

Impluvium, pool or cistern in the centre of an atrium in a Roman house, into which rainwater fell

Incunabulum (pl. incunabula), any book printed in the same century as the invention of movable type (i.e. between 1450 and 1500)

Insula (pl. insulae), tenement house

Intarsia (or tarsia), inlay of wood, marble or metal

Intercolumniations, the space between the columns in a colonnade

International Gothic, painting style characterised by a poised elegance, static but without the rigidity of pure Gothic. There is also a mingling of strong design with loving attention to detail, such as birds, animals and flowers. The style is often called 'courtly', because the natural and the stylised come together in images redolent of medieval courtliness

Intonaco, plaster

Ionic, order of Classical architecture identified by its capitals with two volutes (*qv*)

Juno, the wife of Jupiter and queen of the heavens, Juno was particularly the protectress of married women. As Juno Pronuba she presided over weddings; as Juno Lucina she assisted at childbirth. The cult of Juno Sospita, 'Juno who saves', is of very ancient origin; in this manifestation the goddess is shown clad in a goatskin. Juno Moneta, the 'warning' goddess, also guarded over the state treasury

Krater, antique mixing-bowl, conical in shape with a rounded base

Kylix, wide shallow vase with two handles and a short stem

Laconicum, room for vapour baths in a Roman bath

Latin cross, cross where the vertical arm is longer than the horizontal

Loggia, covered gallery or balcony

Lunette, semicircular space in a vault or above a door or window, often decorated with a painting or relief

Macellum, ancient Roman market hall

Maenad, female participant in the orgiastic rites of Dionysus

Matroneum, gallery reserved for women in early Christian churches

Meta, conical turning-post for chariot races in a circus or stadium

Metope, panel between two triglyphs on the frieze of a Doric temple

Mithraeum, temple of the god Mithras

Monolith, single stone (usually a column)

Mostra, the terminus of an aqueduct, often in the form of an elaborate fountain, used to demonstrate and test the emergent water pressure

Narthex, vestibule of a Christian basilica

Naumachia, mock naval combat for which the arena of an amphitheatre was flooded

Niello, a black inlay into stone, used to pick out an engraved design

Nimbus, luminous ring surrounding the heads of saints in paintings; a square nimbus denoted that the person was still living when the likeness was made

Nymphaeum, a summer house in the gardens of baths and palaces, originally a temple of the Nymphs, decorated with statues, and often containing a fountain

Octastyle, of a portico, having eight columns

Oinochoë, wine-jug, usually of elongated shape, for dipping wine out of a krater (*qv*)

Opus alexandrinum, mosaic design of black and red geometric figures on a white ground

Opus etruscum, type of opus quadratum (*see below*) where the blocks are placed alternately lengthwise and endwise

Opus incertum, masonry of small irregular stones set in mortar (a type of concrete)

Opus mixtum, masonry that is a mixture of brickwork with opus reticulatum (*qv*)

Opus quadratum, masonry of large rectangular blocks without mortar

Opus reticulatum, masonry arranged in squares or diamonds so that the mortar joints make a network pattern

Opus sectile, mosaic or paving of thin slabs of coloured marble cut in geometrical shapes

Opus spicatum, masonry or paving of small bricks arranged in a herring-bone pattern

Opus tessellatum, mosaic formed entirely of square tesserae

Opus vermiculatum, mosaic with tesserae arranged in lines following the design contours

Palazzo, any dignified and important building; the town house of a noble family

Palombino, fine-grained white marble

Pantocrator, literary 'He who Controls All', a representation of Christ in Majesty traditionally featured in the central dome of Orthodox churches and in the main apse of an early Christian basilica

Parian marble, fine white marble from the Aegean island of Paros

Paschal candle, tall candle first lit on Easter Saturday and thereafter at services until Ascension Day

Passion, the sufferings of Christ, ending with His death on the Cross. The Instruments of the Passion are symbols of these sufferings and include the crown of thorns and the column at which Jesus was flagellated

Patera, small circular ornamental disc, usually carved; Greek or Roman dish for libations to the gods

Pavonazzetto, white marble blotched with blue; Phrygian purple

Pax, sacred object used by a priest for the blessing of peace, and offered for the kiss of the faithful; usually circular, engraved, enamelled or painted in a rich gold or silver frame

Pendentive, concave spandrel beneath the four 'corners' of a dome

Pentelic, marble from Mt Penteli near Athens

Peperino, earthy granulated tufa, much used in Rome

Peplos, draped women's woollen mantle made from a single piece of cloth usually open at the side

Peripteral, temple surrounded by a colonnade. The style was common in ancient Greece. Roman temples tended only to have colonnaded porches

Peristyle, court or garden surrounded by a columned portico

Piano nobile, main floor of a palace

Pietà, group of the Virgin mourning the dead Christ

Piscina, Roman tank; a basin for an officiating priest to wash his hands before Mass

Pluteus (pl. plutei), marble panel, usually decorated; a series of them used to form a parapet to precede the altar of a church

Podium, a continuous base or plinth supporting columns, and the lowest row of seats in the cavea of a theatre or amphitheatre

Polyptych, painting or tablet in more than three sections

Porphyry, dark blue, purple or red-coloured igneous rock, much prized in the ancient world and used almost exclusively for imperial commissions

Pozzolana, reddish volcanic earth (mostly from Pozzuoli, near Naples) largely used for cement

Predella, small painting or panel, usually in sections, attached below a large altarpiece

Presepio, literally, crib or manger. A group of statuary of which the central subject is the Infant Jesus in the manger

Pronaos, vestibule or anteroom in front of the cella (*qv*) of a temple

Propylaea, monumental entranceway to an ancient sanctuary

Prostyle, temple with columns on the front only

Pulvin, cushion stone between the capital and the impost block, the block immediately under the architrave (*qv*)

Pulvinar, imperial couch and balcony on the podium of a theatre

Punic Wars, the wars fought between Rome and the Carthaginians between 264 and 164 BC. The second war was led by Hannibal

Putto (pl. putti), sculpted or painted figure, usually nude, of a male, unwinged child (cf. amorino)

Quadratura, painted architectural perspectives, often in *trompe l'oeil* (*qv*)

Quadriga, four-horse chariot

Quadriporticus, four-sided space surrounded by a colonnade

Red-figure ware, ancient Greek pottery style of the 6th–4th centuries BC where the figures appear in red against a black ground

Repoussé, relief-work in metal that has been achieved by hammering from the back, thus punching out the design

Republican period, period of ancient Roman history dating from c. 509 BC to 31 BC (preceding the Imperial period; *qv*)

Revetment, cladding, for decorative or protective purposes, applied to either horizontal or vertical surfaces

Rhyton, drinking-horn often fashioned at

the tip in the shape of an animal's head

Risorgimento, the period when the idea of a united Italy took root (mid-19th century)

Rosso antico, red marble from the Peloponnese; Tenaros red

Rostra, orator's platform; and ships' prows captured in battle, which were often used to decorate these platforms

Sanpietrini (or sampetrini), small rectangular flint paving stones used in Piazza San Pietro (hence the name) but also used in numerous old streets and squares of Rome. Also the name used in past centuries for the workmen employed on the maintenance of St Peter's

Saturnine verse, poetry written in an ancient Latin metre that was current before it was displaced by the hexameter

Schola cantorum, enclosure for the choristers in the nave of an early Christian church, adjoining the sanctuary

Segmented pediment, curved (as opposed to triangular) moulding over a window or door aperture

Sibyl, in the ancient world, a female soothsayer, adopted in Christian iconography as a forerunner of the prophets who foretold the coming of the Messiah

Silenus (pl. sileni), a drunken follower of Dionysus/Bacchus

Sinopia, large sketch for a fresco made on the rough wall in a red earth pigment called sinopia (because it originally came from Sinop, a town on the Black Sea). When a fresco is detached for restoration, it is possible to see the sinopia beneath, which can also be separated from the wall

Situla, water-bucket for ritual use

Skyphos, drinking cup with two handles

Solomonic column, twisted column, so called from its supposed use in the Temple of Solomon

Spandrel, surface between two arches in an arcade or the triangular space on either side of an arch

Spina, low stone wall connecting the turning-posts (*metae*) at either end of a circus

SPQR Senatus Populusque Romanus ('the Senate and the Roman People'), these letters have represented the Romans since the days of the Republic and are now used to denote the municipality

Stamnos, big-bellied vase with two small handles at the sides, closed by a lid

Stele (pl. stelae), upright stone bearing a monumental inscription

Stemma, coat of arms or heraldic device

Stereobate, basement of a temple or other building

Stigmata, marks appearing on a saint's body in the same places as the wounds of Christ (nail-holes in the feet and hands, and the sword wound in the side)

Stoa, a long, narrow colonnaded building, with rooms used as meeting halls or shops opening off the colonnade

Strigil, bronze scraper used by the Romans to remove the oil with which they had anointed themselves before bathing or exercise

Stylobate, basement of a columned temple or other building

Sudarium, cloth with which Christ's face was covered at the Deposition

Synthronon, in an early Christian basilica, semicircular bench on which the clergy sat

Tabernacle, in ecclesiastical furnishings, a casket or box used for the storage of the Host, Communion bread and wine

Tablinum, the reception or family room in a Roman house

Telamones (*see Atlantes*)

Temenos, a sacred enclosure

Tepidarium, room for warm baths in a Roman bath

Term, similar to a herm (*qv*), but different in that the bust and sometimes torso are included as well as the head

Tessera (pl. tesserae), a small cube of marble, glass etc, used in mosaic work

Tetrastyle, having four columns

Theatre, in the ancient Roman world, a semicircular auditorium, as opposed to an amphitheatre which is elliptical and has seats all the way round

Thermae, originally simply baths, later elaborate complexes with libraries, assembly rooms and gymnasia

Tholos, in ancient architecture, a circular building, often funerary

Titulus, the name board fixed to Christ's Cross bearing the letters INRI

Tondo (pl. tondi), round painting or bas-relief

Trabeated, construction where the apertures (doors, windows) have vertical supports and horizontal lintels as opposed to arches

Transenna, open grille or screen, usually of marble, in an early Christian church

Travertine, tufa quarried near Tivoli; the commonest of Roman building materials

Tribune, raised platform or gallery, for watching a spectacle or addressing an audience or crowd

Triclinium, dining-room and reception-room of a Roman house

Triglyph, small panel of a Doric frieze raised slightly and carved with three vertical channels

Triptych, painting or tablet in three sections

Trompe l'oeil, literally a 'deception of the eye'. Used to describe illusionist decoration, painted architectural perspectives, etc

Tropaion (or Trophy), a victory monument

Tumulus, a burial mound

Tuscan Doric, variant of the Doric order (qv) whereby the columns stand on a simple base and the shaft is unfluted

Velarium, canvas sheet supported by masts to protect the spectators in an open theatre from the sun

Verde antico, green marble from Thessaly, Greece; Thessalian green

Villanovan, pertaining to an Iron Age culture of northern Italy

Volute, scroll-like decoration at the corners of an Ionic capital; also typically present console-style on the façades of Baroque churches

Zoöphorus, frieze of a Doric temple, so-called because the metopes were often decorated with figures of animals

Rulers of Ancient Rome

KINGS OF ROME

Romulus	753–716 BC	Tarquinius Priscus	616–579 BC
Numa Pompilius	716–673 BC	Servius Tullius	579–534 BC
Tullus Hostilius	673–640 BC	Tarquinius Superbus	534–509 BC
Ancus Martius	640–616 BC		

ROMAN REPUBLIC (509–27 BC)

Sulla (dictator)	82–78 BC	Julius Caesar (dictator)	45–44 BC
First Triumvirate (Julius Caesar,		Second Triumvirate (Mark Antony,	
Crassus, Pompey)	60–53 BC	Lepidus, Octavian)	43–27 BC
Pompey (dictator)	52–47 BC		

ROMAN EMPIRE (27 BC–AD 395)

Augustus		Lucius Verus (co-emperor)	161–169
(formerly Octavian)	27 BC–AD 14	Commodus	180–192
Tiberius	14–37	Pertinax	193
Caligula	37–41	Didius Julianus	193
Claudius	41–54		
Nero	54–68	**Severans**	
Galba	68–69	Septimius Severus	193–211
Otho	69	Caracalla	211–217
Vitellius	69	Geta (co-emperor)	211–212
		Macrinus	217–218
Flavians		Elagabalus	218–222
Vespasian	69–79	Alexander Severus	222–235
Titus	79–81	Maximinus Thrax	235–238
Domitian	81–96	Gordian I	238
Nerva	96–98	Gordian II	238
Trajan	98–117	Pupienus	238
		Balbinus (co-emperor)	238
Antonines		Gordian III	238–244
Hadrian	117–138	Philip I	244–247
Antoninus Pius	138–161	Philip II	247–249
Marcus Aurelius	161–180	Decius	249–251

Gallus and Volusian	251–253	Galerius	305–310
Aemilianus	253	Licinius	308–324
Valerian	253–260	Flavius Severus	306–307
Gallienus	260–268	Maxentius	306–312
Claudius II	268–270	Constantine the Great	
Quintillus	270	(reunites empire)	306–337
Aurelian	270–275	Constantine II	337–340
Domitianus II (usurper)	270–271	Constans (co-emperor)	337–350
Tacitus	275–276	Constantius II (co-emperor)	337–361
Florian	276	Magnentius (co-emperor)	350–353
Probus	276–282	Julian the Apostate	361–363
Carus	282–283	Jovian	363–364
Carinus	282–285	Valentinian I (in West)	364–375
Numerian (co-emperor)	283–284	Valens (in East)	364–378
Diocletian (institutes tetrarchy)	285–305	Gratian	367–383
Maximian (co-emperor)	286–305	Valentinian II (usurper)	375–392
Constantius Chlorus	305–306	Theodosius I	378–395

WESTERN EMPIRE (395–476)

Honorius	395–423	Anthemius	467–472
Valentinian III	425–55	Olybrius	472
Petronius Maximus	455	Glycerius	473
Avitus	455–456	Julius Nepos	474–475
Majorian	457–461	Romulus Augustulus	475–476
Libius Severus	461–465		

Popes

Antipopes, usurpers or otherwise unlawful occupants of the pontifical throne are given in square brackets.

1. **St Peter**; martyr; 42–67
2. **St Linus**, of Tuscia (Volterra?); martyr; 67–78
3. **St Anacletus I**, of Rome; martyr; 78–90 (?)
4. **St Clement I**, of the Roman Flavian *gens*; martyr; 90–99 (?)
5. **St Evaristus**, of Greece (or of Bethlehem); martyr; 99–105 (?)
6. **St Alexander I**, of Rome; martyr; 105–115 (?)
7. **St Sixtus I**, of Rome; martyr; 115–125 (?)
8. **St Telesphorus**, of Greece; martyr; 125–136 (?)
9. **St Hyginus**, of Greece; martyr; 136–140 (?)
10. **St Pius I**, of Italy; martyr; 140–155 (?)
11. **St Anicetus**, of Syria; martyr; 155–166 (?)
12. **St Soter**, of Campania (Fundi?); martyr; 166–175 (?)
13. **St Eleutherus**, of Epirus (Nicopolis?); martyr; 175–189
14. **St Victor I**, of Africa; martyr; 189–199
15. **St Zephyrinus**, of Rome; martyr; 199–217
16. **St Calixtus**, of Rome; martyr; 217–222
    [**Hippolytus**, 217–235]
17. **St Urban I**, of Rome; martyr; 222–230
18. **St Pontianus**, of Rome; martyr; 21 July 230–28 Sept 235
19. **St Anterus**, of Greece; martyr; 21 Nov 235–3 Jan 236
20. **St Fabian**, of Rome; martyr; 10 Jan 236–20 Jan 250
21. **St Cornelius**, of Rome; martyr; March 251–June 253
    [**Novatian**, 251–258]
22. **St Lucius I**, of Rome; martyr; 25 June 253–5 March 254
23. **St Stephen I**, of Rome; martyr; 12 May 254–2 Aug 257
24. **St Sixtus II**, of Greece (?); martyr; 30 Aug 257–6 Aug 258
25. **St Dionysius**, of Magna Graecia (?); martyr; 22 July 259–26 Dec 268
26. **St Felix I**, of Rome; martyr; 5 Jan 269–30 Dec 274
27. **St Eutychianus**, of Luni; martyr; 4 Jan 275–7 Dec 283
28. **St Gaius**, of Dalmatia (Salona?); martyr; 17 Dec 283–22 April 296
29. **St Marcellinus**, of Rome; martyr; 30 June 296–25 Oct 304
30. **St Marcellus I**, of Rome; martyr; 27 May 308–16 Jan 309
31. **St Eusebius**, of Greece; martyr; 18 April 309–17 Aug 309 or 310
32. **St Melchiades** or **Miltiades**, of Africa; martyr; 2 July 311–11 Jan 314
33. **St Sylvester I**, of Rome; 31 Jan 314–31 Dec 335
34. **St Mark**, of Rome; 18 Jan 336–7 Oct 336
35. **St Julius I**, of Rome; 6 Feb 337–12 April 352
36. **Liberius**, of Rome; 17 May 352–22

Sept 366

[**St Felix II**, 355–22 Nov 365]

37. **St Damasus I**, of Spain; 1 Oct 366–11 Dec 384

[**Ursinus**, 366–367]

38. **St Siricius**, of Rome; 15 Dec 384–26 Nov 399

39. **St Anastasius I**, of Rome; 27 Nov 399–19 Dec 401

40. **St Innocent I**, of Albano; 22 Dec 401–12 March 417

41. **St Zosimus**, of Greece; 18 March 417–26 Dec 418

42. **St Boniface I**, of Rome; 29 Dec 418–4 Sept 422

[**Eulalius**, 27 Dec 418–3 April 419]

43. **St Celestine I**, of Campania; 10 Sept 422–27 July 432

44. **St Sixtus III**, of Rome; 3 July (?) 432–19 Aug 440

45. **St Leo I the Great**, of Tusculum; 29 Sept 440–10 Nov 461

46. **St Hilarius**, of Sardinia; 19 Nov 461–29 Feb 468

47. **St Simplicius**, of Tivoli; 3 March 468–10 March 483

48. **St Felix III** (II), of Rome, of the *gens* Anicia; 13 March 483–1 March 492

49. **St Gelasius I**, of Africa; 1 March 492–21 Nov 496

50. **St Anastasius II**, of Rome; 24 Nov 496–19 Nov 498

51. **St Symmachus**, of Sardinia; 22 Nov 498–19 July 514

[**Laurentius**, Nov 498–505]

52. **St Hormisdas**, of Frosinone; 20 July 514–6 Aug 523

53. **St John I**, of Tusculum; martyr; 13 Aug 523–18 May 526. Died at Ravenna

54. **St Felix IV (III)**, of Samnium (Benevento?); 12 July 526–22 Sept 530

55. **Boniface II**, of Rome; 22 Sept 530–7 Oct 532

[**Dioscurus**, 22 Sept 530–14 Oct 530]

56. **John II**, of Rome; 2 Jan 533–8 May 535

57. **St Agapitus I**, of Rome; 13 May 535–22 April 536. Died at Constantinople

58. **St Silverius**, of Frosinone; martyr; 8 June 536–deposed 11 March 537. Died in exile on the island of Ponza 538 (?)

59. **Vigilius**, of Rome; June 538 (?)–7 June 555 (but elected 29 March 537). Died at Syracuse

60. **Pelagius I**, of Rome; 16 April 556–4 March 561

61. **John III**, of Rome; 17 July 561–13 July 574

62. **Benedict I**, of Rome; 2 June 575–30 July 579

63. **Pelagius II**, of Rome; 26 Nov 579–7 Feb 590

64. **St Gregory I the Great**, of Rome, of the *gens* Anicia; 3 Sept 590–13 March 604

65. **Sabinianus**, of Tusculum; 13 Sept 604–22 Feb 606

66. **Boniface III**, of Rome; 19 Feb 607–12 Nov 607

67. **St Boniface IV**, of Valeria de'Marsi; 25 Aug 608–8 May 615

68. **St Adeodatus I**, of Rome; 19 Oct 615–8 Nov 618

69. **Boniface V**, of Naples; 23 Dec 619–25 Oct 625

70. **Honorius I**, of Campania; 27 Oct 625–12 Oct 638

71. **Severinus**, of Rome; 28 May 640–2 Aug 640

72. **John IV**, of Dalmatia; 24 Dec 640–12 Oct 642

73. **Theodore I**, of Jerusalem (? or Greece); 24 Nov 642–14 May 649

74. **St Martin I**, of Todi; martyr; 21 July 649–exiled 18 June 653–16 Sept 655. Died at Sebastopol

75. **St Eugenius I**, of Rome; 16 Sept 655–2 June 657

76. **St Vitalian**, of Segni; 30 July 657–27 Jan 672

77. **Adeodatus II**, of Rome; 11 April 672–17 June 676

78. **Donus**, of Rome; 2 Nov 676–11 April 678

79. **St Agatho**, of Sicily; 27 June 678–10

Jan 681

80. **St Leo II**, of Sicily; 17 Aug 682–3 July 683

81. **St Benedict II**, of Rome; 26 June 684–8 May 685

82. **John V**, of Antioch; 23 July 685–2 Aug 686

83. **Conon**, of Thrace; 21 Oct 686–21 Sept 687
[**Theodore**, 22 Sept 687– Oct 687]
[**Paschal**, 687]

84. **St Sergius I**, of Palermo; 15 Dec 687–8 Sept 701

85. **John VI**, of Greece; 30 Oct 701–11 Jan 705

86. **John VII**, of Greece; 1 March 705–18 Oct 707

87. **Sisinnius**, of Syria; 15 Jan 708–4 Feb 708

88. **Constantine**, of Syria; 25 March 708–9 April 715

89. **St Gregory II**, of Rome; 19 May 715–11 Feb 731

90. **St Gregory III**, of Syria; 18 March 731–10 Dec 741

91. **St Zacharias**, of Greece; 10 Dec 741–22 March 752

92. **Stephen, pope elect**, of Rome; 23–25 March 752

93. **St Stephen III (III)**, of Rome; 26 March 752–26 April 757

94. **St Paul I**, of Rome; 29 May 757–28 June 767
[**Constantine II**, 5 July 767– murdered 769]
[**Philip**, elected 31 July 768–abdicated 768]

95. **Stephen III (IV)**, of Sicily; 7 Aug 768–3 Feb 772

96. **Hadrian I**, of Rome; 9 Feb 772–26 Dec 795

97. **St Leo III**, of Rome; 27 Dec 795–12 June 816

98. **St Stephen IV (V)**, of Rome; 22 June 816–14 Jan 817

99. **St Paschal I**, of Rome; 25 Jan 817–11 Feb 824

100. **Eugenius II**, of Rome; 21 Feb 824–27 Aug 827

101. **Valentine**, of Rome; Aug (?) 827–Sept (?) 827

102. **Gregory IV**, of Rome; Oct 827–25 Jan 844

103. **Sergius II**, of Rome; Jan 844–27 Jan 847
[**John**, 844]

104. **St Leo IV**, of Rome; 10 April 847–17 July 855

105. **St Benedict III**, of Rome; 6 Oct 855–17 April 858
[**Anastasius**, 29 Sept 855–20 Oct 855]

106. **St Nicholas I the Great**, of Rome; 24 April 858–13 Nov 867

107. **Hadrian II**, of Rome; 14 Dec 867–14 Dec 872

108. **John VIII**, of Rome, 14 Dec 872–16 Dec 882

109. **Marinus I** (Martin II) of Gallesium; 16 Dec 882–15 May 884

110. **St Hadrian III**, of Rome; 17 May 884–17 Sept 885

111. **Stephen V (VI)**, of Rome; Sept 885–Sept 891

112. **Formosus**, bishop of Porto; 6 Oct 891–4 April 896

113. **Boniface VI**, of Gallesium; April 896

114. **Stephen VI (VII)**, of Rome; May 896–Aug 897. Strangled in prison

115. **Romanus**, of Gallesium; Aug 897–end of Nov 897

116. **Theodore II**, of Rome; Dec 897

117. **John IX**, of Tivoli; Jan 898–Jan 900

118. **Benedict IV**, of Rome; Jan 900–end July 903

119. **Leo V**, of Ardea; end of July 903–Sept 903. Deposed and imprisoned
[**Christopher**, of Rome; 903, deposed in Jan 904]

120. **Sergius III**, of Rome; 29 Jan 904–14 April 911

121. **Anastasius III**, of Rome; April 911–June 913

122. **Lando**, of Sabina; end of July 913–Feb 914

123. **John X**, of Ravenna; March 914–May 928. Strangled in prison

124. **Leo VI**, of Rome; May 928–Dec 928
125. **Stephen VII (VIII)**, of Rome; Jan 929–Feb 931
126. **John XI**, of Rome; son of Pope Sergius III and Marozia; March 931–Dec 935. Died in prison
127. **Leo VII**; 3 (?) Jan 936–13 (?) July 939
128. **Stephen VIII (IX)**, of Germany (?); 14 (?) July 939–end of Oct 942
129. **Marinus II** (Martin III), of Rome; 30 (?) Oct 942–May 946
130. **Agapitus II**, of Rome; 10 May 946–Dec 955
131. **John XII**, Ottaviano, of the family of the Counts of Tusculum, aged 19; 16 (?) Dec 955–deposed 14th May 964
132. **Leo VIII**, of Rome, 4 Nov 963–1 March 965
133. **Benedict V**, Grammatico, of Rome; 22 (?) May 964–expelled from the pontifical see 23 June 964; died at Bremen 4 July 966
134. **John XIII**, of Rome; 1 Oct 965–5 Sept 972
135. **Benedict VI**, of Rome; 19 Janm973–June 974. Strangled in prison [**Boniface VII**, Francone, of Rome; June–July 974 for the first time]
136. **Benedict VII**, of the family of the Counts of Tusculum, of Rome; Oct 974–10 July 983
137. **John XIV**, of Pavia; Dec 983–20 Aug 984; killed by Francone (Boniface VII) [**Boniface VII**, Francone; for the second time, Aug 984–murdered July 985]
138. **John XV**, of Rome; Aug 985–March 996
139. **Gregory V**, Bruno, of the family of the Counts of Carinthia; 3 May 996–18 Feb 999 [**John XVI**, John Philagathus, of Greece; March 997–Feb 998]
140. **Sylvester II**, Gerbert of Aurillac, Auvergne; 2 April 999–12 May 1003
141. **John XVII**, Sicco, of Rome; June (?) 1003–6 Nov 1003
142. **John XVIII**, of Rapagnano; Jan (?) 1004–July (?) 1009
143. **Sergius IV**, of Rome; 31 July 1009–12 May 1012
144. **Benedict VIII**, John, of the family of the Counts of Tusculum, of Rome; 18 May 1012–9 April 1024 [**Gregory**, 1012]
145. **John XIX**, of Rome, brother of Benedict VIII; April 1024–1032
146. **Benedict IX**, Theophylact, of the family of the Counts of Tusculum; elected (aged 15) for the first time in 1032–deposed in Dec 1044; elected for the second time 10 March 1045 deposed 1 May 1045; elected for the third time 8 Nov 1047– deposed 17 July 1048
147. **Sylvester III**, John, bishop of Sabina; 20 Jan 1045–deposed 10 March 1045
148. **Gregory VI**, Gratian, of Rome; 5 May 1045–banished 20 Dec 1046; died 1047
149. **Clement II**, Suidger, bishop of Bamberg; 25 Dec 1046–died at Pesaro 9 Oct 1047
150. **Damasus II**, Poppo, bishop of Bressanone, of Bavaria; 17 July 1048–9 Aug 1048. Died at Palestrina
151. **St Leo IX**, Bruno, of Germany, bishop of Toul; 12 Feb 1049–19 April 1054
152. **Victor II**, Gebhard, of Germany, bishop of Eichstätt; 16 April 1055–28 July 1057. Died at Arezzo
153. **Stephen IX (X)**, Frédéric, of the family of the Dukes of Lorraine; 3 Aug 1057–29 March 1058 [**Benedict X**, of Rome; 5 April 1058–deposed 24 Jan 1059]
154. **Nicholas II**, Gérard de Bourgogne; 24 Jan 1059–27 (?) July 1061
155. **Alexander II**, Anselmo of Milan; 30 Sept 1061–21 April 1073 [**Honorius II**, appointed by Imperial Diet of Basle 1061–1072]
156. **St Gregory VII**, Hildebrand di Bonizio Aldobrandeschi, of Sovana; 22 April 1073–25 May 1085 [**Clement III**, Ghiberto; 25 Jan 1080–Sept 1100]

157. **Bl. Victor III**, Desiderio Epifani, of Benevento; elected 24 May 1086, consecrated 9 May 1087–16 Sept 1087
158. **Bl. Urban II**, of Reims; 12 March 1088–29 July 1099
159. **Paschal II**, Rainiero, of Breda; 14 Aug 1099–21 Jan 1118
    [**Theodoric**, Sept–Dec 1100]
    [**Albert**, Feb–March 1102]
    [**Sylvester IV**, 18 Nov 1105–12 April 1111]
160. **Gelasius II**, Giovanni Caetani, of Gaeta; 24 Jan 1118–28 Jan 1119
    [**Gregory VIII**, Maurice Bourdain, of Limoges, 8 March 1118–deposed April 1121]
161. **Calixtus II**, Guy de Bourgogne, of Quingey; 2 Feb 1119–13 Dec 1124
162. **Honorius II**, Lamberto Scannabecchi, of Fanano (Modena); 15 Dec 1124–13 Feb 1130
163. **Innocent II**, Gregorio Papareschi, of Trastevere; 14 Feb 1130–24 Sept 1143
    [**Anacletus II**, Pierleone, a converted Jew; 14 Feb 1130–25 Jan 1138]
    [**Victor IV**, Gregorio da Monticelli, elected 15 March 1138, abdicated 29 May 1138]
164. **Celestine II**, Guido, of Città di Castello; 26 Sept 1143–8 March 1144
165. **Lucius II**, Gerardo Caccianemici dell'Orso, of Bologna; 12 March 1144–15 Feb 1145
166. **Bl. Eugenius III**, Bernardo Paganelli, of Montemagno (Pisa); 15 Feb 1145–8 July 1153
167. **Anastasius IV**, Corrado, of the Suburra, Rome; 12 July 1153–3 Dec 1154
168. **Hadrian IV**, Nicholas Breakspear, of Abbot's Langley (Hertfordshire, England); 4 Dec 1154–1 Sept 1159. Died at Anagni
169. **Alexander III**, Rolando Bandinelli, of Siena; 7 Sept 1159–30 Aug 1181. Died at Civita Castellana
    [**Victor IV** (V), Ottaviano; 7 Oct 1159–20 April 1164]
    [**Paschal III**, Guido da Crema; 22 April 1164–20 Sept 1168]
    [**Calixtus III**, John of Strumio, a Hungarian, Sept 1168, abdicated 29 Aug 1178]
    [**Innocent III**, Lando Frangipane of Sezze, elected 29 Sept 1179, deposed in Jan 1180]
170. **Lucius III**, Ubaldo Allucingoli, of Lucca; 1 Sept 1181–25 Nov 1185. Died in exile at Verona
171. **Urban III**, Uberto Crivelli, of Milan; 25 Nov 1185–20 Oct 1187. Died at Ferrara
172. **Gregory VIII**, Alberto di Morra, of Benevento; 21 Oct 1187–17 Dec 1187
173. **Clement III**, Paolino Scolare, of Rome; 19 Dec 1187–Mar 1191
174. **Celestine III**, Giacinto Bobone Orsini, of Rome; 30 March 1191–8 Jan 1198
175. **Innocent III**, Lotario dei Conti di Segni, of Anagni; 8 Jan 1198–16 July 1216. Died at Perugia
176. **Honorius III**, Cencio Savelli, of Rome; elected in Perugia, 18 July 1216– died at Rome, 18 March 1227
177. **Gregory IX**, Ugolino dei Conti di Segni, of Anagni; elected at the age of 86; 19 March 1227–22 Aug 1241
178. **Celestine IV**, Castiglione, of Milan; 25 Oct 1241–10 Nov 1241
179. **Innocent IV**, Sinibaldo Fieschi of Genoa; 25 June 1243–7 Dec 1254. Died at Naples
180. **Alexander IV**, Orlando dei Conti di Segni, of Anagni; 12 Dec 1254–25 May 1261. Died at Viterbo
181. **Urban IV**, Hyacinthe Pantaléon, of Troyes; elected at Viterbo 29 Aug 1261; died at Perugia 2 Oct 1264
182. **Clement IV**, Gui Foulques Le Gros, of St-Gilles; elected at Viterbo 5 Feb 1265–died at Viterbo 29 Nov 1268
183. **Bl. Gregory X**, Teobaldo Visconti of Piacenza; elected at Viterbo 1 Sept 1271–died at Arezzo 10 Jan 1276
184. **Bl. Innocent V**, Pierre de

Champagny, of the Tarentaise; 21 Jan 1276–22 June 1276

185. **Hadrian V**, Ottobono de' Fieschi, of Genoa; elected at Rome 11 July 1276–18 Aug 1276

186. **John XXI**, Pedro Juliao, of Lisbon; elected at Viterbo 8 Sept 1276–20 May 1277

187. **Nicholas III**, Giov. Gaetano Orsini, of Rome; elected at Viterbo 25 Nov 1277–died at Soriano nel Cimino 22 Aug 1280

188. **Martin IV**, Simon de Brion, of Montpincé in Brie; elected at Viterbo 22 Feb 1281–died at Perugia 28 March 1285

189. **Honorius IV**, Iacopo Savelli, of Rome; elected at Perugia 2 April 1285–3 April 1287

190. **Nicholas IV**, Girolamo Masci, of Lisciano di Ascoli; 15 Feb 1288–4 April 1292

191. **St Celestine V**, Pietro Angeleri da Morrone, of Isernia; 5 July 1294–abdicated 13 Dec 1294. Died in the Castello di Fumone near Alatri 19 May 1296

192. **Boniface VIII**, Benedetto Gaetani, of Anagni; 24 Dec 1294–11 Oct 1303

193. **Bl. Benedict XI**, Niccolò Boccasini, of Treviso; 22 Oct 1303–died at Perugia 7 July 1304

194. **Clement V**, Bertrand de Got, of Villandraut, near Bordeaux; elected at Perugia 5 June 1305–died at Roquemaure 14 April 1314

195. **John XXII**, Jacques d'Euse, of Cahors; elected at Avignon 7 Aug 1316–died at Avignon 4 Dec 1334

[**Nicholas V**, Pietro da Corvara, 12 May 1328–30 Aug 1330]

196. **Benedict XII**, Jacques Fournier, of Saverdun, near Toulouse; 20 Dec 1334–25 April 1342

197. **Clement VI**, Pierre Roger de Beaufort, of Château Maumont, near Limoges; 7 May 1342–6 Dec 1352

198. **Innocent VI**, Etienne d'Aubert, of Mont, near Limoges; 18 Dec 1352–12 Sept 1362

199. **Bl. Urban V**, Guillaume de Grimoard, of Grisac, near Mende in Languedoc; 16 Oct 1362–19 Dec 1370

200. **Gregory XI**, Pierre Roger de Beaufort, nephew of Clement VI, of Château Maumont, near Limoges; elected at Avignon 30 Dec 1370–died at Rome 27 March 1378

201. **Urban VI**, Bart. Prigano, of Naples; 9 April 1378–15 Oct 1389

202. **Boniface IX**, Pietro Tomacelli, of Naples; 2 Nov 1389–1 Oct 1404

203. **Innocent VII**, Cosimo de'Migliorati, of Sulmona; 17 Oct 1404–6 Nov 1406

204. **Gregory XII**, Angelo Correr, of Venice; 30 Nov 1406–abdicated 4 June 1415–died at Recanati 17 Oct 1417

ANTIPOPES

[**Clement VII**, Robert of Savoy, of Geneva; elected at Fondi 20 Sept 1378–16 Sept 1394]

[**Benedict XIII**, Pedro de Luna, of Aragon; 28 Sept 1394–23 May 1423]

[**Clement VIII**, Gil Sánchez Muñoz, of Barcelona; 10 June 1423–16 July 1429]

[**Benedict XIV**, Bernard Garnier; 12 Nov 1425–1430 (?)]

[**Alexander V**, Pietro Filargis, of Candia; 26 June 1409–3 May 1410]

[**John XXIII**, Baldassare Cossa, of Naples; 17 May 1410, deposed 29 May 1415–died at Florence 23 Dec 1419]

----

205. **Martin V**, Oddone Colonna, of Genazzano; elected (aged 50) at Constance, 11 Nov 1417–20 Feb 1431

206. **Eugenius IV**, Gabriele Condulmero of Venice; elected (aged 48) 3 March 1431–23 Feb 1447

[**Felix V**, Amadeus, duke of Savoy; 5 Nov 1439–7 April 1449; died 1451 at the Château de Ripaille on the Lake of Geneva]

207. **Nicholas V**, Tommaso Parentucelli, of Sarzana; elected (aged 49) 6 March 1447–24 March 1455

208. **Calixtus III**, Alfonso Borgia, of Xativa, in Spain; elected (aged 78) 8 April 1455–6 Aug 1458

209. **Pius II**, Aeneas Silvius Piccolomini, of Corsignano (Pienza); elected (aged 53) 19 Aug 1458–15 Aug 1464

210. **Paul II**, Pietro Barbo, of Venice; elected (aged 48) 30 Aug 1464–26 July 1471

211. **Sixtus IV**, Fr. della Rovere, of Savona; elected (aged 57) 9 Aug 1471–12 Aug 1484

212. **Innocent VIII**, G. B. Cibo, of Genoa; elected (aged 52) 29 Aug 1484–25 July 1492

213. **Alexander VI**, Roderigo Lenzuoli-Borgia, of Valencia, Spain; elected (aged 62) 11 Aug 1492–18 Aug 1503

214. **Pius III**, Fr. Todeschini Piccolomini, of Siena; elected (aged 64) 22 Sept 1503–18 Oct 1503

215. **Julius II**, Giuliano della Rovere, of Savona; elected (aged 60) 31 Oct 1503–21 Feb 1513

216. **Leo X**, Giov. de' Medici, of Florence; elected (aged 38) 9 March 1513– 1 Dec 1521

217. **Hadrian VI**, Adrian Florisz. Dedel, of Utrecht; elected (aged 63) 9 Jan 1522–14 Sept 1523

218. **Clement VII**. Giulio de' Medici, of Florence; elected (aged 45) 19 Nov 1523–25 Sept 1534

219. **Paul III**, Aless. Farnese, of Camino (Rome) or of Viterbo (?), elected (aged 66) 13 Oct 1534–10 Nov 549

220. **Julius III**, Giov. Maria Ciocchi del Monte, of Monte San Savino, near Arezzo; elected (aged 63) 7 Feb 1550–23 March 1555

221. **Marcellus II**, Marcello Cervini, of Montefano (Macerata); elected (aged 54) 9 April 1555–30 April 1555

222. **Paul IV**, Giov. Pietro Caraffa, of Capriglio, Avellino; elected (aged 79) 23 May 1555–18 Aug 1559

223. **Pius IV**, Giov. Angelo de'Medici, of Milan; elected (aged 60) 26 Dec 1559–9 Dec 1565

224. **St Pius V**, Ant. Ghislieri, of Bosco Marengo, near Tortona; elected (aged 62) 7 Jan 1566–1 May 1572

225. **Gregory XIII**, Ugo Boncompagni, of Bologna; elected (aged 70) 13 May 1572–10 April 1585

226. **Sixtus V**, Felice Peretti, of Grottammare; elected (aged 64) 24 April 1585–27 Aug 1590

227. **Urban VII**, G.B. Castagna, of Rome; elected (aged 69) 15 Sept 1590– 27 Sept 1590

228. **Gregory XIV**, Niccolò Sfondrati, of Cremona; elected (aged 55) 5 Dec 1590–15 Oct 1591

229. **Innocent IX**, G.A. Facchinetti, of Bologna; elected (aged 72) 29 Oct 1591–30 Dec 1591

230. **Clement VIII**, Ippolito Aldobrandini, of Fano; elected (aged 56) 30 Jan 1592–3 March 1605

231. **Leo XI**, Alessandro de' Medici, of Florence; elected (aged 70) 1 April 1605–27 April 1605

232. **Paul V**, Camillo Borghese, of Rome; elected (aged 53) 16 May 1605–28 Jan 1621

233. **Gregory XV**, Alessandro Ludovisi, of Bologna; elected (aged 67) 9 Feb 1621–8 July 1623

234. **Urban VIII**, Maffeo Barberini, of Florence; elected (aged 55) 6 Aug 1623–29 July 1644

235. **Innocent X**, G.B. Pamphilj, of Rome; elected (aged 72) 15 Sept 1644–7 Jan 1655

236. **Alexander VII**, Fabio Chigi, of Siena; elected (aged 56) 7 April 1655–22 May 1667

237. **Clement IX**, Giulio Rospigliosi, of Pistoia; elected (aged 67) 20 June 1667–9 Dec 1669

238. **Clement X**, Emilio Altieri, of Rome; elected (aged 80) 29 April 1670–22

July 1676

239. **Bl. Innocent XI**, Benedetto Odescalchi, of Como; elected (aged 65) 21 Sept 1676–11 Aug 1689

240. **Alexander VIII**, Pietro Ottoboni, of Venice; elected (aged 79) 6 Oct 1689–1 Feb 1691

241. **Innocent XII**, Antonio Pignatelli, of Spinazzola (Bari); elected (aged 76) 12 July 1691–27 Sept 1700

242. **Clement XI**, Giovanni Franesco Albani, of Urbino; elected (aged 51) 23 Nov 1700–19 March 1721

243. **Innocent XIII**, Michelangelo Conti, of Rome; elected (aged 66) 8 May 1721–7 March 1724

244. **Benedict XIII**, Pietro Francesco Orsini, of Gravina (Bari); elected (aged 75) 29 May 1724–21 Feb 1730

245. **Clement XII**, Lorenzo Corsini, of Florence; elected (aged 79) 12 July 1730–6 Feb 1740

246. **Benedict XIV**, Prospero Lambertini, of Bologna; elected (aged 65) 17 Aug 1740–3 May 1758

247. **Clement XIII**, Carlo Rezzonico, of Venice; elected (aged 65) 6 July 1758–2 Feb 1769

248. **Clement XIV**, Giov. Vincenzo Ganganelli, of Sant'Arcangelo di Romagna (Forlì); elected (aged 64) 19 May 1769–22 Sept 1774

249. **Pius VI**, Angelo Braschi, of Cesena; elected (aged 58) 15 Feb 1775–29 Aug 1799. Died at Valence, France

250. **Pius VII**, Giorgio Barnaba Chiaramonti, of Cesena; elected (aged 58) at Venice; 14 March 1800–died at Rome, 20 Aug 1823

251. **Leo XII**, Annibale della Genga, born at La Genga, near Foligno; elected (aged 63) 28 Sept 1823–10 Feb 1829

252. **Pius VIII**, Francesco Saverio Castiglioni, of Cingoli; elected (aged 69) 31 March 1829–30 Nov 1830

253. **Gregory XVI**, Bartolomeo Cappellari, of Belluno, elected (aged 66) 2 Feb 1831–1 June 1846

254. **Bl. Pius IX**, Giov. Maria Mastai Ferretti, of Senigallia; elected (aged 54) 16 June 1846–7 Feb 1878

255. **Leo XIII**, Gioacchino Pecci, of Carpineto Romano, elected (aged 68) 20 Feb 1878–20 July 1903

256. **St Pius X**, Giuseppe Sarto, of Riese (Treviso); elected (aged 68) 4 Aug 1903–20 Aug 1914

257. **Benedict XV**, Giacomo della Chiesa, of Genoa; elected (aged 60) 3 Sept 1914–22 Jan 1922

258. **Pius XI**, Achille Ratti, of Desio (Milan); elected (aged 65) 6 Feb 1922–10 Feb 1939

259. **Pius XII, Venerable**, Eugenio Pacelli, of Rome; elected (aged 63) 2 March 1939–9 Oct 1958

260. **St John XXIII**, Angelo Roncalli, of Sotto il Monte, Bergamo; elected (aged 77) 28 Oct 1958–3 June 1963; canonised 27 April 2014

261. **Paul VI**, Giov. Battista Montini, of Brescia; elected (aged 65) 21 June 1963–6 August 1978

262. **John Paul I**, Albino Luciani, of Forno di Canale, Belluno; elected (aged 65) 26 August 1978–29 September 1978

263. **St John Paul II**, Karol Wojtyla, of Wadowice (Krakow), Poland; elected (aged 58) 16 October 1978–2 April 2005; canonised 27 April 2014 (feast day 22 Oct)

264. **Benedict XVI, pope emeritus**, Joseph Ratzinger, of Markt am Inn (Passau), Germany; elected (aged 78) 19 April 2005; resigned 28 Feb 2013

265. **Francis**, Jorge Mario Bergoglio, of Buenos Aires, Argentina; elected (aged 76) 13 March 2013

Index

Explanatory or more detailed references (where there are many), or references to places where an artist's work is best represented, are given in bold. Numbers in italics are picture references. Dates are given for all artists, architects and sculptors with works referenced in this guide. Ancient names are rendered in italics, as are works of art.

ROME OVERVIEW

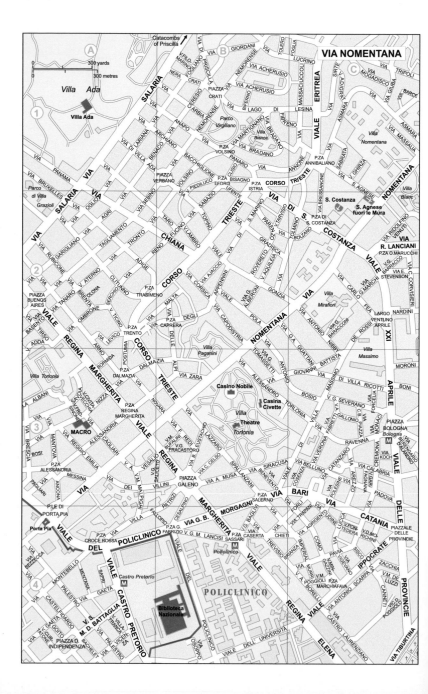

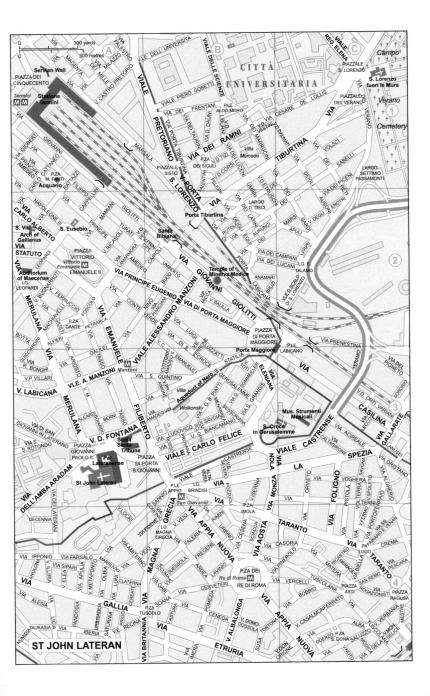

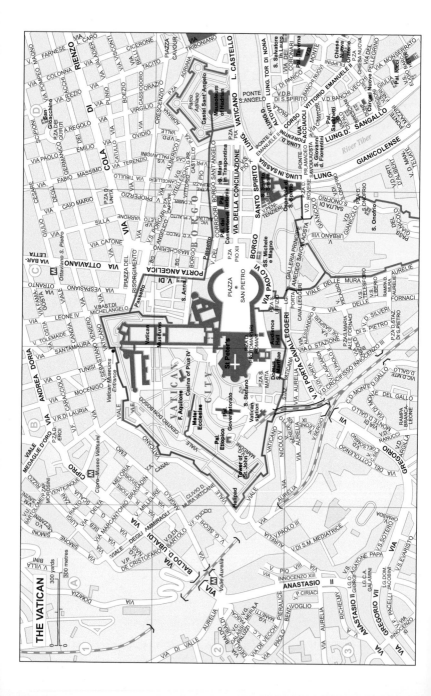

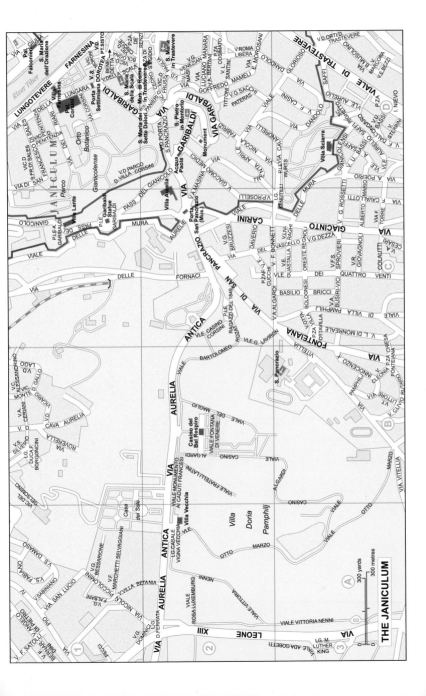

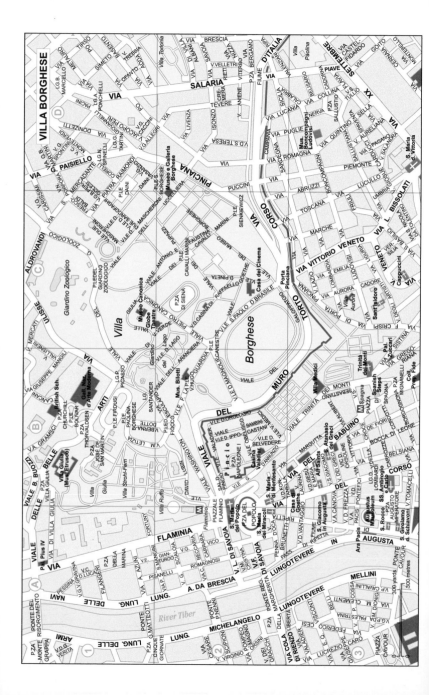

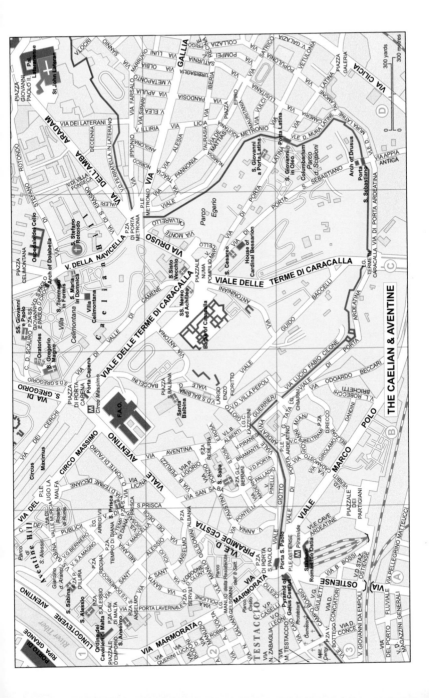

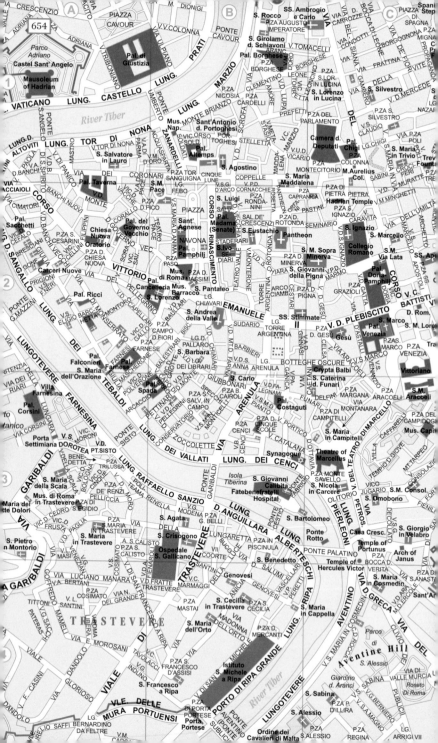